INTEGRATING MARKETING AND SUPPLY CHAIN MANAGEMENT

Successful organisations have long recognised the importance of demand–supply integration to maintaining growth and success. *Integrating Marketing and Supply Chain Management* brings together the two disciplines, marketing and supply chain management (SCM), to provide students with a bird's-eye view of these disciplines and to appreciate their symbiotic relationship to one another.

Taking account of the key strategic priorities from the marketing and supply chain disciplines, the authors demonstrate how both disciplines can be managed synergistically to the benefit of the organisation. Pedagogical features include multiple-choice questions, extended essay questions and learning objectives in each chapter.

Case studies from a range of global industries are incorporated, including shipping, car manufacturing and the retail grocery sector. Overall, this bridge-building textbook is essential reading for students of marketing, logistics, supply chain management and procurement.

Thomas A. Fotiadis is Full Professor of Marketing and Head of the Marketing Laboratory in the Department of Production Engineering and Management at the Democritus University of Thrace.

Dimitris Folinas is Full Professor of Supply Chain Management at the International Hellenic University and Visiting Professor at the Hellenic Open University.

Adam Lindgreen is Full Professor of Marketing at Copenhagen Business School and Extraordinary Professor at the University of Pretoria.

Antonios Gasteratos is Full Professor of Robotics, Mechatronics and Computer Vision; Dean of the Faculty of Engineering; and Director of the Laboratory of Robotics and Automation at the Democritus University of Thrace.

Christos A. Vassiliadis is a member of the academic teaching and research staff of the Department of Business Administration of the University of Macedonia in Thessaloniki.

'This book is a crucial read for both professionals and academics, offering valuable insights into the integration of marketing and supply chain management – two traditionally distinct but interdependent business functions. By addressing the "great divide" between demand generation and supply fulfillment, it provides readers with practical tools and methodologies to enhance organizational performance, foster collaboration, and build resilience in an increasingly complex global market."

Wendy L. Tate, *McCormick Endowed Professor of Supply Chain Management, University of Tennessee, USA*

'It is wonderful to see the publication of this book that manages to build a strong bridge between marketing and supply chain management. For many companies like Apple, these two areas have become core competencies and engines of value creation. What I particularly like about this book is that it builds on a strong theoretical background while focusing on practical solutions. It is great to see that the book also emphasizes sustainable management.'

Andreas Wieland, *Co-Editor-in-Chief,* Journal of Supply Chain Management

'*Integrating Marketing and Supply Chain Management* is a much-needed approach avoiding silo-thinking and broadening the perspective. Students will benefit from the solutions offered, which aim at the joint goal of creating customer satisfaction. It is most welcome that sustainability and corporate social responsibility are key constituents of this integration, ensuring that a wide set of stakeholder demands are considered while at the same time taking up the demands of the ongoing digital transformation.'

Professor Stefan Seuring, *Universität Kassel, Germany*

'A long-awaited book! An integrated approach to marketing and supply chain management has often been called for, and it is this approach that is at the heart of this book. This book shows perfectly how marketing and supply chain management contribute to value creation and how their effective integration can enhance that value creation. The effective integration of marketing and supply chain management as disciplines and areas of activity is becoming increasingly necessary, particularly in today's business world faced with the challenges of sustainability and digitalisation.'

Professor Catherine Pardo, *Emlyon Business School, France*

'Marketing and supply chain management are often treated as separate disciplines, yet their integration is critical for business success. *Integrating Marketing and Supply Chain Management* bridges this gap by offering an original, research-backed perspective on how these two functions interact to create value and enhance competitiveness. The book provides comprehensive insights into strategic alignment, digital transformation, sustainability, and customer-centricity, making it a valuable resource for scholars, practitioners, and students alike. Through real-world case studies and practical frameworks, the book provides valuable guidance for those seeking to better understand the complexities of modern business operations.'

Professor Christian Kowalkowski, *Linköping University, Sweden*

'Marketing and supply chain management are too often treated separately. In an academic setting, they are usually taught in different courses, using different textbooks, often in different departments. But in reality, the two functional areas are strongly connected, and opportunities for integration are superficial or ignored. In this book, Folinas, Fotiadis, Lindgreen, Gasteratos, and Vassiliadis explore the common ground of these functional areas – delivering customer value and achieving customer satisfaction – and present methods, tools, and technologies that facilitate their integration.'

Professor Anthony Di Benedetto, *Temple University, USA*

'*Integrating Marketing and Supply Chain Management* is a significant contribution to integrating our understanding of both marketing and supply chain management. It incorporates all the latest thinking on technological advances made in both fields, such as Industry 4.0/5,0, AI and digital twins. Aimed at the senior undergraduate/postgraduate market, the use throughout this book of case studies, essay questions and online simulation will be significant aids in supporting the learning process.'

Professor Emeritus Peter Naudé, *Manchester Metropolitan University, UK*

'This book examines two scientific areas (marketing and supply chain management), which tend to be considered as separate, but they are very much integrated, interdependent, and intertwined areas, which work together in a symbiotic manner. This book provides novel and important insights extending our knowledge regarding the marketing and supply chain management interface. I am confident that the book will be a great success and enjoyable reading for the academic, student, and practitioner communities.'

Professor Michael Bourlakis, *Director of Research and Director of the Centre for Logistics, Procurement & Supply Chain Management, Cranfield University, UK*

'The book makes a timely intervention into the interaction between supply chains and marketing. With the increasing use of multiple epicenters in business model innovation, the book offers guidance into how, from a marketing perspective, broader value propositions can be designed. The specific intersection between a traditional marketing focus on how products and services are delivered to markets is broadened to consider how innovative channels to customers and consumers can be integrated as value delivery mechanisms. The authors delve deeply into the technology that underpins these new delivery modes allowing readers to visualize broad value proposition development. The book delivers a conceptualization of value creation that extends the traditional remit of marketers and will be of interest to both students of marketing and professional marketers.'

Professor John Nicholson, *University of Huddersfield, UK*

INTEGRATING MARKETING AND SUPPLY CHAIN MANAGEMENT

Converging Paths to Holistic Business Success

Thomas A. Fotiadis, Dimitris Folinas, Adam Lindgreen, Antonios Gasteratos and Christos A. Vassiliadis

Routledge
Taylor & Francis Group
LONDON AND NEW YORK

Designed cover image: Getty Images © Credit: VectorMine

First published 2026
by Routledge
4 Park Square, Milton Park, Abingdon, Oxon OX14 4RN

and by Routledge
605 Third Avenue, New York, NY 10158

Routledge is an imprint of the Taylor & Francis Group, an informa business

British Library Cataloguing-in-Publication Data
A catalogue record for this book is available from the British Library

Library of Congress Cataloging-in-Publication Data
Names: Fotiadis, Thomas author
Title: Integrating marketing and supply chain management : converging paths to holistic business success / Thomas A. Fotiadis, Dimitris Folinas, Adam Lindgreen, Antonios Gasteratos and Christos A. Vassiliadis.
Description: Abingdon, Oxon ; New York, NY : Routledge, 2026. | Includes bibliographical references and index.
Identifiers: LCCN 2025025666 (print) | LCCN 2025025667 (ebook) | ISBN 9781041096146 hardback | ISBN 9781041096122 paperback | ISBN 9781003650973 ebook
Subjects: LCSH: Business logistics—Management | Supply chain management | Marketing—Management
Classification: LCC HD38.5 .F678 2026 (print) | LCC HD38.5 (ebook) | DDC 658.7—dc23/eng/20250905
LC record available at https://lccn.loc.gov/2025025666
LC ebook record available at https://lccn.loc.gov/2025025667

ISBN: 978-1-041-09614-6 (hbk)
ISBN: 978-1-041-09612-2 (pbk)
ISBN: 978-1-003-65097-3 (ebk)

DOI: 10.4324/9781003650973

Typeset in Times New Roman
by Apex CoVantage, LLC

To my daughter, Hermie. . . . Your laughter lights up my world. Your curiosity inspires every page. Thank you for teaching me to dream bigger, love stronger and believe without limits. For you, my little muse – Thomas

For my family, my joy and my trials – Dimitris Folinas

To Thomas and his lovely wife and daughter Maria and Ermylia, with thanks – Adam

To my family, whose unwavering support has been my guiding light, and to my colleagues, whose encouragement and collaboration have turned a researcher's solitary path into a shared journey – Antonios Gasteratos

To all our lovely families and to my friends, who turned this journey into an adventure – Chris

CONTENTS

FIGURES

TABLES

ABOUT THE AUTHORS

Thomas A. Fotiadis is Full Professor of Marketing and Head of the Marketing Laboratory in the Department of Production Engineering and Management at the Democritus University of Thrace in Greece. He holds a postdoctoral degree (postdoc) in contemporary advanced statistical methods for the science of marketing and a Ph.D. in marketing (high technology). In addition, he holds a master's degree in business administration and a master's degree in business computing. His first degree is in economics. Thomas A. Fotiadis has more than 23 years of teaching experience at both undergraduate and postgraduate levels in Greek and international universities and higher technological institutions. His scientific work has been published in journals including *Industrial Marketing Management*, *International Marketing Review*, the *Journal of Applied Business Research*, the *Journal of International Business Review*, the *Journal of International Marketing*, the *Journal of Tourism Management*, the *Journal of World Business* and *Psychology & Marketing*, among others. He has published numerous books, including *Strategic Marketing for High Technology Products* (Routledge, 2018), *Marketing and Supply Chain Management* (Routledge, 2017), *The Customer Value Chain* (Routledge, 2021) and *Industrial Marketing* (Sage, 2023), and he has edited and authored *Marketing* (Kritiki Publishing, 2022), *Marketing in the Public Sector* (Broken Hill Publishers, 2023) and *Marketing of High-Technology and Industrial Products* (Broken Hill Publishers, 2019).

Dimitris Folinas is Full Professor of Supply Chain Management at the International Hellenic University and Visiting Professor at the Hellenic Open University. He holds a Ph.D. in applied informatics from the University of Macedonia, Thessaloniki, Greece, and a master's degree in information systems from the same institution. For more than 20 years, he has held various teaching posts at Liverpool University (UK), Hellenic Open University (Greece), and the University of Macedonia (Greece), teaching mainly information systems, enterprise information systems and logistics and SCM. He is the author and co-author of many research publications and books, and as a researcher, he has prepared, submitted and managed several projects funded by national and European Union research entities. His research interests include logistics and SCM, electronic supply chains, information systems and technologies in supply chains and Industry 4.0.

Adam Lindgreen is Full Professor of Marketing at Copenhagen Business School, where he led the Department of Marketing from 2016 to 2024. Since 2018, Adam Lindgreen has also been Extraordinary Professor with the University of Pretoria's Gordon Institute of Business Science. He has held visiting positions with leading institutions, including Auckland University, Georgia State University, HEC Paris, Melbourne University and Monash University. He received his Ph.D. from Cranfield University and an honorary doctorate from Democritus University of Thrace. Adam Lindgreen's publications have appeared in academic journals including *California Management Review*, the *Journal of Business Ethics*, the *Journal of Management Studies*, the *Journal of the Academy of Marketing Science*, the *Journal of Product Innovation Management*, the *Journal of Travel Research*, the *Journal of World Business* and *Organization Studies*, among others. His 40 books include *A Stakeholder Approach to Corporate Social Responsibility* (with Kotler, Vanhamme and Maon; 2012), *Industrial Marketing* (with Fotiadis, Siomkos, Öberg and Folinas; 2024), *Managing Market Relationships* (2008), *Public Value* (with Koenig-Lewis, Kitchener, Brewer, Moore and Meynhardt; 2019) and *Sustainable Value Chain Management* (with Maon, Vanhamme and Sen; 2013). The recipient of the "Outstanding Article 2005" award from *Industrial Marketing Management* and the runner-up for the same award in 2016, as well as of "Outstanding Published Article [in the *Journal of Management Studies*]" award in 2025 from the International Association for Business and Society, Adam Lindgreen serves on the board of numerous scientific journals. He is co-editor-in-chief of *Industrial Marketing Management* and co-editor-in-chief of Routledge's *Food and Agricultural Marketing*. Since 2017, he has been a member of the Chartered Association of Business Schools' Academic Journal Guide (AJG) Scientific Committee in the field of marketing and, from 2020 to 2025, of Det videnskabelige Råd for Lex.dk.

Antonios Gasteratos is Full Professor of Robotics, Mechatronics and Computer Vision at Democritus University of Thrace; Dean of the Faculty of Engineering; and Director of the Laboratory of Robotics and Automation. He holds an M.Eng. and a Ph.D. in electrical and computer engineering from Democritus University of Thrace (1994 and 1999, respectively). For the past 20 years, he has been the principal investigator on several projects, mostly related to robotics and vision, funded mainly by the European Commission, the European Space Agency, the Greek General Secretariat for Research and Technology and other sources. He has published over 300 papers in peer-reviewed journals and international conferences, and he has written four textbooks in Greek. He is the subject editor-in-chief of *Electronics Letters* and an associate editor with *Expert Systems with Applications*, the *International Journal of Advanced Robotics Systems* and the *International Journal of Optomechatronics*. He is also an evaluator of projects supported by the European Commission and other funding agencies and a reviewer of many international journals in computer vision and robotics. Antonios Gasteratos has served on programme committees of international conferences and as chairman and co-chairman of international conferences and workshops. He is a member of the Plenary of the Hellenic Telecommunications and Post Commission (a national regulatory body in Greece), a fellow member of IET and a senior member of IEEE.

Christos A. Vassiliadis is a member of the academic teaching and research staff of the Department of Business Administration of the University of Macedonia in Thessaloniki. He is a full professor and member of University of Macedonia teaching staff, with more than 20 years of experience working with Greek and non-Greek universities at the graduate and postgraduate levels. His research topics include marketing, tourism management and marketing and services marketing management. His research has been published in various journals. Also, he is a collaborating member of the Greek Open University in the unit of Business Administration and Organisations, and he was a collaborating member of the Open University of Cyprus. He was and is part of the teaching staff of different interdepartmental and master programmes, for example, the postgraduate study in business administration at the University of Macedonia; the International Master Program of Business Administration (IMBA), National Chiayi University; and the Athens University of Economics and Business (MSM-OPA). He has also been the director of the master's programme in tourism management at the University of Macedonia since 2017. He is the author or co-author of the following books: *The Administration and Marketing of Tourism Destinations* (in Greek), *Customer Relationship Management and Marketing of Tourism Destinations* (in Greek), *Principles and Practices of Small-Scale Sport Event Management* (in English), *Marketing: From the Basic Principles to the Contemporary Challenges* (in Greek) and *Event Marketing Management* (in Greek).

PREFACE

The book at hand discusses two of the most prominent business functions: marketing and SCM. A holistic approach is proposed through the systemic survey of the theoretical background and the respective attributes that constitute the context for the fields above. The contribution is solidified under an integrated prism, instead of a self-directive and isolated study of the key areas. Access to various scientific benefits and synergies is revealed, and the outcome considerably surpasses the sum of the respective insights of singular efforts attempted by the theoretical knowledge self-contained in clusters of marketing and SCM.

The distinct fields of application for this systemic viewpoint consist of the conceptual clarification and mapping of marketing and supply chain theoretical background context and the respective interactive correlation of their designated frameworks and goals. It also consists of the systemic approach of the superior customer service orientation; the order's processing operational excellence; the integration of demand-focused and supply-focused processes; sourcing and procurement activities; the distribution channel; management and logistics information systems; and the unified context of services as viewed in an 'out of the box' manner provided by the multilevel holistic delineation.

Furthermore, highly quoted issues like sustainability, green SCM and corporate social responsibility will be discussed and analysed, while a considerable effort will be dedicated towards the resolution of a wide spectrum of green/eco-friendly variables, which comprise the influences of the various stakeholders to and from modern organisations.

This book promotes the idea that for an expanding economy its overall development requires the integration of both paradigms. In the literature, there are many textbooks focused on either marketing or SCM. However, most books (and especially textbooks) take a relatively narrow, functional perspective and neglect the need for integration. This book examines these disciplines/business areas via an integrated approach, providing specific practices and techniques based on well-known philosophies and state-of-the-art technologies.

Let's consider the focus of this book. There is a symbiotic relationship between marketing and SCM within any enterprise. This means that actions in one area directly impact the other. For today's managers to succeed, they must excel in both fields. We therefore begin by exploring the strategic connections and disconnections between SCM operations and marketing/sales through a case study from an operational perspective. This case represents a common scenario that highlights the necessity of integrating these two disciplines.

The key takeaway from the aforementioned case is that the success of one function or department is meaningless if the next department fails. Success depends on the entire organisation working together. We present the key parameters and essentials of marketing and SCM and their contributions to the value chain. The goal is to provide a well-documented cognitive framework for these concepts, aiding readers in navigating the other chapters and equipping them with the necessary conceptual and cognitive tools. Both business functions are structured around a customer-oriented approach, aiming to place the customer at the core of all actions and processes. This approach aspires to achieve maximum customer satisfaction in an effective and efficient manner.

We then examine marketing and SCM, two key business functions often perceived as belonging to different worlds. This perception arises from companies in which the boundaries of their competencies are unclear, creating 'grey' areas in daily activities. Definitions from well-known organisations contribute to this view. The American Marketing Association (AMA) defines marketing as the activity, set of institutions and processes for creating, communicating, delivering and exchanging offerings that have value for customers, clients, partners and society at large. Meanwhile, the Council of Supply Chain Management Professionals (CSCMP) defines SCM as the planning and management of all activities involved in sourcing and procurement, conversion and all logistics management activities. Despite their seemingly different objectives, many researchers and case studies show that the effective coexistence of marketing and SCM fosters proactive demand planning, collaboration and full transparency between marketing and supply chain teams.

The modern business environment is driven by several forces: constant and complex change; a customer-oriented philosophy becoming a crucial strategic factor; market globalisation creating new requirements and challenges; the internet, mobile networks and ubiquitous computing offering new capabilities but also organisational and technological challenges; the recognition of intellectual capital as vital; and strategic alliances with key business partners. These challenges impact how marketing and SCM executives plan and perform their daily activities. They also pose problems for integrating the two functions. We thus address these challenges from an integrated perspective.

Marketing and SCM are two business functions that, despite originating from different fields and employing distinct techniques, share a common goal: achieving customer satisfaction. Both functions are evaluated through this lens, as they contribute to delivering superior value and shaping perceived customer satisfaction. This includes aspects like philosophy, attitude, organisational culture, strategic orientation, vision, mission, processes and functions. Ensuring reassurances and guarantees that enhance customer satisfaction is essential for the long-term survival and performance improvement of an organisation. Accordingly, we aim to identify the key parameters of an integrated approach to marketing and SCM, which can serve as the foundation for examining main business functions.

A distribution channel can be defined as a group of organisations (producers, intermediaries such as wholesalers and retailers, third-party logistics, etc.) involved in the flow of products or services from producers to customers. Therefore, we identify and discuss the key elements of successful distribution channels.

Demand handling in marketing means 'try to increase sales – try to bring in orders!' For SCM, it means 'try to transfer goods to customers' or 'ensure the right product is available in the right quantity, at the right place, at the right time, and at the right cost'. It also involves ensuring there is enough capacity to handle the order. We therefore discuss the main topics of demand handling and forecasting practices and techniques, supported by an online simulation tool.

Finding the right resources and suppliers and maintaining efficient relationships with them are crucial for business success. For new managers, this often means reducing costs and gaining a competitive edge. Successful entrepreneurs must combine the skills of both salespeople and buyers. Company management must quickly realise the importance of procurement and supply chain relationships and treat them with the same importance as marketing and customer relationships. Sourcing is often seen as 'reverse marketing', where marketing and supply departments collaborate to attract and work with suppliers who add value to the company's products and services. This involves using practices and methodologies to find, maintain and grow the customer base, as well as attract loyal customers. There are notable similarities between the relationships with suppliers and customers, which fall under the umbrella of business associate management or relationship management of business partners. This management evolves from opportunity transactions (which may not always benefit both parties) to regular transactions with fixed terms and finally to strategic relationships based on shared opportunities, profits and risks.

We then present the main practices and methods companies use to manage demand. These practices require contributions from managers in the marketing and sales departments, as well as those in logistics and SCM. Approaches such as just-in-time, vendor-managed inventory, efficient consumer response, collaborative planning, forecasting and replenishment, and lean thinking are essential for keeping organisations competitive in today's market.

Following that, we focus on tools and technologies that enable the interdisciplinary integration and systemic approach to marketing and SCM. We also examine e-commerce and e-business technologies, including product auto-identification, customer and supplier relationship management systems, social networks, augmented reality and electronic point of sales. We combine system assessments with theoretical presentations and analyses of practices and methodologies that support the implementation and efficient use of these systems, such as business process management and business intelligence.

Next, we examine the relationships between contracting parties in service management and marketing, focusing on the importance of developing, maintaining and managing their reputations to strengthen these relationships. We highlight the significance of sustainable service supply management, service demand management, service integration management and service coordination management as essential value chain practices in service delivery. Modern economies increasingly require a detailed approach to services that support the introduction and distribution of material goods in demand-driven markets. However, compared to research on supply chains of physical goods, research on service supply chains and the critical role of human capital in service delivery remains underdeveloped. To better monitor and evaluate intangible services, researchers, statistical agencies and literature suggest various classifications of services. The growing contribution of services to gross domestic product (GDP) in developed economies underscores the need to monitor trends and developments in service value chains. Intense global competition necessitates maintaining customer satisfaction to ensure consistent revenue streams. This has led businesses to enhance supporting services for material products, a concept known as the servitisation of goods.

We then consider the characteristics of value chain management in services through four case studies, focusing on companies in catering, transport, tourism and event markets. Understanding the specific factors affecting each service sector helps managers identify potential deviations, problems and opportunities in administrative decision-making related to value chain management. We explore the role of SCM in services marketing, looking at how businesses coordinate their networks of suppliers, partners and customers to create value. This includes integrating marketing strategies within the service supply chain and highlighting emerging trends such as digitalisation, sustainability and customer-centric service design. Studying business sector case studies provides learners and professionals with actionable insights, enhances problem-solving and decision-making skills and prepares them for real-world challenges. These case studies are crucial for understanding the dynamic nature of services, including supply chain sustainability, customer relationships, innovation, operational effectiveness and global strategies. They offer practical lessons directly applicable to solving real-world challenges and driving growth in service industries.

Sustainability is now a key focus in SCM, especially in the service sector, where environmental, social and economic factors are vital for long-term success. We explore best practices for sustainable service SCM (SSSCM) by introducing essential frameworks, models and strategies for creating environmentally and socially responsible supply chains. One core concept is the 'house of sustainable SCM', a structured framework for integrating sustainability into service supply chains. We also examine the triple bottom line approach, which balances economic, social and environmental performance, and the value driver model, which highlights how businesses can incorporate sustainability into their long-term growth strategies. Through case studies and practical insights, we will see how companies across various industries have successfully implemented sustainable practices, including ethical sourcing, green logistics and digital transformation.

Industry 4.0 revolutionised manufacturing with technologies like artificial intelligence (AI), Internet of Things (IoT), smart robotics, big data analytics and simulation, enhancing supply chain integration, logistics, lead times and inventory management. Industry 5.0, the next step, focuses on combining advanced technologies with a human-centric approach for sustainable, personalised and efficient production. This shift prioritises better working conditions, using automation to improve comfort, safety and job satisfaction.

In SCM, Industry 5.0 emphasises strategic coordination and collaboration with external partners to optimise material, information and financial flows. It promotes human–machine collaboration, mass customisation, decentralised production, sustainable solutions, real-time data sharing, resilience and talent development. These strategies aim to enhance operational effectiveness, reduce costs and lead times and improve customer satisfaction. Advanced technologies like AI, IoT, digital twins and extended reality (XR) are crucial for real-time visibility, flexibility and responsiveness in supply chains. AI provides data analysis, predictive analytics and automation, optimising demand forecasting, route planning and inventory management. IoT connects physical objects, offering real-time data on status, location and conditions, improving monitoring and control. Digital twins simulate supply chain operations, identifying issues and optimising processes. XR bridges physical and digital worlds, enhancing human–computer interaction. In conclusion, Industry 5.0 and technologies like AI, digital twins, IoT and XR are transforming SCM, offering opportunities for improved efficiency, agility and customer satisfaction, leading to smart, human-centric supply chains.

Finally, in today's business environment, companies face challenges in improving efficiency, maintaining quality and meeting consumer expectations. Digital technologies offer solutions to these issues, enhancing operations, product integrity and customer satisfaction. Integrating digitalisation, traceability and sentiment analysis into supply chains is crucial for innovation and success. Companies must meet higher expectations for transparency, faster delivery and personalised experiences while adhering to sustainable and ethical practices. Traditional supply chain models are insufficient. Modern supply chains are strategic assets supporting customer-centric models. Digitalisation, traceability and sentiment analysis transform operations, ensuring product integrity, understanding consumer preferences and providing automation and real-time analytics. These elements enhance efficiency, engagement and decision-making. Digitalisation improves operations through automation, data management and analytics, offering benefits like better information access, streamlined logistics, real-time data capture, effective inventory management and increased transparency. Industry 4.0 integrates cyber–physical systems (CPS) for autonomous, interconnected and intelligent operations, enhancing performance and competitiveness. Traceability ensures products are tracked and traced, complying with regulations and standards, verifying origin and quality, and combating malfunctions. Social media enables real-time communication, better coordination and improved product-service quality and efficiency. It fosters information sharing, relationship building and performance enhancement. Sentiment analysis helps businesses understand consumer opinions and align strategies with expectations. Incorporating digitalisation, traceability and sentiment analysis into supply chains represents a significant shift in operations, risk management and customer engagement, driving innovation and sustainability. In summary, integrating these elements into SCM addresses global trade complexities, meeting demands and expectations and providing a competitive edge in customer satisfaction, sustainability and operational effectiveness. The future of SCM lies in enhancing resilience, responsiveness and transparency through digital tools.

1

MARKETING AND SUPPLY CHAIN MANAGEMENT CHALLENGES

Introduction

There is a symbiotic relationship between marketing and supply chain management (SCM) within any enterprise. This simply means that what happens in one area directly affects the other, and, more importantly, for today's managers to succeed, they need to understand that they have to succeed in both fields. This chapter appreciates the strategic connections and disconnections between SCM operations and marketing/sales by presenting and analysing a case study from an operational viewpoint. The case examined can be considered as a common and everyday scenario that reveals the need for integrating the two disciplines.

Learning objectives

After reading this chapter, you will be able to answer the following questions:

- Why is it important for there to be an integrated outlook on marketing and SCM?
- What are the problems and consequences of adopting a non-integrated treatment of the two disciplines?
- What are customers' concerns relating to a low level of service?
- What are the concerns of the management of enterprises – members of a supply chain relating to the low level of collaboration between their logistics systems?

Outline

- Case study
- Customer concerns
- Management concerns
- Theoretical framework/book roadmap

DOI: 10.4324/9781003650973-1

1.1 Case study

In the place of an introduction, we shall present a usual scenario occurring in the market on a daily basis. The chairman of an academic institution decided with the board to procure 100 PCs for the operation of two laboratories. Having visited a trade fair the previous month, he decides to contact three companies that are active in the local market. He arranges three meetings with sales executives from the corresponding informatics companies. In these meetings, the sales executives stress the advantages for the institution to side with them, their many years of experience in the field and the high quality of the systems they sell. The chairman finally decides to go with the supplier-company, which promised a high level of after-sales support and lower maintenance costs. Indeed, as the supplier tries to 'secure' the deal, he promises state-of-the-art systems with higher memory capacities and faster processors, which his company does not possess at the moment and which must be immediately procured.

Ten days later, the chairman telephones the call centre of the company (as agreed with the supplier's head of sales) to be informed on the status of his order. The operator puts him through to the head of sales, who, being unaware of the execution of the order, recommends that the client speak to the accounting department. The accounting department manager informs the client that his order has been received and was forwarded to the production department on the day after the order was placed. Since, however, it was necessary to order the state-of-the-art processors and memory units, the supplies department ordered the required hardware but, due to time constraints, managed to procure them on time, on the one hand, but at a great cost, on the other.

The accounting department employee, assuming that the order has been completed, asks the client to speak with the warehouse staff. The employee in the warehouse informs the client that he has already received part of the order in the warehouse (specifically, 60 PCs). However, he does not know anything about the rest of the order. Consequently, he deems that it is better for the client to contact the production department once more. The head of production reports to the client that the rest of his order has exited the assembly line, and it is only logical that it is on its way to the supplier company. However, he does not know the precise time of delivery for the rest of the order, and for this reason, he takes the initiative to suggest that the client contact the driver of the transportation vehicle himself. The client's 'troubles' end when the driver informs him on the estimated time of arrival for the products in the order.

The scenario above poses the following obvious question:

> Couldn't all of the managers involved in the execution of the order, as well as the employees of the corresponding departments, have collaborated beforehand to better plan the execution of the client's order?

This question also raises concerns from the point of view of both the client and the management of the company. We shall discuss these concerns based on what we know from classic management theory.

1.2 Customer concerns

A simple and unpretentious review of this 'marathon' and virtual (via the telephone) tour of the supplier company almost spontaneously raises a series of thoughts, doubts and concerns to the client:

- Can this really be the same company that was committed to its high after-sales support level – namely, the satisfaction of that factor/prerequisite with added weight, which ultimately shaped the course of action and determined the selection of the supplier? With what assurance? What does all of this say about its reliability, and how could the company respond after the purchase, when it cannot even efficiently and effectively complete a series of routine processes relating to the pre-purchasing stages, within its own house?

- How is it possible for the supplier to claim that they will provide high-efficiency and technology equipment without having previously even considered how the product and/or service would be beneficial for the supplier himself?
- What could a possible future collaboration be, in which its initial stages are characterised by a communication gap and its performance resting on the client's goodwill and patience?
- Who will compensate for the time wasted, or to be wasted in the future if similar conditions and behaviours arise?

In other words, the client experiences an unpleasant state of 'dissonance', which stems from the existence of a divergence between the planned result he anticipated – based on the agreement – and the agreement as it has been realised up to now. Or, even worse (but possibly closer to reality), he experiences a cognitive dissonance and, indeed, a premature one, since this can possibly arise at a post-purchase stage.

In the framework of the client's behaviour, this dissonance relates to the attitudes, emotions, etc., adopted by the client and is, essentially, manifested as an internal and unpleasant state of tension. The theoretical background of 'dissonance theory' was developed by Festinger in 1957, to render the assessment and evaluation of various alternatives clearer and more comprehensible, after a particular choice has been made. While it is typically structured on some form of inconsistency of a psychological nature, stemming from the choice made by the social circle of the consumer, one can, however, see useful parallels and similarities with our scenario, in the context of the processes for the 'resolution' of the purchasing 'problem'.

To render the scope of the components composing the framework of purchasing (and consequently also post-purchase) behaviour clearer, a general model of buyer behaviour is discussed. Figure 1.1 presents the model as a step-by-step process.

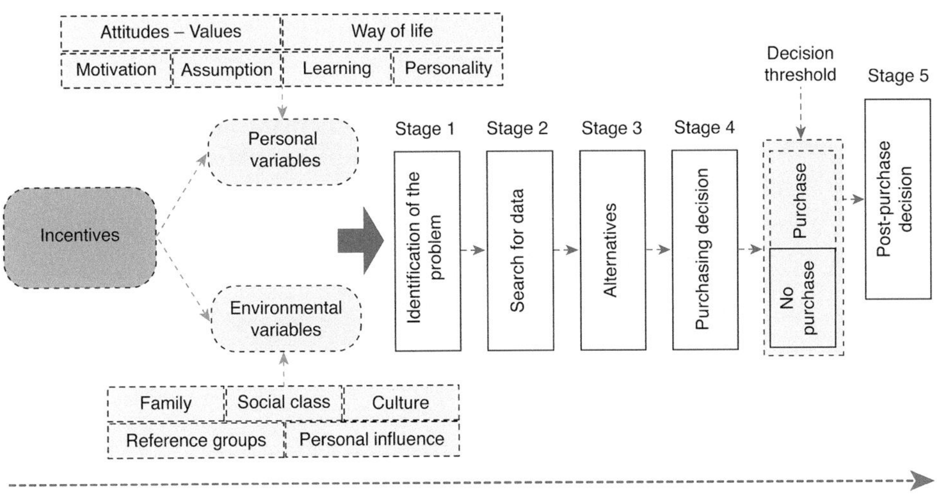

FIGURE 1.1 General model of buyer behaviour in the context of resolution of the purchasing problem

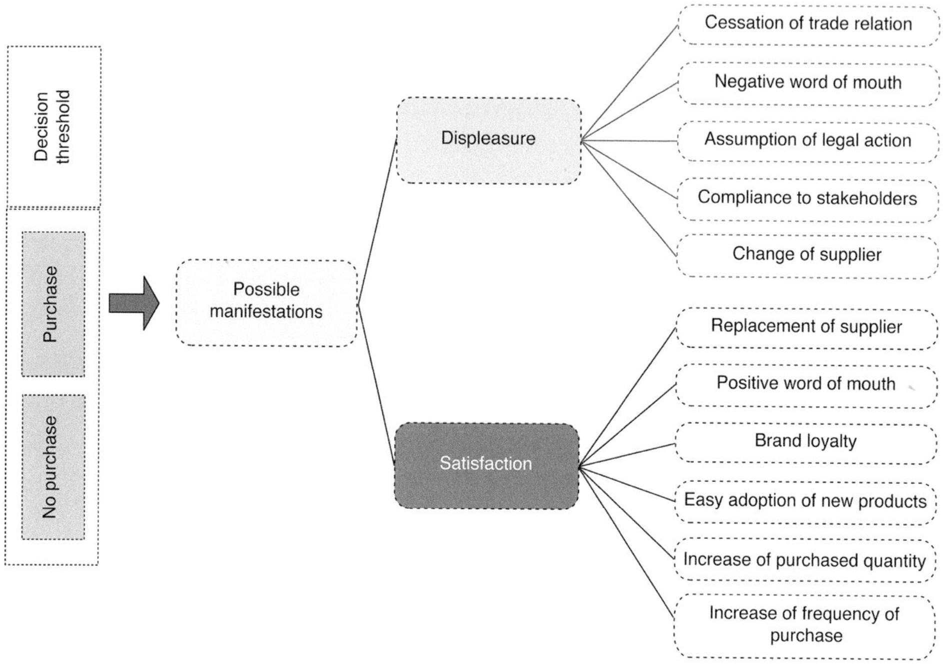

FIGURE 1.2 Possible outcomes after the realisation of a purchase

One can observe that this model essentially attempts to present a wide spectrum of and sometimes perhaps even incongruous and internally competing psychological–personal–social –cognitive parameters, to reflect and describe the influences and processes that take place during the resolution of the purchasing problem. After the realisation of the purchase, the consumer shall ascertain whether the result was worthy of the anticipated level and expectations – as is evident from the above – while the possible manifestations of the post-purchase evaluation are two, each one of which entails its own consequences and extensions (Figure 1.2).

The occurrence of the case where the client in our example shall ultimately pass in the post-purchasing stage is clearly described, since it is evident that his non-satisfaction shall entail unfavourable ramifications also for the supplier. But in this case, the total image emanated by the professional profile of the supplier, as experienced by the prospective client himself, puts the actualisation of the transaction itself in danger. The attribute 'prospective', which characterises the consumer in question at this very moment, is the key for understanding this reasoning. The client is still at one of the stages (between the 2nd, 3rd and 4th) but has yet to cross the differential threshold of realisation of the purchase of the product.

The unpunctuality and unprofessional behaviour on the side of the supplier cause similar conditions of 'discord' or disagreement, and as a result, instead of the course of the decision being linearly and stepwise directed towards the realisation of the purchase (from every previous purchase to every next step), it causes a regression to previous stages and vacillations. That is, there is the risk that the stepwise procedure be interrupted before its 5th stage. And it is obvious that the damage will be exacerbated in such a case. The supplier will be deprived of the income from the purchase and shall suffer the consequences of the client's dissatisfaction – as if the purchase had already been realised.

Naturally what most of us – with or even no experience – can almost self-evidently and intuitively describe is under no circumstances exhausted by the superficial involvement of the theoretical background of consumer behaviour in our example. However, it is indicative of the magnitude of the ramifications, which apparently harmless business attitudes, practices, cultures and philosophies that are alien to marketing may assume.

A more meticulous approach under the light of the theoretical background of marketing decodes, delimits and recommends a more analytical mapping of the framework of variables and components that led to this particular outcome. To take one example: the provider company, to attract the potential (new) client, must offer him 'superior' value, through its product offer. An 'offer' is understood to include all of the tangible and intangible characteristics of a product, the quality thereof, the level of the service rendered and the product's price. The term added value implies that in any possible comparison that the client makes – as an integral part of the 'resolution' of his purchasing problem – with competing offers, he shall decide that this particular product has greater value (Figure 1.3).

The concepts of superior and added value hold a prominent place in a wide array of economic and social sciences and are largely dependent upon (but also constituent elements of) quality. This concept is developed further in the following sections.

The concept of quality emerges as a contemporary managing philosophy, which advocates and pursues the continuous effort to improve all production variables, up to the final stage of the product and/or service (Tenner and Toro 1992).

Lovelock and Wirtz (2004) utilised the shape of a flower in service marketing to introduce the difference between core and supplementary services. According to the authors, the supplementary services that are arranged as petals in a clockwise manner around the core product play a key role by adding value to the service and can assist in differentiating from competitors. These are payment, information, consultation, order taking, hospitality, safekeeping, exceptions and billing (the mentioned sequence shows the likelihood in which they might appear).

Indeed, sometimes in addition to being important variables for taking a purchasing decision, the flower's 'petals' may be rendered even more important criteria for the realisation or not of

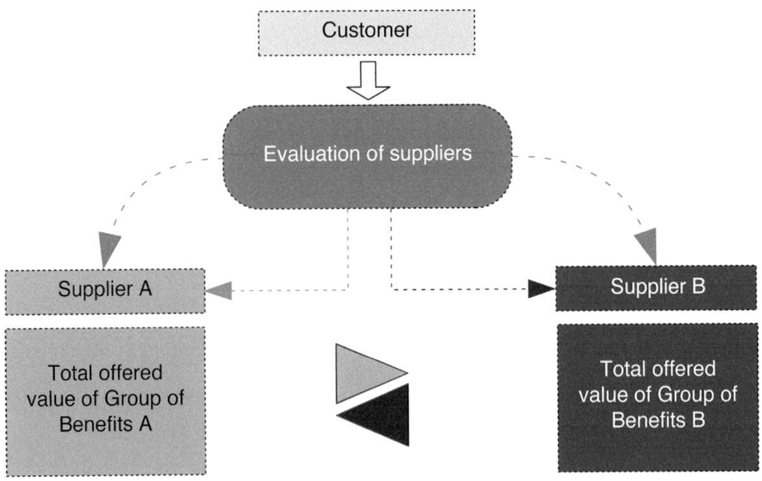

FIGURE 1.3 Comparison of competing product offers for the evaluation and selection of a supplier

the purchase than the principle and obvious reason, namely, the satisfaction of an expressed need, which reflects the core of the flower. This is easily understood should one consider the case of going out for a coffee: evidently the core is, objectively, the consumption of a tasty, invigorating drink with a strong aroma. However, could it be possible that you would be OK with something of less 'quality' as a drink, albeit one that would be served in a more relaxed environment, with a beautiful view, comfortable seating, pleasant music, polite waiters, beautiful cups, complementary snacks and patrons who were more compatible with you?

And despite the fact that the 'flower' was developed to conceptually contribute principally to the theoretical background of services marketing, this does not hinder its contribution to our example.

Important differences differentiate products from services. Most 'material' products include, in most cases, some service element, and, proportionately, services have some element of a product's material substance.

A service (even if purely and exclusively intangible) essentially performs the same function with a material product (namely, anything that may be perceived by more than two senses): it exists to provide a benefit that relates to all utilities stemming from the total product and which is perceived as an 'array of benefits' by the consumer.

But even in the case where there are sufficient guarantees to solidify the purely material nature of a product, the concept of offering greater value via provisions incorporated in the array of benefits of the good may be equally well approached. One of the most prominent marketing scholars, Theodore Levitt (1980), suggested the analysis of a product in five levels. We could illustrate Levitt's concept of various product levels as concentric circles: the inner circle is described as the 'core benefit', and every other following circle that encapsulates the previous one(s) is in following the order: 'basic product', 'expected product', 'augmented product', and 'potential product', which adds a more enhanced set of aspects that further enrich and complete the bundle of benefits offered. Specifically:

1. Core benefit: which the customer essentially buys.
2. Basic product: key components and features of the product.
3. Expected product: features of the product considered as given.
4. Augmented product: features exceeding the customer's expectations.
5. Potential product: anything over and above these features, which may excite the customers.

Given Mundell's (1968) findings and the views put forward by Wentz et al. (1973) that the product is the key weapon against competing enterprises, Figure 1.4 could be developed as in Figure 1.5.

Quality also intrinsically plays a role in the viewpoint advocating the figure above. The British Standards Institution (BSI) considers that quality may be delimited by the set of features and characteristics of a product or service based on their capacity to satisfy expressed and/or latent needs (BSI 1991).

According to Murdick et al. (1990), quality includes the degree by which the constituents of the desired (by the customers) service are attended to closely and are incorporated in the offered product, reflecting the degree of the desired levels, as defined and perceived by the customers. Moreover, should we accept the rationale by Reeves and Bednar (1994) that quality means customer satisfaction and not just safeguarding against unfavourable incidents, then the harmful effects stemming from the company's erroneous/fallacious standpoint with respect to a greater

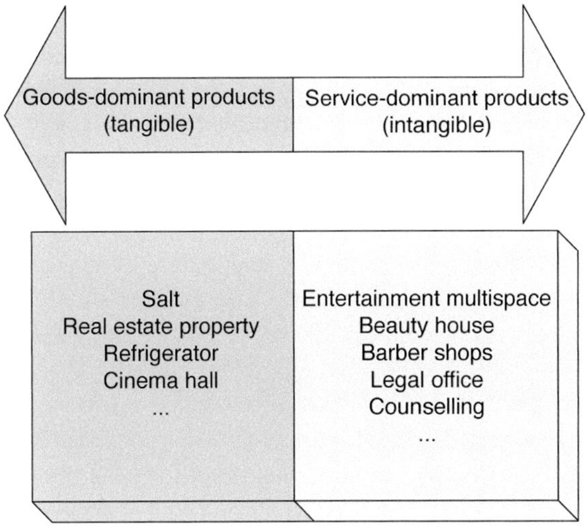

FIGURE 1.4 Service continuum

Source: Adapted from Pride and Ferrell (2014)

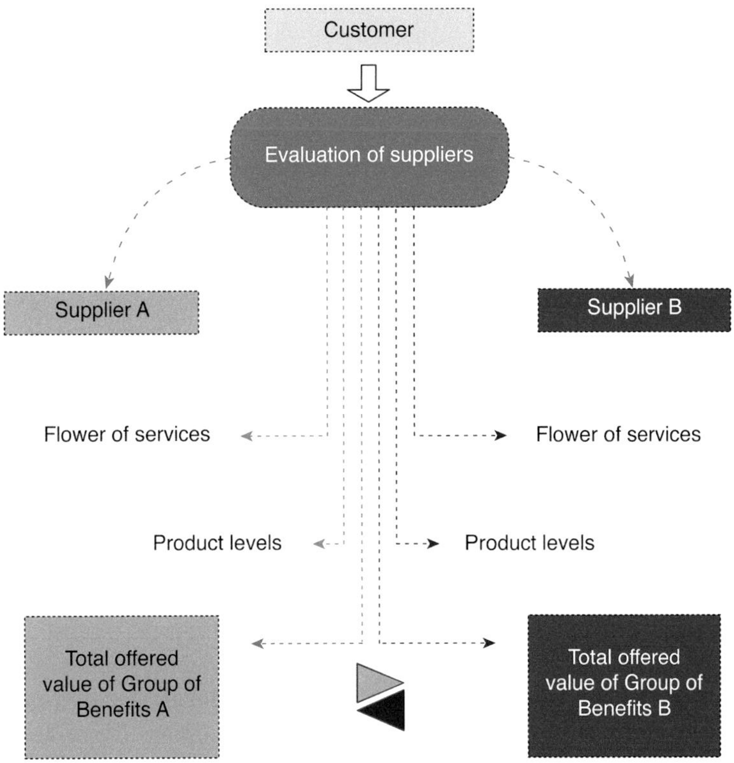

FIGURE 1.5 Comparison of competing product offers for the evaluation and selection of a supplier (fortified)

spectrum of possible consequences become clearer. In a case where the customer's zone of tolerance (the difference between the desired and the acceptable service) is transgressed/exceeded (even if only prematurely, at a pre-purchasing stage), the moment of truth (the contact between the seller and the customer, which offers the opportunity to the customer to come in contact with or evaluate or consume the product) shall be characterised as a 'critical event', namely, as a critically important service moment, not on account of his satisfaction but precisely because of his great displeasure.

Consequently, the selection of this particular supplier by the customer as the provider of the product he will purchase must entail that the 'array of benefits' of this particular offer covers a greater scope and/or greater depth of his needs for the equipment (than that catered for by the competition), and shall be rationally supported, based on the parameters, which have been theoretically developed above. This triangular relation developed between the supplier–competitors–customer is perceptible by this supplier (who, to 'close' the deal, promises more state-of-the-art systems), albeit only partially. Simultaneously, he unfortunately appears to be oblivious to equally important dimensions for its shaping and parameterisation, such as reliability, responsiveness, trust, understanding (concepts and criteria for the evaluation and review of the level of provisions), solvency, time efficiency (which can in some cases be identified with a corresponding cost in money), key variables of cost relating to waiting, concentration, access and accessibility of information that is critical for the transaction, efficiency, and what Kotler and Armstrong (2001) term the 'total acquisition cost' for a good by the customer.

Consequently, he ignores the multi-parametricity of the 'product', which he trades, some dimensions of which relate not only to its material characteristics but also to its intangible dimensions and reflect – and are described as – the special features of services marketing. The hard 'moment of truth', part of which the customer prematurely experiences, is a cumulative consequence of deficient and aimless treatment of the three tips of the amoebic form of the company organisation, which is described by the services marketing triangle (Kotler 1994).

According to Kotler (1994), the three aspects (interfaces) of services among the key constituents could be visually represented as a triangle; each of the main actors/components/constituents (i.e., enterprise, customers and employees) is attributed a vertices of the triangle. The triangle sides represent the respective interfaces formed between those key players. Accordingly, the following types of marketing relation clusters are formed:

- Interactive marketing (the triangle side that correlates the vertices of employees and customers).
- External marketing (the triangle side that correlates the vertices of enterprise and customers).
- Internal marketing (the triangle side that correlates the vertices of enterprise and employees).

Specifically, with respect to employees, external marketing accentuates the importance, which a company must attach when communicating with its customers, since it is essentially via this channel that expectations are shaped, views are formed and the benefits brought by the product, vis-à-vis the competition, become clear. Internal marketing outlines the importance that must be attributed to the relation between management (of the company) and employees, as a mandate for the realisation of the company's commitment towards customers. Interactivity reflects the communication between the customer and the employees, who have been assigned the role of the delivery of the goods and services to the customer. It is the delivery of the realisation of the company's commitments towards the customer, who shall compare it with his conception of service, as formed through the filter of expectations that were shaped by the company. In the case at hand, the 'moment of truth', namely, the dual and fixed time interaction between the supplier and customer (Surprenant and Solomon 1987), even if not already materialised, portends the occurrence of a 'critical incident', which shall be marked as indelible in the mind of the customer in a bad way.

In conclusion, the non-existence or ineffectiveness of structures for the performance of procedures, processes or efficient routines; the lack of structured and cohesive pre-designed and purposeful intra-corporate communications; and the contravention of the principle of the systematic approach act as a barrier for the positive perception of the anticipated benefit from the transaction. They lessen the value for the customer and, in a chain reaction, undermine the possibility for the successful completion or even realisation of the transaction.

And, of course, all of these may simply be the tip of the iceberg, since the dissatisfaction of one customer may cause a chain reaction. Indicatively, an unhappy customer communicates his displeasure, almost vindictively, to the quadruple number of potential customers, compared to a customer whose satisfaction lies within the framework of 'acceptable' boundaries. (In practice, this means that for every unhappy customer, one must create four happy ones.) The supplier switching cost is greater for a customer who is satisfied with his supplier. A satisfied customer shall purchase from his supplier with greater frequency and will order larger quantities, and it is more probable for him to adopt and procure products with which the supplier company expands its product line and to be involved in cross-selling.

A satisfied customer is a loyal customer. Research findings support the existence of influence and the positive relationship between the level of satisfaction and the degree of customer loyalty (e.g., Mittal and Lassar 1998), while, in parallel, the role of satisfaction as the regulator of the disposition towards the frequency of repetitions of purchases is accentuated (Mittal and Kamakura 2001).

Customer experience (namely, what constitutes and composes the total product) is shaped by the system of operation and interaction between the company/supplier and himself. What the supplier fails to understand at the present stage is that the operational/functional system of his company constitutes an integral part, which contributes to and participates in the shaping of the array of benefits offered, by means of the product, as total value to the customer. In the same way that the experience at a restaurant is not determined purely in terms of food quality, the total experience from the product 'equipment' is not exhausted purely and exclusively in terms of state-of-the-art systems with high capacity memory and fast processors.

The customer has already come across a subtotal of the characteristics and features of his total purchasing experience, which offered him value that does not correspond or is consistent with his expressed or implied needs and expectations (and, needless to say, does not exceed them) and is in discord with the initially formed views.

Via the analysis of our example so far, it is clear that marketing is a philosophy, which either due to and via its existence and application, or (unfortunately more frequently) due to and via its absence, runs both horizontally and vertically through every cell of an organisation; participates and contributes to every manifestation of its structures, operations and processes; and projectively flows into what is possibly the most important condition for the viability and prosperity of every organisation: customer satisfaction (see Figure 1.6).

Satisfaction includes, among other things, satisfaction stemming from (i) experience from usage, (ii) the purchasing experience, (iii) the service provided, but also (iv) the procedures for the acquisition and possession of the product. According to Kotler (2003), it may be defined

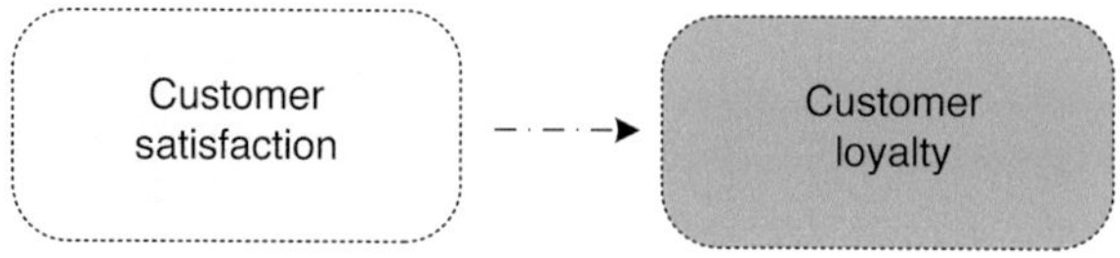

FIGURE 1.6 Relationship between customer satisfaction and loyalty

as the total emotions (positive or negative, of pleasure or displeasure) that ensue as a result of the comparison, by the consumer, of the perceived efficiency of the result and the expectations he himself anticipated from it. The quality of service carries added weight to produce satisfied customers.

1.3 Management concerns

The case presented also renders essential the need for the redesign of the works that comprise the process for the execution of an order, as well as the need for restructuring of the departments involved in this process, under, however, the light of a systems approach.

But in order for the above to occur, it is necessary to design and plan for the entire logistics system and, as an extension, the logistics systems of the businesses that are part of a supply chain (not only of the provider-company that was examined but also of the other business entities with which this company is cooperating). This planning relates to the effective and efficient organisation of all business processes that are included in the execution of an order. These processes are either performed by the various company departments or in common with other entities or members of the supply chain.

> The concept of business process is, in general, a critical parameter for the improvement of the performance of an enterprise. This happens because due to its nature a business process combines important parameters such as the mission and scope of the enterprise, its working positions and structures, the utilised resources, the users, suppliers, produced goods, production time and cost, and goals and objectives.

It is a usual practice for business organisations to rest on their key functions (e.g., sales-marketing, production, financial management, accounting, and HR; see Figure 1.7). This vertical-hierarchical way of organisation has the advantage of easy allocation of competences and responsibilities and facilitates the specialisation of work and the monitoring-supervision of specific activities. Among the shortcomings of this way of organisation, however, we find the establishment of boundaries between the departments, which facilitate the operations, posing obstacles to the realisation, on the part of the company's employees, of their contribution to the ultimate objectives of the company. This result is magnified as we examine and assess the procedures, which are performed in common by the enterprises of a supply chain. For example, the output of a procedure performed by an enterprise is usually the input for the procedure of another.

In the case presented, we saw the need to adopt a new approach for the organisation of the enterprise: one that rests on processes. A process is a structured set of activities (namely, a

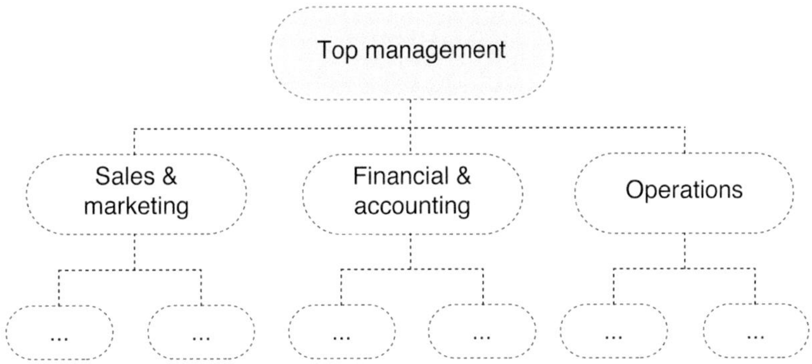

FIGURE 1.7 Business organisation based on functions

set of rationally associated works) that require human resources, information and other business resources in general, and it is designed to produce a specific and desired result for an individual client or market (Davenport 1993). Every activity in a process requires one or more works, which, if individually performed, would offer minimum added value to the company or the offered product-service. Their importance lies in the fact that they provide the framework, which allows the operations or activities of businesses to be consistent and coherent in order for the latter to attain their desired objectives.

Every process consists of three main elements: a specific event that triggers the execution of the process; the processing, i.e., the execution of the process (which usually consists of several steps/tasks that bring additional time and economic costs); and the result (the delivery of the desired product or service) that constitutes not only the goal of the process but also the reason for its existence. For example, the main elements in the 'execution of an order', which constitutes a key process performed by an enterprise daily, are

1. the event of a client placing an order;
2. the processing-execution of the order, which 'passes through' and involves several different departments of the enterprise (specifically, the order is received by the sales department; then moves on to the accounting department for credit control and invoicing; then to the logistics department, which checks the inventories; and, finally, reaches the production department for the production of the goods); and
3. the result, which is the completion of the order (Figure 1.8).

The example shows the need for an enterprise to be organised based on the processes it performs. There is a paradox here, and it lies in the fact that despite the validity of the above, businesses and organisations continue to be organised and to operate based on functions and not their processes. Even today, the dominant view on the organisation of enterprises is with reference to static schema and the typical vertical organisation. This organisation rests on competences and a design of the organisational chart that provides for the necessary administrative entities for the exercise of said competences. Despite its usefulness for the description of the hierarchical structure, the organisational chart does not describe precisely what it is that a company 'does'. Its key deficiency is that it does not cite important elements that relate to the operation of the company, such as its customers, the products and/or services offered to them; neither does it cite

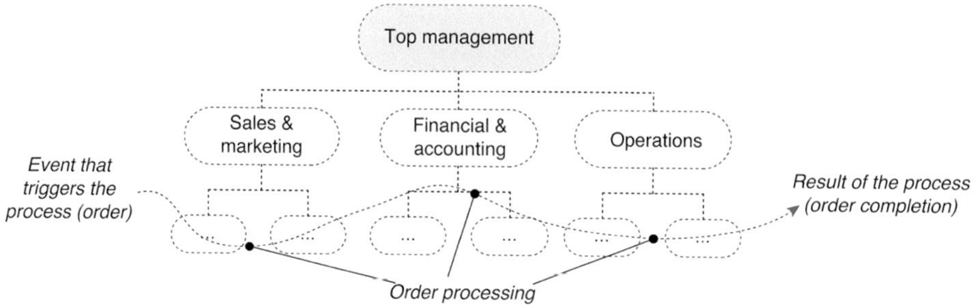

FIGURE 1.8 Example of the execution of a process

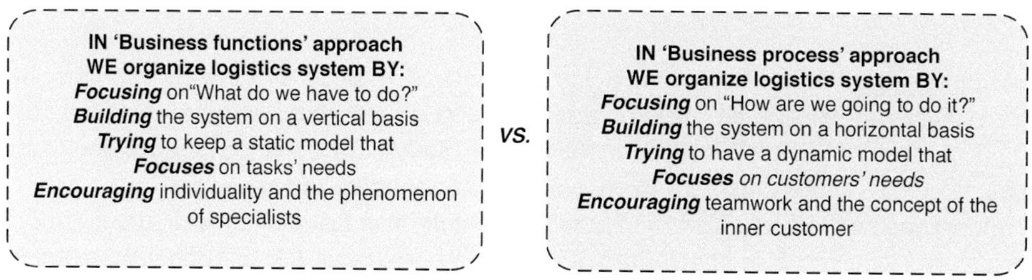

FIGURE 1.9 Business function versus business process approaches

the flow of processes it develops and by means of which it produces and transfers said products to the point where they reach the customer.

The adoption of such practices leads to negative results, such as a lack of coordination and collaboration and an inflexibility with respect to the allocation of competences and personnel that correlates with the principal objectives posed by the company's management. By adopting an organisational scheme based on functions, each company department focuses and cares about the attainment of its own objectives, ignoring on many occasions the possible interdependence between two or more departments. However, the problem emerges and becomes apparent in the case where individual objectives diverge from the common ones, which essentially and practically are to increase the offered level of service and to cut costs.

On the contrary, a modern organisation, in order for it to be able to correspond to the complex problems posed by its external environment, must be flexible, receptive to changes, networked with various bodies from its external environment and able to assimilate information/knowledge and transform it to innovative forms of action.

Figure 1.9 succinctly presents the differences between organising based on functions and on processes.

Modern forms of organising stress the dynamic elements of an organisation, placing emphasis more on the procedures for the operation and planning of action rather than on static organisational schemes. Structures are not an end but a means to an end. Terms like *business process redesign* (BPR) and *business process reengineering* have been employed to describe the change in the way enterprises today regard and treat process change. Modern restructuring methodologies have recognised the need to move away from the traditional approach, based on service units, and to turn to management, via clearly defined processes focusing on clients. To study such processes, their effective management is required, namely, the planning, monitoring and improvement of all critical business processes performed by and in an enterprise.

By focusing on processes, companies' management attempts to resolve many issues caused by the traditional, hierarchical structure, principally since such a focus promotes a philosophy that focuses on the client, manages the 'gaps' between departments and encourages teamwork, the acquisition of knowledge on the part of the employees with regard to what happens beyond their department (business functions) and how this affects and reaches the final customer, who is also the final recipient of the product (Hammer and Champy 1993). Process management includes planning and management of all necessary actions required for the attainment of a high level of performance in a process, and for the determination of opportunities for the improvement of quality, operational efficiency and, ultimately, customer satisfaction.

Of course, all of the above require collaboration between all functions of an enterprise. In the case we examine, for example, the head of sales could collaborate better and more quickly with the head of supplies to avoid the procurement costs for additional hardware. Or the call centre could simply connect the customer directly to only one employee of the company, who could have access to all information relating to the specific order. Thus, the customer would not have to contact employees from different departments.

But this presupposes the planning and performance of a unified business process, which would connect all of the company departments/executives involved in the execution of the orders or, in general, the satisfaction of demand. An ally for this effort would be the existence and use of an information system, which would allow the automatic processing of all the company's departments involved in the process of execution of orders. This would allow a specific company employee, by opening the file with the client's history, to ascertain whether he is a good customer or not, depending on the current order and the orders he had placed with the company in the past, and to see the particulars of the order under examination. He would, then, find out that the order has already been received firstly by the accounting department and then by the production department. After this, he would have also found out that part of the order had already entered the warehouse, and by issuing a simple command, he would have established that the remaining part of the order had been produced, simply by accessing the production lines. Moreover, if the employee had the capacity, using a telematics application, to be informed on the exact point of the transportation vehicle's route, then he could have informed the client with accuracy on the course of his order, so as not to be required by the latter to contact other employees from the departments involved in its execution.

All of the actions recommended above simply constitute a coherent and consistent application of a systemic approach. According to this approach, a business can be considered as a system comprising several specific subsystems. We are not interested in the success of each individual subsystem but, rather, the success of the system as a whole. This is not limited in the context of just one business but in the context of a supply chain.

In the middle of the twentieth century, researchers from different scientific disciplines recognised that an entity can be considered as part of a greater whole. They focused their interest on a set of such entities and their interaction and less on individual entities themselves. This new way of thinking was termed *systems theory*. According to it, the entirety of the entities forms a system, which cannot be dissected without losing its key characteristics and must, thus, be studied as a whole. For example, the human body is a system that depends on the coordinated function of multiple organ systems, such as the heart, the lungs, and the brain. Every part is joined and cannot function by itself. The same happens with a company, which cannot operate without marketing, production, logistics, accounting or human resources. But what we are interested in is the interaction between the departments (subsystems) and not a specific, individual department by itself.

The systems approach is attained with the coordination of the subsystems and their collaboration, aimed at the attainment of the following three objectives (which also constitute the principal goals of the management of a supply chain):

1. maximisation of overall value;
2. minimisation of overall cost; and
3. maximisation of overall profitability.

According to value chain analysis, *overall value* is defined as the difference between what the final product is worth for the customer and the effort exerted by all members in a supply chain for such product to satisfy its needs. The goal of the management of a supply chain is to select companies that can add value to the final product. Overall value is a critical factor for success in the efforts of a company to maximise the offered level of service.

Overall cost, on the other hand, is defined as the following sum: transportation expenses + storage expenses + cost of maintaining inventories + cost for the transportation of products inside the company + order processing cost + cost of buildings, machinery, etc. The goal of SCM is not to minimise the expenses of each activity individually (e.g., to minimise the cost of the management of stock or to minimise transportation costs) but to minimise total expenses (i.e., the cost across the entire supply chain). And overall cost is directly related to the offered level of service. It is impossible to attain a minimum overall cost with the simultaneous attainment of a maximum level of service. Indeed, the relation between cost increase and the increase in the level of service is not linear (it is, rather, exponential at times).

Overall profitability in a supply chain refers to the total turnover that is distributed to all of its members (or is distributed along the length of the entire supply chain). Similarly, that attainment of high overall profitability should not be regarded as the outcome of high turnover from individual businesses in a supply chain but as high profits in its entirety (or, to put it in simpler terms, overall profitability cannot be measured with reference to the individual profits of the businesses-members of the chain in isolation). High overall profitability shall ensue from the proper and efficient management of logistics processes jointly performed by the members of the chain and the flows (product, cash and information flows) between them. Only then can the desired level of service also be attained.

The systems approach can be found behind the attainment of the aforementioned goals. The idea is simple in its conception yet very difficult in its implementation: high overall value, low overall cost and high overall profitability are the results of an effective and efficient interaction of logistics processes and simply the sum thereof. The goal is to improve the system as a whole and not its individual components (system's success versus components' success).

But why is the implementation of the systems approach so difficult? There are two main obstacles: firstly, the conflicting aims/demands of the members of the supply chain. Suppliers, for example, demand from producers orders of fixed and large quantities of specific materials with adjustable delivery times, in contrast to producers who would like to have fixed production times and face an inflexible demand. Moreover, the network of companies cooperating and interacting in the context of a chain is characterised by changes, fluctuations and uncertainty.

This is, on the one hand, due to the constant change of demand, which is, in turn, caused by the changing demands of customers, and, on the other hand, due to the effects of external factors to the supply chain.

1.4 Theoretical framework/book roadmap

In the previous sections and using a case study, we established the need for a unified view of marketing and SCM in a company. Failing this, serious problems are caused, and their principal repercussions relate, on the one hand, to a low level of service for the clients and, on the other hand, to the poor and inefficient collaboration between the departments of a company, as well as between the companies-members of the supply chain.

On the other hand, it is known that *marketing* and *SCM* coexist in every company, since they fulfil the principal cause of existence of every company, which is the satisfaction of demand. These two major business functions demand a detailed conceptual approach under the light, of course, of the objective they are called to accomplish. The main objective of Chapter 2 will be to define theoretically these two disciplines – business functions. The managers of a company acknowledge the need for *coexistence*, which is the main topic of Chapter 3. But today's business arena has been changed dramatically, and it is characterised by challenges and trends not only for the examined functions but also for 'doing' business. Identification of the challenges and trends of marketing and SCM is the main objective of Chapter 4.

This book needs to also treat this relation in an integrated manner, understanding that success is attainable only through *integration*. Especially in a highly competitive and globalised market where low price and high quality are considered as given, the orientation towards the special requirements of every customer is the 'bet' placed by every company. Consequently, the key for success lies in the integration of the two functions, which coexist in every company, but also their joining for a common goal, market orientation, which is the main subject of Chapter 5.

By unifying and changing the orientation, a company revises the way it plans and performs its key activities, such as *distribution channels*, *demand handling* and *procurement*, drastically changing with both *suppliers* and *customers*. Specifically, the management levels of companies have realised that they must treat the management of the relations with the corresponding members of supply chains with the same gravity that they treat the operation of marketing and the relations with their clients.

Enterprises cannot achieve an effective and efficient planning and execution of distribution channels only by applying marketing and SCM practices and techniques of both. Both disciplines' approaches are presented and discussed in Chapter 6.

Demand handling and order execution are both marketing and SCM's main aims. Both areas must work together not only to satisfy market needs but also to reduce the operations cost. Specific techniques and methodologies are presented in Chapter 7.

Presentation and analysis of procurement from the marketing and SCM standpoints is the main objective of Chapter 8.

Typical approaches and *contemporary* ones are both allies to this effort, as are advanced *technologies*. New practices and applications exist today to support the application, on behalf of management, of a harmonious collaboration between these two critical business areas, and these are analysed in Chapters 9 and 10.

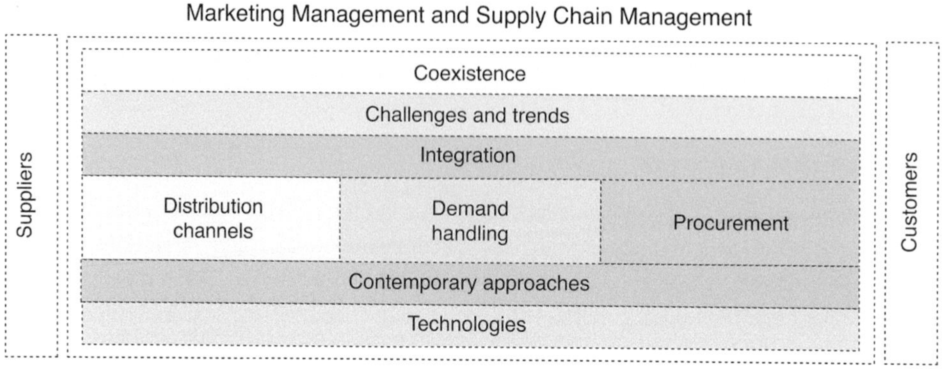

FIGURE 1.10 Theoretical framework and book roadmap

The conceptual framework on which this book is organised is shown in Figure 1.10. This conceptual framework acts as a roadmap for the topics of the book, aiming to give an integrated prism instead of a self-directed and isolated study of the aforementioned key areas.

Synopsis

- The management of the entire process of bringing a product to the market, from its inception to its final sale, is called the marketing management process.
- Logistics management is the next step in marketing, and it involves managing the system that brings products to consumers.
- SCM is the coordination of logistics systems in cooperating companies, forming a supply chain.
- Marketing pursues creating, maintaining and increasing demand (namely, the 'hunt' for order taking from customers), while logistics and SCM pursue the optimal satisfaction of demand, namely, the best execution of orders.
- Consequently, a point of focus for both marketing and SCM is order processing and handling.
- The improper execution of an order raises concerns from both the customer's and management's points of view.
- Firstly, the client experiences an unpleasant state of 'dissonance', which stems from the existence of a divergence between the planned result he anticipated – based on the agreement – and the agreement as it has been realised up to now. Or, even worse but possibly closer to reality, he experiences a cognitive dissonance, and indeed, a premature one, since this can possibly arise at a post-purchase stage.
- Moreover, improper execution of orders renders the need for redesign of the activities comprising the process for the execution of an order imperative. This is also true of the need for restructuring the departments involved in this process, under, however, the light of a systems approach.

Review and discussion questions

- What are the possible outcomes after the realisation of a purchase or not in the scenario cited at the beginning of the chapter?
- How are product and service quality defined in the example at the beginning of the chapter?

- Describe the relationship between customer satisfaction and loyalty using an example from your personal or working experience.
- What benefits will a change of organisation from business functions to business processes bring?
- Describe the systemic approach.
- Discuss ways to improve the internal processes and the way the company is organised to avoid incidences like those in the scenario discussed at the beginning of the chapter. Your response must correlate with the triangle of services marketing and the recommendations of Section 1.3. What are the expected benefits and challenges for implementing the recommendations?

Case studies

Introduction to cases: marketing and SCM

Understanding customer demand is crucial in a competitive supply chain. SCM focuses on aligning supply with demand. The lead time should be as short as possible to reduce resource constraints in the production process and to ensure that customers receive the desired products, thereby ensuring mutual value creation between the customer and the company. SCM operates systemically, meaning that decisions made in one part of the supply chain affect other parts and ultimately the entire supply chain. It is important for a company to understand its role as a link in the supply chain and act accordingly. Sometimes, this requires prioritising the overall goals of the chain over individual goals to avoid sub-optimisation. SCM requires insight, knowledge, information exchange and process integration with other companies in the supply chain.

We have witnessed an accelerating digital transformation that has changed the foundation of customer interactions and business strategies; it has also impacted SCM. However, the transformation of SCM does not stand alone. We have also seen a shift in consumer behaviour. In recent years, the acronyms VUCA – volatility, unpredictability, complexity and ambiguity – and BANI – brittle, anxious, non-linear and incomprehensible – have been used to describe these changes.

We are experiencing that what was once reliable is now vulnerable and can collapse without warning. Consumers no longer just feel uncertain; they have become anxious. Things are no longer merely complex but instead follow non-linear logical systems. Small decisions can have disproportionate effects that can be both beneficial and destructive. What was once ambiguous may now seem incomprehensible. The digital era has pushed expectations for personalisation, speed and service to new heights while also creating a dynamic where customer loyalty seems more fleeting than ever. Everyone talks about customer orientation and customer focus, but it still seems that many confuse these with a one-sided sales orientation rather than focusing on mutual value creation between the customer and the company. The focus, however, should be on the entire customer journey – not only during the sale but also in the delivery and use of products or services.

A series of events has impacted and even changed consumer habits and behaviour. We have experienced the COVID-19 pandemic and the war in Europe, where Ukraine was attacked by Russia in February 2022. Since then, we have seen the war between Israel and Gaza, where Hamas terrorists attacked Israel in October 2023. These wars have left their unfortunate marks on many innocent lives in the affected countries, and territories have also led to an energy crisis and the resurgence of the Cold War. For example, the energy crisis is particularly challenging and is reshaping how consumers use their disposable income. Additionally, there has been an inflation crisis.

It does not take much for an event, such as a ship blocking the Suez Canal, to disrupt global trade, as we saw in the spring of 2021 when the container ship *Ever Given* blocked traffic for 6 days, affecting world trade. At the time of writing, there are challenges in the Red Sea – this time due to attacks from pirates and Houthi forces in Yemen. This has resulted in a halving of the share of sea freight passing through the Suez Canal. The numerous attacks on ships in the Red Sea have led to delays and higher freight costs. Additionally, there are increasing climate changes and challenges these have already caused and will continue to cause in the future. The challenge for companies is that all these are external events they cannot control, yet the companies still require real-time insights and data to provide a solid decision-making foundation and ensure agility in their actions.

VUCA

Crises are coming in waves these days. This presents many challenges for marketing, SCM, sales and service. How should companies change internally and interact with their stakeholders to navigate the rapid changes in consumer behaviour and market conditions? The concept of VUCA clearly sets the stage for working with customers and the market. This concept can be described as follows:

Volatility: The development is both fleeting and unpredictable. The word 'volatility' comes from the Latin *volatilis*, which means flying or fleeting. In the context of change management, volatility is used to describe situations where things happen quickly, and trends can be changing without warning. Therefore, the essence of volatility lies in the high degree of changeability and the fact that it is often unpredictable.

Unpredictability: Nothing is certain, not even what one currently knows. The moment you feel confident in your knowledge and believe you have thoroughly understood things, it is already starting to change. This creates a sense of uncertainty, which can lead to a blockage in how one absorbs new knowledge and in how one communicates knowledge and changes to employees. As a leader of change or associated processes, you may find it difficult to be convincing and motivating when both you and your employees feel that there is significant uncertainty involved.

Complexity: The world and reality we operate in are more complex than before. Many factors come into play, making navigation challenging. For example, there can be political factors, both domestic and international, that affect one's business. Strong, autonomous movements within the general population can also arise, as seen in recent years, with sudden so-called shitstorms on social media and subsequently in traditional media. These various currents can, without warning, alter customers' and other stakeholders' perceptions of the company and its partners, products and services. The currents influence each other and create a reality that cannot be defined or predicted but which leaders must be able to respond swiftly and with the right direction to guide the company and its employees safely through.

Ambiguity: This concept encompasses the duality that developments and changes also create. For example, communication has become easier and faster with digital meetings on Teams, FaceTime and Skype, as well as with emails and smartphones, compared to the past with faxes, letters and long journeys for face-to-face meetings. However, rapid communication can also lead to misunderstandings, create stress or be disruptive in an already busy daily routine. Modern companies must be able to address such paradoxes.

BANI

In relation to VUCA, BANI adds an additional dimension. The concept provides further insight into the challenges that businesses and leaders face in an increasingly volatile and complex world. The factors involved in BANI highlight the fragile balance that must be navigated, and the often ruthless nature of the consequences that follow from missteps or overlooked risks. This concept can be described as follows:

Brittle: Systems, structures or relationships are more likely to break down or fail under pressure than previously assumed. This may be due to excessive optimisation for efficiency at the expense of robustness or an inability to absorb shocks and stress.

Unforgiving: Errors and missteps in today's world can have immediate and severe consequences. This reality underscores the need for careful risk management and often a higher degree of caution in decision-making.

Non-linear: Even small changes in inputs can lead to unpredictable and disproportionate effects. This complicates planning and forecasting and requires a more dynamic and flexible approach to strategy and management. We are shifting from a linear reality to a circular one with feedback loops.

Incomprehensible: This concept describes a dimension of complexity where situations or information can be so intricate or overwhelming that they become difficult to understand and interpret. It points to an environment where traditional methods of making sense and predictions often fall short.

The above can be summarised as follows: if something is vulnerable, it requires focus, resources and resilience; if there is anxiety, it calls for empathy and attention; if something is non-linear, it demands insight, readiness for change and adaptability; and if something is incomprehensible, it requires analysis, transparency and intuition.

Ongoing crises thus sharply highlight the need for marketing and SCM to be flexible, fast and agile as things change. Data and customer insights play a larger and more crucial role in efforts to ensure the company's growth and development. In this process, loyalty has also become a central element. Therefore, access to data and the ability to interact with customers in real time are also critical factors. This places new demands on systems and on ways of working and organising within the company. It is important to focus on what the company can influence and distinguish it from external factors that cannot be directly impacted.

Demands for marketing and SCM

From the company's perspective, one might argue that customers have become uncontrollable. Many businesses are experiencing a scarcity of customers and, for some, also capital, combined with a recognition that the effectiveness of marketing has been declining. It is fundamental that technology is in place so companies can operate in real time. However, this is only one side of the equation. We must also be organised and mentally prepared for this. Our mindset needs to be in sync with customers and the market. This demands much from marketing and SCM.

Changes in the way customers shop, combined with an explosion of customer touchpoints (i.e., the customer journey) and rapidly shifting competitive and technological dynamics, have led to an increased emphasis on agile marketing and, consequently, real-time responsiveness. This can be conceptualised as spanning various organisational levels and has proven to be distinct from related concepts within marketing and similar fields. Marketing agility is about quickly understanding customers and their needs, as well as implementing the necessary marketing decisions.

Marketing agility demands the company's ability to ensure brand consistency, scale agility across the marketing ecosystem and manage data protection issues. It also requires understanding marketing flexibility as a concept and in relation to the hiring of marketing managers and staff (mindset), training and education, and performance goals. However, there must also be a focus on customers, as they, for example, choose the sales channel: Research Online, Purchase Online (ROPO model) versus Research Online, Buy Offline (ROBO model); Buy Online, Pick Up in Store (BOPIS) or ORPO (Offline Research, Purchase Online). Customers' mindset and, importantly, the customer journey should be considered in these deliberations.

Another takeaway is that the agile marketing organisation must shift from a fundamental mindset of working in campaigns to operating through processes and activities. This shift demands changes in the way work is conducted and, importantly, in the competencies and resources available. Many organisations will likely bring tasks in-house from agencies, for instance, to respond in real time, which may present challenges to the usual 9-to-5 work schedule. Global companies will set up 24/7 teams around the world to ensure there are always employees available to monitor activities, such as on social media.

Marketing agility and working in real time have a significant impact on SCM. Both concepts help companies be more responsive and flexible to market and customer needs. Let us now examine how these concepts specifically affect SCM.

Increased demand for flexibility: Marketing agility means that companies must quickly adjust their marketing strategies in response to changes in customer behaviour, trends and competition. This agility puts pressure on SCM to also be able to respond swiftly and flexibly. When marketing changes campaigns or launches new products in real time, the supply chain must be able to rapidly adjust production, distribution and inventory management to accommodate these changes. For example, if a company discovers that a particular product is suddenly trending on social media, SCM must quickly scale up production of that product to meet the increased demand. Products shared on TikTok are a good example of fast-moving trends that challenge the value chain.

Just-in-time delivery and inventory optimisation: Real-time work in marketing means that decisions about production and delivery need to be made more quickly. SCM therefore must adopt just-in-time delivery, where production is streamlined to avoid overproduction and inefficient inventory levels. This minimises waste and ensures that products are always available at the right times, which reduces costs and increases efficiency.

Data-driven decision-making: Real-time data from marketing (i.e., the company) enables SCM to make more accurate and faster decisions. When marketing teams work in real time, they gather data on consumer trends, demand and feedback that can be shared with SCM. This allows for the optimisation of the supply chain based on up-to-date information. For example, if data show that a particular geographic area is suddenly experiencing high demand for a product, SCM can quickly redirect supplies to that area.

Improved collaboration and integration: When marketing and SCM work in real time, it enhances collaboration between the two functions, enabling rapid adaptation and coordinated efforts. This reduces delays and ensures that marketing initiatives are supported by an efficient supply chain. For example, this can result in marketing campaigns being launched with confidence that the supply chain is ready to deliver, preventing situations where there is a shortage of goods when demand peaks.

Increased customer satisfaction: By working agilely and in real time, companies can ensure they meet customers' expectations for fast deliveries and availability. Agile SCM can ensure that products are available when and where customers want them, which increases customer satisfaction and loyalty. For example, rapid changes in delivery schedules or production adjustments based on real-time customer data can ensure that customers have the best possible experience.

Risk management: Real-time work enables SCM to identify and respond to potential risks quickly. These risks could include issues related to suppliers, changes in raw material prices or unforeseen events such as natural disasters. By working agilely, SCM can respond swiftly and adjust its strategies to minimise the impact on the supply chain.

Cases on marketing and SCM

The textbook includes several case studies that provide detailed examinations and context for specific concepts or situations, helping illustrate and explore the theories and practices covered in marketing and SCM. For the case studies, we would like to acknowledge the following contributors:

- Michael Antioco (Purchasing and marketing of social and environmental sustainability).
- Jinsun Bae (Global value chains and supplier perceptions of corporate social responsibility).
- Michael Beverland (Relationship use and market dynamism).

- Misty P. Blessley (A systematic approach to distribution channels; buyer–seller exchange situations; Fulfilling customer demand for fresh convenience foods; relationship use and market dynamism; digital technologies in the food supply chain; technologies for marketing and SCM synergies; the moment of truth in food service: efficient customer co-creation; using the Kraljic matrix to inform synergistic supply chain decisions).
- David B. Grant (Fourth-party logistics management in grocery retailer relationships).
- Martin K. Hingley (Processes and integration in the interaction of purchasing and marketing; supplier–retailer relationships in the fresh produce supply chain; using fourth-party logistics management in grocery retailer relationships).
- Per Østergaard Jacobsen (Destination digital: optimising tourism with data; how SCM determines where customers shop for DIY supplies; Maersk app: integrated logistics in the palm of your hand; using data from toilets to improve service and optimise resource utilisation; Volvo CE: how SCM enhances the value chain).
- Wesley J. Johnston (Configurations of purchasing practices).
- Charles Kane (Fourth-party logistics management in grocery retailer relationships).
- Peter Lund-Thomsen (Global value chains and supplier perceptions of corporate social responsibility).
- François Maon (A model of corporate social responsibility; designing and implementing corporate social responsibility; strategically leveraging corporate social responsibility; tensions in coopetition for sustainable innovation; the organisation as a system).
- Rob Morgan (Processes and integration in the interaction of purchasing and marketing).
- Pauline Munten (Tensions in coopetition for sustainable innovation).
- John Nicholson (Rapidus, IBN and Global Friendshoring).
- Jacquie Pels (Buyer–seller exchange situations).
- Valérie Swaen (A model of corporate social responsibility; designing and implementing corporate social responsibility; tensions in coopetition for sustainable innovation; the organisation as a system).
- Mark Toon (Processes and integration in the interaction of purchasing and marketing).
- Christine A. Vallaster (Corporate brand strategy formation; strategically leveraging corporate social responsibility).
- Remi van der Sloot (Purchasing and marketing of social and environmental sustainability).
- Joëlle Vanhamme (Configurations of purchasing practices; processes and integration in the interaction of purchasing and marketing; tensions in coopetition for sustainable innovation).
- Erik van Raaij (Configurations of purchasing practices).
- Ghasem Zaefarian (Digital transformation in SCM).
- Qi Zhang (Digital transformation in SCM).

Multiple-choice questions

1. What principal concern arises when a company's departments fail to collaborate effectively in order fulfilment?

   A. Increased supplier loyalty
   B. Premature cognitive dissonance

C. Higher employee satisfaction
D. Reduced production costs

2. Which theory explains a customer's psychological tension after a purchase decision?

A. Maslow's hierarchy
B. Cognitive dissonance theory
C. Monopolistic competition
D. Value chain analysis

3. What critical factor differentiates competing product offers in buyer evaluation?

A. Packaging colour
B. Superior perceived value
C. Supplier location
D. Tax implications

4. According to Levitt's product levels, which tier exceeds customer expectations?

A. Core benefit
B. Basic product
C. Augmented product
D. Potential product

5. The 'service continuum' concept primarily distinguishes:

A. Goods versus services
B. Price versus quality
C. Pre-sales versus post-sales support
D. Supplier versus distributor roles

6. What organisational shift minimises departmental silos?

A. Functional specialisation
B. Business process redesign
C. Hierarchical restructuring
D. Inventory centralisation

7. Which objective is NOT part of SCM's systemic approach?

A. Maximising overall value
B. Minimising departmental autonomy
C. Reducing total costs
D. Enhancing profitability

8. Customer loyalty is most directly correlated with:

A. Product availability
B. Post-purchase satisfaction
C. Marketing budget size
D. Supplier lead times

9. The 'moment of truth' in service marketing refers to:

   A. Product launch timing
   B. Customer–employee interaction
   C. Inventory restocking
   D. Supplier contract signing

10. A key deficiency of traditional functional organisation is:

    A. Excessive customer focus
    B. Lack of process visibility
    C. High employee turnover
    D. Overemphasis on innovation

11. Which metric measures supply chain success holistically?

    A. Individual department ROI
    B. Total system profitability
    C. Warehouse capacity
    D. Supplier count

12. The 'zone of tolerance' in service quality relates to:

    A. Geographic delivery ranges
    B. Acceptable versus desired service levels
    C. Inventory buffer stocks
    D. Pricing flexibility thresholds

13. What drives the exponential cost–service level relationship?

    A. Economies of scale
    B. Diminishing returns
    C. Supplier bargaining power
    D. Marketing campaigns

14. A systemic approach prioritises:

    A. Departmental KPIs
    B. End-to-end process success
    C. Short-term cost cuts
    D. Regulatory compliance

15. Which is NOT a post-purchase evaluation outcome?

    A. Repeat purchases
    B. Brand advocacy
    C. Cognitive harmony
    D. Supplier diversification

Essay question

The case study highlights cognitive dissonance arising from misaligned pre-purchase promises and post-purchase experiences, undermining customer loyalty. This dissonance stems from fragmented departmental workflows under functional silos, where sales, production and logistics operate independently. Business process redesign advocates shifting to cross-functional workflows, enabling real-time data sharing and unified customer interaction points. A systemic approach integrates marketing (demand creation) and SCM (order fulfilment) by viewing the organisation as interdependent subsystems. This alignment minimises value gaps, reduces lead times and ensures consistent service quality. Together, these concepts address dissonance through cohesive process management, operational transparency and strategic integration, ensuring customer expectations match delivered value across the supply chain.

2

INTRODUCTION TO MARKETING AND SUPPLY CHAIN MANAGEMENT

Introduction

What should remain at least detectable from the case examined previously is the fact that a function or a department is not worth much if the next department fails. Success does not follow from the success of one function or one department, it depends on the whole. The key parameters and essentials of the contemporary cognitive fields of marketing and supply chain management (SCM) are presented in this chapter, together with their contribution in the value chain. The goal of this chapter is to provide a convincing and documented cognitive framework for the two concepts, which will also function as an aid for navigating the other chapters, equipping the reader's critical thinking with the necessary conceptual and cognitive tools. The rationale on which the two business functions are structured is that they predominantly constitute a customer-oriented approach. As such, it aspires for the maximum possible satisfaction of needs in an effective and efficient manner, always placing the customer at the core of its interest and the ultimate culmination of all of its actions and processes.

Learning objectives

After reading this chapter, you will be able to answer the following questions:

- What are the limits of marketing and SCM?
- What is marketing and what is it not?
- What are the key parameters facilitating the conceptual approach to the function/operation of marketing?
- How is SCM defined?
- How do marketing and SCM affect the definition of value chain?

Outline

2.1 Identifying the limits of marketing and SCM
2.2 What is marketing?

DOI: 10.4324/9781003650973-2

2.3 What is SCM?
2.4 Key parameters and essentials of the contemporary knowledge fields of the areas of marketing and SCM and their constitution in the value chain

2.1 Identifying the limits of marketing and SCM

Every enterprise consists of these main functions (among others): operations management, marketing and sales, and accounting and finance (Figure 2.1).

Operations management may be considered as an umbrella over all disciplines relating to the management (namely, planning, execution, monitoring and control) of all operations, which convert the resources of a business to products and services by implementing its strategy aimed to the satisfaction of demand. Operations management includes scientific fields such as production management, quality management, human resources management, business processes management, logistics management and SCM.

Sales and marketing

Marketing may be delimited as the managerial philosophy, which places customer satisfaction at the centre of its interest and efforts, trying to offer added value products and services. It is an integrated, systematically structured, total system of business activities, designed in such a way so as to satisfactorily cover and cater for certain fields of creation of products, their distribution and pricing, and their promotion.

The set square for the adopted orientation is the undeviating dedication to ensuring the conditions guaranteeing the effectiveness and efficiency of transactions that offer utility–value–usefulness–satisfaction to the consumer. Furthermore, an indivisible part of this customer-oriented approach lies with the fact that the long-term viability and profitability of the enterprise, which rest on the attainment of the goals set, are attainable exclusively only as the result of offering superior value to the customer, satisfied by means of the array of benefits that the company's product offers.

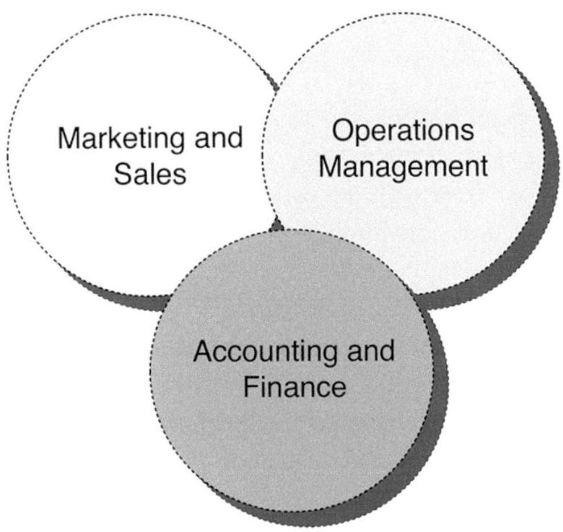

FIGURE 2.1 Main functions of an enterprise

> Despite the fact that sales constitute a subset of marketing and their 'paired' presentation is thus somewhat exaggerated, it shall be employed in this textbook principally based on the assumption of the significant gravity many businesses in the international arena (even in the expression of their organisational charts) place on what they consider (largely erroneously) as the only caterer for the enterprise's revenues.

Accounting and finance

Accounting is the systematic process of identifying, recording, classifying, verifying, summarising, reporting and analysing the financial transactions of an organisation. Financial management is the planning, directing, monitoring, organising and controlling of the monetary resources of an organisation. Accounting is mainly associated with the line managers at the tactical level of the company, while financial management is directly associated with the top management.

2.2 What is marketing?

This section aims to offer a concise, yet simultaneously integrated and multidimensional, introduction to the scientific discipline of marketing. It grants access to the constituent elements that compose the conceptual background required for the initiation of the reader and the firing of the learning procedure of the subject matter. The definition of fundamental concepts – essentially the building blocks for the elementary and basic knowledge and information – first and foremost allows the establishment of a commonly acceptable communication code.

The delimitation, on the conceptual plane, of these key ingredients creates a fertile ground for the understanding, realisation and ability to accept and use the cognitive subject, which this endeavour tackles. A series of widely acceptable assumptions render imperative the need to understand that core material on which the edifice of marketing rests, is structured and is developed (independently of the degree of penetration or the level of specialisation with respect to the intricacies of functional education), with those building blocks acting as catalysts and constituting the *sine qua non* conditions for comprehending and for dwelling deeper in the ideology and the philosophy of the subject matter. These assumptions include the following:

- The fact that marketing, principally in the course of the last decade, has been rendered as one of the most widely popular scientific disciplines in the toolbox of modern strategic-operating and tactical planning, combined with the fact that at the same it continues to be a contested subject with respect to its goals, methodology, effectiveness and – frequently – its scientific merits.
- The in-depth development of subsets – sub-branches or subsections of the edifice of this cognitive subject brought about by a more specialised and targeted-integrated scientific approach to not only existing but also emerging issues and to neighbouring areas.
- The exponentially greater perceived need for the detailed, scientific, systematic and integrated mapping; realised evaluation and, ultimately, utilisation of the common ground established by the creation of points due to the aforementioned investigation and probing of the subject matter and the corresponding validity of the same regime for the development of many other – principally social – sciences.

Regardless of the fact that if someone is engaged with 'services marketing' on account of his professional activity, or studies 'introduction to marketing' as part of his degree, and/or wishes to delve deeper in the interdisciplinary field that is the common ground between marketing and SCM, the elementary understanding of the fundamental conceptual framework is crucial. As a requirement, it precedes any other learning process, while it is also directly correlated with the ability to compose, which is positively related to the effectiveness of the 'cure'.

Someone who is called to put marketing to practice and has a deficient knowledge of the discipline will act in proportion as adversely for his field of action as does, for example, a doctor who recommends a medicine without adequately knowing the qualities and characteristics of its ingredients. The development (but also the application) of 'therapeutic' methodologies for a subject presupposes the existence of understanding of the composition of the elementary particles – concepts that constitute it. The level of efficiency and the very nature of marketing's effectiveness largely depend on the initial understanding of the 'mapping' of its basic structural characteristics, which ultimately compose the nature of its entity and render to it the very reason for its existence.

In addition to the above, the approach of the delimitation on the conceptual level shall act as a touchstone, offering the motivation for consideration and firing the interest for the systemic integration with the principles and 'axioms' from other scientific disciplines, the expected synergies that might potentially ensue, the common aspirations, the complementary means and tools and, in general, the entire framework of this web of cross-correlations, which always begins from the same, common pursuit: *the satisfaction of needs*.

Marketing: An introductory conceptual approach

Most books on marketing usually begin by citing definitions on what marketing is, as part of an effort for an effective fundamental delimitation of the nature and the essential character of the subject matter. There are many valid approaches, which, by sometimes adopting slightly differentiated viewpoints, essentially describe the fundamental characteristics of the scientific background of this cognitive field. They incorporate components and variables, which are the constitutive structures, sometimes of its function, at other times of the ideology and orientation governing its philosophy, and yet other times of the adopted tools and strategies in its quiver – toolbox.

The approach adopted here can be likened to the well-known Socratic *maieutics* method. This approach begins by attempting to make a clear and conscious delimitation of the concepts and of the relations and associations that essentially describe the framework of the not directly visible conventions in which people exist and function as consumer beings. Following this, these fundamental conceptual stones are composed into a greater edifice of whose structure they are integral parts, while the understanding and acceptance of the principles and of the function of the edifice shall be rendered clearer as the analysis and clarification of the concepts progress. What is essentially employed and utilised is the stepwise association of the constituent parts of the 'whole', in an attempt to elicit the conscious framework of acquired knowledge and to shape the thought algorithm so as to converge and conclude freely and seamlessly to the level of composition discussed by the expressed approaches.

It is obvious that the following pages shall not render the reader an expert in marketing. This chapter does not aim to exhaustively cite the full framework of factors, variables, mechanisms, methodology, analytical tools and components that compose the theoretical context of the science in a scholastic manner. This is offered by works that are exclusively devoted to the analysis of the specialised cognitive areas and fields of the science of marketing.

The exploration of marketing will begin by defining and delimiting the concepts of need and desire.

Delimitation of the concept of need

Need possibly plays the key leading role since it constitutes not only the raw material for the entire mental edifice but also the joining web, which connects almost the entirety of all of the associated concepts under a common prism and orientation. As such, it participates in, determines and delimits a wide spectrum of notions, which also outline the way to approach it. It participates in the designation, shaping and clarification of – among others – the concepts of product, benefit and exchange and a wide spectrum of other concepts closely associated with marketing.

Need as the cohesive bond and mobilising force for action

The first characteristic of need is its almost universal participation in the context of marketing's 'philosophy'. This is easy to understand since need essentially constitutes the 'kick in the butt' that mobilises human behaviour for action (motivation), in order for it to be satisfied, fulfilled, staved off or 'smoothened'. It defines a wide spectrum of concepts and actions, which, without exaggeration, one could claim 'make the world round'. It is precisely this characteristic of the cohesive bond that has been placed in the spotlight, but also under the microscope of a dialectical debate. Besides, beyond the motives for a particular behaviour and the taking of action in order for need to cease to exist, there is also a fairly large degree of polemic in the modern vernacular relating to the designation of the 'red lines' between the concepts of need and desire.

Definition of the concept of desire/'gradations' – vagueness of the distinction between need and desire

And while we typically converge to view desire as a vehicle with the capacity to satisfy (in some particular or preferred way) a need, these boundaries are in reality vague and difficult to see, and the discourse takes on an interdisciplinary character. Sociologists, psychologists, human behaviourists and researchers from political and economic sciences ascertain and formulate conflicting, yet frequently complementary, occurrences of the concepts – which reflect on common perceptions. In this context, it is frequent for there to be a common understanding that desire is, subjectively, a less imperative concept (since it involves an element of 'luxury', of the choice for the selected/particular preferred way of catering for a need). Indeed, some invoke Maslow's framework (Maslow distinguishes needs using adjectival designations, e.g., biological, safety and self-fulfilment) to proceed with a differentiation of needs: basic – lack of which entails that a living organism cannot survive – and, therefore, 'genuine' needs and non-basic ones, which, as a consequence and equivalently, are desires (e.g., Maslow 1943, 1970; Maslow and Murphy 1954). The logic of this grading depends on the perceived level of importance but frequently runs up against the multidimensional and multi-parametric texture of the human (and consequently the consuming) substance itself: human beings are multidimensional and manifold beings, distinguished by an extraordinarily indeterminate array of perceived characteristics and qualities. Both the depth and the dynamic of the constituent elements that shape their views render rather fallacious any extortionate and one-sided attempt at a one-dimensional delimitation using strict and hermetic separating limits, which serve conceptual means. Consequently, there can't be a categorisation of needs expressed as steps of desire (the converse is also true: one cannot express desire in scales of need), at least not in a widely accepted, scholastically scientific and/or 'politically correct' way, which would enjoy the same validity regardless of the circumstances. No one can claim with certainty (or, even more, no one can prove) to anybody else whether the feeling experienced is that of need or of desire.

Is it really that difficult to separate need from desire? Is it really that difficult for us to ultimately reach some consensus on this issue? Consider the case of a homeless person who is cold and hungry. Could one claim that such a homeless person 'desires' food and shelter, and not simply that he needs them, such that his need is an imperative? Or, in any case, even if he simply wishes for food and shelter, that the intensity of his desire is more than, say, the intensity with which someone 'desires' (or even has 'the need for') the replacement of his luxurious car with a more expensive model? However, what about the fact that the monks and hermits of almost all religious persuasions renounce the satisfaction of their 'earthly' needs (where such abstinence relates to all four levels of needs based on Maslow's model) to fulfil the need (basic to them) for 'self-fulfilment'. It is obvious that the method of maximisation and overemphasising for reasons relating to clarity of the arguments is not self-evident in as much as reality is seldom equally as theatrical. Reality cannot be described in black or white: it is better to assess it using shades of grey.

Approach of demand and its contribution in the 'entanglement' of need and desire

And it is precisely at this point that things can get more complicated if someone was to incorporate the definition of demand (marketing-wise) to this complex web of inter-associations: 'Demand is the translation of desire when the prospective customer has the resources to pay the price'. What happens in the case where some unpleasant feeling of emptiness cannot be covered due to lack of resources? Does this inability to translate it into demand, due to the inability of being able to pay the price, render it a need or not? Is it a desire or not?

Further approaches to the concepts of need and desire

Reduction to the real world shows that over-exaggeration and simplification are frequently not sufficient and that the intrinsic subjective character that runs through both concepts renders their full and subjective separation largely vague. Nobody will ever be able to adequately set the result by comparing the unpleasant feeling experienced by a family wishing to move to a safer urban complex against the corresponding feeling of a family wishing to upgrade its dietary menu by adding organic products, let alone to characterise either perceived deficit as need or as desire in an absolute way.

According to Kotler and Armstrong (2009), need refers to states manifesting a sense of deprivation, while desire is the form assumed by human needs, such as those shaped by culture and the individuals' personality, while demand is defined to mean needs covered by purchasing power (Figure 2.2). Since, however, further clarification of this division – or even the existence thereof – lies outside the scope and objectives of this work and following the dialectic

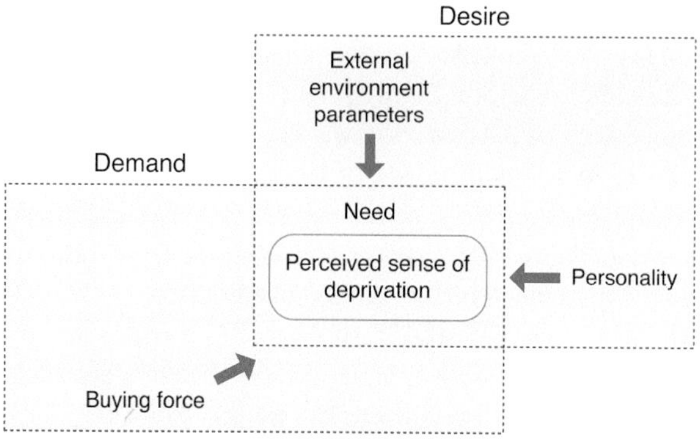

FIGURE 2.2 'Need' as a subset of 'desire' and 'demand'

developed in the context of what mobilises behaviour, the writers adopt the logic, which is schematically presented below and constitutes a more conciliatory proposition, that defines need as the 'unpleasant feeling that I am lacking something'.

'A little of what you fancy does you good', the monkey said, and ate the soap! (Besides, who could possibly blame him for what he fancies? What 'objective' criteria would such criticism rest on? And, moreover, for any criticism, which could be formulated, perhaps, for example, by a person from India, Russia or Greece, what criticisms could correspondingly be raised against, say, curry, vodka or moussaka?)

Independent of whether the delimitation of this concept is a disputed point or the subject/carrier of adjectival designations or even the field of interdisciplinary debate, indisputably the need to, and, to be more precise, the attempt to satisfy it besides 'making the world go round' is also the connecting link for fundamental concepts and positions in marketing.

Delimitation of the concept of product

Another significant concept when attempting to define marketing is product. We adopted a fairly wide definition of need, which ensued largely as the result of a deliberate and 'creative ambiguity' to avoid 'blinker' viewpoints. The concept of product almost directly follows from the definition of need: anything that has the capacity to lessen or stave off the unpleasant feeling that something is missing is considered as 'product'.

The product as a set of benefits

Even though the description above directly delimits its concept, the product, nonetheless, being a key factor, demands further clarification. The newly initiated to this field must avoid a one-dimensional perception of it. Instead, he must consider product as a 'bouquet' – a set/package of qualities and advantages that has the capacity to offer satisfaction (or at a minimum 'soothe' the unpleasant feeling that something is lacking) in various ways through the array of benefits it can offer. To understand this better, one must first understand the concept of need against the broad spectrum of dimensions, which may clad it, and, following this, accept the complexity of the nature of a product as the direct result of the web of interrelations that it carries with it (Figure 2.3).

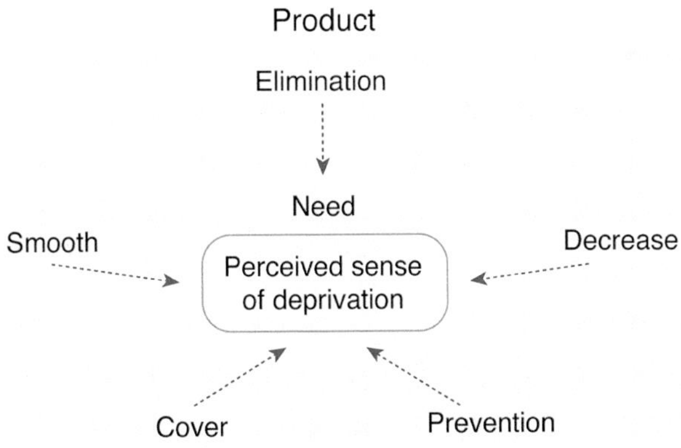

FIGURE 2.3 Sketching the association of 'need' and 'product'

Dimensions of the definition of the concept of product

Consequently, in order for someone to perceive this wide spectrum of factors that constitute a product, one must recompile one's perceptions and comprehend that the array of benefits can refer to or ensue from the covering of needs, which are not manifest on the conscious level by 'everyday' consumers. Specifically, a product is

- one of the four Ps in the marketing mix (see Figure 2.7, p. 37);
- the result of a need being catered for due to its use, and as such, a variable reflecting the efforts that (must) take place to sense and listen to the consumer's preferences;
- the result of a productive process, directed by the producer, depending on the characteristics expressed by consumers (and not the producer himself);
- something that is susceptible to change (Thompson 1962); only if, however, someone accepts the cost entailed. Consumers are a different kettle of fish, since one can only hope to influence them but at a very high cost. Assessing the cost and the feasibility of change for each of the aforementioned variables, one can safely reach the conclusion that the most financially sound, effective and easy way is to do things correctly from the beginning, namely, to determine the needs of consumers and build the satisfaction thereof as structural elements of the product, instead of trying to convince consumers to show a demand for what you produce. Namely, despite the fact that the quiver of marketing's tools offers a multitude of such tools, it is deemed more prudent for the procedure relating to the satisfaction of needs to commence from listening to consumers' needs and for the product to facilitate the catering for such needs. This assumption constitutes a genuine expression but is also a manifestation of the customer-oriented inclination of marketing. In conclusion, a successful product is not sold by producers, it is bought by consumers;
- what the consumer 'sees' (or 'votes for', for one can draw a direct parallel between the voter/consumer and the vote/price, in the sense that in both cases there is an implicit trust by voters/consumers that the 'product' for which they paid the price/cast their votes will cater, as it promises to do, for their needs);
- the reason for the existence of every enterprise;
- the cornerstone of every economic activity;

- that which reflects the efforts by every enterprise to match its resources and abilities with consumers' demands;
- the key tool for pursuing profits on the side of the enterprise, the pole around which all strategies, not only those of marketing but also those of the entirety of symbiotic relations and processes that constitute an enterprise as an organisation, revolve;
- one of the most distinguished factors of marketing according to Thompson (1962), who cites that the two most distinguished factors of marketing are the product and the consumer. The product constitutes a controlled variable, and what is ultimately required is to render feasible the approach between the two;
- the main tool for facing up to the competition, a role that, before the twentieth century, was ascribed to the tool of price (Wentz et al. 1973).

Additionally, however, the product is placed as the key factor at the centre of the discussion, which relates to macroeconomic speculations:

- What will be produced?
- How will it be produced?
- Who will produce it?
- Where will it be produced?
- When will it be produced?
- For whom will it be produced?

The aforementioned are key questions, the answers to which form the subject of the science of macroeconomics.

Moreover, product also refers to the benefit purchased by someone, its characteristic features and advantages as well as anything else that may be offered for purchase, use or consumption that could satisfy a desire or need. It may include, besides its physical characteristics and services, a multitude of other entities that have the capacity of being the subject of satisfaction, such as experiences, locations, ideas, information, organisations and/or individuals.

When two people, in the context of a personal approach and flirting, agree to dine together, then when such exit materialises they do not simply purchase a satisfied appetite but much more: they purchase going out to a pleasant location, the realisation of various manifestations of social life, such as candlelit music, staying in a nice place, the experience of service, the hope of the further fruition of their convergence, the opportunity for discussion and the company of other diners.

Moreover, the product is

- the tangible result of a productive process, in Chamberlin's (1957) view on monopolistic competition (the product is subject to the total utilities it offers, where the physical offer is just one of its ingredients).
- a system of material-intangible elements, which may produce benefits, via the uses it offers;
- the total of technical (tangible) and symbolic (intangible) characteristics;
- a holistic conception of a good, which may shape the corresponding expectation for the satisfaction of needs;
- the array of benefits that stem from its consumption;
- not only and exclusively the benefit that originates from its use but also the hope of potential benefits from it.

The subjectivity of need entails the subjectivity for the perception of a product

In this light, it is easier to understand the difference between the 'uninitiated' and the initiated in marketing. The latter will be easier to understand from the example: when a woman purchases a dress, she does not do so in the narrow context of the satisfaction of her obvious need to keep warm, or not to be naked. Those initiated in marketing could incorporate in the 'array' of benefits also the satisfaction of a set of increasingly obscure and 'hidden' – perhaps even unrealised – needs that may be catered for, such as the satisfaction of the need – existing in many cultures, social environments, independently of how incongruous they may be – for her to be attractive, socially acceptable, 'politically correct', 'in fashion' or even of the need to exhibit her social-economic standing and the power and authority relations, which may characterise her – the status, the commands of her religion, even the catering for the need to state the activities, interests and attitudes she observes.

Levels of product

But the point where our perception will be considerably differentiated and our 'oriented towards marketing' perception will become more acute is that set of potential motivations, subject to a spectrum of viewpoints, that are largely subjective. An astonished sales assistant described the case of one of her 'tougher' customers: the ample-figured lady insisted on asking for a dress several sizes smaller than her body type allowed. After a time-consuming but totally fruitless 'negotiation', where the assistant tried to change the customer's mind, the customer confided to her that 'from Monday I will be on a diet' and that the ultimate purpose of the dress was to initially function as the 'carrot' – hung in a prominent place in the kitchen, next to the fridge, and then to be the trophy, a trophy that she contended and deservedly conquered. Depending, of course, on the product, the historical, cultural, social and religious background, but also on the idiosyncrasy and bio-theory of each individual, the limits for enriching the pool of potential motives are almost indefinable, while they include and transgress variables such as brand, post-sales support or guarantees or auxiliary services.

This expanded view of what a product is was successfully observed and employed by a major car manufacturer to promote one of the vehicles it produces. Should someone adopt the blinkered view that vehicles exist solely to cater for manifestly obvious needs, such as transportation, then they would ignore many – and perhaps more significant – aspects of the package of benefits they offer. And it is obvious that such insistence on the one-dimensional view and delimitation would prove to be very costly, since it ignores multiple parameters and factors for the existence of a product.

The fundamental importance of a product and the multidimensional grid of interrelations reflected in it fed a dialectic centred on the delimitation and clarification of its characteristics and the levels thereof. Levitt (1980) proposes five levels of analysis:

1. The level of the core benefit, which looks at the core of the essence that the consumer expects to acquire through the realisation of the purchase. It is the obvious utility, the catering for the evident need and the principal reason, which constitutes the motive for the purchase (in the example above, someone will buy a car in order – through its utility – to cater for the need of transportation).
2. The core product level relates to the key characteristics and features that the product bears as its constituent elements and without which it cannot exist as a product (the wheels, seats, etc.).

3. The expected product level, which relates to those characteristics or features of the product as perceived by consumers (colour, good condition, functioning seats, etc.).
4. The augmented product level, which refers to those characteristics and features that exceed what is anticipated by the consumer, namely, what is offered beyond that which is expected (e.g., free road assistance for 2 years).
5. The potential product level, which relates to anything additional – beyond those features that are already offered – that would stir the consumer's enthusiasm.

A clarification might be of use at this point. Independent of the point of view adopted above and to approach the concept of a product under the light of marketing, most approaches do not view the concept of product in the severely limiting framework of it being exclusively and only an 'object' (namely, that which is perceived by more than two senses at a time).

Product–service–idea

Even a service or an idea may be considered as a product, however difficult and hard it may be to discern this, especially with respect to the second distinction. This difficulty may be principally attributed to the fact that many 'tangible' products are frequently complemented by a multitude of services (the usefulness of which may in some cases exceed the level of the 'core benefit'), and/or to the fact that many services are, correspondingly, complemented by benefits ensuing from the 'tangible' products accompanying them.

Berry (1980) attempts to accost the intractability of this distinction by adopting the following definitions:

- Goods are particular objects – things, which ensue as the result of the implementation of a productive process on the side of the producer and in which the consumer does not participate and makes no contribution.
- A service is the result of actions and activities implemented by its 'producer' – provider, the performance attained in implementing the aforementioned actions and activities but also the results that entail for the consumer of the service;
- Finally, the term product defines the services, goods or a combination thereof, in the context of an integrated, total offer to the consumer.

It appears that the distinguishing difference is the existence or not of a material essence, which, however, in the case of services is substituted by the experience the consumer derives. The main benefit offered depends on the material or the intangible – principally – nature; one may offer an image of the ranking of the dominance of the material or intangible nature correspondingly.

According to Wirtz et al. (2012), services constitute economic activities, which are exchanged. They are frequently actions of limited duration through the performance/results of which desirable outcomes ensue for those who purchase them or to objects that they possess. Via the exchange of monies, time and effort, consumers aspire to acquire value through the access they are granted to goods, work, vocational skills, facilities, networks and systems. Frequently, however, they do not acquire ownership to any of those elements with a material substance that are involved in the process. This last fact sets a further distinction of products, depending on the nature of the act for the provision of a service and its consumer.

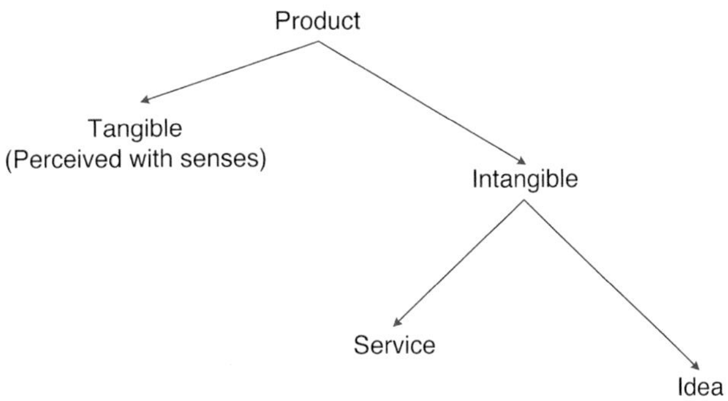

FIGURE 2.4 Product–service–idea: the 'triad'

It is important to realise that in the context of marketing, any form of value offered against a consideration, be it money, time or votes, constitutes a product. The next key concept in understanding marketing is exchange.

Exchange–transaction: fundamental building blocks

The action of an exchange is deemed as the best procedure for the satisfaction of needs and is a central point of reference for marketing, connected with the process for the acquisition of some desirable object by somebody, by offering another object, which functions reciprocally. Namely, the concept of exchange is the common denominator of all those issues that are treated and remedied by marketing. And while exchange constitutes a central concept of marketing, its unit of measurement, transaction, may also be defined as an exchange. Transaction consists of the trade of value among at least two transacting parties. If, for example, we refer to a monetary transaction, then this could be rendered as the act taking place when I pay x euros to acquire object y. It is easy to understand that the monetary transaction is a special category – albeit the most common one – of an exchange, since in a society where money is not used as an alternative mean, I could acquire 3 kilograms of bread by offering 1 kilogram of fish. However, the act of exchange should not be perceived and defined only within the confines of material things but must also be considered under a wider viewpoint: by saying 'objects' we may include other things beyond those which we need two senses to perceive (in direct analogy to products), such as services, views, ideas and even ideologies. With respect to these, the concept of reciprocity may not involve the classic exchange of monies or objects but could take the form, for example, of the subscription to some advocated ideology.

As carrier for the satisfaction of desires and needs, exchange bears a multitude of elements, the roots of which are entangled and interlocked and flow into even the evolution of the human race and culture. People need not know how to do everything to secure all that is necessary for their biological or other needs. The need or desire for exchange is a pillar of social and economic life: it allows the cells of a society to specialise in the production of those products, which they could, on account of their qualities, skills, dexterities and resources, produce more efficiently and which they know they can exchange with those they need. Consequently, exchange reinforces social and economic ties, while at the same time lessening (as contradictory as this may initially appear) dependence for the covering of needs in unacceptable, illegal, immoral or even not-established ways. If the satisfaction of needs is not attained via exchange, then needs may be catered for in unqualified and inappropriate ways, such as violence, war and begging.

Conditions for exchange

In order for an exchange to take place, four conditions must be met:

1. At least two parties, groups, organisations or individuals must participate.
2. Every transacting party must hold something of value and desirable to the other party.
3. Every party must be ready to 'forfeit' this value it possesses to acquire something of value from the other party.
4. Transacting parties must be able to communicate with each other and make their values available for exchange.

Nature and concept of exchange activities

These conditions reflect on the motives that must exist on each transacting side (e.g., that which every party will give up, in the context of its reciprocating offer, shall be of lesser value to the party than that which it expects to gain from acquiring the goods offered by the other party) but also on the bilateral nature of the relation due to the simultaneous (and/or deferred) transaction. Additionally, the significant role played by communication is rendered clear, with respect to both the disclosure of the terms for the exchange and the existence of the disposition and motives for its realisation. Of course, in the framework described, the freedom of will in opting for the decision to realise the transaction is also accentuated, namely, the voluntary nature of the transaction, which shall mobilise behaviour depending on the existence, degree and number of offered incentives, completely free from any type of extortion, coercion or other forms of compulsive intervention. We understand that the intensity and force of the incentives, the efficiency and effectiveness of communication, the existence of reciprocity and of contributory relations in both directions, but also the degree of the freedom of the decision are the catalytic variables that function not only as accelerators but also as multipliers of the possibility for some exchange to take place. It is at this point that the customer-oriented direction of marketing becomes even more evident, as does its social nature being an object, which 'treats' human needs and desires in a legitimate, appropriate and efficient manner.

All parties participating in their free choice, either simultaneously or at different times and to varying degrees (depending not only on the intensity and number of motives but also on other concurrent and contributing conditions), are involved in a procedure, the outcome of which will be the bilateral improvement of the value, utility and benefit for each party. In other words, the transacting parties benefit from the act of exchange – and this is possibly the most significant inferred (perhaps implied) condition of all those that have been cited in order for an exchange to take place. The bilateral improvement offered by value – in any of its equivalent alternative manifestations – is the mainspring that inherently resides behind every transaction, the feeder of the processes and the culmination of the actions of the procedure.

Viewed as a chain reaction, if transactions are seen as sets of activities, behaviour, under the provisos, that create value and offer prosperity at their completion, one could claim that the more of them that take place, the more their positive influence on the groups or individuals participating. In the same way, one could claim that beyond the increase in the frequency of the number of transactions between the same 'players', a positive contribution on the level of the derived benefit for a social group would also ensue from an increase in the number of parties involved.

The marketing mix and uncontrollable variables

Marketing is by definition the catalyst that reinforces and boosts the multiplying results of the derived value. It is the accelerator that, via the viewpoint it adopts and the philosophy and ideology it advocates, supports and applies, turns into the tool for the facilitation and multiplication of transactions. This is precisely and ultimately its quintessence and stands at the core of its contribution to social prosperity. It is the conscious, planned, intended and thought-out series of activities and actions that adopt a social orientation, also via the application of tools shaped by the environment, and create the fertile ground and conditions that allow for an increase of the utility of society. It is the cohesive force assisting in the staving off of 'unpleasant feelings of shortage' and that promotes their resolution by offering benefits that reside in and also satisfy the principle of reciprocity.

Besides being a fundamental conceptual tool, the marketing mix is possibly one of the most obvious and tangible proofs for the above. It is an action plan relating to the four key marketing activities, namely, the creation of the products, their distribution, promotion and pricing in the most suitable way that will satisfy a consumer's needs. These variables are characterised as controllable, since the enterprise is responsible for their parametrisation and this falls under the competence of the marketing department. All decisions taken regarding the preparation of the components for these variables, their degree of participation and the type of tool to be selected on each occasion from marketing's toolbox, but, principally, from the integrated approach and activation of the particular characteristics and qualities such variables have, focus on the consumer. Moreover, the integrated and systemic approach to the mix also serves an additional significant objective. Essentially it is the filter for the external uncontrollable influences to the enterprise from the environment. The external environment consists of factors that are beyond the enterprise's control (at least to the degree it would wish for) and play a determinative role in its survival and profitability since they carry multifaceted and complex influences. In addition,

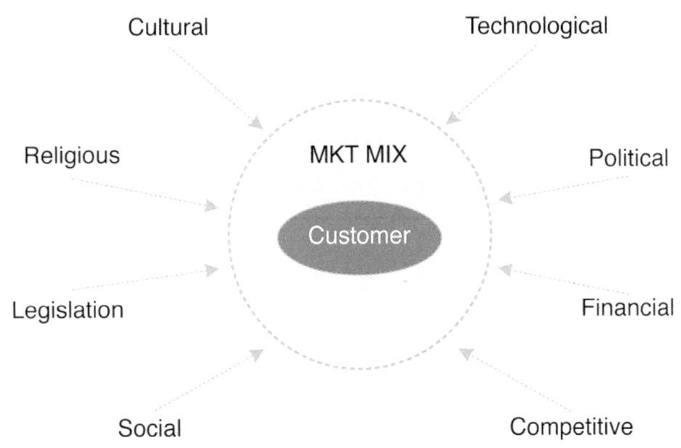

FIGURE 2.5 Uncontrolled variables of the external environment

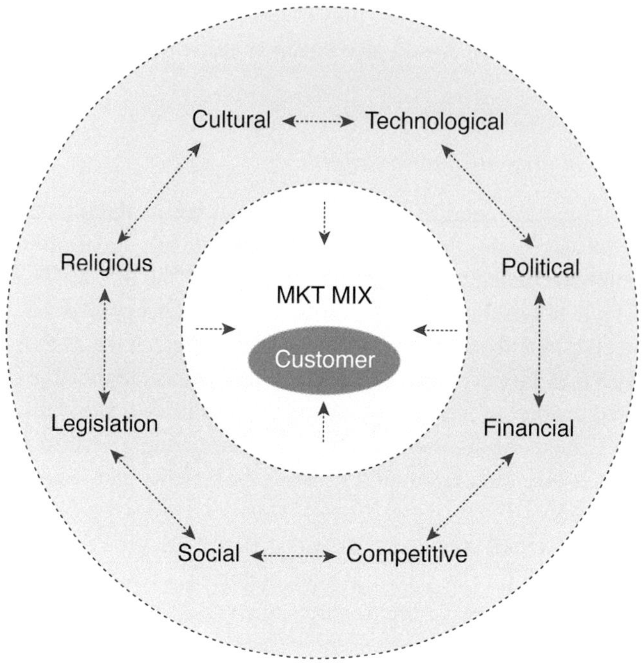

FIGURE 2.6 Dialectic and dynamic interaction of the constituents of the uncontrollable external environment

they are distinguished by the dynamics of their nature, a fact that quickly disdains any attempt at their static 'on-the-spot' depiction. And, even though for methodological reasons of analysis we break down and allocate the external environment into sub-segments/sub-environments, what the enterprise experiences as an incoming influence rarely originates purely from one of any such sub-segments.

These sub-segments intercorrelate, they have a dialectic relation and they exchange influences with one another, a synthesis that increases their degree of complexity. It is precisely this lack of watertight seals between the sub-segments that creates a complex web of intercorrelations that produce and direct towards the enterprise more multivariable influences of a very complex nature.

Of course, the three characteristics regulating and governing this environment (the unavoidable nature of the influences on the enterprise without a corresponding high level of capacity for control thereof, their dynamic nature, and the amalgam and splicing of their qualities due to the interrelations between them) do not always constitute negative variables. They do not always establish what many like to describe as a 'tumultuous' or 'turbulent' or 'volatile' environment. Depending on the nature of their influence to a particular enterprise and within a given time frame, they may be classified as either opportunities or threats.

Should we combine the need or desire, which constitutes a key mobilising force and incentive-shaping factor for human behaviour, with the best, appropriate, legitimate and efficient way to satisfy it – exchange – but also with the objective conditions existing due to their inclusion in the context of the environment, then the marketing mix becomes a fundamentally important catalyst to facilitate and aid the procedure for the covering of needs.

The marketing mix and exchange: close cross-correlation and correspondence

It would be interesting for the reader, following the presentation of a concise description for each element in the marketing mix, to contemplate the conditions that were cited earlier as prerequisites for an exchange and the relation that potentially exists between each one of them with respect to each of the elements in the marketing mix.

The product – more specifically, its 'creation'– as an element of the marketing mix, relates to the investigation of consumers' desires so that what will be created adequately caters for their needs. Marketing, in the context of the shaping of this variable, is responsible for the development of perceptions, which would allow marketers to listen to needs, their limits and nature, regardless of whether such needs can be expressed or the ability to express them is absent, due to the small degree by which the consumer himself realises them – despite their existence. Following this, marketing must find the most efficient way to 'incorporate' the satisfaction of the need in what is called a product. Should someone wish to trade, then they must ensure that their product will be attractive to the other party. If he offers value to the other transacting party, through the existing features (of the 'product') that render it adequate and capable to cater for needs, then, based on the principle of reciprocity with respect to profit in this bipolar relation, he offers an incentive to trade and, thus, to also satisfy his own needs – without a violation of the principle of free will for any of the participating sides.

One could define promotion as the communication process that makes the disclosure of the existence of the aforementioned 'attractive' product among the partakers of the exchange possible. It, principally, relates to actions and procedures that take place in order – besides disclosure – to reinforce the consumer's interest and/or to train him regarding the ways in which the product covers and caters for 'deficits' or needs. However, in order for someone to express an intention to participate in the exchange procedure, to decide if they wish to trade or even to be informed on the terms for the exchange or to, correspondingly, put forward their own terms, there must be communication, which is posed as a prerequisite for the occurrence of an exchange. Let us not forget that there is communication without a sale, but there can never be a sale without communication.

Distribution comprises the performance of all these activities necessary for the subjects of the exchange to reach consumers (and producers) from producers (and, simultaneously, consumers) in the context of their twofold and/or alternating roles. Even if distribution is not included in the wider context of the communication (which consists of suitable and specific channels that render the act of an exchange possible), it is evident that without its contribution no exchange or trade can be ultimately completed either via traditional (physical) or more modern (digital) channels.

Finally, price is defined as that controllable variable of the marketing mix that is shaped by pricing objectives, strategy and policy and is the only one of the elements that functions as the valuable feeder of proceeds for the enterprise. Even if we view the case of an exchange pragmatically as a transaction, price is also present and relevant as an integral and critical factor for the performance and culmination of the procedure. To put it in simpler terms, in this special case money may not subsist as a means for the exchange, but price is clad the role of shaping the units of good x that must be 'sacrificed' to acquire good y. It reflects the perceived value borne by the products under a negotiation for exchange and, ultimately, shapes the expression of the reason for the exchange – the relevant and dependent value-price of one good in relation to the other.

The shaping of these variables, the integrated and systemic approach with respect to the appropriate dose for the ingredients of the mix, ensures the consistency of an adequate response to the consumers' expectations. Simultaneously, it is the most dynamic, clear and explicit manifestation of the customer-oriented viewpoint and orientation adopted by marketing. It ensures that transactions (whether based on money as the medium of exchange, or bartering, either between groups or individuals or between consumers or enterprises) are producers of profit or benefit for each transacting party, in a fair and efficient manner and in the context of decision-making resting on free will and motivated by the maximisation of benefit/utility.

We must, of course, stress the role played by freedom of will. We should note that if removed from the conditions, it would essentially cause the accentuation of the 'P(istol)' as an equivalent constituent – perhaps equally effective but unethical and unfair – replacing every other constituent P that comprises the marketing mix.

We have, however, already underlined that all of the above are valid only in the absence of any compulsive, extortionate or violent admission and manifestation of the carrying out and facilitation of transactions. If we attempted to quantitatively depict the benefit of a transaction, then such depiction must have the form shown in the box below.

Benefit for the seller: product price – product cost.
Benefit for the buyer: benefit from using the product – product price.
Total benefit (value): benefit from using the product – product cost.

Consequently, as transaction we define the activity for the creation of value. Marketing, by means of the orientation it adopts, is the catalyst for the increase in the number and frequency of transactions and therefore – as a chain reaction – the multiplier in the creation of value. Moreover, as we have cited above, it is an aid for the efficient and effective satisfaction of needs due to its function also as a twofold natured filter. Via the shaping of the controllable variables of the marketing mix, it contributes, on the one hand, to the prevention and elimination of negative influences from the external environment (uncontrollable, negative external effects or 'threats'), and, on the other hand, as the receptor that maximises positive external influences (uncontrollable, positive external effects or 'opportunities'). Given the high degree of interaction and influence due to the close interrelation of the 'buyer' and 'seller', the positive consequences of the avoidance-elimination or exploitation-maximisation strategies referred to above, they have a determinative effect on the entire relation.

After this conceptual approach to the concepts of needs, product and exchange, let us attempt to focus on the core of marketing.

Marketing: 'the umbrella'

Consider the following example: an individual (potential consumer) decides to move from point A to point B. The weather is bad: it is raining. As a consequence of biological limitations (if it rains, then it is likely that our individual will catch a cold), social mandates (one is 'decently' dressed when dry) and personal dislike for rain, he realises that he 'needs' to reach point B dry. But the external environment – the natural environment in the case at hand – not only appears to hinder this but is also a factor outside the individual's control and influence to change

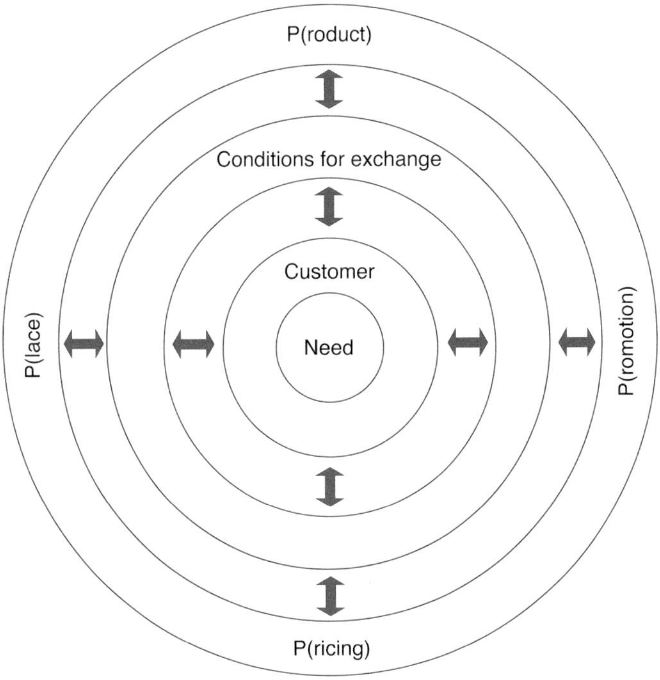

FIGURE 2.7 Four Ps of marketing and customer needs

(i.e., to change rain to sunshine). The moment our individual realises this unpleasant feeling of being wet, he has been rendered a potential buyer of what caters for his need and has, therefore, automatically rendered 'being dry' as a product (we shall not delve into the multitude of objects that have the covering of the need 'being not-wet' built in the core of their aforementioned utility). Marketing is the umbrella that – despite the fact that it cannot affect the external environment – can 'read' it and – having considered and assessed the other parameters and having heard the need – can function as an aid for its satisfaction. In other words, the 'umbrella' facilitated the transactions and successfully dealt with a 'threat' (the uncontrollable variable of the natural environment), offering to the consumer the benefit of being 'dry'. It functioned as a filter for the reflexes of the enterprise, standing between the consumer and the uncontrollable environment.

We could, of course, take our example a step further, by enriching it with other – substantial – details: the umbrella is available in many parallel assumptions (marketing mix), depending on the size, colour, use, price, etc. In this particular assumption, the combination of the above was performed after taking into consideration (indicatively and not exhaustively) the weather conditions in which it would be used; the income of the individual; the cost for the disclosure of its features; the colour and shape dictated by season, fashion and culture of the era; the retail shops, which would sell it; and, evidently, the capacity of the product to render an acceptable benefit also to its producer (in the context of the principle of reciprocity). Let us here not forget the fact that the individual freely decided – without the presence of the pistol (which, despite being illegal and unethical, one could claim is the most adequate means of persuasion in terms of the Ps in the marketing mix) – to move while dry. Now, you'll be the judge of whether the movement was the need and 'dry' was merely the desire.

Our example admits of many more details, which can illustrate other folds of marketing and complete the puzzle of this subject matter in an informed manner. While the 'umbrella' might be the lengthiest expression of the delimitation definition you may have seen, it nonetheless offers a different standpoint, which shall be gradually completed in a stepwise manner and which will be ultimately accompanied by the widespread and accepted definitions.

Building upon the previous example, one could wonder why we defined 'dry' (namely, the elimination of the unpleasant feeling of being wet or, equivalently, the covering of the need to be dry) from the start as a product, while the 'umbrella' was not specifically selected as a means. The umbrella – as with every family of products that bears the characteristics for covering similar needs – constitutes a synthesis of characteristics, features and qualities that – when combined – shape the character of covering needs on each occasion. The value and importance of the umbrella rest only on the capacity of such characteristics to satisfactorily 'quench' such needs (note the use of plural with respect to 'need').

Lockstep viewpoints: marketing's myopia

The umbrella is, therefore, conceived simply as a set of erected, effective and satisfactory responses to needs and only as such can it be highly or lowly assessed – with respect to the degree of its performance. The creation of an umbrella, in other words, does not exist as an end in itself. This would be equivalent to the twisted consideration of first making an umbrella and then figuring out which needs it may correspond to.

The use, of course, of plural with respect to the word 'needs' is intended to sketch the possibility for the existence of other characteristics, which may satisfy a broad spectrum of even incongruous needs (e.g., I am dry, but also in style) and which – as we have mentioned above, sometimes – despite the fact that they indirectly surround the key core of the anticipated benefit, may be assessed and evaluated as more important – and to, ultimately, influence the buying decisions even in a most unexpected way.

Consequently, as such a set of a specific dosage of characteristics and features, the umbrella is part of a greater set of similar and/or completely different compositions of embraced characteristics and qualities, where some string of the web or package/basket of their benefits caters for and covers the need. It would be blinkered and extremely restrictive either for the covering of some need to be a priori and inextricably connected with a specific product or – correspondingly – for a package of offered benefits to be exclusively and only connected with the coverage of one – in indeed aired – need.

In our example, one could easily read a broad spectrum of carriers for the satisfaction of the need to be dry (e.g., one could use a taxi or a bus, wear something waterproof, or wear boots). It would be useful to underline, on the one hand, the reality of the existence of an array of benefits as an accessory of the product and, on the other hand, to incorporate the fact of the participation of the service and the idea (in a competitive and/or complementary manner between different products and/or the same product) as an integral part of the algorithm for our understanding and the role they play in human perception and decision-making (e.g., the individual could have, alternatively, opted for a taxi as he could have reached his destination both dry and well-rested). More important, however, is to unhorse the idea that marketing means that we are tasked with creating products. In marketing, we offer responses to problems, we cater for and cover shortages, we lessen or eliminate unpleasant feelings. To render the adoption of this standpoint possible, one must not narrowly define the coverage of a need exclusively and absolutely only via a carrier or means for its satisfaction but also act in a supervisory capacity and evaluate alternative solutions that are perhaps more harmonised, more compatible and more effective in offering value to consumers. To paraphrase the classic example, we don't sell an umbrella: we sell 'being dry'! Otherwise, we suffer from the ailment of marketing's 'myopia'.

Marketing: a conscious, coordinated and multi-parametric procedure

It is equally interesting also to assess the reasons that led this particular consumer to ultimately choose an umbrella against the great number of other alternatives. A series of parameters, controlled and uncontrolled, were correctly read, and there was also the appropriate response, in the framework of the activities governing the philosophy and orientation of marketing, both of which played a key role.

Obviously, therefore, the creator of the umbrella might have evaluated, among other things, the climate (most possibly, the frequency of rainfall), the economic state of the land (as part for the shaping of the pricing policy), the competition (for its – alternatively – unique value offers), the legal framework (specifications on materials, fabrics, dyes and approved mechanisms), the existence of seasonality (guiding the intensity or not of promotional activities), but also the idiosyncrasy, style, culture, activities and interests of potential customers, in order for the umbrella, after an investigation and evaluation of the alternative solutions offered, after sketching the threats and opportunities, and after assessing the ability to cater for and cover the need, to proceed with an attempt to cover said need with specific product features.

Thus the selection of an umbrella, against, for example, a raincoat, was not purely random. Despite the fact that the system of the requisite perceptions, the evaluation and selection of activities or actions and of decision-making, might seem multi-parametric and complex, even chaotic, it, however, constitutes a coordinated, structured and conscious mechanism and, principally, one way of understanding: in just one word . . . marketing.

Philosophy–ideology–orientation

The managerial philosophy behind marketing's ideology advocates that a company must incessantly and unfailingly satisfy the needs of its customers, through a coordinated series of structured actions, without, however, omitting – in the context of the aforementioned reciprocity – to also satisfy its own needs. This twofold bilateral reciprocal relation appears as a totally dependent system – a network of communicating vessels. If breached, this will signal the end of the symbiotic interrelation.

The attainment of the objectives on the side of the enterprise has a twofold nature. It is, simultaneously, not only a goal for the enterprise (described as a prerequisite for the realisation of the transaction to be attractive) but also the means for the attainment of the goals of the other participant in the transaction. Without the attainment of the goal, the enterprise will not survive in the long run, and, therefore, as a chain reaction it will not be able to build on the satisfaction of needs. The paradox of the simultaneous existence of the symbiotic interrelation, namely, the stipulated condition of the collaboration between the participating parties and the in-parallel competitive hue (who will benefit more), which of necessity it assumes, is the main reason that the existence of benefit for the transacting parties is cited as a condition for the carrying out of a transaction, without the adjective designation 'equivalent'.

Marketing's philosophy constitutes an organisational orientation that, to bear any results besides the bilateral (even if at times lopsided) benefit, must also flow horizontally and vertically across all lengths and breadths of the enterprise. Marketing's value and philosophy are in essence a concept that must run along the entire enterprise and that must be adopted as a business philosophy, the principal characteristics of which lie in the following facts:

- Value is created for the transacting parties – customers and the company – through transactions.
- The understanding on the side of the enterprise is not consumed solely for listening to customers' needs but also in the response to these, taking into account a wide array of the components for building an efficient degree of satisfaction into these. An integral variable that must be taken into consideration is the supremacy of the value offered to the customers, against the alternatives, intertemporally and in a dynamic way.

It is extrapolated that this philosophy has as its touchstone the satisfaction of customer needs (as means and as ultimate goal), which is implemented by the transubstantiation of these needs to product specifications, something that is attained by means of the uninterrupted and unhampered dedication of its business activities to the customer, with the simultaneous, however, awareness of and readiness to respond to the conditions prevailing in the broadly perceived environment (which also includes competition).

From a different viewpoint, a subset of this statement could be the profound awareness and strong commitment on the side of the business to know what it itself can produce with profit that a consumer would wish to purchase. This awareness must guide decision, determine the orientation and be present in the genotype of every cell of the enterprise, must be cultivated and legislated via the acceptance that to produce – greater than the alternatives – customer satisfaction, the indissoluble functional correlation of customer satisfaction, attainment of business objectives must be rendered both goal and experience.

One of the founding stones of this philosophy, besides its market orientation (offer of the maximum potential value to consumers), its orientation towards competition (maintaining the advantages of the offer in a more effective and efficient manner than that of the corresponding offers by competitors), is also its social orientation: marketing activities must be distinguished by their high level of compatibility with the more social objectives of maintaining a rational use of resources. The social dimension of marketing adopts, advocates and incorporates in its mechanisms for strategy-activities and decision-making long-term social interests.

What marketing is: definitions

In the context of the verification and consistency of the structure we have prefatory referred to, we shall cite the definitions formulated with respect to this subject matter. You are undoubtedly adequately equipped to ascertain that they regard different synthetic formulations of what has been cited above – in a more structurally consistent, coordinated and concise expression:

- Marketing may define the entire system of business activities, which is designed as to cover the creation of products, their distribution, pricing and promotion in such a manner so as to ensure that the conditions for effective and efficient transactions inside a dynamically changing environment exist.

- Marketing is a business philosophy focusing on the customer. It presupposes a focus on customer satisfaction, the uninterrupted, uniform, intense and coordinated effort across the entire spectrum of actions and functions of an enterprise, and the conviction that the attainment of the structural objectives may come about exclusively through the satisfaction of customer needs.
- Marketing is the managerial process for detecting, foreseeing and satisfying customer needs, with some profit for the enterprise.
- Marketing is the process for pairing and combining the means of an enterprise with the needs of a consumer.
- Marketing is the specialised managerial philosophy that is related to the common denominator of a transaction, and which aims at the satisfaction of customer and business needs, through its functions.
- Marketing is the development and financial distribution of goods to selected customer segments.
- Marketing is the process in a society by which the structure of demand for economic goods is foreseen and expanded and, subsequently, satisfied by their conception, promotion, transaction and physical distribution.
- Marketing is a managerial orientation or a managerial philosophy.
- Marketing is the activity and the set of institutions and procedures for the creation, communication, provision and exchange of offers, which bear value for customers, consumers, associates and society.
- Marketing is the process by means of which companies create value and build reinforced bridges of ties for and with their customers so as to ensure the return of value from the side of the customers. It is a process that precedes production and produces a set of utilities. More specifically, such utilities can be form-related, transforming the raw materials into something with a useful and attractive form for the customer. Utilities can also be spatial and temporal, relating to the transportation of the product to the market in order for it to be rendered available for consumption at a time and place that suit the customer. Or they can relate to information, namely, to the disclosure of those factors, that support the quality of appeasing needs and ownership, namely, the culmination of the act of transacting.

Finally, marketing is a popular word, however, one that is extremely controversial and at the same time ambiguous – perhaps one that is also exclusively a negative sign for sociologists. It is the subject of criticism and assessment if the dimensions of the capacities it bears to attain all that it (the company) claims exist, or – on the contrary – if it operates as an obstacle to man's bliss. Furthermore, it is subject to the tortures from other types of criticism, which may sometimes be based on (or least be influenced by) political views, religious convictions or philosophical approaches and worldviews.

What marketing is not

The great power of the selective delimitation renders, perhaps, more effective (and certainly more vivid and eloquent) the outlining of the subject matter via a citation of what is erroneously considered as being marketing. Falling into this category of erroneous and disorienting adoptions – besides the myths evolved – are also the one-dimensional assumptions that are strictly focused and persistent and regard only fragmentary illustrations.

So marketing is *not*

- (exclusively and/or only fragmentary) promotion or sales or advertising;
- the one-dimensional view of each of the factors or variables included in the wider context of the market, society, the external and internal environment of an enterprise, or the enterprise itself;
- the unilateral service of the need for the maximisation of profit by business, which is simply clad in a falsified (and devoid of any meaning) modernist neologism fashion;
- the creation of notional needs leading to overconsumption and squandering of resources, and which is characterised by social inertia;
- a smart and scientific-sounding way for the artificial increase of prices;
- an upstart approach that is opportunistically adopted, or stands or bears short-term fruits, resting on the foundations of randomness;
- the unsolicited creation of a product and subsequent attempt to 'push' it to the market;
- that which 'bad' professionals (who may certainly exist) claim to perform;
- a philosophy espoused or used only by charitable institutions;
- a philosophy insistently oriented towards production or a product;
- only cut off from the realisation of desires but also constitutes an integral part thereof;
- a new concept: in its various rudimentary manifestations, it goes hand-in-hand with man from the dawning of civilisation;
- a carrier that advises and promotes the materialistic dimension or bliss through pleasure and raises them to be ends-in-themselves or supreme social values;
- the creator of immoderate cost, which is then passed on to consumers, ultimately making the acquisition of utility or the degree of satisfaction more difficult to attain;
- a function that imposes the production of specific products;
- the promotion of novel but useless features, which mock consumers so as to artificially make them perceive them as necessary and to be lured into purchasing them;
- the use of science to mislead disadvantaged population-consumer subsets;
- a factor of the skewed and vicious influence of the good sense of consumers that leads them to a consuming fit, rendering them as passive and captured puppets in the grip of a continuous and fictitious anxiety for the acquisition of goods;
- the one bearing the responsibility for increasing inequalities, through serving the financially privileged;
- the exclusive engagement in seeking methods, which aim to substitute critical skills and function restrictively as an obstacle in the context of free will and, ultimately, to control and manipulate in reality in a most importunate and repressing manner the (controlled) (il)liberal decision to purchase;
- a counterproductive, useless function that generates only cost or, at least, a function whose only positive contribution lies in the increase of product prices;
- a synonym for the irrational waste of valuable and scarce natural resources.

2.3 What is SCM?

SCM is one of the most crucial business functions and disciplines of operations management. Frequently, SCM is interpreted as the evolution of logistics management. Indeed, even today the concepts of logistics management and SCM are deemed by many as equivalent. This led to a confusion as to their precise designation. In reality, this confusion ensued from the fact that many considered both these two concepts to include the same company activities; however, they must be treated under a different prism.

The way we shall examine these two concepts rests on the systemic approach, which is based on the systems theory. As we have already noted in the previous chapter, according to this theory, an enterprise is a system. It consists of various subsystems that do not operate in isolation but collaborate for the attainment of a common, shared objective. So, *we are not interested in the success of every subsystem individually but in the success of the system as a whole.*

Logistics management: management of the company's logistics system

Perhaps the most widely known definition of logistics management is that first given by the Council of Logistics Management in 1986:

> The process for the planning, implementation and control of the effective and efficient flow and storage of products, services and relevant information from the initial order/production until the final delivery to the end consumer, aimed to fulfil the customer's requirements.

The planning, organisation, operation, monitoring and control of the system for the execution of orders is a 'job' for the logistics system of an enterprise, while the employee to whom we referred at the introduction to this chapter would surely be one of its 'pieces' if not the supervisor of the company's logistics system. Other employees from all the departments referred to above also participate in this system. These employees use tools, machinery and equipment, exchanging information relating to the order. Consequently, the Council of Logistics Management regarded the 'planning, organisation, operation, monitoring and control of the resources of an enterprise (human, machines and information), which are required for the execution of orders or, in general, for the satisfaction of demand'.

Pursuant to the definitions offered above, the subject of logistics management is very wide and covers a wide spectrum of the activities of a company or an organisation. These activities refer to the processes for planning, execution and control of an enterprise (such as procurements, strategy, handling of materials, packaging, distribution channels, number and location of distribution centres, technology, recycling, purchases, transportations, inventory management and customer service). More specifically, the enterprise plans, implements and checks a great number of functions (supplies, handling of materials, forecasting of demand, inventories, order processing, geographic location of facilities and warehouses, storage, packaging, transportation, spare parts and repairs, customer service, treatment of returned products, recycling and waste removal, etc.) to transform raw materials procured from suppliers to ready products offered to clients. In general, a business shall utilise all available resources (natural, financial, human and informational) to optimise the cost–profit ratio and production and delivery flexibility (in terms of time and place), to adjust to the particular needs of clients, which leads to a stronger relation and binding with clients and their better service and acquisition of a competitive advantage. Under this light, SCM includes the planning of four key business functions:

- *Demand planning*, which is the process for planning the prediction for the demand for the products/services. A more precise prediction of customer demand shall improve the service thereof, simultaneously cutting down the costs ensuing from uncertainties concerning demand.

- *Procurement planning*, which is the planning process for the satisfaction of market demand based on the resources and level of inventories available. The covering of replenishment requirements ensures that safety stock is adequate.
- *Production planning*, meaning the planning process, which assesses the available resources and lays out an optimal production schedule, based on the limitations imposed by the boundaries of reality. It may automatically adjust production plans should some suppliers be out of stock or if a key element for production is out of commission.
- *Transportation planning*, which is the planning process for the optimum and cost-efficient method for transportation and distributions, taking into account limitations such as receipt date/time and means of transportation.

SCM: the coordination of companies' logistics systems across the supply chain

In the past decades, the management of companies and organisations has acknowledged the importance of logistics management as a critical factor for their success. At some point, enterprises realised that they are no longer competitively effective in isolation from their business partners. To put it in simpler terms, a business usually does not possess the necessary skills and resources for the management and control of the flow of products/services and information from initial procurements until the final consumption, especially in a competitive and global market. Thus, networks (chains) of business with common goals and benefits were established. Supply chain (SC) is the generally accepted model/framework for the way collaborative relations with other businesses and/or organisations (such as suppliers, wholesalers and retail-sellers) are established. In general, 'SC is considered as the network of organisations or businesses, which participate, via continuous and bidirectional interactions, in processes, which add value to the products/services offered to the final customer' (Ballou 1999: 7).

Based on the above, SCM is the set of approaches and attempts to efficiently unify producers, suppliers, transporters, etc., of a SC so as for the products to be produced and distributed in the correct quantity, quality, time and place, ultimately aiming to decrease total cost and simultaneously to attain high levels of end customer service. Added value offered to customers and their satisfaction are factors that reinforce the competitive nature of the SC and require much more than isolated logistics processes for their attainment. Consequently, it took many years to adopt the view that SCM is more than a new name or synonym for logistics management, namely, that SCM aims to unify and manage basic business processes across the entire SC and not to unify processes at various stages of the SC (i.e., for only one enterprise).

The differentiation above led the Council of Logistics Management to differentiate its original definition for logistics management, rendering it clear that logistics management is a subset/part of SCM. The new definition is the following:

> Logistics Management is that part of SCM, which plans, implements and controls the effective and efficient flow and storage of products, services and relevant information from the initial order/production until the final delivery to the end consumer, aimed to fulfil the client's requirements.
>
> *(Council of Logistics Management 1998)*

According to the systemic approach, we could suggest that every system is inside an environment consisting of other systems with which it interacts, exchanging material and intangible resources. Consequently, for a system to operate, it needs resources, which it procures from its environment as inflows. These inflows are essentially the outflows of other systems. The inflows, which a system takes from its environment, depending on the case, may be capital, materials, equipment, information, etc.

2.4 Key parameters and essentials of the contemporary knowledge fields of the areas of marketing and SCM and their constitution in the value chain

An enterprise can be determined by the set of stepwise processes (or, better, the chain of processes) that are necessary for the implementation of its functions and, more specifically, planning, production, purchases, sales, distribution and service of its customers. The processes above are deemed to be significant strategic factors constituting the value chain and are referred to as added value processes, since they add value to a product or service (Porter 1984).

Porter (1984), to illustrate the value chain in a systemic way, categorised the business processes into two types: main and support processes. Main processes are related to the physical creation of the product, its sale and distribution to the final buyer, and the latter's service. They include the following:

- internal inflow management processes required for the receipt, storage and internal distribution of products/services imported (with respect to an enterprise), such as materials management, checking of inventories, storage and transactions with suppliers;
- functions relating to the production of products/services, such as manufacturing, control and packaging;
- external processes for the management of outflows, relating to the storage and distribution of products/services to customers, such as storage, order taking and transportation;
- sales and marketing, such as advertising, sales, pricing and promotion;
- services relating to the wider service of customers, such as installation, maintenance and training.

Support processes underpin the main processes, providing functions such as the procurement of materials (finished or semi-finished), technological and human resources, and various business functions, which relate to the structure of the enterprise. More specifically, they include

- procurement of materials relating to all processes for the procurement of consumables and equipment (save for those employed in production);
- research/development processes for new products and technologies and the management thereof;
- human resources management processes, such as hiring, training and relocation of personnel;
- processes relating to the general structure of the enterprise, such as segmentation with respect to financing, planning, quality control and assignment of competences to individual departments of the enterprise.

SCM aims to bring value to the market

As can be seen in the figure, the profit margin ensues from all processes (main and secondary). That is, the systemic approach where a company is considered as a system and each of its departments a subsystem is valid. We are not interested in the success of each subsystem in isolation but the success of the system. This success rests on the coordination of the subsystems and their collaboration towards a common goal: the increase in the provided level of service with a simultaneous decrease in cost.

The new conditions in the global market force enterprises to enter into relations and collaborations with other enterprises. Aids to these efforts are new informatics and communications technologies, which allow an enterprise to expand its internal activities beyond those that are clearly its own, relating the enterprise with its external business environment. That is, the implementation of interactions between the value-added processes of one enterprise (e.g., processes relating to the supplies of a customer) and the corresponding processes of its business partner (e.g., a supplier's marketing and sales processes) is supported.

Porter (1981) also tried to describe the integrated value chain as the interrelated processes utilised by an enterprise for the implementation of its transactions for the supply part (including procurement, production and distribution) and the demand part (including marketing, sales and service, and purchase and sale of products and services).

Logistics and SCM have gradually evolved into a major issue, both for the business world and for the academic community. Assessing the relevant bibliography, it follows that in a typical industrial company, the cost of the activities directly related with logistic management processes amounts to 20–25% of the company's turnover and represents 10–15% of the overall cost of the final product (Gattorna and Walters 1996). These percentages include the cost of transportation, management-storage costs for materials and merchandise, costs relating to the management of inventories, the cost of transporting products inside the company, the cost of order processing and personnel expenses. According to the same data, the cost of fixed assets directly relating to logistics management processes amounts to roughly 35–40% of the total fixed assets. This percentage includes building facilities as well as the equipment required for the storage, production, handling and management of materials and merchandise, safety and security equipment, informatics systems, etc. Based on these percentages, the optimisation of cost and investments for logistics management processes, combined with the application of the customer-oriented philosophy (which is the second objective of the science under investigation, besides the reduction of cost), stands as both an opportunity and a challenge for the management of the company.

In addition, company executives over the last two decades have experienced and gone through a period of great changes and new trends. The most significant of these are globalisation and the deregulation of markets, the rapid technological upgrade, the emphasis on the redesign of business processes in the name of relentless competition and the increasing interest in environmental protection, by means of the ever-increasing recall (or recycle) processes for products and materials.

Businesses have to a large extent turned to global resources in order, on the one hand, to ensure their procurements at a lower cost and, on the other, to attain a faster pace of planning and implementation for the products and services they offer. Critical factors in the modern business track and field revolve around the availability of not only capital and the close control of cost but also the quality of the produced products and services. These trends have led to the search for more efficient methods for the coordination of materials and information flows, both internally and externally. A key for such coordination is the orientation towards closer relations with all levels of suppliers and associates. Businesses today compete in relation to both the timing and the quality of their products or services. A business whose SC manages to adjust more expediently to the volatile demands of consumers and which can deliver its product to the customer faster, at a lower cost, without damages and with greater reliability is the one that meets most conditions to win a greater market share.

Moreover, today's global economy is characterised by a commonly accepted term: the continuously increasing value of information, which flows both in the internal and in the external environment of businesses. The deregulation of economies and relaxation of border controls, the enormous spreading and continuous updating of the global web, and the adoption of new technologies by a great number of enterprises have rendered it clear that the competitive advantage for a company rests on and originates from its ability to prudently and correctly manage the enormous volume of information it receives and possesses. Several business informatics systems and technologies have been introduced since the early 1990s. These technologies provide ways to face the new challenge for businesses, namely, to deliver the final product/service to the client at the right time, place, quality and quantity/degree at the lowest possible cost while maintaining minimum levels of inventories.

Simultaneously, the new trend for the recall or recycling of products and materials (reverse logistics) has already been rendered necessary due largely to environmental pollution. Businesses today expand their distribution channels (networks) beyond the final user to include the collection and dismantling of final products to be reused in new products. The operations of such networks include after-sales support, maintenance services and other activities, their main objective being to attain a better control of the flow of products/services, always keeping their customers absolutely satisfied.

As a result of the changes above, today's businesses realise that the activation and expanding competition in the global business arena dictate and impose the development of collaboration networks (supply chains), with mutual targets and benefits, which are possible through the full unification of processes and information flows. The ultimate objective is the full control of the activities of the networks, from the moment the raw material enters until the suitable product/service is delivered/offered to the end consumer.

Synopsis

- Every enterprise consists of three main functions: operations management, marketing and accounting and finance.
- Marketing is the managerial process for detecting, foreseeing and satisfying customer needs, with some profit for the enterprise.
- SCM is a crucial part of the operations management that includes the planning, implementation and controlling of a great number of functions such as sourcing, handling of materials, forecasting of demand, inventory management, order processing, geographical location of facilities and warehouses, storage, packaging, transportation, spare parts and repairs, customer service, treatment of returned products, and recycling and waste removal to optimise the cost–profit ratio, provide flexibility in production and delivery (in terms of time and place), and adjust to the particular needs of clients that lead to a stronger relation and binding with clients and their better service as well as gaining a competitive advantage.
- Both disciplines/business functions aim to create value and build reinforced bridges of ties for and with their customers so as to ensure the return of value from the side of the customers.
- The need to integrate the activities and practices of marketing and SCM is almost mandated by current development. It is estimated that the outcome will surpass, to a considerable degree, the sum of the respective insight offered by singular efforts attempted by the two business functions.

Review and discussion questions

- What is marketing?
- What is not marketing?
- Compare the terms *marketing* and *SCM*.
- Compare the terms *logistics management* and *SCM*.
- What are the main objectives and subject of logistics and SCM? Can these be attained to the maximum degree?
- How can marketing and SCM bring value to the market?
- Define the key pull and push planning philosophies.

Case studies

Case study 1: Processes and integration in the interaction of purchasing and marketing

Marketing and purchasing theories offer alternative viewpoints to traditional economic theories on organisational performance. These theories emphasise breaking down barriers within and outside the organisation to enhance collaboration, improve products and services, and foster value co-creation. Toon et al. (2016) propose a framework focusing on internal organisational integration, especially in purchasing and marketing, examining structural, human and situational dynamics within the firm before discussing strategies for coordination between purchasing and marketing functions.

Internal dynamics of the firm

Below, we discuss structural dynamics, human dynamics and situational dynamics.

Structural dynamics: The integration of purchasing and marketing relies partly on the internal process architecture of the firm, which encompasses both immediate integration of functional activities and broader macro-level integration within the firm. This architecture is derived from the firm's vision and objectives, supporting integration efforts strategically. This strategic integration complements external integration and aids in resource allocation while reducing barriers through clear motivation. Structural dynamics refers to the nature and types of exchange linkages, offering insights into how counterparts interact, as outlined in Table 1.1 as internal dynamics.

Human dynamics: Effective functional integration between purchasing and marketing requires voluntary exchanges among members of both departments. The presence of open communication and goodwill signifies a successful exchange process. However, these exchanges are not purely altruistic. There is an expectation of reciprocity in the future. Knowledge sharing occurs freely, with the anticipation of receiving something in return later on. In the integration process, exchanges take place within a group context, and the group determines the essential conditions of exchange, reciprocity and equivalence. Human dynamics involves trust and norm-based behaviours that shape the exchange process, ranging from collaborative arrangements built on high levels of trust to more transactional relationships governed by norms as the rules of engagement.

Situational dynamics: The organisation's internal factors that shape the functional integration process are referred to as situational dynamics. These dynamics are context-dependent, influencing both the capability and inclination of functions to integrate, thereby affecting the organisation's situational dynamics. These dynamics are a mix of factors reflecting the organisation's institutional position, which collectively act as barriers to internal integration. Three main factors within this mix include physical location and goal orientation, institutional power arrangements and cross-functional knowledge. Differences in physical location and goal orientation may exist between functions; for example, marketing may prioritise quick responses, while purchasing focuses on long-term consistency and SC relationships. Variations in institutional power arrangements can lead to imbalances across functions, reinforcing hierarchical and silo mentalities. Additionally, knowledge of other functions is crucial for collaborative value creation, requiring close integration and contributing at various levels.

Managerial implications: approaches to purchasing and marketing coordination

Below, we discuss transactional approaches, integrative approaches and co-management approaches.

Transactional approaches: This approach to exchange prioritises self-interest over integration with exchange partners, focusing on cost-saving strategies. It aids in effective partner selection, particularly in cost control. However, in the internal environment of a firm, where there's no internal market and limited options for exchange partners, this approach faces limitations. Instead, a transactional approach among functions within the firm may support quality management, with functions acting as exchange partners having specific requirements of their counterparts. For example, procurement must deliver inputs meeting predetermined parameters to operations. While this approach suits direct links between functions, it may not be suitable for all contexts, such as purchasing and marketing interactions lacking direct links. Despite barriers to complex knowledge exchange in transactional scenarios, some industrial contexts benefit from this approach, especially in stable customer requirement settings. A dual focus on supply bases and customers within the supply organisation can offer strategic advantages by addressing customers' cost and quality agendas more effectively.

Integrative approaches: This approach contrasts with the transactional model as it emphasises collaboration among functions, either through dedicated inter-functional teams or regular formal and informal communication. Functional goals align with organisational strategies and prioritise inter-functional cooperation, with one function accommodating some of the partner's priorities. Quality and cost control rely on mutual dependence and relational capital, characterised by high levels of trust governing individual and group behaviour. However, variations in perceptions of trust and the absence of monitoring in relational control processes can limit effectiveness. This approach is less suitable for stable manufacturing environments where volume and cost control are critical, but more adaptable contexts benefit from its flexibility, particularly in rapidly changing product environments. Integrated functions address issues at the design stage, saving time and improving cycle times compared to problem-solving during implementation.

Co-management approaches: This approach to coordinating purchasing and marketing blends integration and exchange, allowing for joint agendas while maintaining function identity and individual goals. Co-management involves structured collaboration through dedicated team meetings and shared agenda items, ensuring cross-functional consideration. It includes dedicated innovation teams for specific projects, feeding back into functional areas with feedback loops for design and operational details. Another co-management pattern involves overlap arrangements where members work across functions, fostering intense exchange, particularly in complex knowledge contexts. Unlike transactional or relational approaches, co-management relies on managerial systems to allocate tasks and ensure accountability without constant monitoring or relational capital development. It efficiently addresses functional distance and strategic goal alignment, accommodating various organisations' integration needs. Co-management balances cost and quality concerns while promoting coordinated value creation across functions, enhancing organisational agility to respond to market challenges effectively. Table 1.1 summarises our discussion.

This case originates from Toon, M., Morgan, R., Lindgreen, A., Vanhamme, J., and Hingley, M. K. (2016). Processes and integration in the interaction of purchasing and marketing: Considering synergy and symbiosis. *Industrial Marketing Management* 52(February): 74–81. Here, the reader can also find additional relevant references to the case and its topic.

TABLE 2.1 Process–interface framework for marketing and purchasing integration

Forms of dynamics	*Theoretical manifestation*	*Managerial approach to purchasing – marketing coordination*		
		Transactional	*Integrative*	*Co-management*
Structural dynamics	Exchanges based on formalisation, joint planning and teamwork	Preexisting work and market systems (e.g., competition) exert positive effects on clusters in the value chain, with applications to integration along the value chain and external to the organisation	Internal functions are co-located, and a set of exchange processes are interwoven	Co-management systems are internal and use organisation-wide knowledge-sharing architectures. Co-management measures may be more successful if extended to more upstream and downstream zones

(*Continued*)

TABLE 2.1 (Continued)

Forms of dynamics	*Theoretical manifestation*	*Managerial approach to purchasing – marketing coordination*		
		Transactional	*Integrative*	*Co-management*
Human dynamics	Trust in exchanges emerges through information sharing and communication that reflects cultural norms	Knowledge exchanges are typically predetermined by contracts. Communication is less frequent than in integration or co-management approaches, and it is mostly formal	Information is shared in an ongoing process, into which both purchasing and marketing feed. This iterative value creation process features continued knowledge exchanges and adjustments	Co-management facilitates the structured inclusion of upstream and downstream external value chain agents to bring about exchange-based adaptation in the process
Situational dynamics	Goal orientation, physical location, institutional power arrangements and cross-functional knowledge	Shared goal orientation assists in value delivery to customers. For example, a dual orientation on customer and supply bases provides strategic assets from which the organisation can attain advantages	The co-location of internal functions and adoption of singular goals support organisation-wide strategic goals. Power is not exercised internally, and cross-functional knowledge develops through close interaction	Physical proximity and integration incentives can facilitate co-management, leading to effective information sharing and aligned decisions

Multiple-choice questions

1. Which element is NOT part of marketing's definition?

   A. Customer satisfaction focus
   B. Resource conversion efficiency
   C. Pricing strategy development
   D. Demand stimulation

2. A 'need' in marketing is best defined as

   A. A culturally shaped desire
   B. A state of deprivation
   C. A purchasing capability
   D. A competitive differentiator

3. Demand is distinguished from desire by

   A. Psychological urgency
   B. Purchasing power
   C. Social influence
   D. Brand recognition

4. According to Levitt, the 'potential product' level includes

   A. Basic features
   B. Future enhancements
   C. Core utilities
   D. Minimum expectations

5. Which is a key role of SCM?

   A. Maximising departmental budgets
   B. Reducing total system costs
   C. Isolating production units
   D. Prioritising shareholder dividends

6. Which of the following is NOT a primary activity in Porter's value chain model?

   A. Inbound logistics
   B. Operations
   C. Human resource management
   D. Marketing and sales

7. The core business process that involves gathering and acting upon market information is called.

   A. New offering realisation process
   B. Market-sensing process
   C. Customer acquisition process
   D. Fulfilment management process

8. Which of the following is NOT one of the core business processes mentioned in the text?

   A. Market-sensing process
   B. New offering realisation process
   C. Customer acquisition process
   D. Supplier relationship management process

9. The process of building deeper understanding, relationships and offerings to individual customers is known as

   A. Customer acquisition process
   B. Market-sensing process
   C. Customer relationship management process
   D. Fulfilment management process

10. Which of the following is NOT a support activity in Porter's value chain model?

    A. Procurement
    B. Technology development
    C. Human resource management
    D. Outbound logistics

11. The value delivery network, also known as the SC, includes

    A. Only the company's suppliers
    B. Only the company's distributors
    C. Company, suppliers, distributors and customers
    D. Only the company's customers
    E. Only the company's employees

12. Core competencies are best described as

    A. Skills that enable a company to deliver fundamental customer benefits
    B. Physical assets of a company
    C. Financial resources of a company
    D. Company's product portfolio

13. Which of the following is NOT a characteristic of a core competency?

    A. It is a source of competitive advantage
    B. It can easily be imitated by competitors
    C. It can be leveraged widely to many products and markets
    D. It contributes significantly to the perceived customer benefits of the end product

14. The concept that a company should view itself as part of a value creation and delivery sequence is known as

    A. Core competency
    B. Competitive advantage

C. Value chain
D. Supply chain management

15. Which of the following best describes the relationship between marketing and SCM?

    A. They are completely separate functions with no overlap
    B. Marketing is a subset of SCM
    C. SCM is a subset of marketing
    D. They are interdependent functions that must work together to deliver customer value

Essay question

Analyse how the concepts of value chain, core competencies and SCM interrelate to create competitive advantage for a company. Discuss how marketing plays a role in integrating these elements to deliver superior customer value.

3

MARKETING AND SUPPLY CHAIN MANAGEMENT COEXISTENCE IN TODAY'S MARKET ARENA

Introduction

Marketing and supply chain management (SCM) are key business functions. Many believe that they belong in different worlds. Indeed, they rest their view on the cases of companies where boundaries with respect to their competences have not been defined with clarity, thus creating 'grey' areas with respect to the performance of daily activities. The definitions offered by official and well-known organisations contribute to this. According to the American Marketing Association (AMA), 'Marketing is the activity, set of institutions, and processes for creating, communicating, delivering, and exchanging offerings that have value for customers, clients, partners, and society at large'. On the other hand, the Council of Supply Chain Management Professionals (CSCMP) defines SCM as the 'planning and management of all activities involved in sourcing and procurement, conversion, and all logistics management activities'. Even if their objectives seem different, many researchers and case studies prove that the effective coexistence of marketing and SCM fosters the proactive planning for demand handling, as well as supporting the collaboration and full transparency among marketing and supply chain teams.

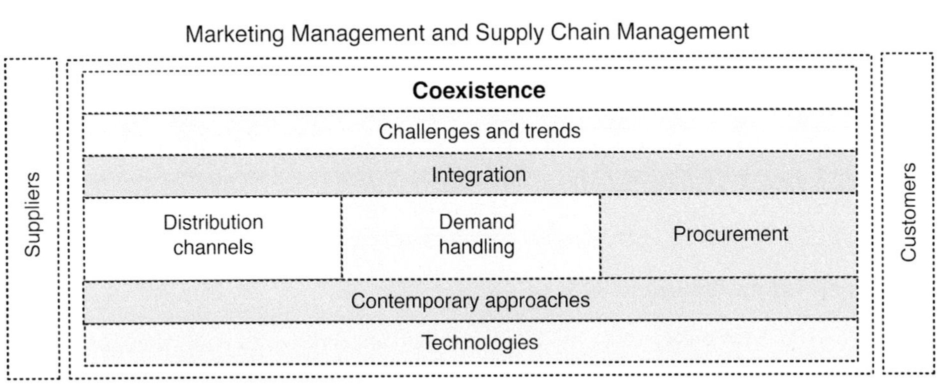

DOI: 10.4324/9781003650973-3

Learning objectives

After reading this chapter, you will be able to answer the following questions:

- What are the similarities and differences between marketing and SCM?
- What is the view adopted by marketing managers on SCM managers?
- How do marketing and SCM collaborate to decrease their lead time and, in general, to satisfy demand?
- Why is communication a critical factor for the success of the effective collaboration of these two functions?

Outline

3.1 Aesop's fable

Aesop, in one of his timeless and always topical fables, refers to a middle-aged man with two mistresses. The fact that lends special value to this myth and, in parallel, the element, which renders it not only timeless but also utilisable in the context of this section, is the directness of parallels that may be drawn for approaching and treating multivariable issues. In every scientific discipline that required the simultaneous aggregation of many factors to attain one objective, equivalent thoughts and speculations take place.

The process for the satisfaction of demand is not a univocal action. It is a multilevel and pre-functional process that requires the splicing, joining and concurrence of efforts, objectives, capacities and capabilities, especially of the operating departments of marketing and SCM, and, therefore, requires the communication and coordination of their actions.

The previous paragraph essentially, descriptively and circumlocutory, photographs the concept of the unification of the two operating departments under the roof of an integrated systems approach, namely, their strategic pairing and the synergies entailed by it, and the most effective use of specialised functional skills and capacities from each department. It is, in simpler terms, the necessary bridge between the specialised parts, which work towards the common direction of demand satisfaction and share the same goals and priorities.

And while it is evident that unification as a concept is complementary of specialisation, it is also true that every operation adopts extreme specialisation approaches (up to the point where there is alienation or even rivalry between the two departments). Communication in such an approach and the safety valves adopted to ensure its effectiveness within such a sector of special characteristics pose intra-business collaboration as a fundamental condition and improve the margins for the correct and expedient management of emerging threats and risks.

3.2 Comparing marketing with SCM

Marketing and SCM are two concepts/functions that are interconnected. Their mutual base is customer service. This initially includes the creation of demand and/or the determination thereof. It also includes the set of the activities by a company that aim to satisfy the customer and are directly related to the execution of orders.

But this is also the subject of SCM: the satisfaction of demand. The survival of a company is possible only when its customers are satisfied. In a market where quality and cost are deemed as given, the responsiveness to customer needs is the 'weapon' in the arsenal of businesses, which wish to increase their competitiveness. Consequently, the attainment of a high level of customer service stresses the close relation between SCM and marketing. Marketing, through advertising, promotion, campaigns, etc., aims to create, maintain and increase demand. SCM aims to satisfy demand via the transportation of the products/services from the company to its customers. The poor execution of orders bears consequences on the level of customer service and, of course, on the level of sales.

In general, three cases for the execution of an order can be distinguished:

- Full execution of an order, when the company possesses all products requested by the customer.
- Partial execution of an order, when the company does not possess all the products requested by the customer but expects them to fully execute the order. This case is called a back order.
- The company does not possess nor will it acquire for disposal the products requested by the customer – a stock-out.

Besides the execution of an order, there are criteria that evaluate the level of service offered by an enterprise (Table 3.1). We can distinguish criteria that may considered as criteria for the evaluation of the logistics systems in a supply chain, but which belong to marketing, and others that belong to both groups.

TABLE 3.1 Evaluation criteria for marketing and SCM

SCM	*Marketing*	*Both disciplines*
Lead time	Resolving time	Financial (gross margin, financial indexes, etc.)
Completed on time	Wait time	Response to questions, queries, complaints
Frequency	Customer satisfaction	External packaging quality
Consistency in delivery	Customer loyalty/retention	Level of service
Extraordinary deliveries when required	Promoters (people who would recommend your business to others)	
Available inventories and uninterrupted feed	Intention/likelihood to reorder	
Full and not partial execution of orders	Complaints	
Informing on shortages		
Ease of placing orders		
Acceptance of orders		
Accuracy of invoices		
Quality of salesmen/agents		
Monitoring of inventories		
Terms of payment		
Labelling		
Collaboration for the introduction of a new product		
Incident volume by channel		

Lead time

It is clear that the time required to execute an order or lead time plays a very important role in client service. This time consists of three sub-times (Figure 3.1):

- The processing time for the order, which commences upon its placement and ends when the product or products requested by the customer are in the warehouse. It is rational to expect that if the company has attended to having the products in hand, this time will be minimum.
- The time for the collection of the products from the points they are located inside the warehouse to the place where they will be ready and packaged to be transported to the customer.
- The time it takes to transport the products from the business to the customer ('door-to-door').

In attempting to reduce its lead time, a company must find ways to reduce each sub-time individually. Ways to reduce each sub-time are recommended in Table 3.2. All these recommendations constitute attempts at the integration of issues and decisions by marketing and SCMs and are analysed in the chapters that follow. They regard themes, which belong to the following business functions: procurements, stock management, storage, distribution networks and transportation, as well as segmentation, targeting, positioning, market research, marketing research, etc.

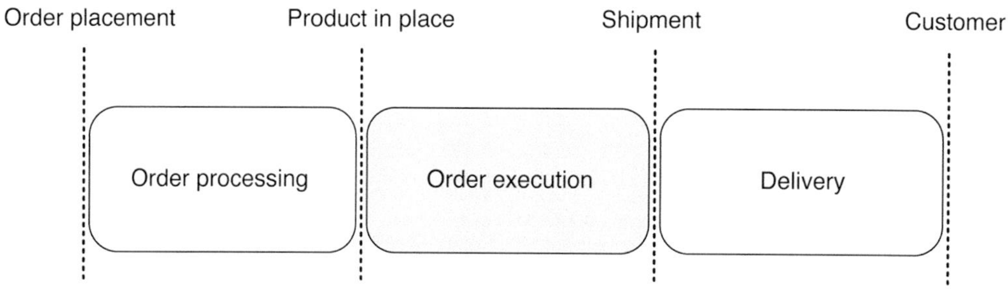

FIGURE 3.1 Reducing lead time

TABLE 3.2 Recommendations and practices to reduce lead time

Sub-time	*Ways and practices for reduction*
Order processing time	Reliable forecast of demand that will assess the products to be required and their quantity based on historic sales data and knowledge of the market Improvement and simplification of the order-taking system Use of an informatics system that will grant immediate access to information relating to the existing stock and the capacity for production and/or procurement of products, if required Organisation of an effective and efficient sales network. For example, the head of sales of a company can request salesmen to visit customers at regular intervals and be informed on possible orders in the near future. Upon their return, salesmen shall inform the relevant company departments, to take care and make available to the customers the products they will ask for

(Continued)

TABLE 3.2 (Continued)

Sub-time	*Ways and practices for reduction*
Collection time	Good organisation of the warehouse, which includes • proper layout of the warehouse, allowing fast access to all products; • 'smart' placement of products in the warehouse. For example, a large retail chain uses the following, simple logic for the layout of products in the storage facilities of its supermarkets. Products are placed in groups (electric appliances, clothes, pasta, etc.) in exactly the same fashion they are placed in the aisles of a supermarket (facing). Products in greater demand are placed closer to the supermarket floor so as to reduce the time it takes to restock the shelves; • use of an informatics system that 'knows' and informs personnel at any time as to where any product is located. It may also offer additional useful information, such as expiry dates, import dates and point for reordering; • use of barcode technology, which will allow the warehouse staff, when used in combination with an information system, not only to know the location, quantity and condition of products in the warehouse but also to perform storage-related actions/works (import, export and inventory) in a short time and, principally, without errors; • use of suitable equipment and means of storage and internal transportation, which facilitate the quick and safe collection of products in demand; • properly defined roles and competences for the staff in the warehouse; • of course, experience on behalf of the staff with respect to storage operations and the use of the infrastructure and the equipment in the warehouse
Transportation time	An organised transportation and distribution network, including • good planning of routes; • proper selection of the transportation means depending on the road network, the morphology and special requirements of the distribution network; • experience on behalf of the drivers and the personnel working in the system for loading the merchandise on the trucks and in the distribution network; • good organisation of the transportation management office (TMO)

Similarities and differences between marketing management and SCM

Similarities

Both constitute two business functions, which, since the reason for their existence is directly related to the customer and the market, are automatically deemed to be necessary. Where there is a market, there are prospective customers from whom a company hopes to take orders – orders that must be satisfied to the maximum degree for the good not only of the customer but also of the company itself. Consequently, marketing management and SCM have a common goal: for the company to survive in the market.

The goal of every company is apparent in the simple formula for profit margin:

Profit margin = income − expenses

We could note that the principal aim of both concepts is the increase of the profit margin. This is their principal and most important similarity. Both these concepts contribute more than any other business function to the success of every company, which is nothing more than the creation of profit. They simply contribute in a different manner. Marketing management aspires to the increase of income, while SCM aspires to the decrease of expenses. But both pursue the increase of the profit margin.

Differences

They have different scope and pursue different (yet similar and counterbalancing) objectives: Marketing management strives to create, maintain and increase demand, while SCM seeks to satisfy that demand through the execution of the respective orders placed.

They operate differently with respect to information management: Marketing management collects necessary information on market research and then informs the market on the products of the company while ultimately aiming to get feedback from customers on the success/suitability or not of the products. SCM informs the customer on the execution of the order and keeps data for the traceability of the products handled.

They consider the importance of marketing's 4Ps differently: The 4Ps (promotion, product, price and placement) or the 7Ps of service marketing (see Table 3.3) are equally important for the head of marketing and sales. Indeed, the head of marketing, when defining strategy, deems that they are all equally important and constitute the key arsenal for the attainment of the objectives of an enterprise.

TABLE 3.3 Definitions and key characteristics of the 7Ps of services marketing

P of services marketing	*Definition and key characteristics*
Product	Investigation of customers' desires, so as for the product to be created by a company to correspond to their needs and desires and, simultaneously, to meet business objectives Key characteristics: • Product mix: range: number of different series of company products; length: total number of goods included in the product series of the company; depth: number of variations for each product in the series; and coherence: degree of connection between different series • Variables: name, firm, trademark, brand, legal–civil liability (e.g., defective products), packaging (functions: protection against spoilage, placement of shelf, ease of distribution, promotion, contribution to building the product's image, contribution to standardisation, e.g., quantity, facilitation of consumption/use, provision of information), label (directions for use, promotion, ingredients, trade name and date of expiry), environmental footprint, social responsibility, support services and style/design
Placement	Establishment of those conditions on the part of the company so that consumers have immediate access to the product, namely, for the product to be made available to them at the time they need it and at an appropriate place for them. Key characteristics: • Distribution mix: number of types of distribution channels; • Variables: type, number of intermediaries (middlemen), type of channels, length–width of channels and the remaining 3Ps;

(Continued)

TABLE 3.3 (Continued)

P of services marketing	*Definition and key characteristics*
	• Functions: transportation, distribution, storage, decrease in the number of transactions, after sales, credit/financing/risk taking, informing, promotion, contact/negotiation, purchase/search, physical possession, ownership, sale/order/payment, packaging and gradation/classification/pairing
Price	Shaping of pricing objectives, pricing policy and the product's price, so as for consumers to be willing to buy it and, simultaneously, to also serve business objectives Key characteristics: • Intra-business factors affecting price: pricing objectives (e.g., market share, increase or decrease in sales, based on competition, maintaining fixed prices, survival and attainment of cost leadership), marketing goals, the remaining P and cost; • Inter-business factors affecting price: competition, nature of market and demand, buyers, macroeconomic figures, legal/institutional/regulative environment and government environment; • Pricing policies
Promotion	Disclosure to or training of consumers or the bolstering of their interest to increase the identifiability of the offered product Promotional mix (advertising, personal sales, sales promotion, public relations and direct marketing) Key characteristics: • Variables: push and pull strategies, marketing goals, the other 3Ps, business resources, type of product, type of demand (e.g., penetration, skimming, status, psychological, indicative price, array and value), type of cost (e.g., fixed percentage above cost, cost and break-even point), type of profit (e.g., pursued profit and pursued profit over sales), type of competition (e.g., same as, over, under, price leadership)
Physical evidence	Environment through which services are offered and which affects customers' perceptions to a large extent • Mix-variables: magnitude, shape, exterior architecture, entrances, lighting, parking, application of corporate identity in the areas where sales take place, displays, shop, reception and waiting room layout, colour palette, smell, illumination, furniture style, heating or air-conditioning, architectural layout and ambience
Process	Structural–functional systems and human resources management in order for the processes performed in the context of service marketing to be effective • Variables: establishment of processes and methods, planning of activities, timely procurement of equipment, materials, evaluation and monitoring of the implementation of the planned for and desirable processes and actions, motivation of human capital and elaboration of process manuals
People	Personnel who come into daily contact with customers and their principal role being the production of services • Variables: job description or specification of skills, evaluation, utilisation, development of human capital, ensuring homogeneous conditions with respect to behaviour and appearance, incentive procedures and feedback • Role: politeness, fast and effective service, consultation – informing, explanations, friendly disposition, understanding, punctuality, confidentiality, initiative taking, etc.

More specifically, the supply chain manager considers promotion as a significant parameter to the planning of which, however, he contributes little. He knows that satisfied customers who have the product they requested at the appropriate quantity, quality, time and cost are perhaps the best advertisement for the company, but decisions relating to promotion are principally taken by the sales manager. The product is very important for the supply chain manager and affects the decisions he takes in issues relating to support, production, materials management, packaging, codification, labelling, storage, transportation–distribution and recycling. It must be noted that a product's features, such as, for example, its dimensions, impose the use of a specific transportation unit, storage system and medium equipment for transportation. The product's price heavily affects its competitiveness in the market; SCM contributes to this by pursuing the reduction of the economic (operating) cost. As we know, economic/net profit is the positive difference between all of a company's income and its economic cost. Marketing management pursues the increase of a company's income, while SCM pursues the decrease of its costs. Both functions, of course, aim to increase profits!

Moreover, the price of a product influences decisions on the equipment and, in general, investments for its storage and transportation. Location is possibly the most critical parameter. The dispatch of the product to the right place is a critical factor for the success of the logistics and supply chain system. Let us consider a simple example: a shipping company is assigned the transportation of a container from one port to a company located inside the industrial zone of a town. Due to poor planning, the truck transports its load to another town. The poor execution of the order 'encroached' SCM's two main objectives, which, as we explained in the first chapter, are the increase in the level of services rendered and the simultaneous reduction of operating cost.

This is also true with respect to serving the market and with cost in particular. The logistics system aims to make available to the market and specifically to the sale points the product in demand at the lowest possible cost (which comprises the entire cost for managing inventories, transportation, storage, execution of orders and administrative cost), thus attaining the desired level of service. This is achieved either by physically transporting the product following an order (make to order) or by accumulating the appropriate level of inventories (make to stock) that the company estimates will cover demand (Stock and Lambert 2001). Indeed, should the company by means of marketing management (namely, the communication channels) collect useful data at the points of sale, it may form a better picture of the market and a better assessment of demand and offer a better service.

They use different tools and practices: Marketing management employs tools such as qualitative tools (e.g., SWOT (strengths, weaknesses, opportunities, threats) and PEST (political, economic, social and technoloigcal) analysis, five forces model, focus group and Delphi method) and quantitative tools (such as exploratory, descriptive and causal analysis). SCM uses practices such as just-in-time, efficient consumer response, collaborative forecasting, planning and replenishment, and vendor-managed inventory.

Systems approach

A systems approach rests on systems theory. This theory treats a company as a system. According to this approach, a company comprises several subsystems, which do not operate in isolation but collaborate towards the achievement of a common objective. We are not interested in the success of every subsystem individually but in the success of the system. And herein lies the problem!

There are conflicting goals between the subsystems of a business; these, however, must be balanced in order for the system to succeed. This fact is amplified by the fact that decisions taken by one subsystem affect all other subsystems. For example, whatever efforts are made to reduce operating costs in SCM processes directly affect the marketing management processes. For example, distribution using a cheap but slow means of transportation (e.g., train and ship) leads to a reduction in cost but increases lead time, the level of inventories and, of course, service time.

3.3 Marketing and SCM managers: how do they feel about each other?

The marketing manager and the supply chain manager coexist in every company. The leading role played by both usually stirs up not only ambiguities as to their precise roles and competences but also tension between them, especially in cases of crises or, in general, when things 'do not go as planned'.

What each of them believes is happening:

- The marketing manager feels that he is unappreciated. It is him who tries the most to increase the profits of the company, and he feels that it is very difficult for him to convince the top management of the company on how much effort succeeding in a sales or maintaining the existing customer base takes.
- The supply chain manager feels that he is unappreciated too. He, too, is the one who tries the most to reduce operating costs and feels that it is very difficult to make the company's management see how great an effort is required and how many individuals must collaborate to execute an order or attain the desired service level.
- The marketing manager accuses the supply chain manager of dealing only with the internal processes of the company to attain an increase in the internal performance indexes. On the other hand, the supply chain manager feels that the only thing the marketing manager cares about is to achieve the targets set for sales and in reality does not really know how the business is running. This view may be generalised as to how the managers above search for new opportunities. Marketing managers seek opportunities in the external business environment without taking account of the capabilities of the company to satisfy and support such opportunities. On the other hand, supply chain managers first assess how well they can support and satisfy whatever opportunities they will then search for in the market.
- The head of marketing considers himself to be an extrovert and social compared to the supply chain manager. This automatically creates problems in certain specific company operations, such as procurements, where the supply chain manager needs the contribution of the marketing manager in searching for the best suppliers, since it is the latter who knows the market better.
- The supply chain manager feels that it is difficult to evaluate his contribution to the company's success (and, in general, to the measurement of its performance). While the performance of the marketing manager is measured in terms of sales (volume and prices), which he attains, the corresponding performance of the supply chain manager relates to the reduction of costs (which is usually a difficult endeavour requiring executives to have know-how and expertise and be fed with appropriate data) and to the availability and strength of the logistics system.

- Marketing managers like to take initiatives and defy risks, as opposed to supply chain managers who do not like being confronted with dynamic situations or taking high-risk decisions.
- The only thing they both agree on is that the company would have been a shambles without them!

It is therefore evident that the success of a business entails and directly depends on the success of the uninterrupted and fruitful collaboration and, ultimately, integration of the departments of marketing and the supply chain.

3.4 Role of communication in the coexistence of marketing and SCM

The key variable and principal factor for success in the daily execution of orders, but also with respect to the satisfaction of demand in general, is interdepartmental collaboration and communication. This has been observed in the majority of both theoretical models and those whose recommendations are derived from empirical research.

The definition of the concept of 'collaboration' is not exhausted in the exchange of information between the inflow and outflow mechanisms and the dialectical relationship existing between them. The lack of communication/collaboration, namely, the non-integration of the departments, ensuing from their individual operational efforts to attain their own – narrowly defined and individual – objectives is a catastrophically destabilising factor intensifying uncertainty and exacerbating most of the other factors that compose the environment for the development of innovative telecommunication products, and in a chain reaction prolongs launching times and drastically contributes to the dynamic negative feedback of the framework in which telecommunication products are developed.

The inadequate or incomplete integration forcefully deviates from the equilibrium that must be attained to dampen or eliminate unfavourable environmental conditions and the destructive results, for the process of launching a new product.

It ought to be stressed that while operating maximisation (under the light of the narrowly and departmentally defined objectives, practices, mentality, etc.) runs counter to and as an obstacle to an all-encompassing, holistic, approach to optimisation and the effective and rational attainment of the common organisational objectives advocated by integration, the concept of maximisation should not be viewed as itself running counter to maximisation. It aims for the same result but treats the system in a more comprehensive and rational way, incorporating in it its own variables and other parameters. As such, this system of understanding and treatment will help one tread the 'foggy' and 'turbulent' landscape more firmly and lead to the faster successful introduction of new telecommunication products.

It is now inconceivable for every operating department of an enterprise to work towards the direction of attainment of the same objectives that constitute its subset.

Example cases of unsuccessful cooperation between marketing and SCM

Case 1: Great product, but not available!

A major seasonal products' wholesaler decided to import synthetic Christmas trees for the holiday season. Two months before Christmas, he concludes an agreement with a supplier for the purchase of a large quantity of Christmas trees at a very good price. Despite the price being very competitive, he decides to realise an advertising campaign for the promotion of the product not only in the local market but also to other markets further away. The advertising campaign turns out to be very successful, and, thus, 1 month before Christmas, he has received orders for all of the trees. Due to poor planning, however, and due to striking a deal with an inexperienced freighter, the trees are delivered 1 day after Christmas Day. In this case, the promotion, advertising and marketing system was very successful in its work. However, the supply chain system failed and took down the entire company with it!

Case 2: To stock or not to stock?

To meet market demand, a company needs to maintain a considerable level of inventory. On the other hand, the cost for acquiring and managing inventory negatively affects its profitability. Moreover, we must also consider the possibility that products are not sold/disposed of or become obsolete. The acquisition and keeping of stock are one of the principle areas of disagreement between the heads of marketing and the supply chain. In a retail chain, each head puts forward his views with respect to maintaining extensive inventories (Table 3.4). Who do you think is right?

Synopsis

- There are similarities and differences between marketing management and SCM. They both aim to satisfy demand by attaining the full execution of orders, decreasing lead time and offering added value products and services.
- On the other hand, they have different objectives and scope; they operate differently with respect to information management, and they consider the importance of marketing's 4Ps in a different manner.
- People from the two business functions coexist in every company. The leading role played by both usually stirs up not only ambiguities as to their precise roles and competences but also tension between them, especially in cases of crises or, in general, when things 'do not go as planned'.
- The successful coexistence of marketing and SCM requires a successful intradepartmental collaboration and communication.
- The inadequate or incomplete integration forcefully deviates from the equilibrium, which must be attained to dampen or eliminate unfavourable environmental conditions and the destructive results, for the process of launching a new product.

Review and discussion questions

- What are the similarities and differences between marketing and SCM?
- You are the marketing manager for a cosmetics firm. What would you recommend reducing – the lead time or response time?
- You are the supply chain manager for a retail chain, responsible for the restocking of the chain's retail outlets from its distribution centre. What would you recommend reducing – lead times or response times?
- What is the attitude of the marketing manager towards the supply chain manager and vice versa? Can you suggest any ways for the gap in the intradepartmental communication to be reduced?

TABLE 3.4 Contrast of marketing and supply chain managers' opinions about holding inventory

Marketing manager	*Supply chain manager*
The company has great capacity and can meet demand	The company is very flexible and maintains the inventory that is needed, when it is needed
It is possible for the company to be out of stock due to a small increase in demand	Stock can become obsolete
The company depends on the capacity of suppliers to supply it with the stock it needs when it needs it	The management of high level of inventories creates high cost
The company can achieve a reduction in the cost for purchasing products from suppliers due to discounts	The management of high levels of inventories can become complex

Case studies

Case: Maersk app: integrated logistics in the palm of your hand

Many argue that shipping companies are conservative, but Maersk proves otherwise. They have developed a cutting-edge app solution for ordering containers, aiming to make it as easy as buying clothes on platforms like Zalando.

Maersk, a Danish-owned company, operates in 130 countries, primarily transporting containers with dry cargo and frozen or refrigerated goods. In 2023, they had sales of USD 51.1 billion. Maersk is an integrated logistics company dedicated to connecting and simplifying global trade for a growing world, with the declared purpose of improving lives by integrating the world.

Revenue from maersk.com increased by 90% from 2021 to 2022, reaching DKK 286 billion. The company has 114,000 unique users. App revenue increased by 300% to 6 billion in 2022. In 2023, there were 301,000 customers for maersk.com and 11,400 mobile customers.

The company holds approximately 15% of the shipping market. It operates 700 owned and chartered container ships with a total capacity of 4 million TEU (twenty-foot equivalent units) and serves 100,000 customers globally. Approximately 12 million containers with 325 tonnes of goods are transported. APM Terminals, an affiliate of Maersk, operates 65 ports and terminals across 33 countries.

Krishnan Srinivasan, SVP Technology & CDO at Maersk, explains, 'Our digital transformation can be described as running a marathon. A few years ago, we started our journey. Now, in 2024, we are beginning to see it come to life and have converted several beta solutions into finished 360-degree solutions in the form of platforms that can handle container transport not only at sea but actually "end to end" all the way to the customer. Our transport services thus include not only transport via our ships but also land transport and air freight. The goal is that customers can manage the entire process digitally, quickly, easily, and simply'.

In developing digital solutions, there has been significant involvement from customers and users, adopting a very agile approach. Continuous feedback from users has ensured that the solutions are user-friendly and relevant.

If companies do not focus on changes in market conditions and customer expectations, they can quickly become shackled by their supplies and demand. Managing logistics across multiple teams, suppliers and borders becomes a challenge that increases in complexity daily.

Maersk app

The app helps customers gain better control over their supply chain. This intuitive app provides real-time updates on everything customers need to keep their logistics in place and ahead of the game. Customers can see where their shipments are and structure their supply chain based on changes or new market strategies.

There is also the option of choosing Value Protect, a simple add-on product, to protect booked cargo. Value Protect applies to all items and can be used in addition to standard coverage. It extends responsibility for transport conditions to aspects not normally covered by traditional terms, such as damage caused by delay or fire. Experience shows that incidents can occur even in the safest hands, potentially impacting goods and business. Value Protect can be added to the contract or shipping with a single click during the booking process, providing extra peace of mind.

Customers can stay updated on their cargo via the app with real-time status updates. Specific shipments can be tracked by marking them as 'favourites' for quick and easy access, allowing customers to follow shipments around the world 24/7. Customers can mark their favourites from multiple bookings and get notified of changes in shipment status. For example, in the ever-changing situation in the Red Sea, real-time information is crucial for keeping everyone in the value chain updated.

The app also helps customers with documentation and invoice issues by gathering all necessary documentation. Customers can view and share information about their shipments with other stakeholders in their network anytime, anywhere. Invoice handling can also be done through the app, allowing customers to download all their invoices and reduce paperwork headaches.

The Maersk app is an excellent example of a solution that supports the increasing need for marketing agility. It is a market-ready solution that empowers customers with greater control over their supply chain.

Multiple-choice questions

1. Which criterion is used to evaluate marketing performance but NOT SCM?

   A. Customer satisfaction surveys
   B. Inventory turnover ratio
   C. Order fulfilment accuracy
   D. Supplier lead time variability

2. What is a primary recommendation to reduce lead time in supply chain operations?

   A. Increase batch production sizes
   B. Implement cross-functional teams
   C. Reduce supplier communication frequency
   D. Centralise decision-making authority

3. Which of the 7Ps of services marketing emphasises the role of frontline employees?

   A. Product
   B. Price

C. People
D. Process

4. Why do marketing managers generally oppose holding high inventory levels?

A. To minimise storage costs
B. To reduce production flexibility
C. To avoid product obsolescence
D. To enhance demand forecasting

5. Which practice aligns marketing and SCM goals in demand handling?

A. Siloed departmental strategies
B. Independent demand forecasting
C. Collaborative inventory planning
D. Decentralised procurement systems

6. What is a critical challenge in integrating marketing and SCM?

A. Overlapping departmental objectives
B. Identical performance metrics
C. Synchronised communication flows
D. Unified customer segmentation

7. Which factor is a key driver of globalisation's impact on supply chain complexity?

A. Reduced transportation costs
B. Homogeneous customer preferences
C. Localised regulatory frameworks
D. Centralised production facilities

8. What distinguishes the 'Process' element in the 7Ps of services marketing?

A. Tangible service environment design
B. Employee–customer interaction protocols
C. Dynamic pricing strategies
D. Geographic distribution networks

9. How does SCM prioritise risk mitigation in inventory decisions?

A. By reducing safety stock levels
B. By diversifying supplier networks
C. By shortening product life cycles
D. By standardising product designs

10. Which trend exacerbates demand volatility in modern markets?

A. Stable economic conditions
B. Homogeneous product offerings

C. Rapid technological advancements
D. Fixed customer loyalty programmes

11. What is a consequence of misaligned marketing and supply chain strategies?

A. Enhanced customer loyalty
B. Synchronised production schedules
C. Increased stockout incidents
D. Reduced procurement lead times

12. Which element of the 7Ps focuses on service delivery efficiency?

A. Physical evidence
B. Promotion
C. Process
D. Place

13. Why do supply chain managers advocate for higher inventory buffers?

A. To minimise warehousing expenses
B. To accommodate demand fluctuations
C. To reduce supplier dependency
D. To streamline production cycles

14. What is a barrier to adopting a global supply chain strategy?

A. Standardised global product designs
B. Localised regulatory compliance costs
C. Centralised decision-making structures
D. Homogeneous cultural preferences

15. Which metric reflects supply chain efficiency but NOT marketing effectiveness?

A. Customer retention rate
B. Order cycle time
C. Market share growth
D. Brand equity index

Essay question

Discuss how the integration of marketing and SCM addresses three interrelated challenges in today's globalised markets: (1) demand volatility driven by technological advancements, (2) conflicting inventory management priorities and (3) the need for glocal adaptation strategies. Support your analysis with specific examples from the chapter.

4

IDENTIFYING THE CHALLENGES AND TRENDS OF MARKETING AND SUPPLY CHAIN MANAGEMENT

Introduction

The modern business environment is characterised by driving forces, such as *change*, which is constant, dramatic, chaotic and complex; a *customer-oriented* philosophy, which tends to become the most crucial and strategic factor; the *globalisation* of the markets, which creates new requirements and, of course, challenges for the management of businesses; *internet* and *mobile networks* and *ubiquitous computing*, which offer new capabilities but also create organisational and technological challenges; and the recognition of *intellectual capital* as a crucial factor and the strategic alliances with key business partners. These challenges have affected the way in which marketing and supply chain management (SCM) executives plan and perform their daily activities. Also, these challenges, either individually or in combination, pose problems to the desire and the process for the integration of the two functions. In the sections that follow, those challenges are addressed under an integrated prism.

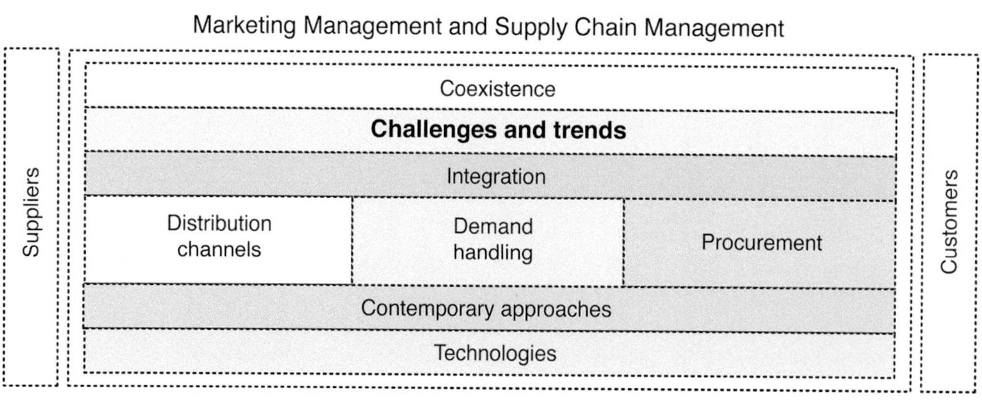

DOI: 10.4324/9781003650973-4

Learning objectives

After reading this chapter, you will be able to answer the following questions:

- What are the challenges marketing managers must address?
- What have been the trends dominating marketing in recent years?
- What are the challenges and trends for SCM in today's market?
- Which are the obstacles for the integration of the two concepts/functional areas?

Outline

4.1 Challenges and trends in marketing
4.2 Challenges and trends in SCM
4.3 Challenges of marketing and SCM integration

4.1 Challenges and trends in marketing

The main challenges of marketing in today's market focus on the following areas:

- green marketing and corporate social responsibility;
- international marketing;
- glocalisation and
- social networks/social media and marketing.

Green marketing and corporate social responsibility

Taking account of the developments in production – but also with respect to the rendering of services – we are in a position to recognise the power and importance of marketing for the survival and operation of businesses. In an era where technological developments are rapid across the entire spectrum of their application, the concepts of borders and geographical limitations with respect to the operation and activity of companies have ceased to exist, and the orientation of companies' strategies itself appears to have shifted on the time frame. Two key 'new'/old trends are dominant and signify both the overall activity of companies and the activity and character of marketing: the first trend relates to the conviction that marketing functions must be governed by sensitivity for the well-being of the natural environment where the company is active, while the second is the perception that business functions (marketing included) must ensure the well-being of the social environment where the company does business. The first regards the concept of green marketing (hereinafter GM), while the second is corporate social responsibility (hereinafter CSR).

These two approaches, although old (the concept of GM is approximately 30 years old, while that of CSR is roughly twice that age), continue to sustain the interest of the academic – and the business – community as if they were only recently developed. Contributing to this is the fact that they are complex concepts, with features, that are not necessarily clearly defined in the bibliography (or least, there is no consensus with respect to what a complete and clear definition of some of their constituent elements can amount to).

On the other hand, world developments (economic, technological and social) by themselves create a fertile ground for the establishment and development of such approaches in our era.

Of critical importance for the accentuation of the aforementioned concepts was the need for businesses to adopt attitudes, strategies and practices that would, on the one hand, be profitable for the businesses while, on the other hand, could limit the consequences and effects that their operations might have either on the natural or the social environment – an observation that gradually aims to define what could be expressed by GM and CSR correspondingly.

GM analysis

The American Marketing Association (2016) provided a definition for GM with a triple nature, depending on the field of action to which one referred.

Firstly, they provided a definition relating to retail sales where GM was considered as the marketing of products that are deemed to be environmentally safe. Then there is a definition in the light of 'social' marketing, where GM refers to the production and marketing of products designed to minimise negative effects on the natural environment or to improve its quality. Finally, with respect to the environment, GM is designated as the efforts by companies to produce, promote, package and reshape their products in such a manner so as to exhibit a sensitivity towards environmental issues. One further definition offered by the American Marketing Association is given also by Li and Cai (2009), by virtue of which GM is defined as the research exploring the positive extensions and negative ramifications of marketing activities on pollution, and the decrease of energy consumption and non-exhaustion of energy reserves.

According to another approach, as expressed by Charter (1992), GM is a holistic process of strategic management, which recognises, foresees, satisfies and realises the needs of 'stakeholders', against a rational consideration, which does not adversely affect the well-being of man or the natural environment. Mintu and Lozada (1993) designated GM as the application of marketing's general principles and tools to facilitate exchanges, which satisfy organisational and individual objectives in a manner ensuring the preservation, protection and conservation of the natural environment. In 1994, Polonsky defined GM as the set of activities designed to realise or facilitate any exchange aiming to satisfy human needs or desires inside the framework where such exchanges have the minimum possible harmful consequences for the natural environment. In 1995 the same author offered a refined version of the definition above, arguing that GM comprises all activities designed and planned to realise or facilitate any exchange aimed to satisfy human needs or desires, in a manner by which the satisfaction of said needs and desires takes place with the minimum negative consequences for the natural environment.

Moreover, Peattie (1995) defined GM as an integrated management process that is implemented for someone to recognise, predict and satisfy what customers or society requests, in a manner that is profitable and viable. A parameter is already added here, which carries the sense of GM closer to the concept of CSR and obviously not without reason – the satisfaction of society's requirements! We shall assess the possible connection in what follows. Fuentes (2014) characterised GM as a complex social, cultural and material creation. The process for the marketing of 'green' products includes rendering them important for consumers while understanding the procedure followed by marketing practices, so as to establish products as noteworthy material – symbolic objects could also reinforce our understanding of how GM operates inside the consumer culture of our times.

Another approach to GM considers it as the expression of marketing strategies that echo the needs and desires of consumers with environmental sensibilities (Mathur and Mathur 2000; Zinkhan and Carlson 1995). The term 'green consumer' is ascribed to consumers with such environmental sensibilities. Chan and Lau (2000) observed that should one wish to understand the 'green movement' in some country, one should begin by assessing how consumers in the country in question treat ecological issues and how the emerging viewpoints reflect consumer behaviour with respect to green issues. Given the importance the consumer holds as the epicentre of the companies' 'attention', we can appreciate the reason for which research relating to consumer behaviour, and indeed that of the green consumer, is broad.

Polonsky (1995) noted the existence of five reasons, to which he suggests increased activity in GM can be attributed:

1. Increased pressure from governmental organisations for increased corporate responsibility.
2. The perception of GM for companies as an opportunity to succeed in their goals.
3. Companies' perception that they are morally committed to be increasingly socially responsible (something that stands as a significant indication of the close relation between CSR and GM).
4. The environmental activity of companies that, in turn, pushes a course of change of the environmental activities of the competition.
5. Elements of cost that relate to waste by-products, which exercise a form of pressure for the redesign of production procedures and of the products themselves.

To sum up: GM is a subset of marketing's general activity, it explores both positive and negative activities, it assesses a limited spectrum of environmental issues, and it assists us in ensuring that the interests of the enterprise and all consumers are protected, that their needs are satisfied, and that GM viewed as a voluntary process of exchange could not exist save only if the buyer and seller would jointly experience a mutual benefit. Adhering to GM's philosophy, we may observe a decrease in cost, satisfaction of the employees, minimisation of waste and well-being in society and the company, suffice that all stakeholders be determined and committed to this (Kumar et al. 2011).

But, there are problems in the case of GM as well, problems emerging as a business is called to implement it. These problems lie in the shaping of strategies, as Mendleson and Polonsky (1995) observe, and emerge due to three principal reasons: the lack of trust on the side of consumers, their cynicism and confusion. The authors suggest that should these issues not be dealt with, it is doubtful that the implementation of GM in its entirety will be effective. Based on their research, they recommend the establishment of strategic alliances with environmental groups as a way to produce benefits for the marketers of consumer products on five levels:

1. Increase in the reliability of green products and the claims complementing them, with respect to consumers.
2. Granting access to companies, with respect to environmental information.
3. Granting access to new markets for marketers.
4. Positive publicity and quieting of criticism from the public.
5. Training consumers with respect to important environmental issues relating to the company and its products.

Stakeholders and stakeholder theory

Having already referred to stakeholders, we must stress the significance of this term for all that will be discussed in what follows. Stakeholders, with reference to the functions of a corporation, constitute an important element relating to the concepts of GM and CSR and refer to all those factors inside and outside the corporation, which have an interest in its operation or are, in some way, affected by it. On the other hand, due to their interaction with the corporation, they are able to, on many occasions, co-shape the conditions under which the company will be active. We must cite at this point 'stakeholder theory', which plays a key role in both the shaping and understanding of the concept of GM, as well as that of CSR correspondingly.

A concise definition for the content of this theory is offered by Businessdictionary.com, which cites that it must be considered as a conceptual framework resting on a combined approach of business ethics and organisational management, which was created to address the moral values and code of conduct of a business or an organisation in general. The way in which management can satisfy the interests of stakeholders with respect to the enterprise is thus delimited. This theory appears appropriate as an approach when we have to deal with GM providing a process that, if adopted, could facilitate the development of a GM strategy, something that would allow the attainment of business targets and the satisfaction of stakeholders (Polonsky 1995). Stakeholders exercise a significant influence on both the company and the market, as Yazdanifard and Mercy (2011) observe, while they are dominant in shaping a GM strategy, provided the enterprise wishes to move accordingly. Jaime Rivera-Camino (2007) suggests that in the case of GM, stakeholders may also include plants, animals and future generations.

A first definition was offered by Carroll (1979). According to this, companies implementing a CSR philosophy serve and facilitate the financial, legal, discretionary and philanthropic expectations that society has of businesses at some given point in time. It is thus supported that businesses are responsible with respect to society and that they ought to do what it expects them to do.

Business in the Community (2005) offered a definition relating to CSR, which cites the management of positive influences the company has on society and the environment through its functions, its products and services, and its interaction with key shareholders, such as its employees, its customers, investors and suppliers.

Holcomb et al. (2007), after citing alternative terminologies for the meaning and contents of CSR – social responsibility, corporate citizenship and corporate sustainability, put forward a definition for the term, which was incorporated and is reflected in the Dow Jones Sustainability Index (2005). According to this definition, CSR is a business approach creating long-term shareholder value, by accepting opportunities to acknowledge elements of risk originating from economic, environmental and social developments. The proponents of corporate sustainability attain long-term shareholder value by appropriately shaping their strategies and the management thereof to tame the potential of the market for sustainable products and services, while simultaneously successfully decreasing and staving off elements of cost and risks to sustainability.

According to Maignan and Ferrell (2004), CSR signifies the duty (jointly motivated by instrumental and moral arguments) to satisfy or overcome stakeholders' rules, by dictating desirable organisational behaviours. Values and rules relating to stakeholder theory are frequently applied in a multitude of issues relating to marketing, such as sales practices, consumer rights, environmental protection, product safety and the rational disclosure of information, as observed by Maignan and Ferrell (2004).

Later, Maignan et al. (2005) presented, among others, a table containing characteristic examples of stakeholder groups affecting the function of marketing and which may need to be attended to during the decision-making process with respect to CSR issues. To summarise the contents of this table, we distinguish six broad stakeholder groups, together with specific points of interest relating to each group:

1. *Employees:* (a) Compensation, benefits; (b) training, development; (c) employee diversity; (d) occupational health, safety; (e) communications with management.
2. *Customers:* (a) Product safety; (b) management of customer complaints; (c) services to disabled customers.
3. *Investors:* (a) Transparency of shareholder communications; (b) shareholder rights.
4. *Suppliers:* (a) Encouraging suppliers in developing countries; (b) encouraging minority suppliers.
5. *Community:* (a) Public health, safety protection; (b) conservation of energy, materials; (c) donations, support of local organisations.
6. *Environmental groups:* (a) Minimising the use of energy; (b) minimising emissions and waste; (c) minimising the adverse environmental impacts of products and services.

Besides all that were cited and the role played by stakeholders in the shaping and implementation of CSR philosophy, Hemingway and Maclagan (2004) assessed the hypothesis that there can be cases of individual executives who, through their personal values, can affect the shaping, adoption and materialisation of CSR policies by enterprises, finding that they play an important role even in those organisations that have not officially adopted a CSR culture or philosophy.

Maignan et al. (2005) propose the use of a stakeholder model when implementing CSR to marketing, observing that marketing's orientation has shifted from the narrow viewpoint of the customer-oriented approach, to another, which includes the management of the relations developed with potential stakeholders, as well as the array of benefits that they enjoy. By characterising the nature of the CSR approach as dynamic and by acknowledging the complexity of the emerging challenges, they stress the need for adequate organisational planning on the level of the enterprise, ensuring adequate resources and a full commitment to this objective. If the effort to invest in CSR is supported, it is expected to bring tangible benefits with respect to issues such as customer loyalty, employee commitment, support and collaboration with suppliers, and corporate reputation. On a different turn of events, the image of the corporation may suffer great losses, endangering even its existence and viability.

Maignan and Ferrell (2004), based on what they observed in their research, present a series of standpoints relating to the consideration of CSR:

- Approaching CSR as a social obligation, which can be further distinguished into different types, such as (a) financial obligations, (b) legal and moral obligations and (c) philanthropic obligations.
- Approaching CSR as an obligation against stakeholders, who can, in turn, be distinguished into four broad categories: (a) institutional, (b) social, (c) regulatory and (d) media.
- Approaching CSR as being dictated by morals, as referenced to the activities of an enterprise with respect to the degree by which they are 'right' or 'wrong' – independent of the type of obligation that they are called to cover.
- Approaching CSR as a managerial process (the term corporate social responsiveness is frequently employed in this context). Three dominant processes are identified, which are considered to be indicative of the term above: (a) monitoring and assessing environmental conditions, (b) attending to stakeholder demands and (c) designing plans and policies aimed at enhancing the firm's positive impacts.

International marketing

For almost eight decades, the issue of standardisation of international marketing has been a focal point of the attention of both the academic community and the practitioners (Ryans Jr. et al. 2003). Jain (1989) define standardisation as a common marketing programme on a worldwide basis. Szymanski et al. (1993) define the term as the 'standardisation of the pattern of resource allocation among marketing mix variables across national markets'. Zou and Cavusgil (2002) considered the term 'global marketing strategy' as the degree by which a company globally generalises its marketing behaviour in various countries, through the standardisation of variables in the marketing mix, the concentration and coordination of marketing activities and the inclusion of competitive moves between markets.

A techno-economic basis is required in order for a marketing strategy to be globalised, a basis comprising traditional economic infrastructures, knowledge creation infrastructures and other infrastructures relating to the modern form of information and communications (Sleuwaegen 1992). The globalisation of support services is also a powerful tool that may contribute towards the direction of expanding on a global scale.

Sleuwaegen (1992) also identifies three important elements relating to the internationalisation of marketing: the role of technology, the role of government (as two forces driving the process of internationalisation) and the adoption of a new, suitable management model, so as to deal with constant changes in the environment, emerging as a response to the two other factors above. With the change and application of the management model, there is a boost towards a new, different procedure for the internationalisation of companies, also including the breadth and multitude of international connections between companies. Governments, in turn, follow developments, attempting to focus on acquiring technology that is necessary to plan for strategic commerce and investment policies, which gradually replace free trade policies. They affect the way by which interstate corporations choose to penetrate foreign markets. From a process of sterilised protection to attain better financial performance, they now move to a different direction, through the provision of incentives for the assumption of technological initiatives and to attract investments from interstate or international companies.

The potential for attaining a scope economy and the diffusions taking place between markets, as a result of the use of technology in different markets, constitute constituents forcing companies to an international expansion process. Scale economies on the corporate level may continue to play a significant role, but they will be more closely related, in this new reality, to scope – product- and geography-wise – economies, rather than the scale economies (relating to products) (Sleuwaegen 1992). Craig and Douglas (2001) identified a challenge in the creation of strategies that respond to and can predict the rapid rate of changes in global markets. They observed that to succeed in this, the needs for information will change, as they become more complex and multifaceted. The need for timely informing (information that is important and time sensitive) also bears more heavily in the daily process of decision-taking but is also aimed at delineating and depicting the course of the company in an environment where the rate of change is rapid and which is turbulent and very competitive.

The new approach, if adopted, shall require increased communication among the R&D, marketing and production departments. There will, in general, not only be an increased need for internal (interdepartmental) communication but also a need to develop synergies (collaborations) across many different fields (Sleuwaegen 1992). On the other hand, the changes observed in the international environment, and the technological developments in data collection, analysis and dissemination, imply (the need for) and dictate the exploration of capabilities in order for the planning, implementation and transfer of research to respond to our modern era. New tools, which incorporate new technologies, will, therefore, need to be created and utilised so as to develop creative approaches for understanding behaviour in cultural contexts, which are differentiated from one another. It is also very important to interpret and incorporate complex data from multiple sources and environments in all this, for there to be recommendations of significance for the company's global marketing strategy (Craig and Douglas 2001).

Zou et al. (1997), referring to the work of Buzzell (1968), cite a series of positive points complementing the adoption of standardisation in international marketing and include decease in cost, consistency with customers, improved planning and distribution, and greater control across national borders. On the other hand, they also cite some negative points in adopting standardisation, which include – in agreement with Douglas and Wind (1987) – that it is attainable only under very specific conditions (the existence of a global market segment, potential synergies from standardisation and the availability of communication and distribution infrastructures), that it implies an orientation towards products and not customers and/or competition, and that it is subject to internal and external limitations with respect to the company itself. With respect to internal limitations, the already existing network of operations might be incompatible with opting for such a strategy. As for the external limitations, they refer to statutory regulations, product safety standards and requirements for local or localised content (Cavusgil et al. 1993; Wind 1986). Another negative point is the resistance from local subsidiary management (Ohmae 1989). Finally, for such a strategy to be implemented, we must assume that there are no major cultural differences.

Following from the above, Zou et al. (1997) propose that companies approach the issue of standardisation with a multidimensional perspective. Moreover, instead of limiting a company's choice between standardisation and adaptation, it could also follow a course for shaping a degree of standardisation on the level deemed necessary or purposeful. Indeed, as Ryans Jr. et al. (2003) observe, the theory on standardisation rests on the hypothesis for the homogeneity of consumers or their tendency towards one. If, on the other hand, we are dealing with heterogeneity – differentiated needs among consumers – the solution proposed as that offering greater value is to use an adaptation strategy.

Glocalisation

According to Svensson (2001), the international strategy of a business group is closely related to its corporate strategy. Corporate strategy guides and leads the generalised business performance of the group as well as the appropriate utilisation of available resources for the attainment of the goals set by the company. Levitt (1983) distinguishes between a multinational business group and a global one. The first is active in several countries and adjusts its products and practices for each one, while the second operates with stability, as if the entire world – or great regions in it – was a uniform entity.

Keegan and Green (2000), as well as Simon-Miller (1986), support the view that the global strategy approach and the globalisation of business activities may bear a considerable competitive advantage inside the market. Segal-Horn (1996) cites the following potential benefits from a global approach to strategy and the globalisation of business activities: reduction of cost and restructuring of the international logistics functions. From this point onwards, such advantages may influence planning, procurements, production operations, packaging, distribution, marketing, advertising, customer service, software development, and the establishment of standardised facilities, methodologies and procedures between locations.

Yip (1992) cites four forces leading to globalisation: a global strategy can improve access to market factors, such as common needs of customers, international customers, international channels, transferable marketing and dominant markets. Companies are also influenced by cost factors, such as economies of scale, scope economies, resource advantages, advantages in procurements and overlapping between the different countries. On the other hand, Jeannet and Hennessey (1992) cite a series of factors that limit an approach such as the one just described. They refer to market characteristics, conditions for industry, organisations associated with marketing and legal limitations.

Svensson (2001), in an effort to explain the view of Yip (1989), argues that, on the one hand, the conditions for the application of a purely multi-domestic strategy exhibit the following features: there is no specific motif for participating in the market, product offer is fully adjustable for every market, the location of the activities offering value are limited inside each country, the marketing approach is localised and competitive moves are individual and targeted for each country. Conditions for a purely global strategy, on the other hand, are characterised by the following: there is no significant participating share in the major markets, the product offer is fully standardised on a global scale, the placement of activities adding value focuses on one activity for every country and the marketing approach is uniform on the global level, while competitive moves are incorporated across all countries. The term glocal strategy (glocalisation) was introduced in an attempt to improve the use of the term global strategy (Svensson 2001). Prakash and Singh (2011) inform us in relation to the origin of the term 'glocal' and the relevant process 'glocalisation' that they ensue from joining the words global and local, referring us to the *Oxford Dictionary of New Words* (1991 edition). With respect to enterprises, this conception was adjusted to refer to global localisation. Raimi (2003) describes that the term invokes the simultaneous presence of trends aiming at the same time to generalise (globalise) and to specialise (localise). Foglio and Stanevicius (2006) refer to the term glocalisation by characterising it as an acceptance and incorporation of globalisation and localisation. The rationale of glocal strategy combines local, international, multinational and global approaches. It differs from the global approach from the moment it explicitly accepts the significance of adjustments on the local level and the tailoring of business activities to the market. Additionally, it contains the rites and issues of international and multinational strategies (Svensson 2001). Svensson concludes that the philosophy behind the term glocal strategy was used to render greater accuracy to the present use of the global strategy approach between scholars and practitioners, while acknowledging the need for balance and harmony between standardisation and adjustment, homogeneity and tailoring with respect to business activities.

A valid glocalisation process will allow the following aims (Stallings 1995; Foglio and Stanevicius 2006): answer to globalisation and to localisation; a counterproposal to the universalism of globalism and opposition to the levelling caused by globalisation; defence of the ethnic, cultural and local particularities; and acquisition of new competitive advantages (glocal advantages) to set up the international process of the enterprise. Furthermore, Foglio and Stanevicius (2006) observe that through the use of a globalisation strategy, the value of the various cultures and traditions and of the identities distinguished on the local level is discovered anew and increases, while these characteristics are placed in the global vision together with their distinctive features. Glocal philosophy includes a process, which is easy to discern compared to the rest. This can be analysed into (a) its global processes, when someone aims to globally expand the product, the market or the marketing strategy, and (b) its local processes, when the increase of the value is pursued and which is aimed at anything that can be characterised as local (product, market and marketing strategy).

The glocal processes are when globalisation processes are applied to something characterised as local and localisation processes are applied to something characterised as global. In this manner, a local product is in a position to reach the niche segments of the global market, while – on the other hand – the globalised product can reach local markets when it undergoes the necessary adjustments. In both cases, we can refer to a glocal market, glocal consumers (or users) and a glocal marketing strategy.

Consequently, should we view the following figures by adhering to the rationale of Foglio and Stanevicius (2006), they can be summarised as follows: the glocal choice is accentuated in the case of a local enterprise, which is interested in the specialised niches inside the global market, when and if, of course, it possesses products that may satisfy these niches (Figure 4.1), or in the case of a global enterprise that is interested in local markets and is willing to actualise the necessary adjustments to satisfy these markets (Figure 4.2).

The same authors finally identify some factors that reinforce the decision to choose glocalisation but also some obstacles during its implementation. The following constitute factors,

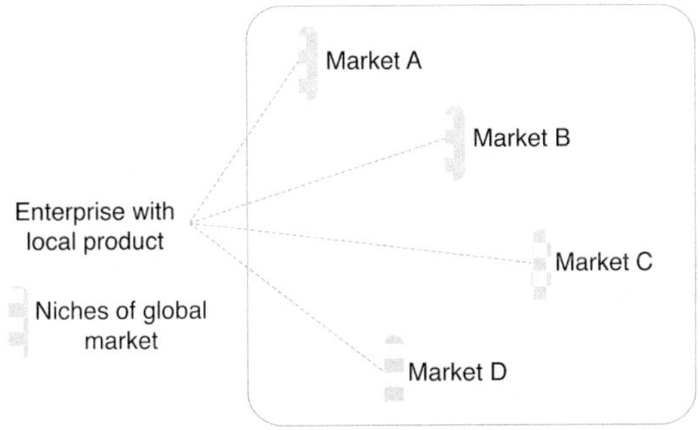

FIGURE 4.1 Glocal way: enterprise with global product addressed to specialised niches of the global markets

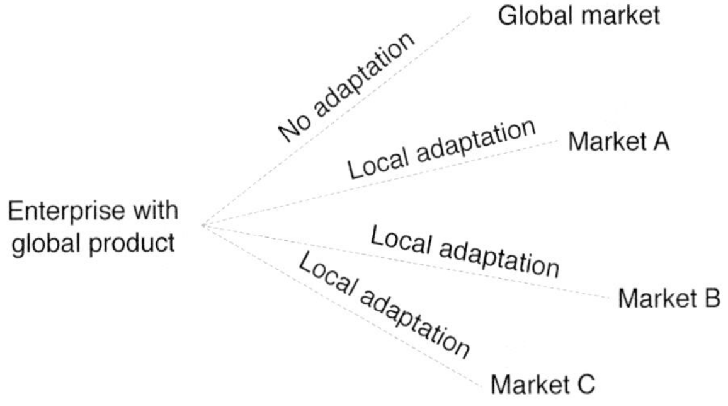

FIGURE 4.2 Glocal way: enterprise with global product addressed to local markets with opportune adaptations

therefore, that support the decision to choose a glocalisation strategy: saturation of the market, presence of a glocal demand (differentiated niches in the global market and local markets), territory and localism, costing, interest in local culture and tradition, increase in the sales, laws and rules, glocal management and glocal marketing. On the other hand, the following are considered to be obstacles to its implementation: geopolitics, the situation of some countries, the mission of the enterprise, conservatism, excessive globalism, excessive nationalism/regionalism, geographical distance, psychological distance, global products that refuse adaptations and typical/local products with poor productive potentiality.

Social networks/social media and marketing

We are in an era where technological developments combined with different needs for communication and the exchange of information/content have led to the creation, establishment and evolution of social networks, mainly via the internet (although there is a trend for the use of social networks over mobile phones). Tussyadiah (2012) argues that online social media will constitute an increasingly key part of marketing's activity, as companies confront the need to incorporate direct communication addressed to targeted customers with indirect communication, which addresses their social networks. Further proof of the power of social media in our era is the observation that they have the capacity to significantly influence the reputation of a company, its sales, even its survival itself (Kietzmann et al. 2011). The following categories of social media are indicatively presented, as such were identified by Constantinides and Fountain (2008):

- Blogs: These are digital periodicals by individuals or companies, which may include podcasts or video.
- Social networks: Applications that allow users to build their own personal web pages, which can be accessed by other users, to exchange personal content and to communicate.
- Content communities: Web pages that organise and disseminate content of a specific type.
- Forums/bulletin boards: Websites for ideas and information exchange – usually revolving around specialised interests.
- Content aggregators: Applications allowing users to fully customise the content of the web pages they wish to access.

Miller et al. (2009) stress that the importance of social network media lies in the communication between consumers and the community and the facilitation of a 'asynchronous, direct, immediate, interactive, low-cost communication'. Social media facilitate the processes for communicating and forming groups inside a multitude of frameworks. The use of mobile devices has helped for such processes to become more direct and effusive (Tussyadiah 2012).

The value of social networks for marketing lies in the fact that these not only constitute networks of interconnected users who are in a position to influence (influencers) by sharing their recommendations but also constitute interconnected, homogeneous ingredients (conformers) seeking recognition from one another (Tussyadiah 2012). The same author also observed the phenomenon of the introduction and inclusion of games in the context of a social network, something that in terms of consumption reinforces the process of competition, which, in turn, leads to comparison and social expansion, which may affect behaviour. He concludes that marketers have utilised this phenomenon to advertise and introduces the term 'advergaming' – the use of games to advertise products and services.

According to Bolotaeva and Cata (2010), social networking sites are tools for the establishment of virtual communities, or social networks, for individuals who share similar educations, lifestyles, interests and activities. Most of these networks can provide other ways for online communication, such as e-mail, messaging, chatting, blogs and discussion groups. Tussyadiah (2012), however, stresses that one of the distinguishing features of such sites is the obvious willingness and abilities of people to communicate their thoughts to others, including people they do not know.

By using a simple SWOT analysis, we can conclude the following:

- Advantages of social network media: Helps raise brand intelligence, comprises a new marketing channel, provides cost savings, creates connections and can raise brand awareness.
- Disadvantages of social network media: Aggressive advertising might lead to loss of customers, lack of e-commerce abilities because the users will not return or stay with the network if there is too much pressure to buy or if the network is viewed as too commercialised, legal issues regarding market research and advertising, lack of brand control and privacy issues on data mining.
- Opportunities of social network media: Public awareness, involvement and mobile handset advertisements.
- Threats of social network media: Economic downfall, ethics, third-party advertisement platforms and user privacy.

4.2 Challenges and trends in SCM

Supply chain managers face the following challenges:

- customers have great expectations;
- networked businesses in networked economies;
- increase of transportation costs;
- segmentation;
- asking for green products and services and
- outsourcing is here to stay.

Customers have great expectations

Many research findings have identified the increase in customer expectations from company logistics and supply chain systems. The factors contributing to this are many; the pressure exercised by customers as well as the other business units/members of the chain can be considered as a key factor not only for better and cheaper products and services but also, mainly, for personalised products and services. Moreover, the florescence of electronic commerce allows, on the one hand, global sourcing and customers, while it increases, on the other hand, the requirements for fast and cheap movement of products around the world. We can also include the demand by the market for the provision of the full picture when an order is executed. Orders made via smartphones will be of special interest in the coming years, as they drastically change consumer behaviour. Finally, the increasing demand for green transportations will reduce the impact on the environment and, in general, for logistics functions with low carbon dioxide emissions.

Networked businesses in networked economies

Today more than ever businesses aim to participate in international networks (improvements in communications and globalisation have played a major role in this). Their management has realised, on the one hand, the opportunities for expanding to and accessing new remote global (both mature and emerging) markets and, on the other hand, their inability to offer 'everything to everybody'. Thus, they collaborate with other enterprises, even competing ones, automatically creating the need to unify their processes and systems. These collaborations range from the collaboration of the members of a supply chain for the fulfilment of partnerships such as collaborative planning, forecasting and replenishment (CPFR) and the assignment of the company's stock management to its suppliers (vendor-managed inventory, VMI), to the global or regional manufacturing consolidation of sales, operations planning, new product design and introduction to market, and channel configuration. Moreover, another challenge with respect to new and emerging markets such as Eastern Europe, China and Africa is their poor transportation infrastructure. One thing is certain: supply chain and marketing are the two areas that are most affected by the global business environment. And volatility due to economic crises and social unrest will be one of the key trends in the new and emerging markets. This fact significantly affects global sourcing, especially from low-cost countries.

Increase of transportation costs

Increase of transportation costs is due to an increase in the price of gas, tolls, etc., but principally due to the dominance of the make-to-order or order-to-order practices and, in general, the trend by companies not to hold stock, but to prefer frequent resupply when necessary, as well as the desire of the market for door-to-door practices.

Segmentation

A classic marketing application is the segmentation of the market by grouping consumers based on their consumer behaviour and their demographic characteristics. But the same is also valid for SCM strategies. In this case, the criteria for customer and market segmentation are operating cost, the demographic and geophysical characteristics of the points for the distribution or sale of the products, and the level of service the company aims for.

Asking for green products and services

The initial 'trend' for sustainability has evolved to a principal market demand. 'Green' transportations refer to the application of practices and technologies, which are aimed at reducing the negative environmental impact of transportations. It belongs to an international economic practice, the application of an energy-efficient and effective system, which will support the economic development of a nation (sustainable development). Furthermore, it involves the implementation of strict environmental standards that will lead to new and innovative business initiatives (sustainability or viability). 'Green' transportations are one part of 'green' practices for the management of logistics processes (green logistics), which focus on the following:

- The design and development of products adopting environmentally friendly practices and materials (such as products manufactured from recyclable materials, organic ingredients and those that use environmentally friendly packaging).

- The selection and collaboration with suppliers who also adopt environmentally friendly production, handling and distribution processes.
- The operation and use of storage facilities that use and utilise energy-saving mechanisms and technologies.
- The use of packaging made from recyclable materials, which do not pollute the environment.
- The more efficient and effective management of returned products (recycling of waste and rejects).
- 'Green' transportation initiatives that aim to change the attitude of businesses and organisation towards major environmental issues, such as climate change and the burdening of the environment due to the irrational use of natural and energy resources. For this to happen, however, management must realise and understand the following:
    - The greatest percentage of total energy consumption originates from transportations (roughly 40%, according to the annual reports by the EU in the past 2 years). Of this percentage, road transportations account for most of the energy consumption (greater than 80%).
    - In all, 20% of the emissions of pollutants and greenhouse effect gases (principally CO_2, but also others, such as CH_4, N_2O, and SO_2) originates from transportations, and 70% of this from road transportations.

A further focus is to identify those functions and daily tasks that encumber the environment directly or indirectly and/or consume large amounts of energy and, finally, to find ways and mechanisms for reducing the above with the simultaneous attainment of financial and social objectives. Consequently, the principal goal of 'green' transportation and SCM in general is to implement a strategy where the economic objectives of a company or an organisation must be connected to the minimum possible burden on the environment.

Outsourcing is here to stay

The decision to assign part or all of some processes that intervene up to the final delivery of merchandise rests on specific benefits for the companies applying such a practice. These benefits are principally associated with the following:

- Lower cost: A business that assigns part of all of its activities to third parties achieves a saving of resources and freeing of capital, since it does not need to invest in infrastructures, equipment, machinery and other information and technology applications to cover its needs, but pays for using those of the third-party logistics (3PL) for as long as it is required. Thus, its fixed costs turn to variable ones, while it is also certain that its operating expenses, including the cost of the personnel required to operate the equipment and machinery, would have been greater than the consideration paid to the 3PL providers. The saving of resources and capital ensuing from collaborating with specialised service providers allows the company to invest in other key objectives and sectors and to develop other activities. Moreover, the risk the company takes is minimal compared to the risk it would have assumed if it purchased, operated and maintained the equipment and machineries itself.
- Better quality: 3PL companies provide resources of skills and knowledge, while, in addition, they have great experience and the appropriate technological infrastructure for the

performance of logistics processes and the expedited offer of services. The upgrading of the level of the quality of the services offered results in the further satisfaction of customers.
- Additionally, the enterprise becomes more flexible and can quickly adjust to the needs of its clients, new practices and the moves by its competitors.

Of course, a partially or totally outsourced supply chain necessitates a planning that would allow and cater for the participation of outsourcing companies, the existence of mechanisms for the monitoring and the measurement of the performance of all members of the supply chain and outsourcing companies in particular, and, of course, IT systems and technologies, which would allow information exchange and transparency across the entire supply chain.

Logistics service providers merge. Most of the logistics service providers believe that the shrinkage of their sector is the most expected fact that will occur in the coming decade. This, all other reasons aside, will single-handedly increase the number of mergers and acquisitions at the sector, offering companies the opportunity to expand their scope across many sectors and regions.

New technologies change everything. As supply chains have become more complex and dynamic, and as the relevant information collected by companies/members of the supply chain from logistics processes, pertaining to traceability and green practices, is so huge, the use of state-of-the-art technologies is recommended as the ideal solution. Some of these technologies are as follows:

- Internet of Things practices and technologies to extract and provide specific functionalities and information that refer to the inner and inter-logistics processes. Specifically, many 3PL companies via their websites extract functionalities from the business information systems either integrated solutions or 'best-of-breed' (enterprise resource planning (ERP), warehouse management system (WMS), etc.), providing access to the customers to (usually big) business data that are maintained in those systems.
- The usage of radio frequency identification (RFID) technology for supporting automating logistics tasks such as routing, scheduling, load planning, and track and trace.
- Business intelligence (BI) capabilities, which capture all the business data from disparate sources and present these to decision-makers in a user-friendly manner (e.g., dashboards) to make business-critical decisions, improve service level and meet customer expectations. BI includes various software applications, practices, technologies and analytical methodologies, which perform big data analysis, and provides real-time visibility and access to useful information (Folinas 2007).

4.3 Challenges of marketing and SCM integration

In the two previous sections, the trends and challenges regarding the two functional areas individually were presented. Their integration, despite its doubtless advantages, is a process that requires a change in a company's/employees' culture and mentality and, of course, must have the support of the top management. Moreover, the following additional challenges must be addressed:

- *Resistance to change:* Resistance by the employees of the two functional areas to the 'opening' of their borders and their collaboration to satisfy demand. This creates the following problem: in wishing to attain their objectives, marketing and sales managers do not take account of the realisation cost and, in general, the requirements in terms of resources. This is especially true in a globalised and volatile market.

- *Lack of trust and mistrust* in the exchange of the information transparency handled by the two departments (silo mentality). This lack of trust can be attributed, on the one hand, to the different objectives of the two functions and, on the other hand, to the sense that the employees have that the exchange of information will stir up problems in their daily tasks and in the attainment of individual objectives.
- *Lack of common considerations for the activities of each function:* For example, common processes and collaborations in key business issues, such as those of the design and development of new products and services, planning, selection and/or production of packaging, demand forecasting, sourcing, etc., are not evident in many enterprises.
- *Lack of common policies and practices* to increase financial results (total profit and turnover). For example, supply chain managers demand that no account is taken of short-term income and short-term and long-term costs when planning and executing an order. Moreover, the need for new costing models is also apparent – costing models that will take account of the costs of the processes of both functions.
- *Lack of common performance measurement indexes:* Every function defines and employs different metrics, and this causes confusion and problems in the measurement of performance. Apparent, therefore, is the need to create new customer-centric performance measurement indexes that will combine the performance of both areas by utilising appropriate business data.
- *Non-support by one function of the practices and philosophies* employed by the other. For example, while the marketing department has designed different practices and policies depending on the particular requirements of market segments, supply chain departments function as if they ignore this, performing the logistics processes in the same manner for everybody. Simultaneously, the practice of just-in-time inventory management that has become, in recent years, the default practice for inventory management and the execution of orders in general, finds, on many occasions, marketing executives in disagreement, these executives perceiving it as an attempt to decrease the dynamics and ability for the effective and efficient satisfaction of demand.
- *Lack of clear and precise job descriptions* in the organisational charts of companies, with respect to the roles and competences of the relevant job positions.
- *Lack of systems, tools and technologies* supporting decisions and taking account of the needs of both functions. We can add to these also the lack of know-how and skills. There are many technologies today that can be applied to support the supply chain and marketing processes. As an example, one can cite auto ID technologies (RFID and QR codes) that can be employed for the handling of materials, the collection and management of stock and the promotion of products, the provision of information and the implementation of interactive advertising.

Synopsis

- In today's business arena, change is the key characteristic; change has proved to be constant, dramatic, chaotic and complex. Moreover, the customer-oriented philosophy, the globalisation of the markets, and the recognition of intellectual capital, new technologies and the strategic alliances with key business partners create not only new opportunities but also challenges for the management of businesses.
- Marketers in today's market face challenges such as GM and CSR, international marketing, glocalisation and social networks/social media and marketing.

- On the other hand, supply chain managers face the following challenges: customers now have great expectations in a global/networking economy, which is characterised by the increase in transportation costs, the segmentation of the markets, the demand for green products and services and the adoption of outsourcing practices.
- These challenges must be taken into account when outlining integration strategies involving marketing and the supply chain and with respect to the design, performance, monitoring and controlling of key business activities such as demand handling, procurement and inventory management.

Review and discussion questions

- How does globalisation affect marketing and SCM?
- What are the effects of an economic downturn in marketing and SCM?
- Discuss the effect of sustainable practices in marketing and SCM.
- Name three challenges to marketing and SCM integration and suggest the corresponding actions to overcome these barriers.

Case studies

Case study 1: Relationship use and market dynamism

An important issue in marketing research is how firms handle growing complexity, dynamism, competitive pressures and evolving market needs. If market relationships help firms navigate these challenges, establishing long-term, mutually beneficial, interactive partnerships with key stakeholders can enhance performance and create tacit competitive advantages.

Beverland and Lindgreen (2004) studied how the changing competitive environment influences the effectiveness of relationship marketing strategies. They identified the contextual factors that affect the motivation, form and intensity of using relationship marketing.

The authors discovered a link between the overall market climate and a firm's strategic adaptations, prompting adjustments in relationship dynamics in response to shifts in competition, opportunities and market conditions. These adjustments are driven by internal strategic decisions like expansion, niche targeting or strategic realignment. Firms often deepen relationships to not only exploit opportunities but also terminate, pause or initiate new relationships in response to market dynamics. Key environmental factors shaping firms' marketing strategies include heightened competition and changes in market growth rates.

Beverland and Lindgreen (2004) identified four marketing practice eras, each representing a dynamic interplay among the environment, strategy and firm structure, akin to gestalts as described by Kazanjian (1988) and Mintzberg et al. (1998). These eras are emergent marketing (1985–1990), order taking (1991–1995), transactions (the 4Ps) (1996–1998), and relationships and the 4Ps (1999 onwards). In each era, changes were observed in relationships' form, intensity and scope, as well as in the systems, structures and strategic posture of successful firms adapting to these shifts.

Figure 4.3 emphasises the importance of niche density and carrying capacity in determining a strategy that aligns with the environment. These concepts, originating from population

		Carrying capacity	
		Low	High
Niche density	Low	Emergent marketing	Order taking
	High	Relationships and the 4Ps	Transactions (the 4Ps)

FIGURE 4.3 Marketing gestalt

ecology (Hannan and Freeman 1977), refer to a niche's ability to accommodate additional production and the number of firms within it, respectively. As a niche approaches its capacity, firms either explore new niches or enhance efficiency in their current one. This adaptation is influenced by each firm's available sources of variation, indicating that firms skilled at niche exploitation can thrive even in challenging environments. However, these efforts only delay the effects of declining growth rates and increased competition, prompting firms to seek new niches for sustainable growth. The interaction of niche density and carrying capacity drives changes in the breadth, form and intensity of relationships firms form with stakeholders. We notice that there are four marketing gestalts:

Emergent marketing: Emergent marketing describes firms operating in environments with few competitors and limited growth rates. Here, low carrying capacity signifies market uncertainty, not low sales volume. Essentially, firms aim to establish a new niche and operate in early-stage markets.

Order taking: Quality improvements and evolving consumer lifestyles drive a notable increase in product demand for firms. Figure 4.3 denotes this phase as 'order taking', marked by a swiftly growing carrying capacity and comparatively low niche density in the environment. In essence, customer demand surpasses supply significantly.

Transactions (the 4Ps): In an order-taking scenario, easily attainable returns attract well-funded new entrants, often larger than existing firms. The success of established firms in establishing a profitable niche results in a swift influx of new competitors. Despite aspiring to produce high-quality products, new entrants may underestimate the challenges.

Relationships and 4Ps: In the absence of new niches, the 4P era emphasises customer retention. Firms aim to enhance the depth and strength of their relationships to adopt a strategic long-term approach. If existing customer relationships are robust, firms decrease efforts to form new relationships, prioritising strengthening current ones before exploring new niches.

Managerial implications

Firms' strategic choices align with their environment's complexity. While the absence or reduction of relationships may be appropriate temporarily, it can have lasting consequences. Early investment in relationships can yield significant advantages, leading to escalating returns and formidable advantages that competitors struggle to match. In mature markets, observing competitors with extensive relationship networks may indicate missed timing advantages. These firms must pursue growth elsewhere while forming relationships defensively.

Beverland and Lindgreen (2004) warn against rigidly applying the model, noting that transitions between gestalts may not always occur predictably. They cite the New Zealand wine industry as an example, where the shift from the 4Ps to relationships and 4Ps wasn't anticipated by wineries or customers. Instead, marketing practices evolved gradually and incrementally, without a clear defining event.

This case originates from Beverland, M. B., and Lindgreen, A. (2004). Relationship use and market dynamism: A model of relationship evolution. *Journal of Marketing Management* 20(7–8): 825–858. Here, the reader can also find additional relevant references to the case and its topic.

Case study 2: Volvo CE: how SCM enhances the value chain

Volvo Construction Equipment (Volvo CE), a leading manufacturer in the construction industry and part of the Volvo Group, develops, manufactures and markets a broad range of machinery, including wheel loaders, excavators, dump trucks, bulldozers and asphalt machines. Renowned for its innovative and sustainable solutions, Volvo CE helps customers enhance productivity and competitiveness. Their offerings include electric machines and telematics systems like CareTrack, which optimise machine monitoring and operations.

This case highlights a growing trend in business-to-business industries, where companies assist customers in optimising logistics and reducing costs. Large construction projects require various machines to meet tight deadlines. Delays often result in financial penalties, making equipment uptime critical from both financial and scheduling perspectives.

Volvo CE provides a wide array of machines to handle these projects, but regular maintenance and occasional component replacements are essential to minimise downtime. To address this, Volvo CE integrated small sensors into its machinery to actively monitor all moving parts. These sensors collect valuable data, which Volvo CE analyses to improve efficiency for both the company and its customers. This data-driven approach has significantly reduced maintenance hours, minimised downtime and increased operational efficiency.

By proactively leveraging these data, Volvo CE can predict and address potential issues before they escalate, leading to substantial cost savings. The data are continuously fed back into their system, enhancing the predictive maintenance model. This ensures machines spend less time out of service while streamlining service operations. Technicians can be dispatched with the right spare parts, reducing unnecessary trips and saving time.

The sensors also help customers optimise machine usage by preventing unexpected breakdowns and operational disruptions. For example, Volvo CE gathers data on load sizes, fuel consumption and performance metrics, allowing customers to adjust machine operation and save up to 20% on fuel without sacrificing efficiency.

Volvo CE has further revolutionised its service model by deploying mobile service trucks that visit customers on-site, eliminating the need for customers to transport machinery to a Volvo CE workshop. They also set up temporary workshops at large construction sites, such as highway or port projects, further improving logistical efficiency. This approach has helped Volvo CE secure contracts over competitors who cannot provide the same level of service.

Data insights have also enhanced customer service offerings. Volvo's data-driven approach enables the company to maintain higher resale values for equipment, allowing customers to secure longer leases, reduce leasing costs and obtain better insurance terms (extending lease periods from 5 to 7 years). This extended lease period is significant, considering the high cost of construction machinery.

Volvo CE has even developed a new business model based on these data. They introduced hourly leasing programmes tailored to customer needs, which have proven profitable. The ability to collect and analyse data enables Volvo to offer flexible leasing solutions while optimising its own logistics.

A major challenge in equipment leasing is managing risk. However, with comprehensive data and insights, Volvo CE has transformed leasing from a potential liability into a business opportunity. Customers can now opt for turnkey agreements with fixed monthly payments, leaving Volvo CE responsible for equipment maintenance. What was once a loss-making service is now a profitable venture, benefiting both the company and its customers.

By helping customers avoid large capital expenditures and offering more flexible financial options, Volvo CE has set a new standard in the construction equipment industry, driven by the power of data.

Case study 3: Rapidus, IBN and global friendshoring

In 2024, US company Rapidus Corporation of Japan announced a significant joint venture to promote upscaling for two nanometre chip semiconductor manufacturing companies in Japan (IBM Newsroom 2024). The political context of this arrangement is illustrative of tensions that have emerged after the global shocks of COVID and the Ukraine war (Witt et al. 2023) alongside ongoing concerns about China's intentions towards Taiwan and other territorial disputes between China and neighbours in the Pacific economic zone. Since 2022, the level of conflict and re-emergence of Cold War-like tensions in the world have brought many challenges to several decades of almost unfettered globalisation in both global value chains and international supply chains. Within this era of globalisation were substantial amounts of offshoring, where key elements of US and European value chains were outsourced to China and other developing economies.

In the early phase of this mass offshoring after 1990, labour cost efficiencies were a driving force, but more recently, the upskilling of value-adding activities in Chinese manufacturing has increasingly made Chinese manufacturers technological rivals to US and European high-tech manufacturers. Even before COVID, commentors spoke of a Thucydides Trap effect occurring, as the rising power of China was challenging the dominant global power of the US (Allison 2017). Observers remark now that global value chains have entered a period of decoupling, defined as bilateral or community–community reduction in interdependencies (Witt et al. 2023). Alongside US policy, there is also a reported sense that China is equally targeting decoupling, for instance through its Made in China 2025 policy framework (Witt et al. 2023). However, reshoring, a return of globally outsourced value chains to a domestic setting, is complicated by the availability of skilled labour.

Post 2020, a number of key sectors have been identified in which increased security concerns are being assessed by the US government, which along with semiconductors include 5G technology, green energy transition technologies including battery manufacture, active pharmaceutical agents and critical minerals (Tran 2022). National security matters in trade policy were strengthened by the Biden administration after October 7, 2023 (CSIS 2023). The US government has since implemented several policy frameworks to encourage domestic growth in chip production. In August 2022, the US Congress passed the Chips and Science Act to promote a security-driven growth in semiconductor production, which includes strong incentives and support for increased domestic production of semiconductors and disincentives for knowledge transfer to non-aligned nations (CSIS 2023). US policy now stipulates a guarantee that any domestic recipients of government funds for domestic semiconductor manufacturing expansion requires the recipient firm to desist from a significant increase in offshored semiconductor manufacturing for a period of 10 years to China, North Korea, Iran and Russia (CSIS 2023).

Within these policy frameworks is also an acknowledgement as to the impracticality of pursuing an all-domestic supply chain for chip production. Concomitantly, a series of arrangements for international collaborations in international supply chains in strategic industries such as chip supply chains have emerged. These include 'the Quad' (i.e., US–Japan–India–Australia's Quadrilateral Security Dialogue); the Chip 4 alliance among the US, South Korea, Japan and Taiwan; and the 14-member Indo-Pacific Economic Framework for Prosperity (CSIS 2023). The Mineral Security Partnership also exists to govern the security of critical mineral, rare-earth mineral supply chains (USDS 2024; Vivoda 2023) and compliments the chip manufacturer arrangements to secure the supply chain for raw materials such as silicon and germanium. In respect of rare-earth minerals, China maintains global dominance in reserves, extraction and processing (Vivoda 2023).

As Japan has been a key military and economic ally of the US since 1945, the IBM alliance with Rapidus has been facilitated by the desire for critical industries to undertake friendshoring arrangements, that is, moving strategic industry value chains to 'friendly' nations, friendly in both political and military alliance dimensions. Friendshoring is therefore one of the three key strategic moves in the value chain to increase security alongside nearshoring and reshoring (Tran 2022). The alliance allows for the transfer of key technologies to upscale two-nanometre chip manufacturing companies. Friendshoring as a matter of strategic foresight in global supply and value chain futures requires, therefore, a sensitivity to the shifting landscape of conflicts and passive alliances in these conflicts, which may be predicted in the flows of defence industry exports, particularly where a shift from US/European defence industries to Russian/Chinese purchases, or vice versa, is apparent. These may be indicators of movements into silos that may predict where friendshoring sensitivity is likely to become a strategic factor (Vivoda 2023; Witt et al. 2023) in the future. Supply chain managers should also increasingly watch which industries are sensitive and increasingly been seen as 'critical' in security contexts.

Multiple-choice questions

1. Which of the following best describes the concept of 'glocalisation' in SCM?

   A. Focusing solely on local markets
   B. Standardising products globally
   C. Adapting global strategies to local contexts
   D. Eliminating international supply chains

2. What is a key challenge of globalisation for SCM?

   A. Reduced product variety
   B. Simplified regulatory compliance
   C. Decreased cultural diversity
   D. Increased supply chain complexity

3. Which trend has significantly impacted both marketing and SCM in recent years?

   A. Decreased use of technology
   B. Rise of e-commerce platforms
   C. Reduced focus on sustainability
   D. Decline in customer expectations

4. What is a primary driver of supply chain volatility in modern markets?

   A. Stable economic conditions
   B. Homogeneous consumer preferences
   C. Rapid technological advancements
   D. Decreased global competition

5. How does the 'long tail' phenomenon affect SCM?

   A. It reduces product variety
   B. It increases inventory holding costs
   C. It simplifies demand forecasting
   D. It decreases transportation needs

6. Which of the following best describes the concept of 'mass customisation'?

   A. Producing standardised products in bulk
   B. Customising products for individual customers

C. Eliminating product variations entirely
D. Focusing solely on niche markets

7. What is a major challenge of implementing sustainability initiatives in supply chains?

A. Decreased consumer interest
B. Simplified regulatory compliance
C. Balancing costs with environmental benefits
D. Reduced competitive advantage

8. How does the trend of 'servitisation' impact traditional product-based companies?

A. It eliminates the need for physical products
B. It reduces the importance of customer service
C. It shifts focus towards service-based offerings
D. It simplifies supply chain operations

9. Which of the following is NOT a typical characteristic of modern supply chains?

A. Increased transparency
B. Enhanced flexibility
C. Reduced collaboration
D. Improved responsiveness

10. What is a key challenge of managing global supply chains in the context of geopolitical tensions?

A. Simplified trade regulations
B. Increased supply chain resilience
C. Reduced need for risk management
D. Potential disruptions due to trade conflicts

11. How does the trend of 'circular economy' impact SCM?

A. It promotes linear production models
B. It reduces the need for reverse logistics
C. It emphasises resource recovery and reuse
D. It increases reliance on virgin materials

12. Which technology has significantly impacted both marketing and supply chain visibility?

A. Fax machines
B. Blockchain
C. Analogue telephones
D. Typewriters

13. What is a major challenge of implementing omnichannel strategies?

A. Reduced customer touchpoints
B. Simplified inventory management

C. Integrating online and offline channels
D. Decreased need for data analytics

14. How does the trend of 'nearshoring' impact global supply chains?

    A. It increases reliance on distant suppliers
    B. It reduces supply chain responsiveness
    C. It brings production closer to end markets
    D. It eliminates the need for international trade

15. Which of the following best describes the concept of 'demand sensing' in modern supply chains?

    A. Ignoring customer preferences
    B. Relying solely on historical data
    C. Real-time analysis of demand signals
    D. Eliminating demand forecasting entirely

Essay question

Analyse how the trends of globalisation, digitalisation and sustainability are reshaping both marketing and SCM practices. Discuss the interconnected challenges these trends present, such as managing increased supply chain complexity, adapting to rapidly changing consumer expectations and balancing economic and environmental considerations. Provide specific examples of how companies can strategically align their marketing and supply chain efforts to address these challenges and create competitive advantages in the evolving business landscape.

5

INTEGRATED FRAMEWORK OF MARKETING AND SUPPLY CHAIN MANAGEMENT

Introduction

Marketing and supply chain management (SCM) are two business functions that stand, as concepts and philosophies, in a constant dialectic cross-correlation. Despite the fact that they emerge from different scientific fields of specialisation, have different cognitive backgrounds and employ different techniques, tools and methodological approaches, the reason for their existence and the degree of their utility are included and correspondingly evaluated through the same common prism: the achievement of customer satisfaction. The provision and ensuring of all kinds of reassurances and guarantees, which shape the delivery of superior value, that contribute, flow into and shape the level of the perceived customer satisfaction (philosophy, attitude, organisational culture, strategic orientation, vision, mission, processes, functions, etc.) are considered to be an undisputed one-way street and the catalytic – essential – condition for the long-term horizontal survival of the organisation and the improvement of its performance. In this chapter, we attempt to identify the main parameters of the integrated approach of both marketing and SCM that could act as the basis for the examination of the main business functions in the next chapters.

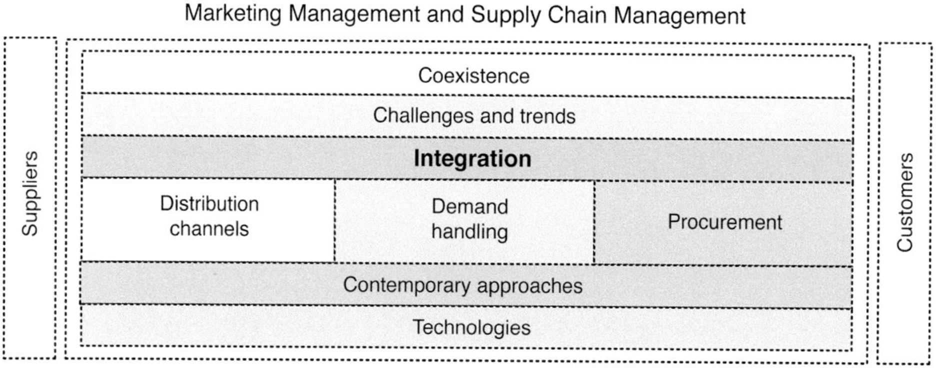

DOI: 10.4324/9781003650973-5

Learning objectives

After reading this chapter, you will be able to answer the following questions:

- What is integration in terms of marketing and SCM?
- What are the obstacles for collaboration and communication among the two disciplines so as to achieve their integration?
- What are the benefits and challenges of the above integration?
- What is the outcome of this integration?

Outline

5.1 Exploration of the integration of marketing and SCM

At a most basic level of delimitation, an organisation can be described as a set of people who have specific knowledge and skills, who are governed by a specific system of values, who have their own attitudes and beliefs and who must work either individually or collectively to play and fulfil the context of the roles assigned to them on each occasion.

By extension, this presupposes the formation of a managerial hierarchy, which is the carrier not only of authority and power but also of responsibility for the attainment of the goals set. To render attainable the effective and efficient realisation of these goals, management designs and plans for the operational units and decides their size, while at the same time shaping and assessing departments, which are specialised carriers of knowledge and simultaneously interdependent structural units. Formulations of the type 'The Marketing department rarely reports what products are needed, but even when it does so, they demand to have them made available yesterday' or 'Marketing is that which you conjure when you can't sell your products' are, unfortunately, aired with increasing frequency.

When 'things' go well and the goals are more or less achieved, it is easier for someone to ignore the issues and symptoms arising from the alienation of the departments, as all are absorbed in the present and disdain having to deal with the future. When time frames are limited by the increase in the gap between what was planned/desirable and what was actualised, and as the accumulative added outcomes of the turbulence are manifestly evident, the failings of the system of the enterprise block and seriously hinder its viability.

Of all the common grounds of special significance that emerge from the operating coming-together of a company's departments, the one that is called to listen to the parameters of satisfaction carried by the product as a vessel of value and also called to deliver such value is deemed to be the most sensitive and critical.

Souder and Chakrabarti (1978) define integration as the symbiotic cross-correlation of two or more entities, which culminates in the production of clear benefits that exceed the sum of net benefits that would ensue from the independent effort by these entities. Lawrence and Lorsch (1967a) define integration as the procedure for the unification of the efforts between various sub-departments for the achievement of the organisational goal. What is seen as the common element of both definitions is the emphasis placed on the result, namely, the additional benefit.

It is well known that an enterprise is characterised by two dimensions of its functions. Due to these, it may be characterised as a closed system but simultaneously as an open one. With respect to this last characteristic, it is considered to be an open system since by necessity it comes into contact with its external environment and is affected by it. One might suggest to record as influences on the business the opportunities or threats that ensue from the almost one-dimensional influence from various and varying sub-environments that frame a business (technological, economic, political, competitive, legal, cultural, etc.). Despite the fact that the company itself 'effuses' influences into its environment (e.g., products and waste), the effects of these – independently of the size of the company – are of much smaller magnitude than those of the corresponding framework of influences the company is subject to from its external environment.

The fact that the external environment is composed of factors that extend much further from the control of the organisation notwithstanding, it is principally their composition, which is that coordinate that must be continuously monitored by the competent executives, be interpreted and decoded by the enterprise, and that feeds it with information and/or feedback. Most organisations claim that they are aware and know the environmental influences they are subjected to, but few are adequately prepared so as to be able to respond to the challenges and their mandates. The majority probably reacts to the emerging needs of customers, rather than attempting to predict them. It is obvious that if the definition ascribed to business management – which poses as its goal the effective handling of the organisation's functions through its manpower – is valid, then it is also true that the organisations ready to change and reorient/redefine themselves towards what is correct, and that can provide motives that are sufficient and adequate to redirect on these lines the entire group of individuals who constitute the enterprise, will have a competitive advantage.

The lack of an orientation for marketing and the ineffectiveness of interdepartmental communication are obstacles for the successful fruition of business efforts. But, as Clarke (1974) notes, marketing is another way of thinking, a different principle, less in terms of detailed accuracy with respect to predictions, which may incorporate both 'exotic' notions (i.e., social conduct and attitudes), while also making use of a different terminology and which incessantly complicates the overall picture of a technically oriented way of thinking.

Too much adherence to fixed and organisationally admissible specialised duties, which follow from the subordination of each employee to some operating department, carries the risk for employees to develop a degree of introversion for the immediate operating group to which they belong. Moreover, they will undoubtedly be led to bolster their faith and trust not only in this specific group but also in the tools it carries in its operating quiver, perhaps in an absolute, unquestioning and one-directionally emphatic manner.

Should all of this be combined also with educational background and natural and perceived tendencies (this may differ, since they contributed to the selection of a different type of specialisation), then it is possible for a web of cross-correlations to be created, cross-correlations that will divert (or at the very least limit) interaction with other executives inside the company, executives belonging to different operating departments.

Having said this, it is clear that there is no one single and unique easy way, nor best and ideal – generally accepted – planning to attain the necessary degree of integration. Some companies seek their radical remake through a small-scale reorganisation and a relaxation of the limitations posed by the existence of interdepartmental boundaries. Communication must be reinvigorated and coordination skills must be considered as an integral part of operational skills.

One of the most frequent problems for the attainment of the synergies entailed by the necessary degree of unification of some interdepartmental functions lies in the following, contradictory fact: in order for operating departments to effectively respond in a timely way to the demands of the modern, dynamic, turbulent, multidimensional and complex business field, they must retain the proofs and 'collaterals' of their personal identity, which is simultaneously delimited, while at the same time defining their specialised skills, knowledge and dexterities. However, in parallel the same executives from various operating departments must be encouraged to take steps towards the (partial) abolition of the mental boundaries of specialisation or the differences in culture, to be effectively oriented towards the realisation of their common organisational objective. Therefore, there is essentially an unrelenting hunt for the golden section between integration and segregation.

As the orientation of businesses tends with increasing stability to adopt marketing's philosophy and incorporate its ideology to the managerial algorithm for taking business decisions, the common perspectives between the marketing and supply chain departments must be explored and investigated, and – to some extent – for some of their activities to overlap.

Throughout the productive procedure, there are many parameters that potentially undermine inter-company communication and collaboration, as well as the commitment of operating units. Managerial decisions are taken in a fluid and rapidly changing framework of imperfect knowledge of technology and markets, and also of human behaviour.

In the primordial forms of economic and administrative organisation, knowledge was held centrally by the business unit, which was frequently identified with one individual (owner) who combined his knowledge of what was needed and of how he could develop that which was needed. The feedback he received from the market was direct, immediate, fast and convincing. This is possible also for modern enterprises, where their size is sufficiently small as to permit it.

In the overwhelming majority of modern markets, businesses must cultivate and guide inter-business/interdepartmental communication. Unavoidably, business development frequently dictates to distinguish roles through the subsumption of specialised skills to operating entities, which necessarily creates a distance between the entities. This distance increases as the specialisation inside the departments increases. The entailed decrease in the communication and contact between the departments causes an at-least-proportional undermining of their capacity to systemically combine their specialised skills.

Marketing and SCM departments are input providers for many activities of the company but simultaneously are responsible for the critical variables of important outflows. The contribution responsibilities for both departments (and, of course, the responsibility to provide their combined capacity) evolve as new technologies become possible and available, as consumers' preferences change, as the competition introduces new ways to offer value to consumers and as limitations on environmental issues or those posed by (inter)national entities change. There is a continuous flow of resources, materials, information and technical specialisation between the borders of two functionally delimited camps, so as to form a well-grounded and forceful response, whose key ingredient will be the competitive advantage ensuing from the combination of forces, with – now – added value.

5.2 Obstacles to achieving cooperation – communication

The following list presents the obstacles for the collaboration and communication that ensued from the analysis in the previous chapters.

- Lack of mutual understanding between marketing and SCM.
- SCM and marketing executives lack experience in other operating areas.

- SCM and marketing executives do not understand each other's work.
- Lack of organising discussions on the same issue.
- SCM and marketing suffer from a communication problem.
- Information exchange between marketing and SCM is inadequate.
- The organisation lacks a systematic method for data collection and the set-up of a common database.
- Marketing is short-term oriented, while SCM adopts a longer-term orientation.
- The temporal requirements of SCM do not fit the times recommended by marketing.
- SCM and marketing set different priorities.
- There are differences in culture between SCM and marketing.
- SCM and commercial employees adopt different thinking models.
- The goals and policies are not in line and frequently are not even compatible.
- SCM and marketing do not adequately comply with the company's general operating strategy.
- SCM and marketing place emphasis on different elements of the company's mission.
- SCM and marketing do not know their precise and corresponding duties or competences.
- SCM and marketing fail to do what they must do, and each of them expects from the other to do more than they must.
- The roles and responsibilities of SCM and marketing are ambiguous and frequently mutually excluding.

In most cases, dissonance is the rule and not the exception. An attempt for an indicative (and not exhaustive) citation of factors shaping the background, perceptions and bio-theory of marketing people follows. Such characteristics may directly contribute to the differences that create the intradepartmental gap and the differences in understanding.

Characteristics of the two disciplines' 'school of thought'

The education and cognitive background of marketing and SCM executives usually originates as the result of their studies in management or economic schools. Their educational background and methodological toolbox usually focus on the solution to general problems where data and information but also intuition are frequently combined to attain successful results. The 'world-view' of marketing executives tends to adopt the short-term horizon of small projects. On the other hand, a high proportion of SCM executives may come from engineering schools or technological or informatics schools.

These characteristics, of course, are not seen across all businesses, nor can someone claim that they underpin or represent the culture of executives. Besides the growth of business schools on the international level and the commensurate huge variety of undergraduate and postgraduate specialisation programmes, the 'sealed features' of the core of such specialised scientific fields tend to be enriched with different viewpoints and principles. Having said this, such particularities in the way of thinking, especially to the degree they constitute clearly seen and concrete features, may potentially provide the 'starting kick' for a chain reaction, which runs the risk for departments to limit and self-determine themselves and, thus, develop self-inclusive 'societies' inside their respective companies. Even in the case where two departments are mature enough and adopt the educational designation of education–knowledge–training–experience, which allows for the conscious understanding that they share the same organisational objectives, the prism through which each department interprets such objectives may itself differ considerably.

Consequently, individual or foreign-to-one-another ways for the collection, processing, evaluation, interpretation and perception of stimuli may, respectively, be translated into difficulties for the perception of objectives, goal-setting and solutions, but also to indecisiveness and inertia with respect to the needs or conditions for trade-offs involving the two departments. And, obviously, this is far removed from the good and unhindered collaboration between departments, which imperatively places the understanding of the manner by which the other department perceives and thinks as a minimum condition.

Obstacles due to different vocabulary/terminology

As a result of the development of different ways of thinking that (by necessity and imperatively) evolve, the verbal obstacles between them also evolve. The marketing and logistics departments each have, employ, evolve and change their own terminology. Each type of terminology is, essentially, the corresponding reflection of their philosophy and scientific principles, positions and achievements and is indicative of their toolbox and methodology, while also constituting from a subset of vocabulary with special connotations, when employed in the narrow scientific frameworks of each specialised group. For example, marketing professionals speak in terms of product value, perceived attitudes and consumer needs and are, in general, familiar with the qualitative aspects that exist as an integral part of their standpoint.

And since terminology, namely, the words (even those with a special and specific meaning), represents thoughts, differences in their denotation, which even render them at times incomprehensible, undermine communication that by definition exists only upon the exchange of thoughts and views.

When there is no effective and efficient communication, the entire organisational structure trembles from the consecutive and unceasing disagreements that get worse with the passage of time, while putting the organisation in a state of awkwardness and distancing it from conceiving

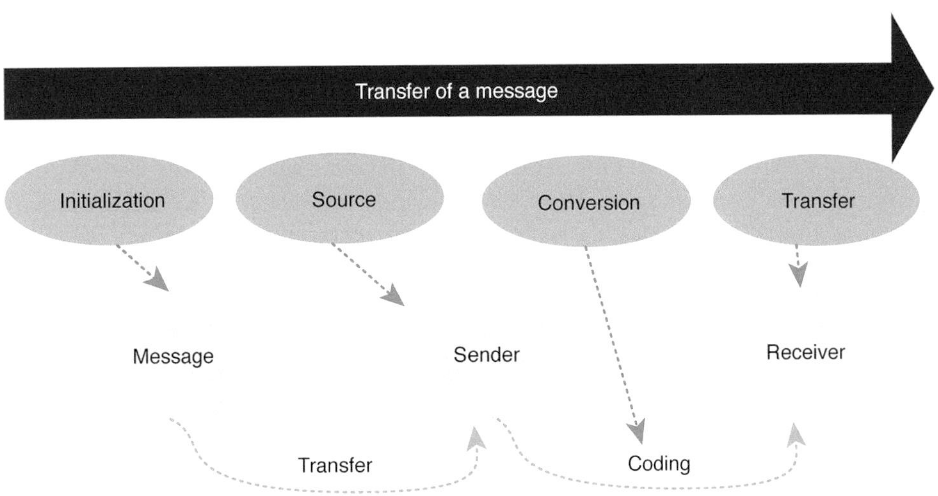

FIGURE 5.1 Process of communication

Sources: Inspired by the Osgood–Schramm model of communication (McQuail and Windahl (2015); Schramm and Roberts (1971); Schramm (1954))

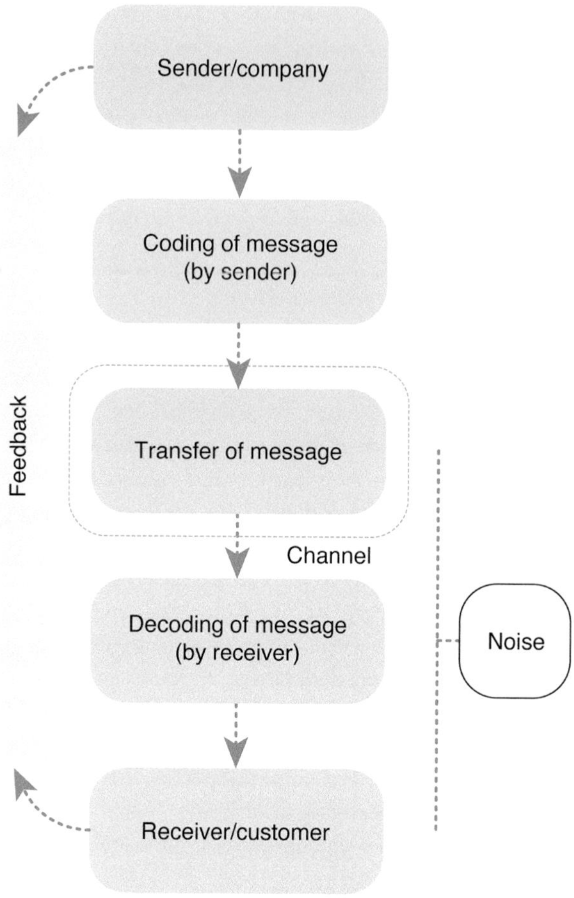

FIGURE 5.2 Transfer of messages in the communication process

Sources: Inspired by the Osgood–Schramm model of communication (McQuail and Windahl (2015); Schramm and Roberts (1971); Schramm (1954))

and realising the optimal results. The ineffectiveness of communication may, in the best case, be characterised as an unbalanced balance, which, if not swiftly resolved, could frequently lead to the dissociation of consumers' needs from the company's value offer. Despite the fact that both (or even worse – more than two) departments may feel that they are talking about precisely the same thing, the absence of cohesive comprehension bonds between the two specialised microcosms operates as an obstacle for the understanding of more specialised concepts (that when used with alternative connotations by different departments may assume a completely different meaning) that are critical for the unique selling proposition for the product. Even small deviations in vocabulary may frequently lead to the recommendation of widely differentiated solutions or proposals and make the difference between a successful and a completely unsuccessful product.

The failure may even lurk on the level of details. Should every operating team be unable to understand customer needs on the level of detail, which is essential to perform its duties and role, this may become the operative event for disappointment during the communication process.

Obstacles due to communication responsibilities

Organisational obstacles can also occur on account of different priorities attributed to goals and competences of operating means for measurement (attaining a market share against the achievement of faster delivery times, maintaining – or not of– inventories to cater for demand, etc.). Typically, the higher levels of managerial hierarchy determine, monitor and adjust such factors, but even the process of organisational change itself, aimed to dampen such interceptions, may sometimes be itself rendered the operative event or obstacle. Middle management executives who attained their promotion via the old established system of rules are hesitant to adopt new organisational tactics, resist changes, classify as foreign and despise anything that goes against the existing or old organisational value system and philosophy. Consequently, here too one can detect a parameter decreasing the levels of intra-departmental cooperation.

Problems due to physical distance

The possibility for two employees to communicate at least once a week decreases dramatically if the physical space separating the facilities/offices of their departments is greater than 10 metres (Allen 1986). Should their operating departments be located in different building facilities or, even worse, in different cities, even if interpersonal communication is assisted by the use of modern technology, essential communication will be even more reduced.

The magnitude of the distance that may render face-to-face communication between the members of operating groups difficult may lead to delays in decision-making. This operating isolation may retrench the different ways of thinking, turn employees to operating introversion, create short circuits across a wide spectrum of their interactions and, ultimately, cause a climaxing of existing perceptions relating to differences on the level of personalities. Senior executives from both disciplines work in the physical space dedicated to management, but this is not the case for middle and junior staff of logistics and SCM departments. These are to be found in the production lines, in the area for packaging, in warehouses and distribution centres, etc. There are, of course, logistics and SCM executives working in the premises for procurement, planning and the organisation of distribution, that is, working in the same managerial premises as those of marketing department executives.

Obstacles ensuing from differences in personalities

Personality differences or stereotypes relating to these or cultural differences or, even, differences detected with respect to the perception of time and temporal orientation may become obstacles to the attainment of the necessary degree of communication. Despite the fact that some of these factors are different in different people (independently of their 'functional' classification), their specialised parametrisation could, however, either compose their inclination towards a specific specialised vocational engagement (and, therefore, also to their inclusion in the corresponding specialised operating department) or be guided and reinforced on account of their engagement in it.

On the practical plane, the above could be summarised, interpreted and described as follows:

- Lack of mutual understanding between operating departments.
- Vagueness with respect to the orientation for delimiting and applying a unified strategy, policies and practices, which are harmonious, contribute to and reinforce the more general organisational orientation, and which are in line with the business vision and mission.

- Vagueness in goal setting, hierarchy and prioritisation for achieving organisational objectives.
- Insufficient attainment of synergies due to the non-application of the systems intra-departmental approach.
- Employees in one operating department lack the experience or are even ignorant of the subject matter of other departments.
- There is no common ground of understanding, which may create a fertile ground to cultivate discussion and collaborations.
- Information travels between departments inadequately or insufficiently and/or in an untimely fashion.
- There is not a systematic approach to the collection of data to build a common database.
- The operating goals posed in a piecemeal manner inside the departments are frequently incompatible and even competitive from an intra-departmental perspective, and as a result, such discordance functions as an obstacle for the attainment of the organisational objectives and hampers the outcome on the business level.
- There are differences relating to the perception and importance attributed to the concept of time, a fact that then affects the mechanism for and actual decision-making.
- There are different thought models that are not included in the framework of a fair symbiotic interrelation.
- Operating departments do not always have a clear, reliable and robust idea on operational strategy and do not always align, in the best and most effective manner, their efforts (either independently as departments, or in cooperation with the other operating parts), so as for the attainment of individual objectives to contribute principally to the realisation of operational ones.
- Different departments place emphasis on different elements of the mission of the business.
- Departments are not absolutely certain on the roles and responsibilities ensuing from their place and have a short-sighted view of their duties and competences – especially with respect to the overall consideration of the organisation as a complex machine of which they are the 'cogs'.
- They frequently fail to do what they must, while each expects the other to do more than it already contributes.

The framework of conditions and constituents, which compose the complex web of interrelations and which designate the critical factors based on which modern businesses are called to develop their activities, has been briefly discussed in the previous sections. It is obvious that this regards a demanding and relatively unwelcoming environment, independent of the theoretical or functional viewpoint for observing it, independent of the definitions and consequent rational associations or even their implicit intrinsic special characteristics.

Independently of the framework adopted on each occasion, which begins with the 'operating' specialised reading and the perceived capabilities of each scientific/theoretical or empirical framework, the common denominator is that the field of activity of modern organisations is fluid, turbulent, dynamic and indeed rapidly changing, and necessitates focusing on the attainment of the maintainable competitive advantage through the goodwill produced from the success in synergies.

Specific characteristics of the modern track and field where companies are active and compete, and which render the need for the systems approach to the operating particularities of these two (at least) departments imperative, are possibly the following:

- The rapid changes in consumers' desires.
- The great number of competitors.

- The fast rate at which technology becomes obsolete and, consequently, the increasingly short product life cycles.
- The greater needs for the inflow-filtering and utilisation of information.
- The imperative or need to adopt a market orientation (with respect to being consumers and competitors).
- The greater needs for the rational and effective management of company resources.
- The degree of complexity and the multidimensional nature of the process for decision-making.
- The frequent change but also sudden alternation of the terms of the competitive 'game' by newcomers and/or the existing actors, but also, generally, of the entire set of requirements that are posed by stakeholders.
- Liquidity.
- Emphasis attributed to competition and its unique selling proposition as such is perceived and interpreted by consumers.
- The frequently observed difficulty on the part of consumers to realise and articulate their needs.
- Changes to perception and what is perceived that ensue from the continuous and wide-spread applications of technology with respect to both the conception and creation of demand for products, as well as their delivery.
- The climaxing of the need for the effective and efficient management of demand.
- Exchange problems.
- Avoiding the trap of the one-dimensional consideration and treatment of competitive advantage, which follows from the up-to-now low priority and importance given to the utility of mapping consumers' desires and delimiting the competition, which the marketing department can offer, and – consequently – its consideration as a second-class department.
- The role of marketing with respect to the constituents of organisational creativity (Hamel and Prahalad 1991).
- The understanding of the manner by which emerging technologies can allow the fulfilment of consumers' unsatisfied needs, or their satisfaction in a more effective manner, which acts as a catalyst for the discovery of a new competitive field.
- The triptych.
- The ability to listen closely to needs and to convey these to the company.
- The ability to interpret and transubstantiate needs to useful and desirable product features.
- To deliver said products in the fastest and most efficient manner that will accentuate and integrate the value offered to the consumer.
- The relentless intensification of competition: the intense competition at times regards changes that take place in the competitive environment (namely, who the competitors are, what is their identity, what tools they use to compete and what is their total product offer), or it may also regard who the potential future competitors may be. The modern business landscape is said to be precipitous also on account of the fact that 'uninvited guests' may also enter (due to globalisation, leaps and the dissemination of technology), originating from other sectors, who can potentially change the standing rules and regulations of the competitive game.
- Additionally, the shorter product life cycle is a fact, which characterises the modern competitive field, at times the result of the now very fast impairment of technological applications due to the continuous development of new technologies and their corresponding applications, and at other times the outcome of the relation of interdependence and interaction between product, as the mean to cover needs, and the ever-shifting borders of desires or needs on the side of the consumers.

The facts above continuously gain ground with respect to the attention shown to them by executives as conscious realisations, which cannot be bypassed unconsidered.

To respect more effectively the commands of the past, some companies try to decrease the interval from listening and the creation of a new product idea until the final product is launched and delivered to the consumer, by applying an in-parallel access and realisation of the intermediate actions, decisions and tactics.

It is obvious that such an approach to the shortening of time until the delivery of the product may, on the one hand, be legitimate and fair, but it presupposes, on the other hand, the effectiveness of the collaboration and the coordination of the entire enterprise. It is deemed inconceivable – for every operating department of a business – not only to work towards the direction of maximising its own individual goal, which is a subset of the operational central goal, but also to collaborate with all other sub-departments so as to render the realisation of the corporate objective attainable. In such an approach, communication and the safety valves adopted to ensure its effectiveness render intra-corporate collaboration and cooperation as an essential condition and improve the margins for the rational and expedient management of the threats and risks that may emerge in time. Time is the dimension par excellence that signifies the dynamics of the modern business environment. Save for its intrinsic participation in the implicit existing characteristics of the environment, but also in the composition thereof, time stands in the foreground as a critical variable for one additional reason.

By compressing time, businesses try to transcend and overcome the obstacles and challenges arising as a chain reaction of the effects that originate from the demanding environment. The traditional accessing on a one-by-one basis of the stages of conception and development and delivery of the products to their end users becomes shorter, while some of the stages in the procedure are omitted and/or abolished, while others are sacrificed on the altar of fast and easy, trouble-free access. In the context of a more effective response to the commands of the modern taxing environment, the decrease of lapse-time is attempted, with quality or the array of benefits ultimately delivered to the consumer frequently being the price. And while shortening times is placed in the foreground as a key variable and may, under specific circumstances, be a useful tool for the successful response to the challenges of the modern competitive environment, with respect to the briefness of product life cycles and in other factors or the effects of factors that act as suppressants to the mission of the company, caution is in order.

Time, and specifically the shortening thereof, cannot be a priori considered as the 'all-subduer', nor can it be rendered (without the parallel and corresponding adoption of safety valves, conditions and qualifications) as the panacea or the generalised wondrous recipe for an integrated, attainable and viable solution to all problems. Perhaps the key condition to guarantee the effectiveness of shortening times (without a parallel 'discount' and compromise for the overall effectiveness of the sequence of processes for the delivery of superior quality to consumers) is the effectiveness of the collaboration and coordination of the entire mechanism of operating specialisations in the business.

Time, therefore, cannot unilaterally and one-dimensionally be considered as the vehicle, which will render the transition to more effective management schema and the more rational approach to the satisfaction of consumer needs possible. It, simultaneously, also is an index of the effectiveness of the tools that were adopted and guided the correctness of the procedure. It is, in other words, a coexisting variable in a multitude of inherent features of modern markets, an intermediary factor leading to consequent effects and an indicative factor of the magnitude of the problem, but also an inextricable ingredient of the system composition of factors that dynamically feed the primary factors of the business field of activity. This is only logical, since it is part of the problem while, simultaneously, being part of its solution. However, it would be more correct to view it – and it is this view that this particular approach adopts – as a goal to attain, the successful outcome of which, however, is directly dependent on the effectiveness of good intra-departmental communication collaboration and coordination, and it represents (while also presupposing) the therapy of intrinsic or is entailed by intrinsic problems, while it may also participate in the constitution of their problematic nature, or it may self-inclusively and independently be the problem itself.

Concisely, the shortening of times is considered to be a fair process and – with other indications and demonstrations – entails and is directly dependent on the success of the uninterrupted and fruitful collaboration and, ultimately, integration of the two operating departments.

5.3 Adopted viewpoint – framework for this work

The long-term success of a company, its prosperity and the attainment of its goals depend on its reliability and the effectiveness of providing superior value to its consumers. Independent of different readings, dimensions and emphases that may vary depending on perceptions and the adopted, on each occasion, viewpoint of every operational corporate determinant, this is neither a one-dimensional action, nor a one-dimensional and unconnected sequence of processes and actions. On the contrary, it is a multilevel and multifunctional procedure that requires compassion, joining of forces and the attainment of synergies with respect to goals, efforts, skills and the capacities of more than one operating departments (in this specific undertaking by marketing and SCM) and, therefore, the uninterrupted communication and coordination of their actions.

To put it in other terms, the partial integration of two operating departments in the context of their systems approach, their strategic fit and consequent synergies, and the more effective and efficient use of their skills show the right orientation. In essence, we describe the bridge between specialised parts, which work towards the common target of the achievement of organisational objectives, have compatible and jointly ordered priorities, and jointly draft their strategy.

And while integration as a concept ought to have been complementary to that of specialisation, it is true that extreme specialisation approaches (to the point of alienation or even rivalry), either resulting from inherent obstacles (mentality, different schools of thought, etc.) or as the result of poor communication and collaboration, sub-optimise the final outcome.

Lack of communication/cooperation – non-integration – as the result of individual and isolated operating efforts for the attainment of the – narrowly defined – goals of some department functions as a destructively destabilising factor that exacerbates the magnitude and effects of the factors that compose the competitive environment for businesses.

The insufficient – or absent – integration deflects the organisation from the balance point that must be attained to stave off unfavourable environmental conditions. It must be stressed that while the attainment of the maximisation of results from an operating perspective (under the light of the narrowly departmental attainment of objectives, adoption of practices and culture, etc.) runs against and is a trammel to a spherical, all-encompassing, approach to the optimisation and the most effective and rational attainment of the common organisational objectives advocated by integration, however, the integration of the departments is not a concept contradicting or competing with maximisation. They aim at the same result, under the proviso of the specific difference that it treats it more spherically, incorporating in the system (besides the pursuit of the operationally defined maximisation) of variables other parameters. Such a system for the perception and treatment may lead to the attainment of the operational objective more forcefully amid demanding conditions and a competitive environment.

It is perhaps inconceivable for every operating department to work towards the direction of attaining the goals, which constitute a sub-set of the central goal, and for it to not collaborate with the other departments to render the realisation of the centrally pursued goal of the company attainable (Schneider 1987; Lawrence and Lorsch 1967a, 1967b). In the context of such an approach, communication and the safety valves adopted to ensure its effectiveness bear intra-corporate collaboration as the fundamental condition and improve the margins for the proper and expedient management of threats and risks emerging over the passage of time.

The definition of the concept of 'collaboration' in the context of this approach is not exhausted in the exchange of information via the inflow–outflow mechanism system or via the dialectic relation only. Besides, the existence of this need is considered more or less self-evident due to the modern view of companies as open systems subject to multivariable influences from their external environment. However, the viewpoint of collaboration and the corresponding documentation of the urgency for the need to attain it and explore it also inside the context of the organisation commences from there.

Marketing, in the framework of delimiting its operating competences, assumes the role not only of listening to customers' needs but also of disseminating and transferring them inside the company. It is, thus, rendered as the carrier and joining link, which discloses facts and inflows information inside the organisation (Gruber 1981; Clarke 1974).

It is clear, however, that the utility of information flow, besides the typical characteristics it must satisfy (being precise, on time and valid) is, ultimately, judged by the degree to which it will be listened, namely, the extent with respect to which it can be included and incorporated in the knowledge depository of the company, to be filtered and processed via the system of accumulated and aggregate experiences, and, ultimately, to be introduced to the organisation's decision-making algorithm. A piece of information – the result of the efficient and structured efforts by the marketing department – is rendered completely useless if it does not affect the direction of the operating alignment with the objectively and mutually accepted goal.

In the chain approach that follows the acquisition of information flows ensuing from listening to consumers' demands, the next step is to transfer and analyse these to transubstantiate them to useful products that will be adopted by consumers as the most efficient and effective way to respond to their needs. And in this case, the time and manner of delivery undoubtedly and essentially contribute to the shaping of the package of offering a superior value from that offered by the competition.

From this reading of the constituent parts, which piecemeal and stepwise compose the value delivered to the end consumer, the common dimension of the expediting importance between the marketing and SCM departments becomes evident.

The delivery of the product at a time and place that suit the consumer is, without doubt, an integral ingredient of the total benefit and utility the consumer will get from the product, and frequently shapes in a determinative fashion his decision to purchase the product or not. The time and place of delivery of the array of benefits are simultaneously and intrinsically existing variables for the perceived value of this array, or, alternatively, of its attractiveness in the judgement of consumers. And while the time and place of the delivery of the product are undoubtedly the most evident field of common points–objectives–pursuits of the two departments, their relation is at the same time characterised principally by an intense trade-off nature.

To make the relation above easier to understand, consider if you will the following simple example. Say that someone wants to buy a bottle of water. The most usual case is for him to be confronted with two choices: he can either buy a bottle from a convenience store in his neighbourhood (that in the majority of cases will be less than 3–5 minutes away), or he can go to a supermarket, which will be 10–15 minutes on foot. In the first case, he will pay a price at least 3–6 times greater than that he would have paid if he purchased the bottle from a supermarket. (Despite varying dependence on the product, country and other factors, the difference in price is an easy-to-perceive and existing differentiation on the level of pricing between the two vendors). Each one of us has certainly realised one or the other purchase from the alternatives presented on multiple occasions. What led us to make one choice on one occasion and a different one on another? The answer is really simple: when time is not the most important variable in the pairing of time and money (time here refers to the place of purchase, on which price depends), namely, whenever we had enough time at our disposal, we traded 'wasting' time for 'saving' price due to the selection of the place (supermarket).

On the contrary, when we judged that the alternative cost was greater than the differential benefit from the lower product price at a remote store, we chose for the 'waste' to burden the variable of price, and, correspondingly, we chose to 'save' in the variable of time, which was deemed as more valuable than the premium on the product's price. The trade-off, that is, involves on each occasion an analysis of the cost–benefits, where difference in cost ensues from the selection made on each occasion and is compared, size-wise, to the difference in benefit, which correspondingly ensues with respect to the other variable of the particular choice made. It is obvious that desirable is that which can be expressed as the desideratum when shaping the marketing mix: the goal of distribution is for the product to be available at a place *and* time convenient to consumers. Note the emphatic undertone of the conjunctive 'and' and the corresponding absence of the disjunctive 'or'!

This simple and characteristic example is indicative of the multiform landscape where the common points between marketing and SCM are borne, and which demand our attention. Just consider how complex a state of affairs becomes if other factors are also involved, factors that frequently participate in operational decisions.

Consider the magnitude of the conflict if, based on all that has been said so far, the marketing department wishes, for example, in this specific circumstance, to place emphasis on place (to show its work and progress as an operating department, it decides to launch promotional activities in store) and – correspondingly – SCM insists that time must take precedence as the crown of all priorities.

The most likely outcome is that the result, with respect to the attainment of the objective posed by the company to which both departments belong and which both serve, will be sub-optimised as a whole, as the result of the aforementioned independent, contradictory and absolutely incompatible unilateral and autonomous pursuit of their individual operating goals. What is possibly easier for one to perceive from this simple example of just two variables falling under the common interests and competences of each of the operating departments is that the interaction between the marketing and SCM departments, besides the symbiosis that must characterise it, is a critical and catalytic factor to attain the delivery of an integrated package of benefits to the consumer. The coordinated unification of efforts is not an optional step but a one-way street and mandate for survival.

The concept of integration is approached as follows. Businesses are structured in a manner similar to any living organism. The cells of the living organism, in the first stages of its life, are differentiated, specialised and organised in groups of tissues, which, ultimately, morph into different organs that must carry out separate and specialised functions. The heart, for example, has its own distinctive and specialised role to play, which is very different from that of the functional role of the lungs or the liver. Within the narrow operating boundaries of function, the ideal function of the heart should produce approximately 70–80 pulses per minute. Correspondingly, the lungs would function 'optimally' by contributing to the oxygenation of the blood, providing a particular quantity of oxygen to the organism – while there are other corresponding optimal values recorded for every organ. What would happen, however, if at some given point and due to external factors (in full correspondence to the uncontrollable factors – influences of the external environment on a company) or internal factors (e.g., some ailment in correspondence with the failings of the internal environment of the company) the organism needed greater quantities of oxygen to better adjust – self-regulate – respond and auto-correct, and the lungs 'refused' to make the adjustment that would branch off their narrowly defined operationally established boundaries of their optimal performance? Or, if the heart – for its own reasons of functional consistency – did not contribute to the distribution of oxygen via the circulation of blood? On the one hand, both organs would continue to function in accordance with medical protocols for physiology and pathology. However, on the other hand, the organism would as a whole collapse, as a result of the non-compliance of its two operating departments with the greater aim: survival. Autonomous priorities set by every operationally specialised system are fair and legitimate only under the condition that not only do they not oppose the common organisational objective, not only do they not constitute an obstacle for its attainment, but they are also compatible with it (under different viewpoints) and contribute to its realisation.

And, provided the parallel above renders the role and importance of symbiotic interrelation in the survival of organisms (living or not) clear, why not go a step further to delimit the viewpoint of integration through an even more brief example? Suppose that a healthy man in a good physical state can run for some minutes at 25 km/h. If this man had one, instead of two, legs, would it be safe to assume that he could run, in similar conditions and without an artificial leg, at half the speed? It is probable that he could not, since running speed is not simply the sum of the work produced by the right leg and that produced by the left leg. It is something more, which lies in and is accentuated by the synergy, collaboration and coordination of both bodily parts (or, more properly, the entire organism that they move).

It is, to put it in other words, the systems approach that may be analysed via integration – at least under the light shed by this work.

Consequently, what is pursued via the integration of the two operating departments is the systems approach to their specialised skills and abilities, so as for the result produced to be greater than the sum of the individual and autonomous efforts by each of them, should such efforts be independently exerted. It is an operating unification to some extent, with respect to the common reading of information inflows, the analysis thereof, and the joint drafting and implementation of a plan and actions on the strategic and tactical level.

It should be noted that the objective is not to abolish one of the two (or, by extension, more) operating departments, or, correspondingly, to discredit their role and competences. Neither is the establishment of a mutated department pursued, a department that will consist of multidisciplinary scientists who will be considered experts on every issue or subject falling under one or the other cognitive field. Something like this would not be prudent (Schneider 1987; Lawrence and Lorsch 1967a, 1967b) on account of the fact that realistically and by definition it would

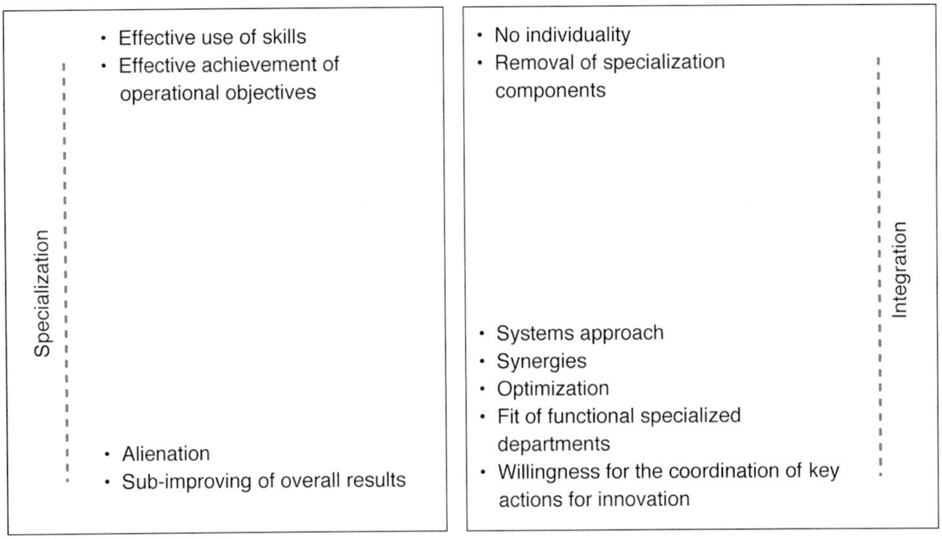

FIGURE 5.3 Specialisation versus integration

amount to the lifting of the notion of specialisation. In other words, it is not rational to abolish specialisation in favour of integration – in the context of the systems approach described.

The aim is to qualitatively increase the magnitude of specialisation, but to do so through integration. What is pursued is to exploit the benefits of both specialisation and integration with the simultaneous – to the extent possible – eradication of their disadvantages, via the interaction, inter-affection and the efficient and effective management and administration of their contact point.

At this point, before we move on, it would perhaps be useful to clarify and further delimit the two concepts: integration and specialisation (see Figure 5.3). The concepts of specialisation (separation – differentiation) of the departments and integration are more complementary than competitive. The existence of both is necessary (Schneider 1987; Souder 1987; Lawrence and Lorsch 1967b). The differentiation is essentially the separation of the organisational system to subsystems (Lawrence and Lorsch 1967a). It is necessary since the outcome of specialisation renders the organisation able to optimise the individual goals that must be attained. On the other hand, integration as a symbiotic relation is considered to be the necessary bridge – the joining ring – of the specialised parts. In other words, the term integration regards the strategic pairing of operationally specialised departments while their individual orientation is still at play.

Its objective or goal is not to dismantle and deconstruct the operating specialisation of departments. The creation of willingness to cooperate and coordinate those strategic decisions and actions, which are critical and essential for the successful delivery of value to consumers, is included in the framework of its objectives. According to Souder (1987), human resources allocated to a specific project are called to play specific roles within these activities (where Souder defines a role as the expected behaviour attributed to a specific place inside a company). These roles are related to a list of information via and with which individuals work to succeed in the proposed goals. All of the human resources, therefore, that have been called upon in the context of a company to complete a project form a working group.

The conception, development and delivery of the means to cater for needs come as the result of information processing by almost all operating departments.

Kotler (1984) suggests that the role of the marketing department includes analysis, planning, application and control of the programmes that have been designed to build and maintain beneficial relations and exchanges with the targeted markets, so as to succeed in the organisational objectives. The function of SCM includes the development and effective use of scientific/technological know-how and of its application to attain the best possible result with respect to the supply of the business and the delivery of the product's value to the consumer with the minimum trade-off between place and time of delivery. The personnel of the marketing department is responsible for providing most of the information relating to users' needs, the competition and resources. The corresponding responsibilities of the SCM department are to provide information not only relating to the tactical side of decisions on distribution and procurement channels but also regarding technologies employed by the competition. Through its competences, it may become the supplier of the raw material for the creation of a competitive advantage, both due to its direct involvement and contribution it may have in decreasing costs and due to the role it plays in shaping the perceived value as the array of benefits enjoyed by consumers as a result of the time and place, and now even the way they are delivered.

One can observe that the kind and qualitative texture of information – but also the way they are used – differ, a fact that is the rational consequence of operational differentiation, which ultimately determines the type of informing and the manner information will be processed and used by operating sub-departments.

The marketing and SCM departments are, therefore, providers or transmitters of retrieved or held information to the departments, which on account of their operating roles do not have access to it, and, correspondingly, are receivers of information from the departments, which, due to their competence, have access to it, while they constantly alternate between the role of the transmitter and the receiver of necessary information. The phenomenon of a posteriori interdependence emerges at the process for the production and delivery of value, precisely because the types and flow of information exist throughout the whole process. Under this light, it is only expected that the integration approach plays a determinative role in business performance (Cheng 1983).

Thus, the high degree of customer orientation poses integration and operational interdependence on the forefront, as critical variables. Through communication and the dissemination of information, team members transfer knowledge to other members. The conveyance of information is rendered the vehicle that grants to the individuals who participate in the organisation access to the information already acquired. Schematically, the proposed approach adopted in the work is illustrated in Figure 5.4.

We propose to maintain the individuality and character of part of the two specialised departments so as to maintain the high level of effectiveness when utilising their skills and also for the attainment of their operational goals to be effective. In parallel, however, it is imperative for such specialisation to be incorporated in a wider framework for the development and exploration of the angle dictated by the integration of the departments. The common ground, the intersection of the two operating sets, is attained by exploring and relaxing their dividing lines (Galbraith 1973), which segment the two operating departments. This type of operating commingling constitutes the base for the appropriate mix that will signify the correct orientation and shall render clear the direction for targeting the common organisational objective, while at the same time also recommending the appropriate and correct means for its attainment.

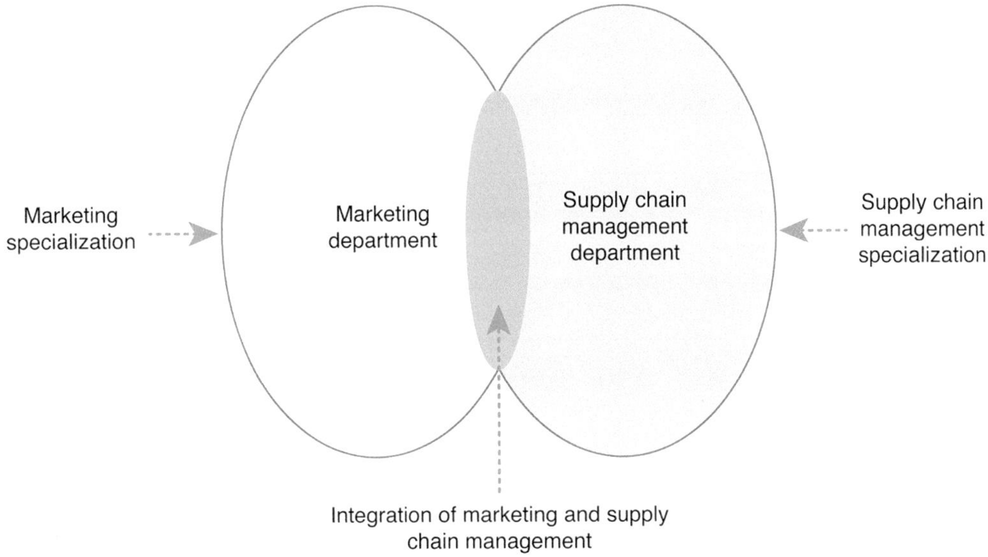

FIGURE 5.4 Diagrammatic illustration of the integration philosophy for the marketing and SCM departments

Under this viewpoint, we aim for the following:

- The strengthening – expansion and reinforcement – of the departments' operationally specialised skills.
- To attain the above in the direction dictated by adopting a systems approach to the two departments, so as for the expansion of their operating skills to be incorporated in the framework of the objectives of integration. Thus, we shall ensure that the expansions of the specialised operating capacities shall dynamically originate as products of the ('partial' or necessary) integration and simultaneously shall directly and also dynamically affect both the qualitative expansion – reinforcement of integration – and its steady establishment and the long-term of the private relation it represents.

Thus, the contribution of the proposed approach for the reinforcement of the operating specialisation of marketing and SCM departments adopts the orientation established by their common organisational objective, via their integration.

Synopsis

- Marketing and SCM departments are input providers for many activities of the company but are, at the same time, responsible for the critical variables of important outflows. The contribution responsibilities for both departments evolve as new technologies become available, as consumers' preferences change, as the competition introduces new ways to offer value to consumers and as limitations on environmental issues or those posed by (inter)national entities change.

- There is a continuous flow of resources, materials, information and technical specialisation between the borders of two functionally delimited camps, so as to form a well-grounded and forceful response, whose key ingredient will be the competitive advantage ensuing from the combination of forces, with – now – added value.
- However, there are many obstacles for the attainment of the desired level of collaboration and communication between the two departments. Obstacles due to different vocabulary/terminology, communication responsibilities, physical distance, ensuing from differences in personalities, etc., hinder this process; however, it is argued that integration is attainable and indeed serves what is identified as their common organisational objective.

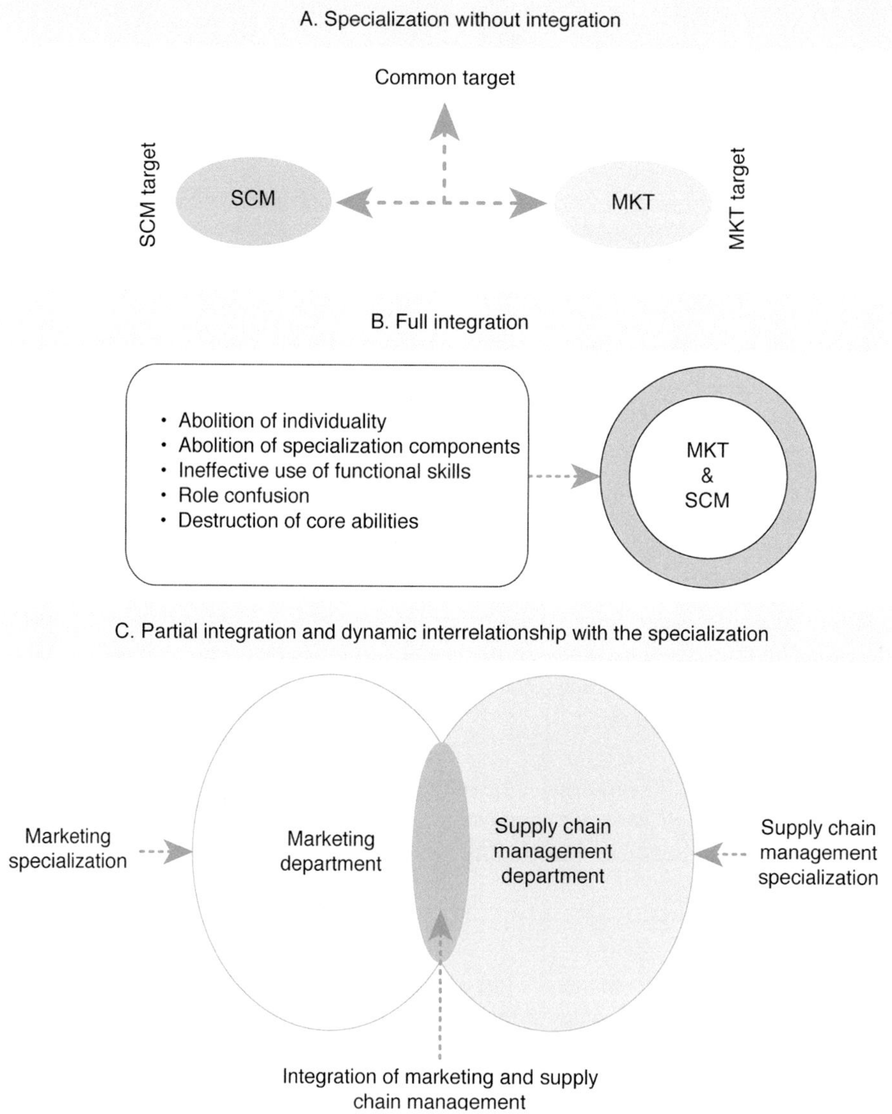

FIGURE 5.5 Specialisation/integration

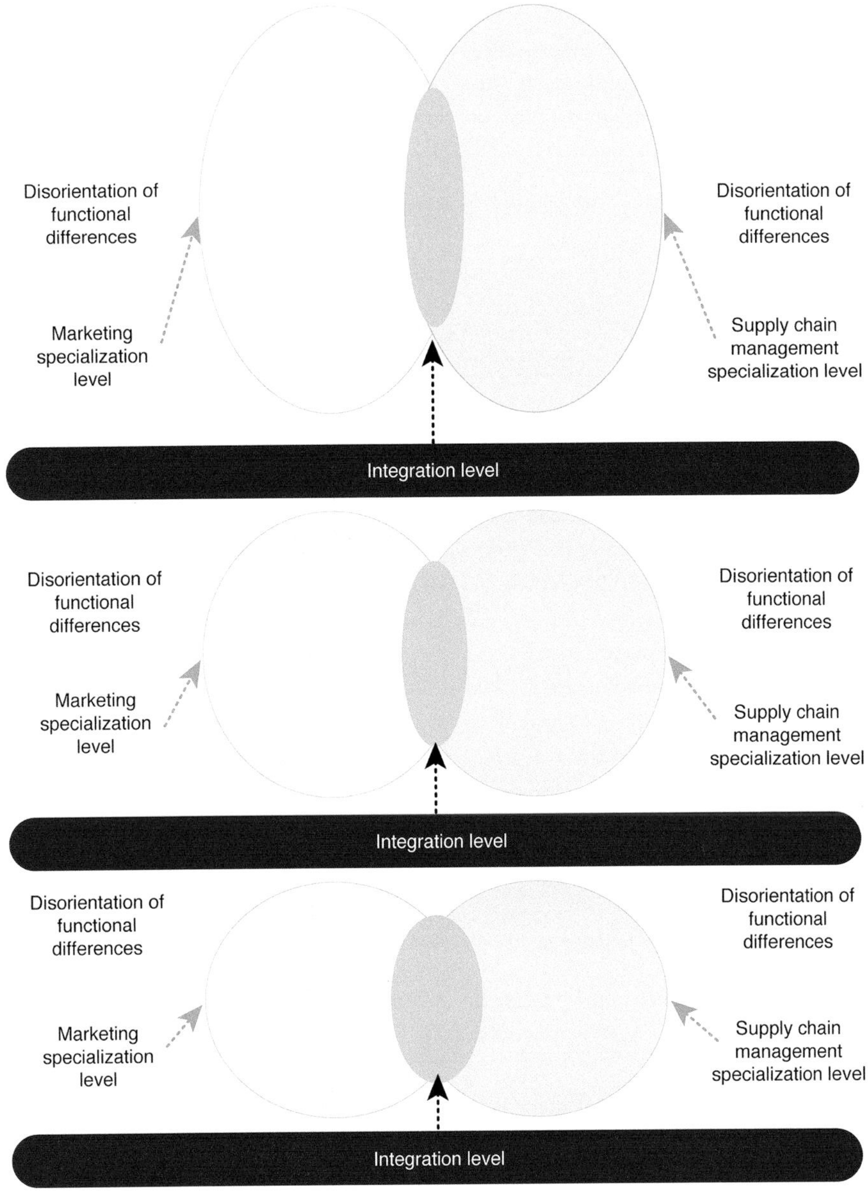

FIGURE 5.6 Positive dynamic interrelation of the two departments with respect to the rational direction for attaining the objective – common organisational goal: positive dynamics

Review and discussion questions

- Describe the essence of the systematic approach using an example and the value chain model.
- Concisely cite the ways in which marketing and SCM can be integrated.
- What are the obstacles for the cooperation and communication of marketing and SCM?
- Based on your personal/working experiences, categorise the obstacles into three categories A, B and C based on their significance.

- What are the obstacles due to different vocabulary/terminology? How can both marketing and supply chain managers confront these obstacles efficiently?
- What are the obstacles ensuing from differences in personalities? What are your thoughts for these obstacles in a multinational environment?
- Describe the types of integration between marketing and SCM departments in an organisation.

Case studies

Case study 1: Corporate brand strategy formation

The significance of corporate branding in the business-to-business realm is growing, with industrial marketers increasingly focusing on developing their brands at the corporate level. Successful corporate branding entails embedding corporate brand values as the organisation's central guiding principle and a filter for employee conduct. Vallaster and Lindgreen's (2011) study sheds light on how business-to-business brand actors engage in the interactive process of brand strategy development. Their research explores the involvement of internal and external brand actors from organisations in shaping brand strategy. Additionally, the study investigates how situational factors influence brand strategy development and contribute to establishing a robust corporate business-to-business brand.

Vallaster and Lindgreen examined the case of HighRingTech, a firm whose performance had consistently lagged behind competitors' for three consecutive periods. In response, HighRingTech introduced a program called 'Customer Orientation First' (UCO) to utilise customer satisfaction reviews as improvement metrics. The company implemented activities aimed at embedding UCO into its organisational culture, aiming to shift employees' focus from a technology-centric mindset to a more customer-oriented corporate brand.

Brand actors and social interactions

The initial activity involves implementing brand leadership practices across all organisational levels (Figure 5.7). The crucial support from top management at the outset of the UCO initiative signalled a commitment to delivering enhanced value to customers. Successful brand strategy formation necessitated collective leadership efforts throughout the organisation, rather than relying solely on individual efforts. To address this, the firm expanded its top and middle management teams and recruited new members who were not attached to previous strategies.

To facilitate the dissemination of UCO principles across the organisational hierarchy, various managers from different levels were selected as champions. These individuals were chosen based on their experiences and personalities, which made them well-suited to advocate for an agreed-upon value system. This system emphasised a commitment to enhancing customer satisfaction, fostering collaboration, promoting professional development and mentorship, and upholding performance standards aligned with the organisation's culture.

Another aspect involves revising communication practices to effectively convey brand strategy formation. HighRingTech aimed to enhance customer visibility not only within internal

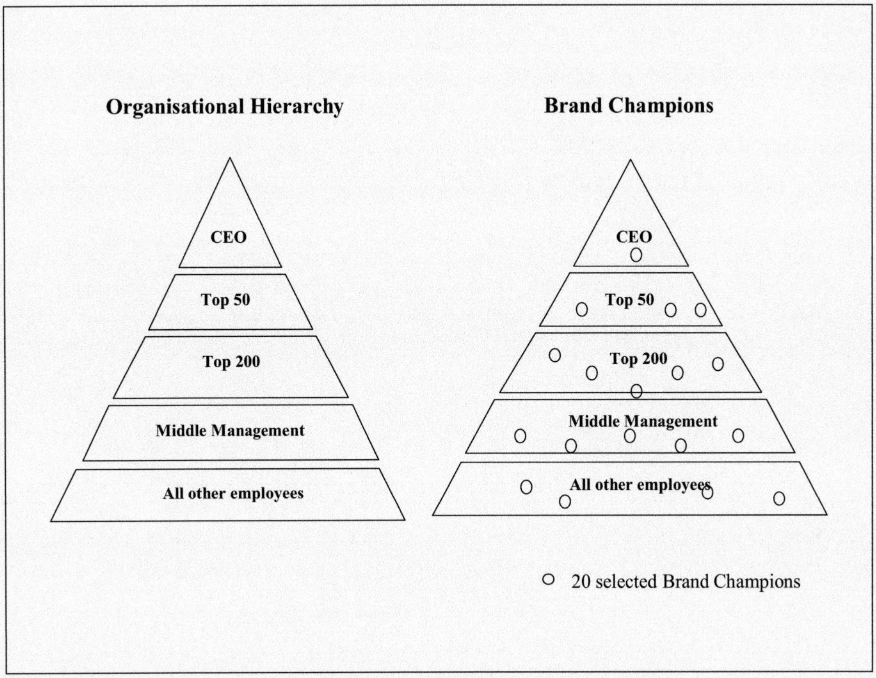

FIGURE 5.7 Brand champions involved in the UCO transfer process

channels but also in offices and production sites. Achieving this required active participation from the human resources and communications department, especially in communicating the significance and essence of the brand strategy to individuals with diverse mindsets.

To mitigate possible conflicts, the key deliberations centred on whether to centrally develop the internal communication campaign or tailor it for individual business segments. Opting for a centralised approach would necessitate recognition from the top management team of each decentralised organisational structure and entail granting considerable entrepreneurial autonomy to various business segments. Failure to engage employees in the communication program posed a significant risk to the success of the UCO initiative as a whole.

Brand strategy formation practices: translating customer requirements into changed processes and operation activities

To improve internal communication and integrate diverse organisational cultures for enhanced learning, HighRingTech initiated a programme named 'Continuous Improvement Processes' (CIP). This programme aimed to promptly and efficiently translate customer needs into operational adjustments. Teams comprising members from various departments and functions collaborated intensively for a few days to devise targeted solutions to specific issues (Figure 5.8).

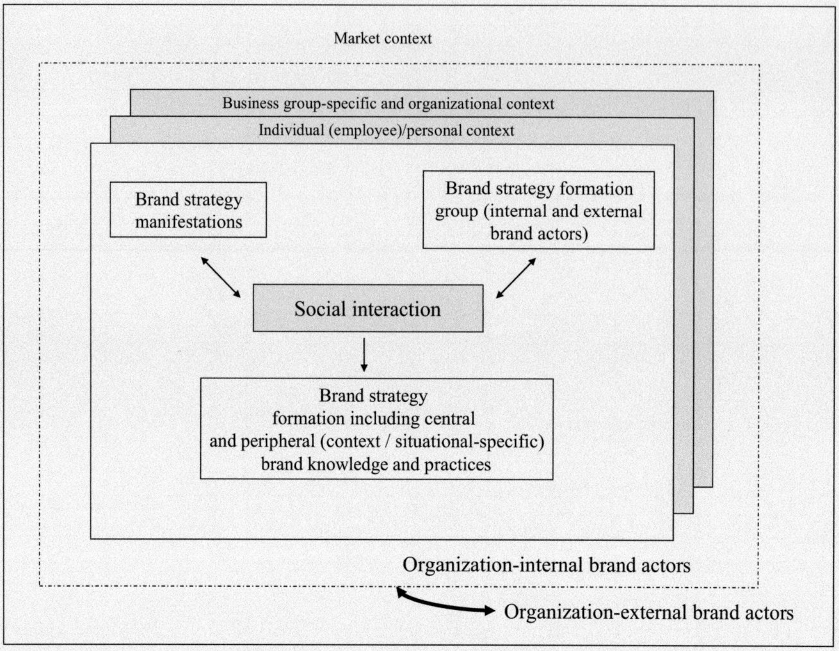

FIGURE 5.8 Brand strategy formation and underlying dynamics

Additionally, 'common issue teams' were assigned to address internal challenges identified through customer satisfaction analysis, including issues like delivery performance, quality defects and innovation lead times. These teams collaborated to enhance underlying processes by strengthening relationships with logistics, suppliers and other stakeholders further upstream in the value chain.

Furthermore, robust collaborative relationships between departments were cultivated, facilitating joint efforts in seeking customer solutions and coordinating relevant information. The outcomes of this collaborative effort were swiftly put into action, with close monitoring of their effectiveness. The teams were granted significant autonomy and decision-making authority, aligning with the firm's overarching objective of delegating more responsibility to employees and fostering a culture of continuous improvement in their daily work routine.

Understanding the influence of the situational context

One context involved cultivating a customer-oriented mindset among employees. However, a challenge arose as many employees didn't grasp the concept of 'customer orientation first'. In response, management renamed the initiative in the local language. Despite this, internal communication efforts alone weren't adequate to foster the desired sensitivity towards customers among employees. To tackle this, the company increased customer visits to production sites to showcase the end use of HighRingTech products.

In the organisational context, addressing employee resistance to customer orientation posed a significant challenge. Management underestimated the difficulty of communicating the guiding principles to the large workforce despite recognising the long-term nature of the UCO brand strategy formation process. Although UCO and related programmes were generally successful, their acceptance varied depending on the effectiveness of information flow for UCO implementation. Motivating resistant employees proved challenging, with different business groups employing various strategies. The workers' committee restricted termination of resistant employees, while some groups applied pressure through performance metrics. However, addressing individual issues like revised reward systems and setting UCO-related goals required personal commitment. Training was deemed effective in enhancing UCO understanding, but some newly hired employees reported receiving no training at all.

In the market context, addressing customer orientation through feedback and satisfaction proved crucial. Initially, there were critical remarks about the items used to gauge customer satisfaction. Despite these comments, a survey conducted 2 years after the UCO initiative showed early success: customers noticed improvements in customer orientation compared to competitors. Biannual customer events like Tech Days and industry forums provided opportunities to engage with customers, partners, consultants and media. These events facilitated gathering feedback on the UCO programme, integrating external perspectives to better meet their needs and fostering networking.

Managerial implications

Vallaster and Lindgreen's (2011) study demonstrates how brand strategy formation involves the active participation of individuals, the tangible outcomes that embody the brand strategy and the contextual factors shaping this continuous, interactive process. Internal and external brand actors engage in social interactions to develop brand strategy manifestations. These manifestations are continuously co-created and implemented, influencing ongoing interactions within the organisation and beyond (refer to Figure 5.8).

Brand strategy formation is a dynamic process characterised by ongoing social interactions, yielding a complex system of brand knowledge. This system comprises both shared and peripheral elements, with consensual core aspects and context-specific peripheral knowledge. These peripheral elements enable flexible adaptation to operational needs without compromising the core strategy. Individual members within the strategy group contribute context-specific brand knowledge, leading to consensus over time. Branding stimuli interpretation is socially constructed through this interaction, providing organisational members with guidance. This complex system of branding knowledge evolves through intentional and unintentional efforts, shaped by and shaping ongoing social interactions.

The brand strategy formation group comprises self-interested and self-selected actors engaged in ongoing interactions centred around strategically relevant brand stimuli. This social interaction is open to interested participants and influenced by organisational structure, prevailing values, norms, management systems, resources and power dynamics. The group is diverse, with varying levels of involvement and roles among participants. Through value-selling training, members introduce and represent stimuli to drive cultural change and influence how issues are understood and addressed through conversations.

In the brand strategy interaction process, members of the brand strategy interest group construct manifestations of the branding strategy, which serve as both practical tools and simplified representations of its meaning, depicted as signs. These signs imbue the organisation with ontological significance, allowing members to comprehend the abstract essence of the brand strategy in tangible organisational terms. Manifestations translate the brand strategy into familiar organisational elements like structures, behaviours, practices and resource allocations, thereby representing the organisational context in which strategically relevant social interactions occur.

This case originates from Vallaster, C. and Lindgreen, A. (2011). Corporate brand strategy formation: Brand actors and the situational context for a business-to-business brand. *Industrial Marketing Management* 40(7): 1133–1143. Here, the reader can also find additional relevant references to the case and its topic.

Case study 2: How SCM determines where customers shop for DIY supplies

On a recent Saturday, while work was being done in the garden, the task of pruning an apple tree became a priority – a task that had been pending for some time. Progress was being made using an electric saw, but suddenly the blade broke, leaving the job half-finished. To complete the task, a replacement blade was needed immediately.

Fortunately, there are three DIY stores within a 5-km radius, so it seemed reasonable to assume that finding a replacement blade would not be too challenging. In the past, this would have required driving to each store without any assurance of product availability. However, with the rise of digital tools, it is now possible to check stock online – at least, that was the assumption.

The search began with the first DIY store, where shopping usually occurred. Unfortunately, the store's website did not provide any stock information. The second store, which was somewhat familiar, offered stock details, but the store's site was not user-friendly. After several clicks, it was determined that the blade was not available at the local branch but could be found at a store located 22 km away – further than desired.

The third store, Jem & Fix, which had not been used before, provided more efficient experience. Jem & Fix is a Danish low-cost DIY store chain that is known for offering a wide range of products for DIY projects at low prices. The stores are self-service stores, which means that customers find and pick up their goods themselves or order via the e-shop for home delivery. The chain is family-owned and has stores in Denmark, Sweden and Norway.

This store's website was easy to navigate, and not only did it show that five blades were in stock, but it also provided specific details about the location of the blades within the store, including the shelf number. This clarity made the decision straightforward, and a trip to this store was the next step.

This experience exemplifies how SCM and digital integration can shape customer behaviour. The availability of real-time data enabled an informed decision about where to shop. Although home delivery was an option, the choice was made to use the 'Buy Online, Pick Up in Store' service to ensure the blade could be obtained immediately and the project completed that day. This combination of digital research and in-store shopping highlights the growing importance of time efficiency in consumer purchasing decisions.

Upon collecting the blade and checking the stock again from the car, the system indicated four blades remaining – demonstrating real-time updates. It is likely that this seamless integration even triggered an automatic reorder of the product. Since then, shopping has been primarily done at this store, with confidence that no trip will be wasted.

While this example pertains to a DIY store, the same principles apply across various industries, including clothing, hardware, groceries, wine and bookstores. The key takeaway is that real-time data and the integration between SCM and customer-facing platforms are crucial in influencing modern consumer behaviour.

Multiple-choice questions

1. Which of the following best describes the concept of 'integrated marketing and SCM'?

   A. Optimising individual departmental functions
   B. Focusing solely on customer acquisition
   C. Aligning marketing and SCM strategies holistically
   D. Prioritising cost reduction over value creation

2. What is a key challenge in implementing an integrated marketing and SCM framework?

   A. Excessive alignment of departmental goals
   B. Overemphasis on cross-functional communication
   C. Resistance to organisational culture change
   D. Simplified performance measurement systems

3. Which element is NOT typically part of the integrated marketing and SCM communication process?

   A. Message encoding by the sender
   B. Channel selection for transmission
   C. Unilateral decision-making by management
   D. Feedback interpretation by the receiver

4. How does the integrated framework address demand variability?

   A. By ignoring market fluctuations entirely
   B. Through rigid, inflexible production schedules
   C. By aligning forecasting with supply capabilities
   D. Focusing exclusively on historical sales data

5. What role does information technology play in the integrated framework?

   A. It is irrelevant to integration efforts
   B. It solely supports marketing functions
   C. It enables seamless data flow and analysis
   D. It replaces human decision-making entirely

6. Which approach best characterises the customer focus in an integrated framework?

   A. Treating all customers identically
   B. Focusing exclusively on new customer acquisition
   C. Segmenting and tailoring value propositions
   D. Prioritising short-term transactional relationships

7. How does the integrated framework impact inventory management?

   A. It eliminates the need for safety stock
   B. It promotes excessive inventory buildup
   C. It balances demand patterns with supply
   D. It focuses solely on just-in-time delivery

8. What is a key benefit of integrating marketing and SCM strategies?

   A. Reduced need for cross-functional collaboration
   B. Increased departmental specialisation and silos
   C. Enhanced overall value creation for customers
   D. Simplified organisational structure and hierarchy

9. Which metric is LEAST relevant in evaluating the success of an integrated framework?

   A. Customer lifetime value
   B. Supply chain responsiveness
   C. Individual departmental profit margins
   D. End-to-end order fulfilment accuracy

10. How does the integrated framework address supplier relationships?

    A. By maintaining arm's-length transactional ties
    B. Through collaborative, strategic partnerships
    C. By frequently changing suppliers to reduce costs
    D. Focusing solely on price negotiations

11. What approach to product development does the integrated framework promote?

    A. Marketing-led design without SCM input
    B. SCM-driven specifications without market consideration
    C. Concurrent engineering with cross-functional teams
    D. Outsourcing all product development activities

12. How does the integrated framework impact pricing strategies?

    A. It focuses solely on cost-plus pricing methods
    B. It ignores supply chain costs in pricing decisions
    C. It aligns pricing with value creation and delivery
    D. It promotes predatory pricing to gain market share

13. Which of the following is NOT a typical barrier to implementing an integrated framework?

    A. Functional silos and departmental rivalries
    B. Lack of top management support and vision
    C. Excessive cross-functional communication and coordination
    D. Incompatible IT systems across the organisation

14. How does the integrated framework address global supply chain challenges?

    A. By avoiding international markets entirely
    B. Through centralised decision-making for all regions
    C. By balancing global efficiency with local responsiveness
    D. Focusing exclusively on domestic supply chains

15. What role does sustainability play in the integrated marketing and SCM framework?

    A. It is considered irrelevant to business operations
    B. It focuses solely on environmental impact reduction
    C. It balances economic, social and environmental factors
    D. It prioritises short-term profits over long-term sustainability

Essay question

Analyse how the integrated framework of marketing and SCM addresses three critical challenges in today's business environment: (1) demand volatility and forecasting accuracy, (2) balancing cost efficiency with customer value creation and (3) achieving sustainability across the entire value chain. Discuss specific strategies and tools within the integrated framework that can be employed to tackle these challenges, and explain how the synergies between marketing and SCM functions contribute to more effective solutions. Support your analysis with examples of how companies might implement these integrated approaches in practice.

6

A SYSTEMIC APPROACH TO DISTRIBUTION CHANNELS

Introduction

A distribution channel can be defined simply as a number of group of organisations (producers, intermediaries such as wholesalers and retailers, third-party logistics, etc.) that are taking part in a process of flow of products or services from producers to customers. In this chapter, the key elements of the successful distribution channels are identified and discussed.

Learning objectives

After reading this chapter, you will be able to answer the following questions:

- What are the differences between value networks – demand chain, supply chain and distribution channels?
- How are distribution, sales and marketing working together to satisfy demand?
- What are the main distribution channel structures?
- What are the critical success factors of marketing distribution systems?

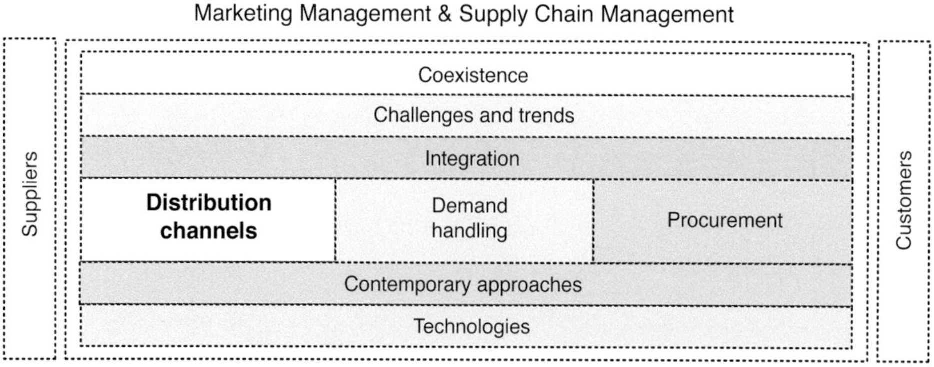

DOI: 10.4324/9781003650973-6

Outline

6.1 Value supply networks – demand chain, supply chain and distribution channels

Up until this point, an effort has been made for the reader to come to an introductory knowledge and understanding of the content, goals and philosophies of the two disciplines – to understand that all actions and activities taking place are ultimately considered useful, tested and are pursued only when aimed to offer value to the company's customers. Indeed, emphasis was also given to the point of view and to the value and power of a systems approach to the special and individual operating capabilities of the operationally specialised departments of a company, and the approach of integration was analysed.

It would, of course, be short-sighted for someone to consider that a business is an autonomous and independent unit and that not only its decisions and capabilities but also its limitations ensue and originate only from inside a sealed framework in which they are active. As was cited above when discussing the systems/integrated intra-departmental approach, organisations function as closed but also as open systems. In the context of this chapter, more emphasis will be placed on their features and the consequences such entail with respect to their aspects as open systems.

To begin with, the term 'open system' directly refers to concepts and rationales relating to interaction, association and interdependence, in other words to a web of dialectical interaction with the environment, beyond and besides consumers. All carriers and environments, either affecting the enterprise or being affected by it, bear their own role and importance and undoubtedly catalytically largely shape the landscape of opportunities and threats that exists for every organisation. There is a direct relation and continuous consecutive movements of action and reaction that must be taken into account. Figure 6.1 could in a sense reflect this framework of cross-correlations that describe and govern the relationship of a company with its environment.

In the context of the analysis and convergence of the two disciplines, emphasis shall be placed on the field that is the common ground of their functions, objectives, pursuits and activities.

What should remain at least detectable from the analysis of Figure 6.1 is the fact that the production and delivery of value to the company's customers are ultimately not a simple and one-dimensional affair but a dependent variable, which is the object of influence of many constituents. From this total of variables that regard and outline the magnitude of the value for delivery, on the one hand, the company actively focuses its efforts towards the set of factors that it itself can control, while, on the other hand, it closely monitors those it cannot control, in order to adjust to any changes to them in a timely fashion. The common place that conceptually, practically and materially connects the two disciplines is the value shaped for delivery to customers. Perhaps this term can be regarded as concisely engulfing the quintessence of the purposefulness for studying the coincidence of the two disciplines. Specifically, should one isolate from Figure 6.1 the context that relates to the subject matter of this book and then focus and amplify the common ground of the value being shaped and delivered, then one would clearly

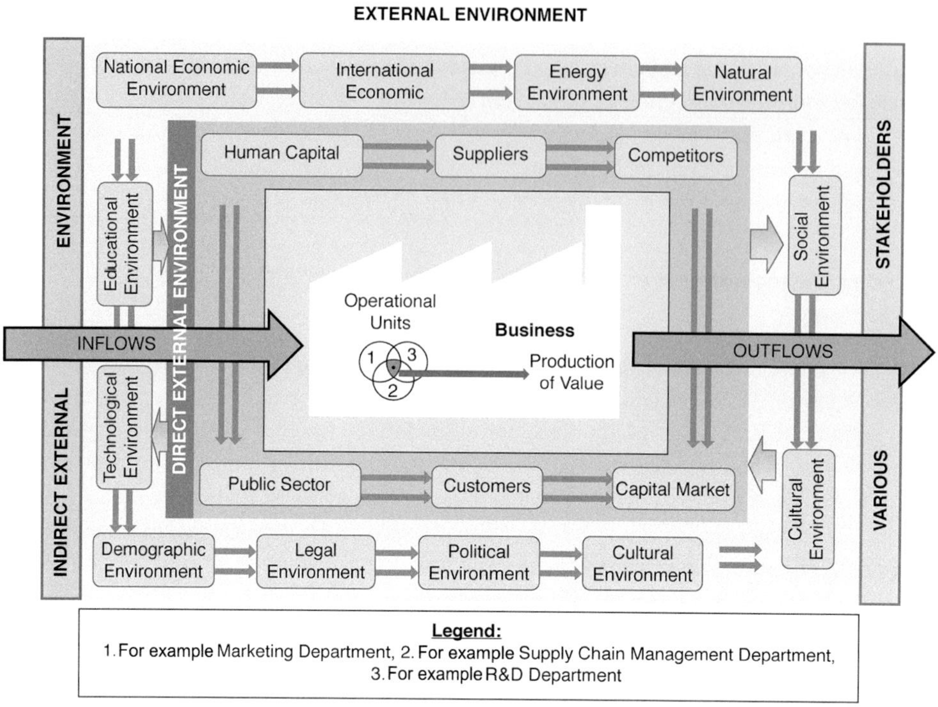

FIGURE 6.1 Relationship between a company and its environment

perceive the specialised axes that govern the relationship between marketing and supply chain management (SCM).

A necessary condition in order for there to be any activity that produces value is the existence of inflows. These may vary depending on the nature of the productive activity, but their existence renders them, *sine qua non*, a prerequisite for (any) productive process.

Indicatively various resources, such as raw materials and structural sub-elements of the product, may be considered as inflows, as are its spare parts, capital, information, know-how and know-why, etc. The carriers who are competent for the actualisation of such inflows are the suppliers of the enterprise. On the other hand, it is easy to understand that the value produced does not essentially exist if not delivered to its recipient or customer. The corresponding associates assigned with this work belong to a subset of the supply chain, which is called a channel, or distribution or handling channel (Figure 6.2).

In more detail, the ascending and descending associates of the company comprise its supply chain. Under the light of a more customer-centric perspective (namely, by removing the somewhat mechanistic stepwise approach for the realisation of the productive process and then the sale and simultaneous 'encasing' of the listening and responding to the needs of customers, the 'demand chain'), it would better reflect the dedication to the creation of the highest value for customers.

The term 'value network' has all players as participants, from suppliers up to the end receivers; that is, it incorporates all variables that ultimately shape and deliver value to the client/consumer.

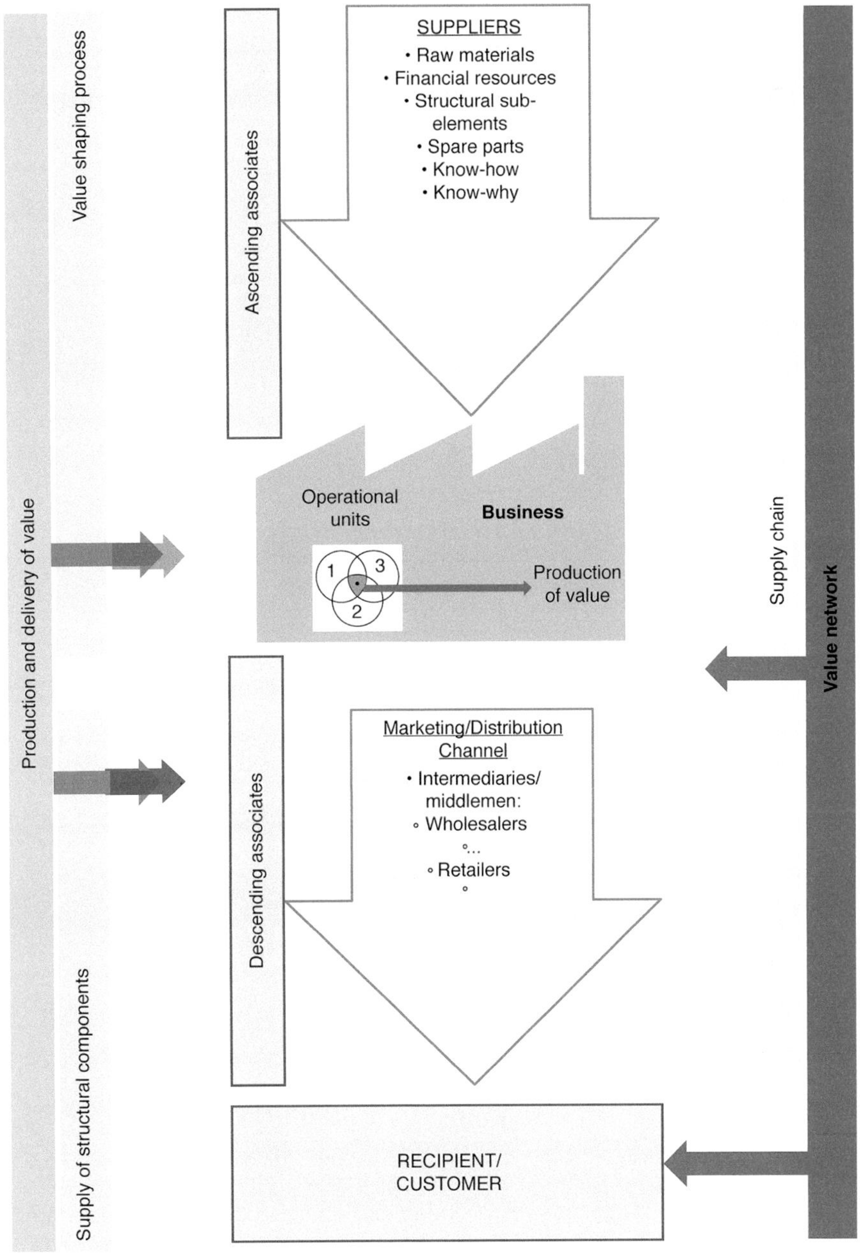

FIGURE 6.2 Graphic representation of a distribution channel

It must be stressed at this point that Figure 6.3 deliberately isolates some variables aiming to emphasise those directly involved in the shaping and delivery of value. The depiction and study of this subset must not under any circumstance divert attention and push towards sidelining or underestimating the other – to a lesser or greater extent – indirect co-modulators of the magnitude of value.

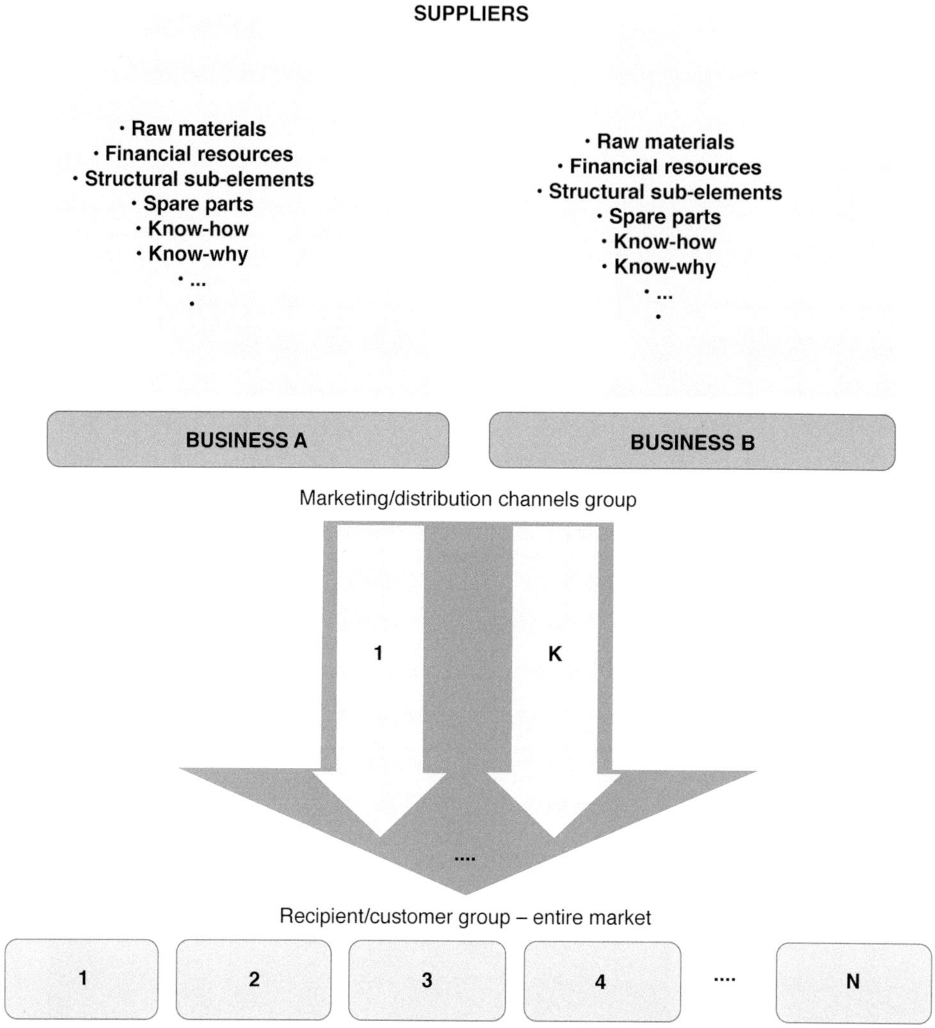

FIGURE 6.3 Value network

For example, given that the competitors of the enterprise – almost self-inclusively – render axiomatically relative the magnitude of the value one offers to his customers (relative since there is always room for comparison, and as it is usually said, 'the enemy of good is the better'), it is imperative that we evaluate supply chains also under the light cast by the terms and the regime of their collaboration with competing companies. Part of even the entire supply chain with which one does business might simultaneously be used as an associate of directly or indirectly competing enterprises (as well as enterprises with which there is no competition whatsoever) and which offer to a greater or lesser extent diversified products.

It is obvious that an integrated approach must take account of the full value network, acknowledging the importance of each and every participant inside and outside the enterprise, in order for both production and the delivery of value to offer to the consumer or recipient the ('relatively') maximum value. This is the principal reason that attention and emphasis on the integrated approach for offering value are reflected on and mandate not only the expanded competences of marketing executives but also their approach through the systems theory adopted in the context of this work.

6.2 Distribution/sales/marketing channels and networks

After theoretically delimiting and sketching the precise place of the marketing channel as a subset of the value network, it is of critical importance to further analyse its role and nature. One of the most important reasons for which this area will be explored is that it is typical for whatever decision taken with respect to channels to have a long-term orientation, which includes terms, agreements and commitments that are unbending to any type of change.

The building of channels is a relatively time-consuming process of a strategic nature. When deciding on those who will participate in the channel, their special function, competences and also the scope of their contribution, account is taken also of the extent by which they serve, converge and are congruent with the objectives and media for the promotion and pricing of the product, as well as of other factors related to its creation and nature. It would not be an overstatement if one claimed that the decisions regarding the structure and function of the channel relate almost in their entirety to the entire spectrum of marketing's actions and activities. For example, one could cite that the decision to create a new product and/or to purchase it (from the company which produces it) depends on whether the members of the channel have the capacity to support this product. Pricing is also directly affected by the distribution channel. Concerns relating to whether the products of the company shall be available in company shops or other national or international distributors are only some of the manifestations of this association. A more integrated approach on the importance of channels would suggest that their relation with the other three ingredients of the marketing mix is a dynamic one.

Marketing channel as a system

Concisely the distribution (or sale, or handling, or trade) performed via channels is a strategically determined function, one of the four Ps in the marketing mix and – equally importantly – stands at a dynamic interaction and cross-correlation with the other three Ps. It recommends the necessary processes that must take place for the product to reach the end consumer in its journey from its original producer. The distribution channel is essentially a chain of carriers–actors–intermediary businesses or institutions that intervene in order for the product to arrive at a time and place convenient for consumers. It is a system whose 'rings' are connected to one another in order to attain the objective laid out above.

Before one delves deeper into the constituent parts of the channel – the intermediaries – and in order to have an overview of the framework of associations and pursuits in which they are active, it would be useful to attempt approaching channels as systems. According to McCammon and Little (1973), marketing channels can be considered as systems, due to the following characteristics:

- The structural elements composing the channel are interrelated and structured in a way that is aimed towards the attainment of specific objectives.
- There is a step-wise performance of activities since each activity is a continuation of the previous one.

- Usually the types of 'acceptable' behaviour by the participants in the channel are established and regulated by some kind of a regulatory code – although it is not rare for some member of the channel to exercise more influence than the others.
- Every member of the channel participates but is also free to leave. This depends, on the side of the participants, on the purposefulness of the benefit they get by participating.
- The formation of the channel rests on the attainment of mutually acceptable objectives.

The last two features in particular allude to a contradiction: the relationship between intermediaries may be collaborative but could, at the same time, be rendered competitive. On the one hand, all intermediaries participating in the channel are structured and assume activities that must bear specific results in the context of the attainment of mutually accepted objective goals. On the other hand, it is clear that participating in the channel takes place and depends on the benefit each participant feels that he can and must obtain, in the form of profits. Should a link deem that he is being hurt, either because of a sub-maximisation of his profits on account of the actions of some other link(s) in the channel, then the competitive leg can supersede on the collaborative structure and interrelation of the channel and lead to conflicts, restructuring or even the collapse of the channel.

These conflicts are deemed unavoidable to some extent, especially when the constituent parts of a channel are enterprises that by definition pursue the maximisation of their own individual/corporate profit. The conflicts are classified into two categories: vertical and horizontal. In the case where the intermediaries from different levels are the leading actors of the conflict, then its direction is vertical. Correspondingly, if the intermediaries engaged in the conflict belong to congener levels, then the conflict is a horizontal one.

Furthermore, the fact that it is typical, as was cited above, for some company member of the channel to manage the channel and, consequently, have greater power will catalytically affect this special relationship that is characterised by the simultaneous existence of cooperation and competition. Inside this given framework of the existing – by definition – interdependence, the conflict is cultivated, climaxes and ensues when some of the parties involved become the subjects of mutual oppression (Stern and Gorman 1969). Consequently, the force may be interpreted as the power to affect towards the direction of the attainment of individual operating objectives and to, therefore, create oppressive forces (e.g., compressing the profits of the other participants). Consequently, all of this can end up in a reaction (i.e., a conflict).

The power of an intermediary participating in the distribution channel grants him the capacity to affect and control it and, perhaps, to impose and force his decisions on some or more of the other members. It usually originates from different skills or abilities, such as the following:

- Expertise: For example, holding specialised knowledge, know-how or technology and/or means or infrastructures allowing the handling of sensitive or fragile products without affecting their quality, or the transportation of, for example, hazardous products in a safe way and without them constituting a threat to public health or safety.
- Reward: Resources that can, for example, be used as reward in order for some participant to complete more expediently or in a different way the performance of his tasks.
- Coercion: Similar to the previous skill but in reverse order. If there is no compliance with respect to the wishes of the one who holds the power (e.g., for the interruption of a simultaneous agreement and collaboration with a competitor), then punitive actions may be enforced, as there is room for the enforcement of power.

- Reference: When, for example, an intermediary wishes to identify its name and image with a participant in the channel, this is a source of power for the second party.
- Legitimation: When, for example, there is a franchise agreement, then the franchisor has the legal powers stemming from the franchise agreement to which the franchisee has consented to.

Conflicts inside a channel are frequent. Factors that act as a catalyst for their manifestation are the conception of a mutually exclusive maximisation of profits in favour of some intermediaries (and not all), differences in the conception of risk taking, 'witch-hunts' taking place when things do not go as planned and, obviously, the size and proportions of the distribution of power.

It ought, however, to be stressed that conflicts are not always unfortunate outcomes, a threat, an irrevocable distortion of strategic planning or a catastrophic event. They may end up reshaping the channel and rendering it a more effective and efficient system, the members of which will be joined by stronger cooperative links and governed by less competitive apperceptions.

Overall, it is important to consider channels as sets of structural subunits on which the degree of cooperation and integration for the effectiveness and efficient operation of the channel as a whole depends. A sub-optimisation ensues from the accumulation of excessive power or by opportunistic behaviours for the unilateral improvement of the position of a participant against the rest. Even in the case where the short-sighted and short-term perspective for the unilateral improvement of the profit gains is not itself the cause of the conflict, one should not forget that the tolerance of a system is limited to (or identified with) the tolerance of its weakest constituent (link). On many occasions when such limits are transgressed, the reshaping or reconfiguration of the channel contributes in a positive manner to the replacement of the unsuitable players and, consequently, to the better operating performance of the channel.

Intermediaries or brokers: role, functions and production of utility

Until now and in the context of an overview of channels, reference was made to the constituent parts as 'structural units' or participants. Moving on to a more detailed assessment of their importance, place and role, intermediaries or brokers are defined as the carriers–enterprises–individuals and/or institutions that are the structural elements of the marketing/distribution channel and which are interposed as intermediaries performing those predefined and objectively necessary functions so as for the product (or service) to be rendered available to consumers for use.
These functions must take place in such a manner that their performance will, obviously, cover their cost and, on the other hand, to render the maximum potential value to it. The most forceful argument in favour of the existence of intermediaries is that they can satisfactorily respond to both of the conditions above. Their contribution is critical and their participation a given, principally due to the following facts:

- They improve the efficiency of transactions by reducing their numbers.
- They facilitate the performance of transactions by dampening the differences in quantity and variety between producers and consumers.

Specifically, with respect to the first feature, consider the following network of contacts that is necessary in order for five consumers to have access to the products of five producers.

To make the products of these five producers available to the five consumers, each of the producers would have to approach each one of the consumers. The number of contacts would, therefore, have been 25.

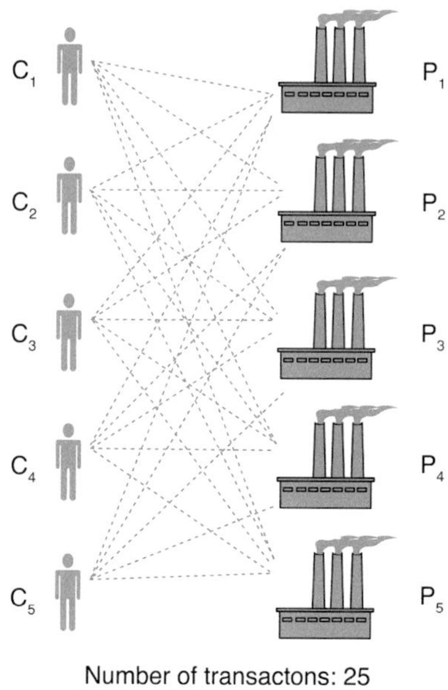

FIGURE 6.4 Number of transactions without an intermediary

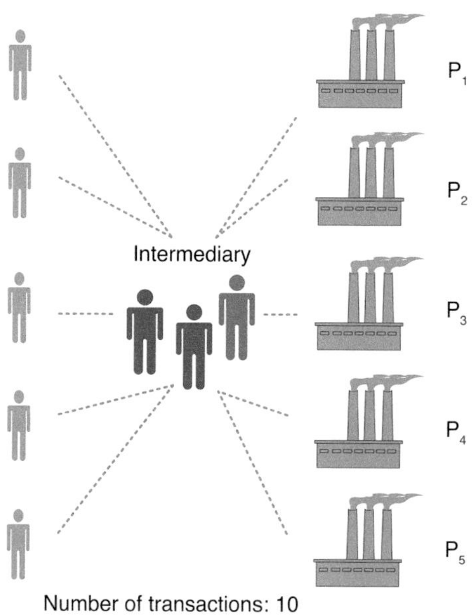

FIGURE 6.5 Number of transactions with an intermediary

In Figure 6.5, the number of producers and consumers remains the same. What differs is the intervention of an intermediary. It is obvious that this intervention creates a more economical environment with respect to the number of contacts (which have now been decreased to just ten!), and, as a chain reaction, this translates into greater effectiveness and efficiency with economic benefits for a number of relevant variables. With respect to the second characteristic, the contribution of intermediaries is also evident from the key assumptions of macro- and microeconomics.

To maximise their benefit, companies aim to produce and sell great quantities of products. This occurs due to a number of reasons, such as, for example, the capacity to purchase raw materials at a lower cost as the quantity supplied increases, the decrease of fixed costs, a greater negotiating power with respect to suppliers, an improvement of learning and experience curves and, ultimately, the attainment of economies of scale.

On the other hand, in order for consumers to maximise their own utility–benefit curve, they prefer to purchase small quantities of a variety of goods and not a limited range of products in great quantities. There is an evident incompatibility between the manner by which producers maximise their profits and the medium for the attainment of the maximum utility–benefit for the consumer (which is defined and limited by his available income). It is precisely this difference that the middleman comes to bridge, intervening as an intermediary and simultaneously satisfying, via his functions, both poles of offer and demand. Through their experience and specialised operation, intermediaries purchase large quantities from producers (serving the ideal of the attainment of maximum potential profits), which they then sell to consumers by segmenting them into smaller ones. Thus, consumers may also be satisfied (the utility curve is improved), since they can direct their income into the purchase of a variety of small quantities of different products. Intermediaries essentially function as converters of the quantities provided by producers to the variety of quantities desired by consumers.

A direct consequence of the above is intermediaries' positive contribution to the procedural section of the consumers' search for products. As a result of the bridging of the gap of pursuits regarding quantity and/or variety, consumers have a wider array of product variety at their disposal, which they can search in a faster and easier manner. The framework above describes the functions of intermediaries and stands as perhaps the most solid acceptance and the quintessence of their contribution and importance.

Their effectiveness is also the principal reason for which businesses accept to assign part of their control with respect to whom and how their products are sold. Intermediaries produce utility that adds value to both the variables posed as the primary goals of distribution: the time and place for the delivery of value. As a result, a reduction in cost is also attained, as is an improvement in the manner. Figure 6.6 accentuates the great array of contribution by intermediaries to the addition of value that takes place as the result of the functions they accomplish. A closer look will also reveal other folds that are located, to a large extent, in marketing's core of functions and sphere of influence and duties.

Intermediaries perform a number of useful functions, including their obvious contribution that relates to the conversion and adjustment of the quantity offered, with respect to both the terms and variety that the side of demand wishes for. They perform this by employing functions that include activities for classification, manufacture, stocking and packaging. In the context of intermediaries, they come in contact, communicate and negotiate with existing and potential buyers. The terms of the agreement – and the subject of the contacts – may cover an array of variables relating to the time, place, cost and status of the transfer of possession or ownership. Of course, contact and communication may also be viewed as promotional activities with respect to both existing and potential customers. Sometimes, due to their role and competences, intermediaries are also assigned with the role of 'front-line staff' in a sense, namely, that they represent the company as the connecting link between it and its customers.

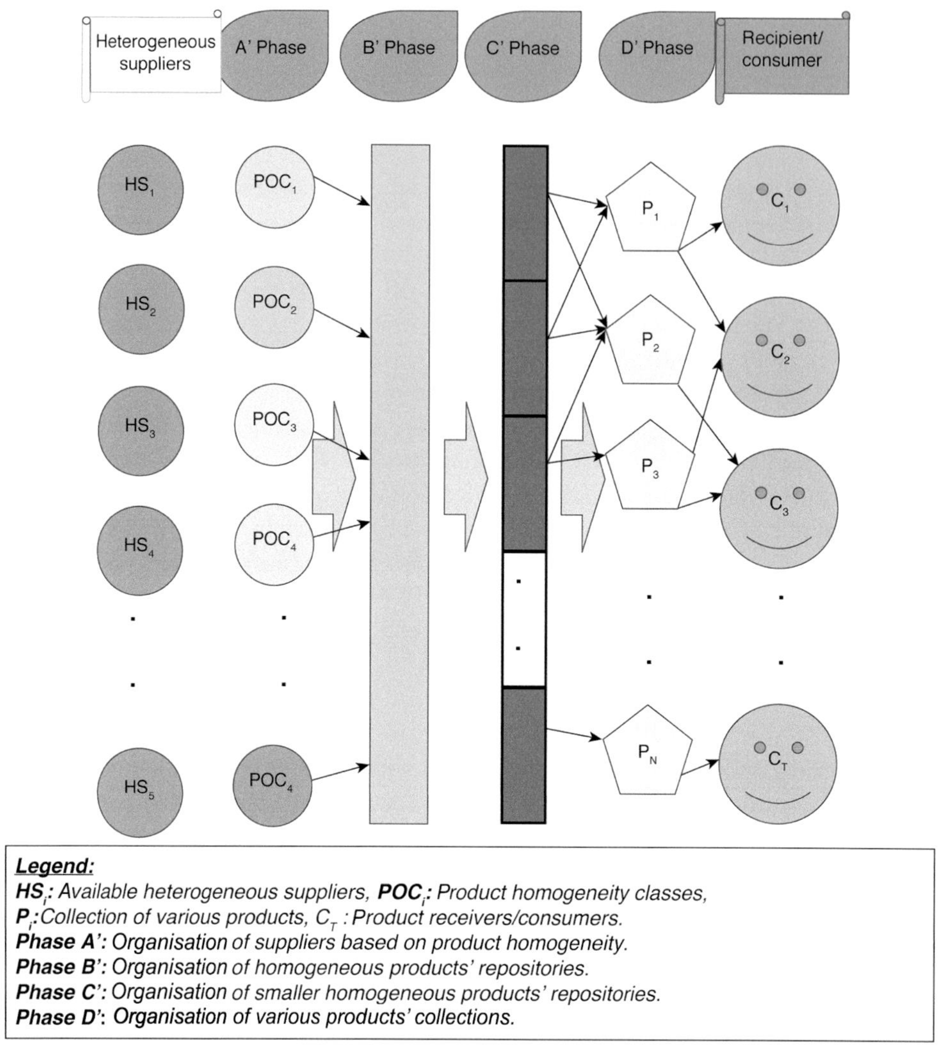

FIGURE 6.6 Contribution of intermediaries in a distribution network

This is logical since as it has been underlined above that intermediaries participate in the building of the total offered value. Communication and contact establish a two-way flow of information, where end users and the environment provide feedback to the company. The field of intermediaries' activities is the par-excellence environment for the emergence of dynamic forces, trends and conditions, the detection, evaluation and dissemination of which inside the company is an aid to strategic planning, organisation, prevention and response. They are, in other words, an integral part of the system for monitoring the environment, where listening closely and assessing are the touchstones for absorbing threats and/or maximising opportunities.

An effort is made in Figure 6.8 to render clear a more integrated picture as possible with respect to functions and the corresponding utility produced by them, as the result of the participation of intermediaries. The order of activities taking place was analysed in a linear and

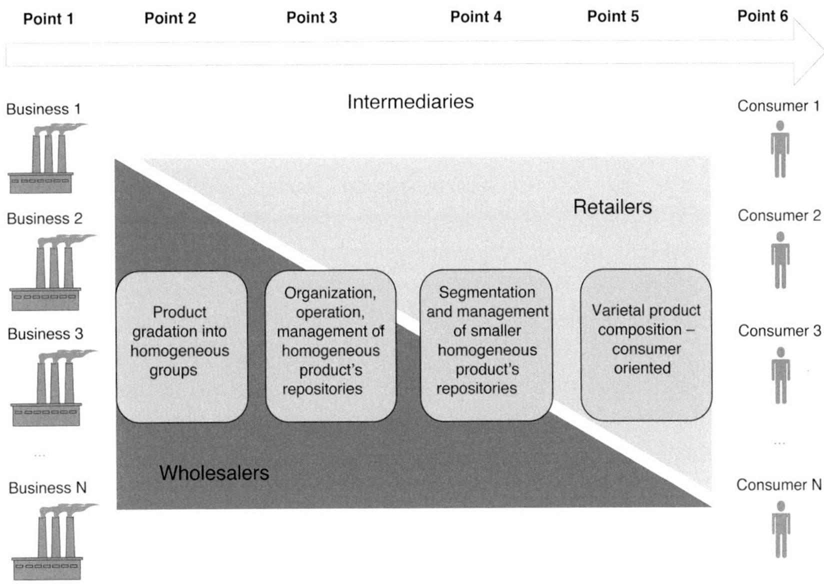

FIGURE 6.7 Field of action of the participants in a distribution network

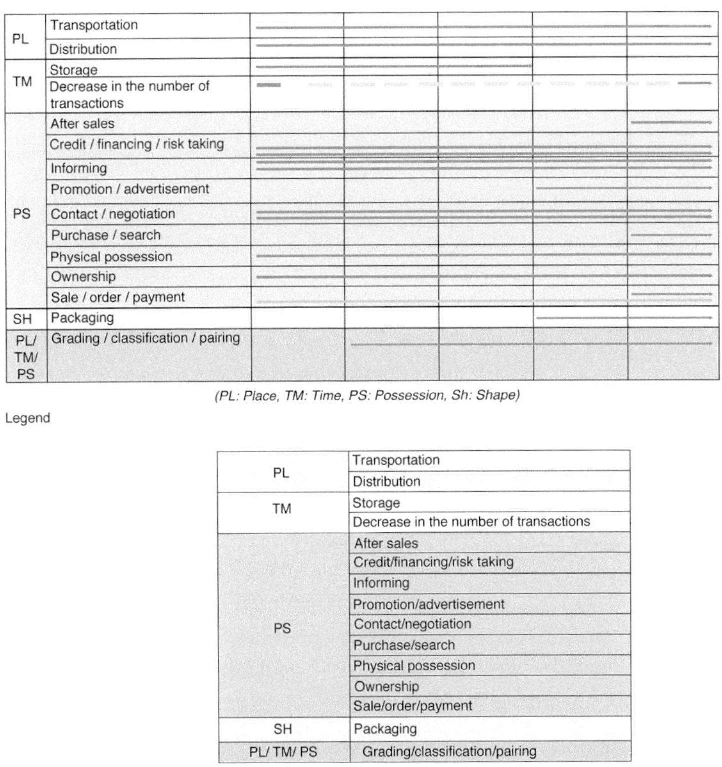

FIGURE 6.8 Field of action of the participants in a distribution network and the various respective flows (taxonomy by utility)

stepwise way in order for there to be a more direct and immediate correlation between functions and activities and to simultaneously underline their usefulness and importance through the connection with the utility produced by each one. In parallel, the entire framework of the participants to the channel remained connected with the external environment that frames it. This was deemed both useful and necessary since – as was noted before – the entire 'marketing/distribution channel' does not exist in a sealed, dissected, independent and sterile sphere. Quite the opposite, it exists as a system that was a multitude of varied contacts and two-way dynamic communication with its external environment (direct and indirect) in the form of (positive or negative) influences (either incoming to it or outgoing from it).

The consideration of the distribution/marketing channel as an integral and irreplaceable part of the supply chain – or to put it in more marketing-oriented terms, the 'demand chain' or, even more integrated, the value network on the one hand and, on the other, its inclusion in the wider network of dynamic interrelations and two-way influences as the result of the business activities in complex environments – accentuates the character of distribution as a system.

Being a system, its effectiveness depends on two variables:

- Its ability to regulate or be structured in such a manner so as for existing balances to be stable and sufficiently oriented towards the attainment of the system's goals (and not the individual goals of its members).
- Its ability to organise, manage and administer effectively and efficiently the functions producing utility. Such functions are formed as flows that penetrate the structural units and representatively sketch the instrumental interfaces between them with respect to competences/activities.

In the context of the recognition of the dynamic nature of functions as well as the system that must cohesively enclose an interdependent set of associates in order to produce, via their symbiotic relationship, a utility greater than the sum of their individual efforts, the use of the term 'flow' is considered justified.

Stern and colleagues (Stern and El-Ansary 1977; Stern et al. 1996) classify flows to three kinds depending on the qualities of their direction:

- Forward flows: Flows that signify movement towards consumers (from producers).
- Backward flows: Flows that signify a movement from consumers (to producers).
- Bidirectional flows: Flows that signify a bidirectional movement from and towards consumers (towards and from producers).

6.3 Types of marketing channel

However a marketing channel is presented, it comprises the structural units participating in it, which are connected to one another as joining links in a chain and, by pursuing mutual benefits, compose systems that perform organic functions. Should the participating members be two (with all that this entails for the completion of necessary functions, its economy quality and its efficiency), then distribution is considered to be direct. If intermediaries other than the producer and the consumer also participate and mediate in the channel, the distribution is indirect.

Table 6.1 depicts the various types, depending on who the participants are and what the structure of the members inside the channel is. In cases where the end recipient of the products

TABLE 6.1 Main types of marketing channels

Type 1: This is a direct channel, which is very rare. It is usual for small producers to be engaged in this form of distribution.	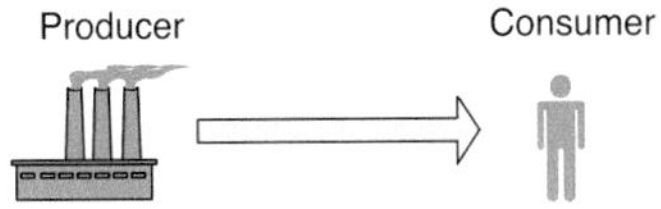
Type 2: This type is principally adopted in economies dominated by large retail chains, which essentially replace part of the functions that would alternatively have been performed by wholesalers. This disadvantage is offset by the existence of more cohesive links in their relation to both producers and consumers	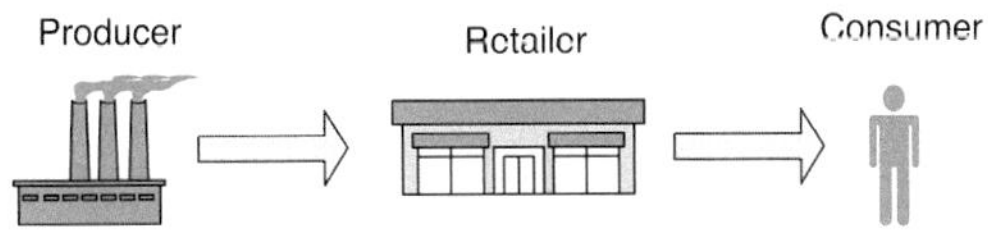
Type 3: The most popular use of this type is for products that in their majority are convenience products, namely, products with a relatively low price and high purchase frequency, which usually do not require involvement in a lengthy decision-making process and are repeated routine purchases	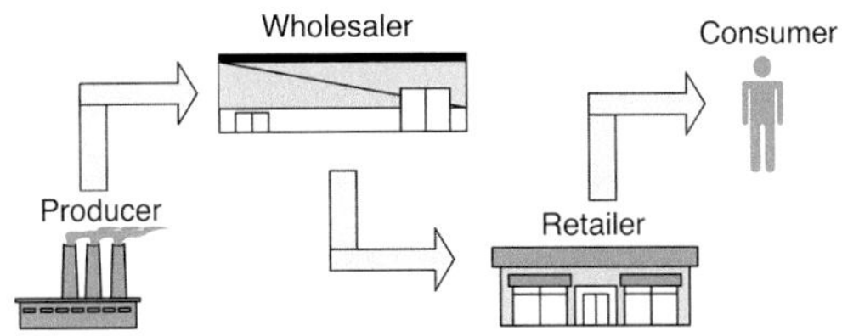
Type 4: The existence of an 'agent' (broker) is usually adopted by channels that operate in fragmented markets. Namely, in cases with increased needs for organisation, management and coordination due to the existence of a large number of small-size producers with increased needs for the development of their sales and, correspondingly, limited capacity to attain that without outside intervention or assistance	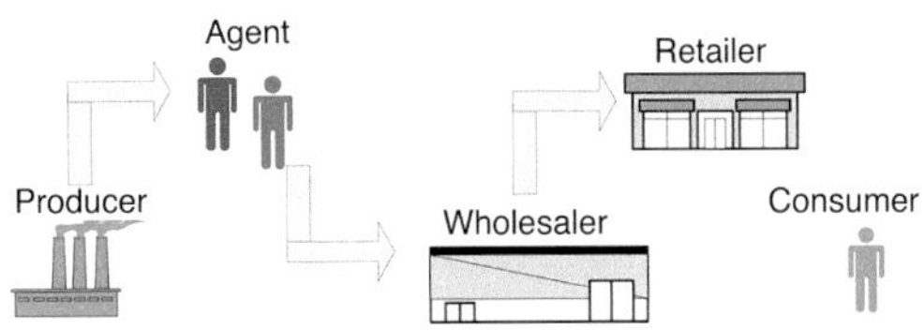

is someone for whom the utility of the product lies in its consumption (consumer market), the various types (direct and indirect) may take the following forms shown in the table.

It is clear that the more one moves towards larger 'multi-member' schema, the more these are rendered more indirect and chain-like and the more the distance of the contact point, bidirectional communication and influence increases. To put it in other terms, as functions are distributed and performed by a greater number of intermediaries, the contact of the original producer and the end consumer is filtered, evaluated and disseminated and ultimately depends on the intermediaries participating in the channel. The way the channel is structured is, of course, not exclusively or solely inside the sphere of the absolute choice of the consumer or the producer. In most cases, it is the golden ratio between the ideal and the attainable.

The point where the minimisation of the distance between the ideal and the attainable appears to depend more heavily on the business side, pinpoints the areas where the business is more influential regarding the shaping of variables that relate to distribution.

The (more) controlled variables are defined to be those areas whose shaping and fine-tuning belong to the competence, jurisdiction and sphere of discretionary power of the strategic and tactical choices of the corporation. One could cite the following as the factors influencing the structure of distribution channels which depend more on the corporation-producer itself.

A. Items that relate to the marketing mix of the business

- Price:

  a. Shaping the price levels

- Product:

  a. Features of the product that pertain to its complexity
  b. Specifications and technical characteristics
  c. Symbolic features
  d. Its classification in the intangibility scale and the entailed consequences regarding its dispensability, perishableness and disunion
  e. Seasonality of the product
  f. Interval – time lapse between its production and consumption
  g. Capacity for standardisation
  h. Mass or customised production
  i. Maintenance needs and specifications
  j. Intended use of the product

- Promotion:

  a. Available budget
  b. Promotion strategy
  c. Promotion goals
  d. Communication mix
  e. Degree of integration of marketing communication

- Placement:

  a. Coherence, complementarity, cohesion and reinforcement of strategic objectives under the umbrella of the integrated systems approach.

B. Factors from management's internal environment

- Wider framework of the adopted strategic orientation, vision and mission
- Depth and breadth of managerial capacities
- Context of the financial capacities and limitation and strategy for the allocation and orientation priorities for resources
- Pursued level of control and disposition towards involvements in relevant trade-offs
- Degree of integration of management functions, but also of the corporation's operations
- Relation to technology, tendency to adopt technological innovation

Moreover, the following factors may be acknowledged to be less controllable or non-controllable by the corporation:

- Consolidated versus fragmented markets
- Level – degree of cohesion and homogeneity of the target markets
- Buyer profile (demographic, psychographic, etc.)

- Attitudes, system of values
- Frequency of purchases
- Quantity purchased
- Human geography structure

C. Intermediaries' factors or components

- Number – rarity
- Fame, identifiability, experience and seniority
- Know-how and expertise, infrastructures
- Specialisation – training, special technical abilities.
- Past or continuing collaborations and relations with other intermediaries on the same level (horizontally) or different levels (vertically)
- Type of link, relation or contact with other collaborating producers who compete directly, indirectly or not at all with the company
- Degree of diversification of the products they already handle
- Negotiating strength, either descending or ascending or horizontally in the channel
- Capacity – intention for development horizontally and/or vertically
- Magnitude and type of power and history of methods for its application.
- Financial capacity and limitations
- Adaptability and availability
- Risk lovers or risk avoiders
- Capacity, levels and compatibility with respect to the auxiliary functions that create synergies and add value
- Existing cost–benefit analysis balance (how much benefit does the intermediary bring compared to its cost – alternative cost)

D. Factors for the remaining stakeholders

- Legal framework
- Government limitation
- Social environment
- Technological environment
- Natural environment
- Energy environment
- Human capital – education
- Buyers' negotiating power
- Negotiating power – number of other competitors
- Obstacles for entering and leaving the market

It must be stressed that classification into one of these categories does not signify or imply full control, on the one hand, and, correspondingly, full inability to participate or shape things. The classification is employed merely to stress the fact that via systematic and careful observation and evaluation of the not-totally (or not at all) controllable variables, one can proactively formulate and adjust those variables over the one that has more control in order to adopt (within what is attainable) the more rational and advantageous decisions that would be closer to the ideal.

One must also note that decisions that relate to distribution channels are of a long-term nature and characterised by their inflexibility, even rigidity, with respect to possible revocations,

TABLE 6.2 Types of channels for industrial products

Type 1(IN): Type 1(IN) is the most frequent form. Principal causes include (a) complexity of specifications and (b) complexity with respect to maintenance. Furthermore, both poles in this collaboration line usually comprise few members with a great geographical concentration, a fact that, combined with specialised specifications and the nature of the products to be handled or transported, dramatically increases the cost of an erroneous choice	
Type 2(IN): In cases where the producer does not have the skills, resources or disposition to engage with industrial buyers, as described in Type 1(IN), the industrial distributor (ID) intervenes, who assumes part of the responsibilities for collecting information, negotiating, promoting and selling	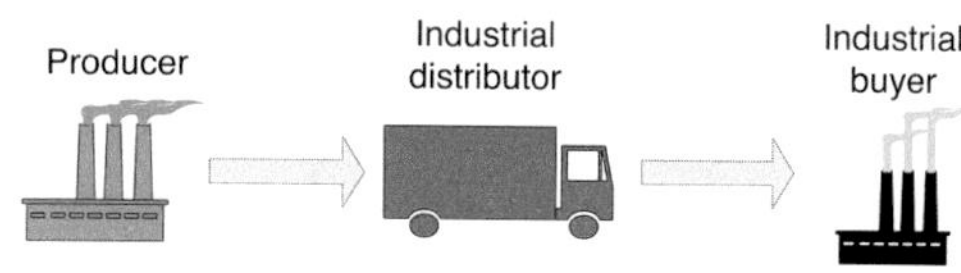
Type 3(IN): This structure is also common when the subject of the production is of relatively small value and/or the number of industrial buyers is large	
Type 4(IN): The structure of this configuration is a combination of Types 2(IN) and 3(IN), and, consequently, it exemplifies some of their characteristics. It is adopted in the case of the export of the manufactured products abroad and, in general, when existing conditions indicate that it is not in the producer's interests to be involved in the processes for the sale/distribution of the product (segmentation of the market, great geographic dispersion, large number of buyers, etc.)	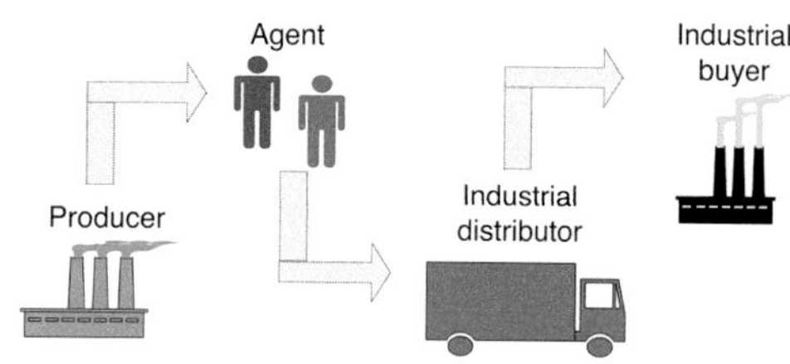

revisions and readjustments. Consequently, the cost (of any type) for dealing with an erroneous decision is insurmountable.

In the event that the final receiver of the products is someone (or some company) for whom the utility of the product does not lie in the use of its consumption, but he purchases it for any other reason, then one refers to the structure of channels for industrial products. The key types can assume the four forms shown in Table 6.2.

6.4 Types of distribution channel structure

Three main types of distribution channel structures can be identified:

1. Hard vertical integration
2. Outsourcing
3. Soft vertical integration

Hard vertical integration

In this case, a member of the distribution channel (or of a supply chain) assumes the planning, execution and implementation of some of the flows in the distribution network between any two levels. For example, in the case of a retail chain, there is a distribution centre that resupplies, by means of a privately owned fleet of trucks, the shops. This solution is acceptable when this particular process (resupply in the example) constitutes for management an added value service, which it does not wish to assign to anybody else. Moreover, the retail chain attains economies of scale with respect to both transportation and storage. In some nations or areas where appropriate third-party companies to assume this role do not exist, the hard vertical integration type appears to be the ideal solution.

However, this solution demands investments for the purchase, installation, operation and maintenance of the appropriate infrastructures and trained personnel with a suitable know-how and expertise. Thus, in several cases this is not possible, and the companies' management realises that the involvement and, in general, the management of flows lie outside their key competence. Such procedures are so complex and demanding that companies cannot assume them.

Outsourcing

Constant changes (technological, economic and social) in the sector of the supply chain for businesses and organisation and the new market requirements as well as the economic crisis have led not only to the revision of logistics services but also to the demand for the establishment of new ones. Logistics services may be performed either by the business entity itself or by assigning part or all of them to a third, independent and specialised company providing logistics services. This process is known as outsourcing, and these companies are called third-party logistics providers.

What?

In general, one can define outsourcing as the assignment of the works of a business to an external associate, who can be either a company specialising in a specific field or even an individual. Companies assign some or the majority of their works from the more principal to the more specialised or secondary works to third parties, from the production of raw materials, packaging and the distribution of products to promotional and advertising activities, holding on to only administration, general supervision and commercial management.

Specifically, in the context of a supply chain, an industrial or trading business (third-party logistics customer) assigns to a 3PL provider the handling of the basic logistics functions with the key objective for the products to reach the end or final customer in the shortest possible time and cost and, thus, provide a greater level of service to the latter. The assignment does not mean that 3PL providers acquire the ownership of the merchandise they store and/or transport, but that they are responsible for the performance of these processes against the final customer.

Why?

The decision to assign part of all of some logistics works until final delivery of merchandise rests on specific benefits for the businesses that adopt such a practice. These benefits are principally related to the following:

- *Lower costs:* A business that assigns part of its activities to third parties manages to save recourses and free capital since it need not invest in infrastructures, equipment and other systems or applications to cover its needs. The saving of resources and capital allows the third-party logistics customer to invest in other markets or products and to develop other business activities. Additionally, operational costs are reduced, since the cost of purchase, operation and maintenance of resources is comparatively greater than the consideration paid to the 3PL provider (or, to put it in another way, fixed costs are converted to variable ones).

- *Improved quality:* 3PL companies provide resources, skills and know-how and additionally have great experience and the suitable modern technological infrastructure for the performance of logistics processes. The upgrading of the level of quality for the services rendered results in further satisfaction of final customers.
- *Faster offering of services:* Upgrading of the level of quality of the rendered services results in further satisfaction of final customers.
- Additionally, the business becomes more flexible and can more quickly adapt to the needs of its customers and new practices, while it can respond more quickly to moves by competitors.

In general, the demand for 3PL companies is influenced by the following factors: (1) the degree of familiarisation of businesses with the advantages of outsourcing logistics services; (2) the complexity of the supply chain in the new, globalised environment; (3) the improved capacities offered by new informatics and communication technologies (the internet in particular) for information exchange between businesses for the more effective and efficient management and handling of inventories and (4) the capacity of some 3PL providers to provide added value services in areas such as the design of the distribution network, the monitoring of the merchandise that is transported, and information on the movement and level of inventories.

Why not?

Besides its advantages, outsources may also incur some risks or problems, such as a decrease in jobs, or the possibility of friction inside the company as the other associates and suppliers may oppose the idea of collaborating with external third-party service providers. Furthermore, the long-term collaboration between businesses and independent associates may bring about a dependence of the first on the second, due to the complacency that results from the gradual loss of their know-how and human resources (or simply, if the third-party logistics customer company chooses to outsource its principal functions, then its ability for innovation and improvement becomes limited). Finally, there is also the possibility that the external associate is unable to ultimately adjust to the particularities of the business, and as a result, the level of its services may not correspond with the expectations of the business.

3PL categorisation

We can categorise 3PL providers based on various criteria, for example, based on the business sector (agribusiness, food industry, etc.), the geographical coverage (on-shoring, off-shoring and near-shoring), number (single or co-sourcing) and the outsourcing level. Based on the last, we can recognise two types: partial and complete. In the first case, there is the assignment of one part of the activities to an external associate (outsourcing), while all others remain in the interior of the business (insourcing). In the second case (complete), all of the activities are assigned, based on an agreement or contract, to a 3PL provider, while the degree of involvement of the business-customer is limited only to the management of the contract.

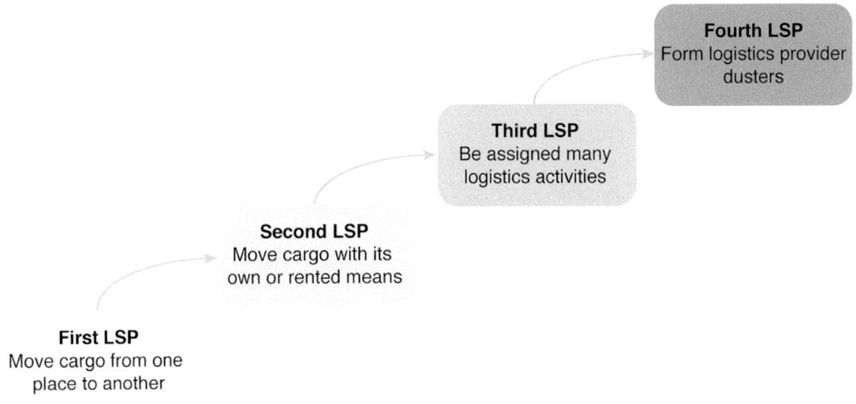

FIGURE 6.9 Types of logistics service provider

A common categorisation that indeed follows the timeline is presented below.
Of special interest are 3PL providers providing a multitude of logistics services, such as transportation, distribution, storage, cross-docking, inventories management, packaging, codification, labelling and execution of orders and fourth-party logistics (4PL), where one provider unifies the services of many 3PL providers (so as to provide integrated SCM solutions by providing consulting services and logistics services as well as infrastructures and technologies and even selecting the spaces (points of sale) and the personnel).

Which logistics processes?

Both primary and secondary logistics processes, such as transportation (domestic and international), warehousing, customs clearance and brokerage, forwarding, shipment consolidation, reverse logistics (returns – repairs), cross-docking, assembly (packaging, labelling and kitting), order fulfilment, costing and ICT management, are assigned to one 3PL provider. Some consider that prosperous processes for outsourcing are those of high priority.

Folinas et al. (2011) propose a step-by-step methodology to ask managers to make the prioritisation of the logistics processes based on specific criteria, such as the following:

- Logistics processes that are essential for the customer and also for the existence of the company. Businesses are usually based on these processes to attain a competitive edge (e.g., the process of picking is critical to the 3PL).
- Logistics processes that cost a lot.
- Logistics processes that are consuming significant resources (informational, financial, technological, human resources, etc.).
- Logistics processes that contribute considerably to the added value of services and products.
- Logistics processes that regularly generate problems, errors and delays.

And since each logistics process does not carry the same importance, managers involved in the logistics process consider them to be of varying significance. The authors in their study proposed possible values for the evaluation of the importance of the above criteria, ranging from 1, no significance, to 7, very high significance.

Which provider?

The selection of the most suitable logistics service provider is a strategic decision. Common decision approaches can be employed, such as the scoring model, analytical hierarchical process and multi-criteria analysis. This section will present a systematic (eight-step) procedure.

1. *Decision:* Each new initiative in the context of entrepreneurship and the planning of a company's activities proves to be very important. At this step, the senior management of the company meets and consults. The existing state of affairs, the expansion of modern views on outsourcing and the presentation of market conditions (opportunities, risks and challenges) constitute the subjects of enquiry. The management of the company must take the strategic decision of choosing outsourcing, by giving credence to the benefits, to the development of the competitive advantage and to ensuring the value of its products, its customers and its shareholders. The authorisation of a flexible project team, which will consist of the CFO, the head of sales and the logistics supervisor, in collaboration with an external consultant, experienced in the outsourcing of logistics issues will signify the commencement of the expansion of the supplier market and the preparation and handling of the survey inside the deadline posed.
2. *Project team:* A project team participates in the process for the evaluation and selection of a provider. The first duty of this team is, after it surveys the needs of the business, to pose clear objectives for the implementation of outsourcing; to assess its impact and consequences on the vision, structure and capital of the business, its competitiveness and human resources; and to speculate on the expected outcomes and the possibility of outsourcing's success. Based on the needs and objectives above, the team will prepare a specifications list and an analysis of the requirements of the project, which will describe in full detail what is to be done and what skills the provider must possess. It would be prudent at this time to utilise some basic criteria for approaching, and for the first evaluation of, a potential outsourcer. These include the profile of the prospective associate – market reputation, information on his facilities, the quality of the services offered, cost and pricing models and the associate's strategy and culture – innovative ideas and development.
3. *Preliminary analysis:* Based on the above criteria, the project team will sound out some suppliers aiming to investigate the prospect for collaborating with them. The approach must be careful and entirely confidential in order to safeguard the uninterrupted continuation of an existing external assignment of this particular project to some other supplier and, on the other hand, the real interest of the prospective supplier at that given time. Very beneficial to this approach would be a quick market survey with some of the customers of the prospective suppliers, who can easily give their opinion and offer their advice on the quality and level of cooperation with the targeted providers.
4. *Initial list of providers:* The above step concludes upon the drafting of a flexible list of prospective associates, which usually includes 5–7 different names. The bulletin containing the specifications and analysing the requirements will be dispatched to them in order for them to prepare and submit their detailed offers/bids.
5. *Evaluation:* The project team accepts the bids from prospective associates, assesses them very carefully and compares them with the detailed evaluation criteria. A visit to the facilities of the providers is deemed necessary to verify some of the criteria. The evaluation relates to both the profile of the business and the offers/bids that have been deposited. Table 6.3

presents indicative criteria and the corresponding detailed evaluation sub-criteria for outsourcing logistics providers.

6. *Selection:* Possible reinsertions of lower financial offers are usually accepted at this stage, while further contacts and negotiation take place and the original expanded working group comes together at the end of this stage in order to survey the materials collected by the project team and to conclude its selection. The external supplier who will assume the activity has been chosen.
7. *Contracting:* After the final choice has been made, it is critically important for the two parties to conclude a contract. Their legal consultants and external outsourcing consultants of the company, in collaboration with those of the supplier and under the directives of the project team, are responsible for drafting a comprehensible and flexible contract. This contract must refer to the objectives of the collaboration, the motives, costs, necessary audit and performance measurement reports, penalties for non-performance of the agreement, changes in the way services are priced and invoiced in cases of changes in the volume and manner of the project, communication between the two parties, as well as the steps and clauses for one of the two parties to exit the agreement. The contract serves to seal the agreement and safeguard the obligations, liabilities and rights of the contracting parties.
8. *Partnership management:* Experience shows that many collaborations resting on a detailed contract, which described in detail both the activities and obligations and liabilities of both parties, ultimately failed due to the lack of communication and relationship development channels. The establishment of the agenda for fixed periodical meetings and reports will help in the resolution of critical and unforeseen problems that will arise. The continuous monitoring of the relations between the executives involved in the collaboration from both sides, and the management of extreme behaviours that function cumulatively and harmfully on the collaboration are signs of a collaborative relationship philosophy that must be built piece-by-piece with the ultimate objective being a long-term collaboration.

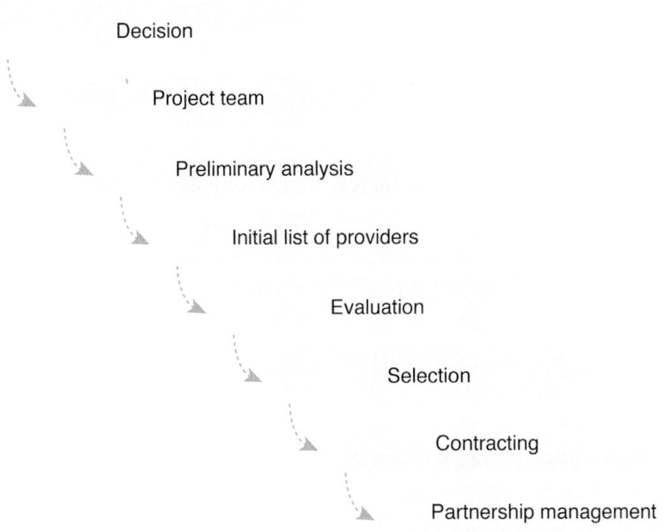

FIGURE 6.10 Selection process of the logistics service provider

TABLE 6.3 Detailed criteria for the evaluation of a logistics service provider

Criterion	*Sub-criteria*
Profile	Experience
	Specialisation in this specific field or sector
	Active clientele
	Experience of executives
	Network of associates
	Reputation
Infrastructure	Size of facilities, location, availability, capacity
	State of equipment in use
	Computers – office automation
	Security systems
Quality of services	Abidance with delivery time schedules (reliability of response times)
	Flexibility in delivery – catering for the customer's special needs
	Lack of errors – delivery quality
	Implementation of quality standard
	Insurance of merchandise
	Recall capacity
Costing of services	Cost per process
	Transparent, clear and easy pricing
	Renegotiation and possible change of agreement
Strategy and development	Existence of overall company strategy
	Bonus malus
	Development tendencies
	Carrier of innovative ideas and technological applications

Note: From the evaluation above, a shorter list of the providers is deduced, who are called for further negotiations.

Soft vertical integration

As a response to the disadvantages exhibited by the two solutions above (hard vertical integration and outsourcing) comes the option of soft vertical integration. In this case, there is collaboration between the members of a distribution network for the planning and performance of the principal flow management activities, such as storage, transportation, promotion and financing. The role for managing this collaboration and coordinating these activities is assumed by one member of the distribution network.

6.5 Strategic planning of the intensity of marketing distribution systems

It has already been stressed that the structure, arrangement, types and number of participating intermediaries in a distribution channel are choices that to a large extent rest on the wider dynamic framework of the company's activity and are influenced by the complex web of interrelations that are designated by the groups of factors that constitute its environment.

It was simultaneously underlined that distribution, which is one of the four elements in the marketing mix, is an area of sensitive importance that can bear a competitive advantage. The apperceptions relating to any decision of a strategic or tactical nature must be distinguished by the dedication to the orientation of the integrated approach, with respect not only to the intrinsic components and variables of distribution but also to the other elements in the mix. This way one could prevent blunders relating to the incompatibility of strategic goals that function competitively and as obstacles for the attainment of the integrated objective and the effectiveness of the systems approach. Additionally, in the light of the philosophy for forming synergies through symbiotic interrelations, the individual goals are not only rendered compatible, but success in one reinforces also the capability for attaining the rest.

Moreover, the choices made (and which ultimately reflect the golden ratio between the ideal and the attainable) have a long-term orientation, are inflexible to changes and, correspondingly, have effects, results and consequences of a strategic and largely permanent nature.

The decision regarding the intensity of distribution is included in the context of the capacity to make strategic choices relating to distribution. Intensity depends on the parallel horizontal existence of a number of intermediaries – principally retailers. The main variable that affects the intensity of distribution is the pursued or desired degree of exposure for the product to the audiences that constitute the target of the company. Of course, this degree depends as a variable on several others, such as the following:

- Status – image of the product
- Pricing policy
- Competition
- Product features
- Human geography
- Frequency of purchases and quantity/purchase
- Pursued geographic coverage of market
- Desired control for, for example, product, retailers, terms of sale and after sales, level of service, promotion, layout of stores and sales practices
- Pursued proximity and relation between retailers and the company
- Identifiability of the product and the level of brand loyalty
- Availability of intermediary retailers

These factors depend on and ensue from the overall strategic planning and the company's environment.

Pursuant to the above, there are three main choices with respect to the intensity of distribution:

- Intensive distribution
- Selective distribution
- Exclusive distribution.

The first choice is adopted when we aim to activate as many points of sale as possible. Usually, an extensive sales network is selected for convenience products or products of impulsive purchases, namely, usually for cheap products that are frequently purchased in small quantities and which do not require the engagement of the consumer in an extensive purchasing decision process. Possible errors here do not expose consumers to great risks. The overall target is for the maximum exposure of the product to consumers.

The second choice includes the participation of a more limited number of intermediaries – retailers. Their number, but also their selection, is performed based on and depending on the pursued shaping of the variables cited above and the expected degree of response and effectiveness of these variables for the attainment of the greater strategic objectives. In schemas of selective distribution, the company maintains a greater control across the entire spectrum of factors relating to distribution and has a more direct communication channel with the corresponding intermediaries. Selective distribution is usually adopted when the products under negotiation are choice products and the availability of retailers is limited based on their geographical distribution.

Exclusive distribution is used for luxury products or products with a high status or the choice of which involves a great degree of engagement by the buyer principally due to the fact that a bad choice will incur a great cost. It is adopted when one wishes for the relationship between the seller and the buyer to be particularly direct. The consequences of such an approach to the intensity of distribution include a greater degree of brand loyalty on the side of consumers, the creation of closer collaboration ties between the producer and retailer, a greater and more dedicated sales approach (even the exclusive sale of this particular product and similar competing ones), greater profit margins for retailers and better control of sales and distribution practices for producers, but also the attainment of a better image for the brand.

Synopsis

- Marketing and SCM share for the distribution channels a common vision, functions, objectives, pursuits and activities.
- The distribution channel is essentially a chain of carriers–actors–intermediary businesses–institutions, which intervene in order for the product to arrive at a time and place convenient for consumers.
- Intermediaries improve the efficiency of transactions by reducing their numbers, and they facilitate the performance of transactions by dampening the differences in quantity and variety between producers and consumers.
- The three main types of distribution channel structures are hard vertical integration, outsourcing and soft vertical integration. In the hard vertical integration, a member of the distribution channel (or of a supply chain) assumes the planning, execution and implementation of some of the flows in the distribution network between any two levels. Outsourcing is the assignment of the works of a business to an external associate, who can be either a company specialising in a specific field or even an individual. In the soft vertical integration, there is collaboration between the members of a distribution network for the planning and performance of the principal flow management activities, such as storage, transportation, promotion and financing.

Review and discussion questions

- Define the value supply networks – demand chain, supply chain and distribution. Channel and identify their main characteristics.
- Name and describe the main roles and tasks of the distribution channels.
- Why can the marketing channel be considered as a system?
- What are the tasks of an intermediary in a distribution channel? Identify the pros and cons of their existence in a channel.
- Describe the different types of marketing channels.
- Name the benefits (and drawbacks) that outsourcing brings to the distribution channels.
- What services are offered by third-party logistics (3PL) providers?
- Describe the types of logistics service providers.
- Describe the selection process of a logistics service provider.
- Cite the criteria for the planning of a distribution channel.

Case studies

Case study 1: A systematic approach to distribution channels

When it comes to distribution channels, marketing and SCM share a common vision, as well as functions, objectives, pursuits and activities. Distribution channels exist to satisfy a firm's customers. How the distribution channel should be configured depends on many factors.

Walgreens, one of the US's largest drugstore chains within the US Retail Pharmacy Segment of Walgreens Boots Alliance, is an integrated healthcare, pharmacy and retail leader serving millions of customers and patients around the world. It uses its retail stores as hubs for home deliveries. A brick-and-mortar retail experience is giving way to customers ordering online, and Walgreens encourages this. Because ship-from-store distribution channels are more efficient than managing separate distribution channels for e-commerce and in-store sales, it makes sense for Walgreens to leverage retail outlets for serving walk-in customers, but also for home deliveries of non-pharmaceutical products (pharmaceutical products are subject to governmental regulations). The firm, however, relies on third-party apps such as DoorDash and Uber Eats, in conjunction with Walgreens' employees picking and packing items for same-day delivery, to process and deliver customer orders.

Walgreens also fulfils customer orders via their 16 distribution centres, providing 2- to 4-day delivery via FedEx. Store fulfilment is offered at the same shipping cost of $5.99, which is free for orders over $35.00. However, customers are incentivised to choose store fulfilment for its 50-minute average delivery, as opposed to 2- to 4-day delivery. Retailers DSW, Macy's, and Target also offer same-day store fulfilment, which McKinsey reports is a retail trend due to rising customer expectations for faster delivery.

The Home Depot Inc., the largest retail home improvement and construction supply company in the world, serves professional and amateur customers via store and distribution centre fulfilment. Unlike Walgreens' promotion of store fulfilment, The Home Depot aims to deliver more professional customer orders directly from its distribution centres to free up store space and employees' time, and to increase in-store product availability at their retail locations. It makes sense for The Home Depot to promote distribution centre fulfilment for its professional customers, but the firm also uses a mix of facility types to fulfil its professional customers' orders. Lumber and other building materials are efficiently picked, packed and shipped from its flatbed distribution centres, while products like flooring, windows and doors are best shipped from direct fulfilment centres.

Distribution channels exist to satisfy the firm's customers, and the objective of this case is to demonstrate some of the many factors that drive how distribution channels should be configured. This case looked at customer type, product type and incentives such as cost and delivery time. There are many factors that a firm must address in configuring distribution channels capable of providing the level of customer service desired.

Reflection questions

- Why is ship-from-store a successful strategy for Walgreens but quite the opposite for The Home Depot?
- Why does The Home Depot benefit by utilising a mix of facilities?
- Think of other firms. Based on their customers and products, how do you think these firms should configure their distribution network?

Multiple-choice questions

1. What is the primary function of a distribution channel?

   A. To maximise producer profits
   B. To minimise consumer costs
   C. To facilitate transactions between producers and consumers
   D. To eliminate intermediaries from the supply chain

2. Which of the following best describes the concept of a 'value network' in distribution?

   A. A system focused solely on cost reduction
   B. A linear chain of sequential value-adding activities
   C. An interconnected set of organisations creating value
   D. A network exclusive to online distribution channels

3. What is the main advantage of using intermediaries in a distribution channel?

   A. Increased control for the producer
   B. Reduced number of transactions
   C. Higher prices for end consumers
   D. Elimination of inventory management needs

4. Which type of distribution channel is characterised by the producer selling directly to the end consumer?

   A. Intensive distribution
   B. Selective distribution
   C. Exclusive distribution
   D. Direct distribution

5. What is the primary goal of channel management in a distribution network?

   A. Maximising the number of intermediaries
   B. Minimising producer–consumer interactions
   C. Optimising channel performance and relationships
   D. Eliminating all forms of channel conflict

6. Which of the following is NOT a typical flow in a distribution channel?

   A. Product flow
   B. Information flow
   C. Ownership flow
   D. Competition flow

7. What is the main purpose of a logistics service provider in a distribution channel?

   A. To manufacture products for the producer
   B. To facilitate the physical movement of goods
   C. To set retail prices for end consumers
   D. To develop marketing strategies for products

8. Which distribution strategy involves selling through all available outlets in a market?

   A. Exclusive distribution
   B. Selective distribution
   C. Intensive distribution
   D. Direct distribution

9. What is the primary challenge of implementing a multichannel distribution strategy?

   A. Reduced market coverage
   B. Simplified inventory management
   C. Potential channel conflict
   D. Decreased customer service options

10. Which factor is LEAST important when selecting a logistics service provider?

    A. Financial stability of the provider
    B. Technological capabilities
    C. Geographical coverage
    D. Age of the company

11. What is the main advantage of vertical integration in a distribution channel?

    A. Reduced control over the supply chain
    B. Increased channel flexibility
    C. Greater coordination and control
    D. Lower initial investment costs

12. Which distribution channel structure is most suitable for highly customised industrial products?

    A. Intensive distribution
    B. Direct distribution
    C. Retailer-only distribution
    D. Wholesaler-dominated distribution

13. What is the primary function of a wholesaler in a distribution channel?

    A. To provide after-sales service to end consumers
    B. To break bulk and assort products for retailers
    C. To manufacture products for the producer
    D. To set retail prices for the market

14. Which of the following is NOT a typical criterion for evaluating a logistics service provider?

    A. On-time delivery performance
    B. Technology integration capabilities
    C. Political affiliations of management
    D. Financial stability and resources

15. What is the main benefit of implementing a just-in-time (JIT) system in distribution?

    A. Increased inventory levels
    B. Reduced transportation costs
    C. Elimination of all supply chain risks
    D. Minimised inventory holding costs

Essay question

Analyse the interconnected challenges of designing an effective omnichannel distribution strategy in today's global marketplace. Your discussion should address the following:

1. The complexities of integrating traditional and digital distribution channels while maintaining channel harmony
2. The role of logistics service providers in facilitating seamless product flow across multiple channels.
3. The impact of emerging technologies (e.g., blockchain and IoT) on distribution channel management and performance evaluation.

In your analysis, consider how these factors influence channel design decisions, partner selection criteria and overall distribution network optimisation. Provide specific examples to illustrate how companies can leverage a systemic approach to distribution channels to create competitive advantages in an increasingly complex and dynamic market environment.

7

A HOLISTIC APPROACH TO DEMAND HANDLING

Introduction

Demand handling for marketing simply means 'try to increase sales – try to bring orders!'. For supply chain management (SCM), demand handling means 'try to transfer goods to customers' or 'try to have the right product, in the right quantity, at the right place, at the right time, with the right cost'. It also means to ensure that there is enough capacity to handle the order. This chapter is focused on this objective. It discusses the main topics of demand handling and forecasting practices and techniques, supported with an online simulation tool.

Learning objectives

After reading this chapter, you will be able to answer the following questions:

- What is demand handling and why is it critical in marketing and SCM?
- What are the main questions that need to be answered regarding demand handling?
- How can the demand handling benefits and challenges of the above integration be identified?

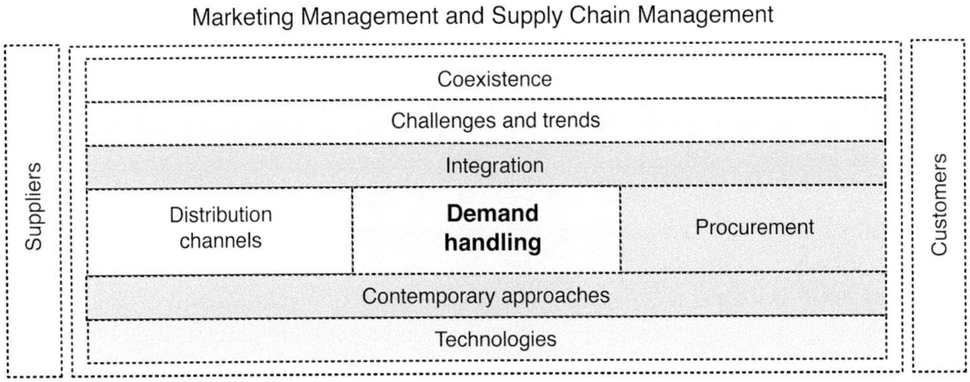

DOI: 10.4324/9781003650973-7

Outline

7.1 Demand handling
7.2 Passive approach/inventory management

7.1 Demand handling

Definition and key features

Demand management can be simply defined as the continuous matching of demand and supply. It is one of the most important 'weapons' in the arsenal of every company not only for its survival but also to acquire comparative advantages against competitors. Indeed, the term demand-driven supply networks (DDSNs) has attracted so much attention in international bibliographies that in some research efforts it is used in much the same way as the term supply chain. DDSNs employ new technologies and processes that sense demand in order for the supply chain network to appropriately respond in real time.

Time is the most critical parameter in demand management. Company executives rest on demand data (sales) from the past, always taking decisions in the present to respond to demand in real time (where demand transmutes to orders), as well as future demand by short-term, medium-term and long-term planning the scheduling of the entire supply chain.

Moreover, demand is led by customers. It is a customer's order that triggers the departments and employees of a company or, in the context of a supply chain, of its members or companies to satisfy it (*pull philosophy*). More specifically, in a supply chain, we do not only observe the collaboration of the companies that constitute it but also the sharing of information in order for the members of the chain to establish, in the best manner possible, the market demand. Companies have, of course, the capacity to produce and stock products to satisfy demand.

A third important parameter of demand management is that it requires cooperation in decision-making by the executive both from supply (SCM) and from the market (marketing and sales). To offer an example, in many cases where companies decide on promotional activities, SCM cannot correspond to the increase in demand, and as a result, such activities fail. Furthermore, it is also associated with inventory management, which comprises the planning, execution, monitoring and controlling of inventories for the uninterrupted satisfaction of demand at the lowest possible cost. It is obvious that inventories and the management thereof are critical factors for the success of a business or organisation. By maintaining inventories, the company can avoid stock-out and back order, reduce its response time (by decreasing processing times) and increase the level of its customer service. On the other hand, maintaining and managing inventories comes at a cost. More specifically, the cost of inventories consists of four individual costs: the cost of purchase (acquiring the products), the cost of storage and maintenance (which includes operating costs, the cost for insuring the inventory, taxes and expenses for the destruction of products), transportation expenses and the deficit cost (the cost of the lost inflow of income plus the cost of losing goodwill).

The fourth important parameter is that demand constantly *changes*. SCM cannot handle such changes by itself. But there are marketing techniques that can regulate/influence demand. Via advertising campaigns, for example, the instruction of new products and the promotion of specific products, demand can be influenced so that its changes can be treated effectively.

One further important parameter for handling demand ensues from the above: the importance of *demand forecasting*. There are many techniques and mathematical models that have been developed for this, supported by corresponding software applications, and employed for the future forecast of demand. Inaccuracies in forecasts by each member of a supply chain, the introduction of new products and the continuous fluctuations of prices, which follow market conditions and trends and the company's pricing policy, the fear of deficits and the grouping of orders (namely, the order of a large quantity one week and its non-order the next), lead to an inefficient management of inventories and low satisfaction of demand.

Finally, many methods have been developed that take into account all of the parameters above, specifically the following:

- Point-of-sale mechanisms that update the databases of the operating informational systems in real time with every product sale. For example, electronic point of sale (EPOS) software utilises the internet to inform all members of the supply chain of demands so that they may successfully be met.
- Auto ID(entification) technologies such as barcodes and radio frequency identifications (RFIDs), which allow for monitoring demand across the entire length of the supply chain.
- Collaborative methods for the management of inventories, such as vendor-managed inventory (VMI) and collaborative planning, forecasting and replenishment (CPFR). In the first case, a close relationship between the supplier and retail seller is developed, where the first manages the inventories of the second. In the second case, all the members of the supply chain collaborate with one another for the planning, execution, monitoring and controlling of the demand forecast and for the replenishment of inventories.
- Customer (market) segmentation in all groups providing a different level of service to each category aiming to maximise profits for every category individually.
- Available-to-promise (ATP) determines what the existing inventories are and which scheduled production or deliveries from supplies are expected to cover the orders that have been placed by customers. If there is no inventory or scheduled delivery, the capable-to-promise (CTP) function establishes when the resources available to the company, its sub-contractors or suppliers can render products able to be produced to cater for the specific orders. The two aforementioned functions are very important in determining the ability of demand to converge to the existing or future supply, while they become even more important in the modern, non-hierarchical collaborative networks of supply, where every member of the supply chain can participate in many other networks and possess its own resources, based on its own interests and less on the interests of the supply chain as a whole.

Types of demand and ways to treat them

There are two types of demand: independent and dependent. Independent demand regards final finished products, while dependent demand is demand for raw materials and semi-finished products required for the manufacture or assembly of final finished products correspondingly.

Consequently, if independent demand and the materials needed to manufacture the final product are known, dependent demand can easily be determined. In Figure 7.1, demand for code A100 is independent demand, while the corresponding dependent demand for its constituent parts can be easily calculated.

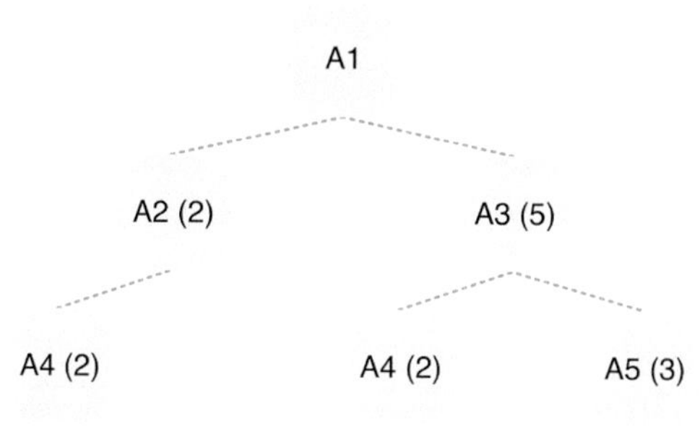

FIGURE 7.1 Production requirements for A1

If, for example, the demand for final product A1 is known to be, for example, ten pieces, then dependent demand is

- 20 A2 and
- 50 A3.

This in turn requires

- 40 A4 (to make the 20 A2) and
- 100 A4 and 150 A5 (to make the 50 A3).

This makes a total of 140 A4 and 150 A5.

Whenever we refer to demand in this chapter, we will be referring to independent demand (for final products). The ways by which a company deals with it are twofold: (1) *active* and (2) *passive*. In active treatment, the company and principally its marketing and sales department attempt – by utilising promotional activities, advertising campaigns, price offers, discounts, motives to customers, training of the employees of the corresponding departments, providing motives to them, etc. – to direct and manipulate demand. In passive treatment, the business does not pursue manipulation but simply the satisfaction of demand. The sections that follow refer to the passive treatment of independent demand.

7.2 Passive approach/inventory management

Inventory management includes all activities, practices, methodologies and systems to deal with all issues relating to the management of inventories to satisfy demand. In this section, we shall present some of these issues and specifically the following:

- Restock from the supplier policy; namely, will the business-customer restock for a fixed quantity or at regular intervals?
- Restock of the customer policy; namely, will the business-supplier restock in greater quantities and less routes, or conversely?
- Policy of selecting products for stocking; namely, what products will the company stock?
- Policy of determining the quantity of products for stocking; namely, what is the quantity of the products that the company will stock?

- Demand forecast based on historic sales figures; namely, how can one forecast demand (usually short-term) using previous demand?
- Demand forecast without utilising historic sales figures; namely, can one forecast demand by utilising his knowledge of the market?

Types of inventories

To begin, the types of inventories must be defined. The example of a hypothetical company will be utilised, say a shop selling a specific model of plasma TVs to cater for the market of a large city. The shop has storage facilities that have a capacity of 750 televisions. The shop manager estimates that 500 television sets will be enough to satisfy demand. To define the types of inventories, let us examine three simple scenarios:

- *Scenario 1: Demand remains constant and equal to 50 sets a day.* In this case, the company's stock will be depleted by the 10th day (50 × 10 = 500). The manager knows that his supplier needs 2 days to restock the warehouse with 500 television sets. Consequently, he orders 500 sets on the 8th day, which arrive on the 10th day to be able to satisfy demand. If demand continues as is on the following days, then the stock will 'run dry' on the 20th day, while the manager must order 500 sets on the 18th day and so on.
- *Scenario 2: Demand increases from 50 to 60 sets a day.* In this case, the stock will have been almost depleted by the middle of the 8th day. If the manager does not realise this in time and misses placing the order with his supplier on day 6, he will run out of stock on day 8 (60 × 8 = 480). In this case, the company will be unable to satisfy demand on the 9th and 10th days. The manager ought to have had 120 more sets (2 × 60 = 120) to meet demand.
- *Scenario 3: 50 sets a day but the supplier delays by 2 days.* The order is placed on the 8th day, but 400 sets arrive on the 12th day. The stock is depleted on the 10th day, and the company cannot meet demand on days 11 and 12. The manager ought to have an additional stock of 100 sets (50 × 2) to meet demand.

The following types of inventories ensue from the example above:

- *Maximum stock:* This corresponds to the maximum number of TV sets that can be stored in the warehouse. In our example, it is equal to 750 and is the capacity of the warehouse.
- *Cyclical stock:* This is the stock the company orders at regular intervals (cyclical) to satisfy demand. In our example, it is equal to 500 sets. In general, it is maintained to cater for average demand throughout the period intervening between successive restocks.
- *Safety stock:* This corresponds to the stock that if the company had it could meet demand (in Scenario 2 it was 120 and in Scenario 3 100 sets). In general, safety stock is maintained to deal with increases in demand, delays in resupply and emergencies (if the two scenarios concurred, the safety stock would have been equal to 60 × 4 = 240 sets). All businesses maintain a safety stock.
- *Stock in transit:* These are orders placed but not yet received. In our example, it regards the 500-set stock in transit from the supplier on days 9 and 10 of the first scenario. The stock in transit belongs to the company but has not been received yet.
- *Seasonal inventory:* This is the stock that relates to products with a seasonal demand (seasonal products). TV sets are not considered to be seasonal products. There are two types of

seasonality: the one occurring once a year (air-conditioners, ice creams, etc.) and the one occurring more than once a year (e.g., retail chains for toys).

- *Speculative inventory:* This is the inventory that the company acquires hoping to profit from it due to a large increase in demand. For example, a major TV event can be the cause for an increase in the sales of TV sets.
- *Obsolete inventory:* This is the inventory corresponding to products not in demand. It is rational for this inventory to be maintained at the lowest possible level, and the business must dispose of it using any means.

Supplier resupply policy

Two options are available: (1) the business is resupplied at fixed intervals but receives a variable quantity on each occasion (the order quantity depends on what demand has been in the previous period) – this system is termed periodic; and (2) the company is supplied with a fixed quantity on each occasion, but resupply occurs whenever needed, namely, at variable times – this system is termed continuous. Consider an example: the owner of a gas station has two options to refill gasoline:

- Once per month, when the owner calls his supplier to 'fill up' his tanks with the quantity necessary each time. The disadvantage of this choice is that it does not take account of the previous demand for gasoline. If, for example, gasoline was not in demand on the previous days, the refill might be for a small quantity or there might be great demand for gasoline in the days to come, and the company might not be able to satisfy demand until the next refill date.
- To utilise some mechanism that would allow him to monitor gasoline levels in the tank. When it falls below a certain point – which is called reorder point – (whenever this happens) the owner orders a specific quantity, same quantity each time. It is manifest that this choice does not exhibit the failing of the previous one. Moreover, in this case one can observe the three principal types of inventory: maximum inventory (tank), cyclical inventory (between the reorder point and maximum reserve) and safety inventory (below the reorder point). This last is used to cater for demand from the moment of the order until the time of resupply.

The conclusion one draws is that the level of inventories must be monitored for all products, especially those in great demand.

Customer resupply policy

Again, two options are available: (1) the company resupplies its customer in great quantities but with a small number of routes and (2) the company supplies small quantities on each occasion but caters for demand by performing many and frequent routes.

Consider the following example: the owner of a pharmacy can restock medicines in two ways: for some drugs in great demand (e.g., cold medicines), the owner orders large quantities at the start of each month. In this case, the restock quantity is great, stock is sufficient to satisfy demand and the business commits capital to acquire it. With respect to the four costs presented in the introductory section of the chapter, purchase and storage/maintenance costs are high, while transportation/sale cost and deficit costs are low. For drugs, on the other hand, for which demand is not fixed or known (e.g., flu medicines), the owner prefers to order when in demand. Thus, the phenomenon emerges whereby many routes are performed with small quantities ever time. This results in costs that are the opposite of those of the first case. The conclusion one can draw is that the constant registering of demand is an imperative, as it would allow the business to choose the policy for its inventories in a more learned fashion.

Policy of selecting which products to stock

This, essentially, regards the known question: 'Which products to stock?' For which codes will one maintain more stock and for which ones less? Or are there any codes for which no stock is to be maintained? The answer is obvious: 'It depends on the sales of these codes! But in terms of pieces, as well as in terms of value'. Codes in great demand and/or of high turnover demand for there to be ample stock to satisfy said demand. On the other hand, codes not in demand should be kept at lower levels. ABC analysis rests on this simple logic. According to this (and in its simplest form), codes are classified into three general categories:

- The codes falling under category A are those in great movement. Namely, the ones where a great number of pieces are in demand (piece-wise) or that bring large profits (value-wise). Businesses aim to maintain high inventories of these codes, considering them to be important for their survival and profitability.
- Category B includes the codes in less demand from those of the previous category.
- Category C consists of those codes that do not 'sell'. It is rational for businesses to try to reduce the inventories of this category as much as they can.

Additional questions of course arise: 'To which category do new products belong?', for which we have no previous sales records, or 'How does one treat products which the company has chosen to promote to the market?' Collaboration with the sales department is needed to answer these questions, as the latter knows the needs of the market and the goals of the company.

ABC analysis rests on Pareto's law, or the 20/80 rule. Vilfredo Pareto, an Italian economist, sociologist and philosopher, observed that 80% of the wealth in Italy (and every country he studied) was held by 20% of the population. The 20/80 rule appears to be valid with respect to a lot of things: 20% of customers account for 80% of total sales; 80% of sales comes from 20% of salesmen; 20% of codes occupies 80% of the warehouse; etc. It appears that the smallest part is the most important one. And it is on this that one must focus: On the 20 per cent of customers, suppliers, codes. Consider an example: presented in the table below are sales for ten codes, their sales as a percentage and cumulatively (they follow if one adds the percentage sales of the previous code).

According to Table 7.1, codes AB458 and DE455 accumulatively account for 78% of total sales and belong to category A. The remaining 80% of codes (and 20% of sales) constitute categories B and C. Graphically Pareto's law is affirmed by Figure 7.2. Consequently, the answer to the original question is obvious: 'I will acquire and maintain stock for codes 1 and 2'. On the contrary, one should not maintain stock for codes 7, 8, 9 and 10.

Policy for establishing the quantity of products to stock

A basic dilemma all logistics executives are faced with relates to the management of inventories: 'What is the quantity that a company must maintain for each code in its warehouse?' There is no easy answer to this question. On the one hand, companies (especially during periods of low

TABLE 7.1 ABC analysis example

Code	*Sales*	*Sales %*	*Cumulative sales %*	*Category*
AB458	4500	49	49	A
DE455	2800	29	78	A
FO007	534	6	84	B
TU148	350	4	88	B
DF378	333	3	91	B
DE500	302	3	94	B
AB912	194	2	96	C
AC611	173	2	98	C
AB191	86	1	99	C
TY775	78	1	100	C
Total	9351	100	100	

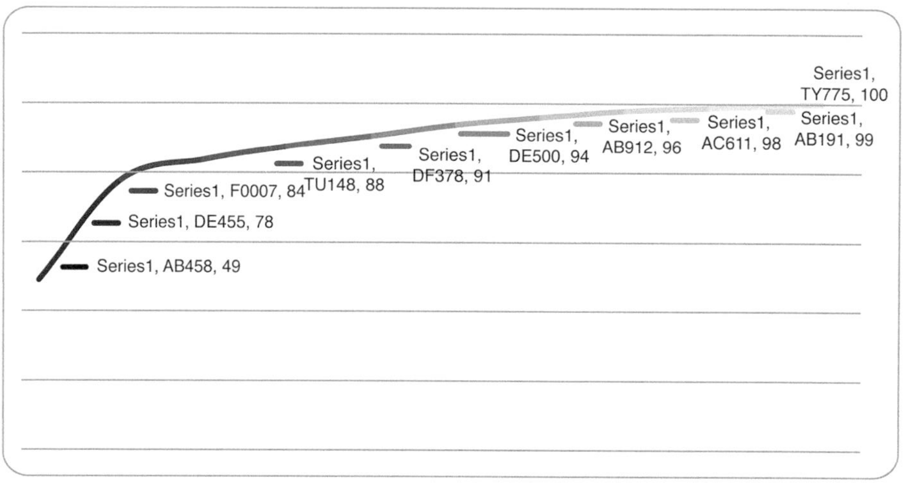

FIGURE 7.2 Example of ABC analysis

demand or economic crises) are pressed to maintain inventories at low levels so as, on the one hand, to decrease the operating cost for maintaining and managing their inventories and, on the other hand, to lower the risk of ending up with unsold stock. On the other hand, the businesses themselves are under pressure to maintain high levels of inventories so as to be able to fully and, more importantly, immediately cater for the market's demand. It is well established that in the case that the order cannot be fulfilled, the customer will contact some other business.

The economic order quantity (EOQ) aims to balance these two pressures by calculating the quantity that corresponds to the lowest possible cost. This cost includes the cost for maintaining inventories and the cost for placing orders. There are strict conditions for the application of the EOQ model. Demand must be fixed, there should be no delays in resupply, there should be no discounts with respect to the quantity ordered and the only costs taken into account, as noted above, are the inventory maintenance cost and a fixed fee per order. Unfortunately, none

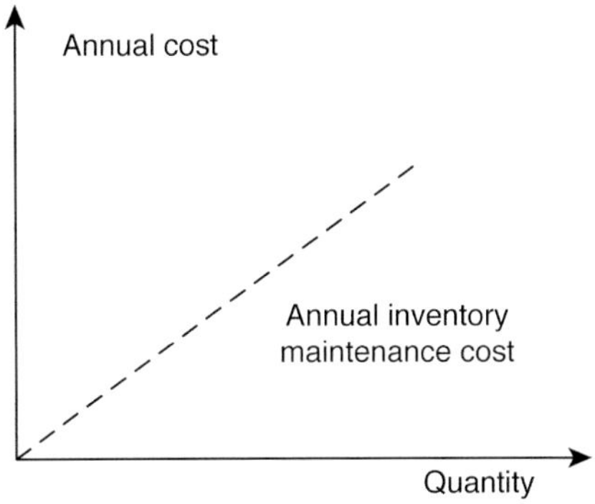

FIGURE 7.3 Annual inventory maintenance cost

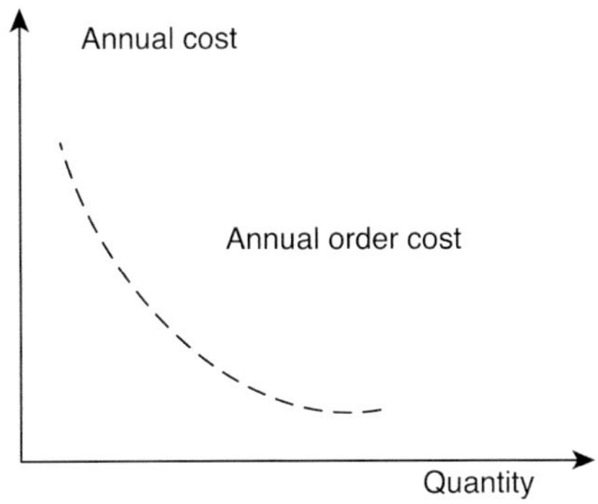

FIGURE 7.4 Annual order cost

of the above is valid in practice. Demand is rarely fixed, and businesses take advantage of scale economies by ordering larger quantities for discounts on the purchase price for the products. Despite all these, the EOQ is a useful and easy-to-apply method for the calculation of the level of inventories and the same for placing the order.

As aforementioned the objective of the EOQ method is to calculate the optimal quantity (Q), which comes at the lowest total cost (C) when it is known that this includes the *annual inventory maintenance cost* (AIMC) and the *annual order cost* (AOC). Figures 7.3 and 7.4 depict these two costs. The AIMC increases linearly as Q increases and is calculated if we multiply the average inventory (in the case at hand, that is $Q/2$) by the cost of maintaining a unit of inventory (H), which is usually calculated as the percentage of the value of the product, since, very simply, the more expensive a product is, the greater the cost for storing it will be. The formula for calculating the AIMC is therefore: AIMC = $Q/(2 \times H)$.

The AOC decreases as the order quantity (Q) increases and is calculated if one multiplies the average number of orders per year (which, in turn, is the ratio of annual demand (D) times the order cost (O), namely, the cost for the execution of one order). The formula for AOC is, therefore: AOC = $D/(Q \times O)$.

As was noted above, total cost = AIMC + AOC, or $C = (Q/2 \times H) + (D/Q \times O)$, while it is graphically depicted as illustrated in Figure 7.5.

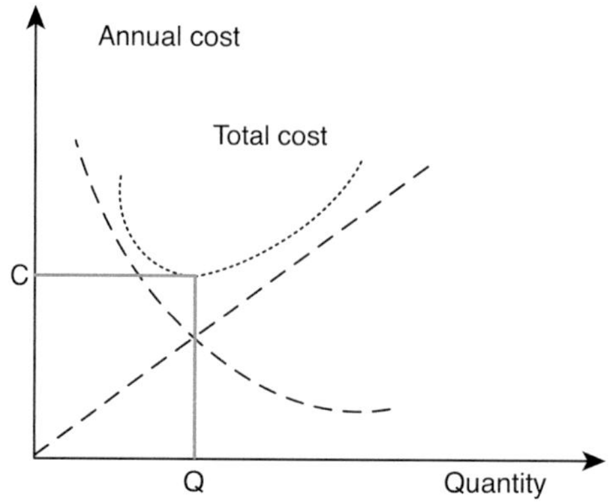

FIGURE 7.5 Total cost

In that chart, we attempt to calculate quantity Q corresponding to the lowest cost C at the point where the two costs are equal – where the straight and the curved lines intersect. We can, therefore, calculate the formula for EOQ, taking the two costs to be equal and solving with respect to Q:

$$\frac{Q}{2}\times H=\frac{D}{Q}\times O \text{ or } Q^2=\frac{2\times D\times O}{H} \text{ or } Q=\sqrt{\frac{2\times D\times O}{H}}$$

Remember that Q is the economic (optimal) order quantity, O is the AOC, D is the annual demand and H is inventory maintenance (storage) cost.

Demand forecast based on historic sales data

The quantity of products that the company will stock is essentially an estimate (forecast) of future demand, either based on demand records for previous periods (namely, using historic sales data) or not. In practice, it is usual for both approaches to be combined. In the case of the launching of a new product to the market, for example, one employs techniques such as market analysis (as there are no historic figures), but in addition data/historic figures for other relevant products, not directly related to the product but which indirectly affect the behaviour of its future sales, can also be used.

The research literature is rife with a multitude of methods that either employ historic data or not. Well known amongst them are the simple or naive forecast, the simple moving average, the weighted average, the exponential method, the adjusted exponential method, the linear oscillation and the seasonal method. Their common characteristic is that they provide a mathematical calculation of demand based on past demand (using time series). Their key elements and subjects of investigation are the trend (positive or negative), seasonality, circularity and fluctuation (due to unforeseen external events).

Depending on the time horizon for the forecast, forecasts are categorised into the long term (over 3–5 years), medium term (1–3 or 1–5 years) and short term (up to 6 months). Before forecast techniques are presented, it is worth noting that all forecasts have errors (forecast errors), and short-term forecasts are more accurate than long-term ones. Some of the methods that do not rest on historic data are the following: executive opinion (directors and personnel), external opinion, expert group, and Delphi method. The methods using historic data are of interest. In the next two examples, we shall present and assess three simple methods: the simple moving average, the weighted average and linear oscillation.

In simple terms, moving average forecasts follow from calculating the average for selected time periods (time series). Used in this technique are the most recent values of real data to shape a forecast (as aforementioned, this type is usually more precise and representative). The average is termed moving since whenever a new observation (or, better, forecast) becomes available, it can be calculated, and thus a new average can be used as a forecast. The forecasts for a time series F*t*, where $t = 1, 2, \ldots, n$, using the simple moving average method are given by the corresponding mathematical formula:

$$F_t = \frac{A_{t-1} + A_{t-2} + A_{t-3} \ldots + + A_{t-n}}{n},$$

where Ft is the forecast for the next period, n is the number of periods in the moving average and At_{-1} is the real value for the period $t - 1$.

Say, for example, that demand for the last 10 weeks is presented in the second column of Table 7.2, while the next two columns show the forecast using the 3-week and 5-week average.

According to Table 7.2, the forecasts for the coming weeks are $F11 = 325$ and $F12 = 343$ by calculating the average for 3 weeks, and $F11 = 329$ and $F12 = 327$ by calculating the average for 5 weeks, correspondingly. Presented in Figure 7.6 are real demand and the forecasts using the moving average for 3 and 5 weeks.

From Figure 7.6 we can see that the forecast for 3 weeks 'follows' the changes in demand but with a 2-week lag, while the forecast for 5 weeks exhibits a much smoother change. In general, an increase in the number of used time periods leads to a greater smoothing of fluctuations, but in the case at hand it is less sensitive to real changes in demand. A key weakness of the simple moving average is the assumption that all past periods carry the same weight, which may lead to erroneous results since it is possible that specific periods may express the current state of affairs better.

TABLE 7.2 Example of the application of the simple moving average

Week	*Demand*	*3 Weeks*	*5 Weeks*
1	346		
2	324		
3	286		
4	275	319	
5	313	295	
6	338	292	309
7	335	309	307
8	289	329	309
9	324	320	310
10	362	316	320
11		325	329
12		343	327

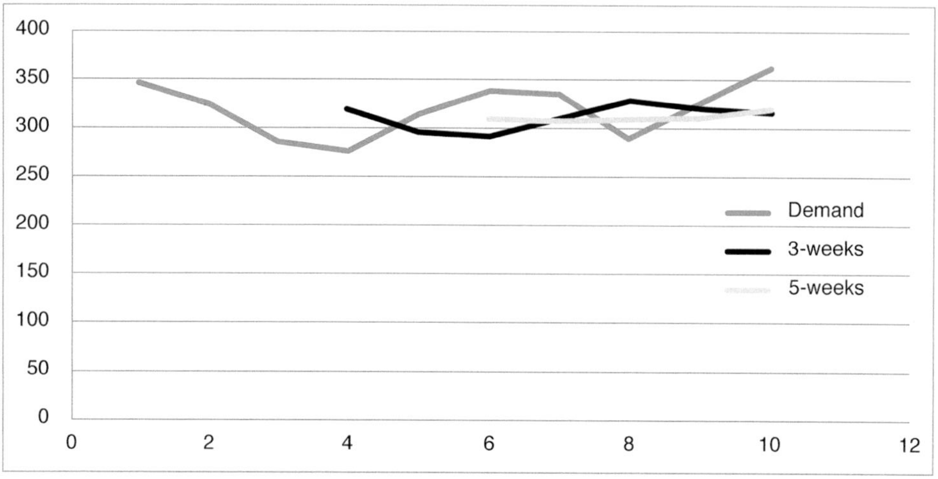

FIGURE 7.6 Example of the application of the simple moving average

Consider, for example, that we ask three sales executives to assess demand for the coming months. It is rational to expect one of them to have greater experience and a better picture of the market. His assessment shall, therefore, carry more weight and is considered more significant. In the case of the weighted average, we establish weights for a specific number of time periods (or, otherwise, weight of these periods) and usually place greater weight on more recent ones.

The forecast for a time series *Ft*, where $t = 1, 2, \ldots, n$, using the weighted moving average is given in the following formula:

$$F_t = w_1 A_{t-1} + w_2 A_{t-2} + w_3 A_{t-3} + \ldots + w_n A_{t-n}$$

Here, *Ft* is the forecast for next period, *n* is the number of periods in the moving average, At_{-1} is the real value for period $t - 1$ and *wn* is the weight of each time period, where it is valid that the sum of the weights is equal to 1 or $\sum_{i=1}^{n} w_i = 1$.

The second column of Table 7.3 presents demand for the past 12 weeks, while the third column gives the weight of each period.

In the example, we shall utilise the last 4 weeks to forecast demand for the next, the 11th week, deeming that recent weeks carry more weight.

By applying the weighted average formula, we get: F11 = $(0.40 \times 977) + (0.3 \times 875) + (0.2 \times 780) + (0.10 \times 904) \approx 900$.

The basic advantage of this technique is that it places emphasis on more representative periods and specifically more recent time periods.

This fact renders this technique more reliable and accurate than the simple moving average. However, it exhibits the following weakness: it does not take account of the difference (deviation) of the forecast from real demand. This is what the next demand forecast technique tries to solve: the exponential smoothing technique.

This method requires just three elements to calculate the forecast: (a) The forecast for the previous period ($t - 1$); (b) the demand for this period (t) and (c) the value of a factor termed the

TABLE 7.3 Demand and weight

Week	*Demand*	*Weight*
1	933	
2	875	
3	773	
4	744	
5	846	
6	911	
7	904	0.1
8	780	0.2
9	875	0.3
10	977	0.4

TABLE 7.4 Demand and forecasting

Week	*Demand*	*Forecasting*
1	933	933
2	875	933
3	773	916
4	744	873
5	846	834
6	911	837
7		860

smoothing factor and symbolised with letter 'α', whose values range from 0 to 1 and are calculated by the formula $\alpha = 2/N + 1$, where N is the number of time periods taken into account in the forecast. The formula for calculating the forecast is: $Ft = Ft - 1 + \alpha \times (At_{-1} - Ft - 1)$, where Ft is the demand forecast asked for time period t, $Ft - 1$ is the forecasted demand in the previous period, α is the smoothing factor ($0 < \alpha < 1$) and At_{-1} is the real demand in the previous period. Table 7.4 presents the forecast for period 7.
Begin by calculating factor α (0.3) and set it as the forecast for the first period, while the corresponding first demand is given by the application of the formula.

The key feature of this method is that as the number of time periods between the forecast and the real value of the time series increases, the weighting factors decrease and indeed dramatically. It is on account of this that the method is called exponential smoothing.

All of these three simple forecasting methods fall under the category of time series analysis, which considers that historic data can be utilised to forecast future data taking account of the trend and seasonality. There are also other well-known methods such as the causal one, which detects factors affecting demand and the way demand is affected. Linear oscillation, for example, examines the relationship but also the possibility for forecasting a variable (in our case demand) based on other variables, such as product price and cost of advertising. The variable to be forecast (dependent) is the function of other independent factors or variables. Econometric standards describing certain sectors of the economy belong to this category, as do other input–output standards that predict the sales in a sector of group of products based on the sales of other sectors, groups, etc.

Assessment of forecasting techniques

After these simple forecasting techniques are concisely presented, a key question emerges: 'which technique do I choose?' (or, in other words, 'Which technique has the smallest forecast error?'). The forecast error is the difference between forecasted and real demand for a specific time period. One can, thus, numerically define the error as: $Et = At - Ft$, where Et is the forecast error for period t, At is real demand value for period t and Ft is forecast for period t.

One can, therefore, calculate the total sum of forecast errors for a time series to which various forecast techniques have been applied, and select as more suitable the technique with the smallest total sum. Moreover, one could also employ the following two indices:

- *mean absolute deviation* (MAD) and/or
- *mean squared error* (MSE).

These two indices are numerically defined as follows: MAD = $\frac{\Sigma | A_t - F_t |}{n}$ και; MSE = $\frac{\Sigma (A_t - F_t)^2}{n}$, where At is the real price for demand in period t, Ft is the forecast for period t and n is the number of time periods that are taken into account for the forecast.

One can assess the accuracy of forecasting techniques using these indices, while one can also select the most appropriate one. Specifically, one should choose the technique whereby the MAD and MSE indices exhibit their smallest value. Consider an example. Presented in Table 7.5 are the period (week), demand and forecasts using three techniques A, B and C. The columns next to them present the initially calculated deviations between real demand and each forecast for every week, then their absolute values and finally the deviations squared.

The MAD indices for each technique are calculated as the average of the absolute prices of deviations, namely, 4.8, 9 and 2.4, respectively. The third technique that exhibits the smaller MAD index is the optimal one. When two or more demand forecast techniques have the same MAD index in some cases, then (and only then) we calculate the MSE indices for each technique as the averages of the deviations squared; that is, the MSE indices for each technique are 37.2, 95.8 and 7.2, respectively. In this case too, we will select the forecast with the smaller value in the MSE index as the optimal demand forecast technique, which shall be employed to forecast the next period.

Forecast of demand without using historic sales data

There are several occasions wherein a company employs qualitative methods resting on opinions of and assessments by individuals either because the corresponding historic sales

TABLE 7.5 Example of the calculation of MAD and MSE indices

Week	*Demand*	*Forecasting*			*Deviation*			*|Deviation|*			*Deviation²*		
		A	*B*	*Γ*	*A*	*B*	*Γ*	*A*	*B*	*Γ*	*A*	*B*	*Γ*
1	33	33	35	33	0	−2	0	0	2	0	0	4	0
2	38	43	27	41	−5	11	−3	5	11	3	25	121	9
3	41	35	49	38	6	−8	3	6	8	3	36	64	9
4	30	32	43	27	−2	−13	3	2	13	3	4	169	9
5	27	38	38	30	−11	−11	−3	11	11	3	121	121	9

data do not exist or because executives feel that they possess the necessary experience and knowledge of the market. Of course, what is usually the case is that both techniques are employed.

The usual methods falling under this category, forecasting without the use of historic sales data, are as follows:

- Market research, wherein utilising specific tools for collecting primary data such as questionnaires and interviews, one attempts to draw conclusions on market conditions. Questionnaires include demographic data and the interest of those filling them for a new product.
- Executive meetings, wherein line level managers meet and exchange views on forecasting demand.
- The Delphi method, wherein a questionnaire is filled out by a team of experts and then amended with respect to the results and is dispatched as many times as it is necessary to draw a commonly accepted conclusion, which, however, did not come about under the pressure of supervisors.
- Grass roots, wherein information originates from individuals who come into direct contact with sales, such as the sales team and merchandisers.

Synopsis

- Demand management can be simply defined as the continuous matching of demand and supply. Time is the most critical parameter in demand management. Demand management is led by customers and its decision-making process requires the cooperation and collaboration of executives from both supply (SCM) and market (marketing and sales).
- There are two types of demand: independent and dependent. Independent regards final-finished products, while dependent is demand for raw materials and semi-finished products required for the manufacture or assembly of final-finished products correspondingly.
- Inventory management includes all activities, practices, methodologies and systems to deal with all issues relating to the management of inventories to satisfy demand.
- Several questions emerge regarding demand handling. These are to do with restock from the supplier policy (will the business-customer restock for a fixed quantity or at regular intervals?), restock of the customer policy (will the business-supplier restock in greater quantities and less routes, or conversely?), policy of selecting products for stocking (what products will the company stock?), policy of determining the quantity of products for stocking (what is the quantity of the products that the company will stock?), demand forecast based on historic sales figures (how can one forecast demand – usually short term – using previous demand?) and demand forecast without utilising historic sales figures (can one forecast demand by utilising one's knowledge of the market?).

Review and discussion questions

- Name the main parameters of market demand.
- Describe briefly the various types of demand.
- What are the key types of inventories?
- Discuss the significance of ABC analysis.
- Explain the assessment of the forecasting methods.

Case studies

Case study 1: Purchasing and marketing of social and environmental sustainability

As advanced medical products become increasingly similar in functional capabilities, suppliers look for new ways to distinguish their offerings. Lindgreen et al. (2008) investigated how organisations grapple with understanding customer perceptions of the environmental and social aspects of sustainability in this context.

The high-tech medical equipment industry, exemplified by Philips Medical Systems' introduction of MRI scanning equipment in 1983, showcases the growing significance of social sustainability. As MRI scanner technologies converge, companies increasingly emphasise social and environmental responsibility standards to impact customer purchasing decisions. MRI scanning equipment is bought by academic, teaching and community hospitals, and by private imaging centres. Across these institutions, the purchasing process is typically similar and influenced by three main stakeholders: clinicians, operators and business managers.

The authors note that stakeholders consider social and environmental sustainability factors when evaluating MRI scanning equipment. There is alignment among customer institutions and the three key stakeholder groups regarding information needs and product criteria. Hence, suppliers of high-tech medical equipment should integrate social and environmental sustainability into their marketing strategies. The study highlights society's influence on individuals and groups involved in the production, usage and disposal of MRI scanners. Additionally, stakeholders express concerns about potential long-term harm, particularly relevant given the technology's hazardous substances and radiation emissions, suggesting broader applicability beyond high-tech medical equipment production.

Managerial implications

Guidelines for incorporating social and environmental sustainability indicators into marketing strategies can be derived from addressing three fundamental questions: (a) who are the primary stakeholders to target? (b) At what stage of the purchasing process should marketing communication take place? (c) How should the communication be conveyed?

The alignment in purchasing processes across institutions and stakeholder groups offers a shared basis for marketing initiatives. Stakeholders should possess a basic awareness of the social and environmental sustainability features of the products. To this end, suppliers' marketing efforts should concentrate on a broader environmental perspective.

Marketing social and environmental indicators should emphasise suppliers' efforts to mitigate potential harm and provide assurance of the safety of scanning equipment, thus instilling confidence in stakeholders. However, the price and image quality of the equipment often have a greater impact on purchasing decisions than social or environmental sustainability factors. Consequently, stakeholders may rely on a company's reputation in these areas to differentiate between products and suppliers. Effective communication of the social and environmental sustainability credentials of MRI scanning equipment requires diverse approaches and careful media selection, tailored to target specific stakeholders involved in the purchasing decision. Suppliers can leverage their brand positioning to reinforce a holistic commitment to sustainability. Trade literature and meetings with stakeholders provide opportunities to communicate the integration of sustainability efforts into business practices. Moreover, specific sustainability indicators should be highlighted to support the sales process, with product brochures and briefing sessions addressing concerns regarding potential harm and risk mitigation strategies.

While the concept of companies prioritising ethical practices forms the basis of social and environmental sustainability, its incorporation into marketing activities offers two commercial benefits. Firstly, it enhances the sustainability of the supplier by boosting product sales.

Secondly, it ingrains these policies within the supplier, fostering a cycle of improvement that reinforces the supplier's reputation and enhances the appeal of its products. In summary, leveraging social and environmental indicators of sustainability can enhance the marketing of high-tech medical products and create differentiation among key customer stakeholders.

This case originates from Lindgreen, A., Antioco, M. D. J., Harness, D., and van der Sloot, R. (2009). Purchasing and marketing of social and environmental sustainability for high-tech medical equipment. *Journal of Business Ethics* 85(Suppl. 2): 445–462. Here, the reader can also find additional relevant references to the case and its topic.

Case study 2: Destination Digital

Destination Digital was an experimental project launched in 2019 with the goal of exploring how data could optimise the tourism value chain. The Danish holiday island of Rømø served as the testing ground for this initiative. Rømø was chosen due to its status as a popular tourist destination and its well-defined geographical area. The project, led by Copenhagen Business School, was carried out in collaboration with the national fund *Dansk Kyst- og Naturturisme* (in English: Coastal Tourism in Denmark), VisitDenmark and several other partners such as NNT Data.

With regard to the partners, *Dansk Kyst- og Naturturisme* is a commercial foundation dedicated to promoting sustainable growth in Denmark's coastal and nature tourism sectors. Established in 2015 as part of a governmental growth plan for tourism and the experience economy, *Dansk Kyst- og Naturturisme* focuses on fostering economic and social sustainability by generating local jobs and vibrant cities. They work closely with municipalities, destination companies and tourism organisations, including VisitDenmark, the country's national tourism body. VisitDenmark's mission is to attract more tourists to Denmark by promoting the nation's attractions, culture, nature and experiences on a global scale.

When the project began, there was limited interest in using data for tourism optimisation. However, researchers from Copenhagen Business School pushed the initiative forward through an open lab where suppliers, businesses, tourist destinations and experts collaborated. Although the project's destination was uncertain at first, it was a risk worth taking. The experiment's success led to its expansion, first along 11 municipalities on the west coast of Jutland and eventually into a nationwide initiative for all Danish tourist destinations. Tourism is significant to Denmark's economy, contributing around 18% of GDP.

The project utilised a wide variety of data sources: traffic data, point-of-sale data from stores, holiday home rental information, weather patterns, social media, mobile data and Internet of Things sensor data. One of the successful outcomes was a predictive model for Fru Dax Café, a well-known café and ice cream parlour on Rømø, which won Denmark's Best Ice Cream Parlor award in 2019.

Fru Dax, a seasonal business with most of its revenue concentrated during summer, faced challenges in staffing, inventory and production due to unpredictable turnover. On busy summer days, up to 30 employees could be needed, but staffing had to be adjusted frequently based on customer flow. Using data on guest numbers, weather, traffic and point-of-sale data, researchers built a model that forecasted daily sales. This allowed Fru Dax to optimise staffing and inventory, reducing food waste and preventing stockouts.

In terms of key findings and innovations, one surprising insight was that Fru Dax had reached its maximum sales capacity relative to demand. The café could not expand its current location, so the decision was made to set up a satellite café near the beach for the next season, allowing them to capture more potential revenue.

Another benefit of the project came from addressing traffic congestion. During holiday home changeover days, long queues would form as everyone arrived simultaneously to collect keys from the rental agency. In later projects, the researchers tested the use of key boxes or digital locks on holiday homes. Guests received a code via text and could go straight to their rental once it was cleaned. This innovation not only reduced traffic and queuing times but also allowed holidaymakers to start their vacations sooner and give thereby a higher service and reduced even CO_2 emissions by having to drive fewer kilometres.

The *Destination Digital* project demonstrates the potential of using data to optimise tourism operations and improve visitor experiences. By leveraging big data, Rømø and other tourist destinations in Denmark can now manage resources more effectively, enhance customer service and support sustainable growth in the tourism industry.

Multiple-choice questions

1. Which of the following best describes the concept of demand handling?

   A. Maximising production capacity
   B. Minimising inventory costs
   C. Balancing supply and demand
   D. Optimising transportation routes

2. What is the primary goal of demand forecasting?

   A. Reducing operational expenses
   B. Predicting future customer needs
   C. Increasing market share
   D. Improving supplier relationships

3. Which forecasting method relies on expert opinions and market research?

   A. Time series analysis
   B. Causal forecasting
   C. Qualitative forecasting
   D. Quantitative forecasting

4. What is a key characteristic of the simple moving average forecasting method?

   A. It assigns equal weight to all observations
   B. It emphasises recent data points
   C. It incorporates seasonal variations
   D. It uses complex statistical models

5. Which of the following is NOT a typical component of time series forecasting?

   A. Trend
   B. Seasonality
   C. Cyclical patterns
   D. Supplier performance

6. What does the MAD measure in forecasting?

   A. Average forecast error
   B. Seasonal fluctuations
   C. Trend accuracy
   D. Demand variability

7. Which inventory classification method categorises items based on their value and usage?

   A. FIFO
   B. EOQ
   C. ABC analysis
   D. JIT system

8. What is the primary purpose of safety stock?

   A. Maximising production efficiency
   B. Reducing transportation costs
   C. Protecting against demand uncertainty
   D. Improving supplier negotiations

9. Which of the following best describes the EOQ model?

   A. A method for classifying inventory
   B. A technique for demand forecasting
   C. An optimal order size calculation
   D. A system for supplier evaluation

10. What is the main objective of the JIT inventory system?

   A. Maximising safety stock levels
   B. Minimising inventory holding costs
   C. Increasing bulk order discounts
   D. Improving long-term demand forecasts

11. Which of the following is NOT a typical benefit of implementing a VMI system?

   A. Reduced inventory costs
   B. Improved supplier control
   C. Enhanced demand visibility
   D. Increased production flexibility

12. What is the primary focus of the CPFR approach?

   A. Internal process optimisation
   B. Supplier performance evaluation
   C. Cross-organisational collaboration
   D. Customer relationship management

13. Which demand handling strategy involves adjusting prices to influence customer behaviour?

   A. Demand shaping
   B. Demand sensing
   C. Demand forecasting
   D. Demand planning

14. What is the main purpose of demand sensing in SCM?

   A. Long-term strategic planning
   B. Real-time demand detection
   C. Historical data analysis
   D. Supplier capacity assessment

15. Which of the following best describes the concept of demand latency?

   A. Time between order placement and fulfilment
   B. Delay in recognising changes in demand patterns
   C. Variation in demand across different markets
   D. Seasonal fluctuations in customer preferences

Essay question

Analyse how the integration of demand forecasting, inventory management and collaborative planning contributes to a holistic approach to demand handling in modern supply chains. Discuss the challenges and opportunities presented by each of these elements, and explain how their synergistic application can enhance overall supply chain performance. Additionally, evaluate the role of emerging technologies and data analytics in improving the accuracy and responsiveness of demand handling processes. Support your analysis with specific examples of how companies might implement these integrated approaches to address the complexities of today's dynamic market environments.

8

PROCUREMENT FROM A MARKETING AND SUPPLY CHAIN MANAGEMENT POINT OF VIEW

Introduction

Finding the suitable and appropriate resources and suppliers for a business, as well as maintaining efficient and beneficial relations with them, is a critical factor for success that cannot be overlooked. For most new managers, just assuming the steering wheel of a company signifies their first move towards deducing cost and gaining a competitive advantage. Experience has shown that a successful entrepreneur of any sector or product must be able to combine the skills of a salesman and a buyer. The management of companies was not slow to realise this and to treat the function of procurements and the relations with the corresponding members of the supply chain with the same gravity they show to the operation of marketing and relationships with customers. Most people consider sourcing as 'reverse marketing', and not unjustifiably so. This means that the heads of the marketing and supplies departments of a company collaborate closely to attract and work with suppliers who are in a position to add value to the products and services offered by the company, by implementing all practices and methodologies used to find, maintain and increase the customer base of the company and, of course, to attract good/loyal customers. Of special interest are the similarities between the types of relations established between both the suppliers and the customers of a business, which drive their planning

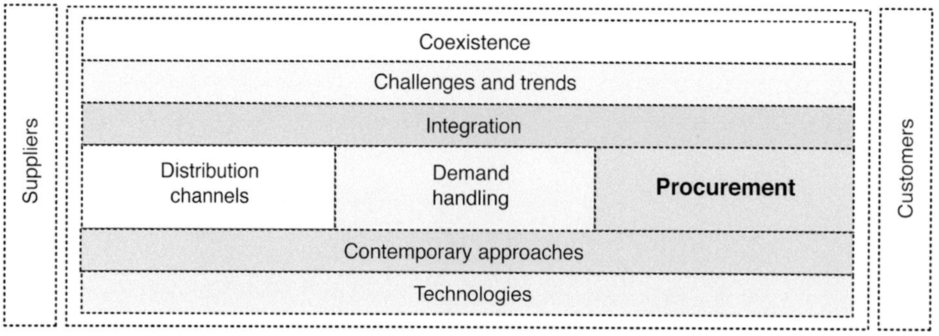

DOI: 10.4324/9781003650973-8

and improvement beneath an integrated 'umbrella', that of the management of business associates or the relationship management of business partners. This management passes through the stages of opportunity transactions without these being necessarily beneficial for both parties ('win–lose') – regular transactions at fixed intervals with fixed terms until the establishment of strategic relationships resting on a relation of sharing opportunities, profits and risks.

Learning objectives

After reading this chapter, you will be able to answer the following questions:

- How do supplies operate from a supply chain management (SCM) and marketing point of view?
- What is the significance of procurement in business success?
- Are there any integrated approaches to the procurement of SCM and marketing in business success?

Outline

8.1 Defining strategic sourcing
8.2 Benefits and challenges of an integrated approach of supplier management

8.1 Defining strategic sourcing

Strategic sourcing from a SCM point of view

Strategic sourcing is a critical function of SCM. It refers to the products (raw materials and semi-finished products) that a company procures to produce the final products – through the production process – that it will then distribute to its clients. Moreover, it refers to the materials procured by the business, which, although it may not use them for the production of the final product, are, nevertheless, indispensable for its operation. The goal for strategic sourcing is aligned with the overall objective of the supply networks of an organisation to constantly reduce operational costs while at the same time maximising value from supplier relationships.

Terms like purchasing, procurement and sourcing are used interchangeably, and to appreciate their benefits, the following questions should be asked:

- What are the differences between purchasing and procurement/strategic sourcing?
- What tasks do they include?
- How can they be improved?
- How can marketing assist in this endeavour?

Answering these questions is the objective of this section.

What?

Purchasing is the transaction between the seller and the supplier that focuses on the acquisition of goods and services. It includes the placement of orders with the suppliers chosen, their payment, the transportation of the products and their delivery to the customers. But procurement is an even wider concept: it includes not only the works that precede but also those that follow purchasing, such as market research, negotiations, selecting the suitable supplier, pricing and concluding deals, monitoring the performance of the supplier and managing risks. The supply cycle presented below includes all of procurement operations. A key feature of the procurement cycle is that it is a systematic process (comprising specific stages) initially for the decision to acquire the products and services, the quality, quantity, price and time of purchase, which are specified as accurately as possible, and to apply rules that will ensure that the goods/services received will fully conform to the required specifications.

Strategic sourcing can be considered as a process that is focused on the strategic level. It can be defined as a systematic, long-term and holistic approach to obtain current and future needs of an organisation at the lowest total cost of ownership (TCO) (which is the purchase price of an asset plus the costs of operation) and lowest risk to the supply network. Therefore, the focus in sourcing includes value creation, risk and uncertainty in the supply chain, and the overall responsiveness and resilience of the supply chain. Furthermore, it also includes the establishment and the overall management and optimisation of supplier relationships and alliances, even for the design of products and the acquisition of strategic sources. At this point, we must stress that the three definitions refer to both products and services.

Why?

Sourcing is one of the most important business functions. The success of any company directly depends on the effectiveness of sourcing management. The influence of an effective sourcing contributes towards the following:

- Decreasing costs, rationalising the large amounts spent on procurements. This is valid since in most cases a material purchased has a value equal to 50–70% of its sales cost. Most of the time companies spend enormous amounts for supplies, which drastically decrease their revenue. This is especially true of industrial enterprises that spend in excess of 50–60% of their income for supplies. But also in the case of commercial companies, it has been demonstrated in practice that a decrease in the cost of the purchased materials is the easiest and most direct way to increase their profitability.
- Increase in the level of service offered by increasing the quality of the purchased materials that comply with strict specifications. The drafting of specifications excludes products that while having an initially appealing and low price turn out to be more expensive in their use (it's not rare for 'cheaper to prove more expensive'), by better utilising working capital and gaining value for money. For example, the greatest percentage of quality issues can be attributed to defects in the materials that have been procured.
- Serving all other business functions of the company and supporting their daily tasks and the goals set by its management. In this case, sourcing objectives are in line with the goals of the other functions, ensuring the acquisition of the required materials/services at the right quality, quantity and time; from a proper source and under the best possible terms.

All of these attest not only to the leading role and great importance of procurement management for modern enterprises but also to the need for its integration with the other functions. The goals remain the same: decrease in ordering times, reliable and timely delivery, completeness of orders, faster response to customer requirements and ability to respond to special requests.

How?

The reasons presented above force businesses and organisations to organise an independent procurement department with specific roles and competences. Moreover, they force such entities to plan and implement an integrated procurement framework where all of the departments participate (and can express a view). The key responsibilities of the department for procurement management initially relate to the management of all stages in the procurement process (namely, the procurement cycle, which will be presented in what follows) and also in decision-making regarding the products (materials and equipment) or services to be acquired, the establishment of their specifications, the implementation of a negotiation or call for tenders procedure, the selection of suppliers, the establishment of a smaller or larger supply base, the decision for own manufacture or not and to seek suppliers or associates in domestic or international markets, etc.

Strategic sourcing cycle

Strategic sourcing is a systematic and integrated process. It includes specific and individual stages that are performed by specific people, following a given timetable, while a specific output ensues at the end of each stage, which is the input for the next stage (Figure 8.1).

Let us consider an example that presents how this is executed in practice. Consider the procurement planning for the next year for a large public hospital that services a major geographical region.

First stage: establishment of strategic objectives and principles for sourcing

Usually at the end of the fiscal year (end of December or early January), the hospital's Procurement Directorate begins planning the scheduling for the materials that need to be procured for

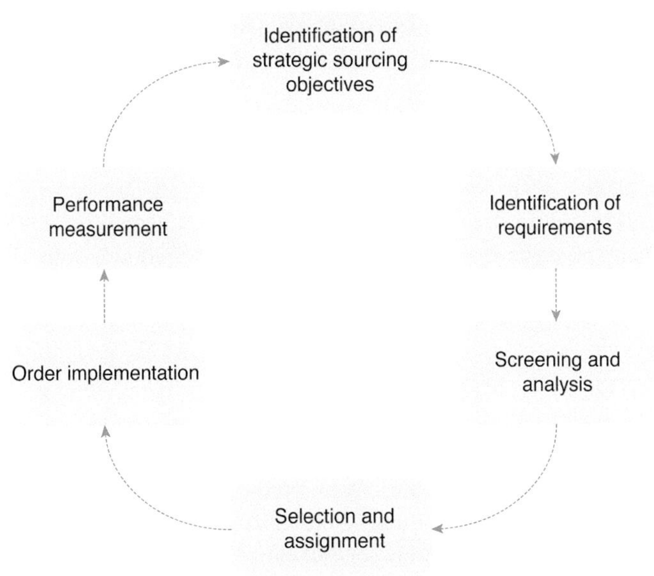

FIGURE 8.1 Strategic sourcing cycle

the next year. The directorate follows the strategy for purchases that has been designed by the management of the organisation, which, in turn, observes the policy of the Ministry of Health. For this reason, a strategic sourcing committee is formed, with the participation of the financial director, the chief financial officer (CFO), the chief procurement officer (CPO), the supply chain manager and, of course, the marketing manager (the quality manager or even the head of production could also be participating in this committee). Decisions such as the maximum limit for the budget; the decision to make or buy; selecting local, domestic or international supply chains; selecting small or large supply base; and going for green or sustainable suppliers fall under the competence of this committee.

Second stage: description and disclosure of requirements

The directorate sends to all departments and supervisions of the hospital a specific document called 'purchase application (or mandate)' and asks that it be filled in. This procedure is usually supported by the health information system (HIS) that is kept by the hospital. The purchase application is an application or mandate for the directorate to procure a specific quantity of a material or a service at a date (or time) and justifies the request for its purchase. To assist the directors and heads of the departments, the directorate usually dispatches the applications for previous years while also helping and advising on how the application is to be filled in. The planning of specifications for the materials to be purchased is especially important. Specifications determine the required quality characteristics and features for the products. They usually relate to certified products or quality standards. The employees of the procurement directorate initially assess the justification for the need to acquire the products and then the accuracy of the drafting of the specifications. Moreover, an initial assessment of prices is also performed at this stage, as well as of the time periods when such materials are required. Concepts such as brand names, sampling (to form a better view of the products to be acquired), and drafting of detailed technical, operational and performance specifications are all common and useful. This stage ends with the preparation by the directorate of the annual procurement planning, which includes all materials to be purchased aggregated and classified per code, as well as the actions to follow.

Third stage: survey of potential suppliers

The third stage includes a market analysis aimed to screen and locate suitable potential suppliers in the market. The survey usually commences with the assessment of the supplier records kept by the company or the organisation, which include information on suppliers for materials procured in past years and the suppliers who collaborated or expressed an interest or desire to collaborate. A proper and updated record will not only provide the contact information but will also inform on possible problems and non-compliance of suppliers observed in the past. Other sources are internet searches, collaborating with the procurement directorates of other hospitals, etc. Reliable information may also ensue from visits and discussions with suppliers, to visits to trade fairs; surveying the relevant bibliography, such as specialised catalogues, newspapers and magazines, and annual reports by commercial and industrial organisations; and visits to international and national procurement institutes, and consulting firms. Today more than ever the problem does not lie with a lack of information but with the over-abundance of it. Moreover, the need is for accurate, valid and updated information, and the principle of garbage-in-garbage-out (GIGO) stands also for procurements. The need to check the reliability and objectivity of the source of information is imperative, as is analysing and interpreting it. And since, as was cited above, information is reused, the need for an organised keeping of supplier records cannot be overstated. The final deliverables of the third stage are the following:

- *Request for information* (RFI): An open enquiry that spans the market seeking broad data and understanding.
- *Request for proposal* (RFP): Sometimes based on a prior RFI; a business requirements-based request for specific solutions to the sourcing problem (terms, conditions, product specifications, delivery, packaging and labelling options) that usually leads to RFP.
- *Request for quotation* (RFQ): A request to potential suppliers to inform about the way they are going to provide their products/services and also information about the corresponding costs.

These will be dispatched to all potential suppliers and published on the hospital's website.

Fourth stage: selection and assignment of suppliers and order

In this stage, interested suppliers send their offers to the hospital's procurement directorate. The directorate, or the sub-committees appointed by the directorate, selects the appropriate suppliers based on specific evaluation criteria and following the legal framework that clearly establishes the manner in which calls for tenders are conducted. The evaluation aims to offer answers to two critical questions:

- From where?
- Why?

These questions will be analysed in the following section.

A key job is to select the proper criteria. Indicatively one could cite the following: after-sales services (such as warranties, maintenance and repairs), the quality of products and services offered (demonstrated by the existence of a quality system and constant checks policy/practices), past experience, investments in research and development, capacity and availability of infrastructures, equipment and systems, reliability (such as guarantee for delivery at the agreed times), adaptability to special requirements and cooperation in functions (such as the design of products and services). There is, of course, also the option of negotiations. In the case of an automatic award procedure (or reverse auction), the final purchase orders will be issued to the suppliers offering the lowest price, to whom the order will be ultimately awarded. The stage is completed by the drafting of the contracts and agreements that put forth the terms for the completion of the order, the levels of services and prices (service level agreements, SLAs), and the relevant market price list for the payment of the suppliers.

At this stage, management must answer the following questions:

- *To negotiate or not?* It depends on various criteria. You are choosing the negotiation in case you cannot accurately estimate the price of products, or the price is low, or there are many criteria that can be taken into account in addition to the price. Moreover, the stage procedure takes on a different form: its duration is much shorter, while material specifications change during the course of the procedure.

- *One or more suppliers?* Each choice has its pros and cons (in this case, the pros of one are the cons of the other). The following are among the pros for selecting one supplier: better prices due to the purchase of large quantities (discounts), lower shipment costs since greater quantities are purchased with fewer routes, and establishment of strategic and long-term relationships. The advantages of going for many suppliers relate to the attainment of better prices and terms for the agreement on account of the competition, increase in the interest and technological evolution of suppliers, and protection against strikes, natural disasters, etc.
- *Local or international supplier?* Similarly, the advantages of choosing one supplier are the disadvantages of another choice. By opting for a local supplier, the company can maintain a smaller inventory due to the small distances involved, the reliability of deliveries, the establishment of strategic and long-term relationships, the satisfaction of extraordinary orders and lower price due to decreased shipment costs. By selecting a supplier from the international market, the business attains better prices, better quality and a greater range of products.
- *Centralised or decentralised?* Two principal models exist for multinational companies: in the first, the centralised model, the supply cycle is performed by the central headquarters of the company, while products are procured from different geographical regions, centrally stored and then distributed to the company's outlets in every country. The biggest advantage of this model is the central control, a fact that renders this model ideal for the public organisations in a country (e.g., hospitals). On the other hand, one can observe an increase in shipment costs and possible tax and customs issues. The management of the cycle in the second, the decentralised model, is performed by the branches in each country, the managers of which choose products and suppliers from the local market. Specifications are usually determined by company headquarters, but the entirety of decision-making is decentralised. The advantages of this model are decrease in shipment costs, improvement of branches' networking and effective flow of information, which strengthen the cultural heritage and also increase their profits.

Fifth stage: collection, checking of products and completion of the order

This stage includes the shipment of products, care of (usually) the suppliers and their qualitative and quantitative check, the check of invoices, accounting monitoring, and the receipt and storage of products by the hospital's staff, and especially its warehousemen, who, in turn, assign the required material to the personnel of other directorates or supervisors when it is so requested of them.

Sixth stage: supplier performance measurement

The procurement directorate monitors collaborations with suppliers and updates the suppliers' records for possible non-compliance with what is provided for in the agreements. Key performance indicators are created and measured, such as quality of products and/or services, on-time delivery, compliance with contract level agreements and/or SLAs, cost savings, procurement lead/cycle time and inventory turnover ratio.

In cases where the procurement of some material or service that was not provided for is requested over the next year, the steps outlined above must be followed again. Consequently, the procedure is repeated in the same manner (i.e., cyclically). This is the reason the procedure is termed the supply cycle.

From where and why?

These questions relate to the evaluation and selection of the appropriate suppliers. A series of individual questions arises from this process.

Are there methods for evaluation and selection?

There are several methods. A simple method for the selection of the suitable supplier is the scoring model. Say, for example, one has three suppliers: A, B and C. The first column in Table 8.1 presents specific evaluation criteria; the second column presents the weight (i.e., importance) of each criterion; the third column presents the mark on a scale of 1–5 (with 1 being the lowest and 5 the highest) for each choice, A, B and C; and the last three columns give the overall scores for choices A, B and C, which are obtained when we multiply the marks of each supplier with respect to a criterion with the weight of the criterion. By adding these products, we get a total score of 445 for supplier A, 340 for B and 355 for C. The supplier with the highest total score is selected, namely, supplier A.

A second popular method is the SWOT (strengths, weaknesses, opportunities, threats) analysis. Figure 8.2 presents an example of the application of SWOT for a particular supplier.

Scoring model

The procedure for the evaluation of suppliers and that for the selection of a suitable supplier to whom the order will be assigned are two of the most important works in the supply cycle. The

TABLE 8.1 Examples of the grading model for the selection of the appropriate supplier

Criterion	*Weight*	*A*	*B*	*C*	*Marks for A*	*Marks for B*	*Marks for C*
Price	40	5	3	4	200	120	160
Response time	30	4	4	3	120	120	90
Infrastructure	20	3	4	3	60	80	60
Market ranking	10	4	3	2	40	30	20
Quality systems	5	5	4	5	25	20	25
Total	105				445	340	355

Strengths	**Weaknesses**
• Good organization • Personnel both trained and willing to collaborate and serve • Good reputation – leadership profile in the market • Oriented towards research and innovation	• The company is expensive with respect to certain products and services • Unsatisfactory coverage network • Non-satisfaction of extraordinary deliveries – direct orders
Opportunities	**Threats**
• Failure of competition to quickly respond to new offers due to decreased liquidity • Construction of national motorways • Increase of living standards in neighbouring nations	• Economic recession • Appearance of major competitor/ multinational company

FIGURE 8.2 Example of SWOT analysis

procurement department is responsible for their performance. Specifically, it is initially responsible for identifying potential suppliers and establishing the general criteria for their evaluation. It will then invite potential suppliers to send their offers or bids.

Interested suppliers will send their offers, and after the company has established the criteria and weight factors for their assessment, it will evaluate suppliers based on their offers and the evaluation criteria. The procedure is completed upon the final selection and award. The scoring model is in general one of the most widely known methods for selecting between alternatives or proposals. In the case at hand (that of public procurements), it relates to the evaluation and selection between prospective suppliers.

The steps for applying this model are as follows:

- Selection of the evaluation criteria.
- Establishing the weight (importance) of each criterion.
- Evaluating every supplier for each criterion based on the measurement scale.
- Calculation of the score for every supplier with respect to all criteria.
- Calculation of total/overall score for each supplier.

We will discuss each of these components in turn. For the *selection of the evaluation criteria*, Dickson (1966) categorises the various supplier selection criteria according to their importance as follows:

- *Extreme:* Quality, distribution – delivery, performance history, warranties and claim policies.
- *Considerable:* Production facilities and capacity, price, technical capability, financial position, procedural compliance, communication system, reputation and position in industry, desire for business, management and organisation, and operating controls.
- *Average:* Repair service, attitude, impression, packaging ability, labour relations record, geographical location, amount of past business and training aids.
- *Slight:* Reciprocal agreements.

It is only logical that the more complex or demanding the services or products are, the more criteria will be required for the evaluation. Furthermore, the selection of the criteria depends on the product, and different criteria will, therefore, be employed for different products. Consider, for example, that for the procurement of a product the head of the supplies department of a company has concluded the following ten evaluation criteria: price–quality ratio, reliability in delivery and distribution, geographical location of the supplier, market reputation, meeting of packaging specifications, performance history, warranties and return policies, facilities, financial position and procedural compliance. The business performs scholastic market research, collecting information and data on those suppliers who expressed their interest by sending bids.

The next step is *establishing the weight (importance) for each criterion.* Not all criteria in the list above carry the same weight for company executives. Some, such as the head of procurements, deem reliability in deliveries and distribution as the most important criterion (namely, that which carries the most weight). For the head of sales and the financial director, the criteria that carry more weight for their decision are market reputation and performance history. But all agree that low price and high quality shall be the principal factors for selecting the best suppliers. After a talk, company executives compile the information in Table 8.2, which presents the

TABLE 8.2 Weight of supplier selection criteria

No	*Criterion*	*Weight %*
1	Price	25
2	(Reliability in) distribution – delivery	15
3	Experience	12
4	Geographical location of the supplier	10
5	Production facilities and capacity	9
6	Performance history	8
7	Attitude	6
8	Packaging ability	5
9	Financial position	5
10	Procedural compliance	5
	Total	100

TABLE 8.3 Evaluation of suppliers with respect to every criterion

No	*Criterion*	*Weight %*	*A*	*B*	*C*
1	Price	25	3	4	3
2	(Reliability in) distribution – delivery	15	5	3	5
3	Experience	12	4	3	4
4	Geographical location of the supplier	10	4	2	4
5	Production facilities and capacity	9	5	4	3
6	Performance history	8	3	3	3
7	Attitude	6	3	3	4
8	Packaging ability	5	5	2	3
9	Financial position	5	4	4	2
10	Procedural compliance	5	5	4	4
	Total	100			

weight for each criterion in a descending order. As the table shows, the first three criteria are the most important ones and correspond to more than 50% of the total weight (note: the total of weights/percentages must be 100).

The third step is the *evaluation of each supplier with respect to every criterion using a measurement scale*. A scale from 1 to 5 will be used for this, where 1 corresponds to the lowest performance and 5 to the highest. For example, say that the company wishes to evaluate three suppliers A, B and C in order to purchase a specific product with the criteria its executives selected in the first step. Table 8.3 presents the result of this process. One can observe that in (most of) the more significant criteria (those with the greatest weight), supplier A has a better score.

The next step is *calculation of the score for each supplier and every criterion*. Now company executives may calculate the score for each supplier by multiplying the score for the criterion with the weight of that criterion, giving the results shown in Table 8.4. We then need to *calculate the total/final score for each supplier*. By adding the products, the executives of a company can select that supplier who has the greatest overall score – that is, in the case at hand, supplier A, as one can see from Table 8.5.

TABLE 8.4 Calculation of suppliers' scores for each criterion A

No	*Criterion*	*Weight %*	*A*	*B*	*C*	*Score A*	*Score B*	*Score C*
1	Price	25	3	4	3	75	100	75
2	(Reliability in) distribution – delivery	15	5	3	5	75	45	75
3	Experience	12	4	3	4	48	36	48
4	Geographical location of the supplier	10	4	2	4	40	20	40
5	Production facilities and capacity	9	5	4	3	45	36	27
6	Performance history	8	3	3	3	24	24	24
7	Attitude	6	3	3	4	18	18	24
8	Packaging ability	5	5	2	3	25	10	15
9	Financial position	5	4	4	2	20	20	10
10	Procedural compliance	5	5	4	4	25	20	20
	Total	100						

TABLE 8.5 Calculation of suppliers' scores for each criterion B

No	*Criterion*	*Weight %*	*A*	*B*	*C*	*Score A*	*Score B*	*Score C*
1	Price	25	3	4	3	75	100	75
2	(Reliability in) distribution – delivery	15	5	3	5	75	45	75
3	Experience	12	4	3	4	48	36	48
4	Geographical location of the supplier	10	4	2	4	40	20	40
5	Production facilities and capacity	9	5	4	3	45	36	27
6	Performance history	8	3	3	3	24	24	24
7	Attitude	6	3	3	4	18	18	24
8	Packaging ability	5	5	2	3	25	10	15
9	Financial position	5	4	4	2	20	20	10
10	Procedural compliance	5	5	4	4	25	20	20
	Total	100				395	329	358

Three points merit attention in the application of the aforementioned procedure:

1. The procedure is simple to use and produces a result quickly, aiming to quantify qualitative characteristics.
2. The selection of the evaluation criteria and the weight assigned to each and the scoring of candidate suppliers on the scale employed are all subjective. It is for this reason that in practice these usually ensue from the collaboration of the executives of a company.
3. Ultimately it may become a way to monitor the performance of the suppliers of a company in the course of the year.

What, how much and when?

For which codes must one keep more stock and for which less? Or are there any codes for which no stock will be kept? The answer is easy: 'It depends on the sales of these codes!' Codes in high demand require the maintenance of sufficient stock to satisfy the demand. On the other hand, codes in low demand must be maintained at low levels. The ABC analysis that will be presented in the next chapter rests on this simple logic.

Make or buy?

Another significant issue for the management of a productive company is the decision of whether products are manufactured by the company or are purchased from third parties (make or buy). A key criterion for choosing is, of course, cost (to own produce or purchase). Businesses that choose to produce their own products do so since this way they align the production objectives with the management's objectives and maintain the control of the productive process, safeguarding the quality of the products produced and the corresponding production know-how. On the other hand, production may be expensive, and purchasing products from third parties may exploit their specialised equipment, personnel and infrastructures.

Make it better?

Electronic procurements

Electronic procurements apply e-commerce technologies and practices attaining communication between the companies participating in the procedure for a supply and contributing towards the decrease of both cost and time of implementation, as well as the simplification and transparency of processes from the description of the procurement requirements until the completion of the order and the payment for the products or services to the supplier.

In general, it may be said that the internet has greatly helped the steps of the procedure presented above that relate to the implementation of an (electronic) auction. An auction is a procedure for the purchase and sale of products or services where participants are willing to offer a specific amount to acquire the product or service on auction. Usually the product is awarded to the supplier making the best offer (highest price). The internet supports the performance of an auction, offering the capability to clients and suppliers to remotely participate in the procedure. In this case, e-auction, suppliers pay the operator of the electronic auctioning house a percentage on the amount of their sales.

The key feature of an electronic auction that differentiates it from traditional ones is that negotiation is effected via the development of competition among suppliers without the intervention of the purchaser, permitting the electronic submission of bids and indeed the submission of multiple bids within a specific and usually brief period. This allows (a) the dynamic pricing of the products (since the procedure of supply is performed in a short period) and personalised pricing according to customers' needs, as well as the capacity provided to suppliers to offer more information to customers; and (b) the elimination of intermediate stages/intermediaries by offering products and services at the lowest price.

In reverse electronic auction, there is a purchasing company and a group of companies-suppliers competing with prescribed specifications and terms and offering consecutive lower prices online and within a specified and usually short period. The purchasing company or the operator of the internet site performing the auction opens it at an initial price and accepts bids at lower prices (the buyer can also set a maximum acceptable price). Suppliers submit offers offering increasingly lower prices. The procedure is completed when no seller is willing to offer a lower price and the one who has offered the lowest one is awarded the procurement.

The expected benefits of a reverse electronic auction are a fall in sale prices, reduction of the time it takes to perform the procurement, better understanding of the needs of specific customers and/or products and, of course, the ability for the participation of small and distant suppliers. Security issues and e-payment-related ones, as well as legal and regulatory issues, can be considered as challenges to electronic reverse auctions.

A typical problem in the aforementioned procedure is the lack of trust due to the lack of reliable information on suppliers wishing to participate in the procedure. Online reputation tools have been developed as a response, which collect and keep feedback from the prior behaviour of the participants in a reverse auction (i.e., when the procedure is completed, both the buyer and the supplier evaluate one another, leaving some comments). Thus, every business that has participated in an electronic reverse auction will have a reputation acquired by its score and the comments, and which is available to all.

In the example shown in Table 8.6, the director of the procurement office in the hospital wishes to procure specialised medical equipment with specific specifications by using a reverse electronic auction.

TABLE 8.6 Traditional procurements versus internet procurements

Stage	*Traditional procurements*	*Digital procurements*
Identification of strategic sourcing objectives	The head of the paediatric clinic fills in the purchase application, entering information on a product, for example, its specifications. He discusses its proper completion with the head of procurements	The head fills in the electronic purchase application form on the informational system by selecting the suitable product from the digital online catalogue. He can search and collect information on the product via internet searches and sources
Identification of requirements	The head of procurements collects all purchase applications filled and creates a new file by grouping the products per code	The head of procurements exports the accumulative file on his preferred file format and automatically uploads it onto the hospital's website. Simultaneously, he informs by e-mail the suppliers with whom he has done business in the past
Screening and analysis	Interested suppliers try to collect all necessary information, by frequently talking to the head of procurements and/or exchanging letters or faxes	Suppliers get all necessary information by downloading the files from the hospital's website and/or by communicating with the head of procurements via e-mail
	Suppliers submit their bids in writing. The two parties communicate using traditional means until the final deadline	Suppliers send their offers electronically or via the hospital's system. They can request any information or clarification by filling out contact forms, while the hospital can upload any change (say with respect to specifications) on its website
Selection and assignment	Bids are evaluated by the departments of the hospital involved based on specific information (usually price)	The bids that were electronically submitted are evaluated, while all talks and negotiations are also conducted digitally. Specifically, suppliers compete with fully established specifications and terms, are informed of each other's bids and compete with multiple bids placed online and offering successive lower prices within a predefined period. The auction ends when there is no one willing to offer a lower price (there are no active suppliers), while the supplier who has offered the lowest price is awarded the contract

(*Continued*)

TABLE 8.6 (Continued)

Stage	*Traditional procurements*	*Digital procurements*
	The supplier who offered the lowest bid is informed on the document he must collect	Communication is effected digitally
	Sends the contract by mail	Sends the contract by e-mail
	Preparation of the order by hand by the employee of the procurement department and dispatch by fax or mail	Creation of the order via the system and dispatch over the internet
Order implementation	Entry of the transaction in the accounting system and of the hospital system and payment by the hospital's accounting department	Automatic registration with the system and electronic payment
Performance measurement	Updating of the suppliers' records and the online reputation mechanisms	When a procurement procedure has been completed, both the purchaser and the supplier evaluate another by also entering comments. Online reputation mechanisms are built this way

Pursuant to what has been cited above, it is obvious that the gains from an electronic procurement system are the following:

- Decrease in the procedural (i.e., performance) costs for procurements. Buy why? First of all, because fewer people are required to participate in the performance of the procurement. Moreover, fewer documents and, in general, less of the traditional ways of communicating (post, fax, etc.) are needed.
- Simplification of the processes, due to their automation and which directly and immediately lead to the shortening of times and the decrease in bureaucracy.
- Increase in productivity and decrease in human errors (by using, e.g., digital catalogues).
- Increase in the transparency of the procedures ensuring the participation of all businesses-suppliers that can be initially informed and also participate in calls for tenders.
- Market increase or expansion, with the ability for remote suppliers to participate.
- Common material codification and common specifications. Ability to export statistical and/or cumulative data for procurements.

Public sector procurements specifically are governed by the following three principles:

1. Principle of publicity, that is, every public procurement must be disclosed to the interested parties.
2. Principle of procedural transparency, that is, the procedure for the performance of public procurements must rest, across all of its stages, on specific and known-beforehand rules, which will be in force throughout the procedure and are complete, comprehensible and clear.
3. Principle of equal treatment, that is, the terminology will be provided to ensure that there is no discrimination against specific businesses or categories of businesses. Electronic

procurement ensures all three principles. However, necessary for the proper and effective implementation of an electronic procurement system are safety technologies and practices, which will reinforce the trust between those involved, the timely and proper briefing and informing of all those involved, common standards, strict regulatory framework and monitoring of the performance of processes so as to attain the required transparency.

Sourcing from a marketing point of view

When implementing the strategic sourcing cycle, marketing executives can help by taking actions advocated in Table 8.7.

8.2 Benefits and challenges of an integrated approach to supplier management

The way sourcing is managed by SCM exhibits many similarities to the way it is managed by marketing.

The similarities can be detected in the following:

- Supply undertakes a 'research of supply sources' in correspondence to marketing's 'customer purchases research'. Consequently, common practices and methodologies can be applied both for the research on sources and suppliers and that on customers. Of special interest is the application of internet and e-commerce tools in general for the promotion of corporate-prospect suppliers and, of course, their more effective search and selection.
- Moreover, common challenges are evident, while there is also a common objective: to find and maintain the best customers and suppliers. The benefits from attaining this objective

TABLE 8.7 Marketing support at the execution of the sourcing cycle

Stage	*Action*
Identification of strategic sourcing objectives	Development of a strategic plan to identify strategically attractive suppliers of a particular market, area, size, segment and commodity
Identification of requirements	Detailed interviews with both procurement managers and potential suppliers conducted throughout the identification and selection of requirements so as include their key opinion; face to face and telephone interviews, online and mail surveys
Screening and analysis	Keeping a supplier database per geographical region and commodity. Moreover, employing on-site visits and evaluation of potential suppliers. To support this, they could organise trade show exhibits or publish leaflets, presentations and sales collateral
Selection and assignment	Marketing and sales executives will participate in the process and support it by means of their very good knowledge of the market
Order implementation	Monitoring logistics processes and developing communication channels between customer and suppliers
Performance measurement	Define common metrics for marketing and create a concept for project workflow to which strategically selected partners can be connected. Also provide trademark assistance and technical and after-sales support

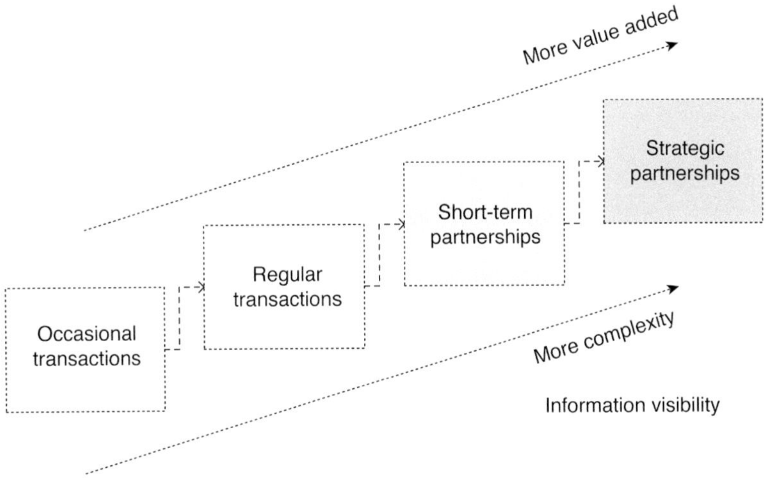

FIGURE 8.3 Supplier relationships

relate, of course, to the success of the entire organisation and ensue from the accumulative benefits of the success of each function.

- Relationship management with respect to suppliers and customers also exhibits several similarities. One can identify four stages from occasional transactions up to a strategic partnership (it must, at this point, be noted that there are many relations between the members of a supply chain; however, all culminate into two key relations: that of the customer and that of the supplier). These stages are summarised in Figure 8.3 and discussed in more detail in the sections that follow.

The internet today offers a great number of tools for the implementation of promotion policies and the creation of contacts for a company. These include, for example, search engine enrolment and optimisation of entries in digital (thematic) magazines (e-zines); the implementation of the ad swap technique, where companies agree to exchange hyperlinks and advertisements or viral marketing techniques; and, of course, the creation, hosting and offering of advertisements from internet sites, which may be either mass or targeted (i.e., to specific economic sectors), and via mobile telephone via SMS/MMS. Finally, social networks (Facebook, Twitter, Google+, Flickr, YouTube, Wikipedia, Blogger, Digg, etc.) allow companies to widely communicate with interested users (via pages), while only authorised and official agents can create such pages, and via groups, which offer to users the capacity to create a space that will allow them to communicate their mutual interests.

Occasional transactions

This can be considered as the simplest relation between the two parties (supplier and customer). Occasional transactions mean one or more transactions pursuing the satisfaction of a specific demand of one from the other (response to some RFI, RFQ, etc.). This relation has three key features: firstly, its time horizon is short. Both parties understand that there is no prospect for a future partnership. This lack of incentives renders this relation as the relation to add the least value. It is obvious that the supplier shall have a low priority for a buyer of this type, while shifting suppliers is easy at no cost for both parties. This also leads to a lack of trust, which hinders the exchange and sharing of information at arm's length between them. Secondly, it regards transactions of standardised and widely consumed products and services, which are on offer by many suppliers. Thirdly, the attempt to measure the performance of the relation is limited to the price, the lead time and the quality of the offered products or services. Any change to the last two of these will automatically lead to the increase of the first (a win–lose relation). Being a member of this type of relationship is not always bad. It mainly depends on the products and services and how both roles perceive them.

Regular transactions

It is common for a customer to frequently order the same products and services from the same supplier (i.e., for this supplier to be his first choice among suppliers). Of course, in their entirety, such transactions are not complemented by some agreement or contract to, thus, be considered as beneficial for both parties. Specifically, the customer's objective is to satisfy his demands, while the supplier's goal is to increase his revenue, not so much due to the low profit margins but due to the increase in the volume of sales. Compared with the previous relation, *regular transactions* exemplify the following characteristics:

- The prospect of new orders and the potential for the establishment of a partnership in the future increase the interest and efforts by the supplier to serve the customer better, while the existence of many transactions creates a climate of trust between them.
- They regard transactions for standardised product and services in wide consumption, offered by many suppliers, where, however, both the selling price and the delivery terms may differ from one transaction to the next.
- The measurement of performance with respect to the application of a small number of performance indices that relate to the key logistics functions and specifically to the degree of responsiveness. Nevertheless, the monitoring of performance indices does not automatically lead to the taking of measures in case of poor performance (consequently the supplier is not considered to be trustworthy). But the purchasing or procurement departments are also involved in this type, as they were in the previous one.

Short-term partnerships

The prospect of a large number of customer orders, on the one hand, and the lack of supplier reliability, on the other, lead to the conclusion of contracts/agreements between them and the establishment of partnerships. The term of contracts is short term (usually between 1 and 2 years). Commensurate to the features of the two previous types, the existence of contracts (a) leads to a better service of customers, as such service is outlined or described by the terms of the contract; (b) regards a wider scope of products compared to the two previous types, where not only price but also products and the quantities thereof may change in the course of the contract, while (c) keeping and tracking of performance indices are not only deemed necessary but are also, indeed, complemented by penalties (and prizes) in cases of non-adherence to what has been provided for (with respect to the performance of the contract). More company departments that belong to higher levels of the company's hierarchy are involved in such relations.

Long-term/strategic partnerships

The next type of partnership is managed by long-term contracts, the performance of the terms of which rests not only on strict clauses and penalties but also on the high level of trust between the two parties. This is implemented, on the one hand, by the distribution of profits, and, on the other hand, by the exchange of information between the parties, information that materially supports decision-making in marketing and logistics. The supplier continuously pursues the improvement of the offered products and services, himself participating in the design, development and implementation of improvement activities, while the customer invests in the long-term collaboration in the certainty that long-term benefits will ensue. The goal, therefore, is to develop solutions that will benefit both parties, that is, one's success 'goes through' the success of the other ('win–win'). This interdependence leads to the obligation that the management of both companies has to collaborate sincerely and invest in the improvement of the offered products and services. This relation assumes a more strategic dimension while decisions are taken mutually by the management of the collaborating parties and relate to the conclusion of agreements and the monitoring of the performance of marketing and logistics activities. This includes the design and application of metrics that measure performance beyond the initial 1–2 years of the collaboration, since the parties are committed to the relation not only on account of the obligations that are dictated by the terms of the agreement but also due to the existence of common goals. All of the activities above assist the parties involved to break out of the short-term project mentality so as to increase their competitiveness and their skills, and to reinforce their market place or to gain access to new markets.

Overall, successful procurement and sourcing require closer collaboration between marketing and SCM. The closer they collaborate, the more efficient, transparent and cost-effective the entire supply chain will be.

Synopsis

- Strategic sourcing is a critical function of SCM. It refers to the products (raw materials and semi-finished products) that a company procures to produce the final products – through the production process – that it will then distribute to its clients.
- The goal for strategic sourcing is aligned with the overall objective of the supply networks of an organisation to constantly reduce operational costs while at the same time maximising value from supplier relationships.
- Strategic sourcing is a systematic and integrated process. It includes specific and individual stages, which are performed by specific people, following a given timetable, while a specific output ensues at the end of each stage, which is the input for the next stage.
- A number of questions need to be answered for a successful sourcing strategy: how will it be applied in practice? From where and why? What, how much and when? Make or buy?.
- Moreover, sourcing can be viewed from a marketing point of view, aiming to create strong partnership relationships in a supply chain.

Review and discussion questions

- Define the terms purchasing, procurement and sourcing.
- Why is procurement a critical business function?
- Identify the stages of the strategic sourcing cycle.

- Describe the steps required based on the supply cycle for the procurement and installation of computers in your company.
- Apply the scoring model in a logistics service provider using the criteria that you think are critical in your decision-making.

Case studies

Case study 1: Supplier–retailer relationships in the fresh produce supply chain

The shift in demand from tinned, frozen or preserved fruits and vegetables to fresh produce reflects changing consumer habits and lifestyles in the UK.

Over the past decade, the UK fresh produce chain, encompassing recently harvested fruits, vegetables and salads, has experienced significant transformations, primarily due to the increasing influence of retailers. Previously, most fresh produce sales occurred through greengrocers, but now, retailers dominate the market, which gives way to their rise in channel power. One supplier commented when asked about their view of the benefits of a partnership between suppliers and retailers, 'Retailers should recognise that we are cheaper and split the difference fifty-fifty. They should recognise we are giving quality and a competitive price and reward us with more business. Retailers are just taking what they want'. Another supplier commented when asked about the problems that are arising, 'The way things are looking at the moment, I think if the supermarkets did not have as much power–and so that the general consensus of opinion coming from the supermarkets was not as one sided and more of a partnership–it would be better'.

Retailers prefer fewer, larger suppliers for partnership, which benefits them by enabling influence over entire food channels through streamlined interfaces. This consolidation not only reduces transaction costs but also fosters closer relationships with 'partner' suppliers, aiding in stringent quality assurance and traceability programmes. Consequently, there is a prevailing trend towards supply chain concentration, reshaping seller–buyer relationships and interactions within the sector. One retailer's comment when asked about how they would describe their relationship with suppliers exemplifies the stakes in the supplier's choice of buying firms. 'Obviously there can be difficulties and issues, such as suppliers supplying a number of retailers, and we will not deal as keenly with them, as we would suppliers who are dedicated to us and who are trying to make us the key winner'. The retailer later acknowledged, 'It is difficult to have a situation where they supply you purely because there comes a day when you cannot take everything they have. We know they have to go to other people and we are flexible about this, but do expect them to prioritise us if we are finding fresh produce sourcing difficult'. Another retailer commented when asked if they feel they are working in a partnership with their suppliers, 'There is cooperation with all of them, but not collaboration with them all. Those we feel we collaborate with more we will reward in terms of volume. We will use suppliers who want to collaborate with us'.

One retailer's comment captures a winning exchange relationship by saying, 'From the supplier's point of view it gives confidence, security. There is a guarantee with a small grower. The business is going to benefit from this, with good returns, etc. From the retailer's point of view, we would develop stronger links with our supply base, and develop the relationship. You work together to help drive up sales of fresh produce. Suppliers and we work together to achieve sales'. The following recommendations can help pave the way for participating firms in the UK fresh produce chain.

Suppliers should do the following:

- Maintain high fresh produce quality and competitive pricing in collaboration with retailers.
- Offer innovative and unique fresh produce along with novel marketing concepts.
- Maintain regular communication with retailers to address any issues.
- Invest in technology and maximise efficiency to deliver top-quality fresh produce to retailers.

Retailers should perform the following:

- Utilise suppliers' expertise and product knowledge to overcome challenges in meeting targets.
- Emphasise regular communication with suppliers, preferably verbally.
- Collaborate with suppliers to address any quality and pricing concerns regarding fresh produce.
- Prioritise fair and meaningful partnerships and recognise suppliers who consistently provide high-quality fresh produce.

This case originates from Hingley, M. K., Lindgreen, A., and Casswell, B. (2005). Supplier-retailer relationships in UK fresh produce supply chain. *Journal of International Food & Agribusiness Marketing* 18(1/2): 49–86. Here, the reader can also find additional relevant references to the case and its topic.

Case study 2: Configurations of purchasing practices

Approximately 35 years ago, a significant transformation unfolded in purchasing and SCM across North America and Western Europe. This revolution shifted supplier relationships from adversarial and distant to closer and more collaborative, often integrated within broader networks involving suppliers, customers and stakeholders. Traditionally, purchasing prioritised individual transactions or short-term contracts, emphasising low prices. However, amid escalating global competition, organisations recognised the strategic value of purchasing and SCM for managing costs, risks and value.

In transactional exchanges, the purchasing organisation and its supplier perceive each other as adversaries in a zero-sum game, with no expectation of ongoing interaction beyond the current contract. In contrast, relational exchanges promote collaboration between the purchasing organisation and its supplier to achieve mutual benefits, involving commitments to specific investments and expectations extending beyond contract terms. This shift towards relational purchasing practices coincided with the emergence of a more strategic role for purchasing, requiring managers to establish integrative partnerships with key suppliers.

Prior studies often dichotomised purchasing practices into transactional and relational categories. However, contemporary practices typically incorporate elements of both, blending arm's-length transactions with close cooperative relationships with suppliers. Yet, managing cooperative relationships can be resource-intensive and increase buyer reliance on suppliers, making them unsuitable for all situations. Thus, it's essential to understand how and why buyers choose specific approaches, exploring their selection and combination of purchasing practices and their impact on organisational performance.

Assessing the impact of supply relationships on organisational performance necessitates measuring the nature and strength of purchasing relationships against specific performance metrics. The forthcoming framework allows managers to identify critical factors distinguishing different purchasing practices, particularly those related to execution and oversight, rather than within the purchasing function itself. Moreover, it facilitates the evaluation of hybrid forms of transactional and relational purchasing.

Purchasing practices framework

One crucial distinction lies in comparing a transaction-focused supply management strategy with one emphasising network coordination, including supply chain integration. Transactional purchasing involves aggressively seeking new suppliers for favourable terms, while network purchasing integrates the organisation within a broader network.

Two alternative practices are available: electronic purchasing and interactive purchasing. Electronic purchasing involves organisations utilising the internet and various one-to-one or one-to-many technologies to facilitate and manage data exchanges with suppliers. On the other hand, interactive purchasing entails direct personal interactions between employees and individual suppliers.

In the purchasing practices framework (see Table 8.8), each of the four practices significantly differs in how the buying organisation manages its relationships with suppliers. For example, communication frequency and interdependency levels vary between transactional purchasing and relational practices like electronic, interactive and network purchasing. Similarly, differences exist within these relational practices themselves.

Eight formative indicators are employed to delineate transactional and relational practices, as outlined in the table. Each purchasing practice can be identified based on a combination of these formative indicators. Additionally, the table incorporates a general indicator that encapsulates the core attributes of each purchasing practice.

The purchasing practices framework enables organisations to excel in specific areas, like excelling in both transactional and electronic purchasing while scoring lower in others. Alternatively, they may score high in relational practices while scoring low in transactional purchasing. Essentially, the four practices are not mutually exclusive. Frameworks categorising supplier relationships as solely type A or type B may overlook diverse existing types. For example, some organisations continuously seek new suppliers for optimal deals, while others combine this with relational approaches, using technologies for data exchange and fostering one-to-one relationships.

TABLE 8.8 Indicators pertaining to purchasing practices

Aspect	*Transactional perspective*	*Relational perspective*		
	Transaction purchasing	*Electronic purchasing*	*Interactive purchasing*	*Network purchasing*
Purpose of exchange: When dealing with our direct suppliers, our purpose is to	Achieve cost savings or other 'financial' measure(s) of performance (monetary transactions)	Create information-generating dialogue with many identified suppliers	Build a long-term relationship with specific supplier(s)	Form relationships with a number of organisations in our supply market(s) or wider purchasing system
Nature of communication: Our communication with direct suppliers can be characterised as	Our organisation using undifferentiated communications with all suppliers	Our organisation using technology to communicate with and possibly among many individual suppliers	Individuals at various levels in our organisation personally interacting with individual suppliers	Senior managers networking with other managers from a variety of organisations in our supply market(s) or wider purchasing system
Type of contact: Our organisation's contact with our direct suppliers is	Arm's-length, impersonal with no individualised or personal contact	Interactive via technology such as the internet	Interpersonal (e.g., involving one-to-one interaction between people)	Across firms in the broader network (from impersonal to interpersonal contact)
Duration of exchange: The type of contact with our direct suppliers is characterised as	Transactions that are discrete or one-off (i.e., not ongoing)	Technology-based interactivity that is ongoing and real-time	Interpersonal interaction that is ongoing	Contact with people in our organisation and wider purchasing system that is ongoing
Formality of exchange: When people from our organisation meet with our direct suppliers, it is	Mainly at a formal business level	Mainly at a formal level, yet customised and/or personalised via interactive technologies	At both a formal business level and an informal social level on a one-to-one basis	At both a formal business level and an informal social level in a wider organisational system/network

(*Continued*)

TABLE 8.8 (Continued)

Aspect	*Transactional perspective*	*Relational perspective*		
	Transaction purchasing	*Electronic purchasing*	*Interactive purchasing*	*Network purchasing*
Managerial intent: Our purchasing exchanges are intended to	Continuously search for new suppliers to find the best deal (i.e., low prices)	Create two-way, technology-enabled data exchanges with our suppliers	Develop cooperative relationships with our suppliers	Coordinate activities between ourselves, suppliers and other parties in our wider purchasing and supply system (e.g., second-tier suppliers, key customers, service providers and other organisations with which we interact through our purchasing activities)
Managerial focus: Our purchasing strategy is focused on issues related to	The purchase item and its price	Managing IT-enabled relationships with many individual suppliers	One-to-one relationships with suppliers, or individuals in supplier organisations we deal with	The network of relationships between individuals and organisations in our wider supply system
Managerial investment: Our purchasing resources (i.e., people, time and money) are invested in	Specifying products, negotiations, ordering and expediting activities	Operational assets (IT, website and logistics) and functional systems integration (e.g., purchasing with IT)	Establishing and building personal relationships with individual suppliers	Developing our organisation's network relationships within our supply market(s) or a wider purchasing system
General indicator: Overall, our organisation's general approach to our direct suppliers (of product-related items) involves	Using aggressive sourcing (continuously search for new suppliers) to obtain purchase items at the most favourable conditions	Using the internet and other interactive technologies to create and mediate data exchanges between our organisation and our suppliers	Developing personal interactions between employees and individual suppliers	Positioning our organisation within a wider organisational system or network

Notes: An additional aspect relating to the managerial level initially appeared in the framework ('In our organization, purchasing activities are carried out by: operational and tactical purchasers [transaction purchasing]; cross-functional buying teams, that is, purchasing specialists with technology specialists and possibly senior managers (electronic purchasing); many employees, that is, across functions and levels [interactive purchasing]; or the managing director or chief executive officer [network purchasing]'). This aspect was later discarded because (a) there was little support for such aspect in the literature and from discussions with practitioners and (b) it had poor external validity. As a complement to the support found in the literature, all practices were checked with both practitioners and academic experts.

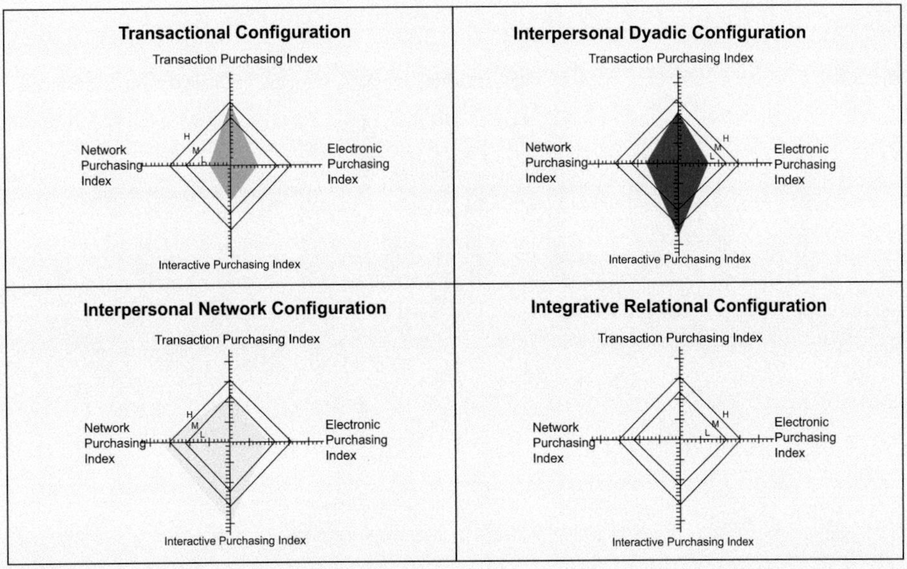

FIGURE 8.4 Four purchasing configurations

Each of the four purchasing practices (transaction, electronic, interactive and network purchasing) is evaluated against eight indicators (purpose of exchange, managerial intent, nature of communication, type of contact, duration of relationship, formality of exchange, managerial focus and investment). These indicators are combined into an index for each practice. As these practices are not mutually exclusive, organisations have their unique combination of scores across them.

Major configurations of purchasing practices

Lindgreen et al. (2013) identified four clusters, each with a unique mix of purchasing practices. One cluster excelled in transactional purchasing but scored low in electronic, interactive and network purchasing (refer to Figure 8.4), labelled as a transactional configuration. Another cluster excelled in electronic, interactive and network purchasing but scored low in transactional purchasing, termed an integrative relational configuration.

Two additional clusters have been identified, both with moderate scores on the transaction purchasing index. The first, termed the interpersonal dyadic configuration, emphasises interactive purchasing but scores lower on electronic and network purchasing. The second, known as the interpersonal network configuration, excels in both interactive and network purchasing but scores low on electronic purchasing.

The transactional and integrative relational configurations can be seen as opposites, with the interpersonal dyadic and interpersonal network configurations in between, as intermediate configurations, with moderate scores on the transaction purchasing index.

Relationships fostered via the internet and interactive technologies, or electronic purchasing, are most effective when combined with interactive and network purchasing. Notably, none of the clusters prioritise network purchasing over interactive purchasing.

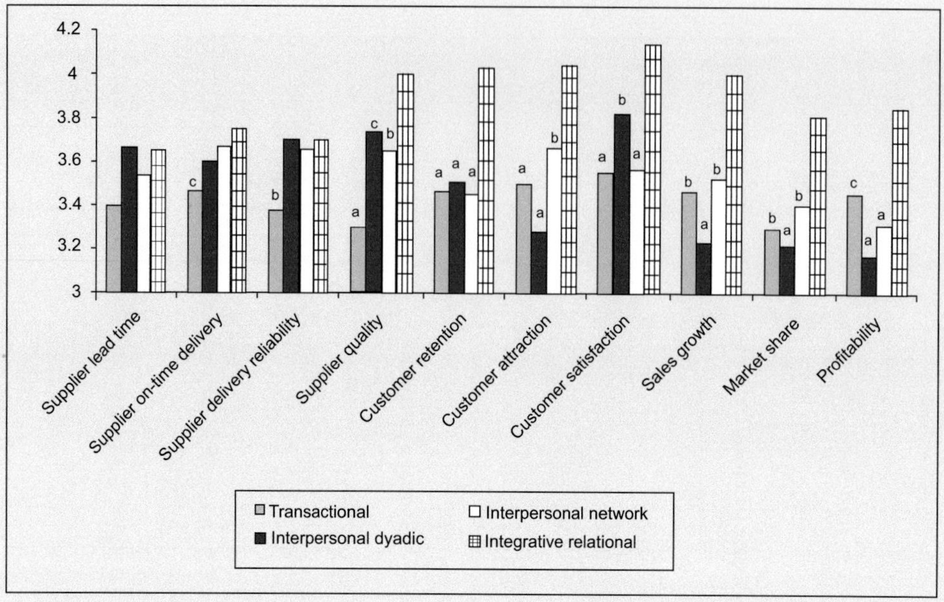

FIGURE 8.5 Differences in performance outcomes between purchasing configurations

Notes: The letters a, b, and c atop the bars signify inferior performance relative to the integrative relational configuration (depicted by the bar with squares on the right side of each group); a: the discrepancy is statistically significant at p1-tail <.01; b: it is significant at p1-tail <.05; and c: it is significant at p1-tail <.10.

Overall, many organisations exhibit pluralistic purchasing practices, often blending multiple approaches.

The study suggests that organisations adopting an integrative relational configuration for their purchasing practices show superior performance. Figure 8.5 compares three clusters with transactional, interpersonal dyadic and interpersonal network configurations to the cluster with an integrative relational configuration.

The comparison highlights that the integrative relational configuration outperforms all others in supplier quality. While it excels in supplier on-time delivery compared to transactional configurations, differences with intermediate configurations are minimal. However, all configurations show similar performance in supplier lead time.

The integrative relational configuration outperforms all others in marketing metrics like customer attraction and retention, satisfaction, sales growth and market share, as well as financial outcomes such as profitability.

Organisations using all three relational purchasing practices (termed integrative relational configuration) show superior performance across seven to nine out of ten metrics compared to those preferring less relational practices (interpersonal dyadic, interpersonal network, and transactional configurations). This superiority is observed across marketing, financial outcomes and up to three purchasing metrics.

The study found no significant differences in the demographics of clusters, such as industry, size, age or business activities. However, organisations with an integrative relational configuration tend to have higher technological intensity and a greater emphasis on the role of technology. In these organisations, information technology goes beyond facilitating current operations; it plays a pivotal role in redefining or driving business activities.

Finally, organisations generally employ more relational purchasing with direct suppliers and more transactional purchasing with indirect suppliers. Interactive purchasing and network purchasing are notably utilised when interacting with direct suppliers, while transactional purchasing is more prevalent with indirect suppliers. However, no significant difference was observed in the use of electronic purchasing across supplier types.

Managerial implications

The study highlights the significant advantage of organisations adopting an integrative relational configuration over others in terms of performance across purchasing, marketing and financial metrics. It underscores the importance of viewing purchasing and supply management as a strategic function, emphasising internal alignment and integration with other functions. Thus, organisations may benefit from fostering collaboration between marketing and purchasing, integrating technology with supplier interactions, investing in interpersonal relationships with suppliers, and managing the marketing–purchasing interface proactively.

The purchasing practices framework, depicted as a radar diagram, can function as a scorecard, providing a simple and accessible tool to monitor and evaluate purchasing configurations. It visually represents the blend of purchasing practices across four clusters of organisations.

An organisation can adapt the assessment tool for individual buyers by having them report on the suppliers they oversee. Scores for each purchasing practice can then be consolidated for each buyer, enabling managers to plot them on buyer-specific radar diagrams. Additionally, buyers often manage various purchasing categories, allowing organisations to assess each category separately and compare their management using radar diagrams. Similarly, multi-unit organisations can use radar diagrams to evaluate how business units manage their supply base.

The four aggregate scores for purchasing practices can be utilised for cluster analysis, especially when dealing with multiple buyers, categories or business units. While an organisation may have limited numbers of buyers or business units, the abundance of purchasing categories often warrants clustering. Using these scores, managers can create radar diagrams for each cluster, depicting the prevalence of each purchasing practice within the cluster, and assess performance outcomes accordingly.

A radar diagram, along with target benchmarks, facilitates focused discussions on strategy improvement by highlighting gaps between current and target levels. It also prompts consideration of resource reallocation for areas surpassing targets. This framework aids organisations in monitoring, evaluating and optimising purchasing practices across different dimensions like buyers, categories and business units, aiding in the selection of appropriate purchasing configurations.

Using performance outcome data, organisations can set strategies, aiding managers in informed decision-making regarding relationships with supplier groups. Goals for purchasing practices and performance outcomes emerge from strategy specification. Subsequently, tracking, monitoring and evaluating purchasing practices follow, akin to the initial mapping process. Managers can then review strategies and apply corrective measures if needed (strategy re-specification), conducted periodically for ongoing optimisation.

Analysing purchasing practices at the industry level mirrors the organisational level, with additional attention to evaluating indicators like direct versus indirect suppliers. This requires separate supplier clustering for chosen variables, adjusting subsequent steps accordingly. Industry-level analysis is commonly performed by entities like chambers of commerce, consulting firms or industry associations.

This case originates from Lindgreen, A., Vanhamme, J., van Raaij, E., and Johnston, W. J. (2013). Go configure: The mix of purchasing practices to choose for your supply base. *California Management Review* 55(2): 72–96. Here, the reader can also find additional relevant references to the case and its topic.

Multiple-choice questions

1. What is the primary goal of strategic sourcing in procurement?

   A. Minimising the number of suppliers
   B. Maximising short-term cost savings
   C. Aligning procurement activities with organisational goals
   D. Standardising product designs globally

2. Which element is NOT typically part of the strategic sourcing cycle?

   A. Supplier performance evaluation
   B. Market research and analysis
   C. Immediate contract termination for underperformers
   D. Negotiation and contracting

3. What is the primary purpose of a SWOT analysis in supplier selection?

   A. Benchmarking competitors' pricing strategies
   B. Identifying internal strengths/weaknesses and external opportunities/threats
   C. Calculating TCO
   D. Assessing supplier geopolitical risks

4. Which metric is most critical for evaluating supplier reliability?

   A. Annual revenue growth
   B. On-time delivery performance
   C. Employee turnover rate
   D. Marketing campaign effectiveness

5. What distinguishes collaborative supplier relationships from transactional ones?

   A. Focus on short-term cost reduction
   B. Joint innovation and risk-sharing

C. Frequent supplier rotation
D. Centralised decision-making

6. Which factor is LEAST relevant in supplier risk management?

   A. Financial stability of the supplier
   B. Supplier's branding strategy
   C. Geopolitical stability of supplier's location
   D. Supply chain redundancy plans

7. What is a key advantage of e-procurement over traditional methods?

   A. Reduced need for supplier audits
   B. Elimination of all contractual negotiations
   C. Streamlined order processing and transparency
   D. Guaranteed lowest prices for all purchases

8. Which criterion is most critical in supplier segmentation?

   A. Cultural alignment with the buyer
   B. Strategic importance and spend volume
   C. Geographical proximity to headquarters
   D. Annual marketing budget size

9. What is the primary focus of TCO analysis?

   A. Initial purchase price minimisation
   B. Long-term operational and hidden costs
   C. Supplier profit margins
   D. Environmental compliance expenses

10. How does supplier relationship management enhance procurement?

    A. By increasing supplier competition
    B. Through collaborative innovation and value creation
    C. By standardising all supplier contracts
    D. Through centralised inventory control

11. Which practice aligns marketing and procurement objectives?

    A. Isolated departmental budgeting
    B. Joint development of supplier sustainability criteria
    C. Separate supplier evaluation frameworks
    D. Independent demand forecasting

12. What is a key challenge in implementing green procurement practices?

    A. Reduced product quality standards
    B. Balancing environmental goals with cost efficiency

C. Elimination of global suppliers
D. Overemphasis on short-term savings

13. Which factor is critical for successful global supplier integration?

A. Homogeneous regulatory frameworks
B. Cross-cultural communication competence
C. Centralised production facilities
D. Fixed pricing strategies

14. What is the main purpose of supplier scorecards?

A. To rank suppliers based on lowest bids
B. To standardise supplier marketing materials
C. To quantitatively evaluate supplier performance
D. To eliminate long-term contracts

15. Which trend has most impacted modern procurement practices?

A. Decreased use of digital tools
B. Rise of sustainability-driven supplier criteria
C. Reduced focus on risk management
D. Decline in global trade agreements

Essay questions

Analyse the interdependencies among strategic sourcing, supplier relationship management and e-procurement in achieving procurement excellence. Discuss how these elements collectively address three critical challenges: (a) aligning procurement with organisational strategy, (b) mitigating supply chain risks and (c) balancing cost efficiency with sustainability goals. Provide specific examples of how integrated procurement strategies can enhance both marketing outcomes (e.g., brand reputation) and supply chain resilience.

9

TYPICAL APPROACHES OF MARKETING AND SUPPLY CHAIN MANAGEMENT SYNERGIES

Introduction

This chapter presents the main practices and methods applied by companies to treat demand. Companies demand the contribution by the managers of the marketing and sales department, as well as those from the logistics and supply chain management (SCM) department in their entirety. Practices such as just-in-time (JIT), vendor-managed inventory, efficient consumer response, collaborative planning forecasting and replenishment and lean thinking are typical approaches for keeping organisations as competitive as today's market demands.

Learning objectives

After reading this chapter, you will be able to answer the following questions:

- How are the practices JIT, vendor-managed inventory, efficient consumer response, collaborative planning forecasting and replenishment, and lean thinking defined, and how do they operate in a modern business environment?
- How significant is the contribution by marketing and SCM to the fruitful and successful application of the practices above?

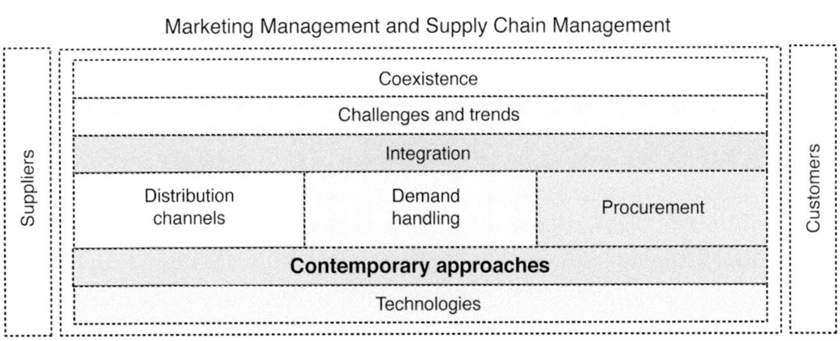

DOI: 10.4324/9781003650973-9

Outline

9.1 Just-in-time

Introduction

In recent decades, most multinational companies, such as Toyota, BMW, Fiat, General Motors, Hewlett Packard, Harley Davidson, Rank Xerox, General Electric, Digital Equipment and IBM, have successfully adopted and applied the *just-in-time* (JIT) philosophy.

JIT expresses the opposite philosophy of *just-in-case*. Resources are acquired at the time of demand (in time) and on schedule in case they are needed. The basic principles are the following:

- The key objective is to minimise inventories and to reduce all types of waste inside the organisation or business.
- The receipt of materials (raw materials or semi-finished products) from suppliers is performed whenever such materials are to be processed, that is, when they are required (at which point only the quantity of goods demanded by the market is produced), while the assembly of the final products is performed only when they are to be delivered to customers.
- Only a small number of suppliers are required, although collaboration with them is on a long-term basis, resting on stringent agreements, while they are frequently located nearby, so as to attain fast replenishment.

The advantages ensuing from the successful application of JIT philosophy practices are the reduction of production and operating costs in general, due to the limitation of inventories; less requirements in terms of materials (raw materials and semi-finished products) and labour; and the limitation of order returns. Moreover, there is also an improvement of product quality due to the high quality of the raw materials, the production process and the final products, as well as the strict agreements with suppliers. Finally, there is the improvement of the level of service for customers, by ensuring flexibility in product delivery and there are no defective products.

Conceptual approach: definition and key features

Initially, JIT referred to the production of final products with accuracy, in terms of time and of quantity and quality sufficient to satisfy demand. Today, JIT is a philosophy recommending methods and tools to attain perfection in a company, that is, aiming for continuous improvement via the continuous elimination of waste. It, of course, does not include only the production line but all activities for the production of the final product, from design to the delivery of the final product, including all corresponding logistics and supply chain stages. It aims, for example, to principally decrease flow times both with respect to production and with respect to the lead time from suppliers and towards customers. JIT philosophy is not something new. Its key principles and ideas originate in the past, and it is simply an improved approach implementing older theories and applications.

In general, just-in-time

- proposes the pull system;
- aims to eliminate waste;
- aims to increase the need for quality of products;
- aims to minimise or even eliminate the inventory;
- proposes the employee-driven nature and
- is based on automation.

These features may be also considered as the principles of the JIT philosophy. Each of these components is discussed in more detail in the following sections.

JIT proposes the pull system

JIT recommends a materials' control system (raw materials, semi-final and final products) by which a link (member) of a supply chain, a part of the production line of a company and, in general, a user signal the supplier, manufacturer or provider that some material is required. Only then does the latter send this material (precisely at the right time, neither earlier nor later, and, furthermore, at precisely the right quantity thereof, no more or less). In such a case, products are produced only when there is demand, and it is for this reason that this system is called produce for demand. In the opposite case (push system – make-to-stock), suppliers, manufacturers and providers supply, manufacture or dispatch materials based on a predefined schedule. This usually ensues either from demand forecast or from the material requirement planning (MRP) system. The issue arises from the fact that such forecasts can frequently be erroneous, resulting in losses for the business.

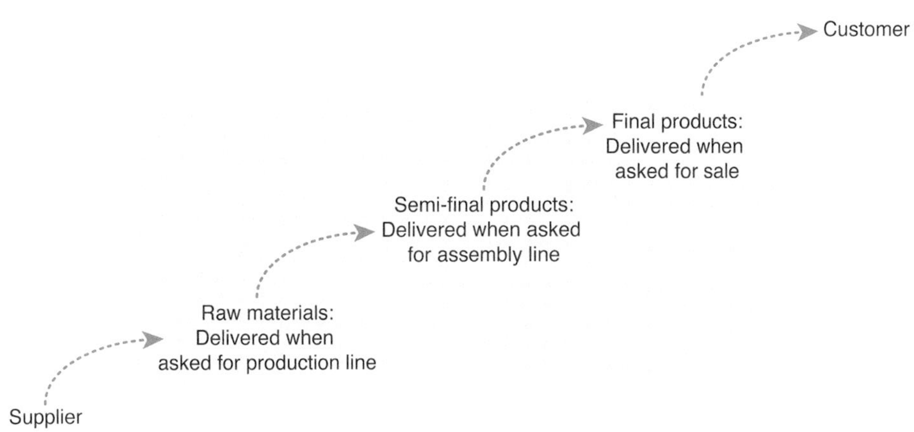

FIGURE 9.1 JIT proposes the pull material control system

In a make-to-order system, the manufacturer does not produce products unless such have been requested of him by his client. The goal of this system is to produce products ready for consumption. The receipt of the product by the customer is immediate from the moment its manufacture is completed. Consequently, each element of the JIT system is produced only at the stage and in the quantity required.

JIT aims to eliminate waste

Waste is a fundamental principle of JIT (and lean thinking philosophy, which will be analysed later on). Any activity or action that does not add value to the product is a form of waste and must be eliminated or minimised. For example, in the warehouse, the customer pays for his/her order execution; everything else must be minimised! Waste includes materials, time and effort spent on the production process and creates cost.

Waste is divided into seven categories (Cheng and Podolsky 1993):

- *Waste from overproduction:* The inventory and investment beyond customer demand. Overproduction is referred to as 'just in case'.
- *Waste of motion:* These motions are the handling and movement caused by overproduction.
- *Transportation wastes:* These result from inefficient plant or cell layout.
- *Processing wastes:* These are processing of some parts unnecessary for production completion or those that do not add value to products.
- *Waste of waiting or queuing time:* This might be caused by inefficient workflow and bottlenecks. This idle time causes increase in production cycle time.
- *Product defect:* These are the products that do not match quality qualifications. This will decrease when inspection work for quality is improved and strengthened.
- *Inventory cost:* Holding inventory costs money through space occupation, extra handling, damage and obsolescence.

The above seven wastes (originated in Japan) are known as 'muda'. They have been categorised by Taiichi Ohno, the father of the Toyota Production System (TPS).

JIT philosophy recommends the following for each of the aforementioned wastes:

- *Waste from overproduction:* JIT is based on the following simple concept: 'Schedule and produce only what can be immediately sold and/or shipped'. This also creates the need for machine changeover/set-up capability. In order for small batches to be produced (so as for there to be no case of producing unneeded quantities), various changes must be affected very fast. It is, thus, imperative that the times for preparing from change to change be as brief as possible so as not to lose valuable time and capacity.
- *Waste of motion:* Due to the precision in the manufacture of products, there are no moves wasted to and from the warehouses and, consequently, no waste of time or energy. JIT proposes the analysis, redesign and improvement of the excessive motions with the involvement of personnel.
- *Transportation wastes:* JIT recommends mapping product flows to determine which processes should be next to each other. Every work station in a JIT system must be ready to serve the next. Consequently, service times should be short or even zero.

- *Processing wastes:* Every workstation/link of the supply chain aims to replenish the stock consumed by the next so as to always be ready to feed the next link with as much supply as it needs and with respect to a specific material. JIT recommends the use of low-cost automation and flexible equipment; creating manufacturing cells while combining steps will greatly reduce the waste of inappropriate processing.
- *Waste of waiting or queuing time:* JIT proposes for processes to be smoothly performed without delays. Linking processes together so that one feeds directly into the next can dramatically reduce waiting. It also caters for the high availability of available resources (e.g., machinery). Given that existing stock is limited, any misfire in the equipment would probably interrupt production and would cause great delays and problems.
- *Product defect:* JIT demands and supports zero number of defective products. A defective product can cause delays in the productive procedure for it to be replaced. When combined with low inventories, this can create the need, on the one hand and initially, for continuous process improvement (CPI), that is, for everything to be produced correctly from the start, and, on the other hand, the existence of strict specifications and clauses on the products offered by suppliers.
- *Inventory cost:* JIT proposes the seamless flow between work centres to improve customer service and slash inventories and their associated costs.

The purpose of JIT is to utilise the minimum possible quantity of equipment, materials and human resources to satisfy demand. With proper maintenance and personnel training, as recommended by JIT, production idle times can be minimised, and the business does not need to buy back-up equipment. Defective products, which demand time and money to be repaired, must be eradicated. Moreover, stock that causes cost increases must also be decreased.

JIT aims to increase the need for quality of products

A critical success factor for JIT is total quality management (TQM). What this means in practice is that 'the importance and need for quality exists in all departments of a company but also extends to its transactions with suppliers'. To attain this goal, quality control processes need to be performed by all members of an organisation. When faults are detected (e.g., a defective product), their cause is established and corrected/repaired as soon as possible. This means that suppliers and the other members of the supply chain must comply with the required and pre-agreed specifications. A principal role for the attainment of the above is played by the mechanisms for the immediate detection of defective or low-quality materials (and of course of the source from which they originate). Consequently, TQM is the integrated commitment for the continuous improvement of products and processes, which is manifested with the participation of everybody so as to absolutely satisfy the ascertained present and future needs of customers.

The general TQM principles are as follows: total quality shapes and drives modern management practices with the following characteristics: the centre of gravity is moved from production to customer needs; communication is now (based on the hierarchy pyramid) from below to above and has assumed the form of a contributory procedure rather than an order; the system becomes horizontal and everybody collaborates with the best service of the consumer as their end objective; everybody participates in decision-making; the assignment of authority and responsibilities between departments is a material imperative; work groups assume some of the departments' roles; employees are trained across different sectors and the subject of their work becomes more flexible.

JIT has proposed several tools or methods to increase the need for quality of products and these can be grouped into three categories:

- creating ideas;
- organising data and
- recognising problems.

Each of these is discussed in more depth below.

Tools for creating ideas

In this category, one finds tools for reading, investigating and presenting (mostly illustrating graphically) problems as well as their possible causes. The goal is to detect their operative events fully and with clarity, a fact that will lead to their timely and effective treatment. The following are the principal tools:

- *Control document:* Every document designed to enter data, for example, a document presenting types of customer complaints.
- *Cartesian chart:* The chart shows the possible relation between two variables, for example, the productivity of the sales department in relation to personnel absences.
- *Cause and effect diagram:* This is a simple technique for assessing a situation and is a good tool to analyse complex problems that are affected by a series of factors. These diagrams provide a useful framework and structure to assess qualitative information, which also includes the human factor. More specifically, a cause and effect diagram is a very useful tool to recognise, explore and graphically illustrate all of the possible causes of a problem so as to render the detection of its operating event possible. Its key advantage is that it helps the team focus on the causes and not the symptoms of the problem. This diagram is also known as the Ishikawa or fishbone diagram since it looks like a fishbone. It is a type of diagram that helps in the analysis of causal relations and the detection of causes for a specific problem and with respect to people, materials, equipment, methods, etc. (see Figure 9.2).

Tools for the organisation of data

The tools of this category are techniques for the organisation of errors, problems or defects as well as the analysis of processes and workflows. They aim to focus on the issue. The following are the tools of this category:

- *Process analysis:* A key feature of quality is to view the activities of an organisation as processes that include inputs and outputs. The key processes of the organisation are initially detected to be analysed and improved so as to maximise productivity and quality. Before, however, a process is measured and evaluated, it must be understood. Process analysis is performed using a simple chart, which detects the key characteristics of a process (Figure 9.3).

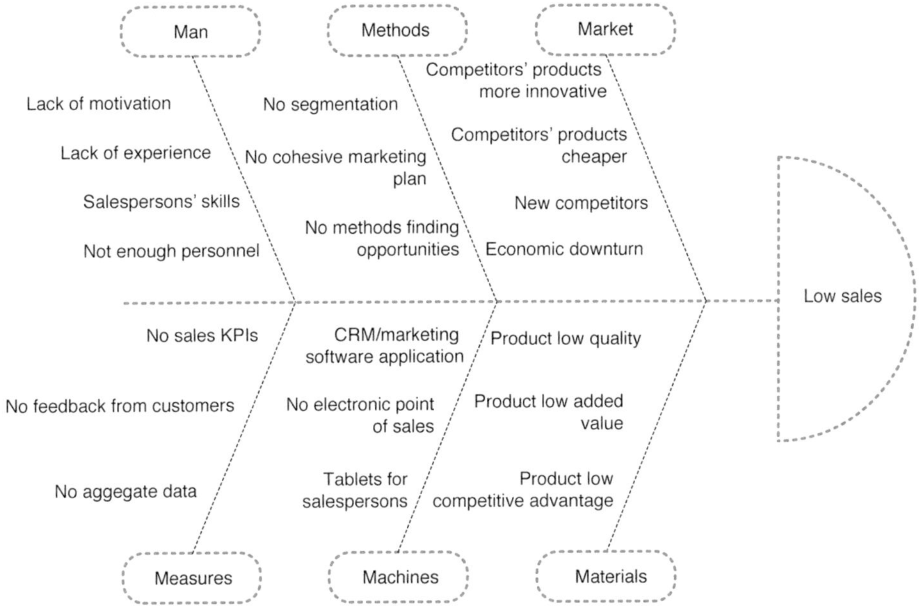

FIGURE 9.2 Fishbone diagram example

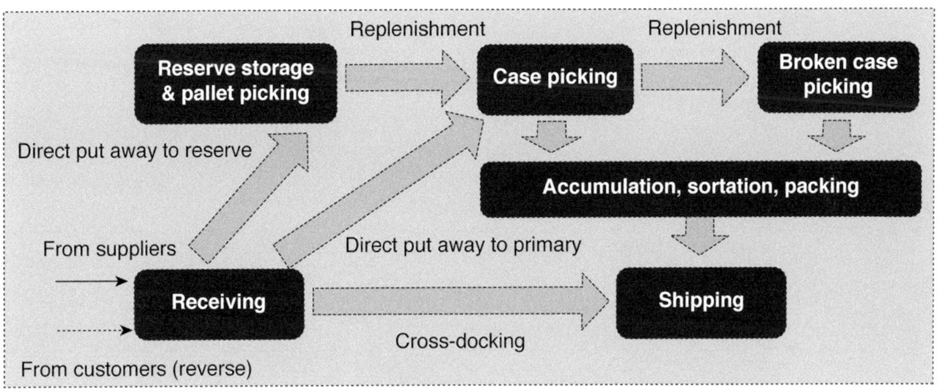

FIGURE 9.3 Process analysis diagram example

- *Flowcharts:* A flowchart traces the flow of information, customers, employees, equipment and materials in a process (Figure 9.4).
- *Pareto charts:* These constitute a method to organise errors, issues or defects, which helps focus on the problem. They are based on Pareto's law that cites that in almost every case, roughly 80% of the problems are due to 20% of the causes. The Pareto chart is a tool widely used to illustrate the results of the analysis for the detection of the more important causes. A Pareto chart graphically presents the relevant frequency or gravity of the causes of a problem, depicting in a simple way how important the effects of a cause are in the creation of a problem compared to the other causes, as well as the percentage improvement that the eradication of each cause would bring. In the chart below, for example, one can see the reasons

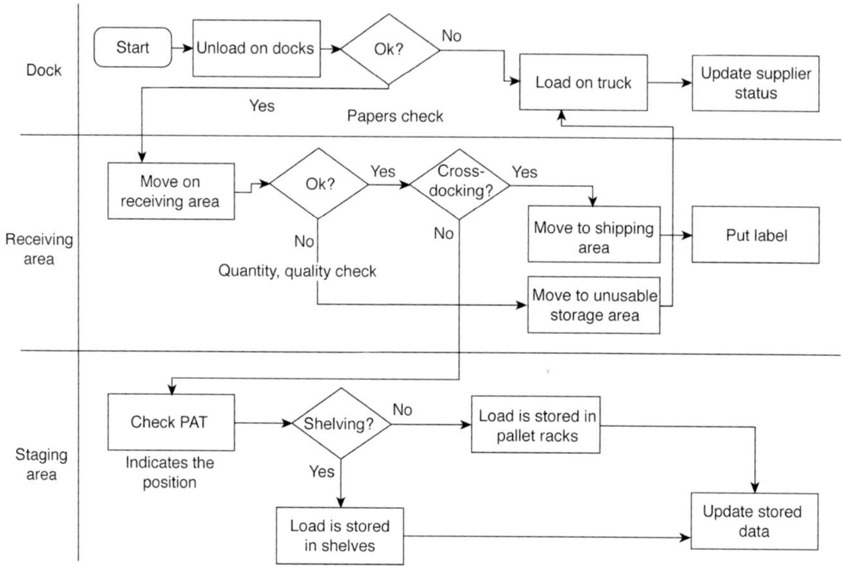

FIGURE 9.4 Flowchart diagram example

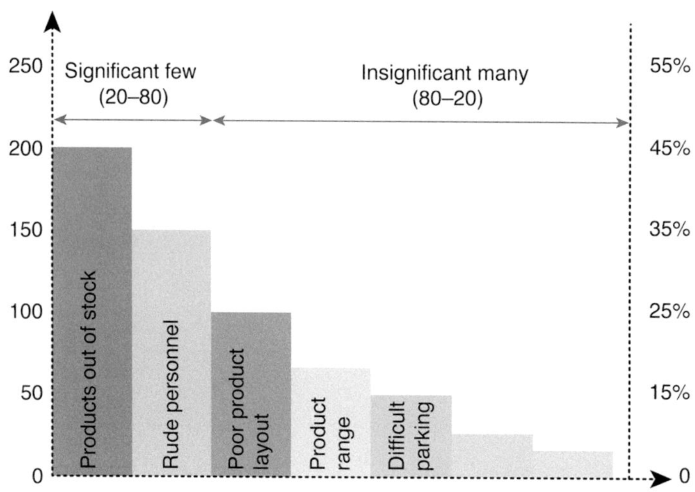

FIGURE 9.5 Pareto chart example

and frequency of the appearance of the causes of a problem on the complaint forms of a shop in a retail chain (Figure 9.5).

Tools for the recognition of problems

Tools for the recognition of problems are employed to record the quality when the product is being produced. They rest on tools and techniques from statistics. These tools offer the capability to a control system to detect products that are not compliant with a prescribed specification easily and at a low cost and thus to activate the processes of the indicated corrective actions that will maintain quality at a competitive level. The quality control includes, among others, the specification of the permissible level for the quality features of the products and measures the performance of the productive process with respect to these.

- More specifically, statistical process control (SPC) consists of a set of methods for the analysis of statistical data aiming to measure, control and maintain processes to fixed quality targets towards their continuous improvement. A primary tool used for SPC is the control chart, which is a graphical representation of certain descriptive statistics for specific quantitative measurements of the process. These descriptive statistics are depicted on the control chart compared to their sampling distributions under control. The comparison detects any unusual fluctuation in the production process, which could exhibit a problem in the process. Control charts have also been used to measure products with the purpose of analysing the capacity of the process and for the CPI efforts. All control charts have three key ingredients: (a) a line across their centre (usually the mathematical average of all samples collected); (b) higher and lower statistical control limits that determine limitations and (c) performance data presented along a time axis. An example of a control chart is shown in Figure 9.6.
- What is checked in control charts? The purpose of this diagrammatic illustration is to assess fluctuations, tracing their special causes and observing their behaviour. The warning limits are used together with some 'rules', which describe contingencies associated with the appearance of special patterns on a control chart. When the contingency described by the rule takes place, it is considered that the process is out of control without necessarily having some point on the chart outside the control limits (upper control level (UCL) and lower control level (LCL)). The benefits of this type of chart may be summarised as follows: it provides supervision and feedback so as for processes to be constantly checked; a problem is revealed in a process when said problem appears; and it traces the causes of fluctuations, decreases the need for inspection, monitors the quality of the process and provides the mechanism to effect changes to the process while also checking the results of such changes.

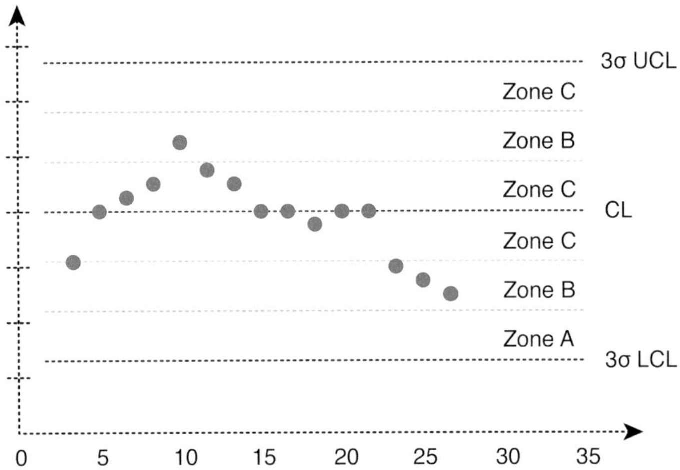

FIGURE 9.6 Control chart example

JIT aims to minimise or even eliminate the inventory

The management of inventories is an important function of the logistics system or the logistics systems of the members in a supply chain. The concept of inventory is general and not limited to the case of raw materials, products and merchandise but covers a wide spectrum of economic phenomena. The decisions taken bear on the success of the systems and the associated enterprises in general. These decisions establish, on the one hand, the level of inventories that must be maintained and, on the other hand, when these inventories must be renewed. For businesses implementing a JIT philosophy, the decisions aim to maintain the precise quantity required and to be replenished exactly when necessary.

Of course, the objectives are the same also in this case: to provide a high level of service at the lowest possible cost. And as these rules cannot in general be attained in the maximum degree but a balance is sought after, also in the case of JIT management of inventories, what is required is a balance between the cost of out-of-stock and that of the surplus of a product. Correct planning and control of inventory management will effectively deal with fluctuations in demand and maintain a smooth production flow, providing a high level of service and decreasing costs.

The JIT philosophy with respect to inventory management was originally focused on the production of final products, while its original aim was to minimise inventories with the ultimate objective of lowering cost. In recent years and within the context of the lean philosophy, the effort to minimise inventories focuses on a set of activities:

- Nullification of safety inventories: It is a fact that both industrial companies, for fear of machine malfunctions, and trade companies, for fear of steep increases in demand for specific codes, were led to maintain significant safety inventories in order for production not to stop or to fully satisfy demand correspondingly. In the case of JIT, the idea is quite the opposite. No safety inventories are maintained since this could mean defective products or hiding a bad supplier. The aim is to continuously produce good products on the first attempt and without errors.
- Strict control of products received by the company that falls under the relations between the company and its suppliers implemented by JIT. The supplier knows that the company or customer does not maintain high levels of inventories and that if defective products are dispatched, it will affect the capacity of its production lines, something that will incur great losses with respect to both service and operating cost. This fact creates the need for a new perception and philosophy for the management of the relations with suppliers with the following key features:
- The company must treat its suppliers as associates, compatriots and not opponents. Consequently, the success of the suppliers 'passes through' the success of the company (sharing risks and benefits).
- Suppliers are close to production lines/points of sales not only for response times to be small but also known (or better, reliably calculable).
- Suppliers have access to the data that relate to demand at production lines/points of sales.
- There is a small supplying basis where in most cases there are one or two suppliers for each code. With fewer suppliers, a company has better control since the order is usually larger and it can, thus, attain scale economies and have greater requirements succeeding in imposing even stricter specifications.
- To attain the above, a company implementing JIT philosophy pursues the creation and maintenance of long-term collaborative relations with its suppliers.

JIT proposes the employee-driven nature

JIT considers the workforce to be the most important business resource. How does this translate to action and what are the ensuing results? Employees have the greatest responsibility not only with respect to the execution but also for the control of the work flow. They also actively participate both in the improvement of business processes and in the quality of the products and services rendered. This responsibility burdens not only senior corporate management but also the lowest administrative level of the company, and for something like this to occur, the management of the company must, of course, shape a working environment that contributes towards the equal participation of everybody and the uninterrupted improvement of the entire system for production and distribution.

The results of this philosophy are fewer and better trained personnel (indeed employees must be trained appropriately so as to be able to handle and operate many machines simultaneously, to transfer from one work station to some other when and where necessary, and to deal with ensuing problems in an expedient manner), while the organisational structure chart proposes less management levels, encouraging horizontal collaboration between employees.

JIT is based on automation

Specifically, JIT is based on automated machines so that one employee can operate more than one machine simultaneously, and because these machines are able to perform problem diagnosis by themselves, delays are avoided that will interrupt the smooth and continuous flow of the productive procedure. The philosophy recommends the implementation of techniques such as knowledge bases. Employees can consult them to resolve potential problems and questions. This automation supports the human-centred nature of companies advocating the JIT philosophy, as it is also supported by the appropriate informational systems that allow employees from all levels to take decisions fast. The same applies in the implementation of intra-corporate communication and the electronic exchange of data between the business and its principal associates.

Pros and cons

When all of the above are successfully implemented, the company adopting them will attain the following:

- High productivity that is attributed to higher reliability, decrease of waste and flexibility of productive processes.
- Better customer service on account of the speed, reliability and flexibility in the execution of orders with a minimum percentage of defective products.
- Lower operating costs due to the decrease in stock and control procedures.
- High quality, which is a continuous effort and the responsibility of all employees and not just quality control executives (total quality management).
- Better use of human resources (and all resources in general), which also encourages its qualitative upgrading.
- Long-term collaborations and win–win relations with suppliers and other members of the supply chain.
- Supports the aims of marketing and SCM to provide the highest possible level of customer service by attaining immediate times for order taking and the delivery of products.

TABLE 9.1 Connecting production with marketing to adopt JIT

Function	*Recommended action*
Production	Costing of product production and the complexity thereof in order to satisfy the particular need of the customers at a profit for the company
Relations with suppliers	Seeking and concluding long-term relationships with suppliers who can make frequent and in-time deliveries whenever needed and can supply high-quality materials and semi-finished products
Relations with customers	Communication and collaboration with customers for a fixed (when possible) rate of orders and production. Additionally, the promotion to the market of the business's environmentally friendly activities through the enforcement of waste-reducing measures

All the above increase the competitiveness of the business and must be appropriately exploited by the marketing and sales department. This requires the coordination of all departments involved and the performance of appropriate actions. Specifically, Table 9.1 presents the actions by the marketing and sales department in support of a JIT philosophy in a productive enterprise.

The advantages of a JIT system are not always immediately obvious. They require time and the support of the company's senior management. On many occasions, production costs may increase for a business, while changes in the way work is carried out and in the culture of employees, the redesign and restructuring or even redistribution of competences, etc., can lead to results that are initially not positive for the business. But even with respect to supply chains, key findings by many studies reveal that supply chains are a complex system that cannot be explained from a single perspective but rather require a more integrated and versatile approach. JIT practices can probably lead to positive business performance, but many factors play a role that may impede the process, while others may diminish its impact on profitability. Furthermore, while low-level inventory plays a critical role in today's economy, some of its issues can also be criticised. The main objective of low-level inventory is reducing inventories to minimise costs and maximise profits. According to many research efforts, it is proven that simply reducing inventories on its own is not enough. To remain competitive in an ever-changing and ever-competitive business environment, a manufacturer must strive for continuous improvement. Moreover, one must understand that customers do not any longer wait to purchase a product if they cannot find it; they will immediately buy the available substitute of a competitor's product. Therefore, regardless of how much a firm exerts efforts to compress its inventory levels to reduce costs and improve profits, these efforts can be eroded if the competitor's product reaches the market first. In other words, theories that support cost reduction and improved profitability because of inventory-level reductions are true, but sometimes only to a certain extent (Folinas et al. 2017).

The disadvantages and possible problems that may follow from the implementation of JIT practices may be summarised as follows:

- In markets wherein demand fluctuates during economic crises, risks for the company are high and it must deal with them in the best manner possible. Steep changes in demand, the closure of productive units or their relocation in neighbouring or distant countries, etc., create an economic environment that does not favour the application of the JIT philosophy, or, in the best-case scenario, time is required for a company to recover to its previous satisfactory state.

- It is difficult for a business to find suitable suppliers that will decide to resupply the company with frequent routes (i.e., with smaller and more frequent orders), to agree to strict clauses with respect to the quality of the materials they will supply or even to move their distribution centres, warehouses, etc., close to the company (the JIT system transfers many responsibilities from the buyer to the supplier). This happens because when distance between the company and its suppliers increases, the delivery times can become more irregular and less predictable.
- The personnel oppose the system. Employees lose their autonomy in the new recommended function, and since they are now treated as a group that must collaborate and not as individuals, they, thus, become less flexible, and this necessitates increased responsibilities and obligations and continuous training.

9.2 Efficient consumer response

Efficient consumer response (ECR) philosophy consists of a set of practices that, assisted by technology (the internet in particular), allows for a close collaboration between the members of a supply chain (and retail in particular) so as to better satisfy consumers' needs, faster and at the lowest possible cost.

In its basic form, the ECR system includes two key functions:

- *The demand side*, which focuses on the development, introduction and promotion of new products by a company that may cater for consumers' needs. Required for this, just as in supply side, is the coordination of all promotional processes for the product, from production until final consumption.
- *The supply side,* which focuses on all points on the supply chain/physical distribution (and the manufacturer's or supplier's warehouse in particular, the distributor's distribution centre, the retail store and the end consumer) that must exchange information and apply effective methods of inventory management to ensure the continuous replenishment of stock and immediate response to the needs of customers and consumers.

These two parts connect the two worlds (those of marketing and of the supply chain) in the best manner possible and operate in direct relation and dependence to one another. Coopers and Lybrand (1996) tried to describe this relation by identifying two barriers: firstly, barriers among internal functions (sales/marketing and production/distribution), and, secondly, barriers among supply chain partners (production/distribution and logistics/stock management). The authors argued that it is the 'enabling technologies' factor that can break down barriers between them.

- *Category management*: This is the demand side of the system aiming to effectively create demand and includes the following activities: product introduction, product promotions and store assortment (continuous presence of a range of products at points of sale, e.g., shelves). These activities cannot be realised unless the members of the supply chain integrate both their internal activities and their external/inter-corporate processes and use their joint capabilities to maximise consumer value. Enabling technologies, as well as communication media, can help attain this goal.
- *Product replenishment:* This regards the supply side of the system. As was mentioned above, the goal is the smooth transportation of products from the production point to the shelves of

the retail seller and the satisfaction of the market, the demand of which is constantly fluctuating while being difficult to predict. Enabling technologies, as well as standardisation of information, can assist in the attainment of this goal.

- *Enabling technologies:* These technologies cater for the exchange of business information both between the various parts of the businesses – members of the supply chain – and among them. They aim to overcome obstacles both for internal functions and for supply chain partners so that they can function effectively and efficiently and perform category management and product replenishment. The point of sales plays a significant role. It is at this point that the necessary data that will effectively support category management and product replenishment are collected, while enabling technologies ensure the uninterrupted flow of information from and to the point of sales (Figure 9.7).

The production and distribution of products rests principally on the data collected at the points of sales in a full application of the pull system. The data collected can assist the decision-making process with respect to planning and forecasting, inventory management, and distribution planning and scheduling. Moreover, the exchange of information in real time by utilising modern IT systems and technologies (e.g., EDI, EPOS and auto ID technologies such as barcodes, QR codes, etc.) and the automation of logistics processes by using common unit load and pallet standardisation contribute to the automation of logistics systems and to the efficient management of the supply chain in general; to decrease complexity, cost and out-of-stock; to best deal with intense fluctuations in demand and to increase customer service and satisfaction levels.

It was noted at the beginning of the section that the ECR philosophy includes a set of practices. In the following sections, we examine what these practices are and how they operate in action.

Continuous replenishment programme

The main characteristic of the continuous replenishment programme (CRP) is the resupply of products in real time and only for the quantity in demand. In its full form, there is no predefined reorder point nor is there a mathematical formula applicable for the calculation of the quantity of the reorder. A simple example to understand the ECR method is the requirement for potable tap water. The moment one requires a specific quantity of water is the moment you consume it.

Of course, this cannot be implemented to the maximal extent on account of place-gap (and the corresponding time-gap) between manufacturers, distributors and stores. What happens in practice is the continuous monitoring of sales at point of sales. As soon as quantity verges on

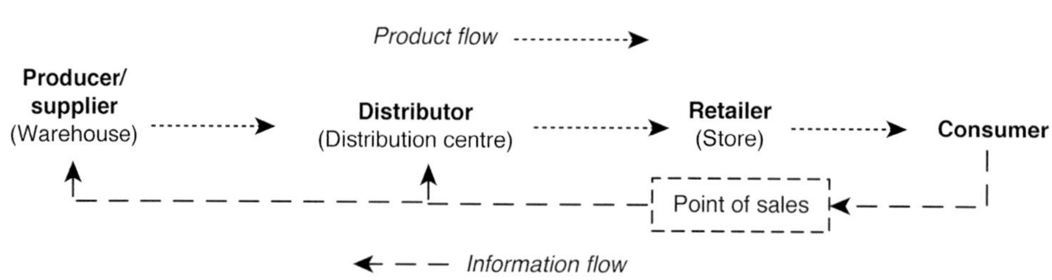

FIGURE 9.7 ECR modules

the order point or the basic inventory as designated by the store, a quantity equal to economic order quantity (EOQ) is reordered. In order for ECR to be successfully and efficiently applied, the entire supply chain must coordinate, being also assisted by the sales department, which will promote certain codes.

Computer-assisted ordering

Computer-assisted ordering provides a cost-effective method by which retailers can accurately predict consumer demand. It aims to tackle two of the most difficult and labour-intensive functions: ordering and consumer response replenishment cycles, as well as controlling inventory.

Cross-docking

Cross-docking is the practice via which the products received are not stored (a fact that is a distinguishing feature of old-school logistics systems) but are transferred from one means of transportation (e.g., truck) to another. Consequently, products transported via trucks (in this case inbound trucks (ITs)) to the entry gates (inbound doors (IDs)) are then unloaded, classified according to the order to which they belong and then loaded onto trucks once more (outbound trucks (OTs)) and pass through the exit gates (outbound doors (ODs)), to be transported to the end receivers (Figure 9.8).

Each IT transfers products from one supplier that are destined for different retail shops, while every OT contains products from different suppliers destined for the same retail shop. The intermediate storage time for the cargo is 24 hours, but most of the time this does not exceed 1 hour. This results in faster delivery of the products to the end customer but also the decrease in storage (the stock kept is zero or close to zero) and transportation costs. Moreover, in the case of third-party logistics (3PL), the provider can store more products and service more customers.

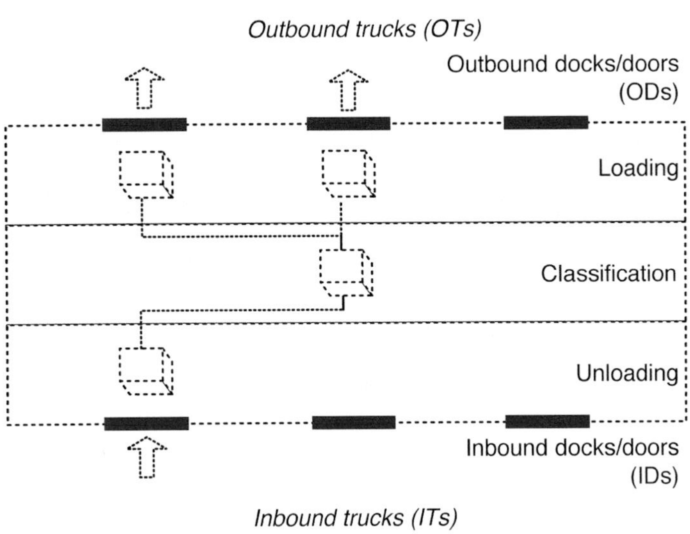

FIGURE 9.8 How does cross-docking work?

Direct store delivery

Merchandisers are the key actors of direct store delivery (DSD). They operate as agents of established and widely circulated products (e.g., carbonated beverages, fresh produce, bread and baked goods, milk, snacks, packaged meat, cheese, beer, frozen foods and candy) that visit every shop on an almost daily basis. Trained employees of the shops monitor the consumption of the products on the shelves and the levels of their stock in the shops' storage facilities. The same individuals are also aware of consumer attitudes and trends, and also have access to a lot of useful sales data that are kept in databases and operational informational systems.

This procedure allows for the fast replenishment of products consumed in large quantities and which have a strong category performance. It is only fair that DSD is considered today as the most effective method that caters for quicker sensing of customer preferences (what customers are buying) at the shelf (i.e., characterised by changing demographics and lifestyle as well as localised assortments), while it streamlines order-to-delivery processes for more responsive delivery to minimise store out-of-stock conditions.

The efficient implementation of a DSD system also requires common collaborative practices and tools, the most significant of which are (a) joint-value creation meetings between the principal suppliers and the retail chain, with the main items on their agendas being product pricing, promotional activities for new and old products, codification of consumer behaviours, the needs in replenishing and resupply, etc.; (b) networking infrastructure for data sharing, data gathered by POS and wireless technologies; and (c) common developed key performance measurement indicators (for marketing/and supply chain operations) for achieving continuous monitoring and pursuing alignment of activities to foster successful relationships among suppliers and sales companies. It is recommended that partners use standard performance definitions and measures.

Activity-based costing

Over the last few decades, a new costing approach has emerged: activity-based costing (ABC). ABC is a method for developing cost estimations in which the project is subdivided into discrete, quantifiable activities or a work unit (Hatzis et al. 2011). Thus, according to the same authors, the activity must be definable clearly, where productivity can be measured in units (e.g., number of orders processed versus man-hours). The next step is the cost estimation for each activity regarding all labour, materials, equipment and subcontracting costs, including overheads, for each activity. Finally, each complete individual estimate is added to the others to obtain an overall estimate. ABC is a powerful tool, but it is not appropriate for all cost estimates as ABC methodology is used when a project can be divided into defined activities.

9.3 Vendor-managed inventory

According to vendor-managed inventory (VMI), the responsibility for the planning, execution and completion of orders and the resupply of stock lies with and is assumed by the manufacturer or supplier and not the company or client. In order, of course, for this to be possible, the supplier must be granted access to the client's data and specifically the levels of his inventory, his sales and the orders he receives. The supplier is responsible for the client's resupply without the client having to resort to ordering afresh. Consequently, the responsibility for the execution of orders taken by the client is transferred to the supplier. This is a great advantage for the company or client, which can now rest on the accumulated experience of the supplier or manufacturer, who has a better picture of the market and access to precise and state-of-the-art tools.

9.4 Collaborative planning, forecasting and replenishment

The most renowned and ambitious system for the collaborative management of inventories is the collaborative planning, forecasting and replenishment (CPFR) system. In simpler terms, in the CPFR system, suppliers and retailers collaborate to plan for and forecast demand to optimise product flow from the production or central distribution points to the points of sale.

While CPFR cannot be considered as the result of the evolution of the previous techniques, one can with certainty accept that it rests on the tools and experience acquired from using them. Where, for example, previous techniques rested on internal or external networks (usually private networks), the CPFR system principally rests on the internet (utilising applications such as EDI, EPOS and cloud computing) and internet tools for collecting data relating to offer and demand, which allows the members of the supply chain to exchange information and know-how and to coordinate their investment policy and smooth product flow along the chain.

Consequently, the subject of CPFR is the uninterrupted collaboration between the parties involved and the exchange of information across the entire supply chain so as to maximise the effectiveness of sales forecasts and to ensure the automatic replenishment of products at distribution centres, warehouses and shelves. The objective is to minimise errors that may negatively affect sales or the profit margin (Figure 9.9).

Just as in the DSD method case, effective implementation of a CPFR system also requires common collaborative practices and tools, networking infrastructure for data sharing and also standardised key performance measurements such as demand forecast accuracy, customer service level, order execution level and accuracy of routing.

By applying CPFR effectively, benefits can be provided to suppliers, retailers and customers, as shown in Table 9.2.

9.5 Demand sensing

Demand sensing is a method for utilising upstream data within the value chain to generate a more accurate unconstrained demand forecast for the organisation. Sensing the customer's

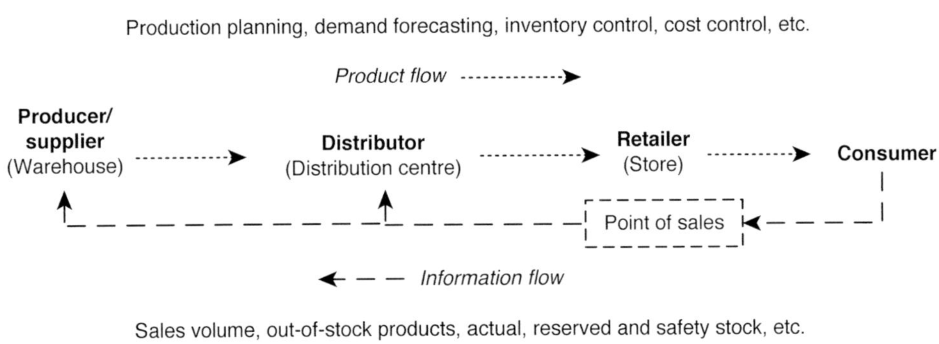

FIGURE 9.9 CPFR operating parts

TABLE 9.2 Benefits of CPFR

Role	*Benefits*
Producers/suppliers	Better production planning and scheduling due to the high forecast accuracy Decrease in inventory levels of raw materials, semi-products and packaging materials Decrease in operation costs (such as warehousing and materials handling)
Retailers	Decrease in out-of-stock products phenomenon Decrease in inventory levels of final products Decrease in operation costs (transportation costs due to better routing and scheduling, warehousing costs, etc.) High flexibility to satisfy unforeseen changes in demand
Customers	Increase in customer level (due to the better sales forecast, access to historical data regarding customer buying behaviour, etc.)

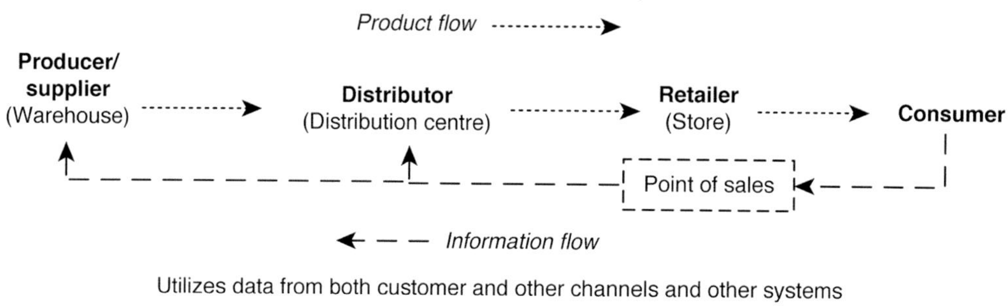

FIGURE 9.10 Demand sensing operating parts

purchase or choice behaviour aims to have a positive impact on the following two critical business areas: on-shelf availability and working capital.

How does demand sensing work?

Demand sensing considers both customer sales data from point of sale and data from other channel, such as sales compensation plans (at the micro level) and weather, geopolitics, social and natural events (at the macro level). It exploits data not only from the retail stores but also from the customer relationship management system, data from the company's website, etc. (Figure 9.10).

The benefits of demand sensing systems can be the understanding of future demand patterns, which can be gleaned from shoppers and suppliers, a more accurate supply response that reflects more accurately demand and improved planning across functions to meet organisational objectives. Hence, the benefits do not just exist within the supply chain functions but also extend to other functions in the organisation and thus cross the entire value. In demand sensing, collaboration and trust are both key success factors in implementing to drive its full benefits to help improve operational effectiveness. Another challenge is data integrity because of the existence of multiple data sources.

9.6 Lean thinking

Lean thinking (LT) is a philosophy that introduces a collection of principles, tools and techniques into the business processes to

- optimise time, human resources, assets and productivity;
- minimise waste (non-value-adding activities: overproduction, waiting, transportation and processing; inventories: raw material, work-in-process and finished goods, moving both operator and machine; defects: defective products or process outputs) (Emiliani and Stec 2004) and
- improve the quality level of products and services to their customers.

Or, in other words, LT can be used to propose a way to 'do more with less'. As Comm and Mathaisel (2005) point out: 'Lean thinking is lean because it provides a way to do more with less – less human effort, less equipment, less time, and less space – while coming closer and closer to providing customers with exactly what they want'.

LT originated from car manufacturing in the 1970s (Taiichi Ohno's TPS, mentioned earlier in this chapter), the aim of which was for production lines to be characterised by continued flow and a high level of waste elimination. According to Liker (2004), the TPS consists of four elements: philosophy (referring to the strategic or long-term decisions), process (supporting the implementation of practices and tools to eliminate non-value added activities), people (emphasising the significance of employees who identify the wastes/problems and suggest incentives for continuous improvement and innovation) and problem-solving (supporting the learning organisation paradigm).

The success of this approach was supported firmly by Womack and Jones (2003), who proposed the following five lean thinking principles: definition of value from a customer's perspective, identification of the entire value stream (VS) and elimination of waste, creation of the VS, production/supply in response to customer demand and pursuit of perfection. Today LT proposes several tools:

- *kanban* for implementing the pull system in the production line;
- *poke-yoke* for an automated defect detection of the products;
- *jidoka* for the inspection of a quality violation;
- *kaizen* that supports continuous improvement via the involvement of all employees at all the organisational level (operational, tactical and strategic) and
- *value stream mapping*, which is a visual representation of processes illustrating how they link to each other, and information such as timing and consumed resources to reveal the non-value added activities, etc.

The above principles and tools can be applied to a large number of industries, both manufacturing and service providers.

Synopsis

- Practices such as JIT, VMI, ECR, CPFR and LT are typical approaches for keeping organisations as competitive as today's market demands.
- In JIT, resources are acquired at the time of demand (in time) and on schedule in case they are needed. The purpose of JIT is to utilise the minimum possible quantity of equipment, materials and human resources to satisfy demand.

- ECR philosophy consists of a set of practices that, assisted by technology (the internet in particular), allows for close collaboration between members of a supply chain (and retail in particular) so as to better satisfy consumers' needs, faster and at the lowest possible cost. A CRP aims to resupply products in real time and only for the quantity in demand. In its full form, there is no predefined reorder point nor is there a mathematical formula applicable for the calculation of the quantity of the reorder. In the VMI, the responsibility for the planning, execution and completion of orders and the resupply of stock lies with and is assumed by the manufacturer or supplier and not the company or client. In the CPFR system, suppliers and retailers collaborate to plan for and forecast demand to optimise product flow from the production or central distribution points to points of sale.
- Demand sensing, on the other hand, is a method for utilising upstream data within the value chain to generate a more accurate unconstrained demand forecast for the organisation.
- Finally, LT is a philosophy that introduces a collection of principles, tools and techniques into the business processes to optimise time, human resources, assets and productivity; minimise waste and improve the quality level of products and services to their customers.

Review and discussion questions

- Identify the key objectives of JIT.
- Can you cite the conditions for the application of JIT?
- Choose a JIT tool and apply it in a specific organisation.
- Do you think that JIT tools require more business than technical capabilities by the decision-makers?
- Name the pros and cons of JIT.
- Describe the key parts and functionalities of ECR.
- Schematically illustrate the differences between ECR, CPFR and demand sensing.
- Identify and discuss the key objectives of the LT philosophy.
- Why are JIT and LT philosophies crucial in today's business environment?

Case studies

Case study 1: Fourth-party logistics management in grocery retailer relationships

The UK grocery retail sector is known for its innovation in logistics and SCM, including vertical collaboration between retailers and suppliers. While efforts towards horizontal and network collaboration exist, they are mainly driven by industry associations. Limited research suggests that external pressures may be necessary to promote horizontal collaboration among retailers. Rising costs and environmental regulations could compel retailers to seek more efficient cost management strategies. The complexity of modern supply chains may also prompt retailers to explore new alternatives. Hingley et al. (2011) examined horizontal collaboration within this sector.

Fourth-party logistics (4PL) involves outsourcing to a neutral provider to oversee the entire logistics process, combining process, technology and management. Unlike 3PL, 4PL

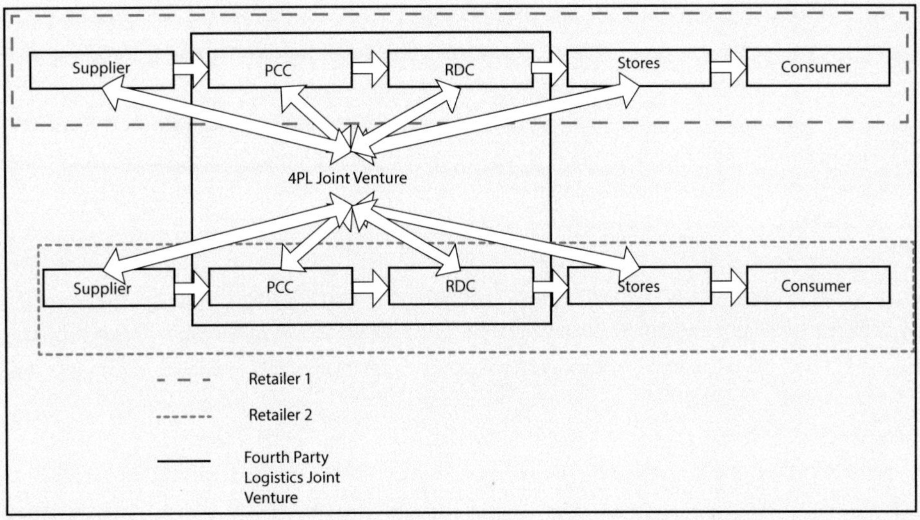

FIGURE 9.11 Structure of a 4PL joint venture

requires all parties to contribute equity and distribution assets, such as systems capability and strategic skills. Physical distribution management staff join the new organisation, viewed as a strategic partner and supply chain orchestrator. The focal organisation manages and integrates the supply chain, engaging specialist logistics providers when needed.

Figure 9.11 depicts a 4PL scenario involving two grocery retailers, their third-party relationships with suppliers and logistics providers. Both retailers have individual supply chains feeding into a joint venture 4PL for store deliveries. This venture encompasses four crucial elements: systems architecture and integration skills, a supply chain control room, effective utilisation of network information and knowledge, and access to top-tier asset providers (Christopher 2005).

The components necessary for 4PL integration, such as existing physical distribution networks and electronic communication systems, suggest few technical obstacles. The main challenge lies in retailers' willingness to adopt 4PL. The specificity of assets involved in joint ventures reduces the risk of opportunistic behaviour. While the automotive industry leads in 4PL, major grocery retailers have adopted innovations from this sector. For instance, General Motors (GM) partnered with Menlo Logistics to form Vector SCM, reducing supply chain costs significantly. Vector SCM integrates technology systems used by GM's 3PL providers and reduces order cycle times and customer lead times, resulting in revenue linked directly to these improvements.

The Vector SCM initiative serves as a 4PL connection between a single company and its 4PL provider. Despite this, the scale and intricacy of its supply chain offer valuable insights into potential outcomes if grocery retailers were to pursue similar ventures. While it might not be feasible to achieve remarkable order cycle time reductions, as grocery retailers already maintain short lead times, moderate reductions and substantial savings through improved asset utilisation remain achievable.

4PL service providers, known for their ability to enhance efficiency, effectiveness and economic performance, could play a pivotal role in leading horizontal collaboration among retailers. Their impartial execution of logistics activities positions them as 'honest brokers' in dealing with individual customers. Consequently, 4PL providers could help overcome barriers to successful collaboration, including parochialism and interfirm conflicts, by coordinating competing interests. These attributes are especially valuable in horizontal collaboration, where scepticism among retailers is prevalent.

Kaufman et al. (2000) proposed a collaboration typology for strategic suppliers, considering collaboration levels and technology. Hingley et al. (2011) suggested that the intensity of collaboration and distribution complexity could serve as a useful typology for assessing the suitability of outsourced logistics, particularly in horizontal collaboration. In cases of low complexity and collaboration, a transactional 3PL relationship may suffice, while increased complexity may warrant a relational 3PL arrangement. However, high intensity may necessitate a 4PL arrangement, where the provider manages physical distribution independently for the customer, either in a less collaborative environment or as a specialised consultant.

Hingley et al. (2011) identified that it was opportune to revise existing physical distribution management structures within UK grocery and retail supply chains. They highlighted potential improvements such as higher asset utilisation and the appeal of environmentally friendly distribution practices. Additionally, less tangible benefits included enhanced reputation from being linked with such innovations. These observations align with existing literature advocating for innovation and horizontal collaboration in retail supply chains.

Hingley et al. (2011) found that while suppliers and logistics service providers were willing to engage in 4PL innovations and horizontal collaboration to enhance efficiencies and customer service while reducing costs, retailers showed reluctance to sustain 4PL operations and collaborate horizontally. This hesitance may stem from power dynamics and control issues, negatively affecting the retailer–supplier relationship. Retailers have predominantly achieved their current positions through horizontal mergers and acquisitions rather than collaborative efforts, possibly reaching a point of horizontal saturation due to competition laws. For retailers, physical distribution management holds significance beyond cost efficiency, emphasising service levels and safeguarding sales information. This value placed on service and data protection makes it unlikely for retailers to collaborate to the extent of sharing physical distribution management.

Retailers, positioned as gatekeepers and leaders in the distribution channel, prioritise safeguards against competition over collaborative cost savings. Hingley et al. (2011) argue that the modified typology in Figure 9.12 offers a practical framework for 4PL operations. However, the lack of retailer support was disappointing, leading them to develop a future structure for retail physical distribution management systems using both 3PL and 4PL, as depicted in Figure 9.13. While a 4PL would still benefit suppliers, either a 4PL or a traditional 3PL provider would need to handle direct and unique deliveries to retailers, despite associated inefficiencies in operations, costs and environmental impact in this final link of the grocery supply chain.

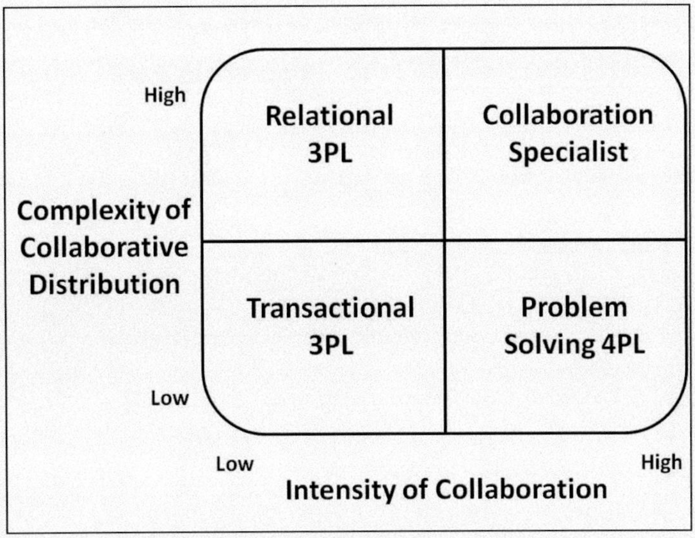

FIGURE 9.12 Proposed typology for 4PL collaboration

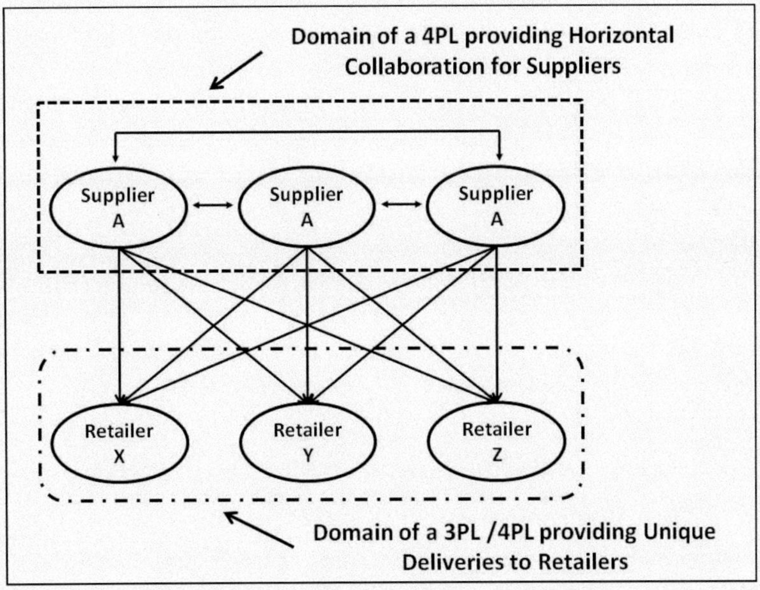

FIGURE 9.13 Possible future structure of 4PL involvement in horizontal collaboration

Prior research inadequately addressed horizontal collaboration in grocery and retail supply chains, focusing mainly on efficiency gains from 4PL without considering retailers' competitive dominance. The emphasis on supply chain secrecy by retailers poses challenges in realising sufficient returns. Hingley et al. (2011) anticipated greater openness and enthusiasm for 4PL and horizontal collaboration. However, the study highlights a critical issue: how can retailers embrace 4PL to reap potential benefits, given their preference for secrecy? The study supports the proposed typology, indicating that as distribution and collaboration operations intensify and become more complex, 4PL specialisation in assets and technology, especially information flow aided by techniques like radio frequency identification, becomes crucial for achieving superior performance.

Managerial implications

The study by Hingley et al. (2011) unveils managerial implications, including the prospect of increased horizontal collaboration, primarily at the supplier level rather than among retailers. While this potential has been tentatively explored by one of the suppliers in the study, further investigation is warranted. Such collaboration presents the advantage of enhancing distribution asset utilisation without jeopardising retailer integrity and service levels, unlike horizontal collaboration between retailers.

Logistics service providers emphasised substantial horizontal collaborations in physical distribution management among major manufacturers, indicating their swift recognition of cost savings and other benefits from such collaborations. In the grocery supply chain, retailers prioritise their own welfare over providing all cost management initiatives. As economic conditions tighten, consumers will demand more competitive pricing from retailers, putting pressure on suppliers. To stay competitive, suppliers should embrace greater horizontal collaboration, presenting an opportunity for smaller producers to enhance cost efficiency as well.

Amid the current economic climate, all participants in the food supply chain face mounting pressure to improve cost efficiency. Despite indications that external pressure has not spurred close collaboration among retailers, its potential impact on effective cost management should not be overlooked.

This case originates from Hingley, M. K., Lindgreen, A., Grant, D. B., and Kane, C. (2011). Using fourth-party logistics management to improve horizontal collaboration among grocery retailers. *Supply Chain Management: An International Journal* 16(5): 316–327. Here, the reader can also find additional relevant references to the case and its topic.

Case study 2: Using the Kraljic matrix to inform synergistic supply chain decisions

To stay competitive in today's market, organisations commonly adopt practices like JIT, VMI, ECR, CPFR, and LT. The Kraljic matrix (Kraljic 1983) is a framework for categorising the items a firm purchases, allowing supply chain managers to apply appropriate SCM practices.

The Kraljic matrix (Figure 9.14) is a two-by-two matrix that categorises items based on their profit potential and sourcing risk. Profit potential refers to the features of the product or service that help the firm maintain a competitive advantage and earn a profit. Risk refers to the challenges in ensuring a steady supply of the item, which can arise for various reasons:

Critical items – high profit potential/high risk: Supply chain managers use practices involving close customer relations, such as CPFR, to ensure a steady supply of critical items by mitigating risk. Sharing more information with trusted partners along the supply chain enhances the efficient flow of items.

Leverage items – high profit potential/low risk: Supply chain managers use practices like LT, as the risk is low and these items drive firm profit. These items are often ubiquitous, reducing the potential for supply chain disruption.

Bottleneck items – low profit potential/high risk: VMI may be a viable option for these high-risk items since the firm cannot function without them, yet they do not require the managerial resources needed for critical items.

Non-critical items – low profit potential/low risk: Supply chain managers may spend little time managing this category. The firm may enter an agreement with a supplier for a set price, allowing authorised members to purchase as needed.

Consider these categories in the context of food items. A chocolatier and a coffee company may view cocoa beans and coffee beans as critical items, requiring long-term communication with distributors and growers. These beans are subject to weather events and require proper handling throughout the supply chain, determining their risk profile. The chocolatier and coffee company cannot produce or sell products without these inputs. Milk may be a leverage item for the chocolatier if there are multiple adequate supply options. Items can switch categories as supply and demand change. For example, a contaminant in milk supply could shift milk from the leverage to critical or bottleneck quadrants. Similarly, during COVID, aluminium single-serve cans moved from leverage to bottleneck due to high demand for hygienic,

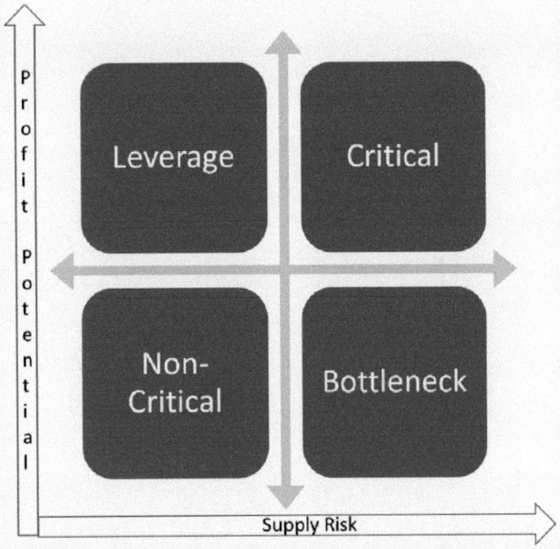

FIGURE 9.14 Kraljic matrix

Source: Adapted from Kraljic, P. (1983). Purchasing must become supply management. Special report: Supercharging Company Knowledge with AI. *Harvard Business Review*, https://hbr.org/1983/09/purchasing-must-become-supply-management (accessed October 6, 2024).

individual servings. Generally, firms should have attractive options for milk and aluminium bottle suppliers, making lean inventories feasible. These items differ from the far-reaching, non-recyclable (aluminium) and multi-intermediary supply chains for critical items like cocoa beans and coffee beans. Branded shrink sleeves for cans and bottles of chocolate milk fall into the high-risk/low-profit (bottleneck) category, where VMI can ensure smooth operations with minimal management. As the chocolatier's demand for milk increases with expansion into chocolate milk, milk may shift from a leverage item to a critical item.

In summary, supply chain managers can use the Kraljic matrix to categorise and manage sourcing strategies, but they must remember that these categories are not static.

Multiple-choice questions

1. What is the primary goal of JIT production?

   A. Maximising inventory levels
   B. Reducing production flexibility
   C. Eliminating waste and inefficiencies
   D. Increasing supplier lead times

2. Which of the following is NOT a key principle of TQM?

   A. Customer focus
   B. Continuous improvement
   C. Centralised decision-making
   D. Employee involvement

3. What does the '5S' methodology in lean manufacturing stand for?

   A. Sort, set, shine, standardise, sustain
   B. Simplify, streamline, synchronise, stabilise, satisfy
   C. Scan, solve, simulate, standardise, scale
   D. Segment, strategise, systemise, synergise, supervise

4. Which tool is used to identify the root causes of problems in quality management?

   A. Pareto chart
   B. Fishbone diagram
   C. Control chart
   D. Flowchart diagram

5. What is the primary focus of ECR?

   A. Maximising supplier profits
   B. Optimising inventory turnover
   C. Enhancing customer satisfaction
   D. Reducing transportation costs

6. Which of the following best describes the concept of cross-docking?

   A. Storing products for extended periods
   B. Direct transfer between inbound and outbound vehicles
   C. Implementing complex sorting algorithms
   D. Maximising warehouse storage capacity

7. What is the main objective of CPFR?

   A. Increasing competition among supply chain partners
   B. Optimising individual company performance
   C. Enhancing supply chain integration and efficiency
   D. Reducing information sharing between partners

8. Which quality management tool is used to graphically represent the sequence of steps in a process?

   A. Histogram
   B. Scatter diagram
   C. Flowchart
   D. Control chart

9. What is the primary goal of demand sensing in SCM?

   A. Reducing product variety
   B. Increasing forecast accuracy
   C. Maximising inventory levels
   D. Slowing down production processes

10. Which of the following is NOT a typical benefit of implementing JIT production?

    A. Reduced inventory costs
    B. Improved quality control
    C. Increased production lead times
    D. Enhanced production flexibility

11. What is the main purpose of the Pareto chart in quality management?

    A. Identifying the vital few causes
    B. Tracking process variations over time
    C. Visualising cause-and-effect relationships
    D. Mapping the flow of production processes

12. Which ECR strategy focuses on optimising product introductions and assortments?

    A. Efficient store assortment
    B. Efficient replenishment
    C. Efficient promotion
    D. Efficient product introduction

13. What is the primary objective of the Six Sigma methodology?

    A. Increasing product defects
    B. Reducing process variability
    C. Maximising inventory levels
    D. Slowing down production speed

14. Which of the following best describes the concept of demand shaping?

    A. Passively responding to market demands
    B. Actively influencing customer preferences
    C. Eliminating all product variations
    D. Ignoring customer feedback entirely

15. What is the main focus of the Theory of Constraints in operations management?

    A. Maximising all resources equally
    B. Ignoring system bottlenecks
    C. Optimising the system's constraints
    D. Increasing work-in-process inventory

Essay questions

Analyse how the integration of JIT production, TQM and CPFR can create synergies between marketing and SCM. Discuss the potential challenges and benefits of implementing these approaches simultaneously, and explain how they contribute to enhancing customer satisfaction, operational efficiency and supply chain responsiveness. Provide specific examples of how companies can leverage these methodologies to align their marketing strategies with supply chain capabilities and create competitive advantages in today's dynamic market environment.

10

TECHNOLOGIES OF MARKETING AND SUPPLY CHAIN MANAGEMENT SYNERGIES

Introduction

The main objective of this chapter is to analyse tools and technologies necessary for the interdisciplinary coexistence and systemic approach to marketing and supply chain management (SCM). Moreover, e-commerce and e-business technologies such as auto identification (auto ID) of product technologies, customer and supplier relationship management systems, social networks, augmented reality and electronic point of sales are also examined. The assessment of the systems is combined with the theoretical presentation and analysis of practices and methodologies supporting the implementation and more efficient use of the systems under assessment, such as of business process management and business intelligence.

Learning objectives

After reading this chapter, you will be able to answer the following questions:

- What are the principal technologies for the auto ID of products and how can they support both marketing and SCM?

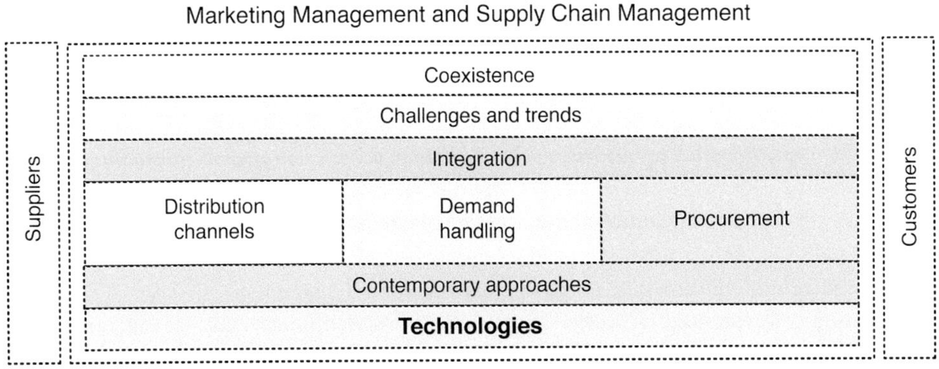

DOI: 10.4324/9781003650973-10

- What are the key business information systems and how are they categorised based on the functions and the decision levels they support?
- How does the evolution of logistics and SCM follow the evolution of e-commerce and e-business?
- How can the internet and e-commerce and e-business technologies and practices support and assist marketing and SCM operations?

Outline

10.1 Auto ID technologies

Barcode is the most widely known automatic identification and data capture technology. Such technologies allow the fast and easy collection and storage of data at the moment such data are created. These technologies also include other widely known and used ones, such as magnetic stripes, radio frequency identification (RFID), quick response (QR) codes, image barcodes, near-field communication, smart cards, voice and vision recognition-identification and biometrics.

The use of such technologies was limited to the support of logistics functions and principally storage and transportation operations. Following the widespread use of smartphones and the entry of new technologies, such as augmented reality, auto ID technologies promise not only to automatically recognise and identify objects but also to access data, data that are stored in remote databases or applications. Moreover, they cater for interactivity, an element that is necessary to support marketing activities.

From barcodes to RFIDs

The barcode was developed and first applied in the US at the end of the 1960s mainly for industrial uses (to cater for material handling needs in large automobile manufacturers) after it was patented by Norman Joseph Woodland in 1952. Its wide application in retail sales ensued in the following two decades, to cater for supermarket needs for faster handling and pricing of goods at the counters. Today barcodes are everywhere. The basic idea of this technology could be summarised in the following two simple steps:

- Data are placed on a label as a succession of black and white stripes that are printed on some product or its packaging. Blanks of variable sizes interject these stripes. The depiction and printing of the stripes follow specific rules established by a national or international organisation, and for each sequence of stripes, there corresponds, one-to-one, a number of letters or characters. Special machines can automatically read this information and transmit it to an information system so that the product can be identifiable, on the one hand, and that all movements relating to this product can be recorded, on the other.
- Information is transmitted by means of special reading equipment (e.g., scanners) to a computer and an information system. This can be performed wirelessly or by cable. The first way

has dominated and is supported by Wireless Local Area Networks (WLANs), in which the transmission can be performed without cables, from a portable terminal to a computer. The data collected are used to make the right decisions.

Let us consider these steps using two simple examples. A supermarket customer gives a product he wishes to buy to the cashier. The product has a code in the form of a barcode. The cashier 'passes' the product over the scanner. The level of the shop's inventories is automatically updated, and a receipt is issued. If the level of inventories reaches the restock point, the shop will order several pieces of the product from the distribution centre or the central warehouse.

Let us also assume that we are responsible for deliveries at a warehouse, and we are expecting the delivery of a carton box of bottled water. Our company has predesignated the precise location where the product will enter the warehouse (using the process we examined in a previous chapter). Upon delivery of the carton box, we scan the barcode on the box and enter the quantity of pieces. We then go to the storage point (shelf) and scan the label of its location, which has also been codified (this is determined by the company itself) and turned into a barcode symbol. The system then knows that this product has entered the warehouse, its quantity and the precise point where it was placed. Other information may also be entered, either automatically (e.g., the date of entry) or not (expiry date, supplier's trade name, etc.). If the product is then requested, we follow roughly the same procedure. We go to the point where the product is located (the system will usually direct us accordingly), scan the location and the product, and enter the number of pieces requested. Thus, the system is updated with the move that just took place and knows the precise number of pieces and their location in the warehouse at any time.

In reality, barcode technology is implemented across the entire spectrum of a logistics system functions, from delivery to loading and inventory-taking: delivery, storage, restock, collection, packaging, loading and inventory. It also extends to the context of a supply chain by supporting traceability in, for example, a food supply chain: harvesting, packing in the field, processing and production, packing in the production line, transportation, storage in the distribution centre, shop and consumer.

By employing barcode technology at every stage of this last example, recording of both business data relating to logistics functions (e.g., quantity, origin, destination, dispatch date, expiry date and transportation and handling conditions), which allows for the quick detection of the location of the product across the supply chain, where it originated from, to where it is going, in case of an emergency need to recall or remove the product from the market, and data regarding quality takes place, allowing us to identify the source, to acknowledge the cause for a potential risk, by knowing the methods of production and processing, storage and handling conditions and other information that accompanies the product if such a system exists, while all of these are available in the case of a dietary crisis.

The most common type of barcode is the one managed today by GS1 organisation, namely, European Article Numbering (EAN). EAN consists of two main parts: the *codification* and the *symbology*. Codification relates to the kind/structure of data to be depicted on the barcode, for example, codification of the country and product, while symbology relates to the way any number or alphanumeric element is depicted in linear form.

The objective is to ascribe a unique number to every product. Specifically, the EAN consists of a 13-digit numerical sequence and can be found in most consumer goods (there are, however, other types of barcodes with more or less digits than those in the EAN standards, which are applicable in other business sectors and/or products). The first number is separate, while

1 234567 891231

FIGURE 10.1 EAN-13 barcode example

TABLE 10.1 Calculation of check digit in EAN-13 barcode

Digit	1	2	3	4	5	6	7	8	9	1	2	3
×	1	3	1	3	1	3	1	3	1	3	1	3
=	1	6	3	12	5	18	7	24	9	3	2	9

the other 12 are divided into two groups of six, one to the left and the other to the right (see Figure 10.1).

The three first digits (123 in the example) stand for the country of origin, while the next four (4567) denote the manufacturer or supplier of the product. The five digits after these (89123) relate to the code of the product, while the last digit (1) is termed a control digit (or check digit) and ensures that reading/scanning was performed correctly. The calculation of the control digit is as follows: firstly, multiply each of the first 12 digits of the product's code by 1 (for odd numbers) and by 3 (for even numbers) (Table 10.1). Then add the products:

$$1+6+3+12+5+18+7+24+9+3+2+9=99$$

The resulting number (99) needs 1 more to make the next ten (i.e., 100), which means the control digit is 1. Consequently, the reading/scanning process is carried out as follows: the EAN code is immediately translated by a scanner to a language that a PC can understand (i.e., 0, 1). The reading of the barcode consists in decoding the reflection of a laser beam that falls on the barcode label. The degree of reflection varies (and is, therefore, unique for every product) as the laser beam comes successively across the white and black stripes. Scanners decode this variable reflection (and convert it into numbers or letters).

When scanning the 13-digit EAN code, the first 12 digits are 'read', and the process described above is used to calculate the control number, which is then compared to the 13th digit on the code. If they are identical, then the scan has been correctly performed, and a distinctive sound is heard. The EAN is a linear barcode type, as are UPC, Interleaved 2 of 5 and Code 128. 2D barcodes are also available, the most notable being Data Matrix, PDF417, MaxiCode and QR codes.

The principal advantages of the application of barcode technology in a warehouse are both evident and significant:

- Increase in entry and exit speed as well as speeding up the movement of the products inside the warehouse. Thus, a decrease in the time needed to collect information is attained.
- Precise informing, since copying and typing mistakes are eliminated. It has been measured that in the manual process, for every 300 characters that are typed, an average of 1 is typed incorrectly. Using the barcode, there is 1 error in every 7,500,000 scans.

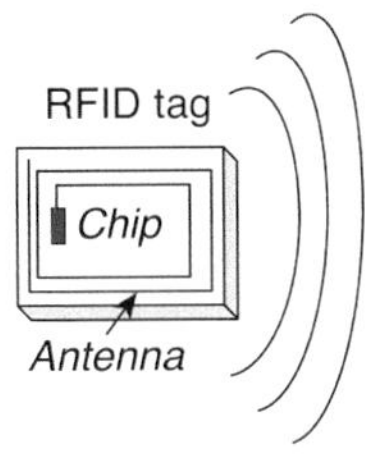

FIGURE 10.2 RFID operation

- Precise knowledge of what and how many products a company keeps in its warehouse and their location at any given time.
- Immediate transmission of the data in real time, if required.

All these lead to significant economic benefits (as a result of good organisation and operation of the warehouse), to a faster and better service in terms of quality serving of customers and, of course, to an overall increase in productivity. The disadvantages include the following: barcodes are expendable and sensitive – that is, they can be easily corroded and destroyed; and direct line-of-sight with the scanning device is required – there is no room to store data and there is no margin for changes to the barcode once it is printed on a product. Many businesses (principally large retail chains) have opted for a new auto ID technology in the last decade: RFID, which uses radio frequencies to read data stored in a small circuit known as a RFID tag.

RFID tags can take on many guises: from a small tablet on a product, to a security tape on an access card. They usually contain a microchip where data are stored and an integrated antenna that allows them to receive and respond to a signal by a RFID reader or interrogators (Figure 10.2).

The reader or interrogator is a device controlled by a computer that transmits radio frequency waves to the tags, which must be located inside a certain radius, so as to detect and activate them. The same device also receives (again via the antenna) and analyses the data contained in each tag and then transfers it to the computer for further processing and storage. Communication between the tag and the transceiver is affected with the antenna. The antenna is usually packaged with the transceiver and a decoder and is converted to a reader that can be a portable or fixed device. The reading device transmits radio frequencies from a distance that varies from some centimetres to several metres, depending on the output power and radio frequency used.

When a tag passes through the electromagnetic field, it detects the activation signal from the reader, while data are transferred to a PC via specialised software, for further use. Consequently, the five key components of RFID are as follows:

- the tag
- the antenna
- the reader
- the software (SW), which manages the date transmitted between the tag, the reader and the computer; and
- the personal computer (PC), where all data are stored (Figure 10.3).

Tags are integrated circuits that can store data ranging from some bits to several kilobytes. Tags can be 'read only', that is, programmed at their production stage without the capacity of

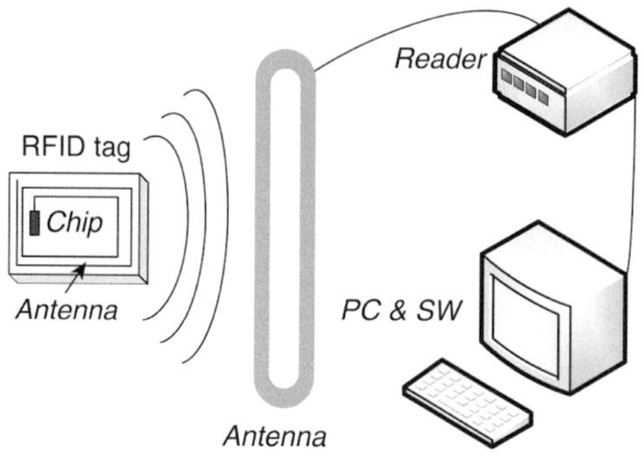

FIGURE 10.3 RFID components

further interventions, or 'read and write', that is, allowing for modifications and amendments to their contents at any time. They can also be 'passive', which are activated when they are inside the field of radio frequencies transmitted by a reader, or 'active', which have a battery and a transponder and transmit themselves the data they contain. RFID tags store data relating to the individuals or objects that carry them. Thus, in practice, they can be applied to a variety of fields where the identification of objects is necessary. One of their most common applications is the handling and transportation of products where they can identify products either at the course of their transportation or inside industrial units, regardless of whether said products are in pallets, warehouses or the shelves of shops, thus replacing barcode technology.

The use of RFID offers significant advantages to the way companies themselves operate, since they can essentially be used to monitor products across the length of their entire supply chain. By using RFID technology, one can attain traceability, thus providing full transparency of the state and status of a product from its production until its delivery to the end consumer. This is for the consumer's benefit, since it continuously offers him high-quality products. Due to their wireless operation, there is no need for direct optical link for the identification of products. This specific function offers the advantage of being able to read multiple tags at the same time. Significant working time is saved this way, since there is a decrease in the time needed to check the incoming and outgoing products. Benefits also ensue from the automation of processes that were manual until now. Businesses expect a fall in their operating cost, since they will engage less personnel and error will also be minimised.

The following are also advantages offered by RFID: precise and informing in real time; that is, the transmission of data to some information system and the capacity of simultaneous reading of multiple tags but also amending the data stored there while being able to operate under adverse environmental and weather conditions. One can also detect some disadvantages that are the reasons RFID is not adopted in practice. These can be classified into technical ones, since the RFID systems employed by various manufacturers are not always compatible with one another; financial, relating to the installation and operating costs; and social, since the use of RFID technology may infringe on sensitive personal data.

At the entry or exit of a pallet with an RFID tag, a unique number for each product is automatically detected, the Electronic Product Code (EPC) number, and the kind of boxes it contains, thus minimising the likelihood for errors. By using RFID systems in storage facilities, one can attain a better management of inventories. The business is not in a position to maintain low levels of inventories, thus saving on storage space. Additionally, it also knows the precise level of inventories for every product it possesses and can better plan its orders. It, therefore, has the advantage to attain high availability of products. The shop can benefit from such high availability because low availability leads to loss of income and has negative repercussions for the establishment's reputation. The reader collects and decodes the data stored on the tags. It then transmits the data to the information system of the enterprise, whether this is an enterprise resource planning (ERP) system or a warehouse management system (MBS), thus attaining precise and real-time updating. Parallel to this, the technology also offers greater security since tags can also be used as theft prevention devices, helping decrease the number of thefts and losses for the business.

Quick response codes

Quick response (QR) codes are essentially a two-dimensional barcode type of label. Their creator (Denso, a subsidiary of Toyota) named this technology to accentuate its main purpose, that is, the fast reading of the label's content. There are, however, two principal differences between linear barcodes and QR codes.

Firstly, the label looks different. Secondly, in contrast to linear barcodes that can store up to 20 digits, QR codes can store more characters (up to 7,089). This allows one to keep and process more information and, of course, decrease the space the QR code takes up in packaging (Figure 10.4).

There are 40 versions of QR codes, each version comprising different modules. The initial version consisted of 21 × 21 modules, while the latest is 177 × 177 modules. As one moves to the latest version, four more modules are added on each side of the QR code (while the information stored increases as well). QR code labels can be used like the other coded labels and tags presented. Of course, due to their high storage capacities, fast reading times and principally the fact that smartphones can also be used to read QR codes, they enjoy a far greater number of applications. What is most interesting are the tremendous abilities that QR codes offer for the retrieval of web pages or files contained in web pages. QR codes can be printed, for example, on any advertising material, such as the pages of magazines, newspapers or posters or even on the packaging of a product, and by scanning the label, the consumer is transferred, via his cell phone, to an internet site offering more information or some advertising message, which may also offer interactivity and engage the user. On the other hand, every movement performed in a logistics circuit (such as the placing of products on the shelves, their collection when ordered, loading and confirmation of delivery) can be identified and automated by using QR code labels.

The potential applications of this technology are practically inexhaustible, at different places and for different reasons. They are, for example, presently employed at bus or metro stations and stops where they can offer information on the time of arrival of the next route. They are also

FIGURE 10.4 QR code

used by museums, monuments and archaeological sites to offer information on the exhibits, or even in the shelves of supermarket chains, offering information on ways to consume the product, such as recipes. The use of QR codes by airline passengers is also an established and very popular practice.

Many hospitals in Japan today print a QR code on a bracelet or card for each admitted patient, to identify the patient and provide information such as the patient's name, date of birth, ward, room and bed, or any other information relating to the patient's medical file. The goal is to ensure that each patient receives appropriate treatment and correct medicine at the correct time. A key feature of QR code technology is its interactivity. Reading a QR code label in an article, for example, can direct a user to a web page/blog where the reader can leave his comments.

Image barcode

The idea behind image barcode technology is that information is incorporated into the packaging of the product, while reading and identification are on the level of the entire product and not just a label. Consequently, the difference is in the reader. Image-based readers work in a different way than traditional laser scanners of 1D or 2D codes because they take pictures of the products as they go, trying to locate the barcode(s) within the image for decoding. Smart software may learn from this process, detecting the basic features of the product's packaging and identifying the product so that they won't need to search for codes next time they identify it. It has been established that by using image barcode technology, the read rate performance is improved, independently of the state of labels or their place on the product's packaging. This technology is presently employed principally at the cashier points of large retail chains. One cannot preclude that the immediate future will not bring applications to support marketing on the product piece level.

Near-field communication

Near-field communication (NFC) is a wireless technology that rests in contact or close approximation (from 5 to 10 cm) of a device containing the NFC chip and a different device equipped with an appropriate sensor.

The operation is simple: the sender device creates a radio frequency field that can be fed to a receiver, allowing quick reading and recording of data on it. Save for smartphones, there are also NFC cards in the form of a smartcard with different storage capacities depending on use (Figure 10.5).

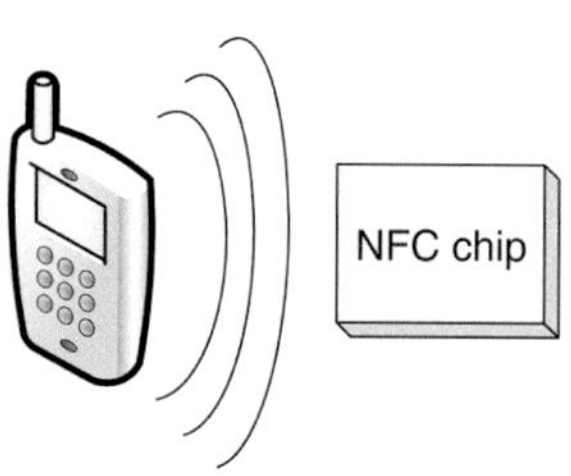

FIGURE 10.5 NFC operation

There are three different modes of operation for NFC:

- Quick read/write mode, where one device is active and the other passive and which allows applications to send and receive data;
- Card emulation, which allows NFC devices to act as a smartcard;
- Peer-to-peer for communicating between devices on the level of the connection.

NFC was created in 2004 as the result of the collaboration of Nokia, Philips and Sony, and new applications have been developing ever since, applications that promise fast reading and writing of data for the performance of daily 'chores', such as the use of virtual credit cards, the certification of products and the activation of services. NFC technology combines older wireless communication technologies, such as Bluetooth and RFID. However, it is differentiated from the first since it allows for bidirectional interaction between electronic devices within a range of some centimetres (while Bluetooth's range extends to 10–15 metres), while less energy is also required. Moreover, and with respect to the second alternative, it requires devices to be adjacent (in RFID, reading can be performed in a radius up to 100 metres) and permits the reading of just one label each time.

The key advantages of the NFC technology are as follows: (a) interactions are simple, only a touch is required for reading or writing; (b) passive NFC can be reused indeed many times; (c) there is no way the data can been intercepted at interaction, due to the proximity of the two sides; and (d) it allows the use of widely popular devices such as smartphones or tablets, easy-to-use devices that cater for interactivity and attain what is known as ubiquitous computing. All the above render this technology prosperous for a multitude of daily uses, such as financial transactions, advertising, smartcards, access and exchange of data stored on remote services. There are, of course, also warehouse applications. An NFC label is placed, for example, on the shelves and keeps information (static and dynamic) on the products located on the shelves. The warehouseman using a smartphone and the corresponding application can read information on a product, check the current level of inventories against the book inventory and, of course, perform his daily duties, such as the placement of products on the shelves or their removal from them for the execution of an order.

Augmented reality

Augmented reality technology allows access to useful information beyond that perceived by the human eye in real time! How does it work? It works by using special devices but also smartphones or tablets that interpose between the user's eyes and the environment and project digital information useful to the user but in actual, physical space. Thus, this is no virtual reality! It is better to describe it as the coexistence of the physical and the digital world that allows one to add data to the already existing environment, thus increasing the information available to the user.

Combining the camera and the GPS of a smartphone in the example above offers information (and specific texts, images, sounds and video) on points of interest (POI) at the geographical location of the user and the direction he points the camera. The viewing of virtual data is possible either using the screen of a smartphone or with special glasses, while it is obvious that virtual objects contain information the user could not have perceived on his own.

The greatest advantage of augmented reality technology is that the necessary hardware and specifically a display (usually a head-up or head-mounted display), detection systems (accelerometers, GPS devices, gyroscopes, RFID, wireless sensors, etc.), input devices (mainly smartphones or tablets) and specialised software are all parts of a smartphone. Augmented reality is by nature a marketing tool exploiting, on the one hand, the modern needs of advertising and product and services promotion (for interactivity and participation), while, on the other hand, it requires only a smartphone, which in some countries can be found in the hands of nine out of ten young people. Its advantages include powerful communication, personalised advertising, ability to send social comments and visualisation of the products.

This technology also promises to effectively and efficiently support logistics operations, such as processes related to collection, shelf placement and last-mile delivery. Moreover, it can support decisions regarding the layout of warehouses, the organisation of the distribution network, the selection of routes, etc. Consider, for example, that the head of the warehouse wishes to apply augmented reality technology for collection. The following are the steps he must follow: initially the areas of the warehouse must be recorded (areas such as the reception area, the storage area and the dispatch area), as must shelves, corridors, equipment, machinery, etc., using a head camera. The next step is to select and accurately mark the locations where the virtual content will be incorporated (virtual labels, GPS, laser, etc.). The link of the locations with the desired content (internet- or database-based) will be the next step, culminating in the use of devices (such as glasses) to project the digital content in the real, spatial areas of the warehouse.

10.2 Customer and supplier relationship management systems

The continuous increase in competition, globalisation of the market and the need to design, develop and offer personalised products and services have forced businesses to develop close ties with both their customers and their suppliers. A potent weapon in their arsenal for dealing with challenges and for the attainment of their strategic objectives is information systems.

The need to establish collaborative relationships, on the one hand, and the wide use of business information systems, on the other, lead businesses to develop new business models resting on trust, joint design, planning and performance of their business processes and on information exchange. This last (the ability to directly communicate and inform) is very important as it leads to productive cooperation, a decrease in cost and response times, and the expansion of the market a company caters for.

Usually, a business installs and operates an ERP system to manage its intra-business processes and information. There are several options if the business wishes to establish collaborative relationships and to have the capacity to exchange information: the company may permit customers and suppliers to have access to its intra-business information and to perform corresponding applications, thus creating an extranet among themselves, to purchase and install information systems that manage its relationships with customers, suppliers, etc. In the last alternative, consolidation with customers and suppliers is realised by connecting the ERP system with its supplier relationship management (SRM) system and its customer relationship management (CRM) systems. Thus, extended ERP or ERP II systems are created.

What does an ERP system ensure? Firstly, it supports the real integration of all functions, departments and employees in a business and covers all the needs of the enterprise; secondly, it operates in real time and guarantees precise and accurate informing on time; and, thirdly, it contains best business practices.

In general, such systems are categorised depending on the following (Folinas et al. 2007):

- Which of the main functions of a company are thus IT supported (namely, supplies, production, inventories, distribution, marketing and sales). IT support attains the following with respect to business processes: automation, simplification, optimisation and reengineering. Automation refers to the standardised ('mechanical') performance of processes that frequently reveals new congestion points and leads to the simplification of operating process standards, i.e., their rationalisation, so that automation can render operating processes more efficient and effective. It also leads to the improvement (i.e., a continuous effort) of parameters such as time, cost, number of errors, delays and tails. A type of more radical change is reengineering where business processes are analysed, simplified and redesigned. Redesign is a far more ambitious goal than rationalisation of processes and demands one to adopt a new viewpoint of the way in which a process is organised.
- Which levels (operating, tactical and strategic) support the *decisions* taken by a company's personnel. The operational level consists of the personnel responsible for short-term decisions (with a time horizon varying from hours to days). The tactical level consists of the personnel responsible for medium-term decisions (with their time horizon being weeks or months). The strategic level consists of the personnel responsible for long-term decisions (their time horizon being months to years). In more detail:
- Operational decisions relate to the daily functions of the company, that is, key functions that must necessarily be performed in order for the company to continue to exist (taking and processing of orders, checking inventories, pricing and invoicing customers, production planning, etc.). Examples of such decisions are: 'How much of this raw material should we order?' 'Is this customer entitled to a 20% discount?' These questions are frequently repeated, and thus, the variables affecting the problem, and their values can be determined. For example, the employees responsible for checking inventories determine the level of inventories below which a specific quantity will be ordered.
- Tactical decisions regard the allocation and control of the resources of the enterprise for the attainment of objective goals. These decisions are usually taken by middle management, responsible for the management of the resources that would allow the attainment of the objectives posed by the senior management of the enterprise. For example, 'What should be the credit limits for each customer category?', 'Which conditions should be in place for customer discounts?' Such decisions are not taken as frequently as operating decisions. The selection of the best raw materials supplier, for example, can be a complex one. Sometimes not all variables are known, nor the values of the variables involved in the problem. A supplier can offer very low prices, but the quality of the materials supplied might be unknown, or the level of service or even his reliability.
- Strategic decisions are decisions that pose the long-term objectives of the enterprise. Such decisions establish the base on which the enterprise will rest and the framework that operating and tactical decisions will observe. For example, 'What strategy will we follow with respect to competition – a low-cost or a differentiation one?' 'Do we compete across the entire country or only in a small part of it?' Such decisions are of a strategic nature, usually very complex, not structured and not repeated. Not all the variables of the problem can be determined, and their values may not even be quantifiable. A lot of the information that is useful relates to factors outside the business, such as competition, suppliers and customers. The uncertainty involved in these decisions is great, since data are vague and causality relations are unknown.

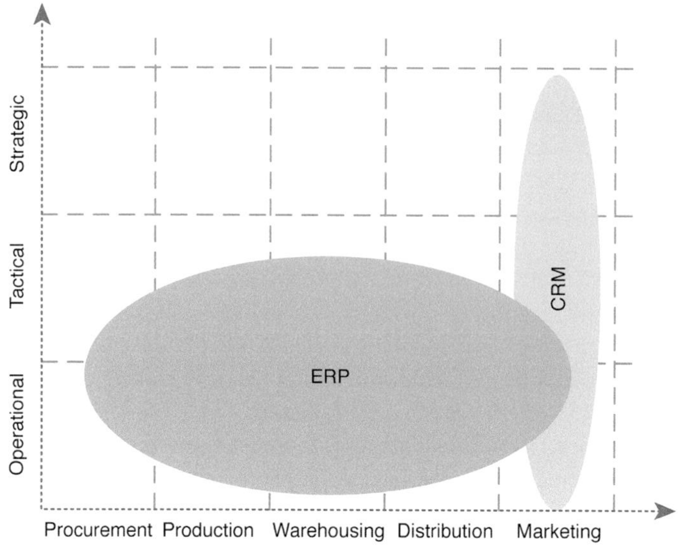

FIGURE 10.6 Framework for the categorisation of business information systems

One can visualise all of the above in Figure 10.6, where the information systems are identified. According to this figure, two main types of business information systems may be identified. Integrated business information systems can support decisions across all levels of the organisation and provide IT support to all functions. In this case, the various operating departments of the information system of a business are interconnected in an entity that exhibits technological integration, integration of the data and the 'logic' (i.e., the way the system operates), and integration of business processes. The design and development of operating departments is performed in the context of a holistic (systems) approach to the information needs of the enterprise.

On the other hand, there are integrated solutions that aim at the automation and optimisation of individual operating areas and in specific enterprises. These systems are either the evolution of traditional systems improved in time, aiming to monitor the transfiguration and reshaping of business processes, or were created as the response to modern market demands. However, they are not operating parts of an integrated business resource management system. The 'best-of-breed' application solutions are the best the market has to offer in their category and usually originate from different developers. These solutions differ considerably from developer to developer and evolve at a rapid pace. For this reason, the brief description that follows will be characterised by their key action axes and the features they offer. Specifically, the 'best-of-breed' solutions assessed below are CRM, WMS and transportation management systems (TMSs).

Business process reengineering

Business process reengineering (BPR) is the best known and most suitable management and organisation methodology to actualise changes to fixed attitudes and create new competitive advantages, which will allow the further development and evolution of a company. Business processes, which run horizontally in classic organisational schema that rest on functions, have a key place in BPR. Frequently the eradication of dysfunctions and increase in the effectiveness of processes are affected by adopting new inter-functional organisation schemes. The result of successful reengineering is the standardisation, simplification and automation of business processes and the transubstantiation of the corporate structure from functions-oriented companies to processes-oriented companies. The successful implementation of reengineering decisions depends on the degree of support from the information system, since it is this system that will ensure their incorporation in the daily operation of the company.

A general definition of BPR could be as follows:

> Radical redesign (redetermination) of business processes aimed to attain dramatic improvements in critical performance factors, such as cost, quality, level of service and speed. The usual practice is the implementation of BPR in parallel with the installation of a Business Information System.

A classic example of the implementation of BPR in a business is the service of a bank customer wishing to secure a building loan (Zigiaris 2000). The process for a building loan application includes three stages:

1. The initial stage (includes checking the information on the application and the customer's creditworthiness);
2. Servicing the loan (includes the calculation of interest and the payment schedule);
3. Marketing (relating to the collection and processing of the customer's particulars for future marketing activities).

Normally, before the implementation of BPR, the customer would have had to visit three different offices to be served. This 'linear' process could last for several days and engage many bank employees. By implementing BPR, the customer needs to contact just one employee, who will fill in the loan application in digital format. A suitable employee will check the application to ensure that all information is completed and correct. The application will then be transferred via the bank's internal network to the officer responsible to ascertain the customer's creditworthiness. If the customer proves to be insolvent, his application will be rejected, whereas if he proves solvent, the application will be digitally transferred to the officer responsible for interest rates, who will calculate the interest rate and establish the corresponding schedule of repayments. The application will then be forwarded for digital signing. Finally, the customer's particulars (personal data, transactions data, etc.) will be stored for future use by the bank's marketing department. The assistance offered by information systems and new technologies for information and document exchange to serve the customer should be evident by this point.

By reengineering the process for issuing building loans, banks have attained noteworthy performance. They were not engaged in the redesign of just one business process, but they reassessed all of the processes that are logically associated with the granting of a building loan. Instead of automating or rationalising the previous method for processing loans, banks designed the entire process from scratch (Zigiaris 2000).

BPR cannot be simply considered a change in the organisation of the company. It aims to improve the processes a company follows, with the objective being the increase in customer satisfaction, the decrease in costs and the improvement of the quality of the services and products offered. Specifically:

- BPR aims to eradicate all unnecessary activities that do not increase the value of the final product for the customer but simply add to time and cost. What is pursued is to eradicate

processes that, for example, encumber the cost of the final product without the customer being at the same time willing to be thus encumbered, or which may possibly increase the average turnover time.
- BPR does not pursue cutting of personnel to attain the reduction of costs. On the contrary, personnel may undergo internal 'movements' to processes that add value to the final product or service.
- BPR is a practice of customer-centric philosophy. It focuses on the customer and offers him products and services with value. The value for the customer can be interpreted as lower cost, higher quality or faster service, and the limiting of complaints.
- BPR lends flexibility and quick adjustment to continuously changing conditions, new market demands and intense competition. Via innovative and original changes, it leads the company in the acquisition of a competitive advantage.
- BPR assists in smoothening the processes of the enterprise, leading to an increase in effectiveness and performance, while integrating the company's systems.
- BPR essentially prepares the business to adopt automations and information support systems. This means that the company must restructure and reorganise its processes before it can move on to the installation of information systems so that it can fully exploit what they have to offer.

Some of the anticipated results and benefits from the application of a BPR technique to a company are as follows:

- The reengineering of processes so that there are fewer resources upon completion, involving the participation of as few employees as possible.
- Unified corporate strategy (e.g., with respect to the sales department in issues relating to 'targeting' per customer, per product and per channel).
- Restructuring of the business organisational plan and upgrading of the role of HR.
- Costing per corporate activity or even by employing activity-based costing (ABC), which principally allocates management and operating costs depending on the contribution of each department or product.
- Direct uniform informing of executives per corporate department or working group.
- Flexible corporate policy for customers and suppliers.

The changes above will bring a reduction in the operating cost of the company and higher quality (with respect to price, readiness, delivery and offer of the relevant services) of products and services offered to customers.

In addition to those methodologies relating to the process for the development of information systems, informatics can also recommend a series of automated tools that can significantly contribute to and assist in the realisation of a BPR project, especially if it is characterised by great complexity and high risk. These tools offer the ability to company employees to function as teams. A concise presentation of these tools follows.

CASE tools

Computer-aided software engineering (CASE) tools are principally employed for the automation and support of system analysis and planning/design. The use of these tools can facilitate modelling of a system, via graphical representation techniques, while the representation of the system can facilitate the automatic production of documentation. These tools were not originally developed to satisfactorily support a BPR project, but their application, even if limited, can substantially facilitate analysis, especially if not focused on functions.

Simulation systems

Simulation may be especially useful for modelling the system and monitoring its operation. The simulation model can refer either to the old system or the system that will ensue after processes are reengineered. The reason for using a model for the simulation of the operation of the system may follow from the need to evaluate the investment for a BPR project, given its high cost and the need to choose between alternative ways for process reengineering (creation and evaluation of 'what if' scenarios). The importance of simulation is more evident if one considers the complexity of the models and parameters included in these.

Project management systems

Automated tools in this category may prove very useful in managing a BPR project, if one considers the complexity and scope of the project. These tools help with organising and coordination, via the facilitation of the distribution of the project, the identification of critical routes and time monitoring.

Group decision support systems

These are applications that connect systems of different user categories. Users share a common 'project' and need a common set of services, even when the applications and architectures of the information systems providing them are heterogeneous and incompatible. Users share a common objective and must work as a team, independently of their geographical location. Focusing on interaction between the users accentuates three points for treatment: communication, collaboration and coordination. Depending on the type of the realised group work, the medium of communication may be sound, text, graphics, images or a combination thereof. Proper collaboration presupposes briefing between the members of a team on each one's work. Thus, information reaches all users regarding the means and the content of the contribution of the other participants in the collective work. Communication and collaboration cannot, of course, ensure the production of an outcome if they lack the coordination of the collaborating parties. A direct categorisation easily ensues from whether the simultaneous interaction of all users with the system is necessary. If it is, then we refer to synchronous systems. If not, we refer to asynchronous systems. If they share elements from both categories, then we refer to mixed systems. Electronic meeting rooms are a classic example of the first category. For asynchronous systems, a well-known application is news bulletin board software. Finally, collaborator writing and designing systems belong to mixed systems.

Digital document management systems

Digital transfer of documents relates to the exchange of documents in digital and strictly standardised formats via communication networks. Its objective is to integrate different functions into one process. The main standards are the EDIFACT, CEFACT and other documents, which were created for e-commerce and e-business initiatives.

Customer relationship management

The term *customer relationship management* (CRM) refers to all those strategies, practices, software applications and set of technologies and tools that assist a business to organise and manage its relations with customers so that they can become relationships of loyalty and trust. The goal of the CRM philosophy is to maximise the value of customers for the business itself. How is this attained? This is attained by a better management of available business resources, such as time, capital, technology and information, and human resources at regular intervals, with the end objective being the optimisation of the value of customers. A result of the adequate management of customer relationships is the minimisation of the cost for acquiring and maintaining such customers and the increase in profits.

It is necessary to stress at this point that CRM is not simply a software application nor an information system. CRM presupposes and supports a change in the philosophy of the business and places the satisfaction of customer needs as the cornerstone of its existence (customer-centric approach). This customer-centric business strategy combined with its set of methodologies, practices, tools and applications constitute CRM.

The truth is that CRM as a philosophy was applied by companies long before the term CRM was invented as an information system! The owner, for example, of a small shop that serves the needs of a neighbourhood applies CRM daily (although he may not be aware of this). This owner knows most of his customers, how frequently and on what days they visit the shop, the number of their family members, their favourite dishes, their habits and their desires. However, such detailed knowledge of hundreds of thousands of customers around the world is something that employees will not and cannot do on their own. That is why companies today rely on new informatics and communication technologies to attain that which eludes the capacity of human intellect.

Which are the characteristics of CRM philosophy? CRM is customer-centric and systemic, meaning that it is individual to each customer, on the one hand, while extending sales from being an individual act of an individual salesman to being a continuous process or continuous effort, with the ultimate objective being to attract and maintain profitable customers. CRM philosophy assists enterprises to identify customers they can attract and maintain at a small cost and who will bring the largest proceeds for each euro spent on marketing or after-sales service. CRM philosophy utilises new information systems and new technologies to detect all the ways a company may interact with its customers, to register the transactions they perform and to analyse these data to maximise intertemporal value and customer satisfaction.

Customer relationship management systems

Customer transactions are realised via a great number of communication channels and contact points. Usual contact points are the salesman (i.e., the interpersonal contact between the seller and the client), telephone, fax, land and electronic mail, call centres, premises or customer service points, etc. CRM systems collect and consolidate data from different customer contact points, data that ensue from the daily transactions with customers, even from the business associates of the company. Such data are entered in a common data repository. The consolidation of data is collection and grouping per customer to ensure and provide a full picture of the company's customers that can be utilised to improve selling procedures and the service of customers.

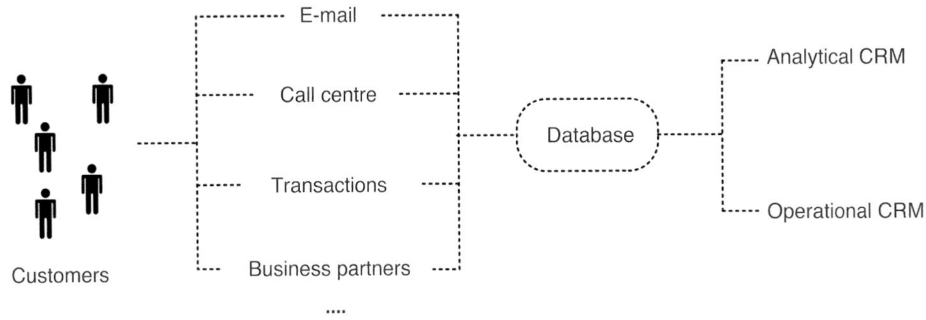

FIGURE 10.7 CRM system architecture

CRM systems, then, provide and disseminate useful information by offering a unique and cohesive picture for each customer that includes all of his transactions with the company – his purchase history, behaviour, complaints and returns. Finally, it permits the *analysis* of all these data from sales and marketing executives for them to gain a thorough understanding of customers' buying behaviour via several tools and reports. Reports may present customer analysis to offer a more accurate and clearer picture of the market with respect to the company's products and services. The goal is to offer better, cheaper and higher-quality products and services to each customer. Figure 10.7 presents the architecture of a typical CRM system.

Data entered in data repositories originate from internal sources (transactions at points of sale, contacts via call centres, e-mails, fax, etc.; transactions or entries in business information systems; contacts on internet sites, e.g., registration, filling-out of forms and order) and external sources (such as data describing the market behaviour of customers that have been collected by specialised market-research companies, customer lists for direct marketing campaigns collected by third enterprises, and statistical and demographic data from public or private Gallop companies). A CRM system can combine and consolidate data originating from the aforementioned sources. The data will be utilised both by operational CRM, such as sales and services, and by analytical CRM that uses complex mechanisms for data analysis to detect and identify possible buying behaviour patterns.

In more detail, operational CRM manages and coordinates the contacts of customers with the enterprise, marketing, sales and servicing. It includes applications that support the interaction between customers and the enterprise over many communication channels, such as the telephone, fax, e-mail, chatting and mobile devices. Analytical CRM regards the entirety of applications for the analysis of data relating to customers by various operating applications in order for information sources to be better 'tapped' so as to better understand customer attitudes and behaviours. More specifically, it includes applications that export data on the customer's history, his preferences and his profitability. This allows the analysis and forecasting of the value and behaviour of the customer, an assessment of demand with great accuracy and, finally, the business to approach its customers with tailor-made offers.

The main benefits that ensue from using CRM systems and of CRM, in general, can be summarised as follows: increased customer satisfaction, decreased direct marketing costs, more efficient marketing and lower cost for the acquisition of new customers. In addition to the considerable benefits brought by the installation of a CRM system at a business, it also poses a great challenge. Integrated CRM systems (operational and analytical) are very expensive and their implementation

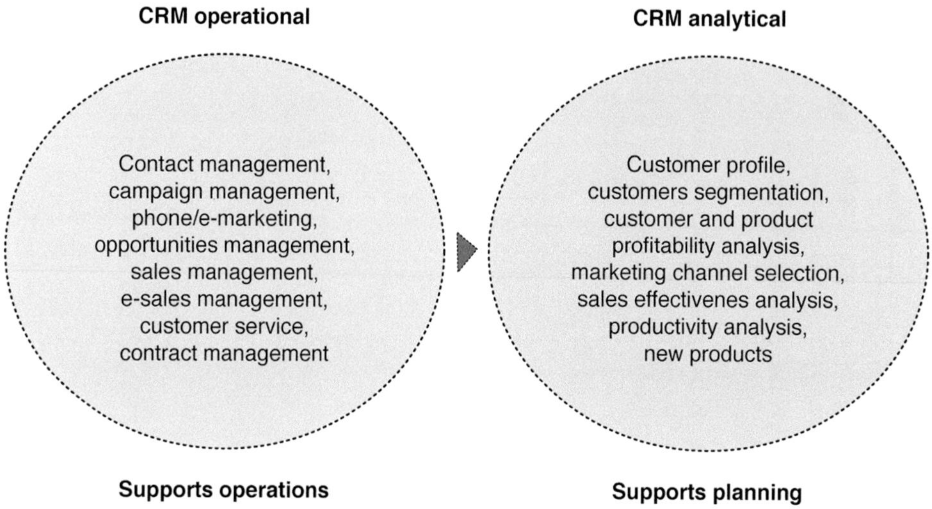

FIGURE 10.8 Operational and analytical CRM

is time-consuming. The percentage of installation failures is very high, due to excessive cost, the challenges to integration and the low acceptance rate of the new system by its users.

Moreover, the installation of a CRM system demands the restructuring of the company and important changes both to the structure and culture of the business, and to business processes regarding customer relations. The restructuring of such processes must aim at the integration of sales, marketing and customer service. This can be attained by consolidating all systems and tools, which will allow the use of information for the optimisation of customer relations. Finally, the installation of a CRM system presupposes also a change in how processes relating to customer relations are performed by personnel assigned with such duties. This change must aim for the development of long-term relations with the customer, an emphasis on maintaining customers against acquiring new ones and the transition from transactions to strategies that rest on customer relations (see Figure 10.8).

Partner relationship management systems

The management of customer relations in a company extends also to its business associates. The use of partner relationship management (PRM) systems aims at the automation of the relations between a company and its suppliers, whereby the use of data and the provision of analytical tools secures the improvement of the coordination of inter-business processes. To attain the aforementioned goals, mechanisms for the collection of data are required, as they are for the conversion of said data to useful information and the provision of tools for accessing and analysing data from a multitude of sides. What is required are the appropriate tools for the most effective and efficient management of knowledge to support decision-making, to resolve problems relating to business processes and to plan and control the offered levels of service with respect to what has been agreed upon.

Similarly to CRM, a PRM system cannot be considered as simply an application but more as a strategy for the reinforcement of collaborating enterprises by providing them with equal

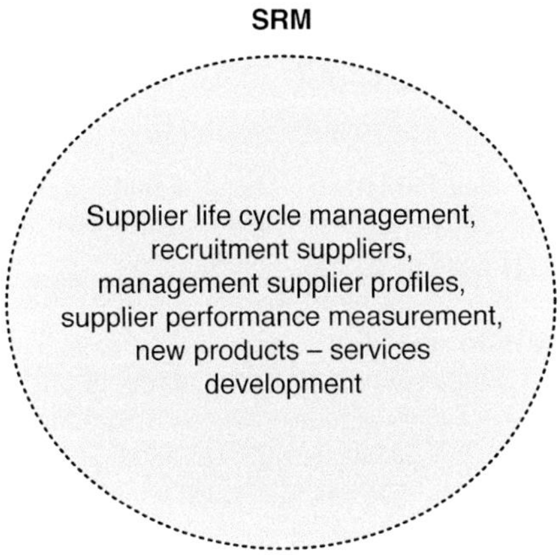

FIGURE 10.9 SRM system

access to data and tools possessed only by the employees of one company, such as information on the product catalogue, education and training, sales techniques, historic data and reports (see Figure 10.9). Each participating member must be in a position to participate on equal terms in the profits so that the expenses and the outcomes of such relations prove profitable for all parties involved. The objective remains the same: maximisation of the offered level of service and minimisation of cost. The provided functions of SRM are a significant factor for the increase in the efficiency and competitiveness of a supply chain.

10.3 Marketing and SCM in the internet era

Although most would agree that the internet and e-commerce/e-business have not affected the fundamental values and philosophies of marketing, they have shaped a multitude of tools and practices, which have been developed specifically with e-consumers in mind. Table 10.2 presents indicative cases of the impact of e-commerce/e-business on services marketing.

The following can be considered as e-marketing tools:

- Creation of electronic customer profiles: The visit of a consumer to the internet site of a company allows the recording of the following information: the IP address, the visitor's identity, the time and duration of the visit, the web pages visited, the recommended means of payment and shipment of the products.
- Electronic pricing offers the following capacities: (i) Continuous informing on the price of a product and briefing the customer who expressed an interest either for the product itself or for something similar; (ii) comparison between products and (iii) different pricing for different market segments and different geographical regions, based on sales history, seasonality, etc.
- Electronic advertising: The internet caters to the creation of low-cost advertisements, offering interactivity, active participation and the personalisation of content and services. A multitude of tools are available to company executives wishing to advertise their products. One can indicatively cite the following: banners, which are the most common tools to attract the consumer's attention and take them to the corresponding web page, pop-up windows, etc.

TABLE 10.2 Impact of the evolution of e-commerce/e-business on services marketing

Seven Ps of services marketing	*Impact of the evolution of e-commerce/e-business on services marketing*
Product	Better detection and targeting, larger volume and type of information (descriptively or via multimedia), inclusion of specialised benefits (market advice, recommendations and critiques)
Placement	New 'space', with the ability to perform orders without time limitations or the need to move spatially
Price	Easy price comparison, greater availability of offer prices and more benefits (personalised delivery conditions and customer support)
Promotion	Easier way to provide better offers or agreements (interconnected sales, suggested sales, discount codes and loyalty discounts), ability to show all offers, and more efficient and effective sale at the purchase point (reminders – prompting at checkout)
Physical evidence	Better fit to the consumer's lifestyle (better penetration in the consumer's reality, daily life and environment)
People	Connection with a wider set of stakeholders, competitors, unions and public bodies
Process	Better response to customer complaints, more effective and efficient feedback process

- The dramatic growth of social media allows marketers to plan promotional activities that are disseminated via the members of such networks or the creation of personal or group pages.
- Digital catalogues that by being digital permit and cater for comparison, filtering and real-time searching, as well as being interconnected with other files or web pages.

E-SCM

The term e-business describes those businesses whose existence and strategy rests on the internet and those businesses that have revised their mission, strategy and operations based on new models for collaboration and modern internet-based practices. It is a wide and encompassing notion that includes the concept of e-commerce. E-commerce refers to companies that employ innovative ICT technologies and more specifically the internet to perform *transactions* and interact with customers. Such transactions (according to the famous Gartner Group's four-phase maturity model that proposes the evolution stages as presence, interaction, transaction and transformation) can include the presentation of products, the attraction of customers (advertising and promotion), interaction with a customer (product catalogues and sales), the processing of orders and sales (taking and execution of orders, delivery and payments), customer support (monitoring the execution of an order, and after-sales service), the electronic exchange of documents and communication with suppliers (Baum and Di Maio 2000; Gartner Group 2000).

On the other hand, e-business (the transformation stage in the Gartner Group's four-phase maturity model) refers to companies that employ ICT technologies and the internet in particular to form collaborations. Such collaborations begin from the interior of the company itself, where operational and geographical boundaries are transgressed, offering the opportunity to employees to utilise and exchange all available information, assisted in this by intercorporate network infrastructure (privately owned corporate computer networks). The result is the allocation of

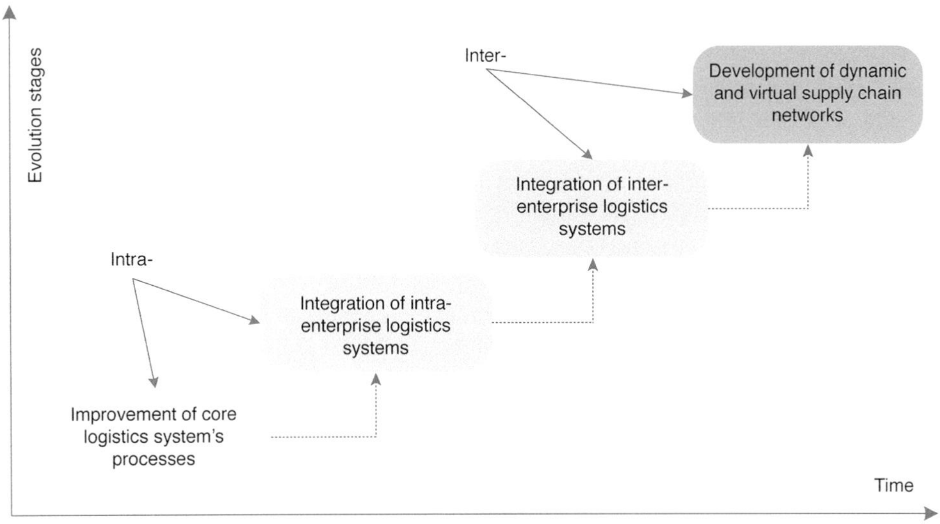

FIGURE 10.10 Evolution stages of logistics management/SCM

Source: Adapted from Folinas et al. (2004).

work (accounting department, production, procurements, sales, HR management, etc.) and the development of collaboration rules, with respect to the allocation of resources and the joint attainment of goals and objectives. Such collaboration may extend also outside the boundaries of a company, including business activities that run along the entire value chain, such as electronic purchases and the supply chain and transactions with business partners. Consequently, e-business pursues the upgrading of the company's relations with all key stakeholders of business processes in both the internal and the external environment of the business.

It is noteworthy to observe that the evolution of e-commerce/e-business (especially with respect to the last stages) is related to the stages of the evolution of logistics management/SCM. Initially logistics management focused on the provision of basic transportation services. Specifically, one can distinguish four stages (as presented in Figure 10.10):

- Stage of improving individual logistics processes.
- Stage of integrating internal logistics system processes.
- Stage of integrating logistics system processes across the businesses and members of a supply chain.
- Stage of establishing dynamic and virtual supply networks.

The first two refer to the interior of a business (internal), while the last two refer to two or more enterprises (external):

- *Improvement of individual logistics processes:* This stage represents the initial attempts by businesses to implement SCM techniques and methodologies aiming to improve specific operations of their logistics system (principally storage, transportation and distribution), pursuing better quality of the services rendered, lower prices for products/services and decrease in inventories and costs. To attain this, companies automate specific functions (of storage, transportation and distribution). The structure is strictly hierarchical, and various departments function as independent entities establishing an environment that consists of 'pockets' of information and decisions. The nature of this stage focuses on individual departments of the organisational structure of a business, and not on the customer or the associate, and on the acquisition of a competitive advantage.

- *Stage of consolidation of internal logistics system processes:* There is collaboration between the departments of the logistics system of an enterprise at this stage, aimed at optimising the enterprise's internal processes and towards its business integration. The first attempts to implement e-commerce applications are also observed, as companies have already developed internal networks and integrated information systems, which permit an increase in the efficiency of the supply chain and the performance of the logistics network. This network now has the capacity to digitally support basic communication and cooperation with suppliers, with respect to the management of distribution and transportation and the coordination of production and supplies. Decisions relating to the planning and operation of the supply chain are in force for the entire corporation and take account of all available resources. Attempts and efforts are focused beyond the optimisation of performance and cost to the better serving of customers, that is, the improvement and faster execution of orders.
- *Stage of consolidation of logistics systems processes between businesses and members of a supply chain:* The orientation of businesses at this stage is to balance an already realised internal improvement with the needs of the external environment of a full supply chain network. External resources are at the disposal of internal teams that pursue the overall improvement of the network and the satisfaction of the end consumer. Synergies are expanded across all levels in this case, and the degree of consolidation and synchronisation of the supply chain is not the most critical factor for the success of a business. To attain this, businesses create strong ties with their key customers by providing customised products/services, value added services, by differentiating their offered services from those of the competition. Innovative internet technologies are applied for the implementation of transactions between different enterprises. The automation of processes for the dispatch of order forms, invoices and other documents is thus supported. Value added collaborations are implemented in a totally functional manner and on separate parts of the chain, in contrast to the dynamic network of the virtual enterprise approach that is characterised by a strategic nature.
- *Stage of the establishment of dynamic and virtual supply networks:* The creation of collaborative models of an electronic supply chain and the establishment of fully interconnected networks are the principal characteristics of this stage. The collaborative virtue networks allow members to jointly collaborate in the design of new products and market demand forecasting, with the aid of the full transparency of information circulating across the entire supply chain, the capacity for flexible use of all available resources and better responsiveness to customers' demands since all members have a more informed and better view of the market. Concepts such as the dynamic management of the supply chain based on modern technology (due to the internet) and the management of external/dynamic networks are materialised. They aim at the optimal exploitation and use of all available internal and external resources, the decrease in the overall cost to the maximum degree possible and the full satisfaction of the end customer. The establishment of this dynamic environment leads to the optimisation of the supply chain and the blossoming of novel e-business applications. All efforts aim to adopt new business models, which are based completely on the internet, and which will assist and lead the business (or, better, the developing network of businesses) to a dominant

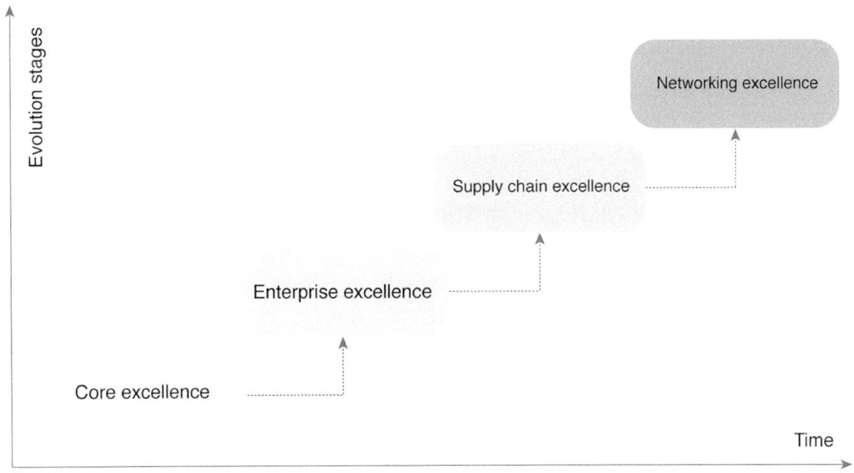

FIGURE 10.11 Evolution stages of e-commerce/e-business and logistics management/SCM interconnection

position in the market. Communities are established at this stage or e-marketplaces or supply chain synergies. Corporations form supply chain networks with one another with common objectives and objective goals. The dynamic nature of networks between companies lends a significant competitive advantage to the participating enterprises and renders them capable to face the new conditions of a globalised market. Emphasis is placed on selecting the suitable associates, which rests on the special skills of each company – member and the high standard of information and process integration among the members, elements that render value to the customer and increase the efficiency of supply chains.

The connection of the evolution of logistics management/SCM, on the one hand, and e-commerce/e-business, on the other, is presented in Figure 10.11. The following sections pursue the theme in more detail.

Core excellence

The first stage focuses on individual logistics processes. A small supplier base and relationships established are characterised by relatively limited trust and the context of specific transactions. The enterprise creates its website for promoting its products and services, and this site is not interconnected with some other specialised business information system. Its key feature is that decision-making is decentralised, departmental and dissected, while the sharing of information between the departments is also limited. Focusing analysis on logistics processes with respect to supplies, purchases are implemented on the level of the department, and the principal objective is to minimise inventories, while the main challenge is the lack of feedback on customer needs.

Enterprise excellence

The second stage focuses on optimising the business as a whole. This observes the strategy for unifying information flows between the different departments of an enterprise, while business decisions are taken collectively and with teamwork. The enterprise communicates with its strategic partners using standardised communication forms for the performance of specific processes. It installs and operates integrated ERP systems that aim to offer functionality, while enterprises usually also implement the restructuring of their business procedures.

To promote their products even further, ERP system manufacturers have adopted and implemented a series of practices and technologies to support e-commerce/e-business activities. Practically all ERP system suppliers have added applications that cater and support processes such as electronic procurements, electronic sales, internet store management (i.e., the presentation of products in electronic catalogues, customer management, basket analysis, payment mechanism, monitoring of orders and customers, advertising mechanisms, personal-customised service and order-taking management). Simultaneously, companies also hope that the expansion of their already existing ERP systems will not only 'positively affect' the investment they made in the ERP solution but at the same time will also accelerate the development of their activities to become involved in e-commerce/e-business.

The installation of ERP systems based on central database systems allows for a unified and uniform business planning and taking of strategic decisions. The logistics processes (supplies, inventory/warehouse management and production scheduling) are treated as an integrated system supported by the ERP system, as are main and daily works, such as product picking, packing and shipping. The existence of a central database also permits the central management of marketing and sales.

Supply chain excellence

The third stage sees the development of electronic collaboration across the entire length of the supply chain by the development of the intra-business organisational structure and decision-making. The exchange is facilitated by standardised documents and jointly planned intra-business processes – one that is based on open standards (EDI-XML).

Electronic Data Interchange (EDI) and *Extensible Markup Language* (XML) technologies are standards for the exchange of business data. EDI technology was the first to emerge, defined as the exchange of structured business data in digital format between the information systems of two or more commercial partners with minimum human intervention. Data relate to accounting and logistics documents (orders, invoices, waybills and dispatch notes). These messages or standards are transferred in a standardised format that must be agreed between the transacting businesses or organisations. The non-existence of common standards for all potential business partners requires new and individual negotiations.

XML emerged later and is the most significant effort today for the digital transfer of data and the automated and real-time execution of business transactions. XML follows on from Standard Generalised Markup Language (SGML – ISO 8879) and aims to organise and structure data so that they can be automatically utilisable by any software or database. It is the new standard that has been developed by the World Wide Web Consortium (W3C). It has been adopted by major international organisations, such as the United Nations Centre for Trade Facilitation and Electronic Business, or UN/CEFACT, research facilities (OASIS, electronic business XML or ebXML, RosettaNet, etc.) and many businesses.

The company aims to integrate either its ERP or devoted information systems with the CRM and/or PRM systems cited above and the SCM systems. Usually all of this is implemented via the internet, which functions as an e-marketplace. Faster processing of the supply procedure is thus attained (which comprises a set of repeated processes), allowing for significant improvements in terms of less administrative and managerial encumbrance, better service quality and faster satisfaction of requirements compared to the previously available costly and time-consuming processes. For buyers, the key advantage offered by this solution is that they can now choose a supplier among many faster suppliers, indirectly and at a lower cost, which results in better product quality and faster delivery. The direct and immediate performance of the suppliers' procedure, electronic negotiation, digital contract signing and cooperation under specifications can contribute to the decrease in both the time and cost of transactions, aiming to fulfil procurement needs. The execution of supply orders is immediate, since all orders and information entered in the internet site are simultaneously shared by all relevant applications at every location of the supplier's enterprise. By having access to the current inventory and the data relating to the supplier's dispatches, the customer can be informed on the status of his order, including availability and expected dispatch dates. Among the benefits for suppliers is the capacity for submitting bids and offers on a global scale, the low cost of submitting an offer and the ability to cooperate with other suppliers. Thus, electronic procurements and the sharing of information offered by an ERP system in conjunction with a subsystem mean that suppliers have the capacity to act fast, directly and effectively with respect to the services they offer and have the ability to offer a high standard of services to the buyers. The application allows suppliers to directly interact with their customers with respect to briefing on the course of their order, the reasons for delays, if there are any, or the renewal of the inventory list. Finally, external sharing of information with suppliers and customers begins, as does decision-making by the intra-business teams that are created.

Networking excellence

The fourth stage sees the culmination of efforts for a dynamic integration of supply chain processes based on knowledge management systems and by employing human resources that specialise in the use of modern technologies. This stage is characterised by the full sharing of processes and information, while there is a high level of trust in the development of collaborative relationships. In addition to knowledge management systems, also encouraged is the use of collaborative methodologies, such as collaborative commerce, virtual organisations and CPFR methodologies. The fourth stage is where information is fully shared and transparent in the context of the dynamic collaborative relationships created. New models for e-business and the corresponding technologies support the successful and effective use of electronic supply overcoming any obstacles that stand between the parties constituting a chain. New business networks (based on the internet) are created, replacing the traditional linear model and exhibiting the following characteristics:

- Full transparency and availability of all information relating to the customer, the product, sales, transactions with suppliers, etc.
- Increased and better relationships with customers, attained via fast, direct and accurate delivery and the integrated servicing services.
- Effective and efficient transactions through the solidification of information flows, financial magnitudes and products/services.

- Flexibility in the adjustment of technological infrastructures and collaborative relations.
- Detailed description and optimisation of the movement of products, of costing and, in general, of the activities required for the satisfaction of demand.
- Environment encouraging joint decision-making and leading to a synchronised supply chain.

The challenges that must be faced for the establishment of an integrated electronic supply chain are many, but the potential benefits are even greater. For this reason, businesses today have realised the need for new business models and real-time information systems. As organisations/businesses enter a new era of competition, the electronic supply chain can play a catalytic role and assist in gaining a larger market share, with the ultimate goals of maximising profitability and customer satisfaction.

The concept of a virtual organisation is approached not as one/autonomous business but as a network of businesses, different and independent businesses, where the use of electronic means and media (most notably the internet) and the sharing of knowledge permit the establishment of dynamic networks, which are in a position to offer more complex products to the market, products manufactured in accordance with their customers' special and specific requirements. Every business or member of the network possesses only part of the skills and resources required for the manufacture and distribution of products or services. The rest come as the result of synergies. A virtual organisation is, therefore, a temporary alliance of businesses, which come to collaborate and share their special skills, resources and competences and have an objective goal: to increase their degree of responsiveness to the business opportunities markets offer (Manthou et al. 2005; Folinas et al. 2003).

The principal features of a virtual organisation include the eradication of geographical boundaries, the absence of boundaries or limits to the movement of information; the liquidity of their organisational form; the high trust and capacity for collaborative and direct synergies; their very high speed and flexibility; and the unity of appearance with respect to customers. More specifically (Folinas et al. 2003), they include the following:

- Absence of boundaries: A network of geographically dispersed companies or company departments is established.
- Emphasis on special skills: Each participating enterprise possesses its special skills, which are complementary to those of the other associates. This fact allows participating enterprises to cater for market needs, offering flexibility in adapting excellent products/services to them.
- Searching for opportunities: A virtual organisation is the temporary collaboration established for a specific business opportunity. Upon its completion, the collaboration ends and the virtual organisation is dismantled. The key feature of this approach is the ability to implement innovative systems, methodologies and practices that are fully customer oriented.
- Dynamic structure: A virtual organisation has a dynamic organisational structure, with rules for administration and management that can easily be readjusted. Thus, a business can enter or exit a virtual organisation at any time, and all of its members usually have the same rights in the absence of a dominant business entity.
- Not fixed or semi-fixed business relationships: Dependence relationships are in place between the members of a virtual organisation, but they can also continue after the completion and dismantling of the virtual organisation.
- Trust: A key feature is the degree of trust between the members of a virtual organisation. The development of a trust that rests on the sharing and allocation of skills and information can replace the traditional form of management and control. This fact is due to the type of relations, the shared skills and knowledge. All of the above require a high degree of trust.

- Technological infrastructure: The technological and communications infrastructure permitting geographically remote companies to collaborate significantly increases the effectiveness of sharing and jointly utilising their available resources, while simultaneously decreasing the corresponding transactional costs.

E-order

The taking and execution of an order include all activities required to offer the ordered products and services to the clients, including after-sales service. In the case of an e-order, these activities are implemented via the internet and by the application of e-commerce and e-business technologies, standards and practices.

> There are two challenges for e-order. Firstly, e-commerce and e-business rest on the pull philosophy, i.e., the activities of order execution begin with an order, usually adjusted (e.g., at the internet sites of Cisco and Smart-car) (in contrast to traditional commerce, which usually begins with production and ends at storage and then is promoted to the customers). Consequently, it is difficult to forecast demand due to lack of experience and the different customer preferences (global market!). Secondly, e-commerce rests on a door-to-door practice; that is, goods are delivered to the customer's door (in sharp contrast to traditional commerce, where goods are manufactured and transported in large quantities to shops' warehouses).

The activities included are the following:

- Checking the completeness and accuracy of an order;
- Credit control;
- Recording of order for execution;
- Checking the availability of the requested products;
- Preparation for the commencement of production (back order) or cancellation of the order;
- Registering the order with the accounting department and charging the customer;
- Execution/collection of order;
- Updating inventories;
- Packaging of order;
- Loading of order;
- Order delivery;
- Management of returns.

As was presented in Chapter 3, these activities make up lead time and are classified into three sub-times (Figure 10.12). Similarly, to decrease the lead time, we have to propose actions to decrease the three sub-times.

1. Reduction of order processing time:
   - *Better forecasting of demand*: The forecast of demand may be frequently performed with collaborating business associates along the supply chain to accurately and correctly

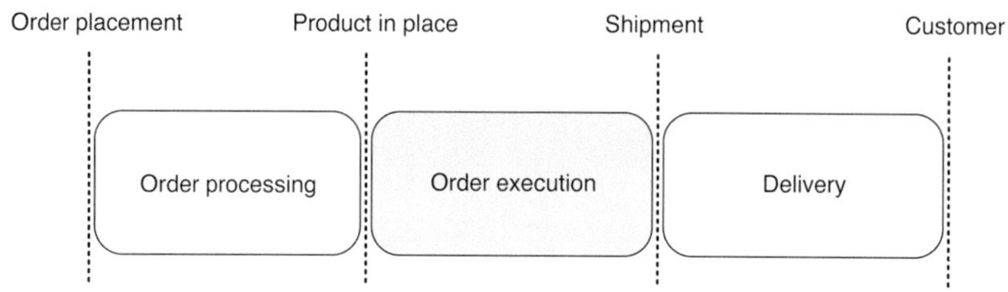

FIGURE 10.12 Decreasing the lead time in e-order

evaluate demand and plan to cover it. Moreover, the application of the collaborative planning forecasting and replenishment (CPFR) technique that was analysed in the previous chapter may help, on the one hand, in the better exploitation of the data available and, on the other hand, in more effective decision-making.

- *Automation of order taking procedure:* More specifically, order taking can be performed using EDI or XML technologies or using digital forms, which cater for a faster, cheaper and more precise procedure. In business-to-business (B2B) transactions, orders can be made and transmitted automatically to suppliers when the levels of inventories fall below a certain level, e.g., by the application of the vendor-managed inventory (VMI) technique that was examined in the previous chapter.
- *Establishment of electronic markets:* An e-marketplace aims to bring together potential suppliers and customers. It is usually set up on an internet site managed by a third business entity that functions as an intermediary. This entity provides appropriate immediate informing and informing with accuracy to suppliers on the demand order, while also informing customers on the course of the execution of their orders.

2. Reduction in time for the execution of an order:

- *Automation of warehouses:* Using automated systems for the collection of products and the use of belts and robotics systems.
- *Use of RFID technology*: This, as was presented in a previous section, allows for the automated and real-time identification of objects and also offers the capacity to monitor objects (static/moving).

3. Use of telematics systems, which transmit data via the internet:

- *Telematics applications:* These in logistics focus on the transportation/distribution of products and specifically on vehicle fleet management. A great number of systems and applications (dubbed by some as 'intelligent transportation systems') are available in the market today, which allow the automatic detection of the vehicle's location in real time, the detection of problems in the vehicle or some system thereof, the ability to navigate the vehicle, the safety of drivers and vehicles and the monitoring of the merchandise's state.
- *GPS/GPRS systems:* These are used for monitoring and locating packages, as well as informing the customers by e-mail on the status of the order and the expected time of arrival of incoming packages.

Figure 10.13 presents the principal users of such applications, e.g., the company employee who sends the merchandise for the execution of the order; the driver of the transportation vehicle; the customer, namely, the recipient of the merchandise; and, finally, the system's manager.

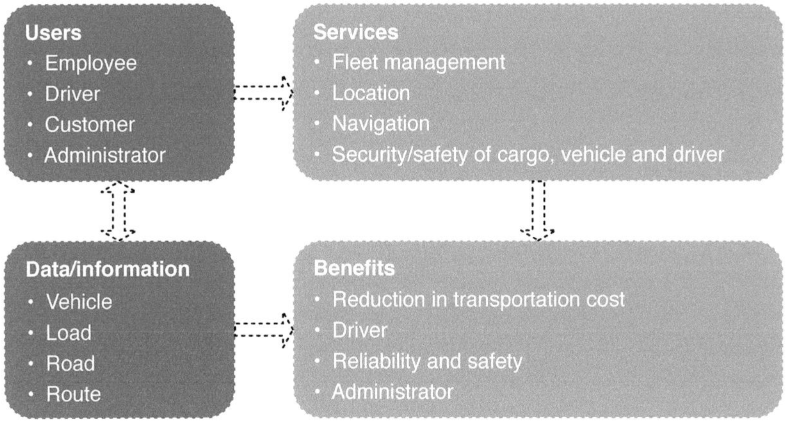

FIGURE 10.13 Framework of telematics applications in transportation

Telematics applications allow the exchange of date in real time between the users mentioned above. Data relating to location and course are collected from the vehicle or other means of transportation, as are data relating to the transportation or distribution itself (such as speed and delivery/dispatch times) and the status of the vehicle and its cargo. The company's employees can give useful information to the driver (on various emergencies, such as accidents or traffic jams) and orders to change course or route.

The recipient can be informed on the location of the merchandise and the estimated arrival time. By collecting the necessary information and printing the appropriate reports, the manager can better plan for routes and the steps for receiving and executing an order. The data are used for the management of a vehicle (or a fleet of vehicles), for tracing its location, for navigation, for the collection of necessary information on the vehicle's safety, and the safety of the merchandise and the driver. The information can be viewed on a mobile phone, a portable computer, a PDA, etc. Finally, the use of such applications leads to a decrease in transportation/distribution costs and an increase in productivity, efficiency, reliability and safety, and the rendering of a high level of service to the customers.

Business intelligence systems

From a business perspective, the true value of any business information system (such as ERP and CRM systems), best-of-breed business information systems (such as the WMS and TMS) and e-commerce/e-business initiatives (e-orders) comes from their ability to reveal to end users the inner workings of business activities and to provide useful insight into corporate transactions (Folinas 2007).

> The most important change that informatics brings to companies is not faster PCs. It is the reassurance it offers to 'labourers' that they have easy access and can utilise the enormous quantities of information stored inside and outside the company (Folinas 2007).

These aforementioned applications provided static reports and insights on transactional data, which were enough for line-level managers, but decision-makers wanted information in a more summarised fashion to perform strategic analyses from huge amounts of data that expanded in a wide time range and from multiple applications (Folinas 2007). The answer to their requests came from the introduction of data warehousing (DW) and the online analytical processing (OLAP) approach. The concept of DW is to simply extract operational transaction data into a separate repository and reorganise data in a renormalised and aggregated fashion that is more appropriate for analysis and performing queries. OLAP provided the tools to perform interactive analysis against DW instead of operational files and databases. DW offered the benefit of integrated source data, which provided better data quality and consistency. It also enabled data to be summarised and kept for historical reporting and analysis. The DW approach also reduced the decision support load on the operational transaction systems. The advantage of DW is that users can query data from across the enterprise. Using the OLAP technique, analysts create complex, multidimensional analyses and deliver to business users meaningful insights that might not be readily apparent (especially when applied with data mining).

> Data mining is the process for searching 'hidden' relations and standards between data kept in data warehouses. These relations and standards represent valuable knowledge for various entities on the database, such as clients, products, suppliers and employees. Examples of such relations may be the response and behaviour of customers to specific offers, the compliance of suppliers to the company's requirements, etc. Specific methodologies, techniques and tools are employed to implement this process, while the ultimate objective is to create models that will represent and be able to forecast reality in the best possible way.

The software applications, technologies and analytical methodologies that perform data analysis and support decision-making constitute the business intelligence (BI) domain. BI captures organisational data from disparate sources and presents it to decision-makers in a user-friendly manner. It can be considered as a value chain converting primary data to information and useful knowledge, useful knowledge leading to informed decisions and actions. It exploits all the software applications, practices, technologies and analytical methodologies that perform data analysis and provides real-time visibility and access to the right information, for the right individual at the right moment and in the right form, wherever he may be, to support enterprise competitiveness.

All of the above would facilitate (a) easy access and collection of primary data from the individual subsystems and external data maintained in the systems of business associates (e.g., members of a supply chain); (b) homogenisation and transformation of primary data to utilisable information, by the application of common business rules; and (c) organisation of information in data structures, which are suitable for multidimensional analysis of a large volume of historic data (Folinas 2007).

In the modern business environment, BI applications are facing significant challenges and are called to satisfy specific demands:

- *Business data are kept everywhere*: They are stored in (a) multiple systems (intra-business, subsystems, associates' systems, internet sites, social networks, etc.) but also (b) in multiple forms (Excel sheets, non-structured documents, e-mails, other formats, e.g., XML, etc.).

- *The significant role of the semantics for business data:* What this means in practice is that an agreement is required to attribute the same meaning/denotation (e.g., common definitions and unified semantics) by all collaborating organisations or businesses or departments and with respect to all business data.
- *Provision of fully parameterised reports on areas of interest:* Specifically, the creation of reports and evaluations based on indices in business areas such as financial analysis, with indices and data relating to basic financial states, and HR analysis, with indices and data relating to productivity, the potential for human resources development, etc., supports function analysis for procurements and supplies with the corresponding performance indices and data for the appraisal of their effectiveness.

Synopsis

- Internet-era tools and technologies support the interdisciplinary coexistence of and systemic approach to marketing and the supply chain. These include e-commerce and e-business technologies such as auto ID of product technologies, customer and supplier relationship management systems, social networks, augmented reality and electronic point of sales.
- The barcode is the most widely known automatic identification and data capture technology, allowing fast and easy collection and storage of data at the moment such data are created. Many businesses (principally large retail chains) have opted for a new auto ID technology in the last decade: RFID, which uses radio frequencies to read data stored in a small circuit known as an RFID tag.
- Business information systems such as ERP, CRM, WMSs and TMSs aim to support the real integration of all functions, departments and employees in an integrated enterprise that covers all the needs of a business operating in real time and guaranteeing precise and accurate informing, while also containing the best business practices.
- All of the above but most of all the internet/e-commerce/e-business have played a crucial role in the evolution of the interconnection between marketing and SCM.

Review and discussion questions

- Identify the areas in which auto ID technologies can be applied.
- Describe the functionalities of barcodes, RFID and QR codes.
- Many believe that the decision to install a business information system is a strategic decision. Do you agree?
- What are the main types of business information systems? You can use the framework for the categorisation of business information systems.
- Why do we call ERP systems integrated resource planning systems?
- Why is BPR crucial in the implementation of a business information system?
- Comment on the following phrase: ‘Choosing to implement an ERP system with changes also leads the organisation to changes in its business processes, while simultaneously forcing the system to change as well’.
- Describe the parts and identify the benefits and drawbacks of CRM systems.
- Describe the evolution stages of logistics management/SCM.
- Describe the evolution stages of the e-commerce/e-business and logistics management/SCM interconnection.
- How do e-commerce/e-business technologies and practices help optimise lead time?

Case studies

Case study 1: Technologies for marketing and SCM synergies

ERP supports the real integration of all functions, departments, and employees in a business and covers all the needs of the enterprise. When IT systems such as ERP systems support a business process, the process should be automated, simplified, optimised and reengineered as needed. The firm's order management cycle is one such process, and, in this case, we are asked to explore it in the context that ensures that each time a firm handles an order, the firm must ensure that the customer is handled at the same time.

Shapiro, Rangan, and Svioloka (1993) challenged firms to staple themselves to a customer's order. This concept was so popular that it has become a classic. In the article, the order management cycle is broken into ten steps, beginning with planning and ending with post-sales service. The steps are as follows:

1. *Order planning*: Designing the order management process.
2. *Order generation*: Determining how and where orders will be solicited and acquired.
3. *Cost estimation and pricing*: Providing price quotes to customers.
4. *Order receipt and entry*: Acknowledging a new order and starting the workflow.
5. *Order selection and prioritisation*: Prioritising orders and how they will be handled sequentially.
6. *Scheduling*: Moving the order into production or distribution.
7. *Fulfilment*: Delivering to the customer.
8. *Billing*: Creating an invoice.
9. *Returns and claims*: Handling any complaints or returns.
10. *Post-sales service*: Service and support activities (warranties, replacement parts, etc.)

Many years later, Gilmore (2010) looks at how the level of automation in the order management cycle has changed since the Shapiro et al. (1992) article was first published. Firms are increasingly faced with handling customer orders in a multichannel environment. In the 1992 article, the ten steps were characterised as having overlapped functional responsibilities, with each step considered the primary responsibility of a given specific department and no step the sole responsibility of any department. Since the order management cycle typically is still not under the purview of a single owner, it is even more important to staple oneself with a multichannel order.

Automation can reveal congestion points and is meant to lead to more simplified and optimised procedures. Where customer orders are falling through the cracks, reengineering the physical process and accompanying information technology may be in order.

Among the takeaways and managerial implications from the above discussion are the following. Firstly, customer orders progress through ten fragmented steps in the process of being fulfilled by a supplier. Also, customer orders can be placed and distributed through multiple channels, making 'stapling oneself to an order' more difficult than in single-channel networks. Secondly, automation can help reveal contagion points that need to be addressed. Finally, managers could benefit by viewing several orders from the perspective of multiple customers as their orders flow through different channels and update accordingly.

Multiple-choice questions

1. Which technology uses radio waves to automatically identify objects and collect data?

   A. QR codes
   B. EAN-13 barcodes
   C. RFID
   D. NFC

2. What is the primary purpose of the check digit in EAN-13 barcodes?

   A. Enhance visual readability
   B. Reduce production costs
   C. Validate data accuracy
   D. Store additional product information

3. Which component is NOT part of an RFID system?

   A. Transponder
   B. Antenna
   C. Magnetic stripe
   D. Reader

4. How does NFC differ from traditional RFID technology?

   A. Requires physical contact for data transfer
   B. Operates at significantly longer ranges
   C. Uses electromagnetic induction for communication
   D. Exclusively supports one-way communication

5. What is the primary function of operational CRM systems?

   A. Long-term customer analytics
   B. Real-time customer interaction management
   C. Supplier performance evaluation
   D. Inventory optimisation algorithms

6. Which technology enables bidirectional data exchange between devices within close proximity?

   A. QR codes
   B. Telematics
   C. NFC
   D. Barcoding

7. What is a critical challenge in implementing SRM systems?

   A. Reducing product variety
   B. Aligning supplier goals with organisational strategies
   C. Eliminating digital payment systems
   D. Standardising global regulatory frameworks

8. Which factor most directly impacts the evolution of e-commerce in supply chains?

   A. Reduced internet penetration rates
   B. Declining customer expectations
   C. Advanced logistics management technologies
   D. Homogeneous cultural preferences

9. What is the primary advantage of telematics in transportation management?

   A. Eliminating driver involvement
   B. Reducing vehicle maintenance costs
   C. Real-time fleet monitoring and route optimisation
   D. Standardising global traffic regulations

10. Which metric is critical for evaluating RFID system effectiveness?

    A. Aesthetic design compatibility
    B. Read-rate accuracy in diverse environments
    C. Colour contrast ratios
    D. Manual data entry speed

11. How do QR codes enhance marketing–SCM integration?

    A. By storing static pricing information
    B. Enabling dynamic customer engagement through mobile access
    C. Reducing product packaging sizes
    D. Eliminating need for inventory tracking

12. What characterises analytical CRM systems compared to operational CRM?

    A. Focus on real-time transaction processing
    B. Emphasis on historical data analysis for strategic insights
    C. Direct management of supplier relationships
    D. Automation of warehouse sorting processes

13. Which trend has accelerated the adoption of SRM technologies?

    A. Decreased supplier competition
    B. Rising demand for transactional buyer–supplier relationships
    C. Globalisation of supply networks
    D. Reduced focus on sustainability metrics

14. What is a key barrier to implementing blockchain in SCM?

    A. Low computational power requirements
    B. Resistance to decentralised data management
    C. Simplified regulatory compliance
    D. Reduced need for partner collaboration

15. How does IoT contribute to demand sensing?

    A. By eliminating historical sales data reliance
    B. Through real-time monitoring of product usage patterns
    C. Reducing warehouse storage capacity
    D. Standardising global pricing strategies

Essay question

Analyse how emerging technologies (e.g., RFID, IoT and blockchain) facilitate synergies between marketing and SCM. Discuss their role in addressing three interconnected challenges: (a) enhancing real-time data visibility across the value chain, (b) improving customer engagement through personalised experiences and (c) optimising logistics operations for omnichannel fulfilment. Provide specific examples of how these technologies create competitive advantages, while balancing implementation costs and organisational adaptability.

11

SUPPLY CHAIN MANAGEMENT IN THE CASE OF SERVICES MARKETING

Introduction

This chapter examines the relationships between contracting parties in service management and marketing, emphasising the importance of reputation management. It highlights sustainable service supply, demand, integration and coordination management as key value chain practices. Modern economies increasingly rely on services to support material goods in demand-driven markets. Services contribute over 70% to European GDP and employment. However, research on service supply chains and the role of human capital is still underdeveloped. Various classifications of services help monitor and evaluate intangible services. The growing contribution of services to GDP in developed economies underscores the need to track service value chain trends (Figure 11.1). Global competition demands high customer satisfaction, leading to the 'servitisation' of goods.

Learning objectives

Upon completing this chapter, readers should be able to answer the following questions:

- What are the fundamentals of service supply chain management (SCM) and how it differs from traditional supply chains?
- How to examine the role of marketing in service supply chains, including the integration of the 4Ps and extended 7Ps framework?
- How to analyse the key challenges in managing service supply chains, such as demand forecasting, quality control and customer expectations?
- What is the level of impact of digital transformation on service supply chains, including the use of AI, big data and blockchain technology?
- How to assess sustainability initiatives in service supply chains and their implications for business strategy and consumer behaviour?
- What are some of the case studies of service-oriented businesses that have successfully implemented innovative SCM practices?

DOI: 10.4324/9781003650973-11

	Social
EU countries	65
Worldwide	62
Ireland	57
Finland	61
Sweden	65
Lithuania	63
Latvia	63
Poland	59
Czechia	60
Slovakia	57
Slovenia	58
Hungary	58
Romania	60
Bulgaria	59
Greece	68
Cyprus	74
Malta	80
Croatia	61
Austria	62
Portugal	67
Spain	69
Italy	65
France	69
Luxembourg	81
Belgium	71
Germany	63
Netherlands	69
Denmark	66

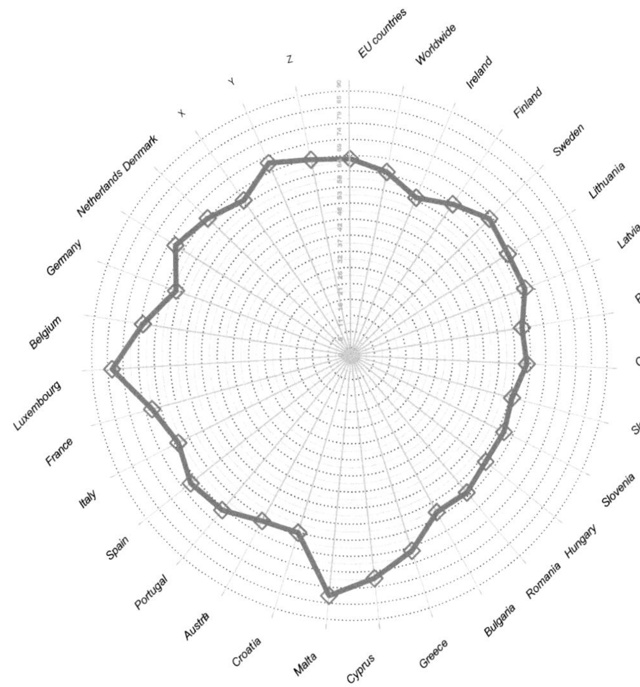

FIGURE 11.1 Contribution of services to EU economies

Note: After processing from the source, CIA (2023), CIA estimations, as indexed on the website, https://www.cia.gov/the-world-factbook/field/gdp-composition-by-sector-of-origin/ (Data on the contribution of services to the GDP of countries/'GDP – composition, by sector of origin').

Outline

11.1 Marketing and supply chain integration in services
11.2 Challenges in managing service supply chains
11.3 Sustainability and value chain management practice
11.4 Future trends and conclusion

11.1 Marketing and supply chain integration in services

The role of the 4Ps and 7Ps in service marketing

Marketing in services involves a comprehensive set of actions known as the marketing mix, which originally comprised the 4Ps: product, price, pace and promotion. As services gained prominence in the 1980s, Booms and Bitner (1981) expanded this mix by adding people, processes and physical evidence, resulting in the 7Ps framework tailored to service marketing.

Hooley et al. (1990) emphasised that marketing should extend beyond departmental boundaries to cultivate a market-oriented culture across the organisation. This perspective aligns with the concept of socially sustainable supply chains, which aim to enhance social welfare while safeguarding stakeholders and the broader society.

Building strong customer relationships is central to modern marketing practices. Ravald and Grönroos (1996) highlighted the role of relationship marketing in enhancing value-based relationships across the value chain. Technological advancements, including AI, big data and predictive analytics, have further transformed marketing, enabling more precise customer behaviour analysis.

Marketing activities intersect with supply chain processes, including sales, procurement, logistics and customer support. This interconnectedness reinforces the view that SCM and marketing are complementary disciplines. Lambert and Cooper (2000) noted that SCM leverages intra- and intercompany integration to optimise performance.

Value supply chains in services versus physical goods

Supply chains for tangible goods typically involve the production, transportation and storage of physical products. In contrast, service supply chains focus on the delivery of intangible offerings, often requiring simultaneous production and consumption. Zhou et al. (2009) highlighted key similarities and differences between these supply chains (Table 11.1).

Service supply chains can be categorised into two types: service-only supply chains and product-service supply chains. The increasing complexity of business environments has driven companies to adopt innovative practices to manage their service value chains effectively (Figure 11.2).

The rapid developments and changes occurring in the external business environment led to the adoption of new practices supported by sectoral activities of the tertiary economic sector. These changes of the external business environment create tendencies for necessary adjustments of the companies active in different business branches. For example, the pandemic period is a good example of how businesses should behave in an uncertain environment through crisis management practices. Globalisation and the development of telecommunication and internet application technology have influenced customers to have the ability to access direct and alternative information about markets, products and services (e.g., buyers, suppliers, end consumers, competitors and players in the industry) internationally.

TABLE 11.1 Similarities and differences between material and services-based supply chains

	Similarities		*Differences*
a.	Procurement decisions	f.	Labour-intensive processes
b.	Causes of errors in delivery process	g.	Customer involvement and service heterogeneity
c.	SCM coordination – information sharing	h.	Service quality is hard to measure and monitor
d.	Bullwhip effect occurrence	i.	Intangibility
e.	Causes of bullwhip effect – demand signalling	j.	Capacity versus inventory
		k.	Simultaneity of production and consumption
		l.	Customer–supplier duality

Source: After use and reformulation from the source (Zhou et al. 2009: 138–139).

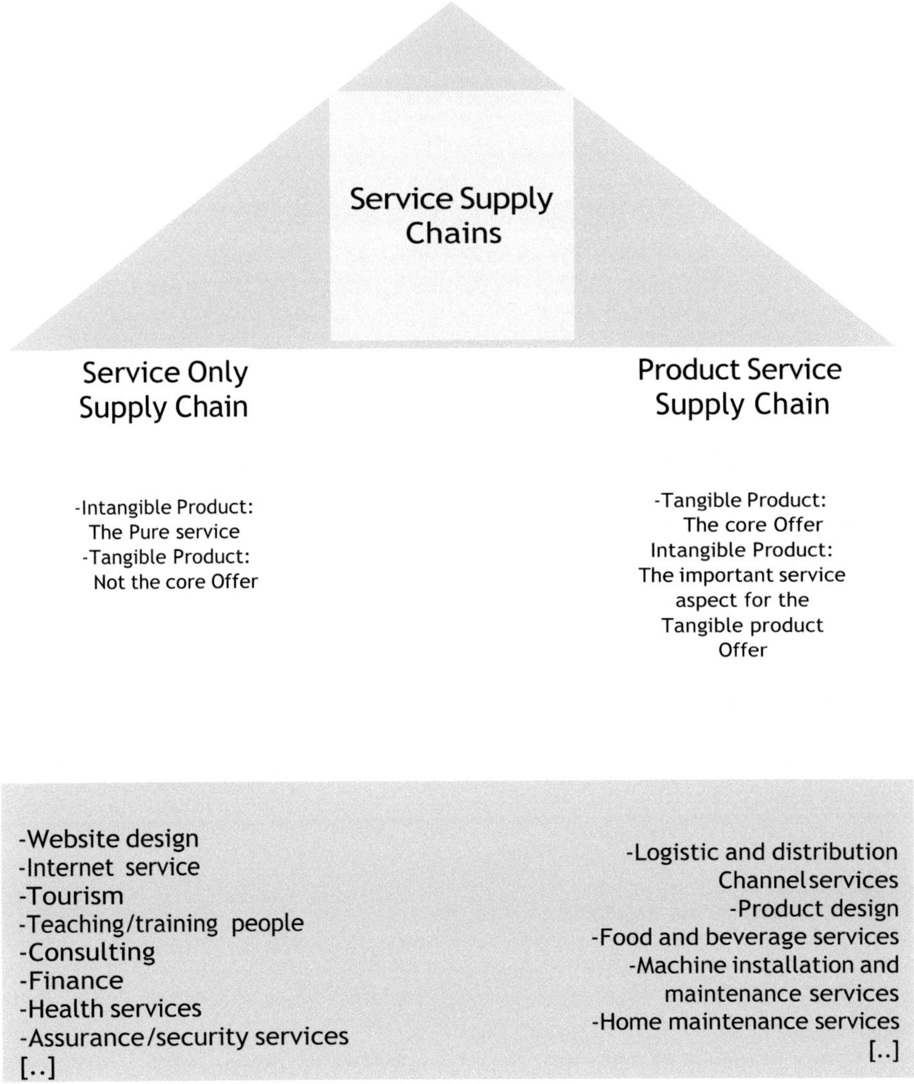

FIGURE 11.2 The service supply chains house

Customer needs vary over time and evolve, while at the same time, together with the evolution of technologies, they signal the need to adapt business operations to achieve sustainable business goals. The internationalisation of activities and the search for rational and innovative solutions for the contracting parties intensify the effort to search for suitable partners and collaborations in the business environment. Thus, the classic processes in the supply chain that referred to service provision procedures such as the management of human resources and material goods, the management of partnerships and distribution channels, and the management of business information systems no longer concern only the relevant department of the company but are undertaken by external partners, from, for example, specialised companies and service organisations that add value to the supply chain.

Business partnerships that support the necessary provision of services are based on increasing core competencies while simultaneously aiming to achieve greater efficiency and effectiveness for the business that selects partners. Therefore, this situation is also an important reason why the service sector has been developing rapidly in recent decades. In still other sectoral activities, cooperation between various parties is necessary for the performance of products and services that require a chain of actions. Thus, in the case of the sectoral activities of tourism, the performance of the related activities judged by the final recipient, who is the buyer or consumer of the goods, requires an effective and efficient cooperation, for example, between the accommodations, passenger transport services, organisers and tourist offices, attractions, event planners, rental services, retailers and shopping centres, and local visitor information and promotion organisations, among others.

Scholars today agree that services are provided along with tangibles through multiple value chains that include the following important actors: suppliers, providers and customers/consumers of services. Value chains in the service industry and, more generally, value chains of material goods that are enhanced with service elements rely on human ability and skill and acquire significant weight in making managerial decisions when these, due to the nature of the services, affect the outcome of providing a service to intermediate and final customers. Thus, in the research literature, the study of the behaviour of human members who come into communication and influence with their behaviour the building of relationships between the members of a service chain is of research interest.

Partner relationships are defined by formal and informal rules that also define the culture of human organisations and companies in providing services and creating value chains. A typical institutional document that defines relationships is the contract that also has legal force. As a contract, one could define 'the relations among parties to the process of projecting the exchange into the future' (Macneil 1980: 4).

Customer relationship management in SCM

The literature review approach to the topic of the main practices of relationship management in supply chains highlights the following key aspects that refer to the effectiveness of relationship management in a chain.

Highlighting confidentiality and trust between members is for many authors an important factor in building trusting relationships between members of a chain. Trust is the cornerstone of strong relationships, reducing perceived risks and fostering open communication. Studies show that trust enhances information sharing, collaborative decision-making and problem-solving.

In addition to trust, another important factor in building relationships between chain members is the development of an effective communication process between chain members. Transparent and frequent communication helps align goals, set expectations and resolve conflict. Digital tools such as SCM software and enterprise resource planning systems facilitate the seamless flow of information.

With the scope, to ensure the confidentiality and substance of the communication between the members of the chain, it is important that the members are involved in the administrative decisions that concern them and that aim at common benefits and pursuits. Thus, the literature indicates that collaborative approaches are important for problem-solving and because they strengthen relationships by demonstrating commitment to mutual success.

The relationship development process should also be supported by the evaluation of the performance of the efforts aimed at quantifying the results of the actions that preceded or will follow. Establishing key performance indicators (KPIs) and common metrics ensures manager accountability as well as supports the continuous improvement effort. An important element for the smooth development of relationships in the chain are the elements of operation supported by the ability of the members to adapt and be flexible to any changes in the business environment. Flexible supply chains (i.e., agile supply chain as a market-sensitive supply chain that is capable of reading and responding to real demand) benefit from partners' willingness to adapt to changing conditions, such as demand fluctuations or disruptions. To achieve all the above, they must be framed by the appropriate culture that promotes cooperation, participation, confidentiality – trust as well as communication and transfer of information between the members of the chain. Shared values and cultural compatibility promote smoother interactions and long-term partnerships.

Strengthening relationships between members is accomplished when there are clear benefits for supply chain participants. More specifically, the benefits of effective relationship management result in four important benefits for partner businesses. The first positive element resulting from the effectiveness of management is the possibility of developing long-term relationships characterised by improved cooperation between chain members. Properly managed relationships result in partnerships that subsequently optimise their supply chain performance.

An important positive element that is also an additional benefit for the members of the supply chain is the possibility of reducing the risk of malfunctions that appear in the performance of the supply chain, due to the changes caused by the external environment of the business or organisation. Strong relationships improve resilience by ensuring reliable communication and coordinated responses to disruptions.

The involvement of the members of the cooperation chain can and does result after coordinated actions in the rational treatment of the economic costs of the operation of the chain. Streamlining can contribute to the efficiency of actions through the monitoring of administrative and operational costs. Thus, reduced transaction costs, minimisation of staff redundancies and more efficient use of resources can come from excellent management of relationships between members of the value chain.

Another positive consequence of the adoption of good practices in the management of relationships between members of the supply chain is the facilitation of the possibility of developing innovations. According to the literature, collaborative relationships promote knowledge sharing and innovation, leading to improved products, processes and technologies.

Great care in managing and controlling the performance of relationships should be given to points of significant control and addressing problems of developing and consolidating relationships, which may be due to various reasons.

There are significant challenges and barriers to the adoption of effective relationship management practices, such as the weakening of trust, cultural differences and contradictions in principles and behaviour among members, tendencies to exercise veto and leadership against softer and weaker members, contradictory systems in the infrastructure and adoption of technology development. More specifically, opportunistic behaviour or failure to meet expectations can damage trust and hinder cooperation. Incorrect values or communication styles can create friction, particularly in global supply chains. Dominant partners may exploit weaker ones, undermining the potential for genuine cooperation, and inefficient or incompatible systems can hinder communication and information sharing.

Value creation in service supply chains

When selecting external suppliers (i.e., business services outsourcing (BSO)) for an organisation that is the buyer of tangible and intangible goods, it may be agreed to offer the service directly to the customers of the organisation that purchased the service. This process, due to the confidentiality shown by the buyer's organisation, may lead the buyer to lack of control over the relationships that develop with their customers and therefore perhaps to customer dissatisfaction due to their possible unsatisfied desires and needs.

The 'service triad' consists of the customer, the provider and the service supplier (Figure 11.3). The members are satisfied when beneficial transactional relationships are developed between them, which are formalised through the management of contract processes. The strategies to deal with the various obstacles are also based on the purpose of the strategic cooperation of the chain parties. Value chain and collaboration networks are based on the efficient management of chain costs, while other forms of service partnerships such as value store-oriented partnerships are based on delivering value to customers and focus on this goal when developing their strategies.

Malhotra and Lumineau (2011) emphasise in their study's conclusions that the greater the number of provisions oriented towards the control of a contract agreed upon between the parties, the lower the degree of trust that is expected from confidentiality between the parties to the contract. Contract content and careful design can influence the degree of trust between parties and the likelihood of continuing a relationship even when it has been weakened by conflict. Control provisions and terms weaken the relationship and create negative tendencies for continued cooperation. As the above authors also mentioned, the willingness to coordinate contract terms and provisions supports the likelihood of continued cooperation between contracting parties even if a crisis has previously occurred in the relationships between the parties in the value chain.

Lacity and Willcocks (2017) note that there are conflicts between contracting organisations that can be categorised into three categories of conflicts. The first refers to 'commercial', the second to 'service provision' and the third to 'relational' conflicts. The commercial ones, called so due to the nature of the agreements, are the most important and can easily create tendencies of increased dissatisfaction in the management members of the collaborating organisations. The findings of the above authors also show that both the collaborative style of developing relationships and the attempt to adopt a transitional style of supporting collaboration can and do support the effort to resolve the fortunate differences and conflicts between the collaborating parties.

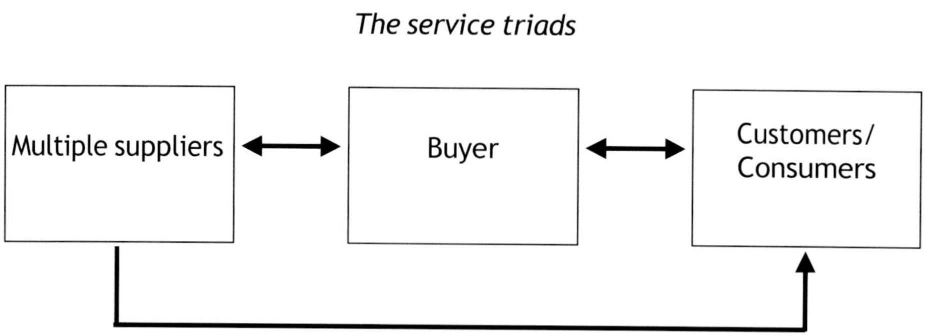

FIGURE 11.3 Service triads' relations: The case of a department store services sales channel

Contracts help build long-term relationships when they clearly clarify the parties' relationships so that potential conflicts are avoided. Contracts should clarify roles rather than focus on the judicial and legal dimensions of their provisions. Therefore, it is important to achieve through the clarity of terms the strengthening of the effort to align the interests of the parties with positive benefits that lead to the avoidance of renegotiation and the strengthening of transactional and relational trust between the parties.

The service triads

The core value proposition that a buyer (e.g., a shopping mall) seeks to create is often based on the contribution of many suppliers that are concentrated in a place of consumption of products and services (Figure 11.3). The ability of the supplier to be hosted in a shopping mall (a place of sale of the buyer's retail services), through its store(s), would simultaneously constitute an opportunity and an investment risk for the buyer.

In cooperation networks, it is important to observe three important conditions for good cooperation. It should, firstly, strengthen the trust between the cooperating parties; secondly, seek to solve problems through the cooperation of the parties; and thirdly share appropriate information for the information and benefit of all interested parties.

Barriers to the development of collaborative networks may arise from cost-related challenges, including the time and financial resources required to establish and maintain such networks.

According to Kern and Willcocks (2002), in the case of BSO, two types of conflicts can be distinguished between parties in the supply chain. The first type involves day-to-day operational issues, while the second pertains to cultural differences, contractual disagreements and broader operational challenges. Hughes and Weiss (2007) emphasise that modern businesses should align alliance management practices with their organisational culture, considering this alignment throughout the implementation process. Building on these insights, the cooperation between value chain partners should be guided by specific principles to prevent potential issues. The first criterion is the clear definition of the cooperation relationship. This involves establishing terms and behavioural practices that promote mutual trust and respect among partners. Supporting procedures should include a detailed description of the decision-making process, resource management and the protocols for exchanging necessary information between the parties.

The second criterion involves ensuring that appropriate mechanisms are in place to measure and assess the progress of the cooperation, allowing for adjustments as needed to maintain alignment and performance. Alliances typically aim for long-term financial returns, which should be clearly defined and communicated among the parties through specific goals and performance measurements. These goals often involve achieving expected outcomes via innovation proposals, the application of know-how and the integration of technology, all supported by the collaborative efforts of the involved partners.

The third condition for successful alliances involves monitoring potential differences in motivation between the parties. Companies frequently form alliances to acquire and adopt their partners' know-how in the future, as well as to gain insights into their markets, customers and suppliers. However, it is crucial to manage cultural differences that could lead to conflicts. The ability to proactively identify the root causes of potential crises is a valuable practice for preventing disruptions in cooperation and fostering value creation within the alliance.

The fourth condition emphasises the need to encourage positive collaboration among the parties. When problems arise, partners should focus on their collective ability to resolve issues, regardless of which party is responsible for the challenge.

The fifth condition relates to the management of internal stakeholders. In cases involving external collaborations, any internal resistance or concerns should be addressed in advance to ensure that all parties work towards shared objectives with active participation and commitment.

A service value chain should also identify and overcome barriers that could undermine supply chain sustainability. According to the literature, Seuring and Müller (2008) identify three primary factors that hinder the development of sustainable practices in service value chains:

1. High costs;
2. The complexity and need for coordinated effort;
3. A lack of communication between value chain members.

Addressing these factors is essential to ensure the sustainability and effectiveness of service value chains.

The management of relationships between members within the value chain is characterised in the modern environment by complex interactions and a greater number of involved members who perform specialised activities that enhance the value of the chain within the now globalised environment of international markets. Emphasising the customer and creating value is a strategic focus effort that involves all members of the supply chain partner network. So, in this way, the diversified requirements of the customers of the service companies are covered more rationally and efficiently. In the continuation of this chapter, key issues, theories and findings related to relationship management practices in the context of SCM are presented.

Relationship management in supply chains can be interpreted from various theoretical approaches that interpret the behaviour and the way of development and strengthening over time of these chains.

According to economic theory, supply chains are based on the economics of transaction cost management (transaction cost economics (TCE)). TCE theory posits that firms seek to minimise transaction costs, which include search, negotiation and enforcement costs. Also, through this pursuit, companies manage to develop strong relationships among themselves, to reduce uncertainty and opportunistic behaviours by aligning their interests with those of supply chain partners.

According to others, relationships are strengthened between members of a group of cooperating supply chain firms because the theory of gaining competitive advantage through leveraging unique resources applies. This theory emphasises the importance of leveraging unique resources and capabilities. Collaborative relationships allow firms to access complementary resources, thereby creating competitive advantages. In fact, one of the special elements of resources that can lead a company to competitive advantages and to the selection of partners and therefore the support of specific supply and value chains is the uniqueness of the resource of social relations also known as 'complex social phenomena or social complexity' (Barney 1991; Porter 1985). In this case, a service business could develop the organisation's culture based on principles, common goals and aspirations through the development of common benefits for all involved members. The ability to adopt a supportive and cooperative team behaviour by managers and staff, the ability to collaborate and participate in decision-making with selected suppliers and the ability to approach customer needs and wants based on benefits and unique offers are a series of social processes relationships that form the unique social complex of cooperation in a supply chain.

According to social exchange theory (SET), members' relationships in a value chain are strengthened when they are based on trust, reciprocity and commitment to maintaining long-term relationships. Also, this theory posits that mutual benefits and a history of positive interactions encourage stronger partnerships.

The service collaborators

In the related literature, it was mentioned that a decisive factor for the effectiveness and long-term maintenance and development of the relationships between the members of the chains is the strategic management of the relationships between customers and the organisation in the provision of services (see Figure 11.4).

The development of human relations between the members of the chains based on trust and coordination is in services one of the main issues for effective and efficient services value chain management. Tonmoy et al. (2020: 1377) present in their research study the concept of service operation function-capability, which is useful for describing any function of modern service operation. The above, extending the idea of interpretation and analysis of the main actors of service production, proposes a new framework for the analysis of value chains of services provided, which consists of four elements of factors, namely, satisfaction feedback (e.g., customers and consumers), the internal and external actors, and the basic process that refers to the three main service providers (Figure 11.5).

The process of collaboration between partners in a value chain requires the predetermination of the benefits of collaboration, which can be based on the following elements:

- Possibility of strengthening the means to achieve easier and more effective access to the market for services and material goods.
- Possibility of achieving economies of scale for all collaborating members.
- Possibility of broader development of capabilities and skills through the collaboration of members.
- Possibility of highlighting their competitive advantages through collaboration.

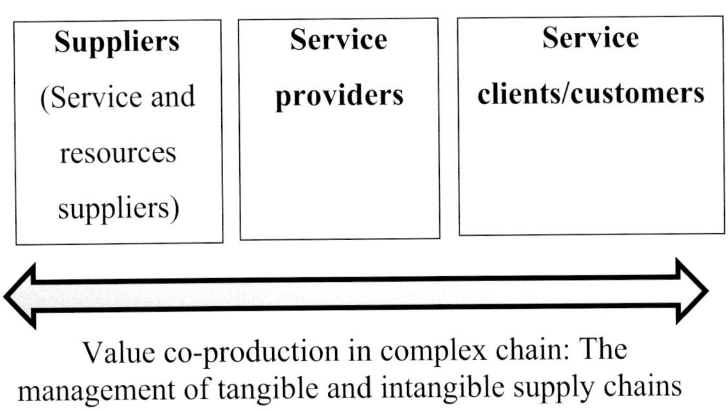

FIGURE 11.4 Collaborators ('actors') in service production

Source: Based on Giannakis (2011: 1810, 1818).

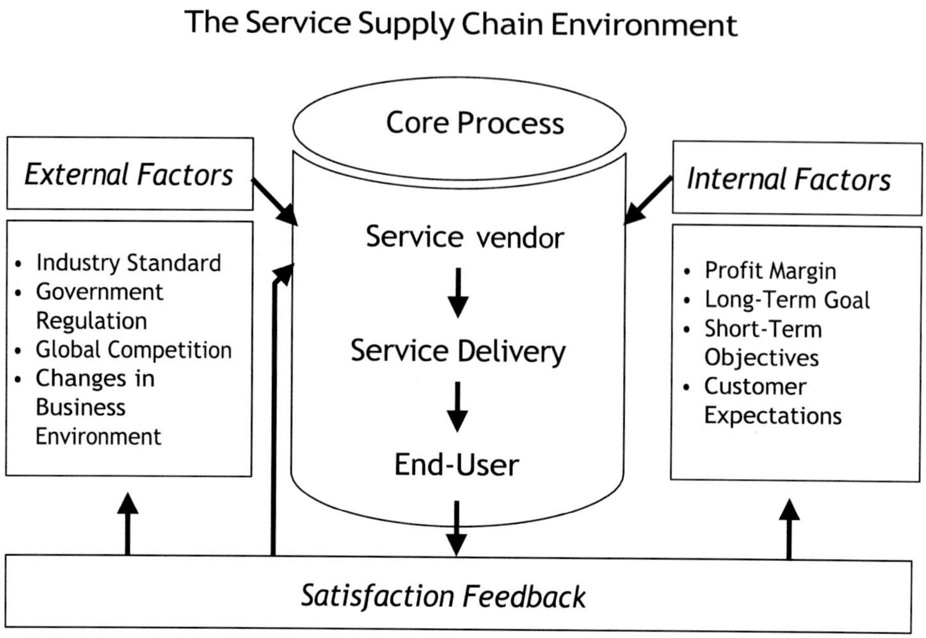

FIGURE 11.5 Concept of the service supply chain micro framework

Source: Retrieved and redesigned from the source Tonmoy et al. (2020: 1377).

The degree of rationalisation, that is, the possibility of high performance with low implementation costs, and the provision of facilities between the members of a value chain define the level of integration adopted in a supply chain. The degree of integration is based on the extent to which a value chain manages to synchronise its operations, coordinate the planning procedures and facilitate the flow of information, be facilitated by operational coordination processes, and aim for a long-term strategic relationship with benefits for all members of the chain. For example, the integration of the chain could be accelerated if the information of each member-partner company of the value chain was channelled in an easier way, for example, through the partnership intranet and through direct communication to all members, immediately and supportively by determining, the sales situation, the ability to support partners with appropriate inventories, the ability to cover orders based on production dynamics and the way to manage shipments and deliveries in the distribution channel. If chain value members communicate and invest time in planning the next common steps and business actions and make this collaboration a prerequisite for achieving long-term goals, then the value chain integration effort is strengthened and takes on a collaborative form in terms of the shared benefit pursuits.

Knowledge management can be a mean to enforce relationships between the members of the value chain network. Collaborations can be hierarchically structured based on roles and goals where mixed patterns of suppliers collaborate to serve customers. Collaborative networks are strengthened when there is a high degree of trust and a long-term commitment to working together to achieve common goals that benefit the collaborating members, often through recurring transactions with customers and suppliers.

Services have a particularity as goods that differentiate them from material goods. Services follow a series of steps and are ultimately processes that include actions and activities. During their provision, they are consumed at the exact same moment so that there is no intermediate period between production and consumption (it is also named as 'inseparability') that could allow for partial consumption and storage. Also, an important characteristic of services is the fact that the customer participates to a significant extent as a co-producer in the process of providing services. According to researchers Parasuraman et al. (1985: 42), services are characterised by three important characteristics that distinguish them from material goods. These characteristics are 'Intangibility;, 'Inseparability' and 'Heterogeneity', for example, the service is perceived differently from person to person due to their different experiences and personal characteristics, for example, interests, beliefs and opinions. Wilson et al. (2012: 15–18) point out these four important elements that differentiate services from physical goods, namely, services are 'intangible', 'ieterogeneous', 'inseparability-simultaneous production and consumption' and 'perishable [.] cannot be saved, stored, resold and returned'.

The characteristics of the nature of services affect both the way in which the management of these goods is developed and their development strategies. The case of value chains in services is significantly differentiated due to the above elements that distinguish services from material goods.

Value chain partnerships

Value chain partnerships benefit the contracting parties since they can strengthen through cooperation the competitive advantages of the product or service they provide, they also help to improve the image and identity of the company and the products and services it offers, but also to ensure in this way its profits and benefits both for the company itself and for all contracting parties. A useful strategic analytical approach to making administrative decisions that supports the development of competitive advantages is the value chain analysis proposed by Porter (1985, 1990).

The value chain analysis technique constitutes a toolbox for the strategist, in terms of analysing the strengths and weaknesses of a company or even other competing companies. In this way, each function and activity of the company can be studied in more detail, as well as determining its impact or relationship in terms of cost and value creation for this company. Companies operating in different industries, such as service industries, can differ in how they gain competitive advantage due to the differentiation of the value chains they adopt.

The possibility of adopting Porter's value chain analysis model can support the strategic management decisions of companies operating in the tertiary economic sector. In this case, some adjustments are suggested due to the service industry and the nature of the services. The following figure and text present the basic components of Porter's value chain analysis model and discuss the significant differences and adaptations compared to the value chains of businesses that produce physical goods (physical/material products). Even if the same service is provided as a process and a series of hierarchical steps repeatedly, the process will differ in terms of the effectiveness and efficiency of the individual processes and therefore the value that will be provided. Each recipient of the service subjectively judges the service that will be provided to him while at the same time being its co-producer. A consumer user of a medical service may judge the provision of the service that will be provided to him differently from the next user because as a co-producer and as an individual he judges subjectively and cannot easily understand which steps he should follow to make an appointment at the same diagnostic-radiological centre of the same hospital. Also, the time-of-service provision varies due to delays, ignorance and additional information and support that will be needed. Moments of time, incidents, situations and events, experiences and behaviours of people have a significant impact and influence the perception, attitude, satisfaction and mood of the co-producer who is also the user-consumer of the medical service. The same user-consumer (client) of the medical service may judge a service provision differently regarding the value chain of the procedures followed. If one provider does not provide him with a parking space during the visit so that he can travel by wheelchair for the MRI, or does not ultimately manage to complete the imaging due to problems with the imaging machine while he paid for the service and is awaiting a refund, then the competing service provider, which may be another nearby diagnostic centre, will manage to satisfy him because the staff, from the first telephone contact, explained the procedure in detail, for example, the possibility of accessing the parking space, the method and time of travel, but also promised him that he does not have to pay, but only when the procedure is completed with the rendering of the medical opinion after the MRI examination.

Observing Figure 11.6 about Porter's concept of the generic value chain and the service sector offer, one realises that the lower area of the figure presents the basic functions or else the 'primary value chain activities' of a business and therefore also those of the service sector. Services are based on a series of activities and inputs and outputs of resources. The following is a presentation of the primary activities of value chain analysis.

The first of the processes below the diagram focuses on inbound logistics. For example, banking and financial services require the support of material and technological resource elements such as computers, high-speed data transmission cables, modems and cloud technology, but also service providers such as website design services, design, development and support of

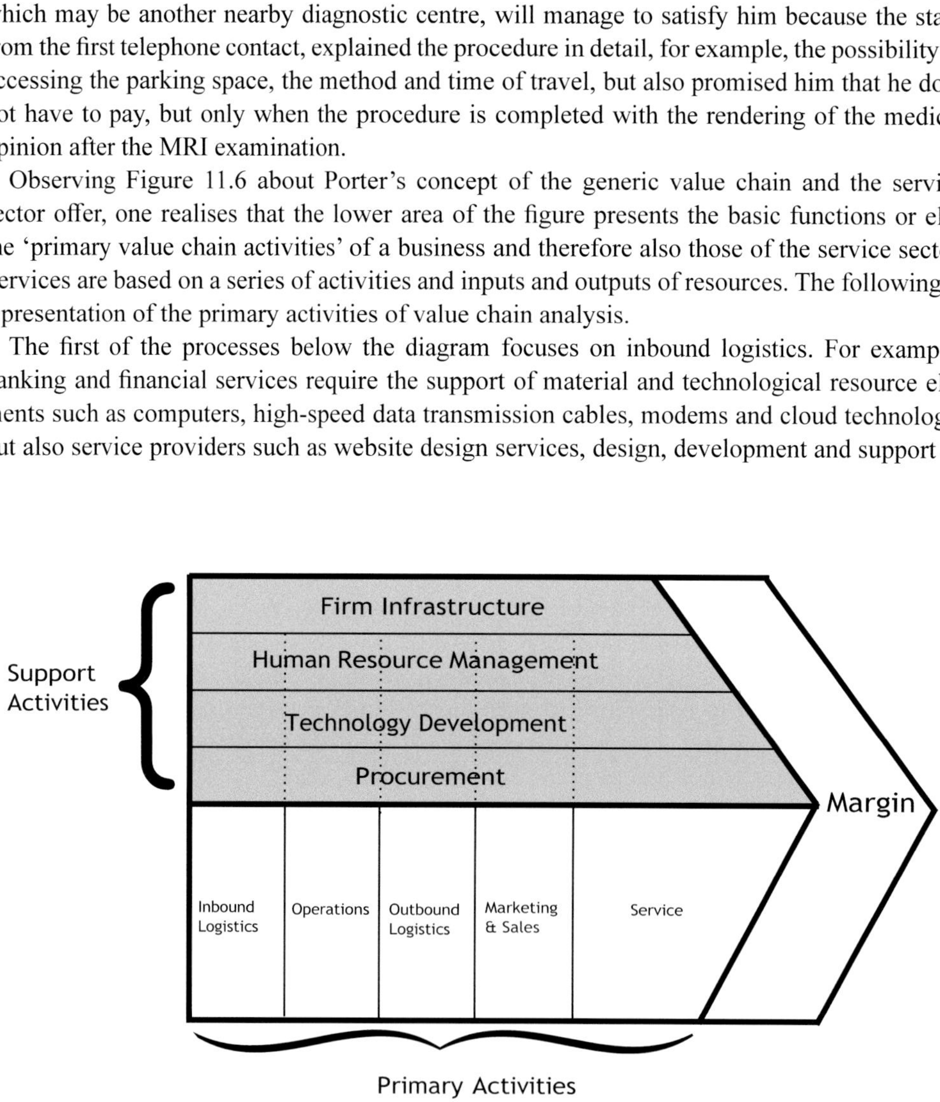

FIGURE 11.6 Generic value chain and the service sector offer: The service value chain analysis

Source: Adapted from Porter (1985: 37).

electronic transactions in digital and mobile application environments, and website user security. A medical centre service provider can include useful facts and advice on ailments from recognised doctors who work with the medical facility and showcase their work or even their private practice. The medical centre's blog also displays, at no extra cost, its certified catering and restaurant services owned by partner suppliers, as well as the excellent quality diagnostic equipment of its radiology department maintained by the relevant internationally renowned quality radiology supplier and maintainer of the equipment. In this way, the services available and displayed by the above companies and service organisations are based on a friendly cooperative system of reception, promotion and support of the incoming services and physical products of their suppliers.

In services, the operations., for example, the series of business processes that consist of different activities to be completed, requires a coordinated execution of activities that result in the transfer of the appropriate service to the end user. The result of these processes is the formation of the purchasing and consumption experience from the consumer's point of view.

Imagine a tourist whose emergency charter flight has been cancelled waiting in uncertainty for hours at the airport as to when and with what he will depart! The experience of this trip will suddenly be negatively affected despite any certified service in the accommodation and organiser in the destination country.

Outbound logistics in the case of services refers to the appropriate and immediate provision of the service to its final recipients. As mentioned above, the previous procedures of the operations aim to create a suitable experience of the end user of the service and therefore aim per offered service at, for example, the speed of execution, at avoiding problems that make the service unsuitable and useless for its recipient, at its qualitative differentiation during execution and distinguishing it from the competition, in the reduction of causes that may burden the provision of the service with additional costs, or the safeguarding of the user (e.g., protection of financial transactions, protection and security during transactions on the internet, and safeguarding of personal data).

The process of sales and marketing from the moment of planning the service until after its immediate consumption requires a different approach due to the additional elements involved in the planning of activities in service marketing. The seven elements that make up the service marketing mix are the following:

- Product-service (i.e., the total perceived product consisting of main and peripheral elements of material and intangible product characteristics);
- Pricing (i.e., the perceived value that constitutes the total cost and effort paid by the consumer to purchase and consume the service in relation to the expected benefits);
- Distribution/place (i.e., the distribution network for the provision of the service in the electronic and conventional environment);
- Promotion (i.e., the communication mix to promote the services provided to the market audience);
- People/participants (i.e., staff who provide services and interact with customers and consumer co-producers);
- Processes (i.e., the actions and hierarchy of actions taken to provide a service);
- Physical evidence (i.e., the surrounding material and physical space where the service is provided).

In services, the producer may not package the product in some metal or paper or plastic boxes and containers but provides his service in a suitably designed environment that includes impressive material elements to highlight the quality of the intangible good. At the same time, the staff is properly prepared for the co-production of the service, smiles, informs and executes with the aim of creating a pleasant shopping experience for the recipient customer. In this effort, the elements of the procedures also converge so that the provision of the service is done without delays and problems for the customers, aiming to provide an exceptional value to them.

Before and after the provision of the service, customers search for or express their experience from the provision of the service. Thus, for example, a medical centre is based in terms of its quality assessment not only on the impressions caused by the services and physical goods it has but also mainly on the man-made environment and the facilities of the services provided. They often evaluate the services by filling out the relevant customer satisfaction forms or by expressing their reviews and comments on the digital website of the business or organisation. In fact, many customers transfer the positive or negative comments to other people through verbal communication, multiplying the formation of the image of the company or organisation in the relevant purchasing decisions of other customers. Usually, unfamiliar customers will want to know the experience of previous active customers, thus reducing any buying risk. The post-purchase approach to customers takes special interest in retaining the organisation's purchases and creating positive experiences for their customers. Many companies and organisations provide maintenance services and customer relations support services as well as special offers to customers who show high loyalty in consuming the products and services.

In service units, the infrastructure plays an important role, which can not only support the services but also facilitate the recognition of the perceived value of their services provided by the customers. The infrastructure in facilities, equipment, services, services and buildings and facilities are important collaborative elements in the effort to highlight competitive advantages. Imagine an inner-city aged care facility with limited car parking or a dilapidated, unsafe and difficult disabled access or no wheelchairs available. Obviously, patients, their companions and the elderly in general avoid units where they are expected to suffer upon their arrival. A sporting event organisation unit is required to have equipment or automation for timing the routes covered by the athletes, real-time visualisation of the spatial and temporal performances of the athletes with GPS systems, coverage, monitoring and surveillance by drone of the flows of the athletes, gates and platform facilities for the start and arrival as well as the awarding of the athletes, facilities for the stay of official and important persons, facilities for sponsors and exhibitors, for the stay of the athletes and attendants, mobile toilets, etc.

Human resource management in services and service value chains and especially in their support activities, requires a different approach that excludes by company and nature of service provision. In the case of patients, care and human presence and communication are irreplaceable elements. Imagine a nursing facility without nursing support or without proper medical staff. Even if physicians have the appropriate expertise, the need for technical associates to support the operation of the radiology equipment, or the need for IT technicians to maintain the applications and databases with appropriate information systems, is a top priority to support the medical diagnosis and opinion. The staff is also an element of the implementation of the MKT services. It is one of the well-known 7Ps of the MKT mix. Therefore training, motivation, reward, development and performance are important elements of investment in the various companies that provide services.

Service companies today rely on the use of smart and innovative technologies that change the intensity of competition in the industry while they can and do influence the service differentiation strategy against the competition. Robotics, nanotechnology, photovoltaic systems, smart and mobile applications, telecommunications and cloud services to access and store large amounts of data are some of the modern technologies that can support service companies. For example, an accommodation unit can gain a technological lead, but also economies of scale, over others if it invests in a suitable application in the electronic environment, which will host the unit and promote it directly and without intermediaries to the interested user-guests (e.g., short-term real estate rentals such as Airbnb type). At the same time, it could invest in nanotechnology in terms of cleaning and waterproofing the external glassing and the internal bathroom facilities of each of its rooms. The robotic technology would enable her not only to answer, 24/7 and without an employee, any questions posed by users on her blog, but also to clean rooms using an electronic robot vacuum cleaner. At the same time, the ability to store a large amount of photos of visitors who share their experiences at the attractions of the area, can be hosted using cloud technology by the owner and become accessible after selection to all interested guests staying in the unit, using wireless technology. The use of smart technology, for example, electric bikes, scooters or even cars, and the use of smart devices and mobile applications for the movement of guests would give a different identity to the accommodation and therefore add value to its value chain.

Choosing the right supplier can help to provide superior quality and at the same time rational use of the cost of providing the services. The hotel units have the need to support the architecture of the internal and external spaces of their accommodation. Also, in the food service (food and beverages (F&B)) areas, the choice of suppliers is decisive for the success and distinction of the services and the smooth operation of the unit. The entire value chain development effort results in a sustainable gross profit margin that allows the company or service organisation to operate and invest with an eye toward its future operational financial viability. Also, this profit margin should aim at the same time to cover the perceived value that the buyer of the service expects, for example, the value that he would like to pay to acquire the good.

11.2 Sustainability and value chain management practices

Service supply management–customer value chain management versus supply chains

Services require the involvement and participation of the consumer/customer in the production process. Without customer involvement during service provision, the production and delivery of services can be compromised. Unlike material goods supply chains, where processes often focus on cost, time and product quality, service supply chains are heavily influenced by customer participation, human resources and real-time interactions.

The material goods chains include elements to assess the appropriate cost time and quality of disposal of the material goods. At the same time, however, they contribute to the creation of value that an organisation/business provides to its customers, differentiating this organisation/business in the eyes of its customers from the competition. The value proposition in chains requires a rational approach to chain management costs. At the same time, the requirement for time management of the processes so that the delivery of the material goods and the provision of the appropriate services at the appropriate place and time becomes possible and leads to the satisfaction of the contracting parties of the supply chain. Creating value for customers is the core purpose of value chains supported by both material and unmaterial resource management and the related supply chains of the final produced goods. Therefore, the management of customer value chains also includes the need to manage supply chains (Figure 11.7). Service supply

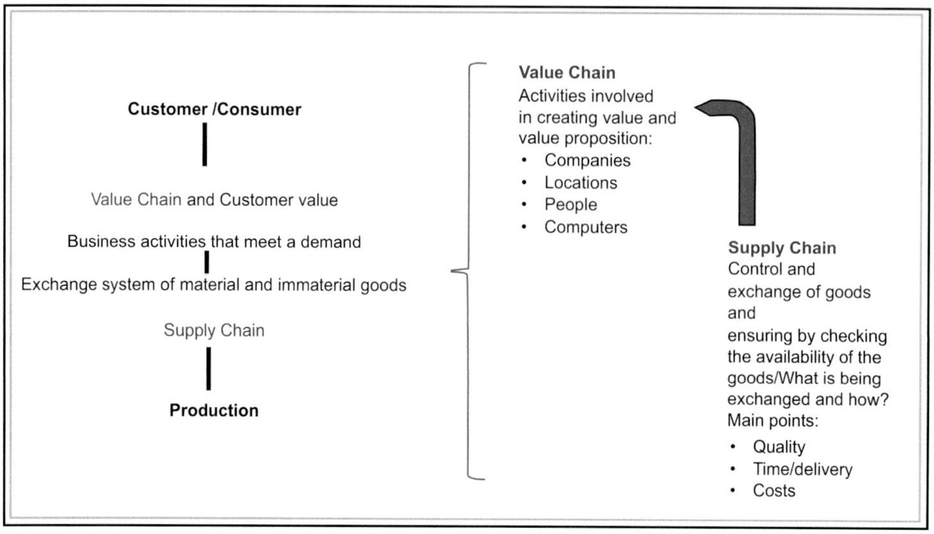

FIGURE 11.7 Supply chain and value chain relation

Source: After adjustment from Wallner, M. (2023): "Value chain vs supply chain: What's the difference? KNΔPP, 4 May 2023 In https://www.knapp.com/en/insights/blog/difference-value-chain-vs-supply-chain/ <last visit at 2 December 2024>.

chains require a focus on human resources. The literature recommends that staff understand the technical and technological aspects of customer service and understanding, while investing in relationship building and physical and electronic customer contact is also considered important to develop and maintain healthy customer relationships.

Blueprinting in services

The systematic series of actions for the provision of services can, with the use of blueprints, be developed in a more detailed way, designed effectively, observed during its provision, and the efficiency and effectiveness of the procedures during the control and redesign process of the development of the actions can be evaluated. As in the case of material goods, so also in the case of intangible goods, for example, services, monitoring the processes of providing the value chain of services through blueprinting in services, facilitates their rationalisation, for example, the management of administrative issues and decisions concerning the delivering maximum value to value chain recipients at the lowest possible cost.

Thus, in services, the elements that make up the service delivery system may include important processes and management elements composed of the following process elements:

- Offer data to the client
- Product offering details
- Offer of facilities
- Management of the procedures related to the execution and provision of the service
- Termination of the service.

These elements are presented indicatively in Figure 11.8.

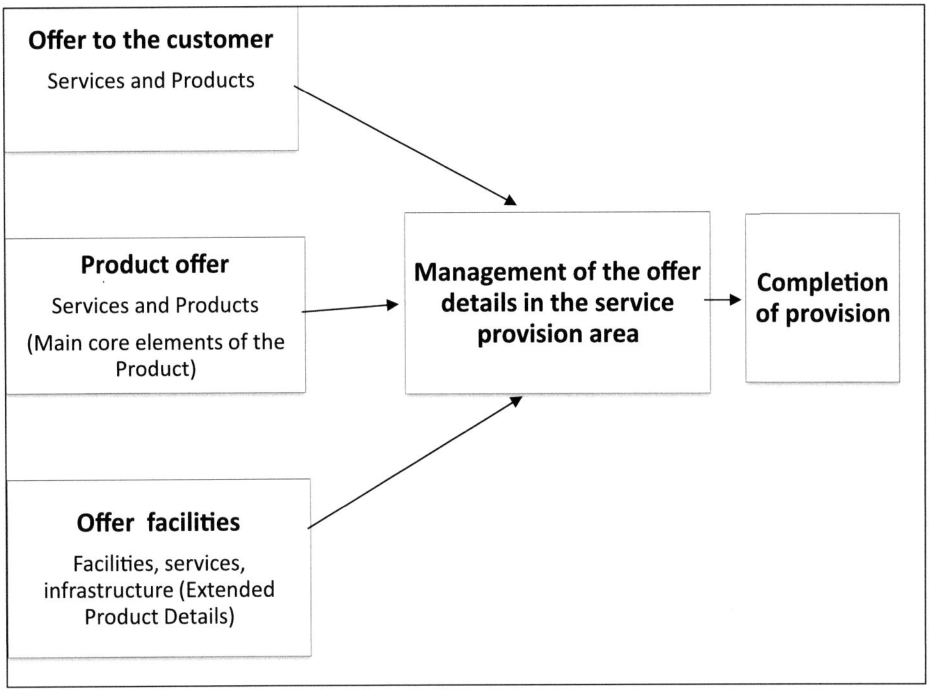

FIGURE 11.8 Elements of the system of procedures related to the provision of services

Product, facility and customer offer

The customer is the source of funding for the business operations of an economic organisation. Thus, customers may vary and may be defined differently in service providers and may concern, for example, the users of the B2B website, the sponsors of an event, the audience of a music event, the visitors of a museum, a clinic or an archaeological site, the students of a theme park, the players of a casino, the visitors of a restaurant or self-service food store, the professional customers of a bank, the students of an educational organisation, the visitors of a professional exhibition or an airline, and the citizens of a public service.

Every customer has some expectations that he expects to be satisfied by the product offer. The procedures to be followed must, always regarding the design of the offer, meet the requirements and characteristics of the request. So, for example, a service that will be addressed as an element of a product offer to a customer group with disabilities should be adapted to its special characteristics and therefore should be accessible so that this group can come into contact and communicate with the resources or service delivery factors. Transport services in an urban centre, taxis, air services at an area's airport and ATMs should be able to accommodate, for example, PWDs who may only be able to move with a wheelchair. In fact, modern societies and economies have adopted the United Nations' Convention on the Rights of Persons with Disabilities (UNCRPD), which is a legally binding act in which the European Union participates since 2011.

In fact, modern societies and economies have adapted the UNCRPD, which is a legally binding act in which the European Union participates since 2011. Thus, according to the legislative act of the convention UN should ensure the protection of the rights of persons with disabilities in each contracting member state or union of states. The expectations of the disabled are therefore also institutionally framed by the provisions of the convention that each member state has signed and should observe in accordance with the programmatic procedures of the UN pact. These expectations also require an appropriate service offering and therefore appropriate service provision procedures and value chain regarding the parties involved during the provision.

Therefore, if the design of the product offer requires the monitoring of transport service procedures, then regarding the group of disabled people the service, the product offer, should be shaped according to the conditions set by the legislative or regulatory framework of a country. The transfer of guests from the airport to the hotel requires in this case air accessibility services that include, in the continuation of the process of providing the transport service, even specially designed taxis for the disabled. For this purpose, relevant regulations have been issued by the EU bodies. Regulation no. 1107/2006 of the European Parliament and of the Council of 5 July 2006 refers to the 'rights of disabled persons and persons with reduced mobility when traveling by air'. The quote from paragraph 5 (EC 2006: 1) is typical:

> Assistance given at airports situated in the territory of a Member State to which the Treaty applies should, among other things, enable disabled persons and persons with reduced mobility to proceed from a designated point of arrival at an airport to an aircraft and from the aircraft to a designated point of departure from the airport, including embarking and disembarking. These points should be designated at least at the main entrances to terminal buildings, in areas with check-in counters, in train, light rail, metro and bus stations, at taxi ranks and other drop-off points, and in airport car parks. The assistance should be organised to avoid interruption and delay, while ensuring high and equivalent standards throughout the Community and making best use of resources, whatever airport or air carrier is involved.

Directive 2019/882/EU, also known as the European Accessibility Act, increases these necessary facilities in terms of infrastructure and structures to facilitate the customers of this group that our example refers to. Thus, through the directive, the adaptation of national legislation is sought by improving the access of people with disabilities to products and services, including the field of information and communication technologies (ICT).

In the directive, priority is also given to digital technologies that are the main objective of this directive, which will be applied to the products and services that will be provided and will be offered after the mid-2030s. The infrastructures and superstructures in products and services related to the access of people with disabilities include a differentiated framework for offering products and services, as stated in the specific paragraph of the directive (EU, 2019; EC-European Accessibility Resource Centre 2024: 3).

Appropriately also accessible and equipped with facilities and services for the disabled, the accommodation could cooperate with the means of transport for the disabled. Passenger transport companies can negotiate which accommodations they will recommend to their customers, as well as promote the accommodations by providing, for example, discounts or even free rides to and from the hotel for customers of these accommodations. We should also note that an uncomfortable accommodation without adequate facilities and services in combination with a tiring route can be negative elements that do not meet the expectations and needs of the target group's customers.

The overall delivered product should be designed for the customer or customer group being served with particular care. As a total customer experience, it should convey additional value that will distinguish the service offering (i.e., the overall product provided) from other competitive products. The airport transport services of the above example should be counted as providing value to the next links of the value chain such as the possibility of finding an appropriately accessible and functional means of transport for the accommodation (e.g., a suitable taxi or public transport) and the possibility of using digital technologies to inform and orient the user of the service from airport, during travel and during the guest's stay at the accommodation, appropriately designed spaces and services within the accommodation.

In the context of the logic of monitoring, a single product experience composed of added values in the process of offering services and material goods to the client, the person responsible for planning the value chains should include appropriate synthetic elements that create tendencies to increase the ultimately contained total value to final and intermediate customers. Facilities in the accommodation such as the provision of smart technology, suitable and quality assured product in food and drinks, appropriately designed and accessible areas, within the accommodation building, for example, elevators, toilets and rooms (e.g., for people with special needs or wheelchair users, or mothers with infants, or the elderly), support the planner's effort to provide high-value services that contribute to the attraction and satisfaction of customers.

Checklists and service mapping models can help in the process of improving the services provided by even preventing any repetition of mistakes. This checklist is useful for the accommodations' CRM practices, for example, to enhance the lodging's reputation because of maintaining a high level of customer service, safety and waste management, and quality standards.

The following is a brief description of the literature review on service design with service blueprinting diagrams and their contribution on value chain creation. This section aims to present key theories, methodologies and empirical studies that illuminate how value chains can be developed and implemented in conjunction with the support of service design tools.

Services blueprints for service design, introduced by Shostack (1982), are a visual tool used to map service processes, allowing organisations to analyse and improve customer experiences. Shostack supports the possibility of developing innovations in services through modelling (visualisation of the delivery system) and mapping their services. Shostack clarifies an alternative way of monitoring the tangible and intangible elements of the whole product offer through the visualisation of the provision processes, giving an example of a shoe cleaning service. The services blueprint as a type of visualised presentation diagram of a provided service, provides information about the elements that the customer perceives through visual approach and contact, but also information about the elements that the customer cannot perceive despite their importance in the provision of the final service and experience that is generally caused to the customers of the service. More specifically, these diagrams highlight the following:

- Customer actions;
- Interactions in the frontstage and backstage;
- Support in the recording and evaluation of intangible goods, processes and physical evidence.

The study of service delivery diagrams such as the services blueprints yields useful information on how customers perceive the service provided, shaping their final overall experience from their points of contact with the service provider. It is therefore also a useful services design tool for identifying any innovations, improvements and novelties that could be supported to better satisfy the needs and desires of customers. The contribution of these diagrams to the coordination of processes between support staff, front-line staff and the process of presenting and providing the service to customers/consumers is also considered important. Their use also facilitates the operational processes of preparation and allocation of resources to create appropriate conditions for the creation of pleasant experiences ('moments of truth') that cause positive experiences in customers/consumers. As the above author mentioned (Shostack 1982: 62): '[.] Moreover, if no blueprint exists and customer behaviour towards the service changes, the marketer will neither be able to account for the change nor scientifically modify the service towards maximum efficiency. [.] Regular reporting systems can easily monitor performance of the service across its distribution system [.]'.

The services blueprint diagram divides the design into two parts. In the 'onstage or frontstage' and in the 'backstage'. The activities in the scene are the activities that are perceived by the customer, while the activities that occur behind the scenes are not observed by the customer. The two parts are separated by a 'line of visibility'. The methodology was later chosen and developed and improved by various authors in the field of service management.

Bitner et al. (2008) highlighted the role of service mapping in the design of service innovations, enabling better alignment between customer expectations and service delivery system. The authors point out that a common diagram of services blueprint includes the five following elements:

1. Activities and actions of the customers/consumers
2. Contact-staffs' visible actions; the onstage
3. Contact-staffs' invisible actions; the backstage
4. Supporting activities and actions
5. Surrounding elements; physical evidence

The 2008 article by Bitner, Ostrom and Morgan can be considered an improved version of Shostack's proposal (1982, 1984). The figure below describes the modules included in the draft proposed by Bitner et al. (2008). An indicative service blueprint diagram adapted to the specifications of a hotel service is the one that follows in the figure below (Figure 11.9).

The triple bottom line approach

Today, societies, governments and broader policy-making bodies and organisations have gradually realised the need for increasing awareness among policy-makers regarding the natural environment. The awareness of environmental degradation, as well as the recognition of the depletion and limited availability of natural resources resulting from intensive consumption, has pushed businesses into a new reality in terms of strategic sustainable decision-making. Sustainable practices are a reality that significantly impacts the development of modern business decisions. Value chain management that includes the coordination of activities throughout the chain from the supply of raw materials to delivery to the end user plays a central role in integrating sustainability into the business activities of all different types of businesses and organisations.

Sustainability in business involves practices that meet present needs without compromising future generations' ability to meet their own. It encompasses three dimensions: environmental, social and economic. The three pillars of sustainability theory, also known as the triple bottom line (TBL) theory or the 3Ps theory (people, planet and profits), is a research proposal and a theoretical construct to identify the key measurable dimensions that impact organisations, planning policies and business activities. Businesses should measure their performance not only in

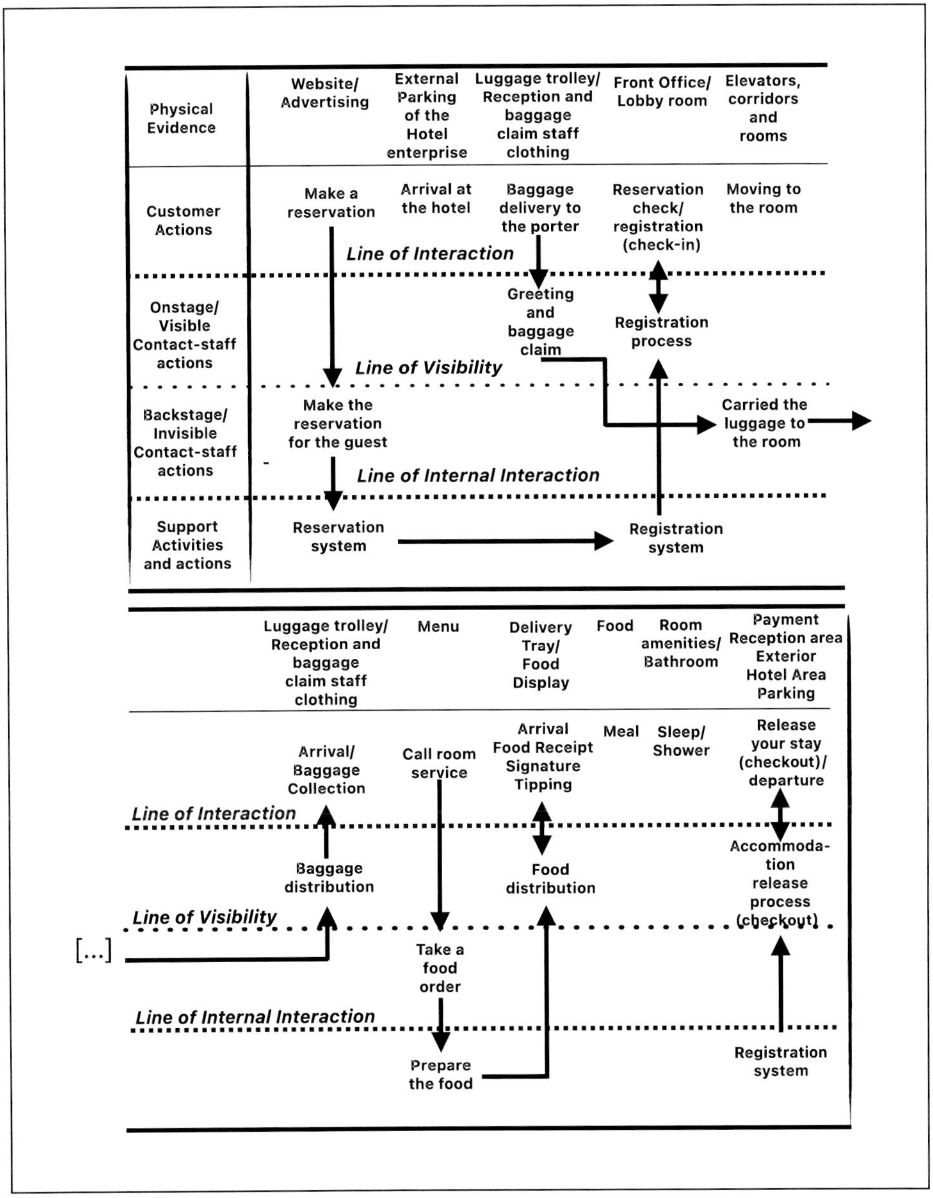

FIGURE 11.9 Basic elements of the services blueprint system: an indicative service blueprint in the case of a hotel service

financial terms but also by their social and environmental impact. Elkington (1994, 1997: 69–96) introduced first the theoretical concept of TBL. Today many companies and organisations adopt the TBL sustainability framework to evaluate their performance. Bansal (2005) highlighted that organisations integrating TBL into their core strategies tend to achieve long-term sustainability and stakeholder trust. The research and study of service chains requires a different approach due to the nature of services. Collaboration between members, the design of service supply chains,

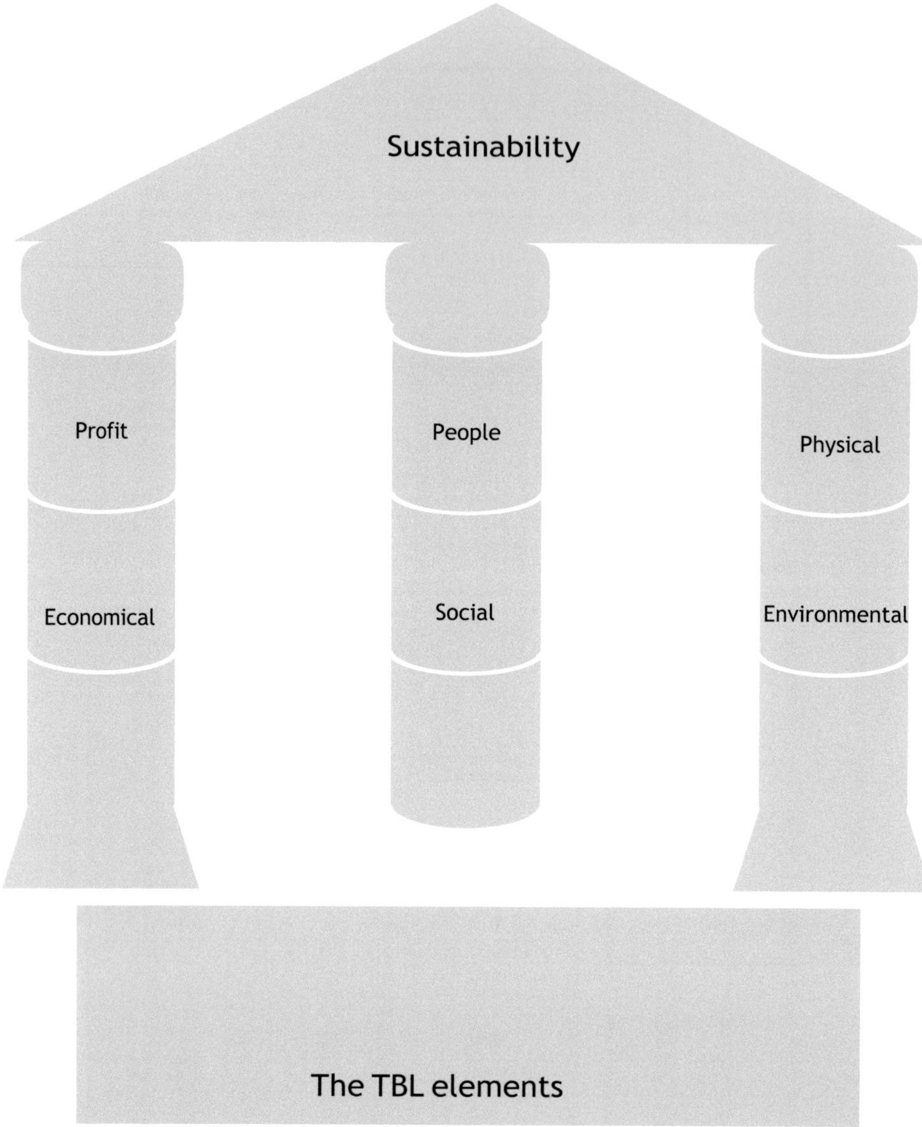

FIGURE 11.10 Triple bottom line sustainability concept

the creation of innovations and the rationalisation of cost structures of different service supply chain networks, and the management of delivery time and the environmental aspects of the service provided are today important points for further research and improvement. The three pillars and their related contents are presented in Figure 11.10.

In a service value chain, we mainly encounter the service providers necessary for the operation of the business, as well as the integrators and customers who express the needs and desires to the intermediate intermediaries (service integrators) who transfer the customer requirements to the relevant suppliers. The adoption of the three pillars of sustainability philosophy is a necessary condition for the success of the venture even when the goods provided are of an intangible

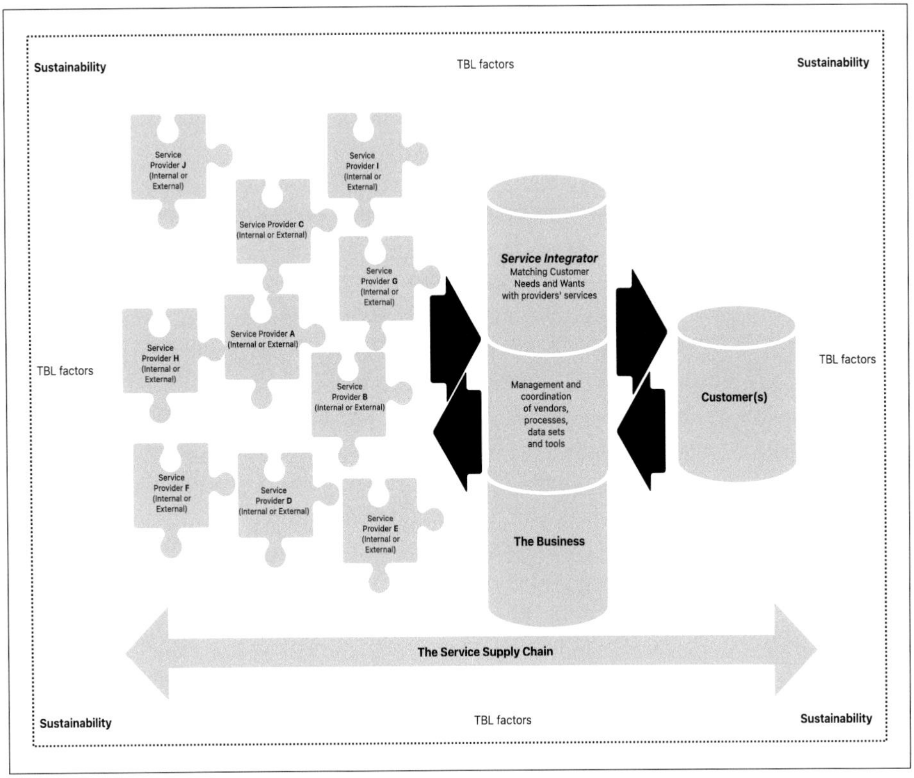

FIGURE 11.11 Service supply chain management and the related contributors

nature. Figure 11.11 provides a summary of the key processes and contracted key members in the service value chain.

11.3 Future trends and conclusion

In summary, the literature emphasises the following elements of developments that make up the current reality that shapes the prospects of the future. The modern reality of digital developments is shaping trends that affect the evolution and development and degree of upgrading of service value chains. More specifically, digital transformation includes automation and the use of AI, at the same time big data and robotics will modify the structure of the business environment and boost further efficiency and customer services and activities. The need to determine the level of demand for the services provided and their accompanying material goods, as well as the need for rational cost management in an internationalised and demanding market, make modern AI technology and machine learning, essential tools for developing the competitive advantages also for a service enterprise. The two-way relationship and communication between suppliers will revolutionise demand forecasting, resource allocation and customer relationship management in service supply chains. Transactions and financial services are now supported by blockchain-type cryptographic systems that secure the transfer of information and add value to transactions that take place in the digital environment. The ability to support customer services and highlight common benefits through cooperative customer–supplier models are elements that contribute to the binding of relationships between chain members and the effort to build long-term relationships with the customers of a service company. Real-time analytics and personalised services will dominate SCM strategies, leveraging big data and customer relationship management systems to create unique customer journeys and experiences.

Sustainability in services supply chain management (SSCM) is based on green SCM principles and is gaining prominence in service industries, with organisations increasingly focusing on energy efficiency, ethical labour practices and minimising carbon footprints. Service companies are likely to adopt circular economy principles to reduce waste and promote sustainability throughout their supply chains (Carter and Easton 2011; Strippoli et al. 2024; UN Tourism 2024). The future of SCM lies in the creation of interconnected ecosystems of suppliers, partners and customers. Shared data and collaborative platforms will enhance agility and responsiveness. Traditional manufacturers are adopting service-centric models, integrating service delivery into their supply chains. This hybrid approach will blur the boundaries between product and service SCM. Baines et al. (2009) discussed the integration of services into traditional manufacturing supply chains, predicting a continued shift towards service-dominant business models. Balancing globalisation with localisation will be critical. Service supply chains should adapt to local market demands while maintaining global efficiency.

Modern development is based on the positive changes that occur in the business environment and include several opportunities to be exploited. Current trends shaping the future of relationship management in supply chains, based on the literature, include the following changes that have occurred and should be considered. The use of blockchain, Internet of Things (IoT) and AI enhances transparency and trust by enabling real-time data sharing and predictive analytics. For example, blockchain facilitates transparent transactions, particularly in financial services, where secure and immutable ledgers are crucial. Similarly, IoT in tourism enables real-time monitoring of customer preferences, enhancing service delivery. Businesses today in the globalised environment of free markets are increasingly prioritising ethical and sustainable practices, requiring closer collaboration with supply chain partners. The debate between global and local supply chains has intensified. Global supply chains benefit from economies of scale, while local models enhance flexibility and responsiveness. For example, local food sourcing in tourism boosts regional economies and reduces environmental impacts.

Sustainable supply chain practices are gaining prominence, driven by environmental regulations and consumer demand. In tourism, for example, local sourcing and eco-certifications help reduce carbon footprints. Circular economy models, focusing on reuse and recycling, are increasingly applied in service industries to minimise waste and promote resource efficiency. The recent COVID-19 pandemic has presented a unique threat but also an opportunity to interpret and control global supply chains. The crisis emergency highlighted practical issues as well as the importance of resilient supply chains, highlighting the need for strong relationship management. Service industries face risks such as supply disruptions, geopolitical changes and pandemics. Strategies such as supplier diversification, real-time monitoring, and agile processes help build resilience. In healthcare, resilient SCM ensures the uninterrupted supply of critical medical equipment during crises, as highlighted by Ivanov (2024a) during the COVID-19 pandemic. Tailoring relationship management strategies to specific partnerships ensures alignment with unique needs and goals ('customisation'), meeting them at a personalised level of service demand. Supply and value chain management includes activities and common practices in which every strategy of a business and more broadly of an economic organisation is developed.

Therefore, the process of achieving environmental and social goals depends on the common adoption of goals and rules of conduct that aim at expected benefits for all members and the network of partners of a supply chain and not only for the main organisation that seeks development based on the dimensions of the TBL theory.

Customer centricity is vital in the service industries. Personalised services and real-time customisation improve customer satisfaction and loyalty. AI-based platforms, such as recommendation systems in retail and tourism, allow businesses to cater to individual needs. The prospects concern the developments in, AI and automation, Predictive analytics and robotic process automation to streamline services, and decentralised supply chains.

In summary, the future of SCM in services will be shaped by technology, sustainability and a relentless focus on customer experience. Companies that successfully integrate digital tools, adopt green practices, and create collaborative ecosystems will thrive in the evolving landscape. As globalisation and service trends intensify, SCM in services must remain agile, customer-centric and innovation-driven practices.

Synopsis

This chapter explores the critical role of value chain management in various service sectors, emphasising its significance in today's service-driven economy. It examines sector-specific approaches, highlighting the unique challenges and opportunities in industries like accommodation, food and beverage, air passenger transport and event management. Through case studies of leading companies such as Marriott International, Espoo Catering, Emirates and the San Martino Festival, the chapter illustrates how businesses can optimise their value chains for sustainability, efficiency and competitive advantage. It underscores the importance of integrating sustainability, digital transformation and customer-centric strategies to achieve long-term success in the dynamic service sector.

Review and discussion questions

- Identify various types of service firms and define the service/product combination.
- How can the recommendations made in this case enhance customer co-creation while allowing operational efficiency?
- Identify service firms where the recommendations made in this case are likely not to be embraced by the customer. What are the characteristics of the service?

Case studies

Case study 1: Using data from toilets to improve service and optimise resource utilisation

Roskilde Festival, one of Northern Europe's largest music and cultural festivals, attracts approximately 130,000 visitors annually to Roskilde, Denmark. Since its inception in 1971, the festival has showcased a diverse range of music genres, featuring over 175 artists across eight stages. In addition to music, the festival offers art installations, workshops and various cultural activities. Organised by a non-profit, the festival donates its profits to charitable causes, particularly those supporting children and youth. Roskilde Festival is also widely recognised for its strong commitment to sustainability.

In collaboration with IBM and other partners, Copenhagen Business School launched a data project at Roskilde Festival, with one sub-project focusing on optimising the festival's toilet system. The festival toilets, which lack direct water connections and exhaust systems, rely on containers that must be emptied regularly. However, predicting when to empty these containers across the vast site presents a challenge. Some toilets fill up quickly, while others remain underused, leading to inefficient route planning for emptying.

To tackle this issue, sensors were installed on the festival toilets. These sensors recorded data points such as the duration of each toilet visit and the weight of waste in the containers. This real-time data collection enabled a better understanding of toilet usage patterns, allowing for more efficient cleaning and emptying schedules.

The system is straightforward: when someone enters a toilet, sensors record the increase in weight and the duration of their visit. These data, processed by a Raspberry Pi and sent to IBM's cloud platform, are analysed through Watson's IoT system. The data are then displayed on a dashboard, showing the number of visits and the current waste level in the container. Once the container reaches an additional 250 kg in weight, an alert is triggered, signalling that the toilet needs to be emptied. Essentially, the festival created a large-scale smart weighing system to manage toilet usage with real-time data, optimising guest experience and the festival's cleaning and energy resources.

For example, peak usage occurred around 11 PM, with 115 visitors per hour, while usage dropped to nearly zero at 3 AM. Another useful metric indicated that if guests were in and out of a toilet quickly, as this was a sign that the toilet likely needed cleaning. By analysing these patterns, the festival could predict when toilets needed service, shifting from reactive to proactive management.

While technology provided clear improvements, it also required a change in mindset. Shifting from traditional cleaning routines to data-driven strategies demanded openness to change and trust in the data.

This project at Roskilde Festival has inspired similar initiatives elsewhere, including at Copenhagen Business School. Sensors installed in soap and paper dispensers in Copenhagen Business School restrooms revealed inefficiencies in cleaning schedules, leading to a complete overhaul of the cleaning process. The result was not only a higher standard of restroom hygiene but also a 20% reduction in cleaning costs. Overall, the project demonstrates how data-driven solutions can transform even the most routine operations, such as toilet maintenance, resulting in improved service and significant cost savings.

Case study 2: The moment of truth in food service – efficient customer co-creation

Products and services differ in several important ways, the most notable characteristic being that products are tangible, while services are intangible. However, many products include a service component, and many services involve delivering a tangible product to the customer. Regardless of the combination, there are interactions between the provider and the customer that are known as moments of truth. The point where the provider and the customer interact is a critical moment of truth, as it shapes the customer's perception of the service they receive.

Another characteristic of services is their variability. Jacobs' Burger and Bourbon, an anchor restaurant at an open-air venue in a beach town, must plan for surges and plunges in customers that vary dramatically throughout the year while staffing with full-time and supplementing with seasonal employees. One customer at Jacob's Burger and Bourbon might have a very different experience from another. The success of the interaction can depend on factors like how the customer places the order, how the server takes it and the quality and freshness of the ingredients used by the chef.

Having customers involved in co-creation, which at Jacob's Burger and Bourbon allows them to take part in crafting their service and meals, can be detrimental to efficiency. Owner A.F. Jacobs must estimate productivity given many variables, and staff accordingly. An article by Tan and Netessine (2020) investigates the impact of table technology on restaurant performance. Tabletop technology is the use of a tabletop device that facilitates the table service process, and such devices are found to increase average sales and decrease the duration of customers' visits. The force behind this finding is that the adoption of tabletop devices provides better service to the customer while increasing operational efficiency for the restaurant. When customers use the tabletop device instead of having a restaurant employee involved, servers have more time to spend on other elements of service, thus increasing the level of customer service.

How can service businesses balance customer co-creation and efficient operations? At the heart of the article by Tan and Netessine (2020) was a device that better served the customer while relieving the service provider of value-added activities (activities deemed to be of value for the customer) so that the restaurant employees could focus on other important activities.

Several recommendations follow from the above discussion. Firstly, in terms of co-creation, for items like burgers, buns, toppings and bourbon, the choices should be simplified. Instead of offering an extensive list of options that can result in numerous combinations, customers should be allowed to select from a curated set of options. For example, toppings could be suggested that pair well together or bourbon flights could be suggested based on distillery or flavour profile. This approach improves portion control, simplifies inventory management and allows customers to participate in co-creation within a manageable framework.

Other operations fall under efficient operations. Automation should be introduced in ways that benefit both the customer and the service organisation. Apps for making or modifying reservations, ordering at the table including the ability to subsequently add second rounds, and the ability to pay and go, provide customers with instant service while enhancing operational efficiency. When these devices work as intended, customers feel served even without direct interaction with a server. For A.F. Jacobs, the benefit of eliminating direct interaction extends to seasonal employees needing less training and less interaction means a great opportunity to spend on value added services that cannot be easily automated.

There are multiple moments of truth, points where the customer interacts with the service provider. These moments can range from a customer's first seeking information about a service organisation to providing feedback on an experience. Each moment of truth is crucial to the overall customer experience. In this case, the focus is on the first moment of truth, where balancing co-creation and operational efficiency is critical to creating a win-win for the customer and the service firm.

Multiple-choice questions

1. What is a key difference between SCM for services and physical goods?

   A. Services are tangible and can be stored for later use
   B. Services are produced and consumed simultaneously
   C. Physical goods require more customer interaction than services
   D. Physical goods are more difficult to standardise than services

2. How does the concept of 'servitisation' contribute to the competitiveness of companies?

   A. By replacing all physical products with digital services
   B. By lowering product quality to reduce costs
   C. By integrating value-added services with physical products
   D. By reducing the involvement of customers in the supply chain

3. What role does human capital play in service supply chains?

   A. It has minimal impact compared to technology
   B. It primarily affects only back-end operations
   C. It enhances customer experience and service quality
   D. It replaces automation in service processes

4. How do the characteristics of services (intangibility, simultaneity and heterogeneity) affect SCM?

   A. They make standardisation easier
   B. They require more customer interaction and flexible operations
   C. They allow for better inventory control
   D. They eliminate the need for demand forecasting

5. What is the role of marketing in strengthening relationships within a service supply chain?

   A. It focuses only on advertising and promotions
   B. It builds trust and fosters collaboration between stakeholders
   C. It eliminates the need for service customisation
   D. It reduces communication between suppliers and customers

6. How does relationship marketing contribute to value creation in service value chains?

   A. By focusing only on short-term sales goals
   B. By reducing customer engagement and retention

C. By fostering long-term partnerships and customer loyalty
D. By minimising customisation in services

7. What is the significance of AI and big data analytics in modern marketing and SCM?

A. They enable demand forecasting and personalised marketing
B. They replace all human decision-making
C. They slow down real-time decision-making
D. They are only useful for product-based industries

8. What are the key components of the 7Ps in service marketing, and how do they impact SCM?

A. Product, price, people and packaging
B. Product, place, price, promotion, people, process and physical evidence
C. Packaging, promotion, pricing and production
D. Profit, processes, procurement and productivity

9. How does supply chain integration affect customer satisfaction in the service sector?

A. It slows down service delivery
B. It improves coordination and enhances service reliability
C. It increases customer complaints due to inefficiencies
D. It reduces the need for supplier collaboration

10. What are the challenges in managing the bullwhip effect in service supply chains?

A. Services have limited inventory buffers, making demand fluctuations harder to manage
B. Services can be stored to compensate for demand surges
C. Demand remains constant, eliminating the bullwhip effect
D. The bullwhip effect does not apply to services

11. How does customer participation influence the service supply chain?

A. It has no impact on service quality or efficiency
B. It increases variability but allows for greater customisation
C. It simplifies service delivery by reducing complexity
D. It eliminates the need for service providers

12. What are the key differences between service-only supply chains and product-service supply chains?

A. Service-only chains focus more on inventory control
B. Product-service supply chains blend physical products with value-added services
C. Service-only supply chains eliminate customer interactions
D. Product-service supply chains do not require human capital

13. What are the main risks businesses face when outsourcing services in a supply chain?

    A. Improved customer satisfaction
    B. Increased control over service quality
    C. Loss of direct customer relationships and quality control
    D. Reduced cost of operations without any trade-offs

14. How does globalisation influence SCM practices in the service industry?

    A. It limits service expansion across regions
    B. It increases cultural and regulatory complexities while expanding market reach
    C. It reduces the need for service standardisation
    D. It makes customer expectations less diverse

15. Why is agility important in service-based supply chains?

    A. Services require rapid response to demand changes and customer needs
    B. It allows businesses to ignore customer feedback
    C. It reduces the need for technology adoption
    D. It eliminates the need for crisis management

Essay question

Discuss the unique characteristics of services. How do intangibility, simultaneity and heterogeneity, impact SCM in the service sector, and what strategies can businesses adopt to enhance efficiency, customer satisfaction and competitiveness in service-based supply chains? Provide some examples of real-world applications and highlight the challenges service organisations may face in implementing these theoretical analytical tools. Finally, suggest strategies for these service organisations.

12

VALUE CHAIN MANAGEMENT IN SPECIFIC SECTORS

Introduction

In this chapter, the reader delves into the characteristics that highlight, in terms of value chain management in services, four case studies or else the practices of those companies that are active in: catering, transport, tourism and event markets. A good understanding of the specific factors that affect each service sector helps the manager study the possible deviations, problems and opportunities that may arise in each different sector application of administrative decision-making related to the management of value chains in services. This chapter explores the role of supply chain management (SCM) in services marketing, examining how businesses coordinate their networks of suppliers, partners and customers to create value. It discusses the integration of marketing strategies within the service supply chain and highlights emerging trends such as digitalisation, sustainability and customer-centric service design. Studying business sector case studies equips learners and professionals with actionable insights, enhances problem-solving and decision-making skills and prepares them for real-world challenges. Service sector case studies are instrumental for understanding the dynamic nature of services, including practices of supply chain sustainability, customer relationships, innovation, operational effectiveness and global strategies. They provide actionable insights and lessons that are directly applicable to solving real-world challenges and driving growth in service industries.

Learning objectives

After reading this chapter, you will be able to answer the following questions:

- What are the fundamental principles of value chain management in service-based industries?
- How does sustainability impact service value chains, and how do businesses integrate environmental and social responsibility into their operations?
- What are the key challenges faced in value chain management across different service sectors, such as catering, transport, tourism and event management?

DOI: 10.4324/9781003650973-12

- How can real-world case studies help identify best practices and lessons learned in optimising service value chains?
- What role does technology and digital transformation play in enhancing value chain efficiency and competitiveness?
- How can theoretical models of value chain management be applied to practical industry scenarios to improve business operations?

Outline

12.1 Sector-specific value chain management approaches
12.2 Accommodation industry (Marriott International case study)
12.3 Food and beverage industry (Espoo Catering case study)
12.4 Air passenger transport industry (Emirates case study)
12.5 Event industry (San Martino Festival case study)

12.1 Sector-specific value chain management approaches

In today's increasingly service-driven global economy, understanding and applying sector-specific value chain management approaches has become vital for businesses seeking sustainable growth and competitiveness.

Value chain management in the services sector involves analysing and optimising each step of service delivery, from initial customer interaction to after-sales support. This tailored approach helps companies reduce costs, improve efficiency and deliver higher-quality services that differentiate them in a crowded marketplace. Furthermore, it fosters stronger relationships across stakeholders, facilitating innovation and enhancing adaptability to economic and market shifts. As services continue to dominate global markets, adopting value chain strategies specific to the sector is essential for driving profitability and long-term success. In summary, focusing on service sector-specific value chain management allows companies to enhance efficiency, profitability and competitiveness in an increasingly service-driven economy. Below are some examples of different business activities related to the service sector and their related supply and value chains.

12.2 Accommodation industry (Marriott International case study)

The following section presents an example of the Marriott International accommodation services provider, which incorporates value chain management practices to improve environmental, social and economic outcomes and deliver related sustainable impacts.

Marriott International has integrated sustainable sourcing practices into its value chain. The company collaborates with local farmers and producers to source fresh and organic ingredients for its restaurants. This approach reduces carbon emissions from transportation while supporting local economies. Marriott also ensures that suppliers adhere to ethical labour practices and environmental standards. The Marriott International hotel group is a typical example of adopting actions that follow the triptych of the TBL theory. Its strategic objectives, which included financial objectives, have now been enriched by objectives that concern the achievement of both environmental and social objectives.

The Marriott International group presents in a relevant report its ambitions and the results of its actions regarding supplier compliance with sustainability certifications, such as the Rainforest

Alliance for coffee and tea, the strengthening actions to support local suppliers and initiatives to reduce the carbon footprint and reduce waste due to surplus food, and the donations to local charities. The 2025 sustainability goals include, among others, reducing carbon intensity per square metre of air-conditioned space by 30% compared to the base year –2016.

The pandemic COVID-19 period positively affected the goal, which was assessed as an opportunity to maintain the new conditions and after the reintegration of the unit's actions in 2022 in conditions of operational normality. Marriott has demonstrated reductions in carbon intensity across all regions since 2016, which has impacted its progress toward this goal. Marriott will continue to reassess its progress as normal operating conditions return and identify opportunities to implement programmes to reduce energy consumption at Marriott hotels. Following the company's submission and approval of its science-based emissions reduction target, Marriott expects to retire its 2025 carbon reduction goal of net zero carbon emissions by 2050 (Marriott 2022).

Marriott International's value chain is a well-integrated system that leverages technological innovation, customer-centric services and a strong brand portfolio to maintain its competitive advantage. By focusing on sustainability, employee satisfaction and seamless guest experiences, Marriott continues to set benchmarks in the hospitality industry. Marriott's value chain refers to the system of activities and processes that the company undertakes to create value for its customers and stakeholders. It encompasses the full range of operations, from procurement and logistics to customer service and feedback (Figure 12.1).

12.3 Food and beverage industry (Espoo Catering case study)

Restaurant services are in modern social reality an important point of reference in the daily life of households and professionals. Practical sustainable value chain activities that have been implemented in the provision of sustainable food services and sustainable value (e.g., in the case of Espoo municipal catering organisation in Finland) are also identified in the literature.

The Espoo city has a special service, the 'Department of Environmental Protection'. This department monitors the progress of the Sustainable Energy and Climate Action Plan and the 'Society's Commitment to Sustainable Development 2050' project (Sitoumus 2050). In Finland, the recent waste management legislation requires that restaurants and catering establishments comply with specific waste and garbage management regulations. Reducing food waste is one of the measures outlined in the Climate Watch of the city of Espoo,[1] which is part of the greater Helsinki Metropolitan Area (UNESCO 2024). Reducing waste and wasteful consumption of food and beverages through resource efficiency also leads to positive economic outcomes for business owners and the economy. Waste separation is therefore mandatory for restaurants that (a) produce at least 10 kg of organic waste, (b) consume 5 kg of FRP and plastic packaging and (c) consume 2 kg of glass packaging per week.

Espoo Catering Ltd, based in Espoo, Finland, is a municipal company specialising in providing food services to schools, daycare centres and other public institutions. The competitive advantage (CA) of the ESPOO catering value chain arises from the integration of effective processes, sustainability initiatives, innovation and customer-centric approaches (Figure 12.2). Their value supply chain encompasses a series of activities designed to deliver high-quality, sustainable and cost-effective catering solutions (ESPOO 2024a). The Espoo catering service, through its actions, strengthens the effort to establish products in the lunch menus of restaurants in the region and promotes products that have been certified as 'Fairtrade'.[2]

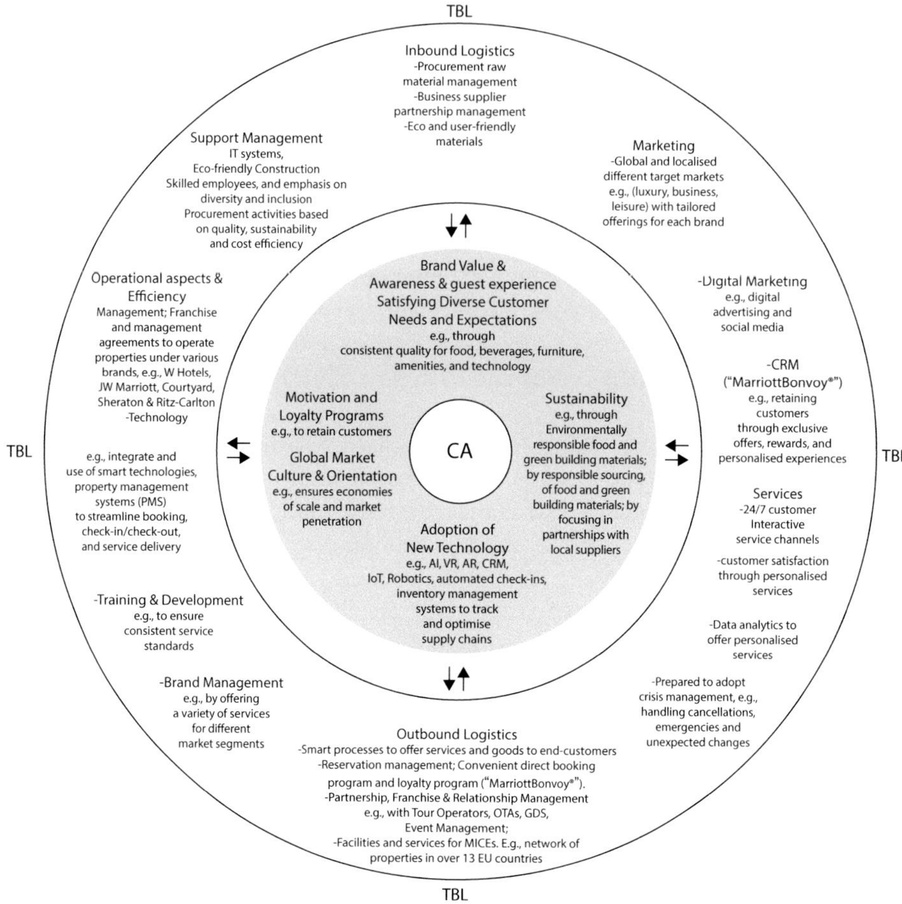

FIGURE 12.1 Marriott's supply and value chain activities

Note: Where, 'CA' = Competitive Advantage, 'IoT' = Internet of Things, 'AI' = Artificial Intelligent, 'AR' = Augmented Reality, 'VR' = Virtual Reality, 'CRM' = Customer Relations Management, 'OTAs'= Online Travel Agents. 'GDS' = Global Distribution System, 'MICE' = Meetings, Incentives, Conferences and Events, '24/7' = 24 hours a day and 7 days a week, &'TBL' = or else the 3Ps; the Triple Bottom Line dimensions i.e., Societal (People), Environmental (Physical) & Economical (Profit), aspects

Espoo Catering's Kilo kitchen is a modern example of a supply chain that prepares, packs and promotes since 2016 more than 8,000 portions daily using digital support tools. As an employment place, it offers jobs for 22 local people. Kilo Kitchen has new infrastructure, modern technology (environmentally friendly and energy efficient) and equipment while covering, with appropriate and sufficient resource potential, the specialised needs of its customers, for example, kindergartens in the area, restaurants and catering areas in hospitals. Espoo Catering Ltd. provides high-quality meal services with a strong emphasis on sustainability. Their commitment to sustainable supply chain management (SSCM) is evident through various initiatives. A decisive point in the selection of Espoo Catering's supply chain is the selection of suitable local suppliers, that is, the selection of suitable quality local wholesalers such as the company Valio Aimo

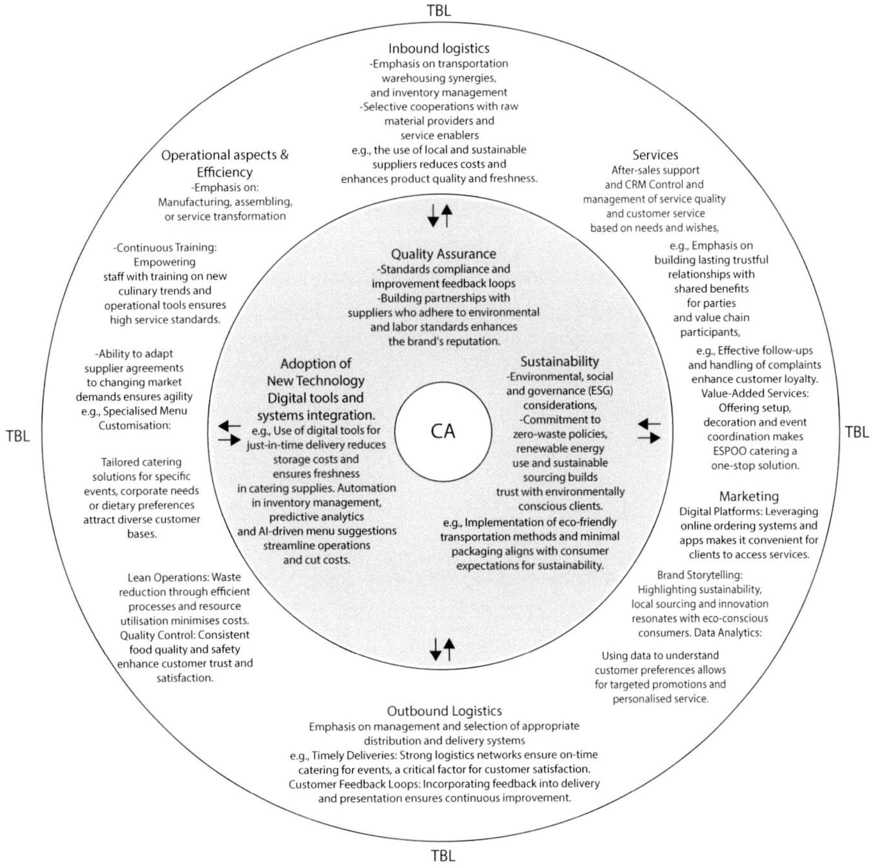

FIGURE 12.2 ESPOO supply and value chain activities

Note: Where 'CA' = Competitive Advantage, 'CRM' = Customer Relations Management, 'ESG' = Environmental, Social and Governance & 'TBL' = or else the 3Ps; the Triple Bottom Line dimensions i.e., Societal (People), Environmental (Physical) & Economical (Profit), aspects

(2024) strengthens its competitive power and also contributes to the strengthening of the local economy by also addressing social problems that are related to the possibility of employment and the well-being of the residents and professionals of the area. In this way, we would say that it also comes close to the basic principle of the three sustainability pillars of TBL.

The company has invested in environmental management by adopting an innovative environmental program focused on SSCM. This programme, as already mentioned, includes the consumption of Fairtrade products, ensuring ethical sourcing and fair compensation for producers.

Espoo Catering collaborates with initiatives like the Future Workshop for Sustainable Development (TUPA) to find practical solutions for reducing and repurposing food waste, further enhancing their sustainability efforts. The TUPA action is part of a wider set of actions for the sustainability and participation of local communities. More specifically, in this action, according to the relevant reference on the organisation's website, it is planned to develop urban solutions for the better treatment of residents, 'the promotion of good governance and the participation of residents' (ESPOO 2024b). The ESPOO catering value chain's competitive advantage is anchored in its ability to offer high-quality, sustainable and customer-tailored services, while leveraging technology and innovation to enhance efficiency and maintain cost competitiveness. These factors create a distinctive value proposition, enabling ESPOO to outshine competitors in the F&B and catering industry.

12.4 Air passenger transport industry (Emirates case study)

International competition and frequent changes in the external business environment (e.g., economic crises, changes in the institutional framework, pandemics and technological developments) bring about necessary adaptations of business functions. Thus, SCM and logistics play an essential role in passenger air services. For example, the services of an airline catering business can affect the cost and quality of airline passenger transport services, thus shifting the focus to rational SCM and the possibilities of improving service efficiency by contributing to the creation of high airline value chains (Rajaratnam and Sunmola 2021). The air passenger transport supply value chain comprises a network of interconnected activities and stakeholders working together to deliver efficient, safe and enjoyable air travel experiences. Below is a detailed breakdown of its components.

Emirates is a Dubai airline that belongs to the government's Investment Corporation group and has been providing air services since 1985 (Emirates 2024a, 2024b). Emirates airlines has been rated and ranked as one of the satellite airlines in the world (SKYTRAX-World Airlines Awards 2024). The company has over time remained operationally viable even in the period of economic crisis, and this has also benefited in part from its excellent value chain (Nataraja and Al-Aali 2011; Kamarudeen and Sundarakani 2019). The company has managed to ensure its long-term competitive advantages through appropriate choices regarding the supply chain. More specifically, the important managerial choices that bring about the excellent performance in its value chain are noted below.

An important initiative of the company is the renewal of the fleet by acquiring suitable aircraft. Emirates has sourced aircraft from manufacturers (e.g., Boeing and Airbus) that effectively manage its maintenance and upgrades. Regarding fuel supply, these come from refineries and are delivered to airports via pipelines or fuel trucks. Also important is the constant preference it shows in choosing and maintaining its relationships with its excellent suppliers. The airline works with suppliers for in-flight meals, cabin materials, spare parts and consumables and with providers of technology systems management, for example, reservations, operational management and ticketing.

Emirates is actively involved in sustainability efforts, including investments in fuel-efficient aircraft and initiatives to reduce environmental impact (Emirates 2024c). Emirates' value supply chain (Figure 12.3) emphasises luxury, efficiency and sustainability, making it a leading player in the global air transport industry.

12.5 Event industry (San Martino Festival case study)[3]

A beneficial business activity that thrives in modern world's economies is that of organising event services. The growth of the events is particularly evident in European countries, followed by the US and Asia/Oceania (Allied Market Research 2024). In the case of events, the success of an event proposal depends on the combination of multiple tasks and actions that should be performed based on a time-schedule. The contribution of the value chain to each event-project

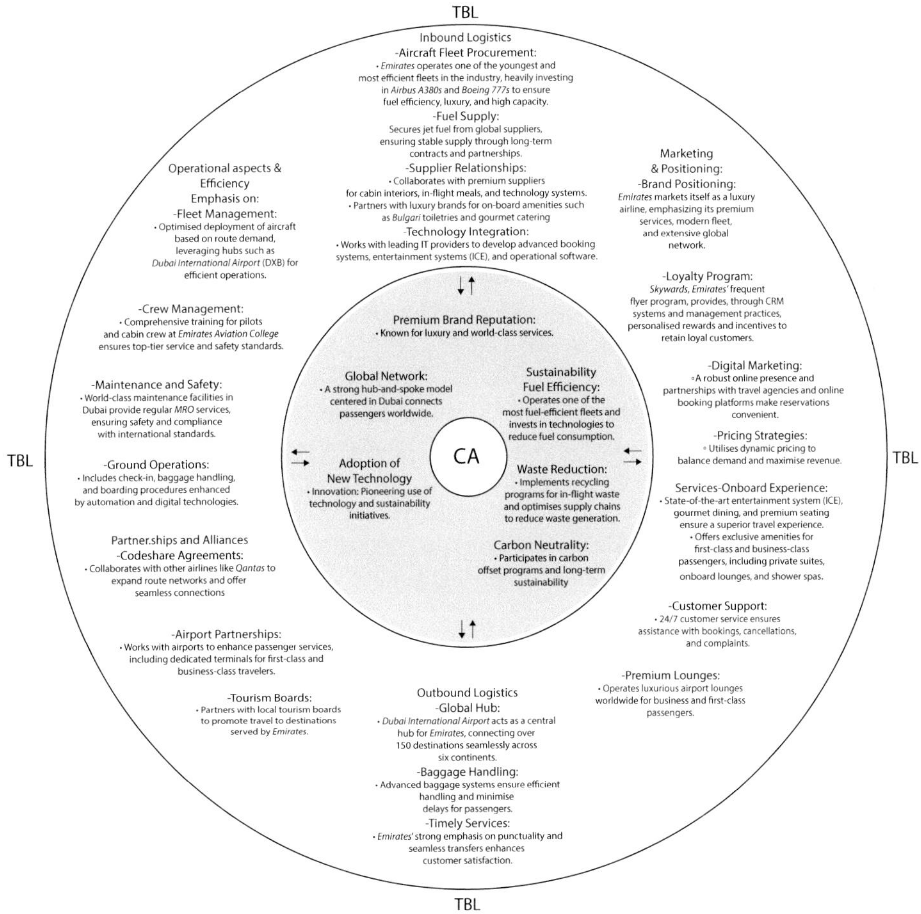

FIGURE 12.3 Emirates' supply and value chain activities

Note: Where 'CA' = Competitive Advantage, 'CRM' = Customer Relations Management, 'IT' = Information Technology, 'MRO' = Maintenance, Repair, and Overhaul services, 'DXB' = Dubai International Airport, 'ICE' = Name of Emirate's entertainment System, '24/7' = 24 hours a day and 7 days a week, & 'TBL' = or else the 3Ps; the Triple Bottom Line dimensions i.e., Societal (People), Environmental (Physical) & Economical (Profit), aspects

is a decisive factor for the success of an event, since it is the connecting link between suppliers and customers of the event organiser. Through the relevant value chains, all important processes of flow of information, material goods and services related to demand (consumers and customers) are adjusted.

SCM offers a dynamic new feature to festival strategy and marketing practice, as collaborative management thinking is the primary tool for the delivery by all chain partners of the exceptional event service value to customers and consumers (Ryan and Kelly 2017). The search for external partners/suppliers (outsourcing) is a common practice of many companies active in the field and gives prospects also for local suppliers with relative benefits for local societies and economies. The development structures of organisations and businesses operating in the events industry may include vertical and horizontal integrations. A music festival organiser may have acquired a supplier of, for example, a musical instrument and equipment company and a customer, for example, the music event venue with its respective infrastructure and superstructure. In this case, vertical management, it could gain competitive benefits due to its cost, consumer/market contact and quality control advantages.

Companies in the industry often collaborate and form groups or are acquired and merged with or by other companies. In this case, for example, international competition due to economies of scale is easier to deal with, and the dynamics of the available resources of the original organiser increases. Industry companies can monitor developments and identify suitable partnerships through industry exhibitions (Pielichaty et al. 2017; Krajewski et al. 2016; Li et al. 2012). An important point of reference is the possibility of standardising the procedures through initiatives of the organisers with certification bodies (ISO 2024) and the Official Bodies' Guidelines on Sustainable Event Organisation (e.g., German Environment Agency; UBA 2020). This ensures continued commitment to sustainable practices and activities by encouraging organisations to responsibly manage social, economic and environmental impacts. This ensures continued commitment to sustainable practices and activities, encouraging organisations to responsibly manage social, economic and environmental impacts. Cooperation with local producers and suppliers can contribute to the reduction of costs, to the quality and availability of the provided services that an organiser seeks, while also having parallel effects that contribute to the reduction of the carbon footprint of the event.

The San Martino Festival (SMF) in Sicily is a significant cultural event that marks the culmination of the agricultural year and the tasting of new wine. This festival not only honours Saint Martin but also plays a crucial role in the local economy by influencing various aspects of the supply value chain, particularly in the wine and food sectors (WineItaly24 2024). Wine producers also participate in wine sustainability programmes such as the 'SOStain' programme, which aims to promote the sustainable behaviour defined by TBL throughout the wine supply chain (Borsellino et al. 2016). The event significantly impacts supply value chain management by driving demand for local products, promoting short supply chains and necessitating efficient logistics and inventory strategies. The festival not only celebrates cultural traditions but also stimulates economic activity, supporting the sustainability and growth of regional industries (Borsellino et al. 2020, 2016). The SMF includes various activities that focus on informing and entertaining the participants. The activities of the SMF during November each year include for the participants the preparation of local agricultural products and their availability to the public, for example, wine tasting, hot roasted chestnuts, local delicacies and entertainment activities, that is, musical dance events and recreational games (SuntripSicily 2024).

The following editor's quote from the 'Grand.News' website is typical (CorriereQuotidiano.it 2024):

> Sicilian wine supply chain turns harvest into festival, reveals rituals between Nero Pachino's glasses and barrels.

As it has been noted in the following Figure12.4, the SMF in Sicily represents a vibrant integration of cultural tradition and modern SCM. By emphasising sustainability, local production and community engagement, the festival not only strengthens Sicily's economy but also preserves its rich heritage. The festival coincides with the end of the grape harvest, a period when vintners prepare new wine for tasting. This tradition encourages local wine production and consumption, fostering a robust market for regional wines (SuntripSicily 2024). In Palermo, 'sammartinelli'

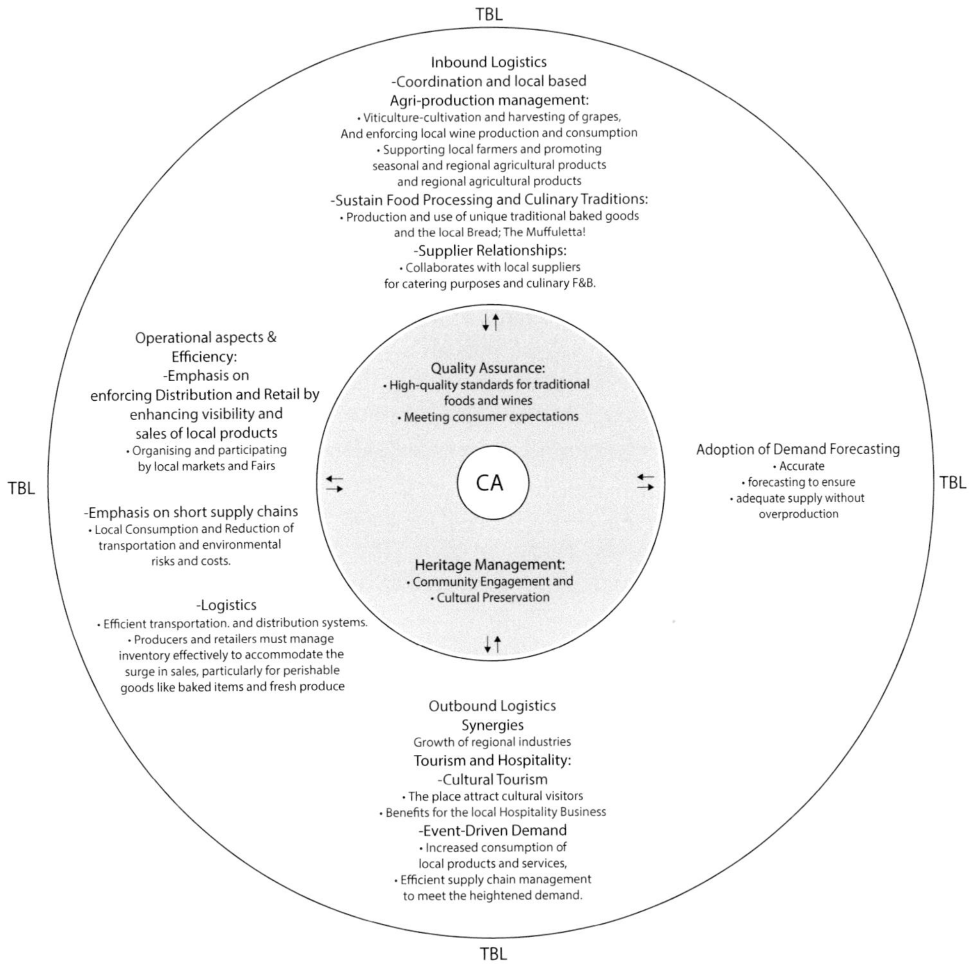

FIGURE 12.4 SMF's event supply and value chain activities

Note: Where, 'CA' = Competitive Advantage, 'FB' = Food and Beverages & 'TBL' = or else the 3Ps; the Triple Bottom Line dimensions i.e., Societal (People), Environmental (Physical) & Economical (Profit), aspects

biscuits are prepared specifically for the festival. These scone-like treats, sometimes filled with ricotta cheese, are traditionally enjoyed dipped in Moscato wine, highlighting the integration of local culinary practices with the festival. Also, Sicilians bake 'La Muffuletta di San Martino', a soft round bread covered with sesame seeds and filled with salumi, cheese or anchovies, showcasing the island's rich gastronomic heritage (deliciousitaly 2023). The festival stimulates economic activity by enforcing the distribution of local products. The SMF participates and use products and services from the local markets where artisans and producers sell traditional foods, wines and crafts, enhancing the visibility and sales of local products (WineItaly24 2024). Also, the SMF and the other business in Sicily emphasise on local production and consumption during the festival, promoting short supply chains and reducing transportation costs and environmental impact while supporting the regional economy (Sicily 2022). The SMF attracts visitors seeking authentic cultural experiences, boosting demand for local accommodations, restaurants and guided tours, thereby contributing to the hospitality sector. The influx of tourists during the festival period leads to increased consumption of local products and services, necessitating efficient SCM to meet the heightened demand (SuntripSicily 2024).

Maintaining high-quality standards for traditional foods and wines is crucial, as the festival serves as a showcase for local products, influencing future consumer perceptions and demand. Efficient transportation and distribution systems are essential to deliver products to markets and venues in a timely manner, maintaining product quality and meeting consumer expectations. The SMF involves community participation in traditional dances, music and culinary activities, preserving and promoting Sicilian cultural heritage (SuntripSicily 2024). Workshops and demonstrations during the festival educate both locals and visitors about traditional production methods, fostering appreciation and continued practice of these crafts.

Each case highlights the importance of value chain optimisation and sustainability, showcasing how businesses can create long-term value for stakeholders while minimising environmental impact.

Marriott International integrates sustainability into its value chain through responsible sourcing, supplier compliance and carbon reduction goals. The company collaborates with local farmers, reduces food waste and aims for net-zero carbon emissions by 2050. Its sustainability efforts align with the TBL framework.

Espoo Catering, a municipal food service provider in Finland, emphasises sustainability through waste reduction, Fairtrade products and collaboration with local suppliers. Its Kilo Kitchen exemplifies efficient and environmentally friendly food production, enhancing both community well-being and economic development.

Emirates Airlines secures a competitive edge through fleet modernisation, supplier partnerships and sustainability efforts. Investments in fuel-efficient aircraft and operational efficiency highlight the company's commitment to reducing its environmental footprint while ensuring luxury service.

The SMF in Sicily demonstrates the interplay between cultural tradition and supply chain efficiency. The festival supports local producers, promotes short supply chains and fosters economic growth. It aligns with TBL principles by emphasising community participation, sustainable agriculture and tourism.

All four case studies emphasise sustainability through environmental, social and economic goals. Marriott, Espoo Catering, Emirates and the SMF adopt practices that align with TBL principles (people, planet and profit).

Reducing waste, lowering emissions and supporting local communities are common across all. Each organisation optimises its value chain by enhancing supplier relationships, improving operational processes and integrating customer feedback. Supplier collaboration and quality control are core practices across Marriott, Espoo Catering and Emirates, while the SMF relies on local partnerships for product supply. Marriott, Espoo Catering, and the SMF actively engage with local suppliers to source products and contribute to local economic development. Emirates ensures strong supplier relationships for its global operations but does not emphasise local suppliers as heavily as the other three. Marriott and Espoo Catering implement waste reduction initiatives, particularly around food waste. The SMF promotes local production and short supply chains, indirectly reducing waste and transportation costs. Emirates focuses more on fuel efficiency and fleet management as part of its waste and emission reduction efforts. Guest experience is a priority for Marriott and Emirates. Espoo Catering emphasises tailored food services for schools and hospitals. The SMF focuses on delivering cultural and gastronomic experiences to attract and satisfy visitors. Marriott and Emirates are large-scale global businesses, while Espoo Catering and SMF are regionally focused. Emirates' value chain emphasises technical efficiency and operational excellence, whereas Marriott, Espoo Catering and the SMF emphasise local supply chain collaboration and sustainability. Espoo Catering and the SMF are more deeply embedded in their local communities, while Marriott bridges global and local supply chains, and Emirates operates primarily on a global scale.

Synopsis

This chapter explores the critical role of value chain management in various service sectors, emphasising its significance in today's service-driven economy. It examines sector-specific approaches, highlighting the unique challenges and opportunities in industries like accommodation, food and beverage, air passenger transport and event management. Through case studies of leading companies such as Marriott International, Espoo Catering, Emirates and the SMF, the chapter illustrates how businesses can optimise their value chains for sustainability, efficiency and competitive advantage. It underscores the importance of integrating sustainability, digital transformation and customer-centric strategies to achieve long-term success in the dynamic service sector.

Case studies

Case study 1: Buyer–seller exchange situations

Since the mid-1990s, it has been argued that both transactional and relational exchanges often coexist in many markets, rather than one prevailing over the other. This perspective, known as the 'pluralistic approach' (Pels et al. 2000), advocates for the creation of a conceptual framework capable of encompassing this diversity.

The pluralistic approach emphasises analysing exchanges from both the buyer's and the seller's viewpoints, suggesting that the choice between transactional and relational exchanges depends on the context and individual interpretations. As a result, diverse exchange scenarios can arise within each market. These scenarios are illustrated in the 'buyer–seller exchange situation matrix', which helps scholars and managers recognise various exchange scenarios a company may face, assisting in deciding when to use a transactional or relational marketing strategy (Figure 12.5). When buyers and sellers both occupy Cell 1 and Cell 4, their demands and offerings for a marketing exchange match. When buyers and sellers occupy Cell 2 and Cell 3, there is a mismatch that must be brought into alignment if a marketing exchange is to be reached.

Flensted Catering, a major Scandinavian salad and potato industry player, embarked upon a relationship marketing programme to mitigate mismatches with their customers. According to Flensted Catering's Marketing Director, 'We believe that a company only improves its capabilities if customers are demanding. This will improve the company. I really believe that we are happy for those customers who are demanding. Often, it is about things that we have not thought about'.

To do so, Flensted first identified the need structure of their diverse customers and then selected those who perceived value in the unique offer proposition that they now sought to

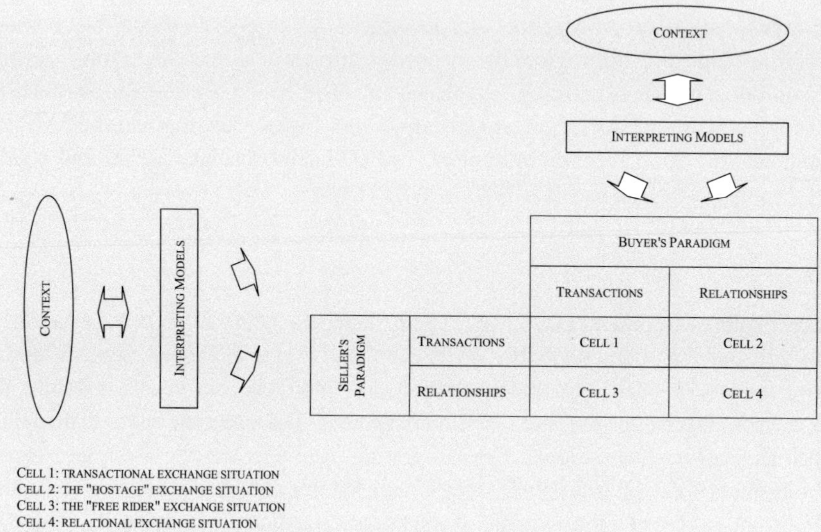

FIGURE 12.5 Buyer–seller exchange situation matrix

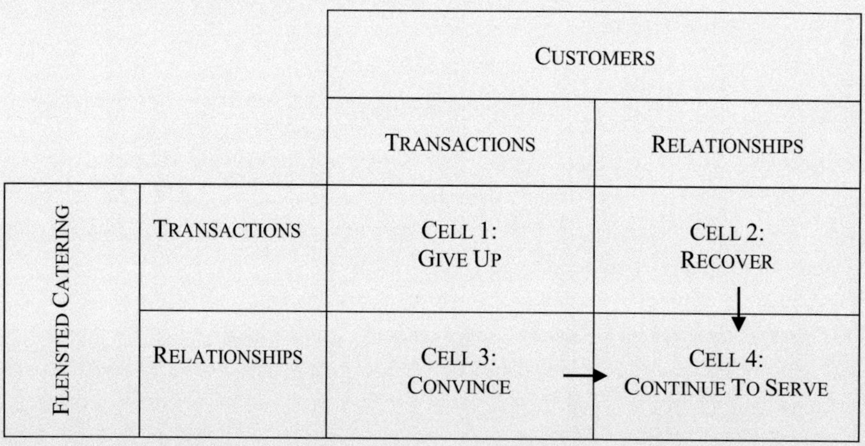

FIGURE 12.6 From different types of customers to Cell 4 customers

focus on. They consciously and intentionally moved from serving all types of customers to concentrating on only those customers who demanded the unique value proposition Flensted Catering sought to serve. When facing the four types of exchange situations they decided to do as follows (Figure 12.6):

- Recover the Cell 2 customers who were not served properly at the moment by proposing the customers a unique offer instead of a generic offer (i.e., a Cell 4 exchange situation).
- Convince the Cell 3 customers that a relationship marketing philosophy (i.e., a Cell 4 exchange situation) is better for both parties with ongoing benefits to both parties.

- Continue to serve the Cell 4 customers as it had previously done.
- Give up the Cell 1 customers.

To understand how different factors influence the exchange scenario, it is essential to take a dyadic perspective. This involves analysing the interaction between the seller's proposal, the buyer's requirements and each party's perceptions of the other:

- What are the potential benefits and costs to Flensted Catering of giving up transactional buyers (Cell 1)?
- How should Flensted Catering convince transactional customers that they would benefit by a relational orientation?

This case originates from Lindgreen, A., and Pels, J. (2002). Buyer-seller exchange situations: Four empirical cases. *Journal of Relationship Marketing* 1(3/4): 60–93.

Reference

Pels, J., Coviello, N., and Brodie, R. (2000). Integrating transactional and relational marketing exchange: A pluralistic perspective. *Journal of Marketing Theory and Practice* 8(3): 11–9.

Case study 2: Global value chains and supplier perceptions of corporate social responsibility

Major global companies enforce corporate social responsibility (CSR) standards within their global value chains (GVCs) by mandating suppliers in developing nations to comply with their corporate codes of conduct. Through CSR, these companies aim to tackle the social and environmental effects of their operations, ensure ethical conduct among business partners, handle relationships with broader societal groups and gain social acceptance. Acting as buyers, these lead firms enforce their codes of conduct on suppliers in developing countries, typically by imposing labour and environmental requirements for continued production contracts.

Suppliers are responsible for implementing buyer-imposed codes of conduct. Bae et al. (2021) explored how suppliers perceive CSR. If suppliers interpret CSR differently from buyers or view it as a form of economic or cultural dominance, misaligned expectations could lead to issues such as symbolic compliance. Additionally, suppliers often face challenges in balancing price pressures, shortened lead times and compliance with multiple buyer-imposed codes.

Bae et al. (2021) investigate the perception of CSR among garment suppliers in Myanmar. The country's garment industry is particularly intriguing due to the country's ongoing transition and evolving role in the global economy, influencing how suppliers understand and implement CSR. The country has become an affordable option for Western clothing brands. However, the introduction of Western corporate codes of conduct by these brands left many suppliers surprised and confused, as they were unfamiliar with how to meet these new requirements.

Bae et al. (2021) propose a more nuanced framework beyond the conventional vertical (buyer–supplier) and horizontal (national institutional contexts) relations to understand how suppliers perceive CSR in GVCs. They advocate considering various combinations of GVC governance modes (captive, modular and market relations) and types of embeddedness (societal, network and territorial). In Myanmar's garment industry, suppliers under captive governance by buyers tend to adopt CSR practices aligned with the norms and values of the buyers' home countries (societal embeddedness). While highly networked, they may become somewhat detached from local employment norms and practices (territorial embeddedness).

Under modular governance, suppliers' perception of CSR mirrors the norms and values of their buyers. However, their network connections within buyer GVCs are looser compared to suppliers under captive governance, resulting in a stronger territorial embeddedness in their CSR practices. Suppliers with a longer history of garment production prior to the country's transition to a semi-authoritarian democracy and the lifting of economic sanctions exhibit a more pronounced territorial embeddedness.

Suppliers under market-based governance by buyers tend to participate in CSR activities that align with their stronger territorial and societal connections. Being small-scale and easily replaceable, they have minimal network connections and are loosely linked to buyer GVCs, thus facing less pressure to adhere to CSR requirements set by their buyers. These findings are summarised in Table 12.1.

TABLE 12.1 Supplier perceptions of CSR: GVC governance and embeddedness

		Buyer governance mode on suppliers' CSR		
		Captive	*Modular*	*Market-based relations*
Embeddedness Type	**Societal**	Supplier CSR perceptions reflect the societal embeddedness of their buyers, embracing codes of conduct and buyers' social audits	Supplier CSR perceptions reflect both the societal embeddedness of their buyers and the suppliers themselves, potentially creating contradictions and supplier discontent	Supplier perceptions reflect mainly the societal embeddedness of suppliers that are local to the country of production
	Network	Suppliers are tightly integrated into the GVCs of their buyers that provide exclusive sourcing relationship in return for demonstrated code compliance	Suppliers are less tightly integrated into the GVCs of their buyers than their peers under captive governance	Suppliers are only loosely integrated into the GVCs of their buyers
	Territorial	Suppliers are, to some extent, territorially disembedded from the country of production	Suppliers display greater levels of territorial embeddedness in the country of production than their peers under captive governance	Suppliers are mainly territorially embedded in the country of production

Managerial implications

The typology of GVC governance and embeddedness aids in identifying and comparing various supplier perceptions of CSR within and across countries. It categorises supplier perceptions and their underlying drivers based on concepts of GVC governance and embeddedness, offering a dynamic analysis that reflects changes in GVC governance modes and supplier embeddedness. Suppliers may encounter different buyer demands for compliance with codes of conduct, serving both types of buyers concurrently. Additionally, the typology acknowledges indigenous perspectives on CSR. The typology thus emphasises the importance for buyers to consider suppliers' CSR perspectives across different contexts.

This case originates from Bae, J., Lund-Thomsen, P., and Lindgreen, A. (2021). Global value and supplier perceptions of corporate social responsibility: A case study of garment manufacturers in Myanmar. *Global Networks* 21(4): 653–680. Here, the reader can also find additional relevant references to the case and its topic.

Multiple-choice questions

1. How does value chain management differ across various service industries?

   A. It is identical across all industries
   B. It depends on customer involvement, service customisation and industry-specific needs
   C. It does not require digital transformation
   D. It is only applicable to manufacturing industries

2. What is one key benefit of analysing industry-specific value chains?

   A. Increased production of raw materials
   B. Lower customer satisfaction
   C. Improved cost optimisation and competitive advantage
   D. Decreased focus on sustainability

3. How does digital transformation impact value chain management in services?

   A. Reduces efficiency and increases costs
   B. Has no impact on value chains
   C. Improves efficiency through AI, automation and real-time analytics
   D. Slows down supply chain collaboration

4. What is a key element of sustainability in service value chains?

   A. Reducing carbon footprints and implementing ethical labour standards
   B. Increasing production waste
   C. Avoiding digital transformation
   D. Eliminating service-based businesses

5. How does Marriott integrate value chain management strategies?

   A. By outsourcing all services without monitoring sustainability
   B. By using only global suppliers to reduce costs

C. By collaborating with local suppliers, reducing emissions and ensuring sustainability compliance
D. By avoiding digital transformation and customer service improvements

6. What is a best practice for value chain management in the tourism sector?

A. Ignoring environmental impact
B. Avoiding collaboration with local businesses
C. Investing in digitalisation and strategic partnerships
D. Eliminating value chain management in tourism

7. How do F&B companies implement sustainability in their value chains?

A. Increasing food waste
B. Relying solely on non-renewable resources
C. Adopting sustainable sourcing, waste reduction and ethical labour practices
D. Avoiding sustainability efforts

8. How does supply chain collaboration benefit service industries like catering and hospitality?

A. It weakens competitive advantage
B. It reduces service efficiency
C. It enhances resource sharing, reduces costs and strengthens competitive positioning
D. It eliminates the need for value chains

9. What is a major challenge transportation companies face in value chain management?

A. Lack of customer demand
B. High fuel costs, regulatory compliance and environmental concerns
C. Reduced need for logistics management
D. Overinvestment in outdated technologies

10. How do case studies help businesses improve value chains?

A. They provide real-world insights into efficiency and innovation
B. They create unnecessary complexity
C. They focus only on past failures
D. They only apply to manufacturing industries

11. How does customer experience influence value chain decision-making?

A. It has no effect on decision-making
B. It drives service design, efficiency and innovation
C. It is irrelevant to value chain management
D. It only applies to physical goods industries

12. What is the impact of supply chain transparency on service value chain efficiency?

A. It increases operational risks
B. It has no impact

C. It enhances trust, accountability and efficiency
D. It slows down decision-making

13. What role does sustainability certification play in managing value chains?

A. It ensures compliance with environmental and ethical standards
B. It reduces brand reputation
C. It discourages sustainable business practices
D. It is not recognised globally

14. How can companies achieve economies of scale through value chain management?

A. By ignoring cost efficiencies
B. By streamlining operations, using digital tools and forming strategic partnerships
C. By avoiding supplier collaboration
D. By eliminating supply chain transparency

15. What is a key lesson from successful value chain management case studies?

A. Sustainability and digital adoption are crucial for long-term success
B. Value chain management has no impact on business growth
C. Customer-centric strategies are unimportant
D. Businesses should avoid innovation

Essay question

Discuss the significance of value chain management in service industries and how it differs from value chain management in manufacturing. How does value chain management contribute to business competitiveness in the service sector? What are the key challenges businesses face in implementing effective value chain management strategies in the service industry? Discuss also the importance of sustainability in the value chain management of the F&B industry, using Espoo Catering Ltd. as a case study.

Notes

1 Climate Watch of the city of Espoo, that is, it serves as a comprehensive open platform for communicating and monitoring the city's climate actions.
2 The label 'Fairtrade' certifies to users that the product follows the framework of international regulations supported by the UN and is about transparency, respect for producers and sustainable development.
3 MICE = Meetings, Incentives, Conferences and Events

13

GOOD IDEAS AND PRACTICES FOR SUSTAINABLE SERVICE SUPPLY CHAIN MANAGEMENT

Introduction

Sustainability has become a crucial focus in supply chain management (SCM), particularly in the service sector, where environmental, social and economic factors play a significant role in long-term success. This chapter explores best practices for sustainable service supply chain management (SSSCM) by introducing key frameworks, models and strategies that businesses can implement to create environmentally and socially responsible supply chains. One of the core concepts discussed is the house of sustainable supply chain management (House of SSCM), which provides a structured framework for building sustainability into service supply chains. The chapter also examines the triple bottom line (TBL) approach, balancing economic, social and environmental performance, and the value driver model, which emphasises how businesses can integrate sustainability into their strategies for long-term growth. Through case studies and practical insights, readers will understand how companies in various industries have successfully implemented sustainable practices, from ethical sourcing to green logistics and digital transformation

Learning objectives

- What are the key principles of SSSCM?
- How does the House of SSCM framework help businesses integrate sustainability into their supply chains?
- What is the TBL approach, and how does it balance environmental, social and economic goals?
- How does the value driver model help businesses measure and improve sustainability performance?
- What are the major challenges organisations face when implementing sustainable service supply chain practices?
- How can businesses leverage technology, such as AI, blockchain and data analytics, to enhance sustainability in supply chains?

DOI: 10.4324/9781003650973-13

- What role do ethics, regulations and corporate social responsibility (CSR) play in building sustainable supply chains?
- How do sustainable supply chain practices contribute to long-term profitability and competitive advantage?
- What are some real-world examples of successful sustainability strategies in service industries like tourism, hospitality and transportation?
- How can businesses develop resilience and adaptability in their supply chains to address environmental and social risks?

Outline

13.1 The house of SSCM framework

The concept of the house of sustainable chain management

The House of SSCM is a conceptual framework that visualises the critical components and principles for building sustainable supply chains. The framework often depicts a structure resembling a house, with the foundation, pillars and roof representing the elements needed to achieve sustainability goals in SCM. So, the SSCM can be used is an idea for key players in SCM practice. Below we analyse the main parts of this theoretical concept.

Elements of the development structure of the house of SSCM

The house of SSCM is a theoretical construction that includes the following.

The first level of the foundation where the basic principles exist

The building is based on the fundamental principles that guide sustainable supply chain practices and more specifically, the theoretical proposition previously mentioned in previous sections about the idea/concept of the TBL, which is developed in the infrastructure elements concerning the 'management risk and compliance'. As already explained, the TBL theoretical approach focuses on balancing environmental, social and economic performance. Also included in this first fundamental level are the ethics standards (i.e., 'laws, standards and regulations') that govern the business implementation of Ensuring fairness, transparency and ethical practices throughout the supply chain. Important aspects are as follows:

- Open communication across the supply chain about environmental, social and economic practices.
- Adherence to moral principles in decision-making, including fair labour practices and anti-corruption measures.
- The ability to adapt to disruptions such as climate change, economic instability or geopolitical risks.

The second level of the pillars that support the roof of the building structure

Each of the three pillars represents a key focus area that supports a sustainable supply chain. The first pillar emphasises environmental sustainability ('environmental performance'), for example, the focus here of the SCM practice can be on physical environmental business practices with positive impact to the natural environment, for example, enforcing means to reduce carbon emissions through green logistics or the smart use of renewable energy sources in production and distribution as well as circular economy practices such as recycling, reuse and waste reduction.

As a second element of the pillar can be considered based on the theoretical idea of SSCM, the social aspects. It is important to recognise during the planning process, the impact of business activities on the local community. An important point of support for sustainable processes, which have an impact on the local community, the wider society and future generations, are the activities developed based on a responsible business culture. The business practice that characterises the responsible activities of an organisation include, among other things, the selection of appropriate suppliers that ensure the standards set by organisations regarding sustainable, ethical and socially useful business practices. In this context, a company can register, certify and ensure that its supply chain is controlled according to the quality assurance criteria of sustainable practices that have a positive impact on society. For a better understanding, we would say that some examples concerning the responsibility in the management actions of a company are as follows:

- The development of fair and democratic, without discrimination and exploitation of human personnel who contribute value to the supply chain, for example, through an ethical approach to labour relations that approach the sustainability values of the UN [17 Sustainable Development Goals (SDGs)].
- The social contribution with CSR business practices, for example, the contribution to support actions aimed at ensuring the health of citizens, the provision of jobs, the securing of employment for members of the local community or professionals and local enterprises, the awarding of students, scholarships, donations to support vulnerable groups, the contribution to infrastructures and constructions that facilitate the daily operation of the community, company–community agreements, etc., can and do arouse the interest of the government, the local governments and of course citizens.

The remaining third pillar concerns the economic benefit and impact of business activities. In the economic dimension of the sustainability house, practices that contribute to the rational approach to costs are considered so that they can become manageable and at the same time contribute to the sustainability and the long-term profitability of the business. The investment policy of businesses and organisations is based on the know-how and technology that contribute overall to the growth and development of the economy. In this context, the business choices made regarding the above factors play a decisive role when it comes to decisions on the management of supply and value chains contributing in micro and macro-economic level to economies of scale.

The management of value chains with the support of innovative technologies, for example, the use of information technology and AI innovative investments, can contribute at a micro-level to faster sales growth and to the development of the level of productivity of the business sector. As highlighted in the relevant literature, it should also be considered that the adoption of innovative technologies, for example, AI does not seem to bring about legitimate changes with a positive impact on business activity, if appropriate organisational structures and changes are not in place.

The third level of the roof of the SSCM house

At the top level, the roof of the sustainable management house includes the elements of expected performance that refer to the predetermined goals and the effort to integrate the organisation and its philosophy and culture. The roof symbolises the primary goals and the integration of sustainability. The framework of goals and the integration of the organisation's aspirations includes the following:

- Determining the organisation's capabilities to adapt to environmental conditions, for example, determining resilience in the event of business-related environmental crises such as economic, health and physical – climatic crises.
- The ability to expand and increase the organisation's performance through appropriate choices in partnerships, for example, selecting appropriate external members such as suppliers and customers as long-term business partners, with the aim of the joint success of the sustainable activities developed by the organisation's value and supply chains.
- The ability to search for external resources and appropriate partners in know-how and technology with the aim of developing innovations and increasing the organisation's efficiency. The contribution of modern technologies to the acquisition of innovations by European companies and beyond is considered great. The EU subsidises the effort and supports it with appropriate financial programs.

The following figure is a presentation diagram of the sustainability management house, which interprets the above elements by integrating them into each level of analysis in a concise manner.

As one can see in Figure 13.1 depicting the house of SSCM, the roof of the house is supported by three pillars of the building's balance, which constitute the dimensions of sustainability in the TBL theory. To balance the building, the pillars rely on the ability to adapt and on the management and prediction of risks. The prediction and diagnosis of risks allows the organisation to understand how to quickly comply with it to avoid or even weaken the impacts of environmental risks. In this way, the organisation manages to approach its desired financial returns in market shares, profits and sales.

The framework for the sustainable operation of the organisation to achieve the above throughout the value chain is defined by the institutional environment (i.e., by laws, regulations and principles/standards of behaviour). At the top, the organisation should have the ability to create a friendly and sustainable culture of sustainability principles, for example, by aligning its activities with the UN principles. The corporate strategy should be supported by an appropriate information system so that the organisation can easily adapt to any changes in line with the standards and principles of sustainability. In this way, difficult situations for the business organisation can be predicted, mitigated or even avoided, protecting the supply chain from external risks.

13.2 The SCM house of value driver model

A useful guide for the adoption of sustainable practices in the case of value chains is that of the United Nations Global Compact proposal (UN-Global Compact and BSR 2015). In the

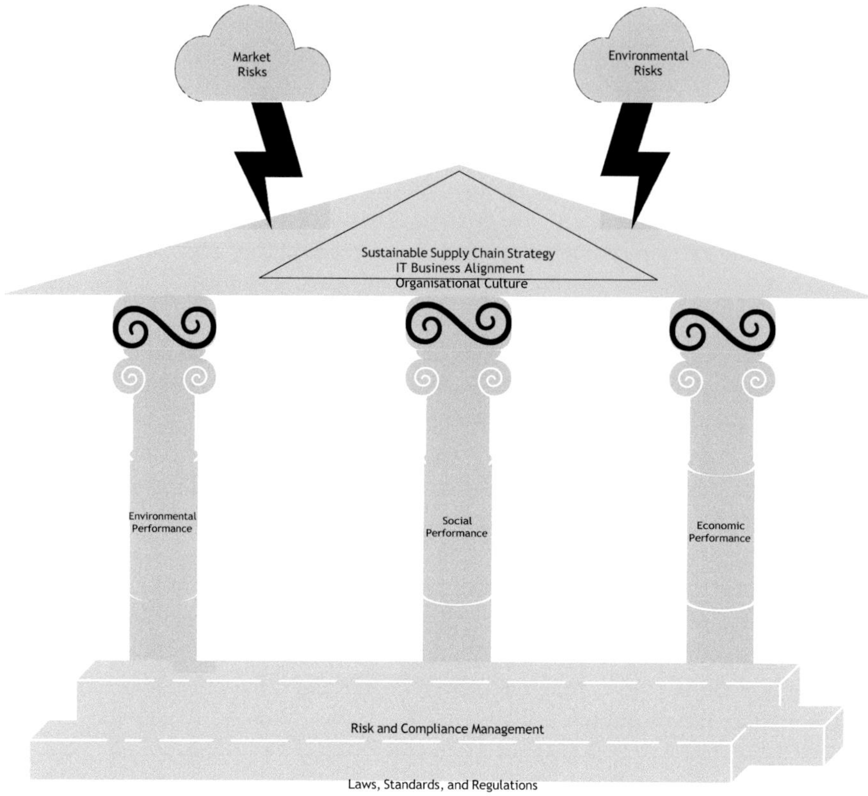

FIGURE 13.1 House of SSCM

Note: Adapted and re-designed from the source Wittstruck and Teuteberg (2011: 333).

section on business applications and cases, the use of the 'value driver model' is suggested (Figure 13.2), which delves into the mode of communication between the cooperating parties, that is, the company and its partners, for example, in a value chain.

The value driver model (Figure 13.2) assumes that when the organisational culture and strategy, as well as the stakeholders who support it, allow for it, then the direct and indirect driver-forces presented in the model proposal can and do contribute to increasing the value of the business and its activities. In this way, the satisfaction of business objectives (goals and objectives) is sought through the corporate culture of enhancing sustainability that also concerns the supply and value chain.

According to the model, business strategies can lead to three desirable outcomes that relate to the elements of the three pillars of the model. More specifically, the three pillars that refer to business growth, business productivity performance and the minimisation or avoidance of risk from the external environment of the business support the sustainability of business activities and the financial performance of the organisation. The model measures the key impacts of value-determining strategies [with measurable elements relating to, for example, revenue for growth, cost for productivity and the TBL and brand value effect for the risk] that drives and

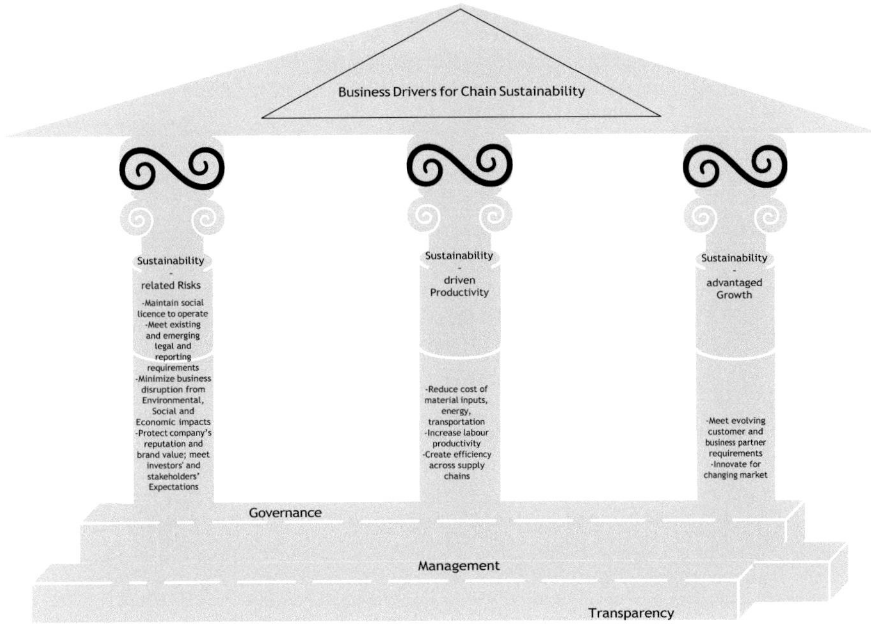

FIGURE 13.2 SCM house of value driver model

Note: Adapted and re-designed from the source 'UN-Global Compact and BSR (2015: 15)'.

impact the creation of overall value performance for the organisation, that is, financial performance relating to value defined as, for example, return on investment/capital or return on equity. Businesses that frequently incentivise partners and members of the value and supply chain should emphasise to their partners the measurable existing and expected benefits by quantifying the results in financial returns. Thus, the current state of revenue, profits and risk management and the current and future performance of the organisation are incentives to upgrade, motivate and energise all members of the value chain.

13.3 The service sustainability SCM model

A supply chain supported by service provision differs structurally from one supported by material goods. Service chains require human involvement with the decisive participation of 'co-producers', that is, customers. The intangible good of service provision includes processes that are adapted without prior standardisation, storage and packaging to the real needs and desires of demand, that is, customers and consumers. In fact, without the involvement of the latter, the provision of the service is not possible, or the desired outcome of the process is affected.

The emphasis on services is given in terms of sustainability to the reduction of unnecessary and environmentally, socially and financially unprofitable processes, for example, reducing the number of garbage trucks, reducing non-conforming passenger transfers and flights, certifying the processes of adopting green practices in the kitchen of a restaurant and adopting quality

TABLE 13.1 Important differences between service supply and manufacturing supply chains

Main factors of differences	*Service supply chain*	*Manufacturing supply chain*
Standardisation	Non-high standardised and centralised procedures (low stability)	High standardised and centralised procedures (high stability)
Control	Mainly ad hoc control procedures: performance evaluation based on service operation with subjective and abstract indicators	Mainly fixed control procedures: performance evaluation based on product operation with objective non-abstract indicators
Resources	Mostly human based	Not only human based
Structure	Can be shorter with important chain intermediary the 'service integrator', for example, P-I-C	Can be long organised and administrated, for example, S-M-W-R-C
Nature of the good	Intangible	Tangible
Co-ordination procedure	Emphasis on capacity and the service plan procedures	Emphasis on production and inventory plan
Service Features	Intangibility, heterogeneity, inseparability and perishability	Tangibility, homogeneity, separability and the chance of storing materials for future use

Note: Above where S = supplier, M = manufacturer, W = wholesaler, R = retailer, C = customer, I = service integrator and P = provider.Sources: Liu et al. (2019: 29–31); Aliakbari Nouri et al. (2020: 817).

recognition marks for services provided in hotels. It should be noted that services are often provided with the support of, or support, tangible goods (Table 13.1). So when providing a service, material elements may also be involved. For example, a dentist or a barber needs the support of equipment and tools that should be selected and maintained by appropriate suppliers. A passenger airline needs the support of suppliers of aircraft fuel and catering A SSSCM is, as in material goods, a chain that focuses the efforts of its members on the triptych of the TBL theory, that is, on reducing (a) environmental and (b) social impacts, while improving (c) the financial results of the organisation, with the scope to run in the long-term manner efficiently the related supply chain operations.

A proposal that highlights the possibility of connecting the dimensions or else the latent variables of sustainability in service value chains and offerings is that of Hussain et al. (2016). The following text will present the dimensions and the usefulness of adopting the model in service value and supply chains (Figure 13.2). The authors present a variation in their proposal with respect to the original proposal of the three pillars/dimensions of sustainability of the TBL theoretical framework that was explained in a previous section. Specifically, the dimension of economic performance that measures the financial performance of a production unit's sustainable practices and activities was replaced by two sub-dimensions that identify the economic dimension in services, that is, the health, safety and risk management and the customer management dimensions.

The authors' proposal is methodologically the result of an extensive literature review that results in four dimensions-modules concerning the degree of development of sustainability in service supply chains. Each dimension related to sustainability includes indicators to identify the variables that measure them, and which concern the practical level of business implementation of sustainable practices in the supply chain of service businesses.

The four dimensions of supply chain sustainability are as follows:

1. Environmental management
2. Social responsibility
3. Health, safety and risk management
4. Customer management

Figure 13.3 provides the theoretical framework for determining the level of sustainability of service supply chains through the application of the four basic dimensions that assess sustainability.

13.4 The service supply chain sustainable operations framework: a proposal

The service supply chain sustainable operations framework according to the authors Aliakbari Nouri et al. (2020) is a useful guide for managers to identify long-term goals that support the expected sustainable practice implementation that will bring multidimensional benefits to society, the natural environment, the business and its supply chain cooperating members. The proposed analytical framework can be adopted in the cases of value chains of various types of services provided with the aim of improving the performance of value chains and modern economies supported by the service sector.

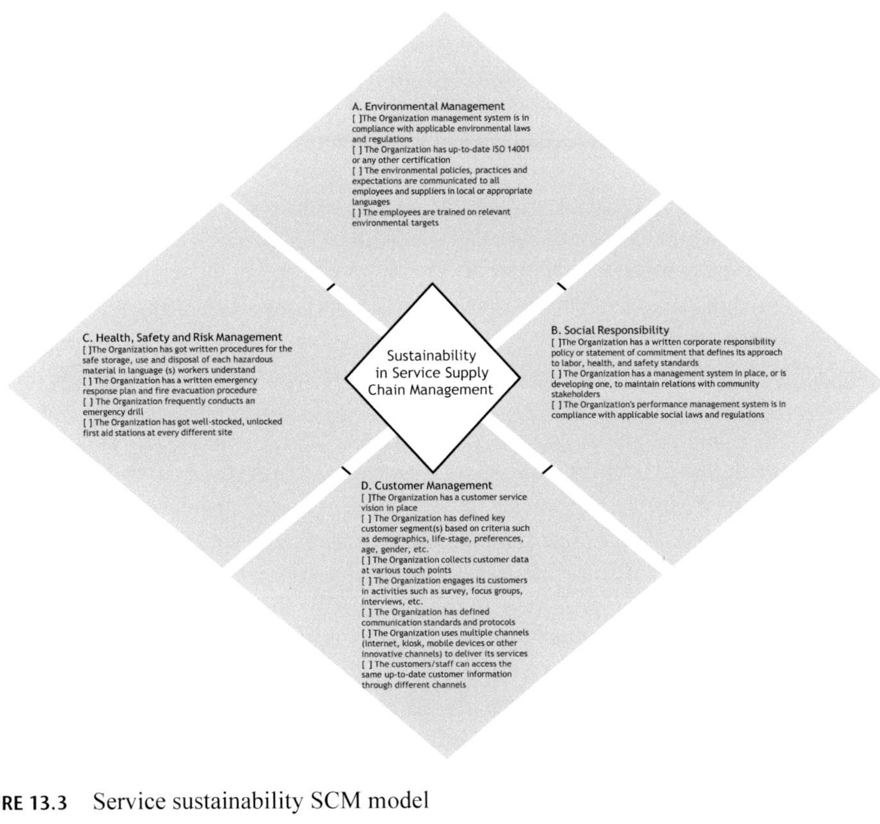

FIGURE 13.3 Service sustainability SCM model

Note: Adapted and re-designed from the source 'Hussain et al. (2016)'.

The approach of the relevant literature led the authors to identify seven important dimensions that affect the different levels of a basic service value chain (Figure13.3). The elements of the seven dimensions are as follows:

1. SSM: sustainable supplier management
2. SEM: sustainable employee management
3. SCuM: sustainable customer management
4. SSPM: sustainable service performance management
5. SSOM: sustainable service operations management
6. SERM: sustainable external relations management
7. SKITM: sustainable knowledge, information and technology management

The approach to each dimension is based on the measurement of relevant variables (SSSC practices) that are included in the seven dimensions above and have been statistically proven to be significant. In more detail, the variable elements that emerged as important for the interpretation of the seven dimensions (SSSC processes) in a service provision application in healthcare services are the proposal of the researchers Aliakbari Nouri et al. (2020). The framework to define the Sustainable Service Supply Chain; SSSC processes is presented in Table 13.2), by describing each of them and their practices.

The research of analysis and study of the management and behaviour of members in service supply chains can include four approaches: (a) the study of the chain's customers, (b) the study of suppliers, (c) the study of integration/provider entities and (d) the study of all the aforementioned processes by all members of the chain (e.g., a comprehensive approach to co-ordinate the chain and its members). The above framework model can contribute to the entire understanding of the operations, the behaviour, the management and administration problematic of the whole service chain and of its parts.

The above research concludes that supply chains focused on sustainability require special attention to the management aspect of developing relationships between the company (integrator), its suppliers and customers. Based on the above-mentioned study, supply chains focused on sustainability require special attention to the management aspect of developing relationships between the company (integrator), its suppliers and customers. Therefore, the necessary contacts and relationships with suppliers and the thorough effort to analyse and manage the relationships between service and material goods providers and the company (integrator) is a process that constitutes an important pursuit, which should be considered by managers and responsible SCM executives (Figure13.3: 'SSM' and 'SERM' processes sections).

The model also mentions the importance of developing relationships with external members (unions, non-profit organisations – international and domestic, associations and public services, etc.) that could positively influence the development of a sustainable chain and its practical processes. These processes are presented in the figure with the label 'SERM'. Services, as already analysed in previous sections, present the particularity of 'co-production' that characterises company-client relationships. Therefore, internal and external customer security issues that refer to the mandatory presence of the customer during the provision of a service should be treated with particular care and sensitivity towards the 'co-producer – client'. People operate in a social system based on rules and accepted principles therefore understanding and recognising the customer about how each member with the organisation should behave affects the success of the goal that refers to the sustainable development of the activities of the business organisation.

TABLE 13.2 SSSC model based on the results of Aliakbari et al. (2020), FDM analysis (i.e., accepted after the analysis items)

The SSM process
1.1[ ]. *Assessing the environmental and social performance of supplier*
1.2[ ]. *Supplier cooperation and contribution*
1.3[ ]. *Supplier technical development*
1.4[ ]. *Supplier human resource development*
2. The SEM process
2.1[ ]. *Training the environmental and social practices to employees*
2.2[ ]. *Employees health and safety systems*
2.3[ ]. *Employees environmental and social performance encouraging system*
3. The SCuM process
3.1[ ]. *Customer safety management systems*
3.2[ ]. *Providing the environmental education programmes to customers*
3.3[ ]. *Customer relationship management*
4. The SSPM process
4.1[ ]. *Implementing environmental and social performance audit and assessment*
4.2[ ]. *Implementing environmental management standards and certificates*
4.3[ ]. *Various pollutions control*
4.4[ ]. *Implementing quality audits to optimise the service delivery process*
5. The SSOM process
5.1[ ]. *Creating the ability to design and develop green product*
5.2[ ]. *Designing the environmental service process operations*
5.3[ ]. *R&D activities*
6. The SERM process
6.1[ ]. *Financial supporting for research institutes and projects*
6.2[ ]. *Government relations management*
7. The SKITM process
7.1[ ]. *Knowledge management systems*
7.2[ ]. *Establishing integrated information tools and systems*

Services, as already analysed in previous sections, present the particularity of 'co-production' that characterises company–client relationships. Therefore, internal and external customer security issues that refer to the mandatory presence of the customer during the provision of a service should be treated with particular care and sensitivity towards the 'co-producer-client'. The internal customer, that is, the company's staff, plays an important role in providing appropriate service to the external customer (the 'SEM' process). The unit of these actions, called in the diagram 'SCM'; 'SCuM' processes and that concern company, staff and customer relationships, require special attention in services such as tourism, hospitality, health, healthcare, passenger transport and museums. The performance of the processes is based on the ex-post understanding and adaptation of customer requirements, needs and desires, which does not help in the standardisation and automation of the processes. Therefore, the appropriate personnel who detect and shape through proposals to the customer the superior value that can be delivered to each

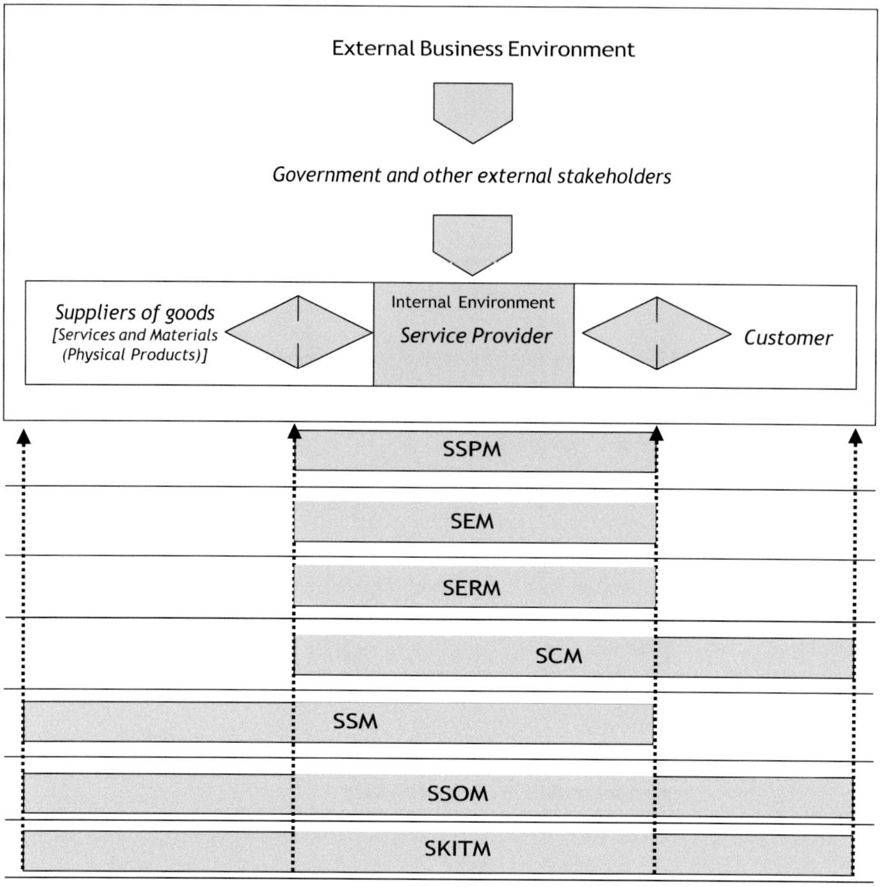

FIGURE 13.4 Service supply chain sustainable operations framework

Note: Adapted and re-designed from the source 'Aliakbari Nouri et al. (2020: 824)'.

individual customer, constitutes the principle for achieving the sustainability of the organisation and contributes to the emergence of competitive advantages for the integrator – enterprise (in the above figure, see the 'SSPM' process). Supporting the business activities that support the supply chain requires the support of flexible, often innovative and relevant services to facilitate the process of providing services. In the context of this effort, the use of appropriate technologies and information systems is considered important for achieving the expected sustainability among all the members of the chain. In the figure, the process is defined as 'SKITM' and together with the coordination of operational processes, they can and do contribute to the adoption of sustainable practices in our modern service provision business.

Synopsis

The chapter emphasises the growing importance of integrating sustainability into service supply chains, addressing environmental, social and economic concerns. It discusses several key frameworks, practices and constructs. Firstly, it introduces a visual framework called the house of SSCM, which represents the foundation (risk management, ethics and compliance), pillars (economic, social and environmental performance) and the roof (resilience, partnerships and performance goals). The chapter also covers the TBL construct, emphasising the balance of environmental, social and economic sustainability for long-term success. Additionally, the value driver model is discussed, demonstrating how sustainability initiatives can drive business growth, productivity and risk reduction, leading to improved financial performance. The SSSCM model focuses on service-based supply chains, highlighting four key dimensions: environmental management, social responsibility, health and safety, and customer management. Furthermore, the sustainable operations framework for service supply chains identifies seven key processes for sustainable operations, including supplier management, employee management, performance audits, external relations and technology integration. Examples from industries like tourism, hospitality and transportation illustrate how sustainable practices can enhance resilience and competitiveness.

Review and discussion questions

- What are the primary components of the house of SSCM framework, and how do they support sustainability goals?
- How does the TBL approach redefine performance evaluation in SCM?
- In what ways does the value driver model link sustainability initiatives to business growth and financial performance?
- Can you identify examples from your own experience or observation where companies applied green logistics, ethical sourcing or digital tools to enhance sustainability in their supply chains?
- How might service supply chains, such as in healthcare or hospitality, face different sustainability challenges compared to manufacturing supply chains?
- What potential benefits and risks come with adopting AI, blockchain and data analytics in sustainable supply chains?
- How can small or medium-sized enterprises (SMEs) leverage technology to integrate sustainability into their supply chains effectively?
- What are some of the most significant barriers companies face when transitioning to sustainable service supply chains?
- How can businesses ensure their sustainability efforts are genuinely impactful and not just ‘greenwashing’ for marketing purposes?
- How can businesses balance short-term profitability with long-term sustainability goals?
- In what ways might the concept of resilience and adaptability become increasingly important for SSCM in the future?

Case studies

Case study 1: A model of corporate social responsibility

Researchers have aimed to redefine CSR with a focus on its practical implementation, seeking to comprehend how organisations adopt CSR and what motivates their involvement in CSR projects.

Maon et al. (2010) propose a comprehensive model of CSR based on stakeholder perspectives. Their model integrates moral, cultural and strategic dimensions of CSR, reflecting how organisations develop and implement CSR initiatives. This approach suggests that an organisation's commitment to CSR is influenced by its stakeholder culture, which shapes its moral, cultural and strategic characteristics. Stakeholder cultures, as defined by Jones et al. (2007), are collective behavioural responses to managing complex stakeholder relationships. This concept helps connect moral, cultural and organisational aspects of CSR across different organisational stages.

The consolidative model outlines a seven-stage journey towards CSR adoption, organised into three phases: CSR cultural reluctance, where CSR is neglected or viewed as restrictive; CSR cultural grasp, where organisations start to understand CSR principles; and CSR cultural embedment, where organisations fully embrace morally driven CSR principles, impacting their outcomes. This model merges organisational values, culture, management practices and operations.

The three overarching phases of CSR culture encompass seven specific developmental stages, each characterised by unique strategic and organisational traits. The CSR reluctance phase includes only the dismissing stage, while the CSR cultural grasp phase comprises the self-protecting, compliance-seeking and capability-seeking stages. The CSR cultural embedment phase encompasses the caring, strategising and transforming stages. Table 13.3 provides an overview of these stages within the CSR cultural phases, highlighting their key features concerning the CSR development process.

CSR cultural reluctance phase

In the initial cultural phase, CSR is viewed as restrictive, leading to active resistance against initiatives that extend beyond financial gains. The organisation disregards its social and environmental impact, challenging stakeholder demands that could limit its operations, despite facing criticism from external sources. The organisation prioritises self-interest, particularly in the short term, emphasising avoidance of constraints and adhering solely to widely recognised shareholder agreements. Within this mindset of prioritising success at all costs, CSR lacks significance in the organisation's core values and beliefs, and its culture fails to endorse CSR efforts.

During the dismissing stage in the CSR cultural reluctance phase, there is a complete lack of motivation for CSR development and a notable absence of any CSR-related actions or initiatives. The organisation takes a closed-off stance towards its external environment, treating relationships with stakeholders purely as contractual obligations.

CSR cultural grasp phase

During the cultural grasp phase, organisations advance towards CSR by becoming more attuned to CSR issues and gradually recognising the importance of CSR concepts and rationale. CSR begins to be viewed as a safeguard for organisational values. There is a growing emphasis on minimising operational risks and preserving the value of assets by reducing environmental and social burdens, with a focus on tangible short-term results and adapting existing processes. While still primarily self-interested, organisations increasingly see stakeholders as instrumental and begin to embrace enlightened self-interest. Compliance objectives and maintaining a license to operate become priorities, leading to the development of efficient management processes aligned with CSR principles. CSR starts to serve as a risk management tool during this phase. Relationships with stakeholders shift from transactional to more interactive, as top management acknowledges the benefits of learning from informed stakeholders. The cultural grasp phase includes stages of self-protection, seeking compliance and building capabilities, all characterised by instrumental stakeholder cultures. This phase marks the integration of CSR into the organisational culture.

During the self-protecting stage, limited awareness of CSR issues leads to sporadic and unstructured CSR activities. The organisation responds to sporadic criticisms from some stakeholders by either denying accusations or making localised fixes. There is no genuine aspiration for CSR, so it is perceived as a constraint on normal business operations or as optional philanthropic endeavours. Management involvement in CSR is minimal, and CSR holds little significance in the organisational culture.

During the compliance-seeking stage, top management becomes more aware of CSR issues and potential risks to the organisation. The focus shifts towards complying with increasingly stringent regulations and meeting minimum industry standards, particularly regarding employment and production practices. The organisation develops policies such as early environmental and safety guidelines and shares them with relevant stakeholders to mitigate risks of penalties. Operating defensively, the organisation prioritises correctness but lacks interactive engagement with the external environment. Concerns about corporate reputation prompt greater integration of CSR into organisational structures and processes. While initially viewed as external requirements, CSR gradually gains internal recognition as a concept worthy of attention.

In the capability-seeking stage, the organisation gains proficiency in managing CSR basics through experience and familiarity with CSR issues. Increased awareness of CSR issues and the risks of neglecting them prompts efforts to showcase societal commitment by engaging new stakeholders. While the business rationale for CSR may still be somewhat unclear, initiatives deemed profitable or beneficial for corporate reputation, especially among key stakeholders, are prioritised. Stakeholder relationships become more interactive, leading to the growing influence of CSR as a core aspect of the organisation's values and beliefs.

CSR cultural embedment phase

During the CSR cultural embedment phase, organisations solidify their CSR progress by expanding their CSR knowledge, strengthening key stakeholder relationships, and mobilising internal resources to proactively address CSR demands. CSR is recognised as a potential creator of value, leading to significant cultural shifts towards integrating stakeholder claims and CSR principles. Decision-making becomes increasingly focused on the well-being of others, demonstrating intrinsic morality balanced with pragmatism, especially concerning derivative stakeholders. Corporate cultures tend towards moral stakeholder orientations, emphasising principles applicable to all stakeholders, not just shareholders. CSR policies transition from short-term, result-oriented approaches to value creation-driven strategies. Stakeholders gain greater influence over decision-making processes, fostering collaborative relationships and durable alliances. Organisations adopt culturally integrated CSR approaches to maximise opportunities and create value through commitments, innovative processes, and collaborations with external stakeholders.

However, viewing CSR as an 'opportunity rather than damage control or a PR campaign' (Porter and Kramer 2006: 91) necessitates a significant shift in mindset. In the CSR cultural embedment phase, recognising the vital connection between CSR and innovation becomes central to the CSR development process. Innovation here refers to creative processes leading to new products and services. Consequently, CSR is increasingly seen as a driver of long-term sustainability by enhancing resource efficiency and product differentiation. Moreover, by emphasising joint innovation, organisations can explore 'new relationships between nature, society, and technology' (Dunphy et al. 2003: 54), fostering creative initiatives aligned with their core business activities.

During the caring stage, top management realises that CSR initiatives extend beyond mere compliance and short-term profits. They recognise CSR issues as long-term challenges requiring more than just compliance or isolated profitable ventures. Instead, they see the potential for long-term improvements and business-wide benefits from cohesive CSR programs. CSR codes of conduct reflect a broader societal focus and long-term perspective. Coordination of CSR policies becomes cross-functional, with core business managers tasked with balancing economic, social and environmental concerns. The organisation begins communicating its CSR reporting efforts publicly and ensures transparency regarding the results of CSR programs. Additionally, it adopts a stakeholder dialogue approach to CSR, gradually integrating CSR into its activities and culture as a distinct attribute.

In the strategising stage, CSR takes on intrinsic importance, recognised as the natural progression of prior advancements. Acknowledging CSR practices as contributors to long-term viability, organisations integrate CSR into their corporate strategy. They leverage implemented CSR systems and initiatives to shape their positioning and earn a reputation as leaders in sustainable practices. Becoming an employer of choice and spearheading innovative initiatives to garner stakeholder support become key objectives. Organisations surpass community expectations, seeking simultaneous social, environmental and economic benefits, shifting towards a value-driven approach to CSR. Codes of conduct evolve into actionable plans, leading the organisation to become proactive in CSR, maintaining transparent dialogues with stakeholders and forming constructive partnerships around key business and societal issues. In this sustainability-focused perspective, CSR becomes the overarching objective guiding all corporate activities.

In the transforming stage, the organisation transcends its traditional business model by fully integrating CSR principles into all aspects of its operations. This entails a profound cultural and strategic shift towards comprehensive CSR, driven by new ethical values prioritising human well-being and ecological sustainability. These organisations are motivated by the belief that sustainability is paramount due to the interdependence of all beings and phenomena. They adopt transparent practices and aim to share their CSR expertise openly. They actively promote CSR both within and beyond their industries, engaging in cross-industry collaborations and forming enduring alliances with community groups, NGOs and public authorities to address societal concerns. Positioned at the forefront of CSR, these organisations adopt a transformative perspective, deeply embedding CSR into their organisational culture.

Managerial implications

From a managerial viewpoint, the consolidative model delves into the multifaceted, cultural aspect of CSR development, going beyond mere policies and practices. It suggests that organisations can leverage their existing strengths and capabilities to advance in CSR, offering constructive starting points for further development. However, managing organisational culture purposefully can be intricate and often yields only surface-level changes. The extent of managerial control over the values, beliefs, and assumptions of organisational members is subject to debate, as existing cultural norms tend to resist deliberate alteration. Nonetheless, unfavourable cultural patterns can be disrupted, and favourable ones nurtured. Thus, embedding CSR into strategy and culture doesn't necessitate direct management and control over organisational culture. Instead, the key challenge lies in creating an environment conducive to CSR awareness and seizing CSR-related opportunities initially, then maximising positive outcomes over time.

This case originates from Maon, F., Lindgreen, A., and Swaen, V. (2010). Organisational stages and cultural phases: A critical review and a consolidative model of corporate social responsibility development. *International Journal of Management Reviews* 12(1): 20–38. Here, the reader can also find additional relevant references to the case and its topic.

Case study 2: The organisation as a system

Identifying and addressing CSR issues is complex due to conflicting stakeholder perspectives. Organisations grapple with prioritising relevant societal concerns. Developing a robust CSR strategy requires managerial insight and interpretation, tailored to each organisation's unique context. This endeavour demands significant resources and adept stakeholder engagement skills.

Organisations operate as interpretation systems, with senior management collectively shaping CSR strategies based on their understanding of events and issues. Influenced by their individual traits, managers play crucial roles in executing CSR initiatives. Maon et al. (2008) offer valuable insights into the organisational processes of crafting CSR strategies, emphasising the importance of managerial perspectives.

TABLE 13.3 A seven-stage CSR development model

CSR Cultural Phase	*Stage of CSR development*	*CSR view & prominence in organisational culture*	*Dimensions of CSR development*										
			Knowledge and attitudinal dimensions			*Strategic dimensions*				*Tactical and operational dimensions*			
			Organisational sensitivity to CSR issues	*Driver of CSR initiatives development*	*Support of top management*	*Social responsiveness*	*Rationale behind CSR initiatives*	*Performance objectives*	*Transparency and reporting*	*Stakeholder relationships*	*Resource commitments*	*Structuring of CSR initiatives*	*Coordination of CSR issues*
CSR CULTURAL RELUCTANCE	1. *Dismissing*	'Winning at any cost perspective'/ none	Active opposition to CSR broader than financial benefits	None	None	Rejection	None	None	Black box	Purely contractual	None	None	None
CSR CULTURAL GRASP	2. *Self-protecting*	'Reputation & philanthropy perspective'/ CSR as marginal	Window-dressing and/or lack of awareness or ignorance about CSR issues	Lack of CSR-orientation perceived as potentially harming business	Piecemeal involvement	Strong defence	Limitation of potentially harming and uncontrolled criticisms	Resolution of problems as they occur	Justifying posture	Punctual	Budget for problems as they occur	Activities	Public relations concern

(Continued)

TABLE 13.3 (Continued)

CSR Cultural Phase	*Stage of CSR development*	*CSR view & prominence in organisational culture*	*Dimensions of CSR development*										
			Knowledge and attitudinal dimensions			*Strategic dimensions*				*Tactical and operational dimensions*			
			Organisational sensitivity to CSR issues	*Driver of CSR initiatives development*	*Support of top management*	*Social responsiveness*	*Rationale behind CSR initiatives*	*Performance objectives*	*Transparency and reporting*	*Stakeholder relationships*	*Resource commitments*	*Structuring of CSR initiatives*	*Coordination of CSR issues*
	3. COMPLIANCE-SEEKING	'Requirements perspective/ CSR as worthy of interest	Growing awareness of CSR-related troubles to be avoided	CSR perceived as a duty and an obligation – Focus on restricted requisites	Involvement in theory/ Professed	Light defence/ reaction	Compliance objectives	Minimisation of harmful externalities/ respect of evolving norms and regulatory requirements	Internal reporting/legal disclosure posture	Unilateral	Limited-minimal funding	Policies	Functional
	4. CAPABILITY-SEEKING	'Stakeholder management perspective'/ CSR as influential	Growing awareness of CSR-related advantages to be gained	CSR perceived as a duty and an obligation – focus on confluent expectations	Fair involvement/ Supportive	Accommodation/ response	License to operate	Anticipating new requirements & expectations/ identification of profitable niches for CSR initiatives	Internal reporting/ Selective disclosure posture	Interactive	Generally sufficient but inconstant funding	Plans of action	Multifunctional

(*Continued*)

TABLE 13.3 (Continued)

CSR Cultural Phase	*Stage of CSR development*	*CSR view & prominence in organisational culture*	*Dimensions of CSR development*										
			Knowledge and attitudinal dimensions			*Strategic dimensions*			*Tactical and operational dimensions*				
			Organisational sensitivity to CSR issues	*Driver of CSR initiatives development*	*Support of top management*	*Social responsiveness*	*Rationale behind CSR initiatives*	*Performance objectives*	*Transparency and reporting*	*Stakeholder relationships*	*Resource commitments*	*Structuring of CSR initiatives*	*Coordination of CSR issues*
CSR CULTURAL EMBEDMENT	5. CARING	'Stakeholder dialogue perspective'/ CSR as embodied	Knowledgeable CSR awareness	CSR perceived as important as such	Commitment	Adaptation	Competitive advantage	Active management of CSR-related issues/ definition of business-wide opportunities	Public reporting posture	Reciprocal influence	Dependable funding	Programs	Cross-functional
	6. STRATEGISING	'Sustainability perspective'/ CSR as prevailing	Leadership objectives on CSR-related issues	CSR perceived as inexorable direction to take	Sound commitment	Strategic proactivity	Value proposition	Leading the pack/ development of sustainable business leverages through CSR initiatives	Certified reporting posture	Collaborative	Substantial funding	Systems	Organisational realignment

(Continued)

TABLE 13.3 (Continued)

CSR Cultural Phase	*Stage of CSR development*	*CSR view & prominence in organisational culture*	*Dimensions of CSR development*										
			Knowledge and attitudinal dimensions		*Strategic dimensions*					*Tactical and operational dimensions*			
			Organisational sensitivity to CSR issues	*Driver of CSR initiatives development*	*Support of top management*	*Social responsiveness*	*Rationale behind CSR initiatives*	*Performance objectives*	*Transparency and reporting*	*Stakeholder relationships*	*Resource commitments*	*Structuring of CSR initiatives*	*Coordination of CSR issues*
	7. TRANSFORMING	'Change the game perspective'/ CSR as ingrained	CSR as an internalised management ideology	CSR as the only alternative considering universal mutual interdependency	Devotion	Proactivity	Enlarged finality – Societal change	Diffusion of expertise/ maximisation of positive externalities	Fully transparent posture	Joint innovation	Open-ended funding and resource commitment	Core integration – CSR as business as usual	Institutionalisation

Systems thinking is a perspective that views the world as interconnected and dynamic, emphasising relationships over isolated entities. It involves identifying the interdependencies within a system and integrating them to understand the system as a unified whole.

Viewed through a systems lens, organisations are dynamic entities operating within uncertain environments. They must adapt to external factors while navigating opportunities and constraints presented by society. Recognising their reliance on stakeholders and interpretations, organisations cannot entirely dictate their actions. Embracing this perspective allows organisations to understand and address CSR challenges across different scales, from local to global.

Critical systems thinking addresses the managerial challenge of identifying stakeholder coalitions and issues. Achterkamp and Vos (2007) introduce a four-phase method (initiation, development/performance, implementation and maintenance) to categorise stakeholders based on their involvement level and timing. Maon et al. (2008) applied this method to CSR stakeholders, treating each CSR issue as a project for effective management. The resulting CSR strategy agenda prioritises projects aligned with corporate goals and potential impact.

Maon et al. (2008) present a comprehensive framework for understanding CSR strategy agendas within organisations (see Figure 13.5). The model features two interconnected loops, connected by two central elements: (a) managerial views on CSR issues and their importance and (b) the integration of these views into an organisational interpretation, shaped by existing organisational traits.

The stakeholder dialogue loop, the initial loop in the model, depicts the ongoing interaction between the organisation and its stakeholders. This structured exchange allows stakeholders to voice their opinions on CSR matters regularly, thereby shaping managers' understanding

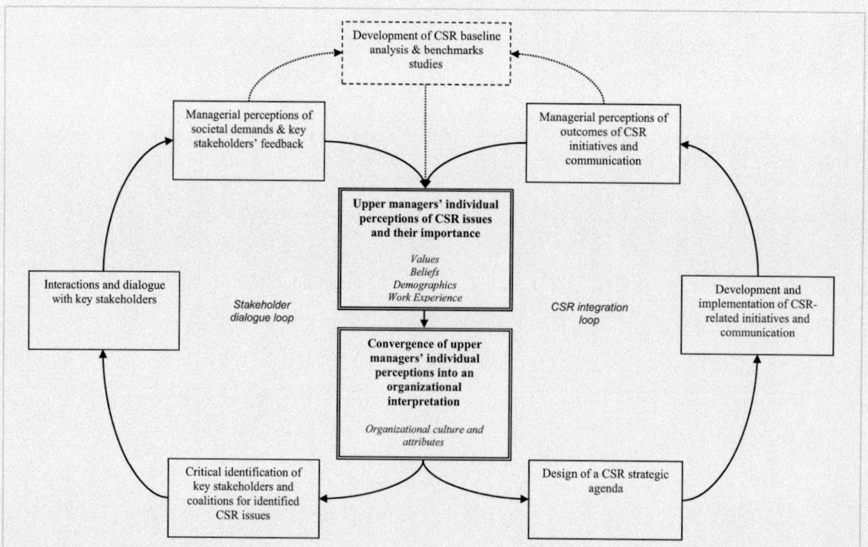

FIGURE 13.5 Dual-loop model for understanding the development of a CSR strategic agenda

of the external landscape and enhancing awareness of CSR issues. Feedback received during these dialogues gradually shapes managers' personal perspectives on CSR matters and their significance for the organisation. The effectiveness of this dialogue and feedback hinges on the resources initially allocated to the process.

The CSR integration loop, the model's second loop, focuses on formulating and executing essential CSR endeavours. Initially, upper managers provide their insights on CSR issues, shaping the organisational interpretation, which forms the foundation for the CSR strategy agenda. Strategically, upper managers evaluate internal CSR capabilities, devise action plans and assess alternative strategies. The implementation of CSR initiatives and progress toward strategic goals subsequently impact upper managers' views on CSR issues and their significance.

Stakeholder feedback, combined with the outcomes of CSR initiatives, shapes managers' perceptions of CSR issues and their importance, influenced by their personal values and beliefs. This iterative process enhances understanding of existing issues and identifies new CSR concerns, necessitating ongoing adjustments to the organisation's CSR strategy agenda. Efficient procedures are crucial for initiating CSR strategy agenda development, particularly in organisations lacking structured CSR policies or systematic scanning processes. In such cases, managers' awareness, knowledge and perceptions are likely limited or tacit, underscoring the importance of establishing formal processes.

Maon et al. (2008) distinguish between two types of CSR issues: generic issues, pertinent to all organisations striving for integrated CSR and industry-specific issues. Generic CSR concerns encompass dialogue with stakeholders, organisational culture, environmental stewardship and employment practices. Industry-specific issues in the pharmaceutical sector include access to medicine, quality management, transparency in clinical trials, ethical product design, supply chain responsibility and marketing ethics.

Figure 13.6 demonstrates how the two categories of CSR issues align with the core functions of business organisations: production, sales and marketing, and research and development.

Maon et al. (2008) present a comprehensive model that illuminates the intricacies of developing a CSR strategy agenda. Their framework integrates systems thinking, CSR theories and organisational interpretation, providing insight into how CSR issues arise, are prioritised and align with organisational objectives. The continuous nature of this process underscores the importance of structured stakeholder dialogue and effective monitoring systems for implementing CSR strategies successfully. The model underscores the necessity of considering stakeholders' needs throughout the development process and adapting strategies accordingly. Additionally, organisations must regularly scan their environments to identify emerging CSR issues and societal/business requirements.

Maon et al. (2008) highlight the significant influence of upper managers and their perceptions in shaping a structured CSR agenda. This insight provides a fresh perspective on how modern organisations develop CSR strategies.

Ultimately, the collective managerial expertise within an organisation serves as a solid foundation for kick-starting a CSR strategy agenda. It is crucial that diverse managerial

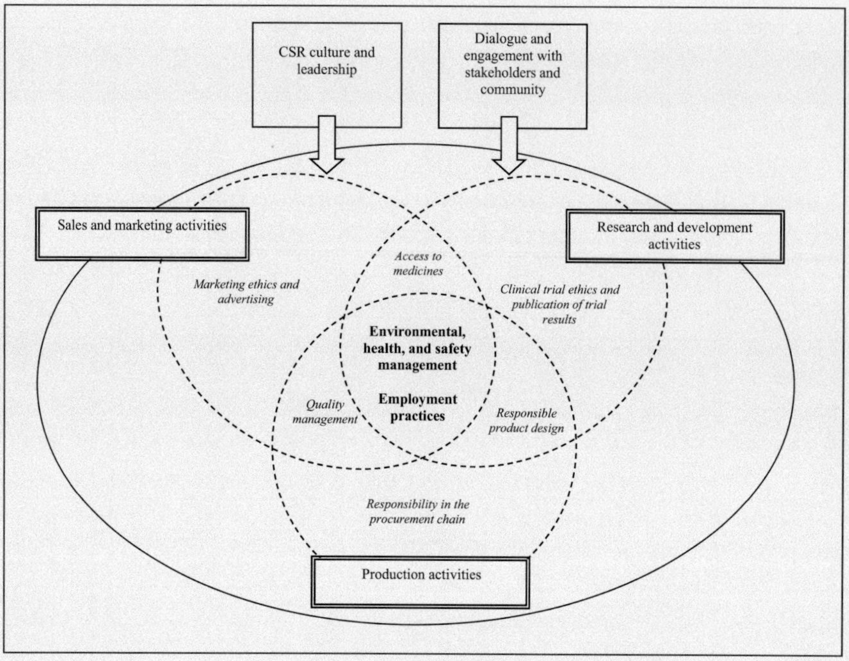

FIGURE 13.6 Key CSR issues in the three spheres of business activity

perspectives on CSR, spanning across departments, converge to provide a comprehensive understanding of the organisation's CSR landscape. CSR concerns are categorised into generic and industry-specific issues, each requiring distinct attention.

Managerial implications

It is possible to suggest simple and practical recommendations in terms of internal processes that organisations should develop:

- A designated CSR facilitator should lead CSR status assessments and oversee the ensuing steps of the process.
- To thoroughly identify CSR issues, it is essential to merge various managerial viewpoints, as managers often have a biased understanding based on their roles. This necessitates pinpointing upper managers from different functional departments who possess deep insight into the organisation's culture and features. Ensuring representation from all key departments facilitates a comprehensive exploration of potential CSR challenges.
- As CSR issues differ across industries, it is vital for a company to consistently compare its CSR approach within its industry while also seeking best practices beyond it. Evaluating the organisation's performance in CSR, both generic and industry-specific, can be done through a straightforward rating system, categorising performance as below average, average or above average.

- Organise cross-functional meetings on CSR issues to foster alignment among managers' perceptions of priority and develop a unified CSR strategy agenda.
- Appointing a CSR champion is crucial, and establishing a CSR committee to create a structured CSR strategy agenda is equally important. This agenda should be informed by the insights and strategic directions identified through the earlier developed simple CSR mapping process.

This case originates from Maon, F., Lindgreen, A., and Swaen, V. (2008). Thinking of the organisation as a system: The role of managerial perceptions in developing a CSR strategic agenda. *Systems Research and Behavioral Science* 25(3): 413–426. Here, the reader can also find additional relevant references to the case and its topic.

Case study 3: Designing and implementing corporate social responsibility

The methods for designing and implementing CSR are not thoroughly investigated. Through a multiple case study, Maon et al. (2009) created a comprehensive framework to aid managers and pinpoint key factors for successful CSR implementation.

The figure's (Figure 13.7) framework employs Lewin's force field model of change, which views change as an imbalance between driving and restraining forces. By shifting this equilibrium in favour of change, managers can enact it. Lewin's model includes three stages: unfreezing, moving and refreezing.

In the initial stage, managers must unfreeze established practices linked to the current state. This involves unlearning ingrained cultural assumptions about operational norms. These deeply held beliefs, often subconscious, need to be brought to the surface through

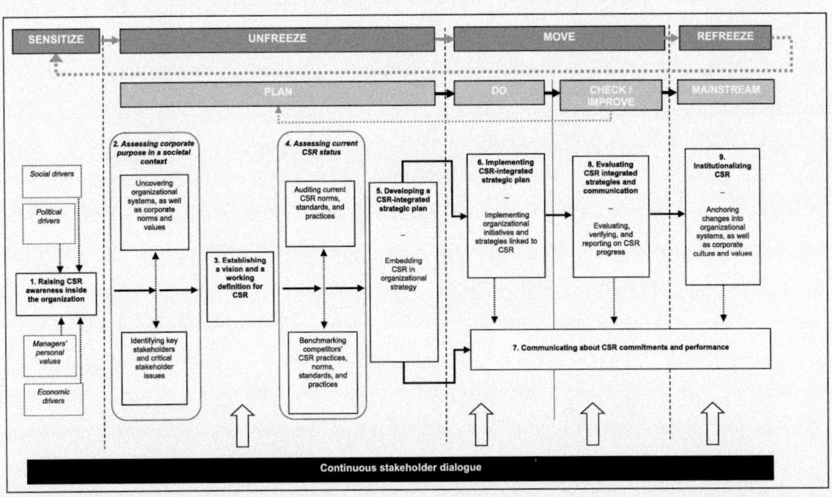

FIGURE 13.7 Proposed integrative framework for designing and implementing CSR

interventions to initiate change. Potential obstacles to developing a CSR mindset include concerns about destabilisation, resistance to change, scepticism regarding the organisation's suitability for CSR, or fears of diverting from core values.

During the second stage (moving stage), the organisation transitions towards new assumptions. Recognising the necessity of embracing a CSR mindset marks the initial phase of change. There are various practices relevant to developing and executing a CSR orientation.

In the third stage, managers must solidify the new cultural norms to establish a lasting state. Depending on the extent of change required, this may entail broader structural adjustments to uphold the new practices. Maintaining a learning orientation is crucial during this phase to embed CSR-focused cultural values effectively. In a learning organisation, employees grasp generative learning, which entails continuous reflection on past strategies, rather than mere adaptation through trial and error.

The framework introduces a fourth stage: sensitising, which occurs before unfreezing. During this stage, top management acknowledges the significance of sustainability concerns and addresses resistance to change.

Together, the four stages encompass nine steps: raising CSR awareness internally, evaluating corporate purpose within societal contexts, defining and envisioning CSR, assessing current CSR status, devising an integrated CSR strategy, executing the strategy, sustaining communication both internally and externally, assessing and refining CSR strategies and communication and formalising CSR policies.

Managerial implications

The framework offers valuable insights into CSR implementation. Firstly, the four-stage change model provides a starting point for managers aiming to integrate CSR effectively. Additionally, organisations undergoing evolutionary change, especially those with existing CSR values but facing implementation challenges, can utilise this framework. For instance, they can address refreezing issues promptly by establishing feedback mechanisms and identifying short-term successes.

Additionally, the framework emphasises the importance of aligning various functions to execute a CSR programme effectively. Managers should invest in internal marketing initiatives to educate organisational members about CSR programme achievements and relevant activities. These initiatives should be supported by revamped human resource control systems to secure commitment to the CSR programme.

Finally, the framework underscores the need for more comprehensive approaches in designing and implementing CSR policies. It represents an outcome of substantial efforts to amalgamate key challenges and facilitators in this process. Moving forward, organisations must elevate CSR practices to a practical and constructive operational level through reflection and action.

This case originates from Maon, F., Lindgreen, A., and Swaen, V. (2009). Designing and implementing corporate social responsibility: an integrative framework grounded in theory and practice. *Journal of Business Ethics* 87(Suppl. 1): 71–89. Here, the reader can also find additional relevant references to the case and its topic.

Case study 4: Strategically leveraging corporate social responsibility

CSR is reshaping branding practices, although the exact mechanisms remain uncertain. Despite some approaches aiming to provide guidance on managing CSR issues, practitioners often struggle to determine how to approach CSR in a manner that enhances both the corporate brand and societal well-being, leading to confusion.

While CSR-based brand management is currently popular, it can be risky. Stakeholders hold diverse expectations regarding CSR, and if claims of CSR as a core value are perceived as insincere, companies face public scrutiny. Attempting to develop a CSR brand requires adapting to the dynamic interactions among stakeholders, which challenges traditional brand management approaches.

A traditional brand strategy prioritises primary stakeholders like customers, shareholders, and business partners, essential for the company's operations. However, building a meaningful CSR brand requires considering secondary stakeholders – individuals and groups affected by the company's activities but not directly involved in transactions. These stakeholders, including social and political actors, tacitly support the company's mission and offer intangible assets like reputation and knowledge. Therefore, a CSR positioning in brand strategy should align with an overarching brand value that resonates with all relevant stakeholders. While maintaining good relations with primary stakeholders is crucial for developing intangible assets, successful CSR branding also hinges on fulfilling promises to each stakeholder and building trust across all stakeholder groups, including secondary ones.

As functional aspects of product differentiation, doubts arise regarding whether CSR can provide sustainable product-level differentiation. Some product categories have turned to CSR-based emotional benefits, yet even this approach faces challenges as consumers become more wary of emotional manipulation. Consequently, companies continue to seek new avenues for differentiation, with many developing corporate CSR brands without fully assessing the implications of this strategy.

When companies publicly espouse CSR values, they face heightened scrutiny and often draw the attention of activists and interest groups intent on challenging their marketing efforts. Marketing, especially branding, can breed distrust, especially when companies make empty promises, exaggerated claims, or provide inaccurate information. Despite efforts towards transparency through increased communication, suspicious consumers remain vigilant. Consequently, discrepancies may emerge between the company's actual CSR attributes and values (actual identity), the communication of its CSR initiatives (communicated identity) and stakeholders' perceptions of the company's CSR commitments (conceived identity). Such discrepancies risk accusations of hypocrisy and public deception.

Vallaster et al. (2012) present a framework for companies to strategically manage CSR and their brands, categorising them as performers, leaders, vocal converts or quietly conscientious based on their level of involvement, integration and the key initiator of CSR focus. The article offers practical recommendations for practitioners aiming to balance stakeholder tensions and achieve consistency in corporate branding and CSR endeavours.

Vallaster et al. (2012) highlight four main approaches companies employ to connect CSR with their brand-building endeavours. They vary in how they respond to different triggers for CSR engagement, their objectives, the integration of CSR into brand identity, and how they measure outcomes:

- Initiators and drivers: Two main types of triggers prompt the use of CSR as a brand strategy: market-driven factors influenced by stakeholders' expectations and market demands, and value-driven factors led by management's aspirations within the company.
- Objectives: Companies utilise CSR and CSR branding to either create or safeguard value. Value creation encompasses economic and social benefits, directly or indirectly influencing brand value development. Conversely, value protection concentrates primarily on safeguarding economic value and securing the company's short-term license to operate.
- Level of integration: Vallaster et al. (2012) distinguish between two levels of CSR integration: ingrained and add-on. For some companies, CSR is deeply embedded within their corporate culture and strategy, including brand values. In contrast, for others, CSR remains peripheral, merely an add-on to be highlighted when necessary.
- Measurement: Measuring the performance of the CSR brand presents an ongoing challenge for companies, with some considering it unattainable. However, most companies with well-defined CSR brand strategies employ multiple tools to assess, maintain and enhance their progress.

Vallaster et al. (2012) present their CSR brand framework in Figure 13.8, which excludes the CSR measurement dimension as it is considered a result of the company's strategic stance rather than a primary determinant. The level of corporate engagement in CSR, whether reactive or proactive, serves as a transversal dimension in their strategic CSR brand framework.

CSR entrepreneurs

CSR entrepreneurs are companies founded with CSR values at their core, shaping their identity and actions. Reflecting the passion and vision of their founders, they integrate CSR beyond structures, embedding it in their culture. Many blend commercial activities with non-profit goals, prioritising authenticity over profit to uphold their non-commercial brand's sincerity. Non-commercial motives often reflect the moral imperative of the corporate brand. However, every decision must balance maximising benefit to the company with maximising benefit to society. CSR entrepreneurs are typically smaller and newer entities. Unlike larger, established companies, they operate without the burdens of size and global presence, allowing them to start with a fresh perspective. However, in recent decades, even traditional companies have adopted the CSR entrepreneurship approach. The rising trend of sustainability has also led to the emergence of impostors making unverified claims about being 'organic', 'natural' or 'sweatshop free'. Genuine CSR entrepreneurs therefore require stringent ethical standards.

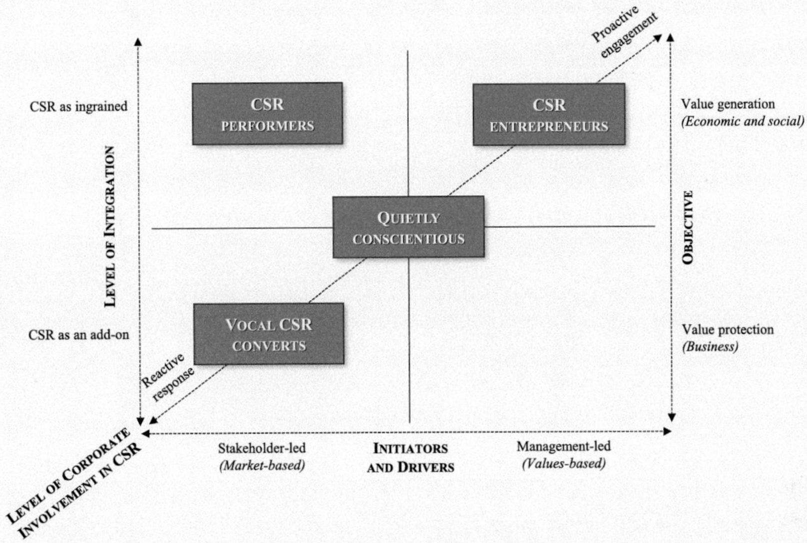

FIGURE 13.8 Strategic CSR brand framework

CSR performers

CSR performers are typically well-established brands known for their strong environmental and social responsibility values, along with the capacity and ambition to revolutionise their industries. While CSR principles are deeply embedded in their organisational culture, their engagement in CSR activities is often driven by external stakeholder expectations rather than internal values. Despite this, publicly owned companies prioritise a short-term perspective, aiming to align their CSR agenda with branding activities to generate profits for shareholders. Managers of such companies encounter pressures related to accountability, resource constraints, and public oversight, leading to direct assessments of the value of CSR investments compared to managers of privately owned firms.

Some companies aim to cultivate a sense of internal ownership of CSR-related brand programs by aligning incentive, training and hiring policies with this objective, ensuring consistent communication about the brand/CSR connection, and implementing systems to integrate CSR into the company culture to some extent. However, many of these efforts are not fully committed. Additionally, CSR performers are not limited to publicly owned companies; privately owned firms with prominent corporate brands in industries under scrutiny by influential secondary stakeholders also fall into this category.

Vocal CSR converts

Some major global brands have recently begun to adopt CSR due to increasing pressure. However, unlike CSR performers, they have not yet convinced the public of the sincerity or long-term nature of their efforts. Whether they are grappling with past issues or facing consumer scepticism that CSR is merely a superficial addition to their brand, these large companies often face backlash when they shift their focus to CSR communications. For companies newly vocal about CSR, a reactive and pragmatic approach focused mainly on business benefits and peripheral CSR initiatives may not be enough to build brand value or overcome a history of irresponsibility, especially amidst rising stakeholder expectations and scrutiny.

Some outspoken CSR converts opt to associate causes with strategic products of their business. However, this narrowed focus on specific CSR-related issues can still lead to stakeholder scepticism and obscure potential advantages for the company. This underscores the necessity for more than just effective public relations to ensure that CSR initiatives and corporate CSR brands remain pertinent for long-term business value.

Quietly conscientious

Many companies promote their CSR activities in hopes of safeguarding or enhancing their corporate reputations and brand value. Conversely, some choose not to publicise their CSR efforts, perhaps due to concerns about potential criticism or because they operate in less visible markets or industries. In the latter scenario, they likely face fewer demands from stakeholders, particularly if they operate in business-to-business settings. These companies quietly undertake initiatives such as reducing carbon emissions, exploring alternative supply sources, influencing supplier practices, optimising production processes or enforcing ethical and social standards. Although sustainability is not explicitly incorporated into their brand identities, all these companies work diligently to minimise negative social and environmental impacts or contribute positively to society.

Quietly conscientious companies recognise that CSR initiatives may not universally enhance brand value; sometimes, they solely benefit the local community or employees. However, these benefits can still elevate corporate reputation and image, attracting talented individuals, investors, and fostering positive relationships with business partners. Similarly, environmentally beneficial CSR endeavours can enhance product-level brand value by reducing costs or enhancing quality. For such companies, targeted communication with specific stakeholder groups is crucial to address legitimate claims and improve their CSR agenda effectively.

Managerial implications

The CSR brand framework offers four suggestions that practitioners should keep in mind:

- Align actions with words: Integrating CSR into the brand fosters trust and credibility. A strategic CSR approach involves aligning competitive strategy, CSR initiatives, and business processes throughout the supply chain. This fosters engagement with employees, customers, and other stakeholders.
- Clarify your strategic goals: Companies aiming for sustainable competitive advantage must pinpoint their CSR priorities and determine whether they aim to set the pace or follow

in those areas. If leading, CSR becomes their main strategic focus; otherwise, various CSR activities can add hidden value that enhances the corporate brand identity without active promotion.

- Allocate resources with foresight: Many companies emphasise eco-friendly practices, social responsibility, honesty and transparency, making it difficult to distinguish themselves. However, practitioners should recognise the differentiation possibilities inherent in this approach. Companies employ diverse strategies to achieve similar goals, leading to variations in execution and nuanced yet significant differences in brand positioning.
- When a company fails to meet a CSR commitment, it has three options: diminish claims, change practices or realign the corporate brand.

This case originates from Vallaster, C., Lindgreen, A., and Maon, F. (2012). Strategically leveraging corporate social responsibility to the benefit of company and society: A corporate branding perspective. *California Management Review* 54(3): 34–60. Here, the reader can also find additional relevant references to the case and its topic.

Case study 5: Tensions in coopetition for sustainable development

Sustainable innovation involves integrating environmental, social, and financial considerations across company processes, spanning idea generation to commercialisation, including products, services, technologies and organisational models (Charter and Clark 2007). It drives institutional change by modifying existing dynamics or establishing new ones, aiming for sustainable development by mitigating production impacts on the environment, bolstering nature's resilience, and promoting responsible resource use (Delmas and Pekovic 2018). Additionally, it seeks to bring about positive social changes.

Sustainable innovation, like any form of innovation, involves intricate processes with uncertain motivations, goals and outcomes, posing risks of negative impacts. It can lead to tensions and clashes of ideas, especially in fast-paced global settings involving diverse business and societal actors. Collaboration among various stakeholders is essential, as sustainability challenges require cooperation within firms and among multiple actors in the value network or broader society (Schaltegger et al. 2013, 2016), although these collaborating actors may also compete.

Coopetition, the simultaneous cooperation and competition within a value network, offers benefits but can also create tensions that strain relationships. In sustainability contexts, where companies already balance economic, environmental and societal goals, coopetition may exacerbate challenges. Some researchers doubt its benefits for sustainability, suggesting that competitive aspects could hinder sustainability objectives, leading to conflicts, opportunistic behaviours and power imbalances – the darker side of business relations in sustainable innovation. Despite some insights, empirical research on coopetition's impact on sustainability remains limited and uncertain, especially regarding its economic, social and environmental outcomes for both firms and society.

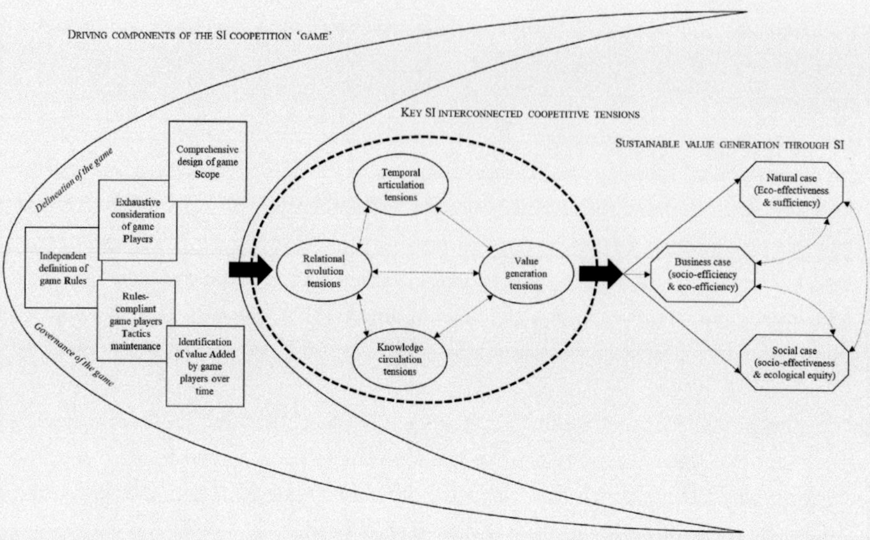

FIGURE 13.9 Taming down coopetitive tensions to generate sustainable value through SI

Munten et al. (2021) conducted a study exploring how sustainability-focused innovation in the automotive sector can lead to both competitive and collaborative tensions within a value network, potentially resulting in negative consequences for participating firms and society. They present a comprehensive framework in Figure 13.9 outlining the essential conditions for achieving positive economic, social and environmental outcomes at both the firm and societal levels.

The authors examine coopetition strategies in sustainable innovation and delve into the tensions arising from the interplay between competition and cooperation in sustainability efforts at both firm and societal levels. They identify four dimensions of tension in coopetition for sustainable innovation: value generation, temporal coordination, relational dynamics and knowledge sharing. Their empirical findings contribute to understanding these tensions, shedding light on the potential negative implications of coopetition in sustainable innovation, highlighting societal risks.

The authors also examine power imbalances in broader business-to-business networks, beyond individual relationships. They find that sustainable innovation can shift power dynamics and dependencies within these networks, influencing how actors balance competition and cooperation. Power imbalances, stemming from factors like economic resources or market position, shape the processes and outcomes of sustainable innovation. Understanding these dynamics helps clarify how various tensions, goals and interests affect sustainable innovation outcomes, including potential negative consequences.

Lastly, practitioners can use these insights to anticipate outcomes of their cooperative relationships in sustainable innovation and work towards resolving tensions to achieve mutually beneficial outcomes for both firms and society.

Value generation

Value generation tensions arise from actors' shared goals of creating sustainable value for stakeholders and society, alongside their individual economic objectives. Sustainable value, encompassing social and ecological aspects, presents a complex challenge due to the diverse expectations and interests of stakeholders and network actors, making it a 'wicked problem' defying straightforward solutions (Dunne 2010). The assessment suggests that value is created or diminished based on how efficiently resources, such as environmental resources, are utilised compared to alternative uses.

The study reveals that coopetition in sustainable innovation frequently involves trade-offs in performance, both real and perceived, concerning the pursuit of multidimensional sustainable value. Sustainable innovation processes create tensions because improving efficiency for one firm may decrease efficiency for others. This dynamic results in varied economic, social, and environmental outcomes for actors within the value network and broader societal ecosystems.

Temporal articulation

Temporal articulation are tensions arising from the need for differentiated positions in the short term to benefit from sustainable innovation, while also requiring an integrative perspective over time to support its deployment for societal-level sustainable change. This duality between separation and integration is crucial in coopetitive processes (Gnyawali et al. 2016). In the study, interviewees emphasised the importance of jointly developing resources and capabilities for sustainable innovation to achieve positive macro impacts. Integration enables actors to meet sustainability demands coherently, consistently and optimally.

Relational evolution

Relational evolution tensions arise when actors in the value network gain new resources and opportunities through sustainable innovation but risk losing control or influence when they become dependent on these innovations. For example, connected autonomous vehicles provide increased comfort and security through features like automatic braking and pedestrian detection. However, if these automation technologies fail, users' sense of safety and autonomy is compromised, highlighting the dual nature of their dependence on the vehicle's capabilities and vulnerability to product failures.

These concerns shift power dynamics in coopetitive relationships for car manufacturers and other stakeholders. The increased reliability of electric and connected autonomous vehicles poses threats to manufacturers' profitability, placing greater emphasis on sales volume and after-sales margins. Consequently, manufacturers employ proactive strategies to leverage the cooperative potential of after-sales services, emphasising the importance of having vehicles serviced or monitored by official brand agencies.

Knowledge circulation

Knowledge circulation tensions arise from the balancing act between sharing and safeguarding data, knowledge, and know-how within the value network. While these assets are vital for competitive advantage, sharing them is crucial for creating broader value and improving environmental and social performance. Interviewees emphasised the significance of knowledge sharing across various levels of the value network, such as manufacturers, suppliers, and subcontractors, for developing services and products. However, they also recognise the risk of data leaks, leading to limited sharing, particularly in relationships involving manufacturers, leasing companies, and connectivity providers.

The above interconnected tensions can diminish the positive sustainability impacts of specific sustainable innovation efforts (see right side of Figure 13.8). When evaluating these tensions, their effects on economic, ecological, and social sustainability, going beyond mere eco- or socio-efficiency, must be assessed. The findings suggest that actors in the value network should consider the natural case for corporate sustainability, focusing on eco-effectiveness and sufficiency, as well as the social case, emphasising socio-effectiveness and ecological equity. Eco-effectiveness involves improving the overall impact of meeting consumer demands on ecological systems, while socio-effectiveness entails reducing harmful social impacts and generating positive social benefits relative to expectations.

Sustainable innovation in the automotive sector may pose risks to future generations and ecological equity. For example, increased waste from obsolete equipment, growing pressure on scarce resources may lead to environmentally and socially harmful mining activities, and a potential widening of the wealth gap due to impoverished labour skills. Limited access to electric vehicles among poorer segments could exacerbate this divide, particularly if fuel alternatives become scarce or heavily taxed. Additionally, actors in the automotive value network have yet to embrace radical sustainability approaches like sufficiency, aimed at reducing overall demand by curbing consumption.

To foster coopetition that drives sustainable innovation, the study refers to the coopetition game outlined by Brandenburger and Nalebuff (1996), comprising five components: players, value, rules, tactics and scope. Defining these components early in sustainable innovation efforts can enhance performance. The value net must encompass all parties affected by sustainable innovation, prioritising those directly involved in the short term while considering potential later entrants. It is crucial to avoid overly narrow scope and ensure equity in defining value contribution from each player. Rule-setting should aim for equitable distribution of gains and equal emphasis on natural, social and business goals, ideally overseen by a neutral, multidisciplinary entity. Explicit rules are essential for enforcement, serving as a societal governance mechanism in coopetition for the greater good (Figure 13.8, left side).

The findings highlight that in the automotive industry, the natural and social cases for sustainable innovation are often implicit rather than explicit goals. Without impartial rules, cooperation is unlikely to align players' self-interest with societal objectives or move beyond solely economic considerations. In essence, relying on Adam Smith's 'invisible hand' alone is insufficient to achieve these goals. Similarly, Hahn and Pinkse (2014) argue that achieving societal objectives in cross-sector partnerships among rival firms hinges on whether competitive forces align with these objectives.

Each party is free to choose their tactics within the rules of the game, with no attempt to alter the rules for personal gain at the expense of others in the value network. Timely and comprehensive disclosure of all ethical considerations is essential to mitigate unequal value distributions in sustainable innovation efforts, driven by power asymmetry among the involved parties. Power dynamics significantly influence value distribution, as the more powerful party may manipulate the game for its own benefit. However, to achieve positive societal outcomes, such power-driven tactics must be restricted and regulated (cf. Hahn and Pinkse 2014).

Managerial implications

Munten et al. (2021) contribute to the understanding of sustainable innovation and coopetition by identifying four key tensions between competitive strategies and cooperation in sustainability efforts at both firm and societal levels. Their study adds to the growing empirical research on coopetition-related tensions. Recognising and addressing these tensions is crucial for promoting sustainable innovation. Failure to do so may jeopardise the success of sustainable innovation efforts and deter future innovations. Therefore, it is essential for firms to innovate judiciously by carefully defining the 'game' and its governance mechanisms.

The study underscores the importance of transparently identifying and comprehensively defining components of the coopetition game for sustainable innovation, considering various outcomes and temporal aspects. It broadens the focus on collaboration beyond individual relationships, addressing conflicts and power imbalances across the entire value network, known as the dark side of coopetition relations. Highlighting the impact of these tensions on societal outcomes, the study emphasises the necessity of adopting a holistic perspective that encompasses the broader network of relationships in sustainable innovation initiatives. It also provides practical and policy insights by identifying key tensions and advocating for holistic approaches and impartial governance mechanisms to ensure positive outcomes for all parties and society.

While the study concentrated solely on the automotive sector, the overarching framework depicted in Figure 13.9 is likely applicable to a wide range of sustainable innovations across different contexts, provided they involve coopetition and collaboration among diverse groups of stakeholders.

This case originates from Munten, P., Vanhamme, J., Maon, F., Swaen, V., and Lindgreen, A. (2021). Addressing tensions in coopetition for sustainable innovation: Insights from the automotive industry. *Journal of Business Research* 136: 10–20. Here, the reader can also find additional relevant references to the case and its topic.

Multiple-choice questions

1. What is the House of Sustainable Supply Chain Management (SSCM)?

   A. A physical building used for logistics operations
   B. A framework organising sustainability efforts into a structured model

C. A set of guidelines only applicable to the manufacturing sector
D. A short-term strategy for cost reduction

2. What are the three main levels of the SSCM house?

A. Ethics, regulations and standards
B. Employees, suppliers and customers
C. Foundation, pillars and roof
D. Technology, innovation and digitalisation

3. What does the foundation level of the SSCM house represent?

A. Short-term profit generation
B. Fundamental principles like risk management, ethics and compliance
C. The application of technology in business
D. Only environmental sustainability

4. How does the TBL framework relate to SSCM?

A. It focuses only on financial performance
B. It ensures a balance between environmental, social and economic sustainability
C. It eliminates the need for risk management
D. It applies only to large corporations

5. Why are ethics, standards and regulations important in SSCM?

A. They help businesses reduce operating costs
B. They ensure fairness, transparency and compliance with laws
C. They prevent companies from expanding globally
D. They are only required for government organisations

6. What is a key reason why risk management is essential in SSCM?

A. It increases company profits in the short term
B. It allows businesses to react to climate change, economic instability and geopolitical risks
C. It only applies to companies working with hazardous materials
D. It is an optional practice in sustainable supply chains

7. What is a common environmental sustainability strategy in supply chains?

A. Increasing carbon emissions
B. Investing in green logistics and renewable energy
C. Reducing collaboration with ethical suppliers
D. Avoiding regulations on environmental impact

8. How does CSR contribute to SSCM?

A. By promoting ethical labour practices and community investments
B. By focusing only on financial growth

C. By reducing corporate donations
D. By eliminating the need for government involvement

9. Which of the following is an example of a socially responsible business practice?

A. Exploiting labour to reduce costs
B. Implementing fair labour policies and ethical sourcing
C. Increasing waste production
D. Avoiding supplier partnerships

10. How does economic sustainability impact long-term business profitability?

A. It reduces financial growth
B. It encourages sustainable business practices that improve efficiency and resilience
C. It only benefits large corporations
D. It eliminates the need for investments in technology

11. How can businesses use technology to enhance sustainability in supply chains?

A. By increasing manual labour and reducing automation
B. By using AI, blockchain and data analytics to track sustainability efforts
C. By avoiding digitalisation to cut costs
D. By focusing only on traditional supply chain methods

12. What is the primary function of the value driver model in SSCM?

A. It aligns business strategies with sustainability goals
B. It replaces financial reporting
C. It eliminates the need for customer engagement
D. It focuses only on environmental sustainability

13. How do service-based supply chains differ from manufacturing-based supply chains?

A. Service supply chains rely more on human involvement and real-time adaptation
B. Manufacturing supply chains focus more on customer interaction
C. Service supply chains do not require risk management
D. Manufacturing supply chains do not require standardisation

14. How do government regulations influence sustainable supply chain practices?

A. By ensuring compliance with environmental and ethical standards
B. By reducing corporate accountability
C. By eliminating the need for green logistics
D. By discouraging sustainable practices

15. How does the SSSCM model help businesses?

A. By measuring sustainability across environmental, social and customer-related dimensions
B. By eliminating government oversight in supply chains

C. By focusing only on financial gains
D. By discouraging technological advancements

Essay question

Discuss the key ideas and best practices for SSSCM as outlined in the chapter 'Good Ideas and Practices for Sustainable Service Supply Chain Management'. How do frameworks such as the House of SSCM, the TBL and the value driver model contribute to sustainability in service supply chains? Provide examples of environmental, social and economic strategies that businesses can implement to enhance sustainability.

14

DIGITAL TRANSFORMATION IN SUPPLY CHAIN MANAGEMENT

Introduction

This chapter explores the transformative impact of advanced technologies on supply chain management (SCM), focusing on AI, IoT, digital twins and XR within the Industry 5.0 paradigm. It highlights the shift towards human-centric approaches, where technology augments human capabilities. The chapter analyses current implementations and future trends, showing how these technologies enhance efficiency, resilience and sustainability. AI revolutionises supply chain processes through advanced demand forecasting, inventory optimisation, logistics planning and predictive maintenance. IoT devices offer real-time monitoring and data collection, providing unprecedented visibility. Digital twins enable simulation and optimisation, allowing improvements without disrupting workflows. XR technologies improve human–machine interaction for more efficient operations. Key findings emphasise the need for a balanced approach, considering technological capabilities, human factors and organisational readiness. Challenges include data security, infrastructure requirements and workforce upskilling. The chapter provides strategic recommendations for leveraging these technologies while maintaining a human-centric approach, ensuring that advancements support human expertise. This work offers valuable insights for practitioners and researchers on integrating modern technologies into supply chain operations.

Learning objectives

By the end of this chapter the reader will be able to answer the following:

- Explain the transition from Industry 4.0 to Industry 5.0 and its implications in SCM.
- Describe how AI, IoT, digital twins and XR can transform supply chain operations.
- Analyse the specific contributions of each technology (AI, IoT, digital twins and XR) to enhancing efficiency, resilience and sustainability in supply chains.
- Answer how AI improves demand forecasting, inventory optimisation, logistics planning and predictive maintenance.

DOI: 10.4324/9781003650973-14

- Explain how IoT enables real-time monitoring and data collection across supply chain operations.
- Define digital twins and their role in simulating and optimising supply chain processes.
- Describe how XR technologies (augmented reality, virtual reality and mixed reality) enhance human–machine interaction in supply chain operations.
- Explore the opportunities for creating more resilient, sustainable and human-centric supply chains through digital transformation.
- Propose approaches for balancing technological advancements with human-centric practices to ensure sustainable and ethical implementation.
- Investigate the potential impact of these technologies on the future of supply chain resilience, sustainability and competitiveness.

Outline

14.1 Transforming technologies

With the aim of advancing manufacturing and industrial practices through the integration of advanced digital technologies, Industry 4.0 brought together several revolutionary innovations, including artificial intelligence (AI), Internet of Things (IoT), smart robotics, big data analytics and simulation. Regarding supply chain optimisation, these technologies enabled more integrated and transparent supply chains, improved logistics, reduced lead times and enhanced inventory management. Industry 5.0, considered being the next evolutionary step in the manufacturing sector, emphasises the integration of advanced technologies with a human-centric focus, aiming to achieve more sustainable, personalised and efficient production processes. This shift is characterised by prioritising improved working conditions for employees, with automation technologies viewed as tools to help people work more easily, comfortably, safely and with greater satisfaction, rather than merely as a means to increase production and profit. To achieve this, the capabilities of AI, IoT, digital twins and other cutting-edge technologies should be leveraged to enhance the efficiency and adaptability of manufacturing and supply chain operations in a human-centred manner. In the context of SCM, Industry 5.0 introduces a paradigm where the strategic coordination of various business functions and collaboration with external partners are crucial. This approach not only seeks to efficiently plan, produce, transport and deliver products or services but also emphasises optimising the flow of materials, information, and finances across the entire supply chain. Through seamless human-machine collaboration, mass customisation of products, decentralised production, sustainable and green solutions, real-time data sharing, resilience and talent development, Industry 5.0 has a profound impact on SCM. It is expected that Industry 5.0 strategies will enhance operational effectiveness, reduce costs and lead times, and improve customer satisfaction through the timely delivery of goods and services.

FIGURE14.1 SCM overview and artificial intelligence are two factors that aim to improve the efficiency and effectiveness of modern business pipelines

Supply constitutes the ring that brings manufacturers and consumers together. As shown in Figure 14.1, its management can be viewed as the strategic coordination and integration of various organisational business functions and collaboration with external partners to efficiently plan, produce, transport and deliver products or services to customers. This involves running a network of interconnected entities, including suppliers, manufacturers, distributors, retailers and logistics providers, to optimise the flow of materials, information and finances across the entire supply chain. The main objectives include enhancing operational effectiveness, reducing costs and lead times and improving customer satisfaction through the timely delivery of goods and services. The integration of hi-end technology within contemporary supply chains is crucial for achieving real-time visibility, flexibility and responsiveness to market demands. Advanced technologies such as AI, IoT and digital twins and extended reality play pivotal roles in enhancing the efficiency and effectiveness of today's supply chains. These technologies enable companies to analyse vast amounts of data and provide better visualisation for improved decision-making, optimise logistics and inventory management, and ensure the traceability and security of goods from production to delivery. Technological integration facilitates a seamless flow of information among stakeholders, allowing for more collaborative and efficient supply chain ecosystems. The adoption of such technologies empowers businesses with better anticipation of market changes, risk mitigation, while they can meet customer demands with greater accuracy and speed. Thereby, enterprises can gain a competitive advantage in the marketplace only by innovating via these cutting-edge technologies.

With a view to keep up with the development of the chapter, let us feature AI, IoT, digital twins and XR as focal points. AI stands at the forefront of transforming SCM by providing sophisticated data analysis, predictive analytics and automation capabilities. AI technologies enable supply chains to become more adaptive and smarter, optimising operations such as demand forecasting, route planning and inventory management for enhanced efficiency and cost-effectiveness. The IoT connects physical objects throughout the supply chain, from manufacturing equipment to products in transit, providing real-time data on their status, location and environmental conditions. This connectivity enables improved monitoring, control and automation of supply chain activities, enhancing efficiency, visibility and responsiveness to changing conditions. Digital twins represent virtual replicas of physical assets, processes or systems, used to model and analyse supply chain operations. By simulating different scenarios and outcomes, digital twins allow companies to identify potential issues before they occur, optimise processes and implement improvements in the real world, leading to reduced downtime and better resource allocation. Last, XR serves as a valuable tool to bridge the physical and digital worlds, offering an immersive experience that strengthens human–computer interaction (HCI) through increased human involvement. With the support of this technology, humans can perceive the output of IoT and digital twins, by visualising symbolic and elaborated operations to upgrade trivial operations in a metaverse's way. In conclusion, Industry 5.0 and the integration of technologies like AI, digital twins, IoT and XR are reshaping the landscape of SCM. These advancements offer unprecedented opportunities for businesses to enhance operational efficiency, agility and customer satisfaction, marking a significant leap forward in the evolution towards really smart anthropocentric supply chains.

14.2 Artificial intelligence in supply chain

We already noted that AI has emerged as a pivotal enabler in modern SCM. In this section let us examine how AI revolutionises traditional processes and bolsters efficiency across various supply chain domains. As firms continue to evolve in the face of globalisation, rapid technological advancements and changing consumer demands, the role of AI in SCM has become increasingly indispensable. In this context, AI encompasses the utilisation of advanced algorithms and technologies to analyse extensive datasets, predict outcomes, optimise operations and mitigate risks. The advent of AI technologies has transformed all the operations across the SCM (see Figure 14.2) by offering unprecedented insights and capabilities. Additionally, AI systems are increasingly expected to embody principles of transparency, fairness, accountability, trustworthiness and explainability. These attributes are crucial for fostering trust in AI-driven decision-making processes and ensuring that AI systems align with ethical and regulatory standards. With the ability to process vast amounts of data in real-time, AI algorithms can extract patterns, trends, and anomalies that might otherwise be overlooked.

In demand forecasting, AI's role can be transformative. Demand is sensitive to several factors, such as seasonality, trends and cycles, influencing forecasting accuracy. Models must effectively capture and incorporate demand patterns into their predictions. By harnessing historical data, market trends and external factors, AI-powered frameworks generate precise predictions, enabling organisations to optimise inventory levels, minimise stockouts and mitigate excess inventory. AI algorithms, such as neural networks and deep learning models, capture complex patterns and data relationships, allowing them to identify non-linear associations and interactions between variables and clusters, leading to more accurate forecasts. Moreover, AI models can adapt to changes in data patterns and trends over time, automatically updating and refining predictions as new data becomes available. AI-driven systems are adept at adapting to dynamic consumer behaviour and seasonal variations, facilitating proactive decision-making to align supply chains with evolving market dynamics and customer demands.

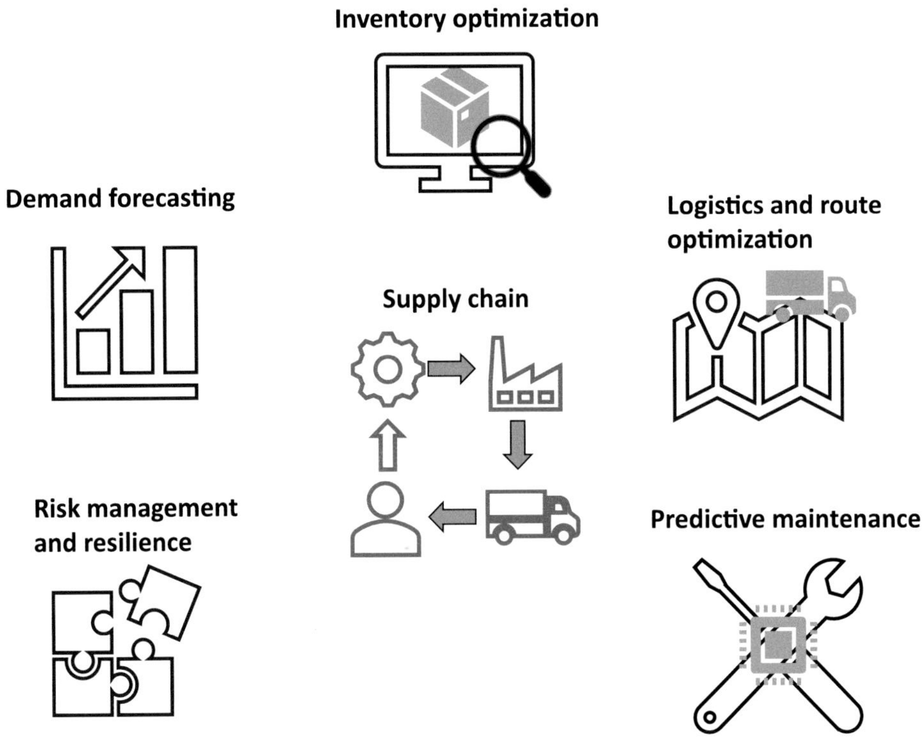

FIGURE 14.2 Artificial intelligence applications in modern supply chains cover the processes of demand forecasting, inventory optimisation, logistics and route optimisation, predictive maintenance, and risk management and resilience

Inventory control and management are domains of prime importance for SCM. Challenges pertaining to inventory management are widespread across various sectors, including production, remanufacturing, repair services and general business operations. Thus, strategically managing and balancing inventory levels, with the aim to maximise efficiency and minimise costs while meeting customer demand, is another critical area where AI demonstrates its competence. Through sophisticated analysis of historical data and customer behaviour, AI algorithms predict demand fluctuations with unprecedented precision. This enables organisations to minimise carrying costs, prevent stockouts and maintain optimal stock levels while enhancing operational efficiency and cost-effectiveness. Additionally, AI-enabled technologies such as machine vision complement these efforts by facilitating real-time monitoring of warehouse capacity and availability, thereby streamlining operations and ensuring timely product availability. AI can boost data accuracy and productivity, help make faster decisions, minimise costs and ensure customer satisfaction.

Contemporary commerce platforms have adopted multi-channel approaches to marketing, leading to increased demand for logistics services. Despite this demand, the logistics industry faces profitability challenges due to substantial capital investments and rising operational costs. Leveraging AI algorithms present a viable solution, as they can optimise transportation routes, minimise fuel consumption and enhance vehicle dispatching efficiency. While existing navigation systems offer route planning capabilities, they often fail to identify a general optimal path. Factors such as traffic congestion during peak hours and real-time weather conditions can significantly impact travel time. By leveraging real-time data and traffic patterns, along with historical information, AI algorithms can generate efficient and adaptive route plans, enhancing delivery speed, resource utilisation and environmental sustainability. Furthermore, predictive analytics empower organisations to swiftly adjust route plans in response to unforeseen challenges, ensuring seamless and optimised supply chain operations. Thus, AI presents a promising solution in logistics and route optimisation.

Predictive maintenance is crucial for the supply chain as it enables enterprises to anticipate and prevent equipment failures before they occur, thereby enhancing supply chain resilience. By maintaining a proactive stance towards equipment maintenance, organisations can better anticipate and respond to unexpected failure events, minimising the risk of disruptions and ensuring business continuity. AI-based solutions facilitate this transition from reactive to proactive maintenance approaches by predicting equipment failures before they occur. Leveraging diverse datasets such as historical performance data, IoT sensor readings and operational patterns, an AI-driven predictive maintenance system creates comprehensive models reflecting equipment condition and usage patterns. This enables precise maintenance suggestions based on real-time operational data analysis. Enterprises adopt this innovation to reduce downtime, extend machinery lifespan, optimise asset performance, enhance safety and reduce maintenance costs. Real-time monitoring capabilities offer valuable insights, enabling strategic scheduling of maintenance activities and efficient resource allocation. Ultimately, predictive maintenance helps organisations maintain operational efficiency, minimise risks and uphold customer satisfaction in their supply chain operations.

The analytical power of AI enables organisations to make informed decisions swiftly, thereby enhancing operational efficiency and responsiveness to market dynamics. Moreover, AI facilitates predictive analytics, allowing organisations to anticipate demand fluctuations, supply chain disruptions, and other critical events with greater accuracy. Thus, AI can play a pivotal role in risk management and resilience, which are paramount in ensuring supply chain stability. By analysing diverse datasets encompassing geopolitical events, market trends, and ad-hoc determined factors, AI-driven tools enable proactive risk assessment and mitigation. Real-time monitoring capabilities empower organisations to make informed decisions swiftly amidst uncertainties, strengthen supply chain resilience against disruptions and enhance supply chain resilience.

Up to this point, we have discussed the employment of AI in supply chains and how it presents promising opportunities for enhancing efficiency and reducing costs. However, we should point out that such a transformation also poses significant challenges across technical, ethical, and operational domains, especially when human-centric and sustainable matters are of primarily concern. To fully realise the potential of AI in creating responsible, resilient and sustainable supply chain ecosystems, organisations must navigate these obstacles with innovative solutions. One of the primary challenges is ensuring data quality and availability, as poor data quality can lead to inaccurate predictions and decisions. Data integration presents another key challenge, as integrating data from various sources within the supply chain can be complex due to siloed data and incompatible formats. Scalability is also a significant challenge, particularly as supply chains grow and evolve, requiring AI-driven systems to handle increased data volumes and transaction complexity without sacrificing performance. The shortage of professionals with expertise in both SCM and AI presents another challenge, along with change management, data security and privacy, interpretation of AI models, infrastructure and costs, alignment with sustainability goals and ethical considerations. Last, we should highlight that the integration of AI into SCM is a multifaceted process encompassing technical, operational and social dimensions, necessitating careful consideration of its implications across various aspects of SCM, including workforce dynamics, decision-making processes and ethical considerations. Despite these challenges, integrating AI with sustainability offers numerous opportunities and benefits. By addressing these challenges with innovative solutions, organisations can unlock the full potential of AI to create responsible, resilient and sustainable supply chain ecosystems.

In conclusion, in the contemporary ever-changing global business landscape, AI-driven optimisation algorithms have drastically enhanced supply chain operations, magnifying efficiency and customer satisfaction. Machine learning and AI algorithms analyse extensive datasets to streamline processes and maximise resource utilisation, whether it is route optimisation for logistics, inventory management or production scheduling. By continuously identifying opportunities for improvement, they minimise costs and ensure timely delivery of products and services. This proactive approach offers unprecedented insights and capabilities, enabling organisations to thrive in a competitive environment. By harnessing the analytical power of AI to predict outcomes, optimise operations and mitigate risks, businesses enhance efficiency, minimise risks and uphold customer satisfaction. As the role of AI continues to evolve, it remains at the forefront of supply chain innovation, driving continuous improvement and competitive advantage. Embracing AI's transformative potential equips organisations to navigate complexities and uncertainties in the global marketplace, fostering innovation, resilience and sustainable growth in supply chain operations. A cautious approach that takes into consideration the guidelines for robust and sustainable AI is warranted in the adoption of AI within SCM to mitigate potential risks and ensure responsible and effective implementation.

14.3 Digital supporting technologies

In this section we attempt to show how other digital transformation technologies enforce change into the today's supply chain landscape. Firstly, we discuss IoT, which pertains to a network of interconnected smart devices, either static or mobile, embedded with sensors and actuators that are operated by software enabling them to gather and exchange real-time data from the physical world. The result of such a technology is to make critical insights available, resulting to enhanced internal operations across diverse sectors, such as healthcare, transportation and manufacturing. In this context, the IoT can be described as an intelligent ecosystem of collaborative devices that seeks to bolster efficiency, convenience and decision-making, striving to address complex processes without direct human intervention. Towards the same direction, digital twins constitute virtual renditions of real systems, that enable live monitoring, examination and refinement thorough data emanating from IoT devices. Moreover, XR technologies are utilised for immersive visualisation, enhancing the connection between humans and IoT-enabled systems. Consequently, attributes, behaviours, and interactions are captured in real-time, thereby enabling improved decision-making, predictive maintenance, warehouse optimisation and operational efficiency when embraced across various industries, including the supply chain.

In particular, within the frame of smart SCM, a digital twin serves to replicate and refine supply chain processes, predict and avert shortages and heighten the effectiveness and quality of services. This virtual counterpart furnishes a meticulous, precise portrayal of the tangible object or system, encompassing its behaviour, functionality and interactions within its surroundings.

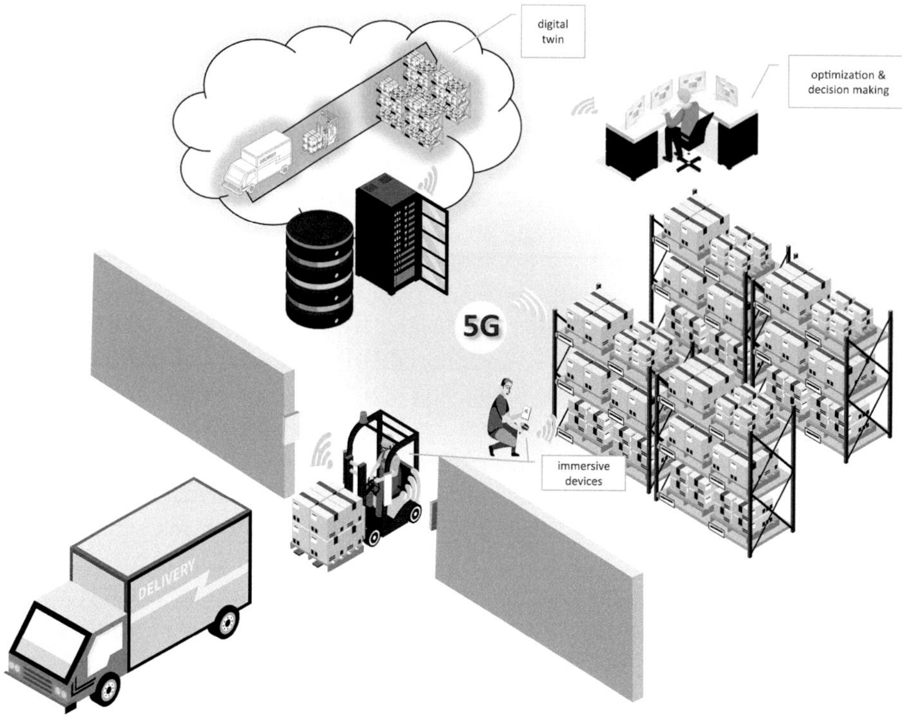

FIGURE 14.3 Smart warehouses utilise digital twins to model the physical space, while edge computing, AI and 5G technologies enable real-time decision making and optimisation. Immersive technologies allow for a seamless human–computer interaction, thus a more efficient interaction between the workers and the smart warehouse.

Employing AI, data analytics and multi-physics simulation, digital twins simulate and scrutinise diverse operational scenarios and external influences on a system. Figure 14.3 portrays the integration of IoT, XR and digital twin technologies in a smart warehouse. The development of digital twins emerges as a pivotal facet of forthcoming technologies poised to impact various global sectors. By carefully examine data from the physical entity, the digital twin delivers real-time insights, monitors its functionality and identifies probable challenges before their display. A digital twin can be harnessed to refine the operation of a physical system by simulating its behaviour and pinpointing areas ripe for enhancement. Corporations can leverage digital twins to model, foresee and refine products and supply chain processes across different sectors, including automotive, power plants and healthcare, prior to investing in tangible prototypes and assets. Consequently, digital twins serve to empower businesses and streamline supply chain processes, fostering better decision-making, cost reduction and enhanced performance across a myriad of sectors and applications.

The creation of a digital twin reduces the time and expenses associated with on-site testing, enabling engineers and designers to explore various scenarios and effect enhancements. The adoption of digital twin technology emerges as indispensable for product manufacturers seeking to bolster the efficiency of their supply chain processes and abbreviate time-to-market. In supply chain contexts, digital twins are crafted by amalgamating real-time data from IoT sensors with models of physical assets and other simulation tools. This amalgamation facilitates real-time monitoring and analysis of equipment and processes, pre-empting potential issues and facilitating data-driven decisions to optimise the supply chain. Through the creation of a digital twin for a component, engineers can visualise through XR and evaluate its performance under diverse scenarios. This enables prognostication of real-world performance, identification of potential issues or shortages and optimisation of design to augment performance. The digital twin confers numerous advantages to smart SCM, facilitating real-time monitoring of supply chain processes and expediting issue resolution. Additionally, it enables product and process testing and refinement before physical production, thereby conserving time and resources. Moreover, digital twins are deployed to ascertain the efficacy of supply chain processes; they facilitate performance monitoring of individual stages on the pipeline, pre-empt issues before they arise and optimise system operations. Additionally, they enable simulation and testing of new processes or equipment prior to implementation, mitigating the risk of costly errors or failures. Digital twins empower supply chain managers to refine models and system performance while unlocking novel commercial opportunities. By spanning the entire lifecycle, a digital twin permits testing and continual improvements at any juncture in the supply chain process within a digital word that is far more cost-effective than the physical one. Some enterprises employ digital twins to simulate entire supply chain lines and pinpoint more efficient methods to enhance part production productivity. Intelligent SCM embodies an approach that incorporates AI, the IoT, and big data analytics technologies to refine supply chain processes and amplify efficiency. The complexity of supply chain environments is mounting, necessitating heightened cognitive and adaptive capabilities in analysing and modifying supply chain processes. It also presents opportunities for product customisation and personalisation, alongside real-time SCM, enabling swift responses to shifts in demand, market trends and consumer preferences. This approach entails leveraging connected devices, automation and real-time data to enhance efficiency, productivity and quality in supply chain operations. The aim is to cultivate a more agile, adaptable and responsive supply chain environment capable of swiftly adapting to evolving market demands and delivering high-quality products at reduced costs. Thus, it integrates digital software tools and data, digitalising every resource for analysis and modification in virtual environments.

Thus, the primary applications of digital twins in smart SCM are status monitoring, simulation and representation. Assets undergo continuous monitoring via the IoT for status updates, while digital twins of physical assets are generated to analyse and refine the mechanisms and processes involved in the supply chain. Goods, systems and equipment are replicated in digital twins for simulation purposes, simulating real operational environments. Moreover, digital twins are essential for predictive maintenance, boosting productivity, facilitating early problem detection and providing new insights for process optimisation. Through the use of machine-specific models generated during production, businesses can more accurately identify the underlying causes of problems. In a nutshell, digital twins facilitate testing of operating conditions and anticipation of results digitally; identification of new revenue streams' reduction of waste, costs, and energy consumption; predictive maintenance of manufacturing processes; improvement of quality and customer satisfaction; tracking of products from production to completion; facilitation of new business models; reduction of time to market and enhancement of part manufacturing productivity. On top of all these, XR supports human-machine collaboration, enabling joint problem-solving for complex tasks, safeguarding anthropocentricism in digital transformation of supply chain. With such tools, new processes can be conceived, developed and refined through virtual simulation prior to deployment on actual physical assets, thereby enhancing performance. Real-time metaverse systems can be seamlessly integrated into digital twins to provide visual tracking and troubleshooting capabilities within operational environments. It is no longer sufficient to view digital twins merely as replicas of physical assets; instead, they should incorporate value-added services that enable physical assets to function as autonomous smart agents in collaboration with human ones.

Thereby, the advantage of digital twins lies in their ability to provide a virtual copy of a physical system, which, along other novel technologies like IoT, XR and edge computing, allow for real-time testing and analysis without disrupting the actual system. The adoption of all these technologies in smart supply chain offer significant benefits in terms of efficiency, cost reduction and product quality, making them indispensable for an enterprise to stay competitive in the global market. However, despite their recognised potential, they have not yet fully gained widespread adoption, which have led to hesitation among consumers and businesses. The reason for this reluctance to innovation is that creating and maintaining digital twins can be costly and time-consuming, necessitating specialised knowledge and expertise. Also, XR devices are still bulky and exhibit limited high-quality virtual content. Besides, in contemporary supply chain systems, more significant obstacles still exist, including connectivity, which can hinder the digital twin's ability to modify processes and XR to visualise them appropriately. The vast amount of data collected poses security vulnerabilities, necessitating the examination and updating of current security procedures before deploying digital twin technology. Advanced AI algorithms are required for analysing and adjusting the supply chain based on data acquired from the IoT sensors. Moreover, real-time 5G-enabled broadband data communication is essential for digital twins to accurately mirror the condition of actual IoT devices scattered around the entire supply chain. Privacy and security concerns regarding data also present challenges in process management using digital twins. Additionally, the lack of stable and sustainable technologies impedes the development of an end-to-end collaborative digital twin system for smart distributed supply chain.

Next, we present a framework for integrating digital twins, XR and IoT into current supply chain operations. We start by presenting the different types of data produced within a smart supply chain ecosystem, which are as follows:

- Supplier data refer to collecting information regarding vendors' dependability, the time it takes to deliver goods and their performance indicators. A comprehensive understanding of suppliers' capacities and constraints permits well-informed sourcing choices.
- Logistics and transportation data encompass information regarding the timing of shipments and the criteria used for evaluating the carriers' performance. This type of information is mandatory, as adequate transportation of commodities from manufacturing plants to distribution hubs and consumers is essential.
- Production data include schedules, capacity planning, work orders, and material invoices. It is worth noting that these data serve as the foundation in the manufacturing process, directing the suitable distribution of industrial resources.
- Market data are derived from customer orders and historical sales. This information enhances strategic decision-making by predicting consumer behaviour shifts, while empowering organisations to adjust to market dynamics and maintain a competitive edge proactively.

Then, we examine the optimisation modules and techniques used by the digital twin, as shown in Figure 14.4 (Tsintotas et al. 2024). The interoperable data space model fosters seamless connectivity and data exchange among stakeholders within the supply chain. More specifically, interoperability is the ability of different systems, applications and devices to exchange and interpret data

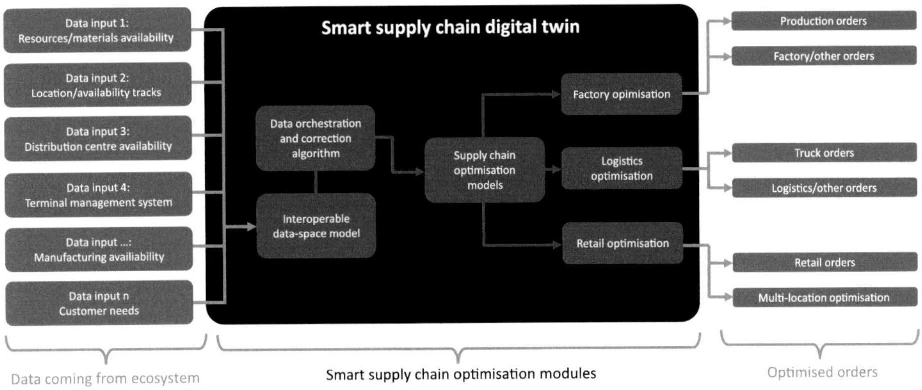

FIGURE 14.4 Smart supply chain framework, comprising three main parts: (a) the data coming from the ecosystem; (b) the digital twin, operating on the information provided by the previous module, to optimise the supply chain models; and (c) the optimised orders

consistently, promoting collaboration between suppliers, manufacturers, distributors and other participants. Its main goal is to overcome the challenges of data silos and incompatibility. Therefore, standardised protocols and data formats are used to facilitate communication while simultaneously enhancing transparency. This empowers supply chain participants to access and share real-time data, leading to better decision-making, reduced delays and increased responsiveness to dynamic market conditions. On the other hand, data orchestration and correction algorithms manage to harmonise and amalgamate information from various data sources, guaranteeing smooth communication and synchronisation. Effective data orchestration is vital for a digital twin, as it seeks to extract patterns to optimise processes. Besides, correction algorithms are used to detect and resolve flaws or inconsistencies in datasets. As in any data-driven set-up, inaccuracies occur due to several factors, for example, human error, technology faults or outdated information, advanced methods, such as pattern recognition, statistical analysis and machine learning, are chosen to identify data anomalies. Since the objective is to guarantee the dataset's precision and dependability, these approaches employ remedial steps to synchronise the data with pre-established regulations once inconsistencies are discovered. When the supply chain optimisation models are treated as different entities, the corresponding branches, that is, the factory operations, its logistics and the retail strategies, permit managers to utilise diverse and customised optimisation models for each entity individually. Factory optimisation promptly identifies and addresses issues by closely monitoring the quality of incoming raw materials, thereby minimising defects and rework. The corresponding digital twin aids in the creation of precise production plans based on demand forecasts, inventory levels and resource availability. Logistics optimisation reduces transportation costs and improves inventory efficiency through network design, routing and warehouse management. The connected virtual model utilises data regarding goods levels, order demand, and transportation costs towards this goal. Furthermore, the digital twin 'oversees' the goods' transportation, monitors delivery schedules and promptly addresses any unforeseen disruptions or complications. Last, retail optimisation uses demand forecasting, assortment planning and promotion models to customise product offerings and increase revenue. The digital twin assists sellers in handling inventory quantities to satisfy customer needs while avoiding expenses associated with stock-holding. This way, precise market prediction and immediate tracking empower businesses to achieve optimal equilibrium between product accessibility and cost-effectiveness.

14.4 Strategic balance

In today's fast-evolving business landscape, the advanced technologies discussed in the previous sections offer significant opportunities for supply chains, enhancing operational efficiency, reducing costs and improving decision-making through real-time insights and predictive analytics. In this section, we aim to explore how digital transformation is reshaping the modern supply chain, highlighting the emerging challenges and opportunities. The success of today's supply chains lies in strategically balancing these challenges with the opportunities presented by digital transformation, which is reshaping traditional models.

Organisations leverage AI to optimise processes, reduce costs and enhance customer satisfaction through predictive analytics, real-time insights and adaptive decision-making, significantly improving overall supply chain performance. The integration of AI into supply chains boosts efficiency, while it improves operational transparency, enabling businesses to gain a clearer understanding of their internal processes and external environments. Improved demand forecasting, streamlined logistics, agile response mechanisms and optimised inventory levels allow businesses to maintain a competitive edge in a rapidly evolving market. Data-driven insights also enable strategic decisions, fostering competitiveness in the dynamic business environment. Additionally, digital transformation tools enhance connectivity across inventory components, aligning resources with production and sales needs, ultimately reducing costs and optimising supply chain operations. This seamless connection across the supply chain improves operational efficiency and also ensures that companies can respond flexibly to fluctuating market demands.

However, these opportunities come with challenges, particularly in integrating AI seamlessly into existing infrastructure, which requires careful planning to avoid disruptions. Companies must ensure that they do not merely add new technologies as a quick fix, only because other do it. Instead, they should thoroughly study the particularities in their business and integrate the modern digital tools in a customised way that supports their long-term operational goals. Inasmuch as privacy and data security is concerned, ethical questions emerge, as vast amounts of sensitive information are processed by AI systems. That is, the digitalisation of supply chains increases their vulnerability to cyber threats, making it essential for businesses to develop robust cybersecurity measures. The potential misuse of customer data can damage the reputation of an organisation, making privacy compliance critical for both ethical and legal reasons. Moreover, organisations must foster a culture conducive to innovation, ensuring that employees, suppliers, and customers are aligned with the company's technological evolution. In this regard, the cultural shift within an organisation is as important as the technological shift – technology can only deliver its full potential if employees are empowered to adopt it effectively. Besides, upskilling and reskilling employees in new technologies is also essential for fully exploiting the benefits of digital transformation. Companies need to invest in training programs to ensure that their workforce is capable of managing and benefiting from advanced digital tools. Moreover, there is a growing need for skilled professionals in AI-based methods, presenting a significant human resource challenge. The development of specialised educational programs and industry collaborations is crucial in addressing this shortage and ensuring a sustainable talent pipeline.

The impact of digital transformation extends beyond operational efficiencies, fundamentally altering business processes, market positioning and relationships within the supply chain ecosystem. AI-driven applications improve demand forecasting, inventory optimisation and logistics, enabling organisations to automate repetitive tasks, optimise workflows and gain real-time insights that reduce lead times and operational costs. Automation frees human resources to focus on higher-level strategic tasks, thereby increasing the value generated by human capital. Risk management and predictive capabilities are significantly improved by the enhanced decision-making enabled by advanced analytics and intelligent strategic decisions provided via immersive visualisations. By the same token, the simulation of various scenarios that leads to optimised supply chain operations drives the precise forecasting of demand and ensures product availability, minimising stockouts and overstock situations, which in turn results to improved customer satisfaction. Optimised logistics and efficient supply chain processes ensure timely deliveries, thereby boosting customer loyalty. The AI-driven personalisation of customer experiences enables companies to cater to individual preferences, further enhancing customer satisfaction and retention. Moreover, the adaptability and resilience of the supply chain are strengthened as organisations swiftly respond to market changes and disruptions by identifying real-time patterns and trends. This adaptability enhances the overall stability and continuity of supply chain operations. For example, during crises, as for example in the COVID-19 pandemic, companies with advanced digital supply chains can pivot more rapidly to address disruptions and shift production strategies. Resilience-building strategies must continue to evolve, preparing supply chains for future disruptions and ensuring business continuity even in unpredictable environments. Finally, cost savings and resource optimisation are achieved through AI's ability to streamline processes, reduce inefficiencies, and optimise resource allocation, creating a more sustainable and cost-effective supply chain ecosystem. Sustainability is a growing concern in modern supply chains, with AI and other digital tools playing a pivotal role in reducing carbon footprints by optimising transportation routes and minimising waste. As businesses aim to meet both financial and environmental goals, digital transformation provides the framework for achieving these dual objectives.

14.5 Future perspectives

This section explores the future trends, challenges and opportunities these technologies present, along with recommendations for stakeholders to effectively prepare for the evolving supply chain ecosystem. AI remains at the forefront of supply chain innovation and as the related models are becoming better and better trained and accurate, they will continue to refine SCM, enabling more accurate demand forecasting, improved logistics and smarter inventory management. Additionally, AI will play a pivotal role in enhancing supply chain resilience by predicting disruptions and providing adaptive solutions. Digital twins are another game-changing trend that enable organisations to simulate and analyse operations in real-time. As digital twin technology advances, we can expect more precise control over supply chain operations, leading to increased efficiency and resilience. The adoption of IoT will further revolutionise the supply chain by enabling the spread of interconnected ecosystems. Moreover, the integration of IoT with AI will enable predictive maintenance, ensuring that machinery and vehicles are serviced well, minimising downtimes and costly disruptions. XR technologies are also set to impact future supply chain operations by providing immersive training for employees, help in warehouse management through AR-guided picking, and even assist in supply chain design and planning by creating virtual environments for testing new layouts and workflows. As XR becomes more integrated into daily operations, it will further improve decision-making and enhance operational efficiency.

One of the primary challenges in the adoption of these technologies in the future is their seamless integration into the today's infrastructures. Many organisations still operate on legacy systems that are not fully compatible with these advanced technologies. The process of upgrading infrastructure to accommodate these technologies is complex and requires significant investment. Moreover, standardisation and interoperability between different systems and technologies remains a concern. Ensuring smooth communication across various digital platforms is essential for maximising the benefits of these technologies. Another key challenge is data security and privacy, as more and more IoT devices are integrated into supply chain networks. The vast amounts of data generated and shared in real-time, though invaluable for optimising operations, pose risks if not properly secured. Organisations must invest in robust cybersecurity measures to protect sensitive information from breaches, unauthorised access and misuse.

In terms of opportunities, probably the most significant one is the ability to create more resilient and adaptable supply chains. The combination of AI's predictive analytics, digital twins' scenario planning, IoT's real-time monitoring, and XR's immersive planning tools will enable businesses to anticipate disruptions, assess risks and adapt swiftly. By simulating various scenarios using digital twins, companies can prepare for potential disruptions, such as supply shortages or market fluctuations and adjust their operations accordingly. Furthermore, sustainability is emerging as a critical factor in SCM. AI and IoT can optimise resource allocation and reduce waste, making supply chains more eco-friendly. For example, IoT-enabled sensors can track energy consumption and emissions throughout the supply chain, while AI algorithms can identify areas for improvement, such as reducing fuel consumption in logistics or minimising waste in production processes. By leveraging these technologies, companies can achieve more sustainable operations, contributing to global efforts to reduce environmental impact. Human–machine collaboration is also a major opportunity, as human workers will gradually focus on higher-order decision-making, creativity, and problem-solving. Upskilling programs are essential to help employees transition to these new roles, ensuring that they work alongside AI systems to drive innovation and improve supply chain performance. XR technologies, particularly AR, can play a key role in this transition by providing immersive training environments for employees, improving skills and efficiency in real-time.

To fully capitalise on these emerging technologies and address the accompanying challenges, stakeholders must take a proactive approach. Next several key recommendations are listed:

1. *Invest in technological infrastructure*: Organisations should prioritise upgrading their technological infrastructure to accommodate digital transformation. This includes ensuring that legacy systems can support the integration of the advanced technologies we have so far discussed and that there is interoperability between different platforms. Investment in cloud-based solutions, big data analytics platforms and cybersecurity measures will be essential to maximising the potential of these technologies.
2. *Develop a culture of continuous learning*: The integration of AI, IoT and other technologies will fundamentally change the nature of work within supply chains. Therefore, companies must foster a culture of continuous learning and provide employees with the training necessary to adapt to new technologies. This includes upskilling and reskilling programs that focus on advanced data analytics and AI. XR can also be leveraged to provide immersive training environments, helping employees gain hands-on experience with new technologies.
3. *Focus on data governance and security*: As the reliance on IoT and AI increases, so does the need for robust data governance frameworks. Organisations must ensure that data collected from IoT devices and AI systems are accurate, securely stored, and used ethically. Implementing comprehensive data governance protocols, including encryption, access controls and transparent AI decision-making processes, will build trust among stakeholders and protect against potential cyber threats.
4. *Prioritise sustainability*: The push for more sustainable supply chains will become even more critical in the coming years. Companies should leverage AI and IoT technologies to track and reduce their environmental footprint, optimise resource usage and minimise waste.

Sustainable practices will not only benefit the environment but also provide a competitive edge, as consumers and partners increasingly favour businesses that prioritise eco-friendly operations.

5. *Enhance collaboration across the supply chain ecosystem*: To achieve the full benefits of interconnected ecosystems, organisations must work closely with suppliers, customers and other stakeholders. AI-powered platforms, coupled with IoT and digital twins, can facilitate better collaboration and real-time data sharing across the entire supply chain. Creating a unified, intelligent network where all parties work together seamlessly will be key to maintaining competitiveness in a rapidly evolving market.

Synopsis

The rapid advancement of digital technologies is reshaping SCM, making tools like AI, IoT, digital twins and XR essential for modern operations. These technologies are revolutionising supply chains by enhancing demand forecasting, inventory management, predictive maintenance, real-time monitoring, simulation, optimisation and human–machine interaction. The benefits include better accuracy in forecasting and inventory control, lower costs, improved logistics, enhanced risk management and greater sustainability. As we move toward Industry 5.0, it's crucial to focus on human involvement, enhancing human skills rather than replacing people. Embracing digital transformation is necessary for businesses to stay competitive. Market pressures, technological evolution and business benefits drive this need. Customers expect faster delivery and personalised services, while competition and demand for sustainable operations are increasing. The advantages include improved efficiency, smarter decision-making, stronger resilience, and enhanced customer satisfaction. Organisations should focus on strategic planning, infrastructure development, workforce development, implementation and continuous improvement. This includes developing a clear digital transformation strategy, investing in necessary technology, training employees and fostering a culture of innovation. The future of SCM lies in integrating advanced technologies with human expertise. Organisations that balance innovation and human-centred approaches will thrive, building competitive, resilient and sustainable supply chains ready for future challenges.

Multiple-choice questions

1. What is the primary focus of Industry 5.0 in SCM?

   A. Complete automation of processes
   B. Human-centric approaches and sustainability
   C. Reducing workforce involvement
   D. Increasing production speed

2. Which technology is primarily used for real-time monitoring and data collection in supply chains?

   A. IoT
   B. AI
   C. Digital twins
   D. XR

3. What role does AI play in demand forecasting?

   A. It replaces human decision-making entirely
   B. It uses historical data and market trends to predict demand
   C. It focuses only on inventory management
   D. It eliminates the need for data analysis

4. What is the main advantage of using digital twins in SCM?

   A. They replace physical assets entirely
   B. They reduce the need for IoT devices
   C. They eliminate the need for human intervention
   D. They allow simulation and optimisation without disrupting physical operations

5. Which of the following is a key challenge in implementing AI in supply chains?

   A. Lack of data availability
   B. Over-reliance on human decision-making
   C. Ensuring data quality and integration
   D. Inability to process large datasets

6. What is the primary purpose of XR in SCM?

   A. To replace human workers
   B. To enhance human–machine interaction and visualisation
   C. To automate logistics processes
   D. To reduce the need for IoT devices

7. Which technology revolutionises predictive maintenance in supply chains?

   A. IoT
   B. AI
   C. Digital twins
   D. XR

8. What is a critical factor for successful digital transformation in supply chains?

   A. Complete elimination of human involvement
   B. Focusing solely on cost reduction
   C. Ignoring data security concerns
   D. A balanced approach considering technology, human factors and organisational readiness

9. Which of the following is not a benefit of IoT in SCM?

   A. Real-time monitoring
   B. Enhanced visibility across operations
   C. Complete automation of decision-making
   D. Improved responsiveness to changing conditions

10. What is the primary goal of logistics optimisation using AI?

    A. To eliminate the need for transportation
    B. To minimise fuel consumption and enhance delivery efficiency
    C. To replace human drivers with autonomous vehicles
    D. To reduce the number of warehouses

11. Which of the following is a key application of digital twins in supply chains?

    A. Replacing physical assets with virtual ones
    B. Eliminating the need for data analysis
    C. Reducing the need for human workers
    D. Simulating and optimising supply chain processes

12. What is a major challenge in adopting digital twins in supply chains?

    A. Lack of interest from businesses
    B. High costs and specialised knowledge requirements
    C. Inability to integrate with IoT devices
    D. Limited use cases in SCM

13. Which technology is most likely to enhance human–machine collaboration in supply chains?

    A. IoT
    B. AI
    C. Digital twins
    D. XR

14. What is the primary benefit of predictive maintenance in supply chains?

    A. Reducing the need for IoT devices
    B. Minimising equipment downtime and extending machinery lifespan
    C. Eliminating the need for human workers
    D. Reducing the need for data analysis

15. Which of the following is a key recommendation for organisations adopting digital transformation?

    A. Ignoring workforce upskilling
    B. Focusing solely on cost reduction
    C. Prioritising sustainability and data security
    D. Avoiding collaboration with external partners

Essay question

Discuss the role of IoT, AI, digital twins and XR in transforming modern SCM. How do these technologies collectively enhance efficiency, resilience and sustainability in supply chains? Provide examples of real-world applications and highlight the challenges organisations may face in implementing these technologies. Finally, suggest strategies for overcoming these challenges to ensure successful digital transformation.

15

DIGITALISATION, TRACEABILITY AND SENTIMENT ANALYSIS

A paradigm shift in supply chain management

Introduction

In the rapidly evolving landscape of international supply chains, integrating digital technologies has become indispensable for enterprises aiming to enhance operational efficiency, ensure product traceability and capture consumer sentiment. This chapter delves into the transformative potential of blockchain, non-fungible tokens (NFTs) and advanced sentiment analysis in redefining supply chain management (SCM) practices. By exploring the technologies of blockchain, NFTs, and advanced sentiment analysis, this study aims to achieve real-time visibility, end-to-end traceability and a deeper understanding of consumer preferences. Specifically, digital passports and NFTs are deployed to secure product information, ensuring the integrity of the supply chain. Additionally, the effectiveness of natural language processing (NLP) techniques in analysing customer feedback across various platforms is emphasised. However, challenges such as data security, technological complexity and workforce upskilling are also examined. The chapter advocates for collaborative efforts involving policy-makers, industry stakeholders and technology pioneers to overcome these barriers and establish benchmarks for the digitalised supply chain. In conclusion, this chapter delves into the transformative impact of the convergence of digitalisation, traceability and sentiment analysis, reshaping the SCM landscape. It highlights the critical importance of digital innovation in supply chains and advocates for further research and development to overcome existing barriers. The future trajectory focuses on digitalised supply chains enhancing efficiency and value creation through customer insights and sustainable methods.

Learning objectives

After reading this chapter the reader should be able to answer the following:

- Explain the fundamental concepts and importance of digitalisation, traceability and sentiment analysis in modern SCM.
- Identify and describe the five key steps in digital transformation of supply chains: establishing a vision, unifying data and processes, automating planning processes, leveraging data and analytics, and aligning people with processes.

DOI: 10.4324/9781003650973-15

- Evaluate the role of emerging technologies in supply chain traceability, including blockchain implementation, digital passports, NFT platforms, and IoT sensors and monitoring systems.
- Analyse how sentiment analysis and NLP contribute to consumer insight gathering, brand reputation management, supply chain decision-making and market trend identification.
- Assess the challenges and opportunities in implementing integrated digital supply chain solutions, particularly regarding data security considerations, workforce skill requirements, technical infrastructure needs and regulatory compliance.
- Demonstrate understanding of how the synergistic integration of digitalisation, traceability and sentiment analysis can enhance operational efficiency, supply chain transparency, consumer trust and risk management capabilities.

Outline

15.1 Transforming technologies

In the constantly evolving business scenery, enterprises grapple with unprecedented difficulties, striving to strengthen operational effectiveness, maintain product quality and meet escalating consumer expectations. The infusion of digital technologies presents a unique opportunity for organisations to confront these challenges head-on. By leveraging these innovations, companies can overcome obstacles and significantly advance their operational capabilities, product integrity and customer satisfaction, setting new benchmarks for success in today's economy. This chapter posits the critical importance of integrating digitalisation, traceability and sentiment analysis into supply chains, asserting that this convergence is advantageous and necessary in modern enterprises that seek to innovate and be successful. Contemporary corporations face heightened expectations regarding transparency, expedited delivery processes and personalised customer experiences. Moreover, governments and regulatory bodies expect corporations to exercise sustainable and ethical practices, and consumers expect high-quality services. It is evident that many adverse impacts, spanning environmental, economic and social dimensions, stem not from direct operations but from end-to-end supply chain activities, including sourcing, production, distribution and logistics. All this complex web of involved parties renders conventional supply chain models insufficient.

Today's supply chains are evolving beyond mere delivery mechanisms to support customer-centric business models, recognised as strategic assets offering competitive advantages. Digitalisation, traceability and sentiment analysis emerge as pivotal instruments to bridge the gap between existing practices and the increased demands of regulatory bodies and consumers. The synergistic integration of supply chain digitalisation, traceability and sentiment analysis can fundamentally transform operational paradigms. Traceability ensures the integrity and transparency of products across the entire supply chain, while sentiment analysis delves into consumer preferences and market trends. Digitalisation provides the framework for automating and real-time data analytics. When employed together, these components form a robust framework that empowers institutions to maximise operational efficiency, foster greater customer involvement and enhance decision quality.

Digitalisation makes operations more efficient through automation, systematic data management and analytics. Thus, it presents numerous advantages for supply chains, including enhanced access to information, streamlined logistics practices, real-time data capture, more effective inventory management and heightened transparency. Broadly speaking, Industry 4.0 denotes the advancement of production and value creation systems in the section of the physical and digital domains. Upon this section, cyber-physical systems (CPS) are seated, which are regarded as pivotal technological breakthroughs of the Fourth Industrial Revolution. Essentially, a CPS comprises an array of enabling technologies put together to form an autonomous, interconnected, and intelligent system, facilitating integration among diverse and geographically dispersed entities. A CPS can essentially provide data acquisition and data generation, as well as data aggregation and data computation, thus facilitating preventive and reliable decisions. Leveraging these technologies, supply chain entities can undergo digital transformation to enhance performance and sustain or enhance competitiveness. Given the escalating interest in supply chain digitalisation within the academic realm, it becomes pertinent to delineate key focus areas to guide future research endeavours. Traceability ensures that products traversing the supply chain are both tracked and traced. Tracking involves monitoring the downstream movement of a product along the supply chain while tracing entails identifying the origin and characteristics of a specific product by referencing records maintained upstream in the supply chain. Tracing the complete history of a product by systematically documenting all related information regarding its way through the supply chain is imperative for modern enterprises. This necessity stems from various factors, including compliance with mandatory regulations; adherence to international standards and certification requirements; implementation of marketing strategies and programmes; verification of product origin, identity and quality; and, notably, the need for effective measures to combat the proliferation of any product malfunction. In a nutshell, traceability advances product safety and authenticity, nurturing confidence and adherence to regulatory requirements. Social media is vital in modern marketing strategies, offering companies new channels to engage with customers and build brand loyalty. Likewise, in the supply chain, social media facilitates real-time communication, enabling better coordination among partners and enhancing overall product-service quality and operational efficiency. By acquiring new business intelligence sources, social media fosters information sharing and relationship building and improves communication, coordination and performance. Sentiment analysis, a technique analysing text to determine whether it expresses positive, negative or neutral sentiment, can help businesses understand opinions, emotions and attitudes expressed in text data. Therefore, utilising data from social media and other digital platforms, sentiment analysis determines consumers' opinions, enabling businesses to align their strategies with customer expectations. Incorporating the aforementioned three elements, namely, digitalisation, traceability and sentiment analysis, into supply chains signifies a substantial paradigm shift in how organisations conduct business, handle risks, and engage with customers. This chapter contends that by adopting these digital tools, organisations can improve operational efficiency and transparency, cultivate a more profound connection with the respective clientele, and stimulate innovation and sustainability in their operations.

In summary, enterprises can confront contemporary global trade's complex web by integrating digitalisation, traceability and sentiment analysis into SCM. This progressive strategy corresponds to present-day demands and expectations. Thus, organisations that allocate resources to these technologies can have an advantageous edge regarding customer satisfaction, sustainability and operational effectiveness. Incorporating digital tools to enhance operational resilience, responsiveness and transparency is where the trajectory of SCM will ultimately lead.

15.2 Transformation of the supply chain through digitalisation

Within the dynamic and constantly evolving business scenery, the digitalisation of supply chains marks a paradigmatic shift towards heightened operational agility, transparency and efficiency. This section delves into the concept of supply chain digitalisation, unravelling its contemporary relevance and the myriad advantages it offers through digital transformation. By showcasing tangible instances, this exploration illustrates how these advancements have significantly elevated operational effectiveness.

The term digitalisation in SCM encompasses the thorough integration of sophisticated digital technologies into all facets of supply chain activities, ranging from product delivery to procurement. This strategic integration of cutting-edge technologies, such as the Internet of Things (IoT), artificial intelligence (AI), blockchain and cloud computing, aims to enhance data precision, optimise operational procedures and significantly improve the overall effectiveness of supply chains. Adopting digital SCM is paramount in its exceptional ability to address and overcome traditional logistical and operational challenges. Historical issues, such as discrepancies between demand and supply, ineffective inventory management and logistical inefficiencies, have hindered business expansion and failed to meet consumer expectations. Digitalisation represents a paradigm shift in addressing these persistent challenges, providing organisations with a means to attain unparalleled operational oversight and command. Through the adoption of digital technologies, organisations gain the capacity to expedite supply chain processes and substantially reduce operational expenses.

Additionally, this digital revolution facilitates a new era of customer satisfaction through enhanced service provision and promptness. The progression towards digitalisation enhances the efficacy and effectiveness of supply chain operations, enabling organisations to navigate the intricacies of the contemporary global market. In doing so, it establishes a new benchmark for gaining a competitive edge, positioning businesses as leaders in terms of consumer engagement and innovation in the era of digitalisation.

The benefits of supply chain digital transformation are revolutionary. The implementation of digital tools throughout supply chains provides stakeholders with an unparalleled degree of visibility into real-time data. This encompasses comprehensive analyses of inventory levels, shipment advancements, and possible disruptions throughout the supply chain. Providing such extensive visibility facilitates proactive management and permits prompt adjustment to ever-changing market circumstances, guaranteeing that decision-makers are equipped with the most up-to-date and accessible information. Moreover, connectivity improves, enabling uninterrupted communication among all stakeholders in the supply chain, such as manufacturers, suppliers and final consumers. By utilising sophisticated digital platforms, organisations have the ability to optimise the transmission of vital data, thereby substantially mitigating the likelihood of inaccuracies and the protracted durations that are customary for manual procedures. Establishing a cohesive communication infrastructure is crucial for constructing supply chains that are both agile and robust. The ability to utilise vast quantities of precise data for the purpose of making informed decisions is fundamental to digital transformation. By leveraging advanced analytics and artificial intelligence, leaders are able to predict forthcoming trends, optimise resource allocation and formulate strategic decisions grounded in a comprehensive understanding of the market's present condition and future forecasts. This capability facilitates operational excellence and establishes a competitive edge for organisations in an ever more intricate and rapidly evolving global market. The ramifications of these benefits transcend ordinary operational enhancements, cultivating a supply chain ecosystem characterised by increased flexibility, ingenuity and efficiency. In such an ecosystem, leaders in the field will be distinguished by their capacity to respond rapidly to changes, anticipate forthcoming obstacles and sustainably optimise operations. For a more intelligent and interconnected global community, the digital revolution in supply chains, driven by cutting-edge 5G/6G communication technologies, transcends mere technological adoption (Taboada and Shee 2021). It entails a fundamental reevaluation and redefinition of SCM principles, harnessing the transformative power of high-speed, low-latency communication networks. The integration of 5G and the anticipation of 6G technologies elevate the efficiency and responsiveness of supply chains, fostering a seamless and agile global network that adapts to the evolving demands of the modern era.

The transformation of a traditional supply chain into a digitalised one is evidently not a straightforward process. It requires a comprehensive examination of the unique conditions and exceptions influencing each case and a profound end-to-end understanding of the supply chain. Nevertheless, one could argue that the following five steps are crucial to ensuring the successful digitalisation of the supply chain (Balaska et al. 2024), as shown in Figure 15.1.

1. *Establish a vision*: Initiating digital transformation within the supply chain necessitates defining a clear vision that aligns with enterprise goals. These objectives should correspond to overarching business aspirations, such as optimising decision-making processes, automating operations and enhancing supply chain visibility. Identify the essential capabilities required to fulfil transformation goals and identify any existing gaps. Ensure that current systems utilise technology that supports new goals. Verify if the technology aligns with business objectives and identify digital solutions and legacy systems contributing to desired outcomes. Assess the capabilities of existing systems in generating, collecting, and analysing data. Ensure easy access to data for actionable insights. Determine if the workforce possesses the necessary skills to work with and adapt to the new business model.
2. *Unify data and processes*: Opt for a unified platform to achieve comprehensive end-to-end visibility across the supply chain. Enhance transparency to streamline core functions, including inventory levels monitoring, supply chain operations and order forecasting. The primary goal is to elevate visibility for every role and process throughout the extended supply chain.
3. *Automate the planning process*: Simplify tasks and extract meaningful insights from large datasets through automated planning. Replace routine or repetitive tasks with automated

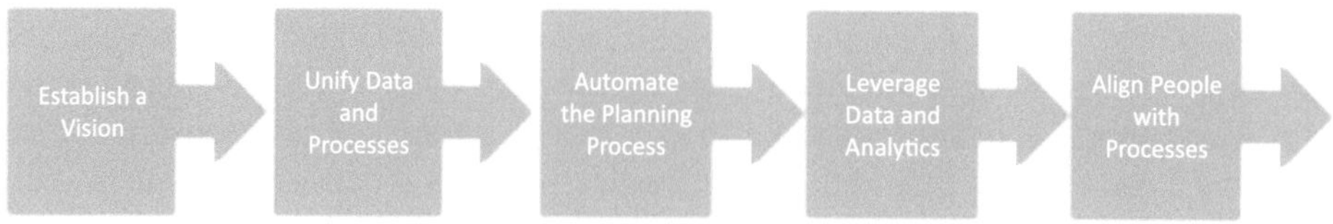

FIGURE 15.1 Five generic steps to digitally transform the supply chain

processes, excluding those involving complex scenarios or necessitating collaboration between planners.

4. *Leverage data and analytics*: Supply chain leaders require real-time access to data for informed decision-making and effective collaboration with partners, suppliers and other stakeholders. Real-time data aids in identifying potential disruptions and enhances overall supply chain visibility. Utilise AI and big data analytics to improve planning processes and derive actionable insights, for example, to prevent stockouts by adjusting inventory levels.
5. *Align people with processes*: Shifting to a digital supply chain is futile unless the workforce is aligned with new techniques and processes. This transition should seamlessly integrate technologies with processes, people and management to ensure teams achieve the desired results in the new business model.

Due to its nature, the supply chain is characterised by vast and complex data produced by monitoring the inventory levels, tracking the production processes, analysing customers' behaviour, overseeing the logistics operations, etc. The analysis of such data can provide unprecedented insights for an organisation. Thus, big data analytics plays a pivotal role in supply chain transformation by digital technologies, ushering in revolutionary benefits. Integrating data analytics tools enables stakeholders to harness vast datasets encompassing various facets of the supply chain. Big data produced by IoT devices empower decision-makers with real-time information, fostering proactive management and timely adjustments to market dynamics. Such data, originating as an extension of data warehouses primarily handling structured data, has introduced new challenges, including data growth, infrastructure, governance/policy, integration, compliance/regulation and visualisation, while offering opportunities for data scientists to develop predictive analytics techniques and uncover unknown dependencies across diverse data sources both within and external to the supply chain, facilitating optimal connectivity. By leveraging digital transformation, organisations enhance communication across stakeholders, creating an uninterrupted flow of information between manufacturers, suppliers and consumers. Implementing advanced digital platforms ensures the seamless transmission of vital data, minimising inaccuracies inherent in manual procedures. This cohesive communication infrastructure is essential to constructing agile and robust supply chains, laying the foundation for enhanced operational efficiency.

Digitalisation in SCM necessitates a cultural shift within organisations, emphasising the need for reskilling and upskilling the workforce. The integration of cutting-edge technologies, such as AI and IoT, demands a workforce equipped with the skills to navigate and leverage these innovations effectively. Reskilling and upskilling initiatives become imperative to ensure that employees possess the digital literacy required for optimal utilisation of digital tools. Furthermore, the cultural change associated with digital transformation transcends traditional supply chain models. It involves fostering a mindset of adaptability and continuous learning, where employees embrace technological advancements as opportunities for growth rather than disruptions. This cultural shift is essential for cultivating an environment conducive to successfully implementing digital strategies in SCM, ultimately leading to increased operational effectiveness.

Digital transformation goes beyond mere technological adoption; it signifies a fundamental reevaluation of SCM principles, leading to the evolution of traditional models into business intelligence-driven frameworks. The amalgamation of digitalisation, traceability, and sentiment analysis fundamentally transforms operational paradigms, positioning organisations to thrive in the intricate and rapidly evolving global market. As a result of digital transformation, business intelligence involves the systematic collection and analysis of data from various supply chain components. This comprehensive approach enhances decision-making capabilities, allowing leaders to predict trends, optimise resource allocation and formulate strategic decisions based on a thorough understanding of the market's present condition and future forecasts. The integration of business intelligence into supply chain models establishes a competitive edge, fostering innovation and sustainability in the era of digitalisation.

15.3 Traceability solutions for end-to-end visibility

This section delves into the evolving area of traceability within the context of digital technologies. We seek to offer a comprehensive insight into the transformative impact of digital technologies on traceability, contributing to a more transparent, efficient and secure global ecosystem through an examination of current trends and expert insights (Chan 2022). Achieving visibility within supply chains is a non-trivial problem marked by various challenges, including the dispersion of visibility data across different enterprises, geographical locations and information systems. Additionally, the need for efficient traceability compounds these challenges, mainly when dealing with disparate legacy enterprise information and communication systems. The heterogeneity of distributed databases further complicates matters, as does the global sourcing and manufacturing landscape, which adds layers of complexity to modern supply chains. Moreover, the nature of visibility data itself adds to the complexity, as it can vary from being lot-based, product class-based, or stock-keeping unit-based for certain products and parts to item-based for others. These complexities underscore the intricate nature of achieving visibility within supply chains and highlight the importance of addressing these challenges to ensure the successful deployment of visibility platforms. The rapid advancements in information and communication technology have catalysed fundamental changes in how products, information and services traverse various sectors. The digital era has ushered in many tools and platforms, including blockchain, digital ledgers, IoT devices and cloud computing, significantly enhancing traceability systems' accuracy, efficiency and reliability. This evolution underscores the importance of leveraging cutting-edge technologies to adapt to the complexities of modern supply chains.

Adopting traceability in supply chains yields several benefits, chief among them being the improvement of end-to-end visibility. Enterprises can now effectively track goods and assets as they navigate through the intricacies of the supply chain, providing real-time insights into order statuses, inventory levels and delivery times. Contrary to barcode and RFID technologies, which are used to track location only, the IoT sensor can be used to additionally provide other modalities information, such as temperature, pressure, exposure to light, vibration and humidity, thus enhancing the visibility of the product through its journey on the supply chain. This heightened enhances operational efficiency and enables proactive decision-making. While the location information can identify potential bottlenecks and swiftly implement corrective measures, the rest of the sensorial information can accommodate product recall if the environmental conditions are unsuitable, especially for sensitive products such as food or pharmaceuticals. Thus, high-end traceability enhances customer satisfaction by facilitating precise and timely updates on order statuses and safety by delivering high-quality products. Both these are prime factors in fostering customer's contentment and loyalty. Moreover, traceability is crucial beyond operational enhancements in ensuring compliance with regulatory standards, particularly in sensitive areas such as food safety and hazardous materials handling. By enabling organisations to adhere to stringent regulations, traceability reinforces consumer confidence in the safety and integrity of products.

Traceability within supply chains has evolved into a fundamental necessity, driven by the intricate web of global trade, burgeoning consumer demands for transparency and stringent regulatory mandates. It goes beyond the simple monitoring of products or components, encompassing an advanced capability to document the complete trajectory of an object, comprising its background, usage and exact whereabouts, through carefully documented identifiers. Traceability, an essential component in contemporary supply chain ecosystems, guarantees operational supervision starting from the point of production and continuing through multiple handling phases until the final delivery. The capability in question possesses a multifaceted significance as it not only enhances standards for product safety and quality control but also facilitates recall processes and strengthens consumer confidence by providing information regarding the origin and path of goods. With the increasing complexity of global supply chains, traceability assumes a more critical role in ensuring product lifecycle management's integrity, accountability and transparency.

Blockchain technology holds significant promise for revolutionising various aspects of supply chain operations, encompassing supply chain provenance, business process reengineering, and security enhancement. The blockchain architecture is designed to ensure the security and transparency of supply chains. In a typical blockchain system mechanism, each block is assigned a 256-bit hash number, generated through a consensus mechanism by a mathematical algorithm. The blocks are interconnected, referencing the previous block's hash, forming a secure and autonomous chain. Prior to inclusion in the blockchain, blocks undergo validation, often through proof of work mechanisms, commonly referred to as 'blockchain mining'. Once validated, a block becomes an integral part of the network's auditable and immutable blockchain ledger.

Additionally, the blockchain incorporates a built-in defence mechanism. Specifically, any detected corruption deemed malicious by the blockchain, including attempts to alter blocks and change hash functions, is identified and addressed. In cases of corruption, the affected block within the compromised node undergoes correction to maintain the integrity of the blockchain. Blockchain technology plays a crucial role in securely documenting and time-stamping every stage of the production and distribution process on a decentralised and tamper-resistant ledger. This feature ensures that stakeholders – consumers, distributors, producers and retailers – have access to accurate and up-to-date data regarding food items' production, management, and movement. The transparency blockchain offers fosters consumer confidence and is a powerful tool for ensuring quality control and compliance with regulations. The implementation of blockchain technology in various industries has significantly reduced fraudulent practices. Due to its immutability, blockchain data guarantees that once information is entered, it cannot be modified, providing a reliable and auditable ledger for each transaction along the supply chain. Furthermore, integrating blockchain technology in the supply chain enhances the efficiency of product recalls related to contamination or safety concerns. By maintaining an up-to-date and accurate log of each product's entire trajectory, stakeholders can promptly identify and isolate compromised quantities, thereby minimising the impact on public health and reducing financial setbacks for enterprises. Incorporating blockchain technology into the supply chain improves overall operational effectiveness and establishes the foundation for trust, transparency, and security.

The introduction of the digital passport, a secure, intangible and portable document, represents a significant advancement in SCM, serving as an extensive repository of essential information, including a product's complete supply chain history, place of origin, and inherent qualities. These digital entities go beyond ordinary informational assets, effectively mitigating risks associated with counterfeit merchandise, ensuring regulatory compliance and facilitating prompt responses to potential disruptions. The importance of end-to-end visibility enabled by digital passports cannot be overstated, providing stakeholders with actionable, real-time insights, ensuring product authenticity, streamlining decision-making processes and substantially improving supply chain efficiencies. Integrating digital passports in the supply chain infrastructures addresses prevalent challenges, including the proliferation of counterfeit goods, safety discrepancies and logistical challenges of recall initiatives. For example, in the extensively regulated pharmaceutical industry, digital passports serve as unequivocal assurances regarding the genuineness and security of medications. Simultaneously, they provide consumers with unprecedented transparency regarding the sourcing and management of a product, ensuring its quality and safety in the food industry. The adoption of digital passports signifies not only technological advancement but also a paradigm shift contributing to the development of supply chains that are more resilient, transparent and consumer-centric. The implementation of digital passports and the trend toward advanced traceability in supply chains evidence an unwavering commitment to achieving high standards in international commerce. This societal movement initiates a paradigm shift where consumer confidence, efficiency and transparency converge, establishing a global supply chain ecosystem that is more dependable, secure and sustainable.

As society increasingly embraces the digital era, the ongoing development and integration of these technologies will inevitably influence the trajectory of SCM, establishing fresh standards for efficient operations and customer contentment. The evolution of digital passports is significantly propelled by technological advancements, notably the incorporation of blockchain technology and the emergence of NFTs, acting as catalysts for transformative changes. The decentralised and immutable nature of the blockchain ledger system enhances the security and integrity of digital passports, creating a highly dependable and tamper-proof framework. The adoption of NFT platforms represents a substantial shift in product authentication and lifecycle management, positioning digital passports at the forefront of technological progress. Visualised in Figure 15.2, the stages

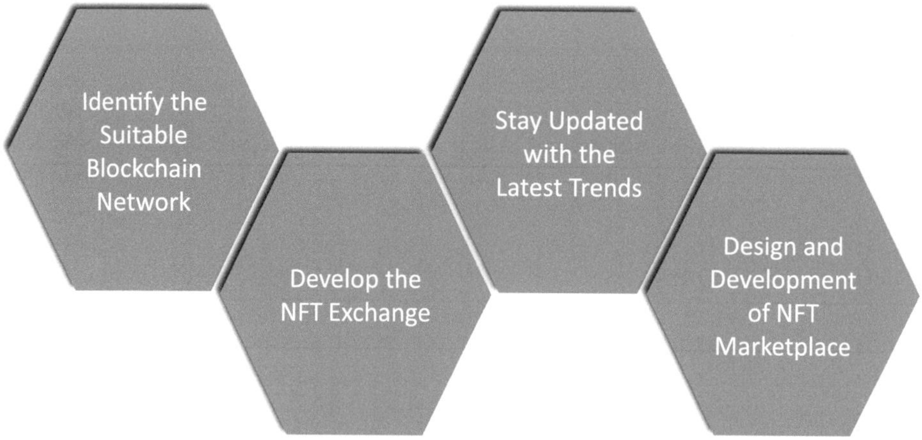

FIGURE 15.2 Stages of creating an NFT ecosystem: (a) identification of the suitable blockchain network, (b) development of the NFT exchange, (c) staying updated with the latest trends and (d) design and development of NFT marketplace

of building an NFT ecosystem highlight the development steps, including identifying a suitable blockchain network, developing an NFT exchange, staying updated with the latest trends and designing and developing an NFT marketplace (Balaska et al. 2024).

NFTs, as unique digital identifiers, introduce a paradigm shift by enabling the creation of digital replicas for tangible merchandise. These digital counterparts serve as enduring digital passports containing a comprehensive and unalterable log of a product's provenance, ownership, and transaction history. The implementation of NFTs in supply chains opens new avenues for product authentication, allowing consumers to verify the authenticity and past ownership of goods with unparalleled precision. Thus, consumer confidence is enhanced, and transparency and security benchmarks are elevated within the supply chain. Moreover, such innovative use of NFTs presents a dynamic approach to overseeing ownership and lifecycles, potentially transforming operational procedures in luxury goods, art and collectibles. NFT-based digital passports offer an innovative solution in industries where the provenance and authenticity of goods are paramount, ensuring the traceability and verifiability of high-value items. The strategic integration of traceability systems, digital passports and NFT platforms is redefining the operational frameworks of supply chains. This integration fosters unprecedented levels of transparency, efficiency and trust among stakeholders and consumers. While the progression of these technologies holds the potential to substantially enhance the security, sustainability, and resilience of supply chains globally, fully exploiting these benefits requires addressing the complexities associated with integration, strengthening data safeguards and prioritising personnel training to navigate these digital environments effectively. The trajectory of SCM in the coming years is closely tied to organisations' capacity to leverage and adapt to these digital transformations, aligning with the ever-changing global trade needs and the rigorous standards set by regulatory agencies. Despite challenges, the path towards fully digitalised, NFT-enhanced supply chains presents a forward-thinking trajectory facilitating the development of a worldwide supply network that is more consumer-focused, transparent, and secure.

15.4 Sentiment analysis

Sentiment analysis, also known as opinion mining, is a domain that utilises NLP, text analysis, computational linguistics and biometrics to systematically identify, extract, quantify and study affective states and subjective information. Consequently, sentiment analysis involves interpreting the emotional nuances conveyed by a string of words to comprehend the attitudes, opinions and emotions expressed in online content. Sentiment analysis has emerged as a prominent approach to tackle the volume, variety and velocity of qualitative data on social media platforms. Sentiment analysis focuses specifically on discerning emotions or sentiments conveyed in online posts, capturing consumers' feelings as expressed in their comments on social media. Businesses employ sentiment analysis to monitor real-time customer feedback, identify areas of dissatisfaction and promptly address them to enhance the overall customer experience. By analysing a product's collective comments and reviews, a firm gains valuable insights into the overall sentiment and perception of the product within the marketplace. A product that fails to gain traction in the market is more likely to face withdrawal. Early indications of reduced impact following a product release may prompt supply managers to adjust their capacity or order commitments that support its manufacturing.

Additionally, discussions surrounding specific product features can inform future product development strategies. Identification of a substantial number of interested consumers may signal imminent large-scale sales. Leveraging sentiment analysis data can also reveal fluctuations in product sales, akin to insights derived from the analysis of point-of-sale data shared across the supply chain.

Thus, the primary objective of this process is to grasp the sentiment of the target audience, significantly influencing marketing strategies. Understanding what resonates or displeases the audience allows marketers to design more effective campaigns, leading to increased engagement and conversion rates. Analysing vast amounts of data from social media, reviews and other textual sources enables businesses to gain insights into customer sentiment regarding products, services or brands. This technology allows automated text analysis and exploration of the emotional tone hidden in the text, providing an efficient and scalable approach to gauge public opinion. Upstream operating enterprises can monitor and analyse consumer sentiments expressed online regarding their products or similar products, allowing them to gauge market preferences and potential changes in consumer behaviour. The fact that such enterprises are involved in manufacturing or distributing products, before they reach the end consumer, allow them the advantage to access valuable data on market-based demand and product reception through sentiment analysis or opinion mining.

The majority of traditional NLP analyses rely on machine learning and AI technologies. In each instance, it is imperative to grasp not only the words themselves but also the underlying concepts and their interconnections to generate meaningful information. The crucial role of AI technologies in obtaining valuable insights into consumer preferences and purchasing patterns and facilitating data-driven business decisions is well-described in Babu et al. (2023). Additionally, applying NLP techniques to unearth consumer-brand relationships from social media data is imperative. A methodological framework proposed for leveraging NLP and machine learning techniques to address challenges in analysing consumer opinions and sentiments from large datasets offers valuable insights for both academic research and practitioners. The integration of sentiment analysis with digitalised supply chains and traceability solutions is increasingly acknowledged as a pivotal strategy for enhancing brand reputation and effectively managing crises. By scrutinising social media and online content, sentiment analysis provides real-time insights into consumer attitudes and perceptions, significantly impacting a brand's image and crisis management capabilities. This integration helps businesses proactively identify and address issues that could harm their reputation, ensuring more responsive and targeted crisis management strategies.

The role of sentiment analysis in enhancing supply chain intelligence, improving collaboration and facilitating information sharing among supply chain members can positively affect supply chain performance. As discussed below, transparency and decision-making are enhanced by integrating sentiment analysis, supply chain responsiveness is improved and brand monitoring in social media is achieved. Applying sentiment analysis in supply chains enhances transparency, enabling better decision-making. Prior research (Wood et al. 2014) explored how sentiment analysis can enhance sales and operations planning by incorporating exogenous information and improving supply chain decisions and performance. By integrating sentiment analysis, supply chains can better respond to market changes. The impact of supply chain integration on performance suggests that strategic collaboration and information sharing are crucial for responsiveness and value delivery (Flynn et al. 2010). Companies can monitor their brand's reputation in real-time through sentiment analysis, identifying and addressing negative sentiments before they escalate into more significant issues. Another study (Tedeschi and Benedetto 2015) proposed a cloud-based extensive data sentiment analysis application for brand monitoring, demonstrating its utility in enhancing brand reputation and tracking. In recent years, deep learning models like bidirectional encoder representations from transformers (BERT) have become commonplace in sentiment analysis, offering valuable insights into customer sentiment and helping identify changing customer trends, patterns, and preferences. BERT allows researchers and businesses to perform better in accurately classifying sentiments, particularly in social media data, which presents unique challenges due to its unstructured nature, informal language, and abundance of noise. A meta-analysis indicates a positive correlation between supply chain integration and firm performance, confirming the beneficial impact of sentiment analysis on the supply chain. Such integration enhances the responsiveness and adaptability of supply chains to market changes, contributing to improved firm performance.

Today, integrating sentiment analysis with large language models (LLMs) marks a significant advance in comprehending consumer sentiments, preferences, and behaviours by analysing unstructured textual data from diverse online platforms. The adeptness of LLMs, reinforced by sophisticated deep learning models like BERT and the application of Recurrent Neural Network (RNN) models with gated recurrent unit (GRU) and bidirectional GRU layers, showcases a profound ability to navigate the complexities of social media data. This evolution in technology amplifies sentiment classification accuracy and broadens the horizon for businesses to derive actionable insights from consumer feedback. Research studies (Jain et al. 2021; Rudra and Gopalakrishnan 2023) emphasise the precision of these models in sentiment analysis, while highlighting machine learning techniques' expansive applicability across various domains. LLMs can look into market trends and supplier performance, helping businesses make informed decisions about procurement and distribution. Moreover, they can analyse sentiment data to forecast demand accurately, enabling businesses to optimise inventory levels and production schedules, and personalise their supply chain strategies based on customer preferences, ultimately improving satisfaction and loyalty. This synergy between AI and sentiment analysis through LLMs hides an unparalleled tool for businesses to monitor brand reputation, tailor marketing strategies, and refine customer experiences in real-time, fostering a deeper connection with their consumer base through data-driven insights.

Therefore, integrating sentiment analysis with digitalised supply chains and traceability solutions is critical for enhancing brand reputation. By leveraging real-time consumer sentiment data, companies can proactively address issues, make informed decisions and maintain a positive brand image. This strategic integration ensures that businesses are both reactive and proactive in managing their brand reputation and responding to market dynamics effectively.

15.5 Advantages and challenges

The collaborative impact of integrated digitalisation, traceability and sentiment analysis has proven transformative across diverse industries, elevating operational efficiency, transparency and consumer understanding. This amalgamation has notably revolutionised the contemporary supply chain, contributing to substantial safety and consumer trust advancements and opening avenues for innovation across sectors. Digitalisation forms the basis for incorporating advanced technologies into business processes optimising data collection, processing and utilisation. Traceability ensures the comprehensive tracking of products throughout the supply chain, guaranteeing quality control, authenticity and compliance with safety standards. Simultaneously, sentiment analysis utilises big data analytics to comprehend consumer emotions and opinions, enabling businesses to tailor their offerings and communications more effectively. The integration of these elements has resulted in noteworthy enhancements in safety standards and consumer trust. Digital technologies powering traceability systems allow rapid identification and resolution of contamination, adulteration, fraud, forgery and other issues, significantly reducing consumer risks. Sentiment analysis tools empower businesses to assess customers' reactions, fostering a more responsive and consumer-centric approach. Several studies (Erevelles et al. 2016; Jin et al. 2016; Kauffmann et al. 2020) have explored the transformative potential of big data analytics, including sentiment analysis, in improving marketing activities and consumer insights through a resource-based framework. Additionally, past research (Buell et al. 2017). (Moussa et al. 2022) has underscored how operational transparency can positively influence customer perceptions, enhance service quality and efficiency, and emphasise the advantages of digitalisation and traceability. The integration of digitalisation, traceability and sentiment analysis can improve operational efficiencies, elevate product quality and deepen consumer insights across sectors like healthcare, manufacturing and retail. For example, tracking patient data and sentiment in healthcare can improve patient outcomes and satisfaction. In manufacturing, the combination of traceability and digitalisation can streamline production processes and enhance product quality. The collaborative integration of digitalisation, traceability, and sentiment analysis has already demonstrated its ability to improve operational efficiency, transparency and consumer insight, especially in the food industry. Its potential for fostering innovation and transformation across various other sectors is substantial. By leveraging these technologies, businesses can enhance operational efficiencies and cultivate stronger consumer relationships through improved transparency and responsiveness.

The convergence of sentiment analysis, digitalisation and traceability presents a promising realm for enhancing operational efficiency, transparency and consumer insights across various industries. However, this integration comes with significant challenges needing resolution to harness its capabilities thoroughly. Key challenges in this domain involve concerns related to data security, the necessity for skilled personnel and the crucial responsibility borne by technology pioneers, policy-makers and industry stakeholders in overcoming these obstacles. The widespread use of digital tools and platforms heightens the susceptibility to data breaches and cyberattacks. The integration of traceability, sentiment analysis and digitalisation involves handling vast amounts of confidential consumer information, necessitating stringent measures to safeguard against unauthorised access and cyber threats. Failure to do so may lead to substantial financial losses, diminished consumer confidence and legal consequences. Policymakers play a pivotal role in establishing a conducive environment for these technologies' expansion and secure integration. This includes implementing data protection regulations, supporting cybersecurity initiatives and promoting research and development investment. Within the industry sector, stakeholders, including trade associations and enterprises, must invest in developing the skills of their workforce to meet the growing demand for technical expertise. Ensuring a continuous supply of proficient professionals requires collaboration with academic institutions to align educational curricula with industry demands. Technology pioneers actively address the technical challenges arising in sentiment analysis, traceability and digitalisation. They can lower adoption barriers for organisations of all sizes by creating more secure frameworks for data processing and intuitive analytics tools.

The integration of digitalisation, traceability and sentiment analysis is expected to drive substantial innovation in the future. Potential developments may include the implementation of AI for more precise sentiment analysis, leveraging blockchain technology to enhance data security and traceability, and crafting personalised consumer experiences through machine learning algorithms. Exploring promising data encryption techniques, developing artificial intelligence models to understand better and predict consumer behaviour, and investigating the ethical implications of using consumer data for business insights are potential research areas. Further research could delve into the potential cross-sector implementations of these technologies, including analysing patient sentiment in the healthcare sector and implementing real-time traceability in SCM.

Synopsis

In the fast-changing landscape of international supply chains, integrating digital technologies like blockchain, NFTs and advanced sentiment analysis is essential for enhancing operational efficiency, product traceability and capturing consumer sentiment. This chapter explores their transformative potential, highlighting key findings and implications for business operations.

The integration of traceability, sentiment analysis and supply chain digitalisation marks a paradigm shift, enhancing efficiency, transparency and consumer insight. Digitalisation streamlines processes, traceability ensures product tracking and sentiment analysis provides consumer behaviour insights. This synergy boosts efficiency, reduces costs and enhances customer satisfaction.

This fusion also fosters transparency, with blockchain creating immutable records of product movements, increasing accountability. Consumers trust brands that can substantiate their products' authenticity and ethical procurement. Sentiment analysis helps businesses understand and predict consumer behaviour, allowing for customised offerings and promotional tactics.

Enterprises should set clear goals for integrating these technologies, align them with business objectives and invest in staff training or hire skilled personnel. Cybersecurity measures are crucial to safeguard digital infrastructure. Collaborating with solutions providers grants access to cutting-edge technologies and facilitates implementation. Policymakers play a role in creating a conducive environment through data protection regulations, cybersecurity support and promoting research and development.

In conclusion, the amalgamation of traceability, sentiment analysis and digitalisation has the potential to revolutionise business operations. Effective implementation requires a strategic approach, investment in capabilities, data safeguarding, cooperation with technology providers and readiness to adapt. The future of SCM is digital, with opportunities for enhancing efficiency, transparency and consumer satisfaction continuing to grow. By staying updated on technological advancements, investing in talent development and fostering industry collaboration, organisations can unlock the full potential of the digitalised supply chain and drive sustainable growth.

Multiple-choice questions

1. Which of the following is not one of the five generic steps to digitally transform the supply chain?

   A. Establish a vision
   B. Unify data and processes
   C. Implement blockchain technology
   D. Leverage data and analytics

2. What is a key advantage of IoT sensors over traditional barcode and RFID technologies in supply chain traceability?

   A. Lower cost
   B. Faster scanning capabilities
   C. Greater scanning range
   D. Ability to monitor environmental conditions like temperature and humidity

3. In blockchain technology, what happens when corruption is detected in a block?

   A. The entire blockchain is deleted
   B. The affected block within the compromised node undergoes correction
   C. The system shuts down automatically
   D. A new blockchain is created

4. What is the primary purpose of digital passports in SCM?

   A. To store a product's complete supply chain history and characteristics
   B. To track employee movements
   C. To replace physical documentation
   D. To manage inventory levels

5. Which technology is crucial for accurately classifying sentiments in social media data?

   A. RFID
   B. NFT
   C. BERT
   D. GPS

6. What is the main advantage of integrating sentiment analysis with LLMs?

   A. Enhanced understanding of consumer sentiments from unstructured data
   B. Reduced operational costs
   C. Improved inventory management
   D. Better supplier relationships

7. In the context of supply chain digitalisation, what is the primary function of cyber-physical systems?

   A. To provide cybersecurity
   B. To facilitate integration among diverse and geographically dispersed entities
   C. To manage employee schedules
   D. To control production machinery

8. What is the main challenge in achieving supply chain visibility?

   A. High cost of implementation
   B. Lack of technology
   C. Dispersion of visibility data across different enterprises and systems
   D. Employee resistance

9. In NFT implementation, what is the first stage of creating an NFT ecosystem?

   A. Developing the NFT exchange
   B. Identifying a suitable blockchain network
   C. Designing the NFT marketplace
   D. Staying updated with trends

10. Which of the following best describes the role of sentiment analysis in SCM?

   A. Managing inventory levels
   B. Tracking shipment locations
   C. Monitoring supplier performance
   D. Understanding consumer opinions and emotions about products

11. What is a key benefit of implementing digital transformation in supply chains?

   A. Reduced need for human workers
   B. Enhanced real-time visibility of operations
   C. Elimination of all manual processes
   D. Decreased technology costs

12 How does traceability contribute to product safety?

   A. By increasing production speed
   B. By reducing transportation costs
   C. By enabling quick identification and isolation of compromised products
   D. By automating quality control

13. What role do policy-makers play in supply chain digitalisation?

   A. Direct implementation of technologies
   B. Providing funding for all companies
   C. Managing day-to-day operations
   D. Establishing data protection regulations and supporting cybersecurity initiatives

14. What is the primary purpose of integrating blockchain in supply chain traceability?

   A. To reduce operational costs
   B. To create a secure and tamper-resistant ledger
   C. To increase production speed
   D. To manage employee schedules

15. Which aspect of supply chain digitalisation requires significant attention to workforce development?

   A. Reskilling and upskilling of employees
   B. Hardware installation
   C. Software updates
   D. Marketing strategies

Essay question

How the integration of digitalisation, traceability and sentiment analysis transforms modern SCM?

In your response, you should discuss on the following:

- The key benefits and challenges of implementing these technologies.
- How these technologies work together to enhance operational efficiency.
- The role of emerging technologies like blockchain and NFTs.
- The impact on consumer trust and satisfaction.
- Future implications for SCM.

Please provide specific examples to support your arguments and consider both the technological and human aspects of this transformation.

BIBLIOGRAPHY

Aaker, D., and Shansby, G. (1982). Positioning your product. *Business Horizons* (May–June): 56–62.

Aaker, D. A. (1989). Managing assets and skills: The key to a sustainable competitive advantage. *California Management Review* 31(2): 91–106.

Aaker, D. A. (2001). *Strategic Market Management* (6th edition). New York: John Wiley & Sons.

Aamer, A., Eka Yani, L. P., and Priyatna, I. M. A. (2020). Data analytics in the supply chain management: Review of machine learning applications in demand forecasting. *Operations and Supply Chain Management: An International Journal* 14(1): 1–13.

Aamer, A., Sahara, C. R., and Al-Awlaqi, M. A. (2022). Digitalization of the supply chain: Transformation factors. *Journal of Science and Technology Policy Management*. https://doi.org/10.1108/jstpm-01-2021-0001.

Abideen, A. Z., Sundram, V. P. K., Pyeman, J., Othman, A. K., and Sorooshian, S. (2021). Digital twin integrated reinforced learning in supply chain and logistics. *Logistics* 5. https://doi.org/10.3390/logistics5040084.

Abolghasemi, M., Beh, E., Tarr, G., and Gerlach, R. (2020). Demand forecasting in supply chain: The impact of demand volatility in the presence of promotion. *Computers & Industrial Engineering* 142: 106380.

Abouzid, I., and Saidi, R. (2023). Digital twin implementation approach in supply chain processes. *Scientific African* 21: e01821.

Adhicandra, I., Tanwir, T., Asfahani, A., Sitopu, J. W., and Irawan, F. (2024). Latest innovations in internet of things (IoT): Digital transformation across industries. *Innovative: Journal of Social Science Research* 4(3): 1027–1037.

Agarwal, M. (1995). Review of a 40-year debate in international advertising. *International Marketing Review* 12(1): 26–48.

Aghdam, N., Rahmani, A. M., and Hosseinzadeh, M. (2021). The role of the internet of things in healthcare: Future trends and challenges. *Computer Methods and Programs in Biomedicine* 199: 105903.

Agrawal, P., and Narain, R. (2023). Analysis of enablers for the digitalization of supply chain using an interpretive structural modelling approach. *International Journal of Productivity and Performance Management* 72(2): 410–439.

Agrawal, P., Narain, R., and Ullah, I. (2019). Analysis of barriers in implementation of digital transformation of supply chain using interpretive structural modelling approach. *Journal of Modelling in Management* 15(1): 297–317. https://doi.org/10.1108/JM2-03-2019-0066.

Alhakamy, A. A. (2024). Extended reality (XR) toward building immersive solutions: The key to unlocking industry 4.0. *ACM Computing Surveys* 56(9): 1–38.

Aliakbari Nouri, F., Shafiei Nikabadi, M., and Olfat, L. (2020). Sustainable service supply chain practices (SSSCPs): A framework development. *International Journal of Productivity and Performance Management* 69(4): 813–833.

Aljohani, A. (2023). Predictive analytics and machine learning for real-time supply chain risk mitigation and agility. *Sustainability* 15(20): 15088.
Allen, T. J. (1986). *Managing the Flow of Technology*. Cambridge, MA: MIT Press.
Allied Market Research. (2024). Events industry market; size, share, competitive landscape and trend analysis report, by type, by revenue source, by organiser, by age group, by origin of attendees, by event location: Global opportunity analysis and industry forecast, 2024–2035. Report Code: A02091. https://www.alliedmarketresearch.com/events-industry-market. Last visited 12 January 2025.
American Marketing Association (AMA). (2013). About AMA: Definition of marketing (approved by AMA Board of Directors, July 2013). https://marketing-dictionary.org/m/marketing/#cite_note-1. Last visited 30 October 2024.
American Marketing Association. (2016). www.ama.org/aboutama/pages/definition-of-marketing.aspx.
Anderson, D. L., Britt, F. F., and Favre, D. J. (2007). The 7 principles of supply chain management. *Supply Chain Management Review* 11(3): 41–46.
Anderson, E., and Coughlan, A. T. (1987). International market entry and expansion via independent or integrated channels of distribution. *Journal of Marketing* 51(1): 71–82.
Angelmar, R., and Pinson, C. (1975). The meaning of marketing. *Philosophy of Science* (June): 208–214.
Ante, L. (2021). Non-fungible token (NFT) markets on the Ethereum blockchain: Temporal development, cointegration and interrelations. *Economics of Innovation and New Technology* 32: 1216–1234. https://doi.org/10.1080/10438599.2022.2119564.
Armstrong, G., and Kotler, P. (2009). *Marketing: An Introduction* [in Greek] (9th edition). Athens: Epikentro Publications.
Avlonitis, G. J. (2001). *Strategic Industrial Marketing* [in Greek] (2nd edition). Piraeus: Stamoulis Publications.
Avlonitis, G. J., and Gounaris, S. P. (1999). Marketing orientation and its determinants: An empirical analysis. *European Journal of Marketing* 33(11/12): 1003–1037.
Avlonitis, G. J., and Papastathopoulou, P. (2004). *The Efficient Management of the Products and Services Portfolio* [in Greek]. Piraeus: Stamoulis Publications.
Awan, U., Kanwal, N., Alawi, S., Huiskonen, J., and Dahanayake, A. (2021). Artificial intelligence for supply chain success in the era of data analytics. In *The Fourth Industrial Revolution: Implementation of Artificial Intelligence for Growing Business Success*, 3–21. Springer.
Aykol, B., and Leonidou, L. C. (2015). Researching the green practices of smaller service firms: A theoretical, methodological and empirical assessment. *Journal of Small Business Management* 53(4): 1264–1288.
Babu, E., Ritvik, K., Sainath, L., and Sai, M. T. (2023). Blockchain-driven agricultural product traceability and supply chain management. In *2023 5th International Conference on Inventive Research in Computing Applications (ICIRCA)*, 1202–1207. https://doi.org/10.1109/ICIRCA57980.2023.10220840.
Babu, S. M., Kumar, P. P., Devi, S., Reddy, K. P., and Satish, M. (2023). Predicting consumer behaviour with artificial intelligence. In *2023 IEEE 5th International Conference on Cybernetics, Cognition and Machine Learning Applications (ICC-CMLA)*, 698–703. IEEE.
Badawy, W. (2023). Data-driven framework for evaluating digitization and artificial intelligence risk: A comprehensive analysis. *AI and Ethics*, 1–26.
Bagozzi, R. P. (1975). Marketing as exchange. *Journal of Marketing* 39: 32–39.
Baines, T. S., Lightfoot, H. W., Benedettini, O., and Kay, J. M. (2009). The servitization of manufacturing: A review of literature and reflection on future challenges. *Journal of Manufacturing Technology Management* 20(5): 547–567.
Balakera, N., Konstantinidis, F. K., Tsimiklis, G., Latsa, E., and Amditis, A. (2023). IIoT network system from data collection to cyber-physical system transmission under the Industry 5.0 era. In *International Congress on Information and Communication Technology*, 929–941. Springer.
Balaska, V., Folinas, D., Konstantinidis, F. K., and Gasteratos, A. (2022). Smart counting of unboxed stocks in the warehouse 4.0 ecosystem. In *2022 IEEE International Conference on Imaging Systems and Techniques (IST)*, 1–6. IEEE.
Balaska, V., Symeonidis, S., Antoniou, S., Fotiadis, T., Chatzoglou, P., and Gasteratos, A. (2024). Digitalising the supply chain for enhanced efficiency and customer satisfaction. In *Olympus International Conference on Supply Chains*, 321–334. Springer Nature Switzerland.
Balaska, V., Tsiakas, K., Giakoumis, I., Kostavelis, D., Folinas, A., Gasteratos, D., and Tzovaras, S. (2022). A viewpoint on the challenges and solutions for driverless last-mile delivery. *Machines* 10(11): 1059.
Ballou, R. (1999). *Business Logistics Management: Planning, Organizing and Controlling the Supply Chain* (4th edition). Englewood Cliffs, NJ: Prentice-Hall.

Baltacioglu, T., Ada, E., Kaplan, M. D., Yurt And, O., and Cem Kaplan, Y. (2007). A new framework for service supply chains. *The Service Industries Journal* 27(2): 105–124.
Bansal, P. (2005). Evolving sustainably: A longitudinal study of corporate sustainable development. *Strategic Management Journal* 26(3): 197–218.
Barney, J. (1991). Firm resources and sustained competitive advantage. *Journal of Management* 17(1): 99–120.
Baryann, G., Validi, S., Dani, S., and Antoniou, G. (2019). Supply chain risk management and artificial intelligence: State of the art and future research directions. *International Journal of Production Research* 57(7): 2179–2202.
Barykin, S. Y., Bochkarev, A. A., Dobronravin, E., and Sergeev, S. M. (2021). The place and role of digital twin in supply chain management. *Academy of Strategic Management Journal* 20: 1–19.
Baum, C., and Di Maio, A. (2000). Gartner's four phases of e-government model. www.gartner.com/DisplayDocument?id=317292.
Bawa, A., and Kansal, P. (2008). Cognitive dissonance and the marketing of services: Some issues. *Journal of Services Research* 8(2): 31.
Bayus, B. L. (1985). Word of mouth-the indirect effects of marketing efforts. *Journal of Advertising Research* 25(3): 31–39.
Beaujean, M., Davidson, J., and Madge, S. (2006). The 'moment of truth' in customer service. *McKinsey Quarterly* 1: 62–73.
Belhadi, A., Kamble, S., Fosso Wamba, S., and Queiroz, M. M. (2022). Building supply chain resilience: An artificial intelligence-based technique and decision-making framework. *International Journal of Production Research* 60(14): 4487–4507.
Belhadi, A., Mani, V., Kamble, S. S., Khan, S. A. R., and Verma, S. (2021). Artificial intelligence-driven innovation for enhancing supply chain resilience and performance under the effect of supply chain dynamism: an empirical investigation. *Annals of Operations Research*: 1–26.
Bell, M. (1982). *Marketing Concepts and Strategy* (2nd edition). Boston, MA: Houghton Mifflin.
Bensaou, M. (1999). Portfolios of buyer-supplier relationships. *Sloan Management Review* 40(4): 35–44.
Benton, R. (1987). The practical domain of marketing: The notion of a 'free' enterprise market economy as a guide for institutionalized marketing power. *American Journal of Economics and Sociology* 46(4): 415–430.
Berger, P. D., and Nasr, N. I. (1998). Customer lifetime value: Marketing models and applications. *Journal of Interactive Marketing* 12(1): 17–30.
Berry, L. L. (1980). The time buying consumer. *Journal of Retailing* 55: 58–69.
Bhakoo, V., and Chan, C. (2011). Collaborative implementation of e-business processes within the health-care supply chain: The Monash pharmacy project. *Supply Chain Management: An International Journal* 16(3): 184–193.
Bigliardi, B., Bottani, E., Rinaldi, M., and Casella, G. (2022). The digitalization of supply chain: A review. *Procedia Computer Science* 200: 1806–1815.
Bikku, T., Jarugula, J., Kongala, L., Tummala, N. D., and Donthiboina, N. V. (2023). Exploring the effectiveness of BERT for sentiment analysis on large-scale social media data. In *2023 3rd International Conference on Intelligent Technologies (CONIT)*, 1–4. IEEE.
Bitner, M. J. (1990). Evaluating service encounters: The effects of physical surroundings and employee responses. *Journal of Marketing* 54(2): 69–82.
Bitner, M. J., Booms, B. H., and Mohr, L. A. (1994). Critical service encounters: The employee's viewpoint. *Journal of Marketing* 58(4): 95–106.
Bitner, M. J., Booms, B. H., and Tetreault, M. S. (1990). The service encounter: Diagnosing favorable and unfavorable incidents. *Journal of Marketing* 54(1): 71–84.
Bitner, M. J., Ostrom, A. L., and Morgan, F. N. (2008). Service blueprinting: A practical technique for service innovation. *California Management Review* 50(3): 66–94.
Blau, P. (1986). *Exchange and Power in Social Life* (2nd edition). Routledge.
Blenkhorn, D. L., and Banting, P. M. (1991). How reverse marketing changes buyer—Seller roles. *Industrial Marketing Management* 20(3): 185–191.
Bliss, P. (1963). *Marketing and the Behavioral Sciences*. Rockleigh, NJ: Allyn & Bacon.
Blythe, J. (2008). *Essentials of Marketing* (2nd edition). Harlow: Pearson.
Bolotaeva, V., and Cata, T. (2010). Marketing opportunities with social networks. *Journal of Internet Social Networking and Virtual Communities 2011*: 1–8.
Booms, B. H., and Bitner, M. J. (1981). Marketing strategies and organization structures for service firms. In J. H. Donnelly and W. R. George (Eds.), *Marketing of Services*, 47–51. Chicago, IL: American Marketing Association.

Borden, N. H. (1964). The concept of the marketing mix. *Journal of Advertising Research* 4(2): 2–7.
Borsellino, V., Asciuto, A., D'Acquisto, M., Di Franco, C. P., Migliore, G., and Schimmenti, E. (2016). Sustainability initiatives and experiences in the Sicilian wine industry. *Rivista di Economia Agraria Anno LXXI*- 2016(1): 67–68.
Borsellino, V., Varia, F., Zinnanti, C., and Schimmenti, E. (2020). The Sicilian cooperative system of wine production: The strategic choices and performance analyses of a case study. *International Journal of Wine Business Research* 32(3): 391–421.
Bosona, T., and Gebresenbet, G. (2013). Food traceability as an integral part of logistics management in food and agricultural supply chain. *Food Control* 33(1): 32–48.
Brancati, E., Brancati, R., and Maresca, A. (2017). Global value chains, innovation and performance: Firm-level evidence from the Great Recession. *Journal of Economic Geography* 17(5): 1039–1073.
Brett, J. M., Behfar, K. J., and Kern, M. C. (2017). Managing multicultural teams. *Harvard Business Review* 95(6): 84–91.
Broekhuis, M., and Scholten, K. (2018). Purchasing in service triads: The influence of contracting on contract management. *International Journal of Operations & Production Management* 38(5): 1188–1204.
Brown, R. (1987). Marketing: A function and a philosophy. *The Quarterly Review of Marketing* 12(3): 25–30.
Brown, S. (1990). The wheel of retailing: Past and future. *Journal of Retailing* 66(2): 143–149.
Brown, S. (1997). Marketing science in a postmodern world: Introduction to the special issue. *European Journal of Marketing* 31(3/4): 167–182.
Brownlie, D. (2002). Environmental analysis. In M. J.Baker (Ed.), *The Marketing Book*. Oxford: Butterworth Heinemann.
Brownlie, D., and Saren, M. (1992). The four Ps of the marketing concept: Prescriptive, polemical, permanent and problematical. *European Journal of Marketing* 26(4): 34–47.
BSI. (1991). *Quality Vocabulary Part 2: Quality Concepts and Related Definitions*. London: BSI.
Buell, R. W., Kim, T., and Tsay, C. J. (2017). Creating reciprocal value through operational transparency. *Management Science* 63(6): 1673–1695.
Burgos Simon, M. A., Garro Crevillen, E., Llacer Sanfernando, M., Blanquer, F., Leino, T., and Konstantinidis, F. (2023). A vision-based application for container detection in ports 4.0. In *Proceedings of the 16th International Conference on Pervasive Technologies Related to Assistive Environments*, 557–561. New York, NY: Association for Computing Machinery.
Business in the Community. (2005). Jargon Buster. www.bitc.org.uk/resources/jargon_buster/cr.html. Last visited 22 September 2005.
Buzzell, R. (1968). Can you standardize multinational marketing? *Harvard Business Review* 49: 102–113.
Cady, J. F. (1984). *Concepts and Tools for Strategic Market Planning: A Course Note*. Cambridge, MA: Harvard Business School.
Carlzon, J. (1987). *Moments of Truth*. Cambridge, MA: Ballinger Publishing Co.
Carroll, A. (1979). A three-dimensional conceptual model of corporate performance. *Academy of Management Review* 4(4): 497–505.
Carter, C. R., and Easton, P. L. (2011). Sustainable supply chain management: Evolution and future directions. *International Journal of Physical Distribution & Logistics Management* 41(1): 46–62. https://doi.org/10.1108/09600031111101420.
Carter, C. R., Ellram, L., Kaufmann, L., Autry, C., Zhao, X., and Callarman, T. (2014). Looking back and moving forward: 50 years of the journal of supply chain management. *Journal of Supply Chain Management* 50(1). SSRN: https://ssrn.com/abstract=2353634.
Carter, C. R., and Rogers, D. S. (2008). A framework of sustainable supply chain management: Moving toward new theory. *International Journal of Physical Distribution & Logistics Management* 38(5): 360–387. https://doi.org/10.1108/09600030810882816.
Cavusgil, S. T., Zou, S., and Naidu, G. M. (1993). Product and promotion adaptation in export ventures: An empirical investigation. *Journal of International Business Studies* 24(3): 479–506.
Chakraborty, S., and Adhikari, S. (2021). Machine learning-based digital twin for dynamical systems with multiple time-scales. *Computers & Structures* 243: 106410.
Chamberlin, E. H. (1957). *Towards a More General Theory of Value*. Oxford: Oxford University Press.
Chan, J. O. (2007). A predictive analytic model for value chain management. *Journal of International Technology and Information Management* 16(1): 31–42. https://doi.org/10.58729/1941–6679.1186.
Chan, K. K. (2022). Supply chain traceability systems-robust approaches for the digital age. In *The Digital Supply Chain*, 163–179. Elsevier.

Chan, R. Y., and Lau, L. B. (2000). Antecedents of green purchases: A survey in China. *Journal of Consumer Marketing* 17(4): 338–357.
Charter, M. (1992). *Greener Marketing: A Responsible Approach to Business*. Sheffield: Greenleaf Publishing.
Cheng, J. L. (1983). Interdependence and coordination in organizations: A role-system analysis. *Academy of Management Journal* 26(1): 156–162.
Cheng, T. C. E., and Podolsky, S. (1993). *Just-In-Time Manufacturing*. New York: Chapman & Hall.
Chesbrough, H. W. (2003). *Open Innovation: The New Imperative for Creating and Profiting From Technology*. Boston, MA: Harvard Business School Press. ISBN: 1-57851-837-7.
Cheung, K. F., Bell, M. G., and Bhattacharjya, J. (2021). Cybersecurity in logistics and supply chain management: An overview and future research directions. *Transportation Research Part E: Logistics and Transportation Review* 146: 102217.
Cheunkamon, E., Jomnonkwao, S., and Ratanavaraha, V. (2023). Measurement model of service quality of tourism supply chains in Thailand. *Anatolia* 34(2): 176–189. https://doi.org/10.1080/13032917.2021.2005646.
Chopra, S., and Meindl, P. (2016). *Supply Chain Management: Strategy, Planning, and Operation* (6th edition). Essex: Pearson Education. ISBN: 97812920093567.
Christopher, M. (2000). The agile supply chain: Competing in volatile markets. *Industrial Marketing Management* 29(1): 37–44. https://doi.org/10.1016/S0019–8501(99)00110–8.
Christopher, M. (2016). *Logistics and Supply Chain Management* (5th edition). London: Pearson.
Christopher, M., Payne, A., and Balantyne, M. (1991). *Relationship Marketing*. London: Heinemann.
Christopher, M., and Peck, H. (2003). *Marketing Logistics* (2nd edition). London: Butterworth-Heinemann.
Christopher, M., and Peck, H. (2004). Building the resilient supply chain. *The International Journal of Logistics Management* 15(2): 1–14. https://doi.org/10.1108/09574090410700275.
Clark, T. (1990). International marketing and national character: A review and proposal for an integrative theory. *Journal of Marketing* (October): 66–79.
Clarke, F. (1974). Three golden rules of contracting. In *Supplement: Contract Research Review*, Vol. 2. London: New Scientist.
Comm, C. L., and Mathaisel, D. F. X. (2005). A case study in applying lean sustainability concepts to universities. *International Journal of Sustainability in Higher Education* 6(2): 134–146.
Comstock, B., Gulati, R., and Liguori, S. (2010). Unleashing the power of marketing. *Harvard Business Review* 88(10): 90–98.
Cooper, R., and Kleinschmidt, E. (1986). An investigation into the new product process: Steps, deficiencies and impact. *Journal of Product Innovation Management* 3: 71–85.
Coopers & Lybrand. (1996). *Efficient Consumer Response – Europe: Value Chain Analysis Project Overview*. Utrecht: Coopers & Lybrand and ECR Europe.
Coperland, M. (1923). The relations of consumer buying habits to marketing methods. *Harvard Business Review* 1 (April): 282–289.
CorriereQuotidiano.it. (2024). Sicily and wine: The festival that reveals the identity of the wine supply chain. *Ground.News Website*. https://ground.news/article/sicily-and-wine-the-festival-that-reveals-the-identity-of-the-wine-supply-chain?utm_source=headline-link&utm_medium=share. Last visited 12 January 2025.
Council of Logistics Management. (1998). CSCMP supply chain management definitions and glossary. http://cscmp.org/imis0/CSCMP/Educate/SCM_Definitions_and_Glossary_of_Terms/CSCMP/Educate/SCM_Definitions_and_Glossary_of_Terms.aspx?hkey=60879588-f65f-4ab5–8c4b-6878815ef921.
Cowell, D. W. (1988). New service development. *Journal of Marketing Management* 3(3): 296–312.
Cox, A. (1999). Power, value and supply chain management. *Supply Chain Management: An International Journal* 4(4): 167–175. https://doi.org/10.1108/13598549910284480.
Coyle, J., Bardi, E., and Langley, C. (1988). *The Management of Business Logistics*. St Paul, MN: West.
Craig, S. C., and Douglas, S. P. (2001). Conducting international marketing research in the twenty-first century. *International Marketing Review* 18(1): 80–90.
Craighead, C. W., Ketchen, D. J., Jr., and Darby, J. L. (2020). Pandemics and supply chain management research: Toward a theoretical toolbox. *Decision Sciences* 51(4): 838–866. https://doi.org/10.1111/deci.12468.
Cruz-Jesus, F., Pinheiro, A., and Oliveira, T. (2019). Understanding CRM adoption stages: Empirical analysis building on the TOE framework. *Computers in Industry* 109 (August): 1–13. https://doi.org/10.1016/j.compind.2019.03.007.

Cudahy, G. C., George, M. O., Godfrey, G. R., and Rollman, M. J. (2012). Preparing for the Unpredictable. *Outlook: The Online Journal of High-Performance Business*. www.accenture.com/us-en/outlook/Pages/outlook-journal–2012-preparing-for-unpredictable.aspx.

Culot, G., Podrecca, M., and Nassimbeni, G. (2024). Artificial intelligence in supply chain management: A systematic literature review of empirical studies and research directions. *Computers in Industry* 162: 104132. https://doi.org/10.1016/j.compind.2024.104132.

Dabbene, F., Gay, P., and Tortia, C. (2014). Traceability issues in food supply chain management: A review. *Biosystems Engineering* 120: 65–80.

Damanpour, F. (1991). Organizational innovation: A meta-analysis of effects of determinants and moderators. *Academy of Management Journal* 34: 555–590.

Dan, B., Zhang, S., and Zhou, M. (2018). Strategies for warranty service in a dual-channel supply chain with value-added service competition. *International Journal of Production Research* 56(17): 5677–5699. http://dx.doi.org/10.1080/00207543.2017.1377355.

Dash, R., McMurtrey, M., Rebman, C., and Kar, U. K. (2019). Application of artificial intelligence in automation of supply chain management. *Journal of Strategic Innovation and Sustainability* 14(3): 43–53. https://doi.org/10.33423/jsis.v14i3.2105.

Davenport, T. (1993). *Process Innovation: Reengineering Work Through Information Technology*. Boston, MA: Harvard Business School Press.

Dawson, L. M. (1971). Marketing science in the age of aquarius. *Journal of Marketing* 35: 66–72.

Day, G. S. (1989). *The Market-Driven Organization: Aligning Culture, Capabilities and Configuration to the Market*. New York: The Free Press.

Day, G. S. (1994). The capabilities of market-driven organizations. *Journal of Marketing* 58(4): 37–52.

De Bruyn, A., and Lilien, G. L. (2008). A multi-stage model of word-of-mouth influence through viral marketing. *International Journal of Research in Marketing* 25: 151–163.

Delcato, M., and Mills, K. G. (2020). The supply chain economy: A new industry categorization for understanding innovation in services. *Research Policy* 49(8): 104039. https://doi.org/10.1016/j.respol.2020.104039.

Deliciousitaly. (2023). Feast of San Martino, delicious Italy website, 30 August 2023. https://www.deliciousitaly.com/lombardia-itineraries/feast-of-san-martino?utm_source=chatgpt.com. Last visited 16 January 2025.

DESA-UN. (2011). *Manual on Statistics of International Trade in Services 2010*. Department of Economic and Social Affairs, ST/ESA/M.86/Rev. 1. Geneva, Luxembourg, Madrid, New York, Paris and Washington, DC. 2012. ISBN: 978-92-1-161542-5. https://unstats.un.org/unsd/tradeserv/TFSITS/msits2010/docs/MSITS%202010%20M86%20(E)%20web.pdf. Last visited 28 October 2024.

Dick, A. S., and Basu, K. (1994). Customer loyalty: Toward an integrated conceptual framework. *Journal of the Academy of Marketing Science* 22(2): 99–113.

Dickson, G. W. (1966). An analysis of vendor selection systems and decisions. *Journal of Purchasing* 2: 5–17.

Douglas, S. P., and Wind, Y. (1987). The myth of globalization. *Colombia Journal of World Business* (Winter): 19–29.

Dow Jones Sustainability Index. (2005). The corporate sustainability assessment at a glance. www.robecosam.com/en/sustainability-insights/about-sustainability/corporate-sustainability-assessment/index.jsp.

Dowling, M. (2021). Is non-fungible token pricing driven by cryptocurrencies? *Behavioral & Experimental Finance eJournal*. https://doi.org/10.2139/ssrn.3815093.

Drucker, P. (1974). *Management: Tasks, Responsibilities and Practices*. New York: Harper & Row.

Drucker, P. (1989). Marketing and economic development. *Journal of Marketing* 22(3): 252–259.

Dutta, P., Choi, T. M., Somani, S., and Butala, R. (2020). Blockchain technology in supply chain operations: Applications, challenges and research opportunities. *Transportation Research Part E: Logistics and Transportation Review* 142: 102067.

Ebinger, F., and Omondi, B. (2020). Leveraging digital approaches for transparency in sustainable supply chains: A conceptual paper. *Sustainability*. https://doi.org/10.3390/su12156129.

EC. (2006). Regulation (EC) No 1107/2006 of the European Parliament and of the Council of 5 July 2006 concerning the rights of disabled persons and persons with reduced mobility when travelling by air (Text with EEA relevance). *Official Journal of the European Union*, 26.7.2006/L 204–1. https://eur-lex.europa.eu/legal-content/EN/TXT/?uri=celex:32006R1107. Last visited 23 November 2024.

EC. (2011). EU ratifies UN Convention on disability rights. IP/11/4. Brussels, 5 January 2011. https://ec.europa.eu/commission/presscorner/detail/en/ip_11_4. Last visited 23 November 2024.

EC-European Accessibility Resource Centre. (2024). Accessible EU final report getting to know the European legislation on accessibility. European Accessibility Resource Centre (AccessibleEU) – Consortium Fundacion: ONCE, ENAT, EASPD, JKU, UNE, 19 April 2024. https://accessible-eu-centre.ec.europa.eu/getting-know-european-legislation-accessibility_en. Last visited 25 November 2024.

Elkington, J. (1994). Towards the sustainable corporation: Win-win-win business strategies for sustainable development. *California Management Review* 36(2): 90–100. http://dx.doi.org/10.2307/41165746.

Elkington, J. (1997). *Cannibals with Forks: The Triple Bottom Line of the 21st Century Business*. Oxford: Capstone.

Elliott, G. R. (1990). The marketing concept: Necessary, but sufficient? An environmental view. *European Journal of Marketing* 24(8): 23–30.

Ellram, L. M., Tate, W. L., and Billington, C. (2004). Understanding and managing the services supply chain. *Journal of Supply Chain Management* 40(3): 17–32. https://doi.org/10.1111/j.1745–493X.2004.tb00176.x.

Emiliani, L., and Stec, J. (2004). Using value-stream maps to improve leadership. *Leadership and Organization Development Journal* 25(8): 622–645.

Emirates. (2024a). About us – Emirates then and now. https://www.emirates.com/english/about-us/timeline/. Last visited 30 December 2024.

Emirates. (2024b). About us – Our business. https://www.emirates.com/english/about-us/our-business/. Last visited 30 December 2024.

Emirates. (2024c). Environment sustainability in operations. https://www.emirates.com/us/english/about-us/our-planet/sustainability-in-operations/?utm_source=chatgpt.com. Last visited 30 December 2024.

Erevelles, S., Fukawa, N., and Swayne, L. (2016). Big data consumer analytics and the transformation of marketing. *Journal of Business Research* 69(2): 897–904.

Espoo. (2024a). ESPOO ESBO municipality website. https://www.espoo.fi/en/news/. Last visited 10 January 2025.

Espoo. (2024b). ESPOO ESBO municipality website. https://www.espoo.fi/en/sustainable-development/future-workshop-sustainable-development-tupa?utm_source=chatgpt.com Last visit on 10 January 2025.

Espoo-catering. (2025). Environmental responsibility. https://www.espoo.fi/en/welcome-espoo-catering/responsibility#practical-responsibility–7999. Last visited 10 January 2025.

Estell, L., and Brewer, G. (1999). This call center accelerates sales. *Sales and Marketing Management* 15(2): 72.

Eteokleous, P. P., Katsikeas, C. S., and Leonidou, L. C. (2016). Review of research on CSR in international marketing: 1993–2013. In M. W. Obal, N. Kray, and C. Bushardt (Eds.), *Let's Get Engaged! Crossing the Threshold of Marketing's Engagement Era*, 683–684. New York: Springer International Publishing.

Eteokleous, P. P., Leonidou, L., and Katsikeas, C. (2016). Corporate social responsibility in international marketing: Review, assessment and future research. *International Marketing Review* 33(4): 683–684.

EU. (2019). Directive (EU) 2019/882 of the European Parliament and of the Council of 17 April 2019 on the accessibility requirements for products and services (Text with EEA relevance), Document 32019L0882. https://eur-lex.europa.eu/legal-content/EN/TXT/?uri=CELEX:32019L0882. Last visited 23 November 2024.

European Commission (EC). (2024a). Internal market, industry, entrepreneurship and SMEs; single market for services. EC; Directorate-General for Internal Market, Industry, Entrepreneurship and SMEs. https://single-market-economy.ec.europa.eu/single-market/services_en. Last visited 29 October 2024.

European Commission (EC). (2024b). Access2Markets-Services; services – Statistics EC; Directorate General for Trade "DG TRADE". https://trade.ec.europa.eu/access-to-markets/en/content/services-statistics. Last visited 29 October 2024.

European Commission (EC). (2025). *The Next Generation Internet of Things*. An Official Website of the European Union. https://digital-strategy.ec.europa.eu/el/policies/next-generation-internet-things. Last visited 13 January 2025.

Fahy, J., and Jobber, D. (2014). *Foundations of Marketing* (1st edition). Maidenhead: McGraw-Hill.

Fang, X., and Zhan, J. (2015). Sentiment analysis using product review data. *Journal of Big Data* 2(1): 5. https://doi.org/10.1186/S40537-015-0015-2.

Festinger, L. (1957). *A Theory of Cognitive Dissonance* (1st edition). Evanston, IL: Row, Peterson.

Festinger, L. (1962). *A Theory of Cognitive Dissonance* (2nd edition). Stanford, CA: Stanford University Press.

Flieβ, S., and Kleinaltenkamp, M. (2004). Blueprinting the service company managing service processes efficiently. *Journal of Business Research* 57: 392–404.

Flynn, B. B., Huo, B., and Zhao, X. (2010). The impact of supply chain integration on performance: A contingency and configuration approach. *Journal of Operations Management* 28(1): 58–71.
Foglio, A., and Stanevicius, V. (2006). Scenario of glocal marketing as an answer to the market globalization and localization. Part I: Strategy scenario and market. *Vadyba/Management* 1(10): 26–38.
Folinas, D. (2004). *E-Logistics Management Model: Supply Chain Integration in Virtual Environment*. Doctoral dissertation. http://thesis.ekt.gr/thesisBookReader/id/13787#page/1/mode/2up.
Folinas, D. (2007). A conceptual framework for business intelligence based on activities monitoring systems. *International Journal of Intelligent Enterprise* 1(1): 65–80.
Folinas, D. (2015). *Logistics Applications* [in Greek]. Athens: Diafantos.
Folinas, D., Fotiadis, T., and Coudounaris, D. (2017). Just-in-time theory: The panacea to the business success? *International Journal of Value Chain Management* 8(2): 171–190.
Folinas, D., Kelemis, A., and Manikas, I. (2011). A generic methodology for the prioritization of logistics processes: The case of the agrifood supply chain. In *Proceedings of the International Conference Management of Technology, Step to Sustainable Production (MOTSP 2011)*, 8–10 June 2011, Croatia.
Folinas, D., Manthou, V., Sigala, M., and Vlachopoulou, V. (2004). e-Volution of supply chain: Cases and best practices. *Internet Research: Electronic Networking Applications and Policy* 14(4): 274–283.
Folinas, D., Manthou, M., and Vlachopoulou, M. (2001). Logistics service management in virtual organization environment: Modeling systems and procedures. In *Proceedings of the 17th International Logistics Congress*, 127–139. Thessaloniki: SOLE.
Folinas, D., Manthou, V., and Vlachopoulou, M. (2003). Modeling business information in virtual environment. In *Proceedings of 10th International Conference on Human–Computer Interaction*, Irakleion, Greece, Vol. 3, 699–703. London: Lawrence Erlbaum Associates.
Folinas, D., Manthou, V., and Vlachopoulou, M. (2007). *Enterprise Information Systems* [in Greek]. Thessaloniki: Anikoula.
Folinas, D., and Rabi, S. (2012). Estimating benefits of demand sensing for consumer goods organizations. *Database Marketing and Customer Strategy Management* 19(4): 245–261.
Ford, D., and Leonidou, L. (1991). Research developments in international marketing: A European perspective. In S. J. Paliwoda (Ed.), *New Perspectives on International Marketing*, 3–32. London: Routledge.
Fornes-Leal, A., Lacalle, I., Palau, C., Szmeja, P., Ganzha, M., Konstantinidis, F., and Garro, E. (2024). Tactile IoT architecture for the IoT–edge–cloud continuum: The assist-IoT approach. In A. Yadav, S. J. Nanda, and M. H. Lim (Eds.), *Shaping the Future of IoT With Edge Intelligence*, 37. Taylor and Francis.
Fosso Wamba, S., Queiroz, M. M., Guthrie, C., and Braganza, A. (2022). Industry experiences of artificial intelligence (AI): Benefits and challenges in operations and supply chain management. *Production Planning & Control* 33(16): 1–13.
Foster, S. T., Sampson, S. E., and Dunn, S. C. (2000). The impact of customer contact on environmental initiatives for service firms. *International Journal of Operations & Production Management* 20(2): 187–203.
Fotiadis, T. A. (2004). *Marketing of High Technology: Development of a Decision Making Procedure for the Introduction of New High Tech Products*. Doctoral dissertation. http://dspace.lib.uom.gr/handle/2159/398.
Fritz, W. (1996). Market orientation and corporate success: Findings from Germany. *European Journal of Marketing* 30(8): 59–74.
Fuentes, C. (2014). Green materialities: Marketing and the socio-material construction of green products. *Business Strategy and the Environment* 23(2): 105–116.
Gagnon, Y. C. (2010). *The Case Study as Research Method: A Practical Handbook*. Quebec: PUQ.
Galbraith, J. R. (1973). *Designing Complex Organizations*. Boston, MA: Addison-Wesley Longman.
Gartner Group. (2000). Gartner's four phases of E-government model. www.gartner.com/doc/317292/gartners-phases-egovernment-model.
Gaski, J. F., and Nevin, J. R. (1985). The differential effects of exercised and unexercised power sources in a marketing channel. *Journal of Marketing Research* 22(2): 130–142.
Gattorna, L., and Walters, D. (1996). *Managing the Supply Chain*. Basingstoke: Palgrave.
German Environment Agency; UBA. (2020). German environment agency (UBA). *Guidelines on Sustainable Event Organisation*. August 2020 (4th updated edition). https://www.bmuv.de/fileadmin/Daten_BMU/Pools/Broschueren/veranstaltungsleitfaden_en_bf.pdf.
Ghabak, V., and Chaugule, R. (2024). Digital twin framework in supply chain governance. In *2024 IEEE International Conference on Computing, Power and Communication Technologies (IC2PCT)*, Vol. 5, 82–89. IEEE.
Ghobakhloo, M., Iranmanesh, M., Foroughi, B., Rejeb, A., Nikbin, D., and Tseng, M. L. (2024). A practical guide on strategic roadmapping for information and operations technology management: A case study on industry 5.0 transformation. *Journal of Industrial and Production Engineering* 41: 1–25.

Giannakis, M. (2011). Conceptualizing and managing service supply chains. *The Service Industries Journal* 31(11): 1809–1823. https://doi.org/10.1080/02642069.2010.503879.

Gierlich-Joas, M., Teebken, M., and Hess, T. (2022). A synthesized perspective on privacy and transparency in the digital workplace. In *55th Hawaii International Conference on System Sciences*, 1–10. ScholarSpace.

Gounaris, S. (2012). *Services Marketing* [in Greek] (2nd edition). Athens: Rosili Publications.

Grant, A. W., and Schlesinger, L. A. (1995). Realize your customers' full profit potential. *Harvard Business Review* 73(5): 59–72.

Grant, C. (1999). Theodore Levitt's marketing myopia. *Journal of Business Ethics* 18(4): 397–406.

Griffin, A., and Hauser, J. R. (1996). Integrating R&D and marketing: A review and analysis of the literature. *Journal of Product Innovation Management* 13(3): 191–215.

Grönroos, C. (1978). A service-orientated approach to marketing of services. *European Journal of Marketing* 12(8): 588–601.

Grönroos, C. (1989). Defining marketing: A market-oriented approach. *European Journal of Marketing* 23(1): 52–60.

Grönroos, C. (1994). From marketing mix to relationship marketing: Towards a paradigm shift in marketing. *Management Decision* 32(2): 4–20.

Grönroos, C. (2000). *Service Management and Marketing* (2nd edition). West Sussex: John Wiley & Sons Ltd.

Grönroos, C. (2015). *Service Management and Marketing; Managing the Service Profit Logic* (4th edition). Haddington, East Lothian: John Wiley & Sons Ltd.

Gruber, W. H. (1981). *The Strategic Integration of Corporate Research Development*. Chicago, IL: Amacom.

Guelzo, C. M. (1986). *Introduction to Logistics Management*. Richmond, VA: Reston Publishing Company.

Gunasekaran, A., and Ngai, E. W. T. (2004). Information systems in supply chain integration and management. *European Journal of Operational Research* 159(2): 269–295. https://doi.org/10.1016/j.ejor.2003.08.016.

Gunasekaran, A., Patel, C., and McGaughey, R. E. (2004). A framework for supply chain performance measurement. *International Journal of Production Economics* 87(3): 333–347. https://doi.org/10.1016/j.ijpe.2003.08.003.

Gunasekaran, A., Patel, C., and Tirtiroglu, E. (2001). Performance measures and metrics in a supply chain environment. *International Journal of Operations & Production Management* 21(1/2): 71–87.

Gupta, C. P., and Kumar, V. R. (2023). Sentiment analysis and its application in analysing consumer behaviour. In *2023 International Conference on Emerging Techniques in Computational Intelligence (ICETCI)*, 332–337. IEEE.

Hakiri, A., Gokhale, A., Yahia, S. B., and Mellouli, N. (2024). A comprehensive survey on digital twin for future networks and emerging Internet of Things industry. *Computer Networks*: 110350.

Haleem, A., Javaid, M., Qadri, M. A., Singh, R. P., and Suman, R. (2022). Artificial intelligence (AI) applications for marketing: a literature-based study. *International Journal of Intelligent Networks* 3: 119–132. https://doi.org/10.1016/j.ijin.2022.08.005.

Hamel, G., and Prahalad, C. K. (1991). Corporate imagination and expeditionary marketing. *Harvard Business Review* 69(4): 81–92.

Hammer, M., and Champy, J. (1993). *Reengineering the Corporation: A Manifesto for Business Revolution*. New York: Harper Business.

Hancock, D. R., and Algozzine, B. (2016). *Doing Case Study Research: A Practical Guide for Beginning Researchers*. New York, NY: Teachers College Press.

Hart, S. L. (1997). Beyond greening: Strategies for a sustainable world. *Harvard Business Review* 75(1): 66.

Hatzis, A., Koulidou, A., and Folinas, D. (2011). Costing logistics services. *Operations and Supply Chain Management* 4(2): 116–122.

Haven-Tang, C., and Jones, E. (2012). Local leadership for rural tourism development: A case study of Adventa, Monmouthshire, UK. *Tourism Management Perspectives* 4: 28–35.

Haywood-Farmer, J. (1988). A conceptual model of service quality. *International Journal of Operations and Production Management* 8(6): 19–29.

Heide, J. B., and Miner, A. S. (1992). The shadow of the future: Effects of anticipated interaction and frequency of contact on buyer-seller cooperation. *The Academy of Management Journal* 35(2): 265–291. https://doi.org/10.2307/256374.

Heinonen, K. (2004). Reconceptualizing customer perceived value: The value of time and place. *Managing Service Quality: An International Journal* 14(2/3): 205–215.

Hemingway, C. A., and Maclagan, P. W. (2004). Managers' personal values as drivers of corporate social responsibility. *Journal of Business Ethics* 50(1): 33–44.

Hendriksen, C. (2023). Artificial intelligence for supply chain management: Disruptive innovation or innovative disruption? *Journal of Supply Chain Management* 59(3): 65–76.

Hirschman, E. C., and Holbrook, M. B. (1982). Hedonic consumption: Emerging concepts, methods and propositions. *Journal of Marketing* 46(3): 92–101.

Hlebeler, R., Kelly, T. B., and Ketteman, C. (1998). *Best Practices: Building Your Business With Customer-Focused Solutions*. New York: Simon & Schuster.

Hoffman, K. D., and Bateson, J. E. (1977). *Essentials of Services Marketing*. New York: Dryden Press.

Hofstede, G., Hofstede, G. J., and Minkov, M. (2010). *Cultures and Organizations: Software of the Mind* (3rd edition). London: McGraw-Hill. ISBN: 978-0-07-177015-6.

Holcomb, J. L., Upchurch, R. S., and Okumus, F. (2007). Corporate social responsibility: What are top hotel companies reporting? *International Journal of Contemporary Hospitality Management* 19(6): 461–475.

Homburg, C., Workman, J. P., Jr., and Krohmer, H. (1999). Marketing's influence within the firm. *Journal of Marketing* 63(2): 1–17.

Hooley, G. J., Lynch, J. E., and Shepherd, J. (1990). The marketing concept: Putting the theory into practice. *European Journal of Marketing* 24(9): 7–24.

Houston, F. S. (1986). The marketing concept: What it is and what it is not. *Journal of Marketing* 50: 81–87.

Hu, W.-C., Wu, H.-T., Cho, H.-H., and Tseng, F.-H. (2020). Optimal route planning system for logistics vehicles based on artificial intelligence. *Journal of Internet Technology* 21(3): 757–764.

Huang, H.-M., and Rust, R. T. (2018). Artificial intelligence in service. *Journal of Service Research* 21(2): 155–172. https://doi.org/10.1177/1094670517752459.

Hughes, J., and Weiss, J. (2007). Simple rules for making alliances work. *Harvard Business Review* 85(11): 121–131.

Husna, A., Amin, S. H., and Shah, B. (2021). Demand forecasting in supply chain management using different deep learning methods. In *Demand Forecasting and Order Planning in Supply Chains and Humanitarian Logistics*, 140–170. IGI Global.

Hussain, M., Khan, M., and Al-Aomar, R. (2016). A framework for supply chain sustainability in service industry with confirmatory factor analysis. *Renewable and Sustainable Energy Reviews* 55: 1301–1312.

ILO. (2025). Supply chains. https://www.ilo.org/topics-and-sectors/supply-chains. Last visited 18 January 2025.

Ilyas, R. M., Banwet, D. K., and Shankar, R. (2007). Value chain relationship – A strategy matrix. *Supply Chain Forum: An International Journal* 8(1): 56–72. https://doi.org/10.1080/16258312.2007.11517176.

ISO. (2024). *ISO-20121: "Event Sustainability Management Systems-Requirements With Guidance for Use"*. International Organization for Standardization. https://www.iso.org/standard/86389.html. Last visited 23 November 2024.

Itoh, H. (2023). What do contracts do to facilitate relationships? *The Japanese Economic Review* 74: 333–354. https://doi.org/10.1007/s42973-023-00132-7.

Ivanov, D. (2024a). Digital supply chain management and technology to enhance resilience by building and using end-to-end visibility during the COVID-19 pandemic. *IEEE Transactions on Engineering Management* 71: 10485.

Ivanov, D. (2023). Intelligent digital twin (iDT) for supply chain stress-testing, resilience, and viability. *International Journal of Production Economics* 263: 108938.

Ivanov, D. (2024b). Conceptualisation of a 7-element digital twin framework in supply chain and operations management. *International Journal of Production Research* 62(6): 2220–2232.

Ivanov, D., and Dolgui, A. (2020). Viability of intertwined supply networks: Extending the supply chain resilience angles towards survivability. *International Journal of Production Research* 58(10): 2904–2915. https://doi.org/10.1080/00207543.2020.1750727.

Jain, P. K., Pamula, R., and Srivastava, G. (2021). A systematic literature review on machine learning applications for consumer sentiment analysis using online reviews. *Computer Science Review* 41: 100413.

Jain, S. C. (1989). Standardization of international marketing strategy: Some hypotheses. *Journal of Marketing* 53(1): 70–79.

Jami Pour, M., Hosseinzadeh, M., and Moradi, M. (2024). IoT-based entrepreneurial opportunities in smart transportation: A multidimensional framework. *International Journal of Entrepreneurial Behavior & Research* 30(2/3): 450–481.

Javaid, M., Haleem, A., Singh, R. P., and Sinha, A. K. (2024). Digital economy to improve the culture of industry 4.0: A study on features, implementation and challenges. *Green Technologies and Sustainability*: 100083.

Javaid, M., Haleem, A., and Suman, R. (2023). Digital twin applications toward industry 4.0: A review. *Cognitive Robotics* 3: 71–92.

Jaworski, B. J., and Kohli, A. K. (1993). Market orientation: Antecedents and consequences. *Journal of Marketing* 57: 53–70.

Jeannet, J.-P., and Hennessey, H. D. (1992). *Global Marketing Strategies*. Boston, MA: Houghton Mifflin Company.

Jin, J., Liu, Y., Ji, P., and Liu, H. (2016). Understanding big consumer opinion data for market-driven product design. *International Journal of Production Research* 54(10): 3019–3041.

Jobber, D. (2003). *Foundations of Marketing*. Maidenhead: McGraw-Hill.

Jobber, D. (2004). *Principles and Practice of Marketing* (4th edition). Maidenhead: McGraw-Hill.

Jocz, K. E., and Quelch, J. A. (2008). An exploration of marketing's impacts on society: A perspective linked to democracy. *Journal of Public Policy and Marketing* 27(2): 202–206.

Johne, A., and Snelson, P. (1988). Success factors in product innovation: A selective review of the literature. *Journal of Product Innovation Management* 5: 114–128.

Jolson, M., and Proia, S. (1986). Classification of consumer goods – A subjective measure? In K. Bernhardt (Ed.), *Marketing: 1776–1976 and Beyond*, 71–75. Chicago, IL: American Marketing Association.

Jones, D. B., and Monieson, D. D. (1990). Early development of the philosophy of marketing thought. *Journal of Marketing* 54: 102–113.

Kamarudeen, N., and Sundarakani, B. (2019). Business and supply chain strategy of flying above the dessert: A case study of Emirates airlines. In *Proceedings of the 9th International Conference on Operations and Supply Chain Management*. RMIT University-Vietnam, 2019. No of the Paper: 18. ISBN: 9786027060470.

Kamdjou, H. M., Baudry, D., Havard, V., and Ouchani, S. (2024). Resource-constrained extended reality operated with digital twin in industrial Internet of Things. *IEEE Open Journal of the Communications Society*. https://doi.org/10.1109/OJCOMS.2024.3356508

Kano, L., Tsang, E. W. K., and Yeung, H. W. (2020). Global value chains: A review of the multi-disciplinary literature. *Journal of International Business Studies* 51: 577–622. https://doi.org/10.1057/s41267-020-00304-2.

Kashyap, D. (1996). Marketing myopia revisited. A view through the 'colored' looking glass of a client. *Marketing and Research Today* 24(3): 197–201.

Katona, G. (1960). *The Powerful Consumer*. New York: McGraw-Hill.

Kauffmann, E., Peral, J., Gil, D., Fernandez, A., Sellers, R., and Mora, H. (2020). A framework for big data analytics in commercial social networks: A case study on sentiment analysis and fake review detection for marketing decision-making. *Industrial Marketing Management* 90: 523–537.

Keegan, W., and Green, M. (2000). *Global Marketing*. Englewood Cliffs, NJ: Prentice Hall.

Kelemis, A., Folinas, D., and Manikas, I. (2011). Identifying key logistics processes. In *Proceedings of the 15th Panhellenic Logistics Conference, 1st Southeast European Congress on Supply Chain Management*, 11–12 November, Thessaloniki, Greece.

Kern, T., and Willcocks, L. (2002). Exploring relationships in information technology outsourcing: The interaction approach. *European Journal of Information Systems* 11: 3–19. https://doi.org/10.1057/palgrave.ejis.3000415.

Khan, H. U., Abbas, M., Khan, F., Nazir, S., Binbusayyis, A., Alabdultif, A., and Taegkeun, W. (2024). Multi-criteria decision-making methods for the evaluation of the social internet of things for the potential of defining human behaviors. *Computers in Human Behavior* 157: 108230.

Kietzmann, J. H., Hermkens, K., McCarthy, I. P., and Silvestre, B. S. (2011). Social media? Get serious! Understanding the functional building blocks of social media. *Business Horizons* 54: 241–251.

Kohli, A. K., and Jaworski, B. J. (1990). Market orientation: The construct, research propositions and managerial implications. *Journal of Marketing* 54(2): 1–18.

Kolmykova, M., Troyanskaya, M., Aralbaeva, G., Seliverstova, N., and Chetverikova, N. (2022). Transformation of management culture in the context of supply chain digitalization. *Human Systems Management* 41(3): 315–326.

Konstantinidis, F. K., Balaska, V., Symeonidis, S., Mouroutsos, S. G., and Gasteratos, A. (2022). AROWA: An autonomous robot framework for warehouse 4.0 health and safety inspection operations. In *2022 30th Mediterranean Conference on Control and Automation (MED)*, 494–499. IEEE.

Konstantinidis, F. K., Balaska, V., Symeonidis, S., Psarommatis, F., Psomoulis, A., Giakos, G., Mouroutsos, S. G., and Gasteratos, A. (2023). Achieving zero defected products in dairy 4.0 using digital twin and machine vision. In *Proceedings of the 16th International Conference on Pervasive Technologies Related to Assistive Environments*, 528–534. Corfu Greece, 5–7 July. https://doi.org/10.1145/3594806.3596554

Konstantinidis, F. K., Kansizoglou, I., Santavas, N., Mouroutsos, S. G., and Gasteratos, A. (2020). Marma: A mobile augmented reality maintenance assistant for fast-track repair procedures in the context of Industry 4.0. *Machines* 8(4): 88.

Konstantinidis, F. K., Myrillas, N., Mouroutsos, S. G., Koulouriotis, D., and Gasteratos, A. (2022). Assessment of industry 4.0 for modern manufacturing ecosystem: A systematic survey of surveys. *Machines* 10(9): 746.

Konstantinidis, F. K., Romanopoulou, E., Koukas, S., Kiritsis, D., and Alexopoulos, K. (2022). Assessment of industry 4.0 for modern manufacturing ecosystem: A systematic survey of surveys. *Machines* 10(9): 746.

Kosnik, T. (1990). The marketing process. In T. V. Bonoma and T. J. Kosnik (Eds.), *Marketing Management: Text and Cases*. Homewood, IL: Irwin.

Kotler, P. (1972a). A generic concept of marketing. *Journal of Marketing* 36(2): 46–54.

Kotler, P. (1972b). *Marketing Management* (2nd edition). Englewood Cliffs, NJ: Prentice-Hall.

Kotler, P. (1973). Atmospherics as a marketing tool. *Journal of Retailing* 49(4): 48–64.

Kotler, P. (1984). *Marketing Management: Analysis, Planning, Control* (5th edition). Englewood Cliffs, NJ: Prentice-Hall.

Kotler, P. (1986). Megamarketing. *Harvard Business Review* 64(2): 117–124.

Kotler, P. (1994). *Marketing Management: Analysis, Planning, Implementation and Control* (6th edition). Englewood Cliffs, NJ: Prentice-Hall.

Kotler, P. (1997). From sales obsession to marketing effectiveness. *Harvard Business Review* 55: 67–75.

Kotler, P. (2003). *Marketing Management* (11th edition). Englewood Cliffs, NJ: Prentice-Hall.

Kotler, P., and Armstrong, G. (2001). *Principles of Marketing* (9th edition). Englewood Cliffs, NJ: Prentice-Hall.

Kotler, P., and Armstrong, G. (2009). *Principles of Marketing* (13th edition). Englewood Cliffs, NJ: Prentice-Hall.

Kotler, P., and Armstrong, G. (2014). *Principles of Marketing* (15th edition). Upper Saddle River, NJ: Pearson Education.

Kotler, P., Armstrong, G., Saunders, J., and Wong, V. (1996). *Principles of Marketing* (European edition). Englewood Cliffs, NJ: Prentice-Hall.

Kotler, P., Haider, D., and Rein, I. (1993). *Marketing Places: Attracting Investment, Industry and Tourism to Cities, States and Nations*. New York: Free Press.

Kotler, P., and Keller, K. L. (2006). *Marketing Management* (12th edition). Englewood Cliffs, NJ: Prentice-Hall.

Krajewski, L. J., Malhotra, M. K., and Ritzman, L. P. (2016). *Operations Management Processes and Supply Chains*. London: Pearson.

Krotov, V. (2017). The internet of things and new business opportunities. *Business Horizons* 60(6): 831–841.

Kumar, D., Kumar, I., Rahman, Z., Yadav, S., and Goyal, P. (2011). Green marketing mix: rethinking competitive advantage during climate change. In *The First International Conference on Interdisciplinary Research and Development*, 31 May–1 June. Thailand, 1–5.

Kumar, V., Petersen, J. A., and Leone, R. P. (2007). How valuable is word of mouth? *Harvard Business Review* 85(10): 139–156.

Kumari, S. (2023). Upskilling/reskilling when implementing value-driven technology. *Journal of Supply Chain Management, Logistics and Procurement* 6(2): 127–139.

Kwon, H., Lee, S., Kim, M., Hahn, C., and Hur, J. (2023). Certificate transparency with enhanced privacy. *IEEE Transactions on Dependable and Secure Computing* 20: 3860–3872. https://doi.org/10.1109/TDSC.2022.3214235.

Kyaw, K. S., Tepsongkroh, P., Thongkamkaew, C., and Sasha, F. (2023). Business intelligent framework using sentiment analysis for smart digital marketing in the e-commerce era. *Asia Social Issues* 16(3): e252965.

Lacity, M., and Willcocks, L. P. (2017). Conflict resolution in business services outsourcing relationships. *The Journal of Strategic Information Systems* 26(2): 80–100. https://doi.org/10.1016/j.jsis.2017.02.003.

Lambert, D., Emmelhainz, M., and Gardner, J. (1999). Building successful logistics partnerships. *The Journal of Business Logistics* 20(1): 165–182.

Lambert, D. M. (1976). *The Development of an Inventory Costing Methodology: A Study of the Costs Associated with Holding Inventory*. Chicago, IL: National Council of Physical Distribution Management.
Lambert, D. M. (1978). The distribution channels decision: A problem of performance measurement. *Management Accounting* (June): 60–63.
Lambert, D. M., and Cooper, M. C. (2000). Issues in supply chain management. *Industrial Marketing Management* 29(1): 65–83. https://doi.org/10.1016/S0019–8501(99)00113–3.
Lambert, D. M., and Knemeyer, A. M. (2004). We're in this together. *Harvard Business Review* 82(12): 114–122.
Larsson, R., Bengtsson, L., Henriksson, K., and Sparks, J. (1998). The interorganizational learning dilemma: Collective knowledge development in strategic alliances. *Organization Science* 9(3): 285–305. https://doi.org/10.1287/orsc.9.3.285.
Lawrence, P. R., and Lorsch, J. W. (1967a). Differentiation and integration in complex organizations. *Administrative Science Quarterly* 12(1): 1–47.
Lawrence, P. R., and Lorsch, J. W. (1967b). *New Management Job: The Integrator*. Boston, MA: Organizational Effectiveness Center and School.
Le, T. V., and Fan, R. (2023). Digital twins for logistics and supply chain systems: Literature review, conceptual framework, research potential, and practical challenges. *Computers & Industrial Engineering*: 109768.
Lee, K. L., Wong, S. Y., Alzoubi, H. M., Al Kurdi, B., Alshurideh, M. T., and El Khatib, M. (2023). Adopting smart supply chain and smart technologies to improve operational performance in manufacturing industry. *International Journal of Engineering Business Management* 15: 18479790231200614.
Lee, W. J., Wu, H., Yun, H., Kim, H. B., Jun, M. B., and Sutherland, J. W. (2019). Predictive maintenance of machine tool systems using artificial intelligence techniques applied to machine condition data. *Procedia Cirp* 80: 506–511.
Leenders, M. R., and Blenkhorn, D. L. (1988). *Reverse Marketing: The New Buyer–Supplier Relationship*. New York: Free Press.
Leenders, R. T. A. (2002). Modeling social influence through network autocorrelation: Constructing the weight matrix. *Social Networks* 24(1): 21–47.
Leonidou, C. N., and Leonidou, L. C. (2011). Research into environmental marketing/management: A bibliographic analysis. *European Journal of Marketing* 45(1/2): 68–103.
Leonidou, L. C., Fotiadis, T. A., Christodoulides, P., Spyropoulou, S., and Katsikeas, C. S. (2015). Environmentally friendly export business strategy: Its determinants and effects on competitive advantage and performance. *International Business Review* 24(5): 798–811.
Leonidou, L. C., Katsikeas, C. S., Fotiadis, T. A., and Christodoulides, P. (2013). Antecedents and consequences of an eco-friendly export marketing strategy: The moderating role of foreign public concern and competitive intensity. *Journal of International Marketing* 21(3): 22–46.
Leonidou, L. C., Leonidou, C. N., Fotiadis, T. A., and Zeriti, A. (2013). Resources and capabilities as drivers of hotel environmental marketing strategy: Implications for competitive advantage and performance. *Tourism Management* 35: 94–110.
Leuschner, R., Rogers, D. S., and Charvet, F. F. (2013). A meta-analysis of supply chain integration and firm performance. *Journal of Supply Chain Management* 49(2): 34–57.
Levitt, T. (1960). Marketing myopia. *Harvard Business Review* 38(4): 24–47.
Levitt, T. (1972). Production-line approach to service. *Harvard Business Review* 50(5): 41–52.
Levitt, T. (1975). Marketing myopia. *Harvard Business Review* 53(5): 26–183.
Levitt, T. (1980). Marketing success through differentiation of anything. *Harvard Business Review* 58(1): 83–91.
Levitt, T. (1983). The globalization of markets. *Harvard Business Review* 61(3) (May/June): 92–102.
Li, H., and Cai, W. (2009). Green marketing and sustainable development of garment industry: A game between cost and profit. *International Journal of Business and Management* 3(12): 81.
Li, L., Ford, J. B., Zhai, X., and Xu, L. (2012). Relational benefits and manufacturer satisfaction: An empirical study og logistics service in supply chain. *International Journal of Production Research* 50(19): 5445–5459.
Liberopoulos, K., and Pantouvakis, A. (2008). *Marketing II: Volume A: Services Marketing* [in Greek]. Patra: Hellenic Open University.
Liker, J. (2004). *The Toyota Way, 14 Management Principles From the World Greatest Manufacturer*. New York: McGraw-Hill.

Lin, C. H., Sher, P. J., and Shih, H. Y. (2005). Past progress and future directions in conceptualizing customer perceived value. *International Journal of Service Industry Management* 16(4): 318–336.
Liu, K. P., Chiu, W., Chu, J., and Zheng, L. J. (2022). The impact of digitalization on supply chain integration and performance: A comparison between large enterprises and SMEs. *Journal of Global Information Management* 30: 1–20. https://doi.org/10.4018/jgim.311450.
Liu, W., Bai, E., Liu, L., and Wei, W. (2017). A framework of sustainable service supply chain management: A literature review and research agenda. *Sustainability* 9(3): 421. https://doi.org/10.3390/su9030421.
Liu, W., Wang, D., Long, S., Shen, X., and Shi, V. (2019). Service supply chain management: A behavioural operations perspective. *Modern Supply Chain Research and Applications* 1(1): 28–53. https://doi.org/10.1108/MSCRA-01-2019-0003.
Loureiro, S. M. C., Guerreiro, J., and Tussyadiah, I. (2021). Artificial intelligence in business: State of the art and future research agenda. *Journal of Business Research* 129: 911–926.
Lovelock, C. H., and Wirtz, J. (2004). *Services Marketing: People, Technology, Strategy*. Englewood Cliffs, NJ: Prentice-Hall.
Lovelock, C. H., Wirtz, J., and Chew, P. (2009). *Essentials of Services Marketing* (1st edition). Englewood Cliffs, NJ: Prentice-Hall.
Luning, S. (2012). Corporate social responsibility (CSR) for exploration: Consultants, companies and communities in processes of engagements. *Resources Policy* 37(2): 205–211. https://doi.org/10.1016/j.resourpol.2011.02.004.
Ma, S., Flanigan, K. A., and Bergés, M. (2024). State-of-the-art review and synthesis: A requirement-based roadmap for standardized predictive maintenance automation using digital twin technologies. *Advanced Engineering Informatics* 62: 102800.
Macneil, I. R. (1980). *The New Social Contract: An Inquiry into Modern Contractual Relations*. New Haven: Yale University Press. https://repository.law.umich.edu/cgi/viewcontent.cgi?article=3862&context=mlr.
Maheshwari, P., Kamble, S., Belhadi, A., Venkatesh, M., and Abedin, M. Z. (2023). Digital twin-driven real-time planning, monitoring, and controlling in food supply chains. *Technological Forecasting and Social Change* 195: 122799.
Maignan, I., and Ferrell, O. C. (2004). Corporate social responsibility and marketing: An integrative framework. *Journal of the Academy of Marketing Science* 32(1): 3–19.
Maignan, I., Ferrell, O. C., and Ferrell, L. (2005). A stakeholder model for implementing social responsibility in marketing. *European Journal of Marketing* 39: 956–977.
Malhotra, D., and Lumineau, F. (2011). Trust and collaboration in the aftermath of conflict: The effects of contract structure. *Academy of Management Journal* 54(5): 981–998. https://doi.org/10.5465/amj.2009.0683.
Malliaris, P. (1990). *Introduction to Marketing* [in Greek] (1st edition). Piraeus: Stamoulis Publications.
Malliaris, P. (2001). *Introduction to Marketing* [in Greek] (2nd edition). Piraeus: Stamoulis Publications.
Malliaris, P. (2012). *Introduction to Marketing* [in Greek] (4th edition). Piraeus: Stamoulis Publications.
Manthou, V., Folinas, D., and Vlachopoulou, M. (2005). Establishing an integrated virtual logistics network. *International Journal of Logistics Systems and Management* 1(4): 354–365.
Marinagi, C., Reklitis, P., Trivellas, P., and Sakas, D. (2023). The impact of industry 4.0 technologies on key performance indicators for a resilient supply chain 4.0. *Sustainability* 15(6): 5185.
Marriott. (2022). Marriott international sustainability report 2022. http://serve360.marriott.com/wp-content/uploads/2022/10/Marriott-2022-Serve-360-ESG-Report-accessible_F.pdf. Last visited 8 January 2025.
Marvin, G., Tamale, M., Kanagwa, B., and Jjingo, D. (2023). Philosophical review of artificial intelligence for Society 5.0. In A. Yadav, S. J. Nanda, and M. H. Lim (Eds.), *Proceedings of International Conference on Paradigms of Communication, Computing and Data Analytics. PCCDA 2023. Algorithms for Intelligent Systems*. Springer. https://doi.org/10.1007/978-981-99-4626-6_1.
Maslow, A. H. (1943). A theory of human motivation. *Psychological Review* 50(4): 370–396.
Maslow, A. H. (1970). *Motivation and Personality* (2nd edition). New York: Harper & Row.
Maslow, A. H., and Murphy, G. (1954). *Motivation and Personality*. New York: Harper & Row.
Mathur, L. K., and Mathur, I. (2000). An analysis of the wealth effects of green marketing strategies. *Journal of Business Research* 50(2): 193–200.
Mayer, R. C., Davis, J. H., and Schoorman, F. D. (1995). An integrative model of organizational trust. *The Academy of Management Review* 20(3): 709–734.
McCammon, B. C., and Little, R. W. (1965). Marketing channels: Analytical systems and approaches. *Science in Marketing* 191: 321–385.

McCammon, B. C., Jr., and Little, R. W. (1973). Marketing channels: Analytical systems and approaches. In B. J. Walker and J. B. Haynes (Eds.), *Marketing Channels and Institutions: Readings on Distribution Concepts and Practices*, 28–29. Columbus, OH: Grid.

McCarthy, E. J. (1964). *Basic Marketing: A Managerial Approach* (revised edition). Homewood, IL: Richard D. Irwin, Inc.

McCarthy, E. J. (1978). *Basic Marketing: A Managerial Approach*. Homewood, IL: Irwin.

McCarthy, E. J., and Perreault, W. D., Jr. (1987). *Basic Marketing*. Homewood, IL: Irwin.

McQuail, D., and Windahl, S. (2015). *Communication Models for the Study of Mass Communications*. Abingdon: Routledge.

Medhat, W., Hassan, A., and Korashy, H. (2014). Sentiment analysis algorithms and applications: A survey. *Ain Shams Engineering Journal* 5(4): 1093–1113. https://doi.org/10.1016/j.asej.2014.04.011.

Mendleson, N., and Polonsky, M. J. (1995). Using strategic alliances to develop credible green marketing. *Journal of Consumer Marketing* 12(2): 4–18.

Menon, S., and Jain, K. (2021). Blockchain technology for transparency in agrifood supply chain: Use cases, limitations, and future directions. *IEEE Transactions on Engineering Management* 71: 106–120. https://doi.org/10.1109/TEM.2021.3110903.

Mentzer, J. T., DeWitt, W., Keebler, J. S., Min, S., Nix, N. W., Smith, C. D., and Zacharia, Z. G. (2001). Defining supply chain management. *Journal of Business Logistics* 22(2): 1–25.

Mentzer, J. T., Gomes, R., and Krapfel, R. E. (1989). Physical distribution service: A fundamental marketing concept? *Journal of the Academy of Marketing Science* 17(1): 53–62.

Merimi, M., and Taghipour, A. (2021). Accelerating the digitalization of the supply chain: An empirical research about covid-19 crisis. In *Digitalization of Decentralized Supply Chains During Global Crises*, 1–24. IGI Global.

Merlino, M., and Sproģe, I. (2017). The augmented supply chain. *Procedia Engineering* 178: 308–318. https://doi.org/10.1016/j.proeng.2017.01.053.

Michman, R. D. (1990). Managing structural changes in marketing channels. *Journal of Business and Industrial Marketing* 5(2): 5–14.

Michman, R. D., and Sibley, S. D. (1980). *Marketing Channels and Strategies* (2nd edition). Worthington, OH: Publishing Horizons.

Miller, K. D., Fabian, F., and Lin, S. J. (2009). Strategies for online communities. *Strategic Management Journal* 30(3): 305–322.

Mintu, A. T., and Lozada, H. (1993). Green marketing education: A call for action. *Marketing Education Review* 3(Fall): 17–23.

Mintzberg, H. (1987). The strategy concept I: Five PS for strategy. *California Management Review* 30(1): 11–24.

Miroudot, S., and Cadestin, C. (2017). Services in global value chains: From inputs to value-creating activities. *OECD Trade Policy Papers, No. 197*. Paris: OECD Publishing. https://doi.org/10.1787/465f0d8b-en.

Mittal, B., and Lassar, W. M. (1998). Why do customers switch? The dynamics of satisfaction versus loyalty. *Journal of Services Marketing* 12(3): 177–194.

Mittal, V., and Kamakura, W. A. (2001). Satisfaction, repurchase intent and repurchase behavior: Investigating the moderating effect of customer characteristics. *Journal of Marketing Research* 38(1): 131–142.

Mohr, J., and Nevin, J. R. (1990). Communication strategies in marketing channels: A theoretical perspective. *Journal of Marketing* 54(4): 36–51.

Mohsen, B. M. (2023). Developments of digital technologies related to supply chain management. *Procedia Computer Science* 220: 788–795.

Morello, G. (1993). The hidden dimensions of marketing. *Journal of the Market Research Society* 35(4): 293–314.

Moussa, O., Alshakhsi, S., Al-Thani, D., and Ali, R. (2022). Can operational transparency enhance the perception of waiting time? A case study from the healthcare sector. In *2022 9th International Conference on Behavioural and Social Computing (BESC)*, 1–7. IEEE.

Moutsis, S. N., Tsintotas, K. A., Kansizoglou, I., An, S., Aloimonos, Y., and Gasteratos, A. (2023). Fall detection paradigm for embedded devices based on YOLOv8. In *Proceedings of the IEEE International Conference on Imaging Systems and Techniques*, 1–6. Copenhagen, Denmark, 17–19 October. https://doi.org/10.1109/ist 59124.2023.10355696

Mundell, R. A. (1968). *International Economics*. New York: Macmillan.

Murdick, R. G., Render, B., and Russell, R. S. (1990). *Service Operations Management*. Boston, MA: Allyn & Bacon.

Musa, A., Gunasekaran, A., and Yusuf, Y. (2014). Supply chain product visibility: Methods, systems and impacts. *Expert Systems with Applications* 41(1): 176–194.
Muthuswamy, M., and Ali, A. M. (2023). Sustainable supply chain management in the age of machine intelligence: Addressing challenges, capitalizing on opportunities, and shaping the future landscape. *Sustainable Machine Intelligence Journal* 3: 3-10.
Narasimhan, R., and Nair, A. (2005). The antecedent role of quality, information sharing and supplychain proximity on strategic alliance formation and performance. *International Journal of Production Economics* 96(3): 301–313. https://doi.org/10.1016/j.ijpe.2003.06.004.
Narver, J. C., and Slater, S. F. (1990). The effect of a market orientation on business profitability. *Journal of Marketing* 54(4): 20–35.
Nataraja, S., and Al-Aali, A., (2011). The exceptional performance strategies of Emirate Airlines. *Competitiveness Review: An International Business Journal* 21(5): 471–486. https://doi.org/10.1108/10595421111171966.
Nicoletti, B. (2023). Industrial revolutions and supply network 5.0. In *Supply Network 5.0: How to Improve Human Automation in the Supply Chain*, 43–101. Springer.
Ning, Y. (2014). Quantitative effects of drivers and barriers on networking strategies in public construction projects. *International Journal of Project Management* 32: 286–297. https://doi.org/10.1016/j.ijproman.2013.04.003.
Normann, R. (1978). *Development Strategies for Swedish Service Knowledge: Report From Multi-Client Study*. Stockholm: Scandinavian Institute of Administrative Research.
Normann, R. (1991). *Service Management: Strategy and Leadership in Service Businesses* (2nd edition), 16–17. Chichester: John Wiley & Sons.
Ohmae, K. (1989). Managing in a borderless world. *Harvard Business Review* (May–June): 152–161.
Oliver, R. K., and Webber, M. D. (1992). Supply-chain management: Logistics catches up with strategy. In M. Christopher (Ed.), *Logistics: The Strategic Issues*, 63–75. London: Chapman & Hall.
Olson, E., Walker, O., and Ruckert, R. (1995). Organizing for effective new product development: The moderating role of product innovativeness. *Journal of Marketing* 59: 48–62.
Osei, M. B., Papadopoulos, Th., Acquaye, A., and Stamati, T. (2023). Improving sustainable supply chain performance through organizational culture: A competing values framework approach. *Journal of Purchasing & Supply Management* 29(2): 100821. https://doi.org/10.1016/j.pursup.2023.100821.
Pagell, M., and Wu, Z. (2009). Building a more complete theory of sustainable supply chain management using case studies of 10 exemplars. *Journal of Sustainable Supply Chain Management* 45(2): 37–56. https://doi.org/10.1111/j.1745–493X.2009.03162.x.
Palmer, A. (1998). *Principles of Services Marketing*. New York: McGraw-Hill.
Pan, S., Trentesaux, D., McFarlane, D., Montreuil, B., Ballot, E., and Huang, G. Q. (2021). Digital interoperability in logistics and supply chain management: State-of-the-art and research avenues towards physical internet. *Computers in Industry* 128: 103435.
Panigyrakis, G. (1999). *International Export Marketing* [in Greek]. Piraeus: Stamoulis Publications.
Panigyrakis, G., and Siomkos, G. I. (2005). *Marketing Cases* [in Greek]. Piraeus: Stamoulis Publications.
Parasuraman, A., Zeithaml, V. A., and Berry, L. L. (1985). A conceptual model of service quality and its implications for future research. *Journal of Marketing* 49(Fall): 41–50.
Park, A., and Li, H. (2021). The effect of blockchain technology on supply chain sustainability performances. *Sustainability*. https://doi.org/10.3390/SU13041726.
Park, S. T., Taeung, K., and Ryang, K. M. (2020). Digitization of supply chain management: Key elements and strategic impacts. *Journal of Digital Convergence* 18: 109–120. https://doi.org/10.14400/JDC.2020.18.6.109.
Parry, M. E., and Song, X. M. (1993). Determinants of R&D: Marketing integration in high-tech Japanese firms. *Journal of Product Innovation Management* 10(1): 4–22.
Patterson, K. A., Grimm, C. M., and Corsi, T. M. (2003). Adopting new technologies for supply chain management. *Transportation Research Part E: Logistics and Transportation Review* 39(2): 95–121. https://doi.org/10.1016/S1366–5545(02)00041–8.
Peattie, K. (1995). *Environmental Marketing Management*. London: Pitman.
Perevozova, I., Horal, L., Mokhnenko, A., Hrechanyk, N., Ustenko, A., Malynka, O., and Mykhailyshyn, L. (2020). Integration of the supply chain management and development of the marketing system. *International Journal of Supply Chain Management* 9(3): 496–507. https://doi.org/10.59160/ijscm.v9i3.4894.
Peter, P. J., and Donnelly, J. H., Jr. (2007). *Marketing Management: Knowledge and Skills* (8th edition). New York: McGraw-Hill.

Petrick, I. J., and Pogrebnyakov, N. (2009). Innovation in distributed networks and supporting knowledge flows. In A. Dwivedi and T. Butcher (Eds.), *Supply Chain Management and Knowledge Management*. London: Palgrave Macmillan. https://doi.org/10.1057/9780230234956_1.

Pielichaty, H., Els, G., Reed, I., and Mawer, V. (2017). *Events Project Management*. Oxon, NY: Routledge.

Pine, B. J., and Gilmore, J. H. (1998). Welcome to the experience economy. *Harvard Business Review* 76: 97–105.

Pitt, B. (2019). *The Study of How XR Technologies Impact the Retail Industry, Now and in the Future*. PhD thesis, University of Dublin.

Polonsky, M. J. (1994). An introduction to green marketing. *Electronic Green Journal* 1(2): 1–10.

Polonsky, M. J. (1995). A stakeholder theory approach to designing environmental marketing strategy. *Journal of Business and Industrial Marketing* 10(3): 29–46.

Porter, M. (1985). *Competitive Advantage: Creating and Sustaining Superior Performance*. New York: Free Press.

Porter, M. (1990). *The Competitive Advantage of Nations*. New York: Free Press.

Porter, M. (2024). *The Value Chain*. Institute of Strategy and Competitiveness-Harvard Business School. https://www.isc.hbs.edu/strategy/business-strategy/Pages/the-value-chain.aspx. Last visited 30 December 2024.

Porter, M. E. (1981). The contribution of industrial organization to strategic management. *Academy of Management Review* 6(4): 609–620.

Porter, M. E. (1984). *Competitive Advantage*. New York: Free Press.

Porter, M. E. (1985). *Competitive Advantage: Creating and Sustaining Superior Performance*. New York: Free Press.

Porter, M. E. (1996). What is strategy? *Harvard Business Review* (November–December): 61–68.

Porter, M. E., and Linde, C. V. D. (1999). Green and competitive: Ending the stalemate. https://hbr.org/product/green-and-competitive-ending-the-stalemate/an/95507-PDF-ENG.

Prahalad, C. K., and Hamel, G. (1990). The core competence of the corporation. *Harvard Business Review* 68(3): 79–91.

Prakash, A., and Singh, V. B. (2011). Glocalization in food business: Strategies of adaptation to local needs and demands. *Asian Journal of Technology and Management Research* 1(1). www.ajtmr.com/papers/vol1issue1/GLOCALIZATION%20IN%20FOOD%20BUSINESS.pdf.

Praveen, U., Farnaz, G., and Hatim, G. (2019). Inventory management and cost reduction of supply chain processes using AI-based time-series forecasting and ANN modeling. *Procedia Manufacturing* 38: 256–263.

Pride, W. M., and Ferrell, O. C. (2014). *Marketing* (International edition). New York: Houghton Mifflin Company.

Priya, C. S. R., and Deepalakshmi, P. (2022). Study on online review-based consumer sentimental analysis using machine learning approaches. In *2022 IEEE World Conference on Applied Intelligence and Computing (AIC)*, 610–616. IEEE.

Qiao, H., Lin, X., Zhou, X., and Jiang, M. (2022). Research on joint decision-making of timely delivery, product quality and marketing in supply chain based on differential game. *Sustainability* 14(17).

Rada, J., and Vandermerwe, S. (1988). Servitization of business: Adding value by adding service. *European Management Journal* 6(4): 314–320.

Rahmanzadeh, S., Pishvaee, M. S., and Govindan, K. (2023). Emergence of open supply chain management: The role of open innovation in the future smart industry using digital twin network. *Annals of Operations Research* 329(1): 979–1007.

Raimi, S. (2003). Glocalization. http://searchcio.techtarget.com/sDefination/0,sid19_gci826478,00.html.

Rajaratnam, D., and Sunmola, F. (2021). Supply chain management in airline catering service: Characteristics, challenges and trends. In *Proceedings of the International Conference on Industrial Engineering and Operations Management*, 1831–1842. Rome, Italy: IEOM Society International, 2–5 August 2021.

Rane, N. (2023). Enhancing customer loyalty through artificial intelligence (AI), internet of things (IoT), and big data technologies: Improving customer satisfaction, engagement, relationship, and experience. *Internet of Things (IoT), and Big Data Technologies: Improving Customer Satisfaction, Engagement, Relationship, and Experience*, 13 October 2023.

Rane, N., Choudhary, S., and Rane, J. (2023). *Sustainable Tourism Development Using Leading-Edge Artificial Intelligence (AI), Blockchain, Internet of Things (IoT), Augmented Reality (AR) and Virtual Reality (VR) Technologies*. Blockchain, Internet of Things (IoT), Augmented Reality (AR) and Virtual Reality (VR) Technologies.

Ravald, A., and Grönroos, C. (1996). The value concept and relationship marketing. *European Journal of Marketing* 30(2): 19–30. https://doi.org/10.1108/03090569610106626.

Razak, G. M., Hendry, L. C., and Stevenson, M. (2023). Supply chain traceability: A review of the benefits and its relationship with supply chain resilience. *Production Planning & Control* 34(11): 1114–1134.

Reeves, C. A., and Bednar, D. A. (1994). Defining quality: Alternatives and implications. *Academy of Management Review* 19(3): 419–445.

Reichheld, F. F. (1992). Loyalty-based management. *Harvard Business Review* 71(2): 64–73.

Reinartz, W. J., and Kumar, V. (2000). On the profitability of long-life customers in a noncontractual setting: An empirical investigation and implications for marketing. *Journal of Marketing* 64(4): 17–35.

Reinartz, W. J., and Kumar, V. (2003). The impact of customer relationship characteristics on profitable lifetime duration. *Journal of Marketing* 67(1): 77–99.

Reinhardt, F. L. (1998). Bringing the environment down to earth. *Harvard Business Review* 77(4): 149–157.

Rejeb, A., Rejeb, K., Simske, S., and Keogh, J. G. (2023). Exploring blockchain research in supply chain management: A latent Dirichlet allocation-driven systematic review. *Information* 14(10): 557.

Rese, M. (2006). Successful and sustainable business partnerships: How to select the right partners. *Industrial Marketing Management* 35(1): 72–82. https://doi.org/10.1016/j.indmarman.2005.08.009.

Reuter, C., Iacono, L. L., and Benlian, A. (2022). A quarter century of usable security and privacy research: Transparency, tailorability, and the road ahead. *Behaviour & Information Technology* 41: 2035–2048. https://doi.org/10.1080/0144929X.2022.2080908.

Rinehart, L. M., Cooper, M. B., and Wagenheim, G. D. (1989). Furthering the integration of marketing and logistics through customer service in the channel. *Journal of the Academy of Marketing Science* 17(1): 63–71.

Rivera-Camino, J. (2007). Re-evaluating green marketing strategy: A stakeholder perspective. *European Journal of Marketing* 41(11/12): 1328–1358.

Robinson, J. (1932). *The Economics of Imperfect Competition*. London: Macmillan.

Rogers, E. M. (1962). *Diffusion of Innovations*. New York: Free Press.

Rosenbloom, B. (1987). *Marketing Channels: A Management View*. Hinsdale, IL: Dryden.

Rudra, R. I., and Gopalakrishnan, A. K. (2023). Sentiment analysis of consumer reviews using machine learning approach. In *2023 20th International Joint Conference on Computer Science and Software Engineering (JCSSE)*, 49–54. IEEE.

Russell, R. S., and Taylor, B. W., III. (2008). *Operations Management Along the Supply Chain* (6th edition). Hoboken, NJ: John Wiley & Sons.

Rust, R. T., and Huang, M-H. (2014). The service revolution and the transformation of marketing science. *Marketing Science* 33(2): 206–221. https://doi.org/10.1287/mksc.2013.0836.

Rust, R. T., and Oliver, R. L. (2000). Should we delight the customer? *Journal of the Academy of Marketing Science* 28(1): 86–94.

Ryan, W. G., and Kelly, S. (2017). Chapter 8: The effects of Supply Chain Management (SCM) activities and their impact on music festival management and the customer experience. In Alan Jepson and Alan Clarke (Eds.), *Power, Construction and Meaning in Festivals* (1st edition). London: Routledge. http://dx.doi.org/10.4324/9781315161181–8.

Ryans, J. K., Jr., Griffith, D. A., and Steven White, D. (2003). Standardization/adaptation of international marketing strategy: Necessary conditions for the advancement of knowledge. *International Marketing Review* 20(6): 588–603.

Saberi, S., Kouhizadeh, M., Sarkis, J., and Shen, L. (2019). Blockchain technology and its relationships to sustainable supply chain management. *International Journal of Production Research* 57(7): 2117–2135. https://doi.org/10.1080/00207543.2018.1533261.

Saeed, S., Altamimi, S. A., Alkayyal, N. A., Alshehri, E., and Alabbad, D. A. (2023). Digital transformation and cybersecurity challenges for business resilience: Issues and recommendations. *Sensors* 23(15): 6666.

Sahin, F., and Robinson, E. P. (2005). Information sharing and coordination in make-to-order supply chains. *Journal of Operations Management* 23(6): 579–598. http://dx.doi.org/10.1016/j.jom.2004.08.007.

Sarkis, J. (2021). Supply chain sustainability: Learning from the COVID-19 pandemic. *International Journal of Operations & Production Management* 41(1): 63–73. https://doi.org/10.1108/IJOPM-08-2020-0568.

Schiegelmilch, B. (1998). *Marketing Ethics: An International Perspective*. London: International Thomson Business Press.

Schiffman, L., and Kanuk, L. (1993). *Consumer Behavior* (3rd edition). Englewood Cliffs, NJ: Prentice-Hall.

Schlemitz, A., and Mezhuyev, V. (2024). Approaches for data collection and process standardization in smart manufacturing: Systematic literature review. *Journal of Industrial Information Integration* 38: 100578.

Schneider, S. C. (1987). Information overload: Causes and consequences. *Human Systems Management* 7(2): 143–153.

Schramm, W. (1954). *How Communication Works: The Process and Effects of Mass Communication*. Urbana, IL: University of Illinois Press.

Schramm, W., and Roberts, D. F. (1971). *The Process and Effects of Mass Communication*. Urbana, IL: University of Illinois Press.

Scott, R. A., and Marks, N. E. (1968). *Marketing and Its Environment*. Belmont, CA: Wadsworth.

SECAP. (2019). Sustainable Energy and Climate Action Plan (SECAP) of Espoo under the Covenant of Mayors (CoM) – ESPOO ESBO. https://static.espoo.fi/cdn/ff/IVFPqlaf1L8WqBKsXWoCg4l-R1cnZJfdfrRVY87BI89c/1629719566/public/2021–08/SECAP-raportti_Espoon%20kaupunki%20%28ei%20saavutettava%29.pdf. Last visited 12 December 2024.

Segal-Horn, S. (1996). The limits of a global strategy. *Strategy and Leadership* (November/December): 12–17.

Seklouli Sekhari, A., Hossain, S. A., Bouras, A., and Santiteerakul, S. (2020). Sustainable supply chain management from the perspectives of risk management. In *APMS2010, Competitive and Sustainable Manufacturing, Products and Services*, October 2010, Cernobio, Italy. Conference Paper. (hal-00527359). https://www.researchgate.net/publication/47441524_Sustainable_Supply_Chain_Management_from_the_Perspectives_of_Risk_Management.

Selcuk, S. (2017). Predictive maintenance, its implementation and latest trends. *Proceedings of the Institution of Mechanical Engineers, Part B: Journal of Engineering Manufacture* 231(9): 1670–1679.

Senge, P. M. (1990). *The Fifth Discipline: The Art and Practice of the Learning Organization*. New York: Doubleday Currency.

Serradilla, O., Zugasti, E., Rodriguez, J., and Zurutuza, U. (2022). Deep learning models for predictive maintenance: A survey, comparison, challenges and prospects. *Applied Intelligence* 52(10): 10934–10964.

Seuring, S., and Müller, M. (2008). From a literature review to a conceptual framework for sustainable supply chain management. *Journal of Cleaner Production* 16(15): 1699–1710. https://doi.org/10.1016/j.jclepro.2008.04.020.

Seuring, S., Sarkis, J., Müller, M., and Rao, P. (2008). Sustainability and supply chain management – An introduction to the special issue (Editorial). *Journal of Cleaner Production* 16(15): 1545–1551. https://doi.org/10.1016/j.jclepro.2008.02.002.

Shang, D., Hu, Z., and Wang, Z. (2021). Mining consumer brand relationship from social media data: A natural language processing approach. In *Artificial Intelligence and Security: 7th International Conference, ICAIS 2021*, 553–565. Springer.

Shapiro, B. P. (1988). What the hell is market oriented? *Harvard Business Review* 66: 119–125.

Shapiro, B. P., Rangan, V. K., and Sviokla, J. J. (1993). Staple yourself to an order. *Harvard Business Review* 70(4): 113–122.

Sharma, A. (2018). Role of digitalization in improving supply chain management: A quantitative investigation. *Information Technology in Industry*. https://doi.org/10.17762/itii.v6i1.829.

Sheffi, Y. (2005). *The Resilient Enterprise: Overcoming Vulnerability for Competitive Advantage*. Cambridge, MA: MIT Press. ISBN: 9780262195379.

Sheth, J. N., and Sisodia, R. (1995). More than ever before, marketing is under fire to account for what it spends. *Marketing Management* 4(2): 13–14.

Shipley, D., and Prinja, S. (1988). The services and supplier choice influences of industrial distributors. *Service Industries Journal* 8(2): 176–187.

Shostack, G. L. (1977). Breaking free from product marketing. *Journal of Marketing* (April): 73–80.

Shostack, G. L. (1984). Designing services that deliver. *Harvard Business Review* 62(1): 133–139.

Shostack, G. L. (1985). Planning the service encounter. In J. A. Czepiel, M. R. Solomon, and C. F. Surprenant (Eds.), *The Service Encounter*, 243–254. Lexington, MA: Lexington Books.

Shostack, G. L. (1987). Service positioning through structural change. *Journal of Marketing* 51(1): 34–43.

Shostack, L. G. (1982). How to design a service. *European Journal of Marketing* 16(1): 49–63. https://doi.org/10.1108/EUM0000000004799.

Shultz, T. R., Léveillé, E., and Lepper, M. R. (1999). Free choice and cognitive dissonance revisited: Choosing 'lesser evils' versus 'greater goods'. *Personality and Social Psychology Bulletin* 25(1): 40–48.

Sicily. (2022). *Sicily – Soul of the Mediterranean Gastronomy*. Sicily Region of Italy, Assessorato Regionale Agricoltur, 31 December 2022. https://svilupporurale.regione.sicilia.it/wp-content/uploads/2024/09/European-Region-of-Gastronomy_Sicilia-candidate–2025.pdf?utm_source=chatgpt.com. Last visited 17 January 2025.

Sigala, M. (2020). Tourism and COVID-19: Impacts and implications for advancing and resetting industry and research. *Journal of Business Research* 117: 312–321. https://doi.org/10.1016/j.jbusres.2020.06.015.

Simchenko, N., Tsohla, S., and Chyvatkin, P. (2019). IoT & digital twins concept integration effects on supply chain strategy: Challenges and effects. *International Journal of Supply Chain Management* 8: 803–808.

Simon-Miller, F. (1986). World marketing: Going global or acting local? Five expert viewpoints. *Journal of Consumer Marketing* 3(2): 5–7.

Sinclair, D., Hunter, L., and Beumont, P. (1996). Models of customer-supplier relations. *Journal of General Management* 22(2): 56–75.

Siomkos, G. I. (2013). *Strategic Marketing* [in Greek] (3rd edition). Piraeus: Stamoulis Publications.

SKYTRAX-World Airline Awards. (2024). The world's Top 10 Airlines of 2024 voted for by travellers around the world. https://www.worldairlineawards.com/worlds-top-10-airlines-2024/#google_vignette. Last visited 12 January 2025.

Slaper, T. F., and Hall, T. J. (2011). The triple bottom line: What is it and how does it work? *Indiana Business Review* 86(1): 4–8. http://www.ibrc.indiana.edu/ibr/2011/spring/article2.html. Last visited 1 January 2025.

Sleuwaegen, L. (1992). Advances in international marketing. *International Journal of Research in Marketing* 9(4): 319–323.

Smith, N. C., Drumwright, M. E., and Gentile, M. C. (2010). The new marketing myopia. *Journal of Public Policy and Marketing* 29(1): 4–11.

Sobb, T., Turnbull, B., and Moustafa, N. (2020). Supply chain 4.0: A survey of cyber security challenges, solutions and future directions. *Electronics* 9(11): 1864.

Sofia, M., Fraboni, F., De Angelis, M., Puzzo, G., Giusino, D., and Pietrantoni, L. (2023). The impact of artificial intelligence on workers' skills: Upskilling and reskilling in organisations. *Informing Science: The International Journal of an Emerging Transdiscipline* 26: 39–68.

Solomon, M. R., Surprenant, C., Czepiel, J. A., and Gutman, E. G. (1985). A role theory perspective on dyadic interactions: The service encounter. *Journal of Marketing* 51(1): 99–111.

Soori, M., Arezoo, B., and Dastres, R. (2023). Digital twin for smart manufacturing: A review. *Sustainable Manufacturing and Service Economics*: 100017.

Souder, W. E. (1987). *Managing New Product Innovations*. Lexington, MA: Lexington Books.

Souder, W. E., and Chakrabarti, A. K. (1978). The R&D/marketing interface: Results from an empirical study of innovation projects. *IEEE Transactions on Engineering Management* 4: 88–93.

Sousa, R., and da Silveira, G. J. C. (2019). The relationship between servitization and product customization strategies. *International Journal of Operations & Production Management* 39(3): 454–474. https://doi.org/10.1108/IJOPM-03-2018-0177.

Stabell, C. B., and Fjeldstad, O. D. (1998). Configuring value for competitive advantage: On chains, shops, and networks. *Strategic Management Journal* 19: 413–437. http://dx.doi.org/10.1002/(SICI)1097–0266(199805)19:5<413::AID-SMJ946>3.0.CO;2-C.

Stalk, G., Evans, P., and Shulman, L. E. (1991). Competing on capabilities: The new rules of corporate strategy. *Harvard Business Review* 70(2): 57–69.

Stallings, B. (1995). *Global Change, Regional Response: The New International Context of Development*. Cambridge: Cambridge University Press.

Stanton, W. (1991). *Fundamentals of Marketing*. New York: McGraw-Hill.

Stern, L. W., and El-Ansary, A. I. (1977). *Marketing Channels*. Englewood Cliffs, NJ: Prentice Hall.

Stern, L. W., El-Ansary, A. I., and Coughlan, A. T. (1996). *Marketing Channels* (5th edition). Englewood Cliffs, NJ: Prentice-Hall.

Stern, L. W., and Gorman, R. H. (1969). Conflict in distribution channels: An exploration. In L. W. Stern (Ed.), *Distribution Channels: Behavioral Dimensions*, 156–175. Boston, MA: Houghton Mifflin Co.

Stevens, G. C. (1989). Integrating the supply chain. *International Journal of Physical Distribution & Logistics Management* 19(8): 3–8.

Stock, J. R., and Lambert, D. M. (2001). *Strategic Logistics Management* (4th edition). Singapore: McGraw-Hill.

Stone, J., Beauvois, J. L., and Joule, R. V. (1998). A radical new look at cognitive dissonance. *The American Journal of Psychology* 111(2): 319–326.

Strippoli, R., Gallucci, T., and Ingrao, C. (2024). Circular economy and sustainable development in the tourism sector – An overview of the truly-effective strategies and related benefits. *Heliyon* 10(17): e36801. https://doi.org/10.1016/j.heliyon.2024.e36801.

SuntripSicily. (2024). San Martino festival. *SunTripSicily.com*. https://www.suntripsicily.com/38-events_in_sicily-san-martino-festival.php. Last visited 15 January 2025.

Surprenant, C. F., and Solomon, M. R. (1987). Predictability and personalization in the service encounter. *Journal of Marketing* 51(2): 86–96.

Svensson, G. (2001). 'Glocalization' of business activities: A 'glocal strategy' approach. *Management Decision* 39(1): 6–18.

Swain, A. K., and Cao, R. Q. (2019). Using sentiment analysis to improve supply chain intelligence. *Information Systems Frontiers* 21: 469–484.

Szymanski, D. M., Bharadwaj, S. G., and Varadarajan, P. R. (1993). Standardization versus adaptation of international marketing strategy: An empirical investigation. *Journal of Marketing* 57(4): 1–14.

Taboada, I., and Shee, H. (2021). Understanding 5G technology for future supply chain management. *International Journal of Logistics Research and Applications* 24(4): 392–406.

Tagarakis, A. C., Benos, L., Kateris, D., Tsotsolas, N., and Bochtis, D. (2021). Bridging the gaps in traceability systems for fresh produce supply chains: Overview and development of an integrated iot-based system. *Applied Sciences* 11(16): 7596.

Taghipour, A., Lu, X., Derradji, M., and Sow, A. D. (2022). The impact of digitalization on supply chain management: A literature review. In *Proceedings of the 12th International Conference on Information Communication and Management*. https://doi.org/10.1145/3551690.3551702.

Tapscott, D., and Tapscott, A. (2016). *Blockchain Revolution: How the Technology Behind Bitcoin is Changing Money, Business, and the World*. New York: Penguin.

Tedeschi, A., and Benedetto, F. (2015). A cloud-based big data sentiment analysis application for enterprises' brand monitoring in social media streams. In *2015 IEEE 1st International Forum on Research and Technologies for Society and Industry Leveraging a Better Tomorrow (RTSI)*, 186–191. IEEE.

Temitayo, O. A., Tolulope, O. A., Kenneth, C. N., Ummulikhaeri, T. I.-L., Emmanuel, A. I., and Daniel, I. E. (2024). The rise of the "smart" supply chain: How AI and automation are revolutionizing logistics. *International Journal of Science and Research Archive* 12(2): 790–798. https://doi.org/10.30574/ijsra.2024.12.2.1304.

Tenner, A. R., and De Toro, I. J. (1992). *Total Quality Management: Three Steps to Continuous Improvement*. Reading, MA: Addison-Wesley.

Terpstra, V. (1972). *International Marketing*. New York: Holt, Rinehart & Winston.

Thomas, H., Bowman, E. H., and Singh, H. (2002). The domain of strategic management: History and evolution. In A. Pettigrew, H. Thomas, and R. Whittington (Eds.), *Handbook of Strategy and Management*, 31–51. London: Sage.

Thompson, S. (1962). *How Companies Plan*. AMA Research Study No. 54. Chicago, IL: American Marketing Association.

Tikkanen, I., and Jaakkola, L. (2019). Sustainable value chain activities towards sustainable food services: A case study from Finland. *Journal of Hospitality and Tourism Insights* 2(4): 409–424. https://doi.org/10.1108/JHTI-12-2018-0086.

Tikkanen, I., and Varkoi, T. (2011). Consumption of Fairtrade products in a municipal catering organisation. *Nutrition & Food Science* 41(3): 183–190. https://doi.org/10.1108/00346651111132457.

Tonmoy, T. C., Sanjoy, K. P., Humyun, F. R., Zhenguo, J., and Nagesh, S. (2020). A systematic literature review on the service supply chain: Research agenda and future research directions. *Production Planning & Control* 31(16): 1363–1384. https://doi.org/10.1080/09537287.2019.1709132.

Trucker, W. T. (1964). *The Social Context of Economic Behavior*. New York: Holt, Rinehart & Winston.

Tsang, Y. P., Yang, T., Chen, Z. S., Wu, C. H., and Tan, K. T. (2022). How is extended reality bridging human and cyber-physical systems in the IoT-empowered logistics and supply chain management? *Internet of Things* 20: 100623.

Tseng, M.-L., Lim, M., Wong, W.-P., Chen, Y.-C., and Zhan, Y. (2016). A framework for evaluating the performance of sustainable service supply chain management under uncertainty. *International Journal of Production Economics* 195: 359–372. https://dx.doi.org/10.1016/j.ijpe.2016.09.002.

Tsintotas, K., Moutsis, S. N., Kansizoglou, I., Konstantinidis, F., and Gasteratos, A. (2024). The advent of AI in modern supply chain. In *5th Olympus International Conference on Supply Chains*, Katerini, Greece, 24–26 May 2024.

Tussyadiah, I. P. (2012). A concept of location-based social network marketing. *Journal of Travel and Tourism Marketing* 29(3): 205–220.
Tzortzakis, K., and Tzortzaki, A. (2002). *Principles of Marketing: The Greek Approach* [in Greek] (2nd edition). Athens: Rosili Publications.
UN Tourism. (2024). Global roadmap for food waste reduction in the tourism sector. https://www.unwto.org/sustainable-development/food-waste-reduction-in-tourism. Last visited 23 November 2024.
UNCRPD. (2024). UN convention on the rights of persons with disabilities (UNCRPD). https://www.un.org/disabilities/documents/convention/convoptprot-e.pdf. Last visited 23 November 2024.
Undell, J. G. (1968). Towards a theory of marketing strategy. *British Journal of Marketing* 2(4): 298–303.
UNESCO. (2024). Espoo climate watch project. *UNESCO-Institute for Life Learning*, 31 July 2024. https://www.uil.unesco.org/en/articles/espoo-climate-watch-project. Last visited 12 January 2024.
UN-Global Compact & BSR. (2015). *Supply Chain Sustainability: A Practical Guide for Continuous Improvement* (2nd edition), June 2015. United Nations Global Compact Office & BSR. https://d306pr3pise04h.cloudfront.net/docs/issues_doc%2Fsupply_chain%2FSupplyChainRep_spread.pdf. Last visited 20 November 2024.
UN-Global Compact LEAD & PRI. (2013). The value driver model – A tool for communicating the business value of sustainability. Final Version of the Interim Report Released at the UN Global Compact Leaders Summit 2013: Architects of a Better World, December 2013. https://d306pr3pise04h.cloudfront.net/docs/issues_doc%2FFinancial_markets%2FValue_Driver_Model%2FVDM_Report.pdf. Last visited 15 January 2025.
UNIDO. (2025). Sustainable supply chains. https://www.unido.org/our-priorities/sustainable-supply-chains. Last visited 19 January 2025.
Uzzi, B. (1997). Social structure and competition in inter-firm networks: The paradox of embeddedness. *Administrative Science Quarterly* 42(1): 35–67. https://psycnet.apa.org/doi/10.2307/2393808.
Valentin, E. K. (1996). The marketing concept and the conceptualization of market strategy. *Journal of Marketing Theory and Practice* 4(4): 16–27.
Valeonti, F., Bikakis, A., Terras, M., Speed, C., Hudson-Smith, A., and Chalkias, K. (2021). Crypto collectibles, museum funding and openglam: Challenges, opportunities and the potential of non-fungible tokens (NFTS). *Applied Sciences* 11(21): 9931.
Valio Aimo. (2024). Hello, I am Aimo the wholesaler. Nice to meet you! https://www.valioaimo.fi/valio-aimo-in-english/. Last visited 11 January 2025.
Varadarajan, P. R., Clark, T., and Pride, W. M. (1992). Controlling the uncontrollable: Managing your market environment. *Sloan Management Review* 33(2): 39–47.
Vargo, S. L., and Lusch, R. F. (2004). Evolving to a new dominant logic for marketing. *Journal of Marketing* 68(1): 1–17.
Varriale, V., Cammarano, A., Michelino, F., and Caputo, M. (2023). Industry 5.0 and triple bottom line approach in supply chain management: The state-of-the-art. *Sustainability* 15(7): 5712.
Wakili, A., and Bakkali, S. (2024). Internet of things in healthcare: An adaptive ethical framework for IoT in digital health. *Clinical eHealth* 7: 92–105.
Wall, E. A., and Berry, L. L. (2007). The combined effects of the physical environment and employee behavior on customer perception of restaurant service quality. *Cornell Hotel and Restaurant Administration Quarterly* 48(1): 59–69.
Wallner, M. (2023). Value chain vs supply chain: What's the difference? *KNΔPP*, 4 May 2023. https://www.knapp.com/en/insights/blog/difference-value-chain-vs-supply-chain/. Last visited 2 December 2024.
Wang, B., Kang, Y., Childerhouse, P., and Huo, B. (2018). Service supply chain integration: The role of interpersonal relationships. *Industrial Management & Data Systems* 118(4): 828–849. https://doi.org/10.1108/IMDS-02-2017-0062.
Wang, L., Wang, D., Long, S., Shen, X., and Shi, V. (2019). Service supply chain management: A behavioural operations perspective. *Modern Supply Chain Research and Applications* 1(1): 28–53. https://doi.org/10.1108/MSCRA-01-2019-0003.
Wang, Q., Li, R., Wang, Q., and Chen, S. (2021). Non-fungible token (NFT): Overview, evaluation, opportunities and challenges. ArXiv, abs/2105.07447.
Ward, S., and Lewandowska, A. (2008). Is the marketing concept always necessary? The effectiveness of customer, competitor and societal strategies in business environment types. *European Journal of Marketing* 42(1/2): 222–237.
Webster, F. E. (1976). The role of the industrial distributor in marketing strategy. *Journal of Marketing* 40(3): 10–16.

Webster, F. E. (1997). Chapter 3: The future role of marketing in the organization. In D. R. Lehmann and K. Jocz (Eds.), *Reflections on the Futures of Marketing*. Cambridge, MA: Marketing Science Institute.
Webster, F. E., Jr. (1992). The changing role of marketing in the corporation. *Journal of Marketing* 56(4): 1–17.
Webster, F. E., Jr. (2002). The role of marketing and the firm. In B. A. Weitz and R. Wensley (Eds.), *Handbook of Marketing*, 66–82. London: Sage Publications.
Wentz, B., Eyrich, I., and Stevenson, K. (1973). Marketing of products. In H. Britt (Ed.), *The Marketing Manager's Handbook*. Chicago, IL: Dartnell Corporation.
Wheelwright, S., and Clark, K. (1992). *Revolutionizing Product Development*. New York: The Free Press.
Wieland, A. (2020). Dancing the supply chain: Toward transformative supply chain management. *The Journal of Supply Chain Management* 57(1): 58–73. https://doi.org/10.1111/jscm.12248.
Williamson, O. E. (1985). *The Economic Institutions of Capitalism; Firms, Markets, Relational Contracting*. London, New York: The Free Press.
Wilson, A., Zeithaml, V. A., Bitner, M. J., and Gremler, D. D. (2012). *Services Marketing; Integrating Customer Focus Across the Firm* (2nd European edition). Singapore: McGraw-Hill.
Wind, Y. (1986). The myth of globalization. *Journal of Consumer Marketing* 3 (Spring): 23–26.
WineItaly24. (2024). Feast of San Martino in Italy: A journey through traditions and legends, 10 November 2023. https://www.wineitaly24.com/wine-and-more/wine-and-culture/feast-of-san-martino-in-italy-a-journey-through-traditions-and-legends–3534.html. Last visited 23 November 2024.
Wirtz, J., Chew, P., and Lovelock, C. (2012). *Essentials of Services Marketing* (2nd edition). London: FT Press.
Wittstruck, D., and Teuteberg, F. (2010). Ein Referenzmodell für das sustainable supply chain management. *Zeitschrift für Management* 5(2): 141–164.
Wittstruck, D., and Teuteberg, F. (2011). Development and simulation of a balanced scorecard for sustainable supply chain management – A system dynamics approach. *Wirtschaftinformatik Proceedings* 2011. Paper 86. http://aisel.aisnet.org/wi2011/86.
Womack, J., and Jones, D. (2003). *Lean Thinking: Banish Waste and Create Wealth in Your Corporation* (2nd edition). New York: Productivity Press.
Wood, L. C., Reiners, T., and Srivastava, H. S. (2014). Sentiment analysis in supply chain management. In *Encyclopedia of Business Analytics and Optimization*, 2147–2158. IGI Global.
Wood, L. C., Reiners, T., and Srivastava, H. S. (2016). Think exogenous to excel: Alternative supply chain data to improve transparency and decisions. *International Journal of Logistics Research and Applications*. https://doi.org/10.1080/13675567.2016.1267126.
Woschank, M., Rauch, E., and Zsifkovits, H. (2020). A review of further directions for artificial intelligence, machine learning, and deep learning in smart logistics. *Sustainability* 12(9): 3760.
Wyner, G. A. (1996a). Customer profitability: Linking behavior to economics. *Marketing Research* 8(2): 36–38.
Wyner, G. A. (1996b). Which customers will be valuable in the future? *Marketing Research* 8(3): 44.
Wyner, G. A. (2006). Moment of truth. *Marketing Management* 15(1): 8–9.
Xenia Team. (2024). Hotel opening & closing checklist. https://www.xenia.team/templates/hotel-opening-closing-checklist. Last visited 30 November 2024.
Yaqub, M. Z., and Alsabban, A. (2023). Industry–4.0-enabled digital transformation: Prospects, instruments, challenges, and implications for business strategies. *Sustainability* 15(11): 8553.
Yazdanifard, R., and Mercy, I. E. (2011). The impact of green marketing on customer satisfaction and environmental safety. In *2011 International Conference on Computer Communication and Management*, 637–641. Singapore: IACSIT Press.
Yip, G. S. (1989). Global strategy: In a world of nations? *Sloan Management Review* (Fall): 29–41.
Yip, G. S. (1992). *Total Global Strategy: Managing for Worldwide Competitive Advantage*. Englewood Cliffs, NJ: Prentice-Hall.
Yoder, R. T. (2019). Digitalization and data democratization in offshore drilling. In *Offshore Technology Conference*, D032S058R008. OTC.
Zaheer, A., McEvily, B., and Perrone, V. (1998). Does trust matter? Exploring the effects of interorganizational and interpersonal trust on performance. *Organization Science* 9(2): 141–159. https://doi.org/10.1287/orsc.9.2.141.
Zeithaml, V. A. (1988). Consumer perceptions of price, quality and value: A means–end model and synthesis of evidence. *Journal of Marketing* 52(3): 2–22.

Zeithaml, V. A., Berry, L. L., and Parasuraman, A. (1988). Communication and control processes in the delivery of service quality. *Journal of Marketing* 52(2): 35–48.

Zeithaml, V. A., Berry, L. L., and Parasuraman, A. (1993). The nature and determinants of customer expectations of service. *Journal of the Academy of Marketing Science* 21(1): 1–12.

Zeithaml, V. A., Parasuraman, A., and Berry, L. L. (1985). Problems and strategies in services marketing. *Journal of Marketing* 49(2): 33–46.

Zhang, G., Yang, Z., and Liu, W. (2023). Blockchain-based decentralized supply chain system with secure information sharing. *Computers & Industrial Engineering* 182: 109392. https://doi.org/10.1016/j.cie.2023.109392.

Zhou, G., Zhang, C., Li, Z., Ding, K., and Wang, C. (2020). Knowledge-driven digital twin manufacturing cell towards intelligent manufacturing. *International Journal of Production Research* 58: 1034–1051.

Zhou, H., Shou, Y., Zhai, X., Li, L., Wood, C., and Wu, X. (2014). Supply chain practice and information quality: A supply chain strategy study. *International Journal of Production Economics* 147: 624–633.

Zhou, M., Park, T., and Yi, J. (2009). Commonalities and differences between service and manufacturing supply chains: Combining operations management studies with supply chain management. *California Journal of Operations Management* 7(1): 136–143.

Zhu, X., Zhao, Q., and Yao, X. (2024). How inventory flexibility affects productivity: The moderating roles of digital transformation and supply chain concentration. *Journal of Manufacturing Technology Management*. https://doi.org/10.1108/JMTM-03-2024-0110.

Zigiaris, S. (2000). Business process reengineering. www.adi.pt/docs/innoregio_BPR-en.pdf.

Zinkhan, G. M., and Carlson, L. (1995). Green advertising and the reluctant consumer. *Journal of Advertising* 24(2): 1–6.

Zou, S., Andrus, D. M., and Wayne Norvell, D. (1997). Standardization of international marketing strategy by firms from a developing country. *International Marketing Review* 14(2): 107–123.

Zou, S., and Cavusgil, T. (2002). The GMS: A broad conceptualization of global marketing strategy and its effect on firm performance. *Journal of Marketing* 66(4): 40–56.

MULTIPLE-CHOICE ANSWERS

Chapter 1

1. What principal concern arises when a company's departments fail to collaborate effectively in order fulfilment?

   B. Premature cognitive dissonance

2. Which theory explains a customer's psychological tension after a purchase decision?

   B. Cognitive dissonance theory

3. What critical factor differentiates competing product offers in buyer evaluation?

   B. Superior perceived value

4. According to Levitt's product levels, which tier exceeds customer expectations?

   C. Augmented product

5. The 'service continuum' concept primarily distinguishes:

   A. Goods versus services

6. What organisational shift minimises departmental silos?

   B. Business process redesign

7. Which objective is NOT part of SCM's systemic approach?

   B. Minimising departmental autonomy

8. Customer loyalty is most directly correlated with:

   B. Post-purchase satisfaction

9. The 'moment of truth' in service marketing refers to

   B. Customer–employee interaction

10. A key deficiency of traditional functional organisation is

    B. Lack of process visibility

11. Which metric measures supply chain success holistically?

    B. Total system profitability

12. The 'zone of tolerance' in service quality relates to

    B. Acceptable versus desired service levels

13. What drives the exponential cost-service level relationship?

    B. Diminishing returns

14. A systemic approach prioritises

    B. End-to-end process success

15. Which is NOT a post-purchase evaluation outcome?

    D. Supplier diversification

Chapter 2

1. Which element is NOT part of marketing's definition?

   B. Resource conversion efficiency

2. A 'need' in marketing is best defined as

   B. A state of deprivation

3. Demand is distinguished from desire by

   B. Purchasing power

4. According to Levitt, the 'potential product' level includes

   B. Future enhancements

5. Which is a key role of SCM?

   B. Reducing total system costs

6. Which of the following is NOT a primary activity in Porter's value chain model?

   C. Human resource management

7. The core business process that involves gathering and acting upon market information is called

   B. The market-sensing process

8. Which of the following is NOT one of the core business processes mentioned in the text?

   D. Supplier relationship management process

9. The process of building deeper understanding, relationships and offerings to individual customers is known as

   C. Customer relationship management process

10. Which of the following is NOT a support activity in Porter's value chain model?

    D. Outbound logistics

11. The value delivery network, also known as the supply chain, includes

    C. The company, suppliers, distributors and customers

12. Core competencies are best described as

    A. Skills that enable a company to deliver fundamental customer benefits

13. Which of the following is NOT a characteristic of a core competency?

    B. It can easily be imitated by competitors

14. The concept that a company should view itself as part of a value creation and delivery sequence is known as

    C. Value chain

15. Which of the following best describes the relationship between marketing and SCM?

    D. They are interdependent functions that must work together to deliver customer value

Chapter 3

1. Which criterion is used to evaluate marketing performance but NOT SCM?

   A. Customer satisfaction surveys

2. What is a primary recommendation to reduce lead time in supply chain operations?

   B. Implement cross-functional teams

3. Which of the 7Ps of services marketing emphasises the role of frontline employees?

   C. People

4. Why do marketing managers generally oppose holding high inventory levels?

   C. To avoid product obsolescence

5. Which practice aligns marketing and SCM goals in demand handling?

   C. Collaborative inventory planning

6. What is a critical challenge in integrating marketing and SCM?

   A. Overlapping departmental objectives

7. Which factor is a key driver of globalisation's impact on supply chain complexity?

   C. Localised regulatory frameworks

8. What distinguishes the 'Process' element in the 7Ps of services marketing?

   B. Employee–customer interaction protocols

9. How does SCM prioritise risk mitigation in inventory decisions?

   B. By diversifying supplier networks

10. Which trend exacerbates demand volatility in modern markets?

    C. Rapid technological advancements

11. What is a consequence of misaligned marketing and supply chain strategies?

    C. Increased stockout incidents

12. Which element of the 7Ps focuses on service delivery efficiency?

    C. Process

13. Why do supply chain managers advocate for higher inventory buffers?

    B. To accommodate demand fluctuations

14. What is a barrier to adopting a global supply chain strategy?

    B. Localised regulatory compliance costs

15. Which metric reflects supply chain efficiency but NOT marketing effectiveness?

    B. Order cycle time

Chapter 4

1. Which of the following best describes the concept of 'glocalisation' in SCM?

   C. Adapting global strategies to local contexts

2. What is a key challenge of globalisation for SCM?

   D. Increased supply chain complexity

3. Which trend has significantly impacted both marketing and SCM in recent years?

   B. Rise of e-commerce platforms

4. What is a primary driver of supply chain volatility in modern markets?

   C. Rapid technological advancements

5. How does the 'long tail' phenomenon affect SCM?

   B. It increases inventory holding costs

6. Which of the following best describes the concept of 'mass customisation'?

   B. Customising products for individual customers

7. What is a major challenge of implementing sustainability initiatives in supply chains?

   C. Balancing costs with environmental benefits

8. How does the trend of 'servitisation' impact traditional product-based companies?

   C. It shifts focus towards service-based offerings

9. Which of the following is NOT a typical characteristic of modern supply chains?

   C. Reduced collaboration

10. What is a key challenge of managing global supply chains in the context of geopolitical tensions?

    D. Potential disruptions due to trade conflicts

11. How does the trend of 'circular economy' impact SCM?

    C. It emphasises resource recovery and reuse

12. Which technology has significantly impacted both marketing and supply chain visibility?

    B. Blockchain

13. What is a major challenge of implementing omnichannel strategies?

    C. Integrating online and offline channels

14. How does the trend of 'nearshoring' impact global supply chains?

    C. It brings production closer to end markets

15. Which of the following best describes the concept of 'demand sensing' in modern supply chains?

    C. Real-time analysis of demand signals

Chapter 5

1. Which of the following best describes the concept of 'integrated marketing and SCM'?

   C. Aligning marketing and SCM strategies holistically

2. What is a key challenge in implementing an integrated marketing and SCM framework?

   C. Resistance to organisational culture change

3. Which element is NOT typically part of the integrated marketing and SCM communication process?

   C. Unilateral decision-making by management

4. How does the integrated framework address demand variability?

   C. By aligning forecasting with supply capabilities

5. What role does information technology play in the integrated framework?

   C. It enables seamless data flow and analysis

6. Which approach best characterises the customer focus in an integrated framework?

   C. Segmenting and tailoring value propositions

7. How does the integrated framework impact inventory management?

   C. It balances demand patterns with supply

8. What is a key benefit of integrating marketing and SCM strategies?

   C. Enhanced overall value creation for customers

9. Which metric is LEAST relevant in evaluating the success of an integrated framework?

   C. Individual departmental profit margins

10. How does the integrated framework address supplier relationships?

    B. Through collaborative, strategic partnerships

11. What approach to product development does the integrated framework promote?

    C. Concurrent engineering with cross-functional teams

12. How does the integrated framework impact pricing strategies?

    C. It aligns pricing with value creation and delivery

13. Which of the following is NOT a typical barrier to implementing an integrated framework?

    C. Excessive cross-functional communication and coordination

14. How does the integrated framework address global supply chain challenges?

    C. By balancing global efficiency with local responsiveness

15. What role does sustainability play in the integrated marketing and SCM framework?

    C. It balances economic, social and environmental factors

Chapter 6

1. What is the primary function of a distribution channel?

   C. To facilitate transactions between producers and consumers

2. Which of the following best describes the concept of a 'value network' in distribution?

   C. An interconnected set of organisations creating value

3. What is the main advantage of using intermediaries in a distribution channel?

   B. Reduced number of transactions

4. Which type of distribution channel is characterised by the producer selling directly to the end consumer?

   D. Direct distribution

5. What is the primary goal of channel management in a distribution network?

   C. Optimising channel performance and relationships

6. Which of the following is NOT a typical flow in a distribution channel?

   D. Competition flow

7. What is the main purpose of a logistics service provider in a distribution channel?

   B. To facilitate the physical movement of goods

8. Which distribution strategy involves selling through all available outlets in a market?

   C. Intensive distribution

9. What is the primary challenge of implementing a multi-channel distribution strategy?

   C. Potential channel conflict

10. Which factor is LEAST important when selecting a logistics service provider?

    D. Age of the company

11. What is the main advantage of vertical integration in a distribution channel?

    C. Greater coordination and control

12. Which distribution channel structure is most suitable for highly customised industrial products?

    B. Direct distribution

13. What is the primary function of a wholesaler in a distribution channel?

    B. To break bulk and assort products for retailers

14. Which of the following is NOT a typical criterion for evaluating a logistics service provider?

    C. Political affiliations of management

15. What is the main benefit of implementing a JIT system in distribution?

    D. Minimised inventory holding costs

Chapter 7

1. Which of the following best describes the concept of demand handling?

   C. Balancing supply and demand

2. What is the primary goal of demand forecasting?

   B. Predicting future customer needs

3. Which forecasting method relies on expert opinions and market research?

   C. Qualitative forecasting

4. What is a key characteristic of the simple moving average forecasting method?

   A. It assigns equal weights to all observations

5. Which of the following is NOT a typical component of time series forecasting?

   D. Supplier performance

6. What does the Mean Absolute Deviation (MAD) measure in forecasting?

   A. Average forecast error

7. Which inventory classification method categorises items based on their value and usage?

   C. ABC analysis

8. What is the primary purpose of safety stock?

   C. Protecting against demand uncertainty

9. Which of the following best describes the EOQ model?

   C. An optimal order size calculation

10. What is the main objective of the JIT inventory system?

    B. Minimising inventory holding costs

11. Which of the following is NOT a typical benefit of implementing a VMI system?

    D. Increased production flexibility

12. What is the primary focus of the CPFR approach?

    C. Cross-organisational collaboration

13. Which demand handling strategy involves adjusting prices to influence customer behaviour?

    A. Demand shaping

14. What is the main purpose of demand sensing in SCM?

    B. Real-time demand detection

15. Which of the following best describes the concept of demand latency?

    B. Delay in recognising changes in demand patterns

Chapter 8

1. What is the primary goal of strategic sourcing in procurement?

   C. Aligning procurement activities with organisational goals

2. Which element is NOT typically part of the strategic sourcing cycle?

   C. Immediate contract termination for underperformers

3. What is the primary purpose of a SWOT analysis in supplier selection?

   B. Identifying internal strengths/weaknesses and external opportunities/threats

4. Which metric is most critical for evaluating supplier reliability?

   B. On-time delivery performance

5. What distinguishes collaborative supplier relationships from transactional ones?

   B. Joint innovation and risk-sharing

6. Which factor is LEAST relevant in supplier risk management?

   B. Supplier's branding strategy

7. What is a key advantage of e-procurement over traditional methods?

   C. Streamlined order processing and transparency

8. Which criterion is most critical in supplier segmentation?

   B. Strategic importance and spend volume

9. What is the primary focus of TCO analysis?

   B. Long-term operational and hidden costs

10. How does SRM enhance procurement?

    B. Through collaborative innovation and value creation

11. Which practice aligns marketing and procurement objectives?

    B. Joint development of supplier sustainability criteria

12. What is a key challenge in implementing green procurement practices?

    B. Balancing environmental goals with cost efficiency

13. Which factor is critical for successful global supplier integration?

    B. Cross-cultural communication competence

14. What is the main purpose of supplier scorecards?

    C. To quantitatively evaluate supplier performance

15. Which trend has most impacted modern procurement practices?

    B. Rise of sustainability-driven supplier criteria

Chapter 9

1. What is the primary goal of JIT production?

   C. Eliminating waste and inefficiencies

2. Which of the following is NOT a key principle of Total Quality Management?

   C. Centralised decision-making

3. What does the '5S' methodology in lean manufacturing stand for?

   A. Sort, set, shine, standardise, sustain

4. Which tool is used to identify the root causes of problems in quality management?

   B. Fishbone diagram

5. What is the primary focus of ECR?

   C. Enhancing customer satisfaction

6. Which of the following best describes the concept of cross-docking?

   B. Direct transfer between inbound and outbound vehicles

7. What is the main objective of CPFR?

   C. Enhancing supply chain integration and efficiency

8. Which quality management tool is used to graphically represent the sequence of steps in a process?

   C. Flowchart

9. What is the primary goal of demand sensing in SCM?

   B. Increasing forecast accuracy

10. Which of the following is NOT a typical benefit of implementing JIT production?

    C. Increased production lead times

11. What is the main purpose of the Pareto chart in quality management?

    A. Identifying the vital few causes

12. Which ECR strategy focuses on optimising product introductions and assortments?

    A. Efficient store assortment

13. What is the primary objective of the Six Sigma methodology?

    B. Reducing process variability

14. Which of the following best describes the concept of demand shaping?

    B. Actively influencing customer preferences

15. What is the main focus of the Theory of Constraints in operations management?

    C. Optimising the system's constraints

Chapter 10

1. Which technology uses radio waves to automatically identify objects and collect data?

   C. RFID

2. What is the primary purpose of the check digit in EAN-13 barcodes?

   C. Validate data accuracy

3. Which component is NOT part of an RFID system?

   C. Magnetic stripe

4. How does NFC differ from traditional RFID technology?

   C. Uses electromagnetic induction for communication

5. What is the primary function of operational CRM systems?

   B. Real-time customer interaction management

6. Which technology enables bidirectional data exchange between devices within close proximity?

   C. NFC

7. What is a critical challenge in implementing SRM systems?

   B. Aligning supplier goals with organisational strategies

8. Which factor most directly impacts the evolution of e-commerce in supply chains?

   C. Advanced logistics management technologies

9. What is the primary advantage of telematics in transportation management?

   C. Real-time fleet monitoring and route optimisation

10. Which metric is critical for evaluating RFID system effectiveness?

    B. Read-rate accuracy in diverse environments

11. How do QR codes enhance marketing-SCM integration?

    B. Enabling dynamic customer engagement through mobile access

12. What characterises analytical CRM systems compared to operational CRM?

    B. Emphasis on historical data analysis for strategic insights

13. Which trend has accelerated the adoption of SRM technologies?

    C. Globalisation of supply networks

14. What is a key barrier to implementing blockchain in SCM?

    B. Resistance to decentralised data management

15. How does IoT contribute to demand sensing?

    B. Through real-time monitoring of product usage patterns

Chapter 11

1. What is a key difference between SCM for services and physical goods?

   B. Services are produced and consumed simultaneously

2. How does the concept of 'servitisation' contribute to the competitiveness of companies?

   C. By integrating value-added services with physical products

3. What role does human capital play in service supply chains?

   C. It enhances customer experience and service quality

4. How do the characteristics of services (intangibility, simultaneity and heterogeneity) affect SCM?

   B. They require more customer interaction and flexible operations

5. What is the role of marketing in strengthening relationships within a service supply chain?

   B. It builds trust and fosters collaboration between stakeholders

6. How does relationship marketing contribute to value creation in service value chains?

   C. By fostering long-term partnerships and customer loyalty

7. What is the significance of AI and big data analytics in modern marketing and SCM?

   A. They enable demand forecasting and personalised marketing

8. What are the key components of the 7Ps in service marketing, and how do they impact SCM?

   B. Product, place, price, promotion, people, process and physical evidence

9. How does supply chain integration affect customer satisfaction in the service sector?

   B. It improves coordination and enhances service reliability

10. What are the challenges in managing the bullwhip effect in service supply chains?

    A. Services have limited inventory buffers, making demand fluctuations harder to manage

11. How does customer participation influence the service supply chain?

    B. It increases variability but allows for greater customisation

12. What are the key differences between service-only supply chains and product-service supply chains?

    B. Product-service supply chains blend physical products with value-added services

13. What are the main risks businesses face when outsourcing services in a supply chain?

    C. Loss of direct customer relationships and quality control

14. How does globalisation influence SCM practices in the service industry?

    B. It increases cultural and regulatory complexities while expanding market reach

15. Why is agility important in service-based supply chains?

    A. Services require rapid response to demand changes and customer needs

Chapter 12

1. How does value chain management differ across various service industries?

   B. It depends on customer involvement, service customisation and industry-specific needs

2. What is one key benefit of analysing industry-specific value chains?

   C. Improved cost optimisation and competitive advantage

3. How does digital transformation impact value chain management in services?

   C. Improves efficiency through AI, automation and real-time analytics

4. What is a key element of sustainability in service value chains?

   A. Reducing carbon footprints and implementing ethical labour standards

5. How does Marriott integrate value chain management strategies?

   C. By collaborating with local suppliers, reducing emissions and ensuring sustainability compliance

6. What is a best practice for value chain management in the tourism sector?

   C. Investing in digitalisation and strategic partnerships

7. How do F&B companies implement sustainability in their value chains?

   C. Adopting sustainable sourcing, waste reduction and ethical labour practices

8. How does supply chain collaboration benefit service industries like catering and hospitality?

   C. It enhances resource sharing, reduces costs and strengthens competitive positioning

9. What is a major challenge transportation companies face in value chain management?

   B. High fuel costs, regulatory compliance and environmental concerns

10. How do case studies help businesses improve value chains?

    A. They provide real-world insights into efficiency and innovation

11. How does customer experience influence value chain decision-making?

    B. It drives service design, efficiency and innovation

12. What is the impact of supply chain transparency on service value chain efficiency?

    C. It enhances trust, accountability and efficiency

13. What role does sustainability certification play in managing value chains?

    A. It ensures compliance with environmental and ethical standards

14. How can companies achieve economies of scale through value chain management?

    B. By streamlining operations, using digital tools and forming strategic partnerships

15. What is a key lesson from successful value chain management case studies?

    A. Sustainability and digital adoption are crucial for long-term success

Chapter 13

1. What is the House of SSCM?

   B. A framework organising sustainability efforts into a structured model

2. What are the three main levels of the SSCM house?

   C. Foundation, pillars and roof

3. What does the foundation level of the SSCM house represent?

   B. Fundamental principles like risk management, ethics and compliance

4. How does the TBL framework relate to SSCM?

   B. It ensures a balance between environmental, social and economic sustainability

5. Why are ethics, standards and regulations important in SSCM?

   B. They ensure fairness, transparency and compliance with laws

6. What is a key reason why risk management is essential in SSCM?

   B. It allows businesses to react to climate change, economic instability and geopolitical risks

7. What is a common environmental sustainability strategy in supply chains?

   B. Investing in green logistics and renewable energy

8. How does CSR contribute to SSCM?

   A. By promoting ethical labour practices and community investments

9. Which of the following is an example of a socially responsible business practice?

   B. Implementing fair labour policies and ethical sourcing

10. How does economic sustainability impact long-term business profitability?

    B. It encourages sustainable business practices that improve efficiency and resilience

11. How can businesses use technology to enhance sustainability in supply chains?

    B. By using AI, blockchain and data analytics to track sustainability efforts

12. What is the primary function of the value driver model in SSCM?

    A. It aligns business strategies with sustainability goals

13. How do service-based supply chains differ from manufacturing-based supply chains?

    A. Service supply chains rely more on human involvement and real-time adaptation

14. How do government regulations influence sustainable supply chain practices?

    A. By ensuring compliance with environmental and ethical standards

15. How does the SSSCM model help businesses?

    A. By measuring sustainability across environmental, social and customer-related dimensions

Chapter 14

1. What is the primary focus of Industry 5.0 in SCM?

   B. Human-centric approaches and sustainability

2. Which technology is primarily used for real-time monitoring and data collection in supply chains?

   A. IoT

3. What role does AI play in demand forecasting?

   B. It uses historical data and market trends to predict demand

4. What is the main advantage of using Digital twins in SCM?

   D. They allow simulation and optimisation without disrupting physical operations

5. Which of the following is a key challenge in implementing AI in supply chains?

   C. Ensuring data quality and integration

6. What is the primary purpose of XR in SCM?

   B. To enhance human–machine interaction and visualisation

7. Which technology revolutionises predictive maintenance in supply chains?

   B. AI

8. What is a critical factor for successful digital transformation in supply chains?

   D. A balanced approach considering technology, human factors and organisational readiness

9. Which of the following is not a benefit of IoT in SCM?

   C. Complete automation of decision-making

10. What is the primary goal of logistics optimisation using AI?

    B. To minimise fuel consumption and enhance delivery efficiency

11. Which of the following is a key application of Digital twins in supply chains?

    D. Simulating and optimising supply chain processes

12. What is a major challenge in adopting Digital twins in supply chains?

    B. High costs and specialised knowledge requirements

13. Which technology is most likely to enhance human-machine collaboration in supply chains?

    D. XR

14. What is the primary benefit of predictive maintenance in supply chains?

    B. Minimising equipment downtime and extending machinery lifespan

15. Which of the following is a key recommendation for organisations adopting digital transformation?

    C. Prioritising sustainability and data security

Chapter 15

1. Which of the following is not one of the five generic steps to digitally transform the supply chain?

   C. Implement blockchain technology

2. What is a key advantage of IoT sensors over traditional barcode and RFID technologies in supply chain traceability?

   D. Ability to monitor environmental conditions like temperature and humidity

3. In blockchain technology, what happens when corruption is detected in a block?

   B. The affected block within the compromised node undergoes correction

4. What is the primary purpose of digital passports in SCM?

   A. To store a product's complete supply chain history and characteristics

5. Which technology is crucial for accurately classifying sentiments in social media data?

   C. BERT

6. What is the main advantage of integrating sentiment analysis with LLMs?

   A. Enhanced understanding of consumer sentiments from unstructured data

7. In the context of supply chain digitalisation, what is the primary function of cyber-physical systems?

   B. To facilitate integration among diverse and geographically dispersed entities

8. What is the main challenge in achieving supply chain visibility?

   C. Dispersion of visibility data across different enterprises and systems

9. In NFT implementation, what is the first stage of creating an NFT ecosystem?

   B. Identifying a suitable blockchain network

10. Which of the following best describes the role of sentiment analysis in SCM?

    D. Understanding consumer opinions and emotions about products

11. What is a key benefit of implementing digital transformation in supply chains?

    B. Enhanced real-time visibility of operations

12 How does traceability contribute to product safety?

    C. By enabling quick identification and isolation of compromised products

13. What role do policy-makers play in supply chain digitalisation?

    D. Establishing data protection regulations and supporting cybersecurity initiatives

14. What is the primary purpose of integrating blockchain in supply chain traceability?

    B. To create a secure and tamper-resistant ledger

15. Which aspect of supply chain digitalisation requires significant attention to workforce development?

    A. Reskilling and upskilling of employees

INDEX

Page numbers in **bold** type indicate tables; those in *italics* indicate figures.

For Product Safety Concerns and Information please contact our EU representative GPSR@taylorandfrancis.com Taylor & Francis Verlag GmbH, Kaufingerstraße 24, 80331 München, Germany

Batch number: 10753441

Printed by Printforce, the Netherlands